D1603031

HOSPITALITY AND TREACHERY IN WESTERN LITERATURE

HOSPITALITY AND
TREACHERY IN
WESTERN LITERATURE

James A. W. Heffernan

Yale

UNIVERSITY

PRESS

New Haven & London

Published with assistance from the
Mary Cady Tew Memorial Fund.

Yale University Press books may be purchased in quantity for
educational, business, or promotional use. For information, please
e-mail sales.press@yale.edu (U.S. office) or sales@yaleup.co.uk
(U.K. office).

Set in Electra type by IDS Infotech Ltd., Chandigarh, India.
Printed in the United States of America.

Library of Congress Cataloging-in-Publication Data
Heffernan, James A. W.
Hospitality and treachery in western literature / James A. W.
Heffernan.
pages   cm.
Includes bibliographical references and index.
ISBN 978-0-300-19558-3 (alk. paper)
1. Hospitality in literature. 2. Betrayal in literature. 3. European
literature—History and criticism. I. Title.
PN56.H66H44 2014
809'.93355—dc23   2013030741

A catalogue record for this book is available from the British
Library.

This paper meets the requirements of ANSI/NISO Z39.48-1992
(Permanence of Paper).

10 9 8 7 6 5 4 3 2 1

In Memoriam
Half and Susanne Zantop

CONTENTS

ACKNOWLEDGMENTS

This book began with a paper on hospitality in Homer and Joyce that I gave at the biennial meeting of the International James Joyce Association held in Dublin in June 2004 to coincide with the hundredth anniversary of Bloomsday. Two years earlier J. Hillis Miller and Karen Lawrence had stirred my interest in Joycean hospitality by presenting papers on this topic at the IJJA meeting in Trieste, Italy. Since that time, Hillis Miller has supported my project with extraordinary generosity and warmth, not only offering specific advice on several chapters (especially chapter 3) but also recommending the book to Yale. One or more versions of the chapter on classical hospitality were read by Charles Beye and two Dartmouth classicists, Edward Bradley and James Tatum, all of whom kindly offered their counsel, and to Jim I also owe special thanks for strongly supporting the whole project. Stephen Prickett vetted the chapter on biblical hospitality. Robert Hollander scrutinized my brief discussion of Dante at the end of chapter 2. Peter Saccio read and commented on two versions of the Shakespeare chapter, which was also read by Julia Lupton, whose work on hospitality—especially in *The Winter's Tale*—I have found extremely helpful. Kenneth Johnston helped me greatly with chapter 5, and Jack Stillinger thoughtfully read chapter 6. Paul Hunter and Robert Polhemus both examined the chapter on fiction from Fielding to James and gave me extensive comments. Colette Gaudin, who read the Proust chapter, carefully explained to me the nuances of such key words as *patronne*. And Suzette Henke was gracious enough to advise me on the final chapter even though it occasionally questions her reading of Woolf's *Mrs Dalloway*.

Anyone familiar with the lectures on *Ulysses* that I made in 2001 for the Teaching Company (which distributes them on CD and DVD) may perceive that in the final chapter I have adapted material from a few of these lectures. My thanks to the company for allowing me to do so.

While writing this book I frequently used the resources of Baker Library at Dartmouth College and of Alderman Library at the University of Virginia, and I thank the staffs of both libraries for their courteous and timely help.

In the late fall of 2011, when I was completing this book, the Bogliasco Foundation granted me a month's residency at its elegant villa on the Ligurian coast near Genoa. With its lovely surroundings and its large, beautifully furnished rooms, the villa is the perfect setting in which to think, read, write, and rewrite. For their exceptionally gracious hospitality I warmly thank the entire staff at the foundation and in particular Ivana Folle, Alessandra Natale, Valeria Soave, and Pasquale Pesce. I also thank my fellow residents for their stimulating company, and, for the recommendations that led to this residency, I am grateful to James Tatum, J. Hillis Miller, Paul Hunter, Robert Fogelin, and W. J. T. Mitchell.

Before I reached Bogliasco, I was the only one who had ever read the entire manuscript. But there every word of it was read by my wife, Nancy Coffey Heffernan, who gave me sound advice on how to cut and reshape each chapter. Once again, as with all my previous books, she has proven to be an ideal reader.

I owe special thanks to Eric Brandt, my editor at Yale University Press, who has warmly supported this project; to his able assistant Erica Hanson; to Lawrence Kenney, who meticulously copyedited the book; to Mary Valencia, who designed it; and to Margie Towery, who compiled the index.

For last-minute help with Pushkin's Russian and the names of Proust's characters I thank, respectively, Barry Scherr and Robert Brawer.

I dedicate this book to the memory of Half and Susanne Zantop, whose warmth and genuine hospitality will never be forgotten by anyone who knew them.

Hospitality and Treachery in Western Literature

INTRODUCTION:
CROSSING THE THRESHOLD

This book considers what hosts, hostesses, and guests do for and to each other in works of literature ranging from Homer's *Odyssey* to Albert Camus's short story "The Guest."

At their best, as most of us know from experience, the pleasures of hospitality approximate the pleasures of love. Few other stimuli can match, let alone surpass, the taste of a good meal in the house of old friends or convivial new ones. Ancient literature pays tribute to such pleasures. In the *Odyssey* hospitality and love quite literally converge when the shipwrecked hero is lavishly entertained by the king and queen of Phaeacia just as their lovely daughter Nausicaa is falling in love with him. Even without an erotic charge, hospitality in the *Odyssey* can poignantly signify devotion. When Odysseus finally reaches his native Ithaca after ten years of fighting in Troy and ten more of voyaging, he has changed so much that he cannot be recognized by even the most loyal of his servants, the swineherd Eumaeus. But since Eumaeus believes that "every stranger and beggar comes from Zeus" (14.57–58 / F 14.66), he feeds and shelters this would-be stranger without hesitation, partly as an act of loving homage to the master he has never forgotten, the man he believes to be still voyaging home.

Yet if hospitality can occasionally furnish something like the pleasures of love, it also resembles love in exposing all of its parties to the perils of intimacy. To fall in love is to give someone the power to break your heart. To ask one or more people into your home, whether to dine at your table, sleep under your roof, or simply converse, is to give them the power to complicate your life right up to the act of taking it. Bizarre as the latter may sound, it is precisely what happened some years ago to two Dartmouth professors at their home in Etna, New Hampshire, just a few miles from my own. About noon on the final Saturday of January 2001, two preppie-looking teenage boys knocked on their door, got in by pretending to be conducting a survey, and then—for the sake of their ATM cards—fatally stabbed both of them.[1] Half and Susanne Zantop paid the ultimate price for their hospitality. If they had not been instinctively welcoming, if they had refused, like others before them, to let two complete strangers into their house, they would almost certainly be alive and well today. What they experienced was something wholly unexpected and yet disturbingly common in the history of literature: hospitality ambushed by treachery.

By this I do not mean that literature offers only a series of cautionary tales on the perils of hospitality. In the *Odyssey* alone, the stories of encounters between hosts and guests range all the way from the cannibalism of Polyphemos to the graciousness of the Phaeacians. Since literature thrives on conflict, since it cannot long endure or sustain the spectacle of perfect contentment, it tends to favor the darker end of this spectrum. But we will also find that it ranges from one end to the other. In doing so, it shows how delicate is the line between loving communion and social friction, how subtly hosts and guests may betray each other without drawing a single drop of blood.

As a theme in literature and a fact of life, hospitality is at once ancient, modern, and ubiquitous. In the book of Genesis, Abraham runs from the doorway of his tent to offer food and water to three strange men who suddenly appear before him and then turn out to be angels (Gen. 18:1–8). In the *Odyssey* Eumaeus offers wine, food, and shelter to the returning Odysseus even though he fails to recognize him. In the penultimate chapter of James Joyce's *Ulysses*, Leopold Bloom ushers Stephen Dedalus into his home, gives him a cup of cocoa, and invites him to become a more or less permanent house guest. Strange as these episodes may seem, they involve something as quotidian and familiar as our very own doorways: the giving and taking of hospitality.

In spite of its ubiquity and its pervasiveness in literature, hospitality has long been slighted by literary theorists and critics. But in his final years Jacques Derrida began to talk and write about it. He observed not only that hospitality is "culture itself,"[2] but also that the very words *host* and *hospitality* drag behind them a tangled etymology and radiate a bewildering complex of meanings.[3] The English word *host* looks as if it came from the Latin word *hostis*, but *hostis* means first of all "stranger" and then "enemy"—whence the English word *hostile*. The word *host* springs not from *hostis* but from its cousin *hospes*, which means first "stranger" and then "guest." From *hospitis*, the genitive of *hospes*, come the words *hospitality* and also *host*, which Derrida nonetheless traces to the Indo-European *hosti-pet-s*, meaning one who has power in the household (*OH* 5).[4] So the Latin roots of *host* and *hospitality* are at least partly entangled with words meaning "stranger" and "enemy." Still more problematic is the Greek word *xenos*. It can mean either "guest" or "host"; it can designate a friend with whom you have a hereditary treaty of hospitality, such as the child of someone whom you once entertained or who once entertained you; it can mean anyone who is entitled to the rights of hospitality simply because he or she is a stranger; or it can denote a complete stranger, a *barbaros*, or foreigner.[5] But in English the word *xenos* seems to leave but a single trace: xenophobia, fear of strangers, which can all too easily turn into virulent hatred of them.

Derrida's theory of "absolute hospitality" would banish this hatred by a kind of decree, by what he calls, *tout court*, "*the law* of hospitality" (*OH* 77, emphasis added). While conventional hospitality is conditional, based on laws of reciprocity and mutual obligation between individuals or groups, absolute hospitality is unconditional. It requires, says Derrida, "that I open up my home . . . to the absolute, anonymous other, and that I give place to them, that I let them come, let them arrive, and take place in the place I offer them, without asking of them either reciprocity (entering into a pact) or even their names."[6] Something close to this kind of hospitality turns up in the Gospel of Luke, where Christ tells the Pharisee who asked him to dine one Sabbath day not to invite anyone who could invite him in return, but only "the poor, maimed, lame, and blind. Then you will be blessed, because they cannot repay you, for you will be repaid at the resurrection of the upright" (Luke 14:12).[7]

Possibly even this formulation would have failed to meet Derrida's standards since Christ assures the host that his generosity will be ultimately repaid. But whether or not hospitality can ever be absolute, whether or not it can ever banish the expectation of repayment, it cannot forestall the possibility of fraud or violence or both. Derrida frankly admits that anyone who offers unconditional hospitality takes a gigantic risk. "Unconditional hospitality," he says, requires "that you give up the mastery of your space, your home, your nation. It is unbearable. . . . For unconditional hospitality to take place you have to accept the risk of the other coming and destroying the place, initiating a revolution, stealing everything, or killing everyone" ("HJR" 71). Spoken in 1999, Derrida's last two words chillingly adumbrate what happened to the Zantops in January 2001. Yet their last act of hospitality was not unconditional. The boys who killed them entered their house only after identifying themselves and posing as dutiful students working on a class project, their pretext for gaining admission. Conditional or unconditional, hospitality can never be purged of risk.

This point was brutally confirmed on September 11, 2001. Less than nine months after the Zantops were killed in their home by unexpected guests, nineteen Middle Eastern men who had legally entered the United States and who had legally boarded four planes at three airports hijacked the planes, flew two of them into the World Trade Center towers in New York, one of them into the Pentagon, and a fourth into a field in Shanksville, Pennsylvania, killing altogether nearly three thousand people. Time has given us the means to see this episode in something like its proper scale. Vicious as the 9/11 hijackers were, they stopped far short of doing everything that the beneficiaries of Derrida's "unconditional hospitality" might have done: destroy the place (our space, our home, our nation), initiate a revolution, steal everything, or kill everyone. While many people felt that everything changed on 9/11, and while the attacks of that day most certainly led to the long wars in Afghanistan and Iraq and a great deal of suffering elsewhere, America did not suddenly lock its doors to all foreign visitors. Not even the wave of xenophobia loosed by the attacks, which prompted immigration officials to seize hundreds of foreign-born residents for trivial infractions, could drown this nation's hospitality. In an article on suicide bombers that appeared soon after 9/11, Joseph Lelyveld wondered "how you could smash terrorist networks in conditions of an open society, which allow them to operate on our ground far more confidently than they ever could on their own" (Lelyveld 79). Whatever happens, our bureaucratic machinery seems inalterably set to extend a welcoming hand. On March 11, 2002, it was reported, "precisely six months after the WTC disaster, Huffman Aviation International, a flight school in Venice, Florida, received notice from the Immigration and Naturalization Service that the two Saudi Arabians who had hijacked and then piloted jetliners into the World Trade Towers of New York— Mohammed Atta and Marwan Alshehhi—had been awarded student visas that had been approved the previous summer" (Eggen and Thompson A13).[8]

We can now see clearly, then, that the attacks of 9/11 fell far short of exemplifying the price to be paid for taking the risk of absolute, unconditional hospitality. Shattering as they were, the attacks took place within the framework of conditions then prevailing for what might be called official hospitality: legal entry to the United States, provision of student visas, authorized access to flight schools, and the right to board commercial airplanes. These conditions could not and did not prevent the treachery that may undermine any act of hospitality, regardless of the law or laws that govern it. Nevertheless, Derrida broached his theory of hospitality—and never disavowed it, even after 9/11—to combat what he saw as the greatest threat to humanity in our time: not terrorism but xenophobia. Nation-states, he wrote, have been treating foreigners, immigrants (documented and undocumented), refugees, the homeless, and stateless persons of all kinds "with unprecedented cruelty" (*Adieu* 64). Deploring "the crimes against hospitality endured by the guests and hostages of our time, incarcerated or expelled day after day, from concentration camp to detention camp, from border to border, close to us or far away from us" (*Adieu* 71), Derrida proposed a radical alternative. Founded on what Emmanuel Levinas has called the "ethics of hospitality," his law of absolute hospitality defies xenophobia by overturning the laws and conventions that govern the admission of strangers to our nation and our homes.[9]

The law of absolute hospitality and the laws of conditional hospitality need each other, Derrida says, because they define each other by opposition and are "thus both contradictory, antinomic, *and* inseparable" (*OH* 81). Absolute hospitality, which is unprompted by any sense of duty and which neither expects nor asks anything of the stranger, not even his name, defines itself precisely by transgressing the laws of conditional hospitality. But I believe the two regimes—the law and the laws—are bound by more than dialectical polarity. In practice they are bound by exposure to risk as well as by the virtual impossibility of banishing all conditions from the act of crossing a threshold.

Consider first a law of hospitality that makes room for terrorists. Shortly after the attacks of 9/11, President George W. Bush told the nations of the world that "if you harbor a terrorist, you're just as guilty as a terrorist" (qtd. Safire 34). This shortly became known as the Bush doctrine. But Taliban leaders defied this doctrine to honor a much older one:

> In refusing to surrender Osama bin Laden to American hands, the Taliban leaders of Afghanistan were following the laws of their Pashtun tribe, which anthropologists consider one of the oldest on earth. Pashtuns live by the Pashtu Wali, or Code of Life. According to this code, the law of *badal* obligates members of a tribe to exact revenge for wrongdoing—like the American attack on other members of the tribe. And the law of *milmasthia* requires tribal members to serve a guest and to give sanctuary to anyone who requests it, even an enemy. Though the host can evict a guest if he creates trouble for the family while he is in the house, the Taliban evidently decided not to do so. (Bragg B5)

Among the Taliban the law of hospitality trumps all other obligations, even the demand to give up someone who had murderously exploited the official hospitality of the United States.[10] Their law has classical as well as tribal precedent. Near the end of Homer's *Iliad*, when Achilles receives as a guest his mortal enemy Priam, the old king is likened to a murderer seeking refuge in a foreign land (*Iliad* 24.480–84). Though the murderer here is Achilles, who has just killed Priam's son Hector, these two dare to behave as host and guest, breaking bread together, sleeping under the same roof, and suspending their enmity for the sake of hospitality. That Osama bin Laden remained alive for nearly ten years after plotting the attacks of 9/11 testifies, among other things, to the power of an ancient law that might almost be construed as absolute in its unrestrictiveness, its openness to "anyone who requests [hospitality], even an enemy." Yet the law that protected bin Laden is not *the* law of hospitality but *a* law, one of many, of the Pashtu Wali. And in obeying this Pashtun law the Taliban leaders risked arousing the wrath of the most powerful nation on earth.[11]

Like the attacks of 9/11, then, the Taliban's treatment of bin Laden suggests that grave risk and transgression, two of the most distinguishing features of absolute hospitality, also vex the workings of conditional hospitality. Treachery, which is always transgressive, presupposes a set of conditions. Consider what is perhaps the founding instance of treacherous hospitality in Western literature: the murder of Agamemnon. Just after returning to his Mycenaean kingdom after ten years of fighting in Troy, he and his men were butchered while feasting as guests at the house of Aigisthus, who had become the lover of Agamemnon's queen and who conspired with her to kill him. Rending the fabric of trust woven by the laws of hospitality as well as by marriage, the murder of the homecoming Agamemnon is so often recalled throughout the *Odyssey*—in steadily more graphic terms—that it burns its way into our minds.[12] The final version of the story, the most graphic of all, is told by the shade of Agamemnon himself to Odysseus, who meets him in Hades while en route to his kingdom in Ithaca and who thereby learns just how dangerous homecoming can be. By Agamemnon's account, its perils rival the worst ordeals of voyaging.

The murder of Agamemnon not only exemplifies the perils of homecoming but also takes its place in a sequence of injury and retaliation that radically reshapes the bedrock condition of hospitality in Homer's world: reciprocity. On one hand, when Eumaeus tells the returning Odysseus, whom he does not recognize, that "every stranger and beggar comes from Zeus" (14.57–58 / F 14.66), he breathes something like the spirit of absolute hospitality. But if Zeus avenges any wrong toward strangers and suppliants, as Odysseus elsewhere tells the monster Polyphemos (9.271), we may infer that Zeus punishes those who treat strangers and suppliants badly and rewards those who treat them well, just as Christ promises to repay us in heaven for entertaining those who cannot repay us on earth. Either way, hospitality prompted by divine authority cannot be absolute in Derrida's sense, for it is conditioned by fear of divine retaliation or desire for ultimate reward. In Odysseus's appeal to Polyphemos it is precisely the threat of divine retaliation that enforces the law of hospitality and makes it conditional.

Retaliation is the dark double of reciprocal giving. In the giant's cave the spirit of benign reciprocity that animates prior scenes of hospitality, such as Telemachus's reception of Mentes/Athene, instantly gives way to the malign reciprocity of injury and revenge, as we will see again in *Beowulf*. More than anything else, this malign revision of hospitable exchange turns the whole story of Odysseus's encounter with Polyphemos into what has been called a grotesque "parody of a hospitality scene" (Reece 126).

Though no other literary host (so far as I know) devours his guests, the hosts and guests of literature repeatedly spurn benign reciprocity in favor of retaliation. This collapse of one into the other exacerbates the problem of formulating, let alone enforcing, any law of hospitality itself, whether absolute or conditional. On the one hand, hospitality presupposes law. Odysseus can imagine no hospitality without justice, which is why he wants to know if the Cyclopes are "violent, savage, [and] lawless" *or* "friendly to strangers, god-fearing men" (9.175–76 / F 9.194–95). Likewise, when Aeneas and his men are blown off course by ferocious winds in the first book of the *Aeneid*, they are dumbfounded to be denied "hospitio . . . harenae," the right to land on the beach.[13] This is the right that Immanuel Kant envisioned when he proposed the law of universal hospitality, meaning "the right of a stranger not to be treated as an enemy when he arrives in the land of another" (Kant, *Perpetual Peace* 320). On the other hand, justice may transcend any particular body of laws.[14] Hospitality itself breeds conflicting laws, as we have seen in the conflict between absolute and conditional versions of it. If Pashtun law requires a tribe "to serve a guest and to give sanctuary to anyone who requests it, even an enemy," must tribal members risk their lives to do so? Or would such a risk make the guest troublesome enough to justify eviction? If Lot in the book of Genesis is willing to sacrifice the virginity of his daughters in order to forestall an attack on his guests, does the law of hospitable protection trump all other obligations, even within the family? In the story of Lot, which I will examine in detail, the relation between a host and his guests becomes not just familial in its intimacy but usurpative, preempting the bonds between a father and his daughters. It also illustrates a problem inherent in Derrida's concept of absolute hospitality, which seems to require that we hold nothing back from anyone who comes to us for help.

What happens when the state comes calling in the form of surveillance, when the uninvited guest is a spy eavesdropping on telephone calls or mining data from e-mails? Derrida answers as follows: "Wherever the 'home' is violated, wherever at any rate a violation is felt as such, you can foresee a privatizing and even familialist reaction, by widening the ethnocentric and nationalist, and thus xenophobic, circle: not directed against the foreigner as such, but, paradoxically against the anonymous technological power (foreign to the language or the religion, as much as to the family and the nation), which threatens, with the 'home,' the traditional conditions of hospitality" (*OH* 53). Here Derrida finds himself compelled to qualify the absoluteness of his absolute hospitality. Having sought to vanquish xenophobia by positing a hospitality of total, undemanding, unquestioning openness to all strangers, he nevertheless sanctions the individual's right to protect his or her private domain from the estranging inquisitiveness of the state. So far from urging us to open ourselves unreservedly to the state or to anyone else, he attacks Kant for demanding that we tell the truth to anyone who asks for it, even to a murderer seeking his would-be victim in our house.[15] In Derrida's opinion, Kant's imperative destroys, along with the right to lie, any right of keeping something to oneself, of

> dissimulating, of resisting the demand for truth, confessions, or public openness. . . . In the name of pure morality, from the point where it becomes law, he introduces the police everywhere, so much and so well that the absolutely internalized police has its eyes and its ears everywhere. . . . And there is also nothing fortuitous, it seems to me, if in [Kant's essay] the privileged example . . . refers to a situation of *hospitality*: should I lie to murderers who come to ask me if the one they want to assassinate is in my house? Kant's response . . . is "yes" [i.e., no], one should speak the truth, even in this case, and thus risk delivering the guest to death, rather than lie. It is better to break with the duty of hospitality rather than break with the absolute duty of veracity." (*OH* 71)

Unlike Kant, Derrida believes that the "absolute duty of veracity" must bow to "the duty of hospitality." He therefore commends Lot for putting "the laws of hospitality above all, in particular the ethical obligations that link him to his relatives and family, first of all his daughters" (*OH* 151). But two things complicate Derrida's argument. One is that Lot does not lie to save his guests; he offers his daughters to a gang of rapists. The other, deeper problem is that Derrida's concept of absolute hospitality is just as hard to sustain as Kant's concept of absolute veracity, or "pure morality." If Lot's action exemplifies absolute hospitality, or the triumph of hospitality over veracity, it nonetheless entails acceptance of rape. And if absolute hospitality requires unconditional openness to all visitors, it cannot remain absolute without authorizing state surveillance, the political invasion of the private domain. In short, as Derrida himself seems to recognize, there is no hospitality that cannot be undermined by treachery, no law or laws of hospitality that can preclude every form of subversion or perversion.[16] Here is the truth, though I stop short of calling it absolute, that Western literature repeatedly affirms.

This literature includes the Old and New Testaments, especially the latter, wherein Christ makes the eternal fate of everyone wholly dependent on our hospitality to strangers. At the Last Judgment, he says, when all nations are divided into the saved and the damned, the saved will be those who housed, fed, and slaked the thirst of strangers, no matter how humble, and thereby accommodated God himself, who will tell them, "in so far as you did it to one of the humblest of these brothers of mine, you did it to me." Conversely, Christ says, God will tell the others that "in so far as you failed to do it for one of these people who are humblest, you failed to do it for me" and will condemn them to everlasting punishment (Matt. 25:34–46). In light of this statement it is scarcely possible to overstate the moral importance of hospitality in the New Testament. In making our response to needy strangers on earth the *sole determinant* of our eternal life, Christ places hospitality at the very center of his teachings. As the pivot point for the starkest of choices, it also plays a crucial role at the Last Supper, when he himself plays host to his apostles and foresees that one of his guests will betray him, turning host into *hostia*, sacrificial victim.

Literature has never tired of reenacting the ways in which hosts and guests betray each other. In Dante's *Inferno* the circle of treachery at the bottom of hell is occupied not only by Judas but also by men who have arranged the murder of their guests, as Fra Alberigo did in 1285 when he invited two of his relatives to a banquet at which they were butchered by his servants. In Shakespeare's *Macbeth* the heinousness of regicide is amplified by its fusion with something equally outrageous: the murder of a guest by his host. In recasting the historical facts about King Duncan, who, according to Holinshed's *Chronicles*, was killed in an ambush near Inverness, Shakespeare makes the violation of hospitality central to his play, which repeatedly invokes the rites and pleasures of conventional hospitality even as it undermines them. Viewed through the lens of hospitality, even the shooting of a bird can be a heinous crime. In Samuel Taylor Coleridge's "Rime of the Ancient Mariner" the mariner and his shipmates welcome an albatross "with great joy and hospitality" when it first appears as the only living thing in an Antarctic world of fog and ice. But after they hail it "as if it had been a Christian soul, / . . . in God's name" and feed it daily for a time, the mariner suddenly and "inhospitably" shoots the bird with his crossbow ("Rime" 63–82), leading all of them into a hell of desolation and thirst that only the mariner survives.

In the fiction of the past two centuries the treachery of hosts and guests grows less violent, more subtle, but also more disturbing. Just as heroism becomes demilitarized and domesticated, treachery learns how to strike without drawing blood. While visiting Dorothea in George Eliot's *Middlemarch*, Will Ladislaw annihilates her husband, his absent host, by simply casting doubts on his scholarship. In Henry James's *Portrait of a Lady*, Isabel Archer is betrayed by those who know just how to manipulate a guest and disempower a hostess. In the final volume of Marcel Proust's *À la recherche du temps perdu*, the Baron de Charlus and his hostess fight a duel of betrayal that ends with the titanically arrogant baron psychically shattered. And in Joyce's radical reimagining of Homer's epic voyager, an urban wanderer survives both Dublin's anti-Semitism and the perils of an Odyssean homecoming without ever resorting to violence. In the "Cyclops" chapter of *Ulysses*, Leopold Bloom fights the bigotry of the citizen with the weapons of language alone. Even when threatened with crucifixion as well as a cracker box, he never actually comes to blows with the citizen or anyone else, and he decisively rejects the idea of taking violent revenge on Blazes Boylan for adulterously bedding Molly. Yet while pacifism is one of the many things he shares with his would-be son, Stephen Dedalus, his hospitality to Stephen will turn out to be motivated by treacherous designs. In spite of his best intentions Bloom will unwittingly try to betray his guest in the name of domesticity.

Hospitality, we shall see, reverses the uncanny. In the words of Friedrich Schelling, the uncanny, or *unheimlich*, "is the name for everything that ought to have remained . . . hidden and secret and has become visible."[17] Amplifying this definition, Sigmund Freud argued that the uncanny springs from the return of the repressed: "nothing new or foreign, but something familiar and old-established in the mind that has been estranged only by the process of repression" ("The 'Uncanny'" 394). While the uncanny thus exposes the threatening strangeness of what has been hidden by custom, familiarization, and domestication, hospitality yearns to domesticate the stranger, to take him in as if he were part of the family, to vanquish and absorb his otherness. Even Derrida's unconditional hospitality depends on the stranger's acquiescence to domestic containment, familiarity, and familial cohabitation, however temporary they may be. And it is precisely this prospect that estranges Dedalus from Bloom, who to Stephen is at once the most gracious and most threatening of hosts.

In works ranging from *Ulysses* and Albert Camus's "The Guest" to the contemporary play called *Omnium Gatherum*, the literature of the twentieth and twenty-first centuries continues to stage the seemingly insoluble problem of domesticating the stranger, absorbing the other in one's home or one's town or one's homeland. But in the United States at least, the word *homeland* has been bolted to *security*, and in the wake of 9/11 public debate about immigration has been largely hijacked by xenophobia. Those who clamor for greater enforcement of the borders, especially of the Mexican border, see illegal immigrants not just as low-wage workers bent on stealing American jobs and overloading public services but also as potential terrorists threatening our lives. Could we allay these fears by admitting Latin American laborers as guest workers here only for a limited time, long enough to do the work most American citizens will not do, such as picking grapes, but not for good? Unfortunately, this formula crumbles as soon as we apply it. Even if it somehow vanquished the fear of being terrorized, it could not ensure that these new guests would not join the estimated eleven million plus immigrants who have come to this country with no invitation and are at all costs determined to stay.[18] At best the phrase *guest worker* is a euphemism for the exploitation of unskilled laborers so desperate to work for a living wage that they will forgo everything else, above all the hope of staying permanently, in order to get it.[19] However benign the intentions behind them, guest worker programs betray the very meaning of the word *guest*.[20]

I do not treat such programs in this book because my subject is literature, more precisely the practice of hospitality in Western literature. At times I invoke the independent history of hospitality, as when I link the New Testament to the Roman law of *hospitium* and Shakespeare's *Macbeth* to the Glencoe massacre of 1692. I also occasionally refer to what has been called the hospitality industry: the business of furnishing food or lodging or both to paying visitors who are typically called guests.[21] But this book is not a history of hospitality and certainly not of the process by which it became a commercial transaction. The hosts and guests who meet one another in the literature I examine are typically bound by ties of reciprocity, as I have explained, but not by any obligation that could be discharged by the payment of a bill.

The sense of obligation bred by traditional hospitality runs too deep for accounting but not for literature, which thrives on peril and paradox, on threats both overt and subtle, on the juxtaposition of extremes. On the one hand, literature offers us moments of hospitality at its most generous, gracious, and self-less, as when Abraham entertains the anonymous angels and Eumaeus receives the would-be beggar Odysseus. But literature also shows how rare and precarious these moments can be: how often and easily the fabric of trust that hospitality weaves can be rent by suspicion, resentment, misunderstanding, and treachery. When globalism promises to flatten the world and leap national boundaries even as terrorism fans the flames of xenophobia, we more than ever need to understand what literature teaches us about the delicate process of receiving a guest or crossing another's threshold. If there is no hospitality without risk, as literature shows again and again, the same could be said of life itself, which for most people would be inconceivable without hospitality. That is why it permeates literature and why I have taken the risk of writing about it.

This book examines the literature of hospitality from Homer to Camus, with a coda on a play written in our own time. Given the ubiquity of my theme, I can hardly exhaust it, and those looking out for lacunae will find them readily enough. A whole book could be written about hospitality in nineteenth-century English fiction, which I have treated in parts of just one chapter.[22] As for the staging of hospitality, which likewise deserves a book, I have largely confined myself to what Shakespeare does with it. Within the past ninety years alone, hospitality and its discontents have been dramatized in plays ranging from George S. Kaufman's and Edna Ferber's *Dinner at Eight* (1932) to Edward Albee's *Who's Afraid of Virginia Woolf?* (1962), John Guare's *Six Degrees of Separation* (1990), Yasmina Reza's *God of Carnage* (2006–9), and, most recently, Ayad Akhtar's Pulitzer Prize–winning *Disgraced* (2012). Hosts and guests have also menaced each other in films ranging from Buster Keaton's *Our Hospitality* (1923) to Lars von Trier's *Dogville* (2003).[23] Besides dealing with works such as these, a comprehensive treatment of hospitality in modern literature, broadly considered, would also have to reckon with its place in the modern library of etiquette manuals, which begin at least as early as Mary Elizabeth Wilson Sherwood's *Etiquette, The American Code of Manners* (1884) and extend through the works of such *arbitri morum* as Emily Post and Amy Vanderbilt to the books of Judith Martin, the superlatively wise and witty Miss Manners of our time.

I say all this in part to justify the length of this book. Though its topic is far too big for a single volume, I have tried to show how deeply and widely the theme of hospitality permeates the history of Western literature, how each new work of literature reconceives and restages the conflict between hospitality and treachery, and, finally, how inexhaustible the topic is.

This book aims to reach a wide variety of readers. Given the range of literary works I consider, I could not write for specialists in any one of them or in the period it exemplifies, and while I cite a number of critics I can hardly claim to have grappled with all available criticism on each of the works I treat. Nevertheless, since my topic has been largely neglected by literary critics and scholars, I hope that even specialists may be drawn by the light it sheds on their respective fields. Also, since I cannot presume specialized knowledge of any text, I have tried to make each of them as accessible as the concept of hospitality itself. During the years I have spent working on this book I have been pleasantly surprised by the quickened reaction of many people, in and out of the academy, to whom I have mentioned its topic. Since nearly everyone has firsthand experience of hospitality and its discontents, they tell me they would like to know more. Very well, then, here is my answer.

CLASSICAL HOSPITALITY

The final book of Homer's *Iliad* contains one of the most extraordinary scenes of hospitality ever written. When Priam visits the Greek camp to ransom the body of Hector, he seeks hospitality from his son's killer. He not only clasps the knees of Achilles but kisses the very hands that took Hector's life, "the man-killing hands / that had slaughtered Priam's many sons in battle" (*Iliad* 24.478–80 / F 24.560–62).[1] Yet as Priam enters the tent of Achilles, he is himself compared to a killer: a murderer seeking refuge in a foreign land from a wealthy lord who is amazed to receive him (24.480–84). Though Priam has killed no one, his desperation recalls that of Patroclus, who, long before this time, came as a boy to the house of Achilles' father after thoughtlessly killing the son of Amphidamas (23.86–87). Furthermore, although Achilles and Priam are mortal enemies, grief makes them sharers in hospitality. With courageous sympathy they dare to behave as host and guest, breaking bread together and sleeping under the same roof. During the eleven-day period of mourning and burial for Hector, Achilles pledges even to defend the Trojan king as a host defends his guests:

> "All will be done, old Priam, as you command.
> I will hold our attack as long as you require."
> With that he clasped the old king by the wrist,
> by the right hand, to free his heart from fear.
> (24.669–72 / F 24.786–89)

In Western literature, this is the primordial instance of a principle that survives to this very day in Arab culture: since hospitality requires a suspension of violence, a man must protect anyone who becomes his guest—even his mortal enemy.[2] In taking Priam's right hand, a sign of hospitality that repeatedly recurs in Virgil's *Aeneid*, Achilles briefly restores the bonds of hospitality that Paris long before severed by abducting Helen from her husband Menelaus when he was their guest. Though Achilles and Priam forge nothing like a peace treaty between their respective peoples, who are fated to fight to the immolation of Troy, they nonetheless achieve a temporary cease-fire sanctioned by the laws of hospitality. Hospitality thus seems to furnish a respite from war, a moment of sympathy which, however fleetingly, transcends the murderous hatred and bitter resentment of the other, the stranger, the alien, the enemy.

Nevertheless, classical hospitality entails three kinds of peril. First of all, whenever hosts or guests mistreat or offend one another, the system of benign reciprocity that governs hospitality as an exchange of benefits can all too readily turn into its dark double, retaliation. Second, hospitality that turns seductive can trap a traveler and detain him indefinitely, making him (he is always male) forget his home or his mission or both. Third, the very act of eating together, which might seem to epitomize the communal spirit of hospitality, can be riven by violence, debased by cannibalism, or otherwise haunted by the specter of mortality.

RECIPROCITY AND RETALIATION

Classical hospitality sometimes approximates Derrida's absolute hospitality. In the *Iliad* feasting involves men who know and owe each other for services rendered or who belong to a circle of feasting companions.[3] In the *Odyssey* hospitality is often blind, for the master of a household is expected to feed and entertain a stranger before even asking him who he is, that is, before learning anything about the stranger's claims on the host's hospitality. Just as Telemachus feeds Athene, who is disguised as Mentes, before knowing anything about him or what he wants (1.122–24), Nestor prompts both Telemachus and his friend Peisistratos to eat and drink heartily before asking them who they are and whether they are traders or piratical "sea-wolves raiding at will, who will risk their lives / to plunder other men" (3.71–74 / F 3.79–83).

The latter prospect reveals the disturbing consequences of blind hospitality. As Steve Reece observes, "A proper host like Nestor was obliged to offer hospitality to his guests regardless of who they were, even to pirates" (Reece 63). Yet this obligation might be construed as something driven by a general or even universal principle of reciprocity. When Telemachus and Peisistratos reach the palace of Menelaus, the king's henchman, Eteoneus, stiffly asks the king if the two should be admitted. Exasperated with the man, Menelaus says, "Just think of all the hospitality we enjoyed / at the hands of other men before we made it home" (4.33–36 / F 4.38–39). Menelaus posits something like the golden rule: as others have fed us, we should feed them, regardless of who those others are. In spite of its occasional blindness, therefore, the hospitality practiced in the *Odyssey* entails a history of prior benefits directly or indirectly exchanged between host and guest, or the expectation that a guest will repay his host. Nestor feeds Telemachus and Peisistratos without knowing who they are, but as soon as he learns that Telemachus is "the dear son of Odysseus," whom Nestor warmly recalls as a master strategist of war (3.120–22), he insists that they sleep in his palace (3.352–55). Likewise, Odysseus himself is lavishly fed by the Phaeacians, who owe him nothing for past favors, but he begins his long after-dinner story by giving his name to his royal host, King Alcinous,

> so you may know it well and I in times to come,
> if I can escape the fatal day, will be your sworn host,
> your sworn friend, though my home is far from here.
>   (9.16–18 / F 9.17–20)[4]

A few centuries after Homer's *Odyssey*, the reciprocal structure of ancient Greek hospitality was strikingly dramatized in Euripides' *Alcestis*, first produced in 438 BC. Behind the play stands a history of hospitality. When Apollo was exiled from Olympus for nine years, he spent them with Admetus, king of Pherae in the land of Thessaly, who treated him so well that Apollo obtained for him, by way of recompense, a respite from death. But though Apollo persuaded the Fates to let Admetus live beyond his allotted time, the king could do so only on condition that someone else take his place when Death came for him. In other words, the exchange of hospitality for extended life actually required an exchange of one life for another.

When the play begins, Queen Alcestis is near death because she has offered to die in place of her husband. But on her deathbed she too asks a recompense: Admetus must never remarry. And by way of further recompense Admetus vows to spend the rest of his life in mourning and to renounce the hospitality for which he has been so well known: no more "revelry and entertainment," no more flowers and music, no more sounds of the flute and lute (ll. 343–46).

Yet he forgets his promise as soon as Heracles arrives at the palace. Though he does not know that Heracles has come (as Apollo earlier predicted) to wrest Alcestis from the clutches of Death, he feels bound to receive and thereby repay a man who once entertained him. When asked how he can possibly entertain a guest while his wife is dying, he says he cannot bear to be "inhospitable" to one who is not only his best friend but also his "host / whenever I go to Argos, which is a thirsty place" (ll. 556, 559–60). For Admetus, then, the duty to repay hospitality trumps even his vow of perpetual mourning.[5] Pretending that he and his servants are all mourning some strange woman, he orders his servants to welcome Heracles and say nothing about the death of their queen.[6]

Admetus's order shortly proves too much for his servants to bear. Incensed by Heracles' drunkenness and wild singing as well as by his insistence that they shed their gloom, one servant blurts out the truth—whereupon Heracles resolves to save Alcestis so as to "pay Admetus all the kindness that I owe" (l. 842). In recompense for what this "hospitable man" (l. 830) has done for him under such painful conditions, Heracles saves her in a way that reaffirms the value of hospitality. When he presents the king with a veiled young woman whom he claims to have won as a prize and whom he asks Admetus to keep as a servant, Admetus balks. Aghast at the idea that this strange woman should somehow replace his wife, whom she resembles and whose very bed she might enter, he tells Heracles to take her away. But when Heracles insists that the king take her by the hand, he does so, and just as Heracles removes her veil to reveal the living Alcestis, he tells Admetus, "Some day / you will say the son of Zeus came as your generous guest" (ll. 1119–20). Finally, after telling the king to lead her in, Heracles says, "For the rest of time, / Admetus, be just. Treat your guests as they deserve" (ll. 1147–48).

From before its beginning to its very end, then, this play makes hospitality virtually synonymous with reciprocity. Apollo prolongs the life of Admetus because the Thessalian king once entertained him for years; Admetus feels bound to receive Heracles, even in a house of mourning, because Heracles has entertained him in Argos; and Heracles restores the life of Alcestis because this son of Zeus is a "generous guest" who knows how to recompense his host. The sequence of hospitality and reciprocation here is enriched and complicated by an exchange of sacrifices, or proffered sacrifices. Having seen Alcestis give up her own life to save his, Admetus vows to give up entertaining, which he seems to love almost as much as life itself. But the guest he feels bound to receive and for whom he thereby breaks his vow repays his hospitality by reviving his wife and thereby reaffirming the value of hospitality, of a "good man's welcome to [his] guests."

Besides dramatizing the fundamentally reciprocal structure of hospitality, *Alcestis* ties it firmly to the gods. In seeking to show Admetus that "the son of Zeus is a grateful guest," Heracles implicitly reminds us that Zeus himself is the god of guests, protector of their right to hospitality. But in the *Odyssey* the gods themselves can be dangerous, turning hospitable reciprocity into brutal retaliation. Just after the Phaeacians send Odysseus off with gifts and have him swiftly rowed back to Ithaca, their ship is literally petrified while returning to its own port. It is turned to stone by Poseidon, god of the sea, because he resents the Phaeacians for conveying all men "without hurt" across his realm (13.172–74). By no coincidence, Poseidon causes nearly all the sufferings of Odysseus during his ten-year voyage home from Troy, and since these sufferings are divine punishment for Odysseus's blinding of Polyphemos, his monstrous host, they exemplify the retaliation that strikes by turns both the hosts and guests of the poem.

The *Odyssey* as a whole culminates in a sequence of reciprocity and retaliation. Near the end of the poem, the old swineherd Eumaeus warmly receives a man whom he takes for a stranger but who is actually his old master Odysseus estranged by all he has suffered in twenty years of fighting and voyaging. Sharing Odysseus's belief that "every stranger and beggar comes from Zeus" (14.57–58 / F 14.66) and imagining Odysseus himself as a wanderer needing substance (14.42–43), Eumaeus vicariously entertains his long-absent master, the generous source of "goods that a kind lord will give a household hand / who labors for him, hard" (14.62–63 / F 14.74–75). Yet just as the moment of peace so remarkably achieved by Achilles' hosting of Priam cannot erase the memory of war or forestall the prospect of still more fighting and dying, Eumaeus's touching eagerness to treat a stranger as his guest cannot forestall the violence of what Odysseus must do to reclaim his palace and his wife: kill the suitors who have besieged her in his absence, slaughter the would-be guests who have grossly abused his hospitality by devouring his substance and ravishing his serving women, and thereby gain vengeance on them all.

Like Achilles' reception of Priam, Eumaeus's heartfelt reception of Odysseus seems a respite from hatred and violence. Yet the very words of Eumaeus hold the seeds of retaliation. When Eumaeus says that "every stranger and beggar comes from Zeus" he reminds us of what we have learned already, which is that Zeus *Xenios* is god and protector of guests. If all strangers and beggars are sacred to Zeus, one might infer that Zeus will repay or at least look kindly upon anyone who treats them well.[7] But besides protecting the rights of guests, Zeus avenges any wrongs done to them. On first meeting the giant Cyclops who is called Polyphemos, Odysseus says,

> "Respect the gods, my friend. We're suppliants—at your mercy!
> Zeus of the Strangers guards all guests and suppliants:
> Strangers are sacred—Zeus will avenge their rights!"
> (9.269–71 / F 9.303–5)[8]

Here the polytropic Odysseus—the man of many turns—makes a two-sided appeal for hospitality. In the name of Zeus *Xenios* he begs and threatens at once, asking for gifts and promising divine vengeance if he does not get them: a high-stakes version of trick or treat. This ostensibly pious appeal for help entails a kind of reciprocity quite different from what the poem has shown before in Telemachus's visits to Nestor and Menelaus. The spirit of benign reciprocity that drives these earlier scenes of hospitality now gives way to the malign reciprocity of injury and revenge, which goes hand in hand with a determination to enforce the law of hospitality.[9]

Ironically enough, however, Odysseus expects to receive hospitality even while breaking its rules. When he and his men enter the giant's cave after finding it unoccupied, they violate the rule that requires a guest to wait for an invitation before crossing the threshold of a would-be host (Reece 15). They also build a fire, make sacrifice, and help themselves to the cheeses they find, acting a little like the suitors devouring Odysseus's own goods in his absence. Even though Odysseus will not let his men steal the giant's livestock and sail away, even though he insists on waiting for the giant's return to see "what gifts he'd give" (9.229 / F 9.258) beyond what they have already taken, the very act of occupying the cave shows reckless presumption.[10] It is not the action of a prudent or considerate guest.

Yet if Odysseus bends the rules of hospitality, the giant openly defies them, goading his guest into retaliation. Odysseus not only knows the rules of hospitality and remembers them throughout his ordeal; he also knows how to repay the treachery of a host. As Homerists have long known, the story of Polyphemos combines at least two widely distributed folktales about a hero's encounter with an ogre, but not one of the more than two hundred other versions of these tales refers to hospitality (Reece 126). Homer foregrounds it. Odysseus visits the land of the Cyclopes precisely to learn whether they are savage or hospitable, and in telling the story of Polyphemos to the Phaeacians he highlights the savagery and violence of the giant by framing them within the conventions of hospitality. In doing so, as I have already noted, he creates what Reece calls a grotesque "parody of a hospitality scene" (Reece 126).

Central to this parody is the question of identity, which is always at stake in the *Odyssey* whenever a stranger is entertained. First of all, as soon as the giant returns to his cave and discovers the men inside it, he blocks the exit with a vast boulder, turning his unexpected guests into prisoners.[11] Then, after silently milking his sheep and goats, he asks the men who they are and where they have come from. The content of his question is perfectly proper, for it echoes verbatim the question Nestor puts to Telemachus, quoted above (3.71–74). But in asking his visitors to identify themselves *before* he has welcomed, entertained, and fed them, he unwittingly breaks one of the first laws of Greek hospitality, which requires the deferral of interrogation. Derrida overlooks this point. When he writes that absolute hospitality asks nothing of the visitor, not even his name, he forgets that this is itself a convention of hospitality in Homer's world, where the proper host asks nothing until the guest has been graciously received. Only then is he asked for his name, which is not only a "countergift for a host's hospitality" (Reece 27) but also a promissory note for reciprocal hospitality to come.

Rather than giving his name to Polyphemos, who forfeits all claim to countergifts by eating two of his guests each night, Odysseus calls himself *Outis*, "nobody," as part of a scheme to outwit the monster.[12] But cunning does not keep Odysseus from being reckless. Even after he and his men have cleverly escaped from the cave and rowed out to sea, he thoughtlessly endangers them all by taunting the giant and at the same time casting himself as an avenger. Reminding the monster that Zeus punishes those who mistreat their guests, he implicitly defines himself as the nameless, invisible agent of divine vengeance:

> Your filthy crimes
> came down on your own head, you shameless cannibal,
> daring to eat your guests in your own house—
> so Zeus and the other gods have paid you back!
> (9.478–79 / F 9.533–36)

If Zeus protects guests and strangers, Odysseus might well feel that Polyphemos has been justly punished for devouring his guests. But in implicitly defining himself as the nameless agent of divine vengeance, Odysseus makes himself the target of Polyphemos, who desperately seeks his own vengeance and who, though he cannot see Odysseus, can readily track the sound of his voice. Ironically, Odysseus himself is blind to the danger here: not just the immediate threat of being struck but the long-term price to be paid for exposing his identity to a host who will use it against him, thereby proving that he too can play the game of vengeance. Even after the monster hurls a huge rock into the sea ahead of them and drives their ship back toward the shore, even after they manage to thrust off again and row through the breakers, Odysseus insists on leaving his calling card. He takes full credit for blinding the giant, sharing none with the gods or even with the men who helped him do it. In this transaction, then, a conventional ritual of hospitable exchange—giving one's name to one's host—becomes a vindictive taunt:

> Cyclops—
> if any man on the face of the earth should ask you
> who blinded you, shamed you so—say Odysseus,
> raider of cities, *he* gouged out your eye,
> Laertes' son who makes his home in Ithaca!
> (9.502–5 / F 9.558–62)

Rejoicing in vengeance, boasting of what he has done to Polyphemos's eye, Odysseus blinds himself to the prospect of retaliation. If Zeus avenges all injuries done to suppliants and strangers, will nothing happen to a guest who blinds his host? Not if the giant can help it. After trying in vain to lure the Greeks back with the treacherous promise of another "guest gift" (9.517 / F 9.574) and a prayer to his father Poseidon for their safe passage home, the giant turns the prayer into a curse. He begs Poseidon to ensure that Odysseus never gets home or at best reaches it alone, with all his shipmates lost, "and let him find a world of pain at home!" (9.531–35 / F 9.588–95).

By a final irony, the stone the giant throws to punctuate this curse—a stone far bigger than the first—falls just behind the Ithacans' ship and drives them forward to the island where their companions await them. But if Odysseus twice dodges a boulder, he will nonetheless pay a gigantic price for the momentary, self-indulgent thrill of trumpeting his name to the giant. After losing all his men and his ship and suffering excruciating delays, he will come home to find in his house something like what Polyphemos finds in his cave: strangers bent on devouring his food and attacking their long-absent host.

In taking a terrible vengeance upon these guests, Odysseus rewrites the story of another homecoming warrior, Agamemnon. Having survived all the perils of fighting and voyaging, Agamemnon deserved to be welcomed and entertained like a distinguished guest, like the guest-stranger (*xenos*) that the long-absent Odysseus becomes when he stands, not yet recognized, before his wife Penelope (19.253). But Agamemnon's end poisons the very idea of homecoming. To see just how, as well as how often, Homer tells the story of Agamemnon's end is to see how he makes it unforgettable.

In the council of the gods that begins the narrative of the *Odyssey* we first hear the story from Zeus, who mentions the price Aegisthus paid for marrying Clytemnestra and killing her homecoming husband. In thus defying the will of the gods, who warned him against both deeds, Aegisthus drove Agamemnon's son Orestes to take his revenge. Yet the story of Aegisthus encloses the story of Agamemnon's end, and that story serves as a cautionary tale to any homecoming traveler who might expect to be welcomed like a special guest. For it is precisely *to* travelers that the story is later retold: by Nestor to Telemachus, who has set out to learn from his father's old war comrades what they know of him; by Menelaus, passing on to Telemachus what he has learned from Proteus, the old man of the sea; and finally by the shade of Agamemnon himself when Odysseus meets him in the underworld.

As we move from one version to the next, as we hear the story from Nestor (3.193–98), from Menelaus (4.521–37), and finally from the shade of Agamemnon

(11.409–26), his death grows ever more horrible. The final and most authentic version, Agamemnon's own account of his death, plainly shows that this home-coming feast exemplified hospitality at its most treacherous. Whereas Menelaus says that Aegisthus ushered Agamemnon into a banquet and killed him there, Agamemnon plainly declares that Aegisthus "invited me to his palace" (11.411 / F 11.460), and the description of the butchered bodies grotesquely mingles food and gore: mixing bowl, loaded tables, sprawling bodies, and blood streaming over the floor.[13]

Dreadful as this murder is, to look beyond or rather behind what we learn about it from the *Odyssey* is to see that it too takes its place in a sequence of injury and retaliation and ultimately springs from a still more ghastly crime against hospitality. From Aeschylus's *Agamemnon* (though not from Homer) we learn that the Mycenaean king infuriated his wife by killing their daughter Iphigenia—sacrificing her at Aulis to gain fair winds for the Greek fleet's voyage to Troy. Besides sacrificing his daughter, Agamemnon inherited the sin of his father or (in some versions) grandfather Atreus, who served his brother and rival Thyestes a dish of exquisite cruelty: the diced bodies of his children, which he unwittingly consumed. On learning what he had done Thyestes cursed the house of Atreus and fled the kingdom with his surviving son Aegisthus. In this light, Aegisthus's murder of Agamemnon at a feast becomes an act of revenge for the gruesomely treacherous hospitality of Agamemnon's forebear. In turn, as we shall see, Odysseus's slaughter of the suitors obliquely avenges the slaughter of Agamemnon even while directly avenging their abuse of his household. Insult and retaliation thus take the place of hospitable exchange.

Beyond taking its place in a sequence of injury and retaliation, however, Agamemnon's picture of himself as a man turned into bloody meat while he dines holds special meaning for Odysseus. In saying that Aegisthus cut him down "as a man cuts down some ox at the trough!" (11.412 / F 11.461), Agamemnon echoes what Proteus told Menelaus in book 4 (535 / F 602); but in saying that Aegisthus and Clytemnestra slaughtered him and his companions "just like white-tusked boars . . . for a wedding, banquet, or groaning public feast" (11.419–20 / F 11.468–70), Agamemnon unwittingly compares the murderous pair to the giant Polyphemos, who not only killed but devoured several of Odysseus's companions, literally turning them into food. This is just one of several points at which the stories of Agamemnon and Odysseus converge. Agamemnon himself warns Odysseus to beware of his wife, and though Agamemnon promptly admits that Penelope is too good to murder him, the story of what Aegisthus did to Agamemnon prefigures what awaits Odysseus in Ithaca. Already pressing his wife to marry one of them and literally devouring his livestock, the suitors gathered in his house would murder him if they caught him returning.

Odysseus's final slaughter of the suitors, therefore, is first of all a preemptive strike against those bent on murdering him and a fittingly treacherous response to their flagrant abuse of his hospitality. In presuming to devour his goods and appropriate his wife, they usurp his role as master and host even as they blindly take him for no more than a beggar when he returns in the guise of one: a beggar to be scorned and struck with a footstool when he asks Antinous for food (17.460–63) and mockingly pelted with the "guest-gift" (*xenios*) of an ox hoof flung at his head (20.296–300). Worse still, the suitors are ready to reenact the crime of Aegisthus and Clytemnestra. Self-appointed hosts in the palace of Odysseus, they would not hesitate to kill him at his own table once they recognized him or once he revealed his identity, as a guest was traditionally expected to do after being welcomed and fed. But the would-be beggar reveals his true identity in the very act of stringing the great bow of Odysseus and turning it into a weapon of vengeance. He not only takes vengeance for what the suitors have done to him and his wife and his household but also strikes a retaliatory blow on behalf of all returning travelers who, like Agamemnon, might be treacherously invited to a feast of blood. Having strung the great bow, Odysseus catches Antinous at the very moment when, with no thought of danger or death, he is lifting to his lips a fine two-handled gold goblet of wine; when an arrow driven straight through his neck makes blood spurt from his nostrils, he drops the cup, kicks away the table, and "food shower[s] across the floor, / the bread and meats in a swirl of bloody filth" (22.14–21). This vivid picture of spilled wine, spurting blood, and scattered food plainly recalls what Agamemnon told Odysseus in Hades. If reciprocity is the essence of Homeric hospitality, the treacherous abuse of hospitality can be reciprocated only by retaliation.

SEDUCTIVE HOSPITALITY: CIRCE, CALYPSO, DIDO

As an epic of hospitality, the *Odyssey* tells how a homecoming warrior tests his mettle and identity against a series of hosts ranging from the man-eating Polyphemos to Alcinous and Arete, the impeccably gracious king and queen of Phaeacia. Given the obvious difference between these two kinds of hosts, it is tempting to infer that they are polar opposites: either brutally murderous or graciously receptive. But between these two extremes, the hospitality granted to epic travelers can be dangerously seductive. Consider how Circe entertains her guests. When Odysseus, with the aid of Hermes, foils the magic that would have turned him into a beast, she promptly draws him into her "luxurious bed," and after she restores his men to their true forms (from the pigs she has made of them) they all spend a whole year feasting and drinking with her (10.480–86 / F 10.529–35). Much more than bestializing metamorphosis, this kind of hospitality subtly endangers her guests. Just as the drugged wine that Circe gives to Odysseus's men makes them forget their homes as well as turning them into pigs, the charms of this enchanting hostess make Odysseus himself forget his home — until his men tell him that he must leave if he hopes to see his land and house ever again.

He is very differently treated by the Phaeacians at the last stop on his long journey home. Since these people actually speed him on his way after welcoming him with great kindness, their hospitality seems altogether benign. After seeing that he is bathed, lavishly fed, entertained, and comfortably bedded, they give him clothing, precious gifts of bronze and gold, and swift conveyance home by means of a ship that is rowed while he sleeps. In so doing they answer the prayer he makes in his very first speech to Queen Arete, when he clasps her knees as a suppliant and asks only for "rapid convoy home / to my own native land" (7.151–52 / F 7.179–80).

Yet for all the graciousness of their hospitality, the Phaeacians pose a threat that Odysseus links with the captivating charms of Calypso. As he explains when Queen Arete asks who gave him the mantle and tunic he wears, he landed on Calypso's isle under circumstances very like those that brought him to the Phaeacian island of Scheria: shipwrecked, alone, and exhausted after days in the water.[14] What he says of Calypso could also be said of the Phaeacian princess Nausicaa, for like Calypso she welcomed Odysseus, cared for him, and gave him clothing (7.255–96). No matter how hospitable these gestures may seem, anything that reminds Odysseus of Calypso must pain him. Since Calypso made him her prisoner without ever winning his heart, he wept with impatience for seven years, drenching the very clothes she gave him (7.259–60). He tells this poignant story right after twice begging, first of Arete, then of King Alcinous, that they speed him home (7.151–52). It may seem captious to fault Alcinous, for Odysseus himself admits that he must eat before he does anything else, and in response to his second request — that he be launched homeward "at the first light of day" (7.222 / F 7.257) — the king promises conveyance "tomorrow" (i.e., one day later) by means of his highly accomplished oarsmen (7.318–28). But just before saying this the king wishes out loud, in what is really a prayer to the gods, that the stranger could marry his daughter and remain in Scheria. He even offers the stranger a house and great wealth. So while firmly refusing to hold the stranger against his will, he obviously wants him to stay.

It is hardly surprising that Odysseus does not even acknowledge the king's offer. Behind its generosity lurks the threat of yet another entrapment, yet another obstacle to his return, yet another temptation to forget his identity as king of Ithaca and husband of Penelope. But the charms of Nausicaa can allay his impatience no more than the charms of Circe or Calypso. When the princess bids him farewell and asks him to remember that she saved his life, he prays first that Zeus may grant him a return to his home and only then pledges to pray to her there (8.466–68). Not even the pleasures of feasting can check his impatience to leave. Banqueting and listening to the song of the bard, he says at one point, "is the best that life can offer" (9.5–11 / F 9.5–11). But this statement is merely a prelude to the long story of his "bitter pains" (9.12 / F 9.12), a story he tells precisely to answer Alcinous's question about why he has been weeping (8.577–79 / F 8.647–48). In other words, he must review and relive the entire ordeal of his travels before he can be on his way. Only after he finishes his long story and the night gives way to another dawn (13.18–19), a full day after his ship was ready to go, does he board it for the voyage to Ithaca.

Seductive hospitality in the *Odyssey*, however, is chiefly something offered to the hero by supernatural women, Circe and Calypso. In the *Aeneid* these two are reborn within a mortal woman, Dido, who is herself subject to the manipulation of the gods, or rather goddesses, as well as to the irrepressible yearnings of her all-too-human heart. In receiving the shipwrecked Aeneas and his men, Dido combines the graciousness and generosity of the Phaeacians with the allure of Homer's two enchantresses, but even though she does all she can to detain her guest, she is finally made to seem much less the agent of treachery than its victim. Unlike Circe and Calypso, who each entrap Odysseus for a time without ever abandoning themselves to him, Dido is fatally consumed by her passion for Aeneas.

At first she seems the reembodiment of Phaeacian hospitality. As soon as she learns that Trojans have been shipwrecked on her shores, she invites to her palace all the Trojans she finds in her temple and holds a luxurious banquet for both Trojans and Tyrians, her own people. In the midst of the feast she offers a toast that seems to epitomize hospitality at its most inclusive and respectful, asking Jupiter, who gives "laws . . . to hosts and guests" (hospitibus . . . jura), to make this day joyous for Tyrians and Trojans alike and memorable for their descendants (1.731–35).[15] Dido seems hospitality personified. If her overzealous frontier guards have offended the god of guests by mistreating the Trojan sailors, as Ilioneus tells her (1.539–43), her wholehearted warmth and generosity now make amends for their dereliction. Who could fault her or mistrust her?

This would-be rhetorical question can be answered in just four words: anyone who distrusts Juno. Besides being the patron deity of Carthage, which is even now building a temple to her, Juno is the implacable enemy of the Trojans, as we learn from the opening lines of the poem.[16] Just as Poseidon makes Odysseus wander for years, Juno unrelentingly keeps Aeneas and his men at sea, and in Juno's hands even hospitality can be menacing. As Venus tells Cupid, she fears what may come of "Junonian hospitality" (Junonia . . . hospitia, 1.671–72) as Dido holds and detains Aeneas with stroking words ("tenet . . . blandisque moratur / vocibus," 1.670–71). As the goddess of love, Venus knows how easily a traveler may be led astray or led to stay by a seductive woman, especially one devoted to Juno. In voicing her fear of Junonian hospitality, Venus echoes what Laocoon, the Trojan priest of Neptune, says of the gigantic wooden horse left by the Greeks just outside the walls of Troy: "I fear the Greeks, even when bearing gifts" (Timeo Danaos, et dona ferentes, 2.49).[17]

Because it instantly evokes the episode in which a *hostis* (enemy) treacherously masquerades as an appreciative *hospes* (guest), this line is probably the most famous of all in the story that Aeneas tells Dido about the Trojan war. The gift of the horse was the brainchild of Ulysses, and the Trojans were led to accept it by the duplicity of Sinon alone, with no intervention from the gods. But to read the story of Aeneas and Dido in light of the wooden horse is to see how the gods themselves turn the rites of hospitality into a duel of seduction. Since Junonian hospitality calls for Dido's stroking words to detain Aeneas, Venus fashions Cupid into something like a wooden horse, bearer of dangerous *dona*. Just before Venus talks to Cupid, Aeneas asks Achates to fetch Aeneas's son Ascanius and also, as gifts for Dido, two precious relics of Troy: a robe embroidered with gold figures and a veil woven with acanthus flowers. But these lovely garments are tainted. Made in Greece, they were both worn by Helen when she left Mycenae and her husband Menelaus to sail for Troy and her "inconcessos . . . hymenaeos" (1.643–51), her adulterous union with Paris. Now these garments play their part in promoting a new kind of adultery. To keep Juno from turning Dido against Aeneas, Venus tells Cupid to impersonate Ascanius in bearing Aeneas's gifts to the queen and at the same time to inflame the queen with love for her guest, making her forget her dead husband, Sychaeus. Before Juno can act, says Venus, "I plan to trap the queen with trickery [dolis] and bind her with flame [flamma]" (1.673).

It is scarcely possible to overstate the resonance of *dolis* and *flamma*, trickery and flame. Laocoon says of the wooden horse, "Do you think any / treats from the Greeks can come without tricks?" (ulla putatis / dona carere dolis Danaum, 2.42–44).[18] Just as the Greeks used a would-be gift horse to invade Troy and set it on fire, Venus uses Cupid in disguise to deliver gifts that will help ignite a blaze of lust: a passion so fiery it will end up leaving Dido literally in the flames of her funeral pyre, the *flammis* in which the *moenia* (walls) of Carthage glow as Aeneas looks back on the city from his departing ship (5.1–4). That final view of Carthage in turn recalls Aeneas's picture of his native city on its fiery deathbed: "Then it seemed to me that all Ilium was sinking into the flames" (Tum vero omne mihi visum considere in ignis / Ilium, 2.624).[19]

The first book of the *Aeneid*, then, marks Dido as a woman doomed to immolation, like Troy, by the treachery of a would-be *hospes*.[20] Aeneas's intentions are anything but treacherous, especially in his capacity as a guest. We have no reason to doubt his sincerity when he tells Dido that he cannot fittingly thank her for her hospitality and that wherever he goes he will always praise and honor her for it (1.600–610). Regardless of his own intentions, however, he cannot help but serve those of Venus, who, with Cupid acting as her irresistible aphrodisiac, does everything possible to rouse Dido's desire for him. Though Dido has firmly vowed, as we later learn, never to take a second husband (4.15–18), Cupid knows how to make her forget the first "little by little" (paulatim) and replace him "with a living love" (vivo . . . amore) (1.720–22).

Thus aroused, Dido is the perfect audience for Aeneas's story of the fall of Troy, which is enclosed within a story of seductive hospitality. Aeneas tells the story at a banquet given by Dido and specifically in response to her request for it. Having drunk deep of desire for him ("longum . . . bibebat amorem," 1.749) and having repeatedly plied him with questions about Priam, Hector, and the Greek warriors, she finally asks her guest, whom she calls "hospes," for the whole story of "the treachery of the Greeks" (insidias . . . Danaum) and the sufferings of the Trojans (1.753–55). In this pregnant passage the words *hospes* and *insidias* jostle each other like unborn twins writhing in the womb. Embedded in a story of hospitality betrayed, of a guest who unwittingly but also insidiously rouses the passion of his hostess, Aeneas's account of the treachery of the Greeks may well be read as a story of insidious guests, *hostes* masquerading as *hospites*, strangers whose would-be gift to the city turns out to be the ancient forerunner of the battlefield tank.[21]

The interwoven stories of Dido's passion and the fall of Troy both radiate fire. On the night of the banquet the hidden fire Cupid breathes into Dido makes her burn with gazing ("ardescit . . . tuendo") on the boy and his gifts (1.713–14). In Aeneas's story of Greek treachery, fire becomes literal, culminating in his vision of the whole city sinking into flames (2.624–25).[22] In response to this narrative Dido burns again with a hidden fire ("caeco . . igni") in the very first lines of book 4 (4.1–2); later on, her body feeds the flames of the funeral pyre that she wants her cruel guest to see from the deep. And just after she falls on her sword, the impact of her suicide on Carthage itself is explicitly compared to a fiery invasion of it (4.668–71).

In light of this comparison, the story of the fall of Troy that Aeneas tells in book 2 might be read as a prefiguration of Dido's fiery end.[23] Conversely, as Sarah Spence suggests, to read Dido's fiery end as a metaphorical reenactment of the fall of Troy is to turn Aeneas from a victim of Greek guile into the perpetrator of it, with Dido as his victim (Spence 87). But neither of these two victimizes or seduces the other. On one hand, we have no access to Aeneas's libido and no evidence of his desire for Dido; he burns ("ardet") only when Mercury tells him he must leave Carthage to found a new kingdom in Italy, and what fires him is simply a passion to flee this all-too-seductive land ("abire fuga dulcisque relinquere terras," 4.279–82).[24] On the other hand, Dido never sets out to deceive or entrap Aeneas, not even as an unwitting agent of Juno, who is herself outwitted by Venus. Dido is manipulated by supernatural powers she cannot resist, for she is emotionally ambushed by no fewer than three deities, including her very own patroness.[25] First, under orders from Venus, a Cupid masquerading as the sweet little son of Aeneas wipes out "little by little" the vow she has made to a dead husband, obliterating it with a "living love." Then Juno herself is tricked into playing a further trick on the queen: sending the thunderstorm that drives her and Aeneas into a cave.[26] How could Dido withstand this combination of divine trickery and her own reawakened desire? With scarcely any consciousness of volition or consent, she is made to play the role of a seductive hostess.

In response, Aeneas can hardly bear to behave as a treacherous guest. But nothing he says to Dido can dissuade her from seeing him that way. When she learns that he and his men are secretly arranging to leave Carthage, she tells him,

> Traitor! Did you really hope you could hide [dissimulare] such a crime,
> and silently steal away from my land?
>
> (4.305–6)

Dido's "dissimulare" echoes a key word in Aeneas's account of the fall of Troy. While building the wooden horse, the Greeks conceal its real purpose with a cover story. They pretend—"simulant" (4.17)—that it is an offering left to secure their safe return, and to make the Trojans think they have left for Mycenae, they hide their ships behind an island. Aeneas aims to conceal only his departure plans, and he has no intention of destroying the city built by his hostess. Yet Dido feels he is betraying her: denying their love, breaking his marriage vows, and abandoning her to the doom of a wretched death. Poignantly she asks,

> To whom do you leave my dying self, guest,
> since this name alone remains now that "husband" is gone?

[cui me moribundam deseris, hospes,
hoc solum nomen quoniam de coniuge restat?]
(4.324–25)

In Dido's eyes Aeneas has become her husband, for she has called their relationship "conjungium," marriage (4.172). But since Aeneas never considered them married, she ruefully reaffirms their original relationship: queen and guest, *regina* and *hospes*.[27] As a guest he lauds her generosity. Since she has asked his pity if ever she deserved well of him ("si bene quid de te merui," 4.317), he says he will never deny ("nunquam . . . negabo") that she deserves everything she can name ("quae plurima fando / enumerare vales," 4.333–34). But his language is formal and rhetorically hedged. Right after saying she deserves everything she can name, he denies her claims that he is her husband and that he hoped to hide his flight by stealth. The second denial is questionable. Though he rightly claims he never made a marriage vow, we know very well he ordered his plans for departure to be kept at least temporarily hidden, especially from Dido. Up to now she has had no way of knowing he ever intended to tell her himself.

Sweeping past this problem, he takes the high ground of abstract rights and divine orders. From far above the pit of her anguish, he asks: if you as a Phoenician can set up a kingdom in Carthage, why can't Trojans settle in Italy? We too have the right to seek a kingdom in a foreign land ("et nos fas exterra quaerere regna," 4.350). Here he claims a right that Dido never questioned and that has nothing to do with her desperate appeal for his pity.[28] But in any case, his abstract rights are guaranteed by divine orders: Jove's command that for the sake of Ascanius he must press on to Italy and its predestined lands ("fatalibus arvis," 4.355). Having thus laid out his lofty arguments, he concludes by trying to silence hers: "Cease inflaming both of us with your complaints. / Not of my own will do I seek Italy" (desine meque tuis incendere teque querilis. / Italiam non sponte sequor, 4.360–61).[29]

But nothing he can say will quench her flames. On the contrary, the verb "incendere" cruelly anticipates what she will literally do when Aeneas leaves. She can no more cease to inflame herself than Aeneas can give up his voyage to Italy. In her eyes, he is "perfide" (4.365), a traitorous guest, because he has utterly failed to reciprocate her hospitality. Though he says he will never deny that she deserves everything she can name, he denies the name she applies to him: *conjunx*. But if he can legitimately claim that he never took a marriage vow, she can just as rightfully remind him how much he owes to her hospitality:

Nowhere is faith [fides] safe; thrown on my shore, destitute
I took him in and recklessly set him up in part of my kingdom;
his missing fleet I recovered and saved his men from death.

(4.373–75)

Hospitality is nothing if not an act of *fides*, faith and trust in the responsiveness of a guest. In recalling what she has done for Aeneas and his men, Dido clearly implies her belief in a gigantic quid pro quo. Even though she originally told the Trojans, just before meeting Aeneas, that she would send them all off to Italy with an escort if they wished to go there (1.571), she has forgotten that pledge just as she has abandoned her vow of fidelity to the ashes of Sychaeus.[30] Having given up everything else for Aeneas, she has obviously been expecting him to give up everything else for her and believing he would do so. That is the faith he has betrayed. He has undermined the faith that he himself, by becoming her lover, has unwillingly roused in his hostess. At this point, then, the benign reciprocity of hospitable exchange once more gives way to the lust for retaliation. Just as Polyphemos flings a curse at the departing Odysseus, she begs the gods to punish Aeneas:

Truly I hope that midway on the rocks, if the upright gods have any power,
you will drink your punishment and often call on Dido's name . . .
my shade will haunt you everywhere. You will pay, villain!
I will hear, and the story [of your undoing] will reach me in the underworld
below.

(4.382–87)

Aeneas himself brings her the story of his anguish. Some weeks after his departure, when he and Achates find the shade of Dido in the underworld, he pours out his heart to her. After repeating his earlier excuse—that he left her against his will, at the gods' commands ("iussa deum")—he comes close to expressing remorse. "I could not believe," he tells her, "that my leaving would bring you such misery" (6.463–64). But Dido has nothing more to say to him. She simply disappears, and since he never heard her second curse—the one she flung at his departing fleet—he does not know how bitterly she renounced the hospitality with which she first welcomed him and his men. On celebrating their arrival she prayed to Jupiter that the descendants of Tyrians and Trojans alike might remember the joy of their gathering (1.731–35). But after Aeneas sailed away, she exhorted her people to nurture nothing but hatred of his descendants (4.622–24): a recipe for endless war between Carthage and Rome.

Arguably, then, all the later sufferings of Aeneas himself and of his descendants spring from what Dido sees as his unforgivable crime against hospitality. Since she yearns to make both Aeneas and his line pay for this crime, she prays to Juno, Hecate, and the Furies that Aeneas be violently resisted in Italy, that he be wrenched from the arms of his son, and that he be made to beg for help and see his friends die shamefully (4.615–18). She also calls on some avenger ("aliquis . . . ultor") to rise from her ashes and pursue the Trojan settlers with fire and sword (4.625–26). The avenger will come when Hannibal invades Italy many centuries after Aeneas founds a new kingdom there (Knox, "Introduction" 26). But much of her curse proves prophetic for Aeneas himself.

In leaving Carthage under her curse rather than with her blessing, Aeneas breaks a pattern of clear-cut contrasts set by the first part of his voyage: by the stories he tells to Dido about the range of receptions he has met in other lands. En route from Troy to Carthage, the Trojans are either graciously received or savagely rebuffed. At the "most peaceful" (placidissima) island of Delos (3.78), for instance, they are warmly welcomed by King Anius, who runs to meet and greet them when he recognizes Anchises: "We join hands in hospitality" (iungimus hospitio dextras, 3.80–83), says Aeneas. By contrast they are horrified to learn that the king of Thrace, long a welcoming refuge for Troy ("hospitium antiquum Troiae," 3.15), has broken every bond of hospitality ("fas omne abrumpit," 3.55) by killing Priam's youngest son, who had been sent to him for rearing.[31] As soon as the Trojans learn of the murder they all leave this sinkhole of rotten hospitality ("pollutum hospitium," 3.61).[32]

Dido's treatment of Aeneas fits nowhere in this dyad of contrasts because it tangles them in knots. It binds the most loving and generous hospitality with the deepest sense of betrayal and the most excoriating curses and it predetermines what Aeneas must suffer in the second half of the poem. As Dido predicts, the Trojans meet violent resistance to their settlement of Italy when Turnus, the leader of the Rutulians, attacks the Trojans precisely because he resents the warmth of the welcome they get from Latinus, king of Latium, who wants his daughter to marry Aeneas rather than Turnus himself. Once again, hospitality sets the stage for betrayal.

In killing Turnus at the very end of the poem, Aeneas kills the man who sees every foreigner as an enemy and all hospitality as treachery. Is Turnus, then, the barbarous enemy of civilization justly trampled by its forward march? Though it is hard to escape this conclusion, we must remember that he is defined this way by a poem written to glorify the Roman empire and above all the reign of Augustus. Since hospitality leads to treachery again and again in the poem, Turnus has good reason to conflate them, especially since Aeneas must seem to him—as to Latinus's Queen Amata—a second Paris, an alien prince bent on seizing the woman meant for Turnus himself. Seen from the viewpoint of the Rutulians, Aeneas and his men are reenacting the Greek invasion of Troy for imperial ends. Having invaded Italy, they will subject its inhabitants to the rule of a new kingdom that will eventually become an empire. This is a biased viewpoint, for according to Jupiter, the natives of Italy will keep their language and culture and the Trojans will merely sink ("subsident") into a mixture that generates a surpassing new race (12.834–40). But since Aeneas is fated to be the new king of Italy, it is hard to escape the conclusion that the newcomers will dominate the kingdom as well as drive the march to imperialism.

Virgil does not always find this march a glorious thing. As Bernard Knox observes, two of the farmers in Virgil's *Eclogues* express their dismay at being thrown off their land when it is confiscated to reward veterans of the armies of Octavian and Antony after the battle of Philippi (Knox 4–5). Meliboeus, for instance, describes the soldier who will get his farm as "impius" and a "barbarus" to boot—a foreigner (Virgil, *Eclogues* 1. 71). Losing one's would-be bride to a foreign king is not the same as losing one's farm to a foreign soldier, but in each case the native is made to bend to a destiny forged by outsiders. For all its celebration of that destiny, Knox hears in the *Aeneid* "a constant and vibrant undertone of sympathy for and identification with the Italians" (Knox 3). I do not argue that this sympathy extends to Turnus, but in his doomed resistance to the invaders—to the idea that these Trojan guests have been divinely authorized to subjugate their Italian hosts—Turnus combines brutality and pathos.[33]

Only when we realize that the principle of hospitality in this poem rests on the ideological foundation of empire—Rome's manifest destiny—can we see how this principle vindicates Aeneas's killing of Turnus. Aeneas's sword avenges not just the death of Pallas but all injuries done to the pact that binds the Trojans to their Arcadian hosts, and beyond that all injuries done to them as foreigners newly arrived in Italy. Through the machinations of Juno and Allecto and the rage of Queen Amata, the Latins are roused to make war on their Trojan guests in an act so revolting that King Latinus cannot bear to look at it, much less endorse it. But even when the Latins break the pact of hospitality made by their king, Aeneas holds no grudge against them. On the contrary, he persuades them to make a truce and thus restore, at least in part, the bonds of hospitality. Evander likewise venerates those bonds. Even when his son dies fighting for his Trojan guests, the king blames neither them nor the pact they made nor the right hands they joined in *hospitio* (8.169) when they first met. On the contrary, the pact gives him the right to ask for vengeance—by means of the very right hand that shook his own.

On the other hand, no such pact explains the fate of Dido. If the killing of Turnus can be justified by the imperialized principle of hospitality or by a guest's obligations to his bereaved host, what can justify her suicide? Here we pass from hospitality to *eros*, for Dido's passion rends the delicate membrane separating a host or a guest from a lover.

History and literature alike furnish telling examples. Behind the story of Dido and Aeneas and the whole Trojan war, as noted above, lies Paris's abduction of the wife of his royal host Menelaus—a flagrant violation of hospitality. In the late sixth century BCE, long after the time of Aeneas and Dido, an exemplarily chaste Roman matron named Lucretia was raped in her own house by Tarquinius Sextus, son of Tarquinius Superbus, Rome's last king, who is briefly mentioned in Virgil's account of the prophetic scenes on the shield that Vulcan sculpts for Aeneas (8.646). According to Livy, the younger Tarquin raped Lucretia in her bedroom after she hospitably welcomed him one night while her husband Collatinus was away. When Lucretia told her father and husband what had happened and then killed herself in shame, Collatinus's friend Brutus swore to avenge the outrage by overthrowing the Tarquin dynasty and founding a republic.[34]

Had Virgil himself told the story of Tarquin and Lucretia, it might have taken its place in his shield-preview of the history of the Roman republic. Brutus's vengeance for Tarquin's betrayal of hospitality would then prefigure Aeneas's vengeance for Turnus's murder of Pallas (an act prompted by his hatred of hospitality), and both events would point the way toward the triumph of peace and liberty as well as of hospitality in Rome. But Virgil makes no mention of Lucretia, and the sequence of historical events that are sculpted on the shield culminates not in the triumph of liberty but in the glory of empire personified by Augustus, the emperor for whom the *Aeneid* was written. In any case, the story of a wife who commits suicide after being raped by her guest strays uncomfortably close to the story of a widow who commits suicide after being abandoned by her guest-turned-lover.[35] No matter how carefully we distinguish these stories, to see Aeneas and Dido in the infrared light cast by the story of Tarquin and Lucretia is to see why Aeneas cannot simply be viewed as a heroic defender of *hospitium*, a champion of the bonds handwoven by hosts and guests. He is not a rapist, of course, but he becomes his hostess's lover willingly, feeding a desire that he knows—as a traveler bound for Italy—he must eventually thwart. Are the ties woven by the embrace of lovers less sacred than the bonds woven by the joined hands of hosts and guests? Or is Aeneas simply a ship blown alternately off course and on his way, drawn by Dido and driven by deities ranging from Cupid to Jupiter? However we judge him, one thing is clear: his long voyage to Italy and his struggle to launch a kingdom there make him not only face the perils of war but also walk the perilous ground where hospitality meets treachery and reciprocity becomes retaliation.

DINING, DEATH, AND TRIMALCHIO'S FEAST

In classical literature as well as in scripture, modern literature, and life itself, nothing so well exemplifies the communal spirit of hospitality as the sharing of a meal. Whether enjoying a lavish banquet or a simple repast, hosts and guests who dine together generate among them a kind of familial intimacy. It is no accident that the central ritual of the Christian faith, the Communion service, reenacts the Last Supper; and shortly after the crucifixion Christ revealed his identity to two of his followers by the simple act of breaking bread with them. But the Last Supper, at which Christ asks the apostles to consume his body and drink his blood, is shadowed by the imminence of betrayal and death. Classical literature is likewise rife with stories of dining that turn cannibalistic, lead to death, or plainly foreshadow it.

Tantalus, king of Sipylos, gave a feast for the gods at which he served them the flesh of his son Pelops, whom he had butchered and cooked. This kind of hospitality was repeated by his grandson Atreus, king of Mycenae and father of Agamemnon. When Atreus learned that his brother Thyestes had cuckolded him, he invited Thyestes to a banquet at which, as noted above, he served him the diced bodies of his own children, which Thyestes unknowingly ate. But the most cannibalistic of all hosts is surely Homer's Polyphemos, who prepares dinner in his cave by seizing two of Odysseus's men, bashing their brains out all over the floor, then tearing them "limb by limb to fix his meal" (9.291 / F 9.328). The last phrase exemplifies Homer's wit at its blackest, for as Reece notes, it dresses cannibalism in the conventional diction of hospitality (Reece 25). Just as Odysseus and Telemachus will later stand in Eumaeus's hut "cooking supper" (16.453 / F 16.504), Polyphemos readies his meal before eating it. In Odysseus's whole account of his sojourn in the cave, nothing is more startling than the consistency with which he recalls the rituals of hospitality even as they are savagely violated.

Elsewhere in the *Odyssey*, killing dinner guests can be something like turning them into food. When Agamemnon tells Odysseus that Aegisthus and Clytemnestra slaughtered him and his companions at the dinner table "like white-tusked boars . . . for a wedding, banquet, or groaning public feast" (11.419–20 / F 11.468–70), he implicitly compares the murderous pair to Polyphemos. Likewise, at the last supper of the suitors, when the unrecognized host drives an arrow straight through the neck of Antinous, the bread and meats of the feast are "caught up in a swirl of bloody filth," a mélange of human and animal flesh.

At first glance these ghastly episodes of cannibalism and violence seem a world away from the story of Trimalchio's feast in the *Satyricon* of Petronius. Rather than harming his guests in any way, Trimalchio aims to dazzle them with a parade of elaborate, astounding, and extravagant culinary marvels. Nevertheless, since the *Satyricon* was written in the middle of the first century of our era, during the time when the Gospels and Epistles of the New Testament were produced, the story of Trimalchio's feast presents a radically different way of seeing what hospitality might have meant for a certain class of people in pagan Italy or, more precisely, in the world ruled by Nero, emperor of decadence as well as persecutor of Christians. It is also startling to set Trimalchio's feast beside the Last Supper. Different as they are, these two extraordinary meals are both haunted by the specter of death. And in each case, the act of dining is linked not only to death but also to the communal consumption of a human body.

If the *Satyricon* was written by Gaius Petronius Arbiter, as is commonly thought, it sprang from the imagination of one whom Tacitus called "a man of refined luxury." Having proved himself both energetic and effective as proconsul and then consul of Bithynia, he became an intimate friend of Nero, who made him *elegantiae arbiter*, arbiter of elegance, and we are told that the emperor "thought nothing charming or elegant in luxury" unless Petronius approved it. His final party proved him a master of entertainment right up to the end of his life. Accused of conspiring against the emperor and placed under house arrest at his villa in Cumae, he held a dinner party at which he slowly committed suicide by cutting and binding up his veins while eating and drinking, conversing with his guests, and listening to the recitation of light, amusing verse. "He dined, indulged himself in sleep," writes Tacitus, "that death, though forced upon him, might have a natural appearance" (*Annales* 16.18–19, in *Works* 408–9).

This man who combined eating, entertaining, and dying at his own final party has left a work in which all three activities are mixed and seasoned with rhetoric, the food meant for hearers and readers. The *Satyricon*, which survives only in fragmentary form, begins with a quoted declamation in which the narrator attacks the bloated rhetoric of his time. Speaking in an outdoor colonnade to an audience that includes his teacher Agamemnon, he deplores the eclipse of chaste speech ("pudica oratio"). The understated speech of old Greek masters like Plato and Demosthenes, he says, has given way to windbags of verbal fluff ("tumor rerum"), empty thunderclaps of opinion ("sententiarum vanissimus strepitus"). Speech has grown fat and feeble:

Great style—by which I mean understated style—is neither blotchy nor bombastic, but arises from natural elegance. Lately that windy and gigantic verbosity has migrated to Athens from Asia; on the yearning spirits of the young, spirits reaching up toward greatness, it blew like some pestilential star, and once broken, the standard of eloquence stood fixed and dumb. After that, who achieved the majesty of Thucydides or who the fame of Hyperides? Not even poetry radiated the flush of health, but all the arts, as if fed on the same diet, lost the power to grow old and turn white.

[Grandis et ut ita dicam pudica oratio non est maculosa nec turgida, sed naturali pulchritudine exsurgit. Nuper ventosa istaec et enormis loquacitas Athenas ex Asia commigravit animosque iuvenum ad magna surgentes veluti pestilenti quodam sidere afflavit, semelque corrupta eloquentiae regula stetit et obmutuit. Quis postea ad summam Thucydidis, quis Hyperidis ad famam processit? Ac ne carmen quidem sani coloris enituit, sed omnia quasi codem cibo pasta non potuerunt usque ad senectutem canescere.] (Petronius 2.14–24)[36]

Here is a curious way of decrying rhetorical decadence. At the beginning of this satire, a word that evokes both *satura* (mixed dish) and *satyr* (hybrid of man and animal), Encolpius spouts not the chaste simplicity of "pudica oratio" but a veritable ratatouille of tropes: gigantic verbosity, Asian wind, a blowing star, a broken standard silenced (can a *regula* be silenced?), and malnourished poetry denied the power to age, as if caught forever in its youth or doomed to early death. In other words Encolpius serves up a mixed dish of figures. Though his teacher Agamemnon commends him for speech of rare flavor and good sense ("sermonem . . . non publici sapores" and "bonam mentem," 3.3–5), Encolpius's declamation scarcely exemplifies the style it ostensibly recommends. Instead it broaches one of the major themes of the *Satyricon:* the alignment of bloated rhetoric with overeating—or malnutrition—and death. It thereby leads the way to the central event of the *Satyricon*, the *cena*, or feast, given by the fabulously wealthy Trimalchio.

To this feast Agamemnon himself, by way of his servant, invites Encolpius and his young boyfriend, Giton, along with two others, a poet named Eumolpus and an itinerant preacher named Ascyltos. The lives of Encolpius and his friends seem at first to revolve around Priapus. The older three compete for the favors of Giton, who has evidently run away from his master, and early in the *Satyricon*, after being accused of intruding on secret devotions in the chapel of Priapus, they are led into Priapic rites, both homosexual and heterosexual, by a priestess named Quartilla. But Encolpius suffers from impotence. His "frigida" member (20.6–7) cannot rise to the touch of Quartilla's maid Psyche, and later on he kills one of three sacred geese who suddenly attack him. Since the goose is a bird sacred to Priapus, he is denounced for his deed, and in a poem he recites shortly after, he imagines the wrath of Priapus following him over land and sea just as the wrath of Neptune (Homer's Poseidon) pursued Ulysses. This passage hints, as one commentator notes, that the whole *Satyricon* may be driven by the wrath of Priapus.[37]

But given the salience of Trimalchio's *cena*, sexual activity in the *Satyricon* is at least rivaled in importance by feasting. Both are shadowed by death. Just as Encolpius's groin cannot be roused by Pysche because it has been chilled by a thousand deaths ("mille . . . mortibus," 20.5), Trimalchio turns his dinner party into a funeral banquet for himself. He announces the terms of his will, stipulates precisely how his tomb should be carved and inscribed, and even weeps over the inscription (71–72). This passage anticipates the ending of the *Satyricon* (or what we have of it), where Eumolpus declares that his heirs will get his money only if they cut his body into pieces and eat it right in front of a crowd ("astante populo comederint," 141.6–9). Eumolpus thus literalizes a metaphor that later recurs in the literary representation of inheritance, as when Shakespeare's Lear tells Cornwall and Albany to "digest" what he had meant to give Cordelia (1.1.128) and Dickens's Miss Havisham predicts that her greedy heirs will come to "feast upon [her]" when she is laid out on her dining table (Dickens 72).[38] But in the *Satyricon*, as Gian Biagio Conte observes, the revolting grotesqueness of literal anthropophagy is made palatable by an art that is at once rhetorical and culinary (Conte 135).

The man described as ready to manage the funeral of Trimalchio is called Gorgias, a name clearly meant to recall the teacher of rhetoric in Plato's dialogue of that name. From his interrogation of Gorgias in the dialogue Socrates infers that rhetoric is an art of flattery, deception, and sham. Like cookery, which "pretends to know what food is best for the body," and tailoring, which invests the body with a "spurious beauty," rhetoric "aims at pleasure without any thought of the best" (Plato 1.522–23 [Gor. 464–65]). The Gorgias of the *Satyricon* perfectly expresses this kinship of rhetoric and cookery. Anticipating the disgust that might be provoked by the prospect of eating a corpse, he tells his hearers that "we," that is, he and presumably his unnamed fellow chef, will find some sauce that might transform the revolting taste of rotting human flesh ("aliqua . . . blandimenta, quibus saporem mutemus," 141.24–25). For no flesh, he says, pleases by itself, but only by means of the art with which it is amended and hence reconciled to the nauseated stomach ("Neque enim ulla caro per se placet, sed arte corrigitur et stomacho conciliatur averso," 141.26–27). Rhetoric and cookery serve as metaphors for each other. Before speaking of cookery Gorgias tries to overcome resistance to the very idea of cannibalism by inviting his hearers to shut their eyes and imagine they are devouring a million sesterces: a heady image of their legacy.[39] Having metaphorically sweetened human flesh by the art of rhetoric, he turns literal, promising to find a sauce that will make it physically palatable. Then he returns to rhetoric, his metaphorical sauce. To his anxious hearers he serves a bountiful platter of precedents: three cases in which people felt driven to cannibalism by famine or war, with no legacy in prospect. In the most gruesome of these cases, some of the mothers of Numantia, long besieged by Scipio Aemilianus, were found holding the half-eaten bodies of their infants.

Since this ghastly image of infanticidal cannibalism marks the very end of what remains of the *Satyricon* — itself half eaten or at least partially consumed by the rude wasting of old time — it reinforces the theme of cannibalism that subtly infects the narrative as a whole. Behind its decadent world of luxurious feasting and rampant sexuality lurks the specter of Homer's Polyphemos. Whether or not he and his cave are pictured among the unnamed scenes from the *Iliad* and *Odyssey* that adorn Trimalchio's hall (29), two of the chief characters in this story seem preoccupied with the Cyclops. Their thoughts about him sometimes take a playful turn. When a crowd comes looking for Giton at the inn where Encolpius is staying (a reward of one thousand pieces has been offered to anyone who tracks him down) Encolpius tells him to hide under the bed and cling to the ropes supporting the mattress, just as Ulysses evaded the Cyclops by clinging to the belly of a ram. In evading the crowd by this means, says Encolpius, Giton beat even Ulysses at his own tricks ("Vlixem astu simillimo vicit," 97.16). But when Giton's sneezing leads Eumolpus to pull off the mattress, Giton saves himself only by his capacity to feed the appetites of lust: to Eumolpus he's a tasty treat, "a Ulysses whom even a hungry Cyclops could have spared" (Vlixem, cui vel esuriens Cyclops potuisset parcere, 98.21–22). But Giton is no Ulysses. If a hungry Cyclops could have refrained from literally devouring him, it would only be to reserve him for sexual consumption.

In the *Satyricon* Ulysses is made to signify not just the threat of being devoured but also the treachery of a host who would willfully and perhaps fatally overstuff his guests. By this means Trimalchio compounds the suffocating effect of all hospitality that buries a guest in excess.[40] After his servants present and then remove a dish marked with signs of the zodiac and filled with rich delicacies, Trimalchio scorns the idea that he would have offered his guests no more than that. "Is this the Ulysses you know?" he asks them (Sic notus Vlixes?, 39.7). In quoting the words of Laocoon from the *Aeneid* (2.44), Trimalchio aligns himself with Virgil's Ulysses, who, in the eyes of the Trojan priest Laocoon, epitomizes the treachery of the Greeks. Denouncing the would-be gift of the great wooden horse left outside the gates of Troy, Laocoon scornfully asks his countrymen if

Ulysses is known for sincere generosity. He thereby intimates what his countrymen discover only too late: that the horse has been packed with armed men
bent on breaking out of its belly and sacking the city. Trimalchio has no such
wicked designs, for he thinks himself a benign trickster bent only on surprising
and amusing his guests. But in offering them first an enormous boar and then a
gigantic pig that are each cut open to release what has been stuffed inside, he
presents spectacles of what might be called abdominal explosion. When a hunting
knife was plunged into the side of the boar, we are told, thrushes flew out of it:
"evolaverunt" (40.21–22). When the cook slit open the pig, sausages and giblets
flowed out ("effusa sunt," 49.27–28) like warriors spurting from the Trojan horse.[41]
Between these two explosions or eruptions of overstuffed beasts, a guest named
Seleucus speaks of human death in similar terms. The fine Chrysanthus, he says,
"made his very soul boil over" (animam ebulliit, 42.6–7) and then adds, "We are
walking windbags worth no more than bubbles" (Utres inflati ambulamus. . . .
non pluris sumus quam bullae, 42.8–11).[42] Chrysanthus, to be sure, did not die of
overeating, for he neither ate nor drank anything during the five days before his
death (42.11–12). But Trimalchio seems bent on stuffing his guests just as he stuffed
his great boar and pig and thus hastening the day of their mortal explosion.[43]

   While Trimalchio's table tricks recall the Virgilian mastermind of the Trojan
horse, later episodes in the *Satyricon* recall the Ulysses (Odysseus) of Homer
and specifically the man who proved his mettle against the Cyclops. Even the
ship that Giton and the others board to escape his pursuers proves something
like a floating cave. When Giton and Encolpius say they are terrified of dying
on this ship, Eumolpus assures them that Lichas, its owner and captain, is
"verecundissimus," a supremely respectable man bound to market with his
cargo (101.15–16). "This," says Eumolpus jokingly, "is the Cyclops and pirate
king to whom we owe our passage" (Hic est Cyclops ille et archipirata, cui
vecturam debemus, 101.19–20). Eumolpus thus invites his friends to savor the
irony of a would-be Cyclops who speeds them on their way. But when Eumolpus
adds that Lichas's cargo includes a wanton beauty named Tryphaena, Giton
explains that Lichas and Tryphaena are just the pair that he and Encolpius are
running away from.

   Suddenly unhinged, Eumolpus now evokes the Cyclops in deadly earnest.
"Imagine," he says, "that we've entered the Cyclops' cave. Some means of
escape must be found, unless we suffer shipwreck and free ourselves from every
peril" (Fingite antrum Cyclopis intrasse. Quaerendum est aliquod effugium,
nisi naufragium patimur et omni nos periculo liberamus, 101.26–29). Darkening
in this way from playful to fearful, the repeated references to the Cyclops gradually intensify the sense of entrapment felt by all three characters. Paulo Fedeli

links these references to the "labyrinthine patterns of action" that drive them.[44] But a labyrinth, whether Cretan or not, differs greatly from the cave of the Cyclops. In repeatedly using the story of this cave to signify his characters' fear of entrapment, Petronius subtly binds that fear to the prospect of being devoured: precisely what Eumolpus decrees as the fate of his own corpse.[45]

In sum, Trimalchio's feast epitomizes the theme of mortality. Dominating a narrative that ultimately identifies the act of eating with death and cannibalism, the feast repeatedly presents itself as a memento mori. Even before the first main course arrives, we are told, a slave brought in a silver skeleton ("larvam argenteam attulit," 34.28–29) so well articulated that its joints and sockets could be moved in every way. Thrown down more than once on the dining table so that its supple limbs assume a variety of postures ("aliquot figuras," 34.32), it apes the living even as it unmistakably prefigures death and draws from Trimalchio himself three lines of sepulchral verse:

> Alas for us wretched ones, that all humankind is nothing,
> So shall all of us be, after Orcus has carried us off,
> Then let us live, while we can be / eat well.

> [Eheu nos miseros, quam totus homuncio nil est,
> Sic erimus cuncti, postquam nos auferet Orcus,
> Ergo vivamus, dum licet esse bene.]

(34:34–36)

As Catherine Connors notes, the poem exemplifies the interchangeability of life, death, and food, for "esse" means at once "to be" and "to eat," the infinitive of "edo" (Connors 52). The very dish, or *ferculum*, which is brought in at this point amplifies the note of mortality Trimalchio has just sounded. "The *ferculum* too," writes Connors, "is itself a coded figure for mortality because it depicts the zodiac. For astrologers and those who believe them the position of the stars at a person's birth holds the secret of his death because the death of an individual was astrologically determined by the alignment of the zodiac at the moment of birth. . . . Thus the zodiac dish which is carried in itself reaffirms the inevitable fact that death carries us all off, as Trimalchio had asserted with his silver skeleton and his poem" (Connors 52). In this light, the whole of Trimalchio's feast becomes a proleptic funeral banquet for his guests as well as himself. At once funereal and cannibalistic, Trimalchio's orgy of consumption is made to signify not just the inexorability of death but the inevitability of being devoured.

Classical hospitality is as polytropic as Homer's Odysseus. In the last book of the *Iliad*, when Achilles admits to his tent the father of a man he has just killed, hospitality furnishes a precious, albeit fleeting, respite from war. In the *Odyssey*, when Eumaeus entertains the homecoming Odysseus without knowing or at first even asking who he is, the swineherd radiates something like the unconditional receptivity that would make his hospitality absolute in Derrida's sense. But sooner or later Eumaeus and all of Homer's other hosts interrogate their guests so as to elicit information, at the very least, in return for the food and lodging they provide. Classical hospitality, in short, always entails reciprocity, a history or expectation of benefits directly or indirectly exchanged. But it also entails peril of three different kinds. First, when guests or hosts mistreat each other, the system of benign reciprocity can turn into its dark double, retaliation. Second, whenever hospitality turns seductive, as it does when dispensed by figures like Circe, Calypso, and Dido, it threatens to detain a traveler indefinitely, to make him forget his home or his mission or both. Third, the very act of eating together, which might seem to epitomize the communal spirit of hospitality, can turn funereal or even cannibalistic. Trimalchio's feast may therefore be read as the pagan counterpart of the Last Supper, wherein the convener is at once the host and the *hostia*, the sacrificial victim who offers his body and blood for consumption just before he is betrayed by one of his guests.

2

BIBLICAL HOSPITALITY

PROLOGUE: MILTON'S GENESIS

In the poignant last lines of *Paradise Lost*, his epic reshaping of the book of Genesis, Milton describes how the fallen, exiled Adam and Eve walk out of the Garden of Eden:

> They, hand in hand, with wandering steps and slow
> Through Eden took their solitary way.
>
> (*PL* 12.648–49)

With great reluctance they leave the quarters furnished for them by God, the most powerful and generous of all hosts. During their brief time in Eden they themselves play host to Raphael, whom they lavishly feed when he comes to remind them of their duties to God and to warn them against Satan. But having failed to heed his warnings, they forfeit both Eden and immortality by eating the fruit offered to them by Satan, the most treacherous of hosts.

Satan not only masquerades as their benefactor; he loves to play the role of host. Even before the creation of the world and the beginning of time as we know it, when God first proclaims the divinity of his Son, Satan launches a rebellion against the two by summoning his band of angels to a meeting at which, he says, they will prepare "fit entertainment" for the new king (5.690). By this sly joke he means that they will plot to overthrow both the old king and the new one, Father and Son, in a gigantic war against the angels who remain loyal to God. To Satan, waging war is like giving a party. On the second day of battle he mockingly "entertain[s]" his angelic adversaries with gunpowder that blows them away as they approach (*PL* 6.582–617). Though he and his army kill none of these indestructible foes, suffer crushing defeat, and are condemned forever to hell, he can never stop thinking of himself as a host, even if he is simply the host of hell. Almost immediately after finding himself prone and chained to a burning lake, he takes mental charge of his new surroundings. By a startling act of will, he calls himself not the prisoner of hell but its "new possessor" (1.252), the monarch of an infernal empire. And when he learns that God has resolved to create a new race of humans to fill the vacancy left by the expulsion of the rebel angels, he talks his way out of hell, flies to earth, and sneaks into paradise to lure humankind into his new domain—precisely by playing the treacherous host. Apostrophizing Adam and Eve in a soliloquy just after first spying them in paradise, he offers them his own diabolical hospitality:

> League with you I seek,
> And mutual amity, so strait, so close,
> That I with you must dwell, or you with me
> Henceforth; my dwelling haply may not please,
> Like this fair Paradise, your sense; yet such
> Accept your Maker's work; he gave it me,
> Which I as freely give: Hell shall unfold,
> To *entertain* you two, her widest gates,
> And send forth all her kings; there will be room,
> Not like these narrow limits, to receive
> Your numerous offspring; if no better place,
> Thank him who puts me loth to this revenge
> On you who wrong me not for him who wronged.
>
> (4.375–87, emphasis added)

Since Satan's speech is scripted for him by an expert Latinist, his way of using "entertain" unearths its root meanings (*inter* + *tenere*) to imply that once the gates of hell have opened for Adam and Eve they will close again to *hold* the pair *among* its prisoners. (We have seen in the *Odyssey* how easily a guest may become a prisoner.) Though Satan knows full well that hell cannot furnish anything like the pleasures of paradise, he perverts the principle of hospitality that later prompts Adam and Eve to entertain Raphael when he is sent to warn them against Satan. Just as they offer to God's *angelos*, his messenger, a portion of the gifts God has given to them, Satan will "freely give" them the hell God made for him. Turning hospitable reciprocity into revenge, Satan will pay back God by giving hell, quite literally, to his creatures, and even now he boasts of its capacity to accommodate them and all their descendants. No one knows better than Satan how to "entertain" his guests. In book 9, the pivotal book of the whole epic, he not only enters the body of a serpent but also casts himself as the counterfeit host of Eden, offering to Adam and Eve the "mortal taste" (1.2) of its deadliest fruit.

Spared immediate death and sentenced instead to a life of toil on earth, the fallen couple become wanderers and thus initiate the history of humankind. Whether its wandering is construed as a quest to regain paradise, a migration to more habitable lands, a journey toward some ideal city, or a pilgrimage to a sacred place, the lust or compulsion to move drives human beings just as powerfully as the yearning to settle and build. Since much of the Old Testament tells the story of a wandering people, it features some remarkable episodes of hospitality, beginning with a major one in the life of Abraham.

ABRAHAM AS HOST OF THE ANGELS

In the book of Genesis the story of Abram (as he is called at first) begins in earnest only when God tells him to move for the second time. Having already emigrated from Ur to Haran with his father, wife, and nephew, he is ordered to travel again: "Leave your land, your relatives, and your father's home, for the land that I will show you; and I will make a great nation of you; and I will make your name so great that it will be used for blessings" (Gen. 12:1–2).[1] When Abram reaches the land of Canaan, God promises it to his descendants (12:7), and many years later, renamed Abraham, he is told that his descendants will be as numberless as the stars (15:5). But he is also told that neither he nor his descendants will possess Canaan until they have lived for centuries as immigrants there and in Egypt, where they must spend four hundred years as slaves. "Know this for certain," God says, "that your offspring shall be strangers [gerim] in a land that is not theirs" (17:8, 15:13–15).

Abraham's life as a wandering stranger is as remarkable as his superannuated paternity. In the course of his travels this hitherto childless old man begets nations by fathering two sons: Ishmael, born of his wife's Egyptian maid Hagar when Abraham is eighty-six, starts a line that, according to Muslims, leads to Mohammed and the founding of Islam in the seventh century of our era; and Isaac, born to Abraham's wife Sarai (renamed Sarah) when he is ninety-nine and she ninety, begets Esau and Jacob, who in turn beget, respectively, the nation of Edom (36:1–8) and the patriarchs of the twelve tribes of Israel (35:23–26). By this means Abraham becomes "the father of three religions," as Derrida says ("Hostipitality" 369), begetter of Islam as well as of Judaism and its heir, Christianity. These three religions all derive from a patriarch who, in Derrida's words, "came to earth as a 'stranger, a hôte, *gêr*' and a kind of saint of hospitality."[2]

Abraham plays all of these roles. Though he lives in Canaan as an immigrant, an alien, a sort of guest, he proves himself a consummate host one day at the small tree (terebinth) of Mamre, where "the Lord" appears to him as "three men" standing near his tent in the heat of the day.[3] Rising from the tent door, he runs to meet them, bows before them, and begs them to stretch out under the tree while their feet are washed and they are refreshed with food. Rushing back to the tent, he tells his wife Sarah to make cakes "quickly" from three *seahs* of the best flour; then, after picking out from his herd a plump, tender bullock for a servant to prepare, he sets it before the strangers along with milk and curds, and waits on them as they eat (18:1–8).

At this point the story turns its focus on Sarah. When the visitors ask Abraham, "Where is Sarah thy wife?" he points to the door of the tent behind him, where she stands and hears the visitors, now shrunk to a single "he," tell Abraham that his aged wife will bear a son. Earlier, when God said this to Abraham, he "laughed, and said in his heart, Shall a child be born to him that is an hundred years old? and shall Sarah, that is ninety years old, bear?" (17.17). Though God promptly answered this question for Abraham, Sarah learns only now that she will bear a child and then reenacts Abraham's response: she "laughed within herself, saying, After I am waxed old shall I have pleasure, my lord being old also?" (18.12). Like Abraham, who questioned the news "in his heart," Sarah laughs and questions it internally, "within herself." But unlike Abraham, she is chided for her laughter because it implies that she doubts the omnipotence of God, and when she fearfully denies having laughed, he insists that she did: "Nay; but thou didst laugh" (18.15).

What does this laughter—or more precisely Sarah's echoing of Abraham's laughter—tell us about their hospitality? According to Tracy McNulty, their hospitality is true because it opens itself to the unknown: Abraham welcomes the strange visitors before he knows who they are. Though Paul much later claims that Abraham and Sarah alike show "unquestioning faith" in God's promise of a son (Rom. 4:19–21, Heb. 11:11), neither immediately recognizes the identity of their visitors, and Sarah's laughter reveals her total ignorance of them. Their ignorance, McNulty notes, makes amends for the sin that drove Adam and Eve from the hospitable precincts of paradise: the desire to know "as gods" do (Gen. 3:5). "In the act of hospitality," says McNulty, "the patriarch compensates for the sins of Eden and Babel, or the attempt to 'know' God, precisely by failing to recognize the guest, and thereby altering his sublime alterity. His narrative tells us that human hospitality will redeem the loss of divine hospitality—or paradise—by relinquishing the prideful fantasy of knowing and coming to accept the discontinuity between them" (McNulty 9).

Nevertheless, Sarah's response to the visitors exemplifies what McNulty calls "an ethics of unlimited receptivity to the Other" that is both distinctively feminine and potentially subversive. Once Israel becomes a monotheistic nation with a Decalogue and a code of other laws, she argues, indiscriminate receptivity to the unknown can expose it to peril: foreign nations, foreign gods, everything that may subvert Jewish identity and adulterously threaten Israel's "marriage" to the one true God.[4]

McNulty seems to me right on two points. Against the Pauline claim that Abraham and Sarah both show "unquestioning faith" in God's promise of a son, she rightly recalls their initial laughter at it, and she is equally persuasive in stressing the risks of unlimited receptivity to strangers. But she is far less persuasive in claiming that Sarah exemplifies such receptivity simply because she does not know who the visitors are.

Just how receptive is she? First of all, though she instantly obeys Abraham's command to make cakes for their visitors, she has nothing to do with welcoming them and offers not one word of greeting even after she is presented to them, or rather to the one whom they become just as Abraham points her out.[5] Instead of welcoming this one, she simply laughs "within herself" at his promise, an act of internal resistance to its plausibility. Second, when God asks Abraham why she laughed, in other words how she could doubt his power to give her a child, she denies having done so, "for she was afraid" (Gen. 18.15). Can denial and fear signify openness? Just as her laughter shows her ignorance of God's power, her denial shows her ignorance of his omniscience, his knowledge of everything she thinks, feels, and does "within herself." In responding to their divine visitor with a sequence of incredulity and fear, she embodies, I believe, anything but "unlimited receptivity to the Other."

As for Abraham himself, does he really fail to recognize the divinity of his guest(s)? He might well have done so when the three men dissolve into a single he who predicts that Sarah will have a son, for Abraham has already heard this from God earlier, and this time he accepts it without question. He might also have perceived the divinity of his visitor(s) just as soon as they ask about Sarah by name, for, as Robert Alter notes, this is something ordinary strangers could not know (Alter 86n). By the very act of *not* asking them how they knew it, he seems to accept their divinity. He may even have recognized it at once. *Pace* St. Ambrose, he could not knowingly have honored the Trinity by simply serving up one slaughtered calf and three measures of meal.[6] But since "Mamre" means "vision" or "sharpness of sight," Origen contends that Abraham's purity of heart enabled him to see God.[7] Augustine likewise thought he could not misconstrue the light of divinity. While Abraham, and later his nephew Lot (Gen. 19:305), served "human nourishment to them as men who needed it," Augustine writes, the strangers radiated "something so excellent that those who showed them hospitality as men could not doubt that God was in them."[8]

Divinity likewise radiates from the central figure in Rembrandt's oil painting of this episode, *Abraham and the Angels* (fig. 1). Following the example of earlier artists such as Lucas van Leyden, whose engraving of ca. 1513 shows three young angels standing close together with Abraham kneeling before them (Ackley 214), Rembrandt puts wings on all three visitors, who are raised above a half-kneeling Abraham. Rembrandt also distinguishes one of the three as God. While the other two are shadowed, with cropped heads, wings furled or half folded, and bodies limned in profile or from behind, the central figure, poised slightly above the others, displays a full face and shoulder-length hair between extended wings, and the light emanating from the ample folds of his white robe dominates the picture. Yet Rembrandt carefully humanizes all three. Rather

Figure 1. Rembrandt van Rijn, *Abraham and the Angels* (1646). Oil on panel. (Aurora Art Fund, Bridgeman Art Library International, New York)

than standing stiffly over Abraham, as in van Leyden's engraving, they sit comfortably before him on a low, carpeted platform, and the angel shown in profile is plainly tucking food into his mouth.

More remarkably, the central figure thrusts a bare and all-too-human foot toward the kneeling Abraham, who holds in his hands a pitcher and basin as he looks at the foot. Rembrandt here depicts an incident that Genesis mentions only in passing, when Abraham orders that "water be brought to wash [their] feet"— without saying who will wash them. In performing this quintessentially hospitable act himself, Rembrandt's Abraham prefigures Christ, who at the Last Supper poured water into a basin so that he could wash the feet of each disciple (John 13:5–6).[9] Visually, the youthful, long-haired, white-robed central figure who signifies the God of the Old Testament anticipates Christ, the God of the New. But, just as powerfully, Abraham prefigures the wingless Christ who insisted on performing, as his nearly final act, what was probably the humblest duty of an ancient host. With Sarah looking on shyly from the half-opened doorway in the background, Abraham treats the three with the kind of deference that scripture, Old and New alike, defines as due to *any* guest, not just to God and his angels.

Ten years after painting this picture Rembrandt took up its subject again in an etching, *Abraham Entertaining the Angels* (fig. 2). The three visitors in this picture look quite different from their predecessors. Having studied the depiction of Near Eastern clothing in early seventeenth-century Indian miniatures for what he thought were visual clues to biblical dress, Rembrandt clothes the three like Indian elders and adorns the head of the largest figure, who is seated between the other two, with a folded headdress secured by what seems to be an ornamented pin. The large white beard of this figure evokes the God portrayed a year earlier in Rembrandt's etching of Daniel's apocalyptic dream (Ackley 210, 214), and the carpeted platform or porch on which he sits with the other two raises them once again over Abraham, who stands, apparently on the ground below, with pitcher in hand and head bent deferentially toward them. But this time Sarah looks down on all three figures from the half-opened doorway. More surprisingly, the apex of the triangle formed by the heads of Abraham and his visitors is occupied not by God, as in the etching of Daniel's dream, or even by an angelic cherub, but by a young boy drawing a bow from his perch on the top of a wall. He is doubtless the thirteen-year-old Ishmael, soon to be displaced by the birth of Isaac (Ackley 214). But Rembrandt's playful inclusion of this figure, who is nowhere mentioned in the story of Abraham and his visitors, works to humanize and domesticate the scene. Anyone who has ever tried to entertain guests while young children crawl all over the furniture can readily see what is happening here.

Figure 2. Rembrandt van Rijn, *Abraham Entertaining the Angels* (1656). Etching and drypoint on Japanese paper. (Saint Louis Art Museum, funds given by the Sidney and Sadie Cohen Foundation in memory of Ilene Cohen Edison)

Besides keeping the visitors below Sarah and the playful boy, Rembrandt gives two of them—the two on either side of the largest figure—receding hairlines and small black beards. But these two figures, who look like middle-class merchants seated for midafternoon tea, bear wings, as if to suggest that any guest, no matter what he or she looks like, may be an angel in disguise. The large figure seated between them is wingless, but, like the gesture of Abraham in the painting, his gesture prefigures Christ. At once the guest of Abraham and the God who would ultimately become the host of the Last Supper as well as the sacrificial host, he holds a cup in one hand and with the other blesses or offers to the others the bread placed in the bowl set before him. So even as it signifies the superhuman status of the three visitors, Rembrandt's etching makes them human, or at the very least suggests that Abraham experienced them *as* human before he found out who they really were.

The timing of Abraham's recognition, however, matters less than the simple fact of its occurrence. Regardless of just when Abraham recognized the angelic or divine perfection of his visitors, the whole story of his encounter with them exemplifies a theme as common in classical literature as it is in scripture: the sanctity or even divinity that may lurk in the humblest of strangers.[10] In the first book of the *Odyssey* Telemachus is scandalized by the sight of a stranger standing at the doors of the palace and being ignored by the suitors; only after welcoming this stranger and making sure that he is lavishly served does Telemachus discover first his would-be earthly identity as Mentes, a guest-friend of Odysseus, and then her divinity as Athene, goddess of wisdom (1.119–88, 319–23).

Another story of divinity masquerading as humanity turns up in book 8 of Ovid's *Metamorphoses*. After coming in mortal form to Phrygia and finding "a thousand houses / Shut in their face" (*Met.* 8 / H 200), Jove and his son are welcomed into a cottage by a poor old couple named Baucis and Philemon, who manage to provide them with a bountiful meal of good, simple fare served on rustic earthenware with a bowl of wine. When the wine bowl miraculously refills itself, the couple beg to make a better meal, whereupon the gods drop their mortal disguise, condemn this "wicked neighborhood" (*Met.* 8 / H 202), and lead the couple up a mountain from which they see a flood sheeting their neighbors' houses and leaving only their cottage, which becomes a temple with marble pillars and a golden dome.

Stories like these may have helped to initiate the Graeco-Roman practice of setting out couches for the gods and serving food to them—what the Greeks called *theoxenia* (Visser 94), treating a god as a guest. In any case, these stories not only feature divinity masquerading as visiting humanity but also tend to identify hospitality with piety. "Glad to receive strangers," writes Ambrose, Abraham was also "faithful to God and tireless in his service," which manifests itself in his zeal to serve his guests ("On his Brother, Satyrus" 2.98, ACC 61). He thereby sets a standard of hospitality that his nephew Lot strives to meet while living among the Sodomites, but with far more complicated results.

HOSPITALITY AMONG THE SODOMITES

Like Abraham, Lot entertains angels. Unlike Abraham, he is living in Sodom at the time he plays host: living in a city whose men are vicious, impious, and barbarously inhospitable. Besides making no effort to welcome the angels to their city, the Sodomites demand to rape them as soon as they become the guests of Lot (Gen. 19:1, 5). Like the neighbors of Baucis and Philemon, who are punished with a flood for their inhospitality, the Sodomites are punished first with blindness and then with the fiery devastation of their city (19.23–25). But for his singular hospitality to the visiting angels, Lot is rewarded with the chance to escape to a nearby town (19:19–22). Together, then, the stories of Lot and Abraham suggest that hospitality brings both earthly and heavenly rewards. "Hospitality," writes Ambrose,

> is a good thing and it has its recompense: first of all the recompense of human gratitude and then, more importantly, the divine reward. In this earthly abode we are all guests; here we have only a temporary dwelling place. We depart from it in haste. Let us be careful not to be discourteous or neglectful in receiving guests, lest we be denied entrance into the dwelling place of the saints at the end of our life. . . . Moreover, while we are in this body, there often arises the necessity of traveling. Therefore that which you will have denied to others, you will have decided against yourself. You must show yourself worthy of that which you will have offered to others. If all decided not to receive guests, where would those who are traveling find rest? Then we would have to abandon human habitations and seek out the dens of the wild beasts. ("On Abraham" 1.5.34, ACC 64)

In this journey of our life, this *cammin di nostra vita*, we may grant hospitality not just to regain it from others in this world or the next but also to confirm our humanity and express our piety. In the *Odyssey*, as we have seen, Eumaeus welcomes the disguised Odysseus without yet knowing who he is because, he says, "all vagabonds / and strangers are under Zeus," whom he later calls "the god of guests" (14.57–58, 389). This belief in the sanctity of wandering strangers, whether they be gods in disguise, angels in disguise, or simply the adopted children of a protective divinity, permeates the Old and New Testaments alike. In the New Testament Paul alludes to Abraham when he counsels the Hebrews, "Do not forget to be hospitable to strangers, for by being so some, without knowing it, have had angels as their guests" (Heb. 13:2). Reversing this allusion in his commentary on the Abraham story, Caesarius of Arles ties it directly to the words of Christ. "Behold," writes Caesarius, "while blessed Abraham welcomed those men warmly, he merited to receive God in consideration of his hospitality. Christ further confirmed this in the Gospel when he said, 'I was a stranger, and you took me in'" (Matt. 25:35; Sermon 83.4 in ACC 64–65).

The famous line Caesarius quotes comes from a long sermon in which Christ describes the ending of the world and the Last Judgment, when the Son of man, Christ as the new king of heaven, will separate all nations into the saved and the damned, sheep on the right and goats on the left. Remarkably enough, this sermon makes our eternal fate *wholly* dependent on our hospitality in this life. To those on the right, says Christ, the new king will say,

> Come, you whom my Father has blessed, take possession of the kingdom which has been destined for you from the beginning of the world. For when I was hungry, you gave me food, when I was thirsty you gave me something to drink, when I was a stranger, you invited me to your homes. . . . Then the upright will answer, "Lord, when did we see you hungry and give you food, or thirsty, and give you something to drink? When did we see you a stranger, and invite you home . . .?" The king will answer, "I tell you, in so far as you did it to one of the humblest of these brothers of mine, you did it to me." Then he will say to those at his left, "Begone, you accursed people, to the everlasting fire destined for the devil and his angels! For when I was hungry, you gave me nothing to eat, and when I was thirsty, you gave me nothing to drink, when I was a stranger, you did not invite me home. . . ." Then they in their turn will answer, "Lord, when did we see you hungry, or thirsty, or a stranger . . . and did not wait upon you?" Then he will answer, "I tell you, in so far as you failed to do it for one of these people who are humblest, you failed to do it for me." Then they will go away to everlasting punishment, and the upright to everlasting life. (Matt. 25:34–46)

In light of this statement, it is scarcely possible to overstate the moral importance of hospitality in Christ's evaluation of souls. In making our response to needy strangers on earth the sole determinant of our eternal life, Christ confirms the implications of what he earlier told the apostles when he sent them off to preach. To maximize their dependence on hospitality, he bade them take with them nothing at all—no money, bag, or extra clothes—and to stay with "some suitable person" in each town or village they visited, blessing each house that receives them. But he also said, "Where no one will welcome you, or listen to you, leave that house or town and shake off its very dust from your feet. I tell you, the land of Sodom and Gomorrah will fare better on the Day of Judgment than that town" (Matt. 10:14–15).[11]

In the eyes of Christ then, nothing—not even depravity—is worse than inhospitality. Insofar as we can read the Old Testament in light of the New, the

Sodomites doom themselves on both grounds, first by refusing to welcome their angelic visitors and then by demanding to rape them. Their behavior starkly contrasts with that of Abraham, whose hospitality at Mamre signally helps to define him as a precursor to Christ. In offering his visitors a "tender and plump" calf, says Origen, Abraham prefigures the father of the prodigal son, who kills a fatted calf to celebrate the son's return (Luke 15:22–24). Further, notes Origen, Christ offers himself as a fatted calf when he declares, "No one can show greater love than by giving up his life for his friends" (John 15:13–14). Abraham stops well short of this when he prepares to sacrifice Isaac at God's command (Gen. 21:9–11). But in having the feet of his visitors washed, he anticipates, as I noted above, what Christ does at the Last Supper.[12] Though it is evidently Abraham's servants who wash his visitors' feet while he fetches their food (Gen. 18:4–5), his eagerness to have this done for them adumbrates Christ's insistence on washing the feet of every disciple, including Peter, who cannot bear to let Christ wash his feet until he is told that otherwise he "will have no share with" him (John 13:5–9). Christ performs this service precisely to set an example for his disciples so that they might wash each other's feet (John 13:14–15).

Yet just as hospitality presupposes its opposite, Christ reveals, even as he washes his disciples' feet, that not all of them are spiritually clean (John 13:11). One of them, he says, will betray him (John 13.21), and in John's Gospel he identifies the betrayer by giving to Judas Iscariot a piece of bread that has been dipped in a dish (John 13:26). In the Old Testament, Ishmael, son of Nethaniah, breaks bread at Mizpeh with Gedaliah, the newly appointed governor of Judah, just before standing up with ten other men and killing him as well as all the Jews who were with him (Jer. 41:1–3). But Christ rewrites the story of Gedaliah even as he recalls it. Unlike Gedaliah, Christ foresees the treachery to come, and he signifies the traitor by means of a quintessentially hospitable gesture: feeding a guest.

No treachery mars the meal that Abraham graciously serves to his angelic guests. But shortly afterward, when Lot seems to reenact Abraham's hospitality by welcoming two angelic visitors to his house in Sodom, the harmony of the occasion is threatened by the aggressive lust of the Sodomite men, who surround Lot's house and demand to know his guests carnally (Gen. 19:4–5), that is, to rape them. "In the ancient Near East outside Israel," writes one modern commentator, "homosexual acts between consenting adults do not seem to have been banned, but homosexual rape was, except to humiliate prisoners of war. Everywhere it would have been regarded as abhorrent to treat guests in this way, rather, there was a sacred duty to look after them" (ECB 53).[13] Shockingly enough, Lot tries to discharge this duty by playing the part of a pimp. Stepping outside his house and shutting the door behind him, he tries to buy off the Sodomites with a heterosexual treat. If they will curb their "depraved" appetites and leave his male guests alone, "inasmuch as they have come under the shelter of my roof," he will bring out his two virgin daughters for the Sodomites to do "what [they] like with them" (Gen. 19:7–8).

Possibly because the Sodomites do not even consider this offer, patristic commentators on Lot's hospitality have absolutely nothing to say about it. Generally, in fact, they conclude that he acquits himself well, even if he earns no Michelin stars for his cuisine. Caesarius of Arles, for instance, faults him for not killing a fatted calf and serving only unleavened bread, not cakes made of fancy flour.[14] But, adds Caesarius, "since he offered what he could in a kindly spirit, he merited to be freed from the destruction of Sodom" (Sermon 83.3, ACC 66). Chrysostom goes much further, insisting that Lot exemplifies hospitality at its most zealous and vigilant. He is waiting at the gates of Sodom in the evening when the angels arrive (Gen. 19.1). Eagerly rising to greet them (19.2), he shows an alacrity that ought to shame "those ... given to repulsing" importunate callers, and with "exceeding humility" he begs these "unknown, unprepossessing wayfarers" to spend the night at "your servant's house" (Gen. 19.2). Persistently generous, he will not take no for an answer to his invitation. Finally, pressing the strangers until they comply and enter his house, he "occupie[s] himself in attending on them, providing something to eat and giving evidence of respect and attention to [them]" (Chrysostom, Homilies on Genesis 43.12, ACC 74–75).

If Chrysostom is right, Lot exemplifies a model of hospitality second only to that of Abraham. But since neither Chrysostom nor any other learned Father of the Church says anything about Lot's offer of his daughters, we must look else-where for light on this problematic point. One modern commentator thinks Lot is bluffing. Since he knew the Sodomites were homosexuals, he is said to have reasoned that they would have "no interest in his daughters and might be shocked to their senses by his offer."[15] But would any man bent on raping another man be shocked or deterred by the chance to rape a woman? It seems to me more plausible to argue, as other modern commentators do, that Lot's proposal reflects both his desperation and the supremacy of "a moral code, repulsive to the modern reader, which put the duty of hospitality above any other" (*ECB* 53, *OBC* 52).[16] But can we stomach the repulsiveness of this code? Even though the daughters later choose to copulate with their father after getting him drunk (Gen. 19:32–37), his offer usurps both their bodies and their wills.[17] It stirs just the kind of discomfort we feel in trying to reconcile the morality of the Old Testament and sometimes that of the New with moral stan-dards that are now considered universal and indisputable, but have actually been forged in our own time.[18] Given all the ways in which contemporary feminism has redefined the role and the rights of women, we can scarcely imagine excusing a man who would sacrifice the virginity of his daughters, let alone citing him for his exemplary hospitality, as Chrysostom does.[19]

But is Lot's willingness to sacrifice the virginity of his daughters any more repugnant than Abraham's willingness to take the life of his only son, Isaac (Gen. 22:2)? Søren Kierkegaard construes this state of mind as a "teleological suspension of the ethical" in which God's demand for the sacrifice of Isaac—as a test of Abraham's obedience—trumps all moral obligations, no matter how potent or familial they may be (Kierkegaard 46–58). Something like this principle might be applied to the offer made by Lot. Though God does not demand that he make it, his sense of duty to his guests, whom he has up to now treated with faultless solicitude, evidently makes him feel he has no other choice.[20] Is it not possible that Lot's hospitality is tested by his angelic visitors just as Abraham's obedience is tested by God? In both cases a good man's willingness to make a morally repugnant sacrifice for the sake of what he believes to be a higher good is rewarded by angelic intervention that precludes the need for sacrifice. And in each case the intervention is perfectly timed. Just as the angel of the lord stops Abraham's hand only at the moment when he reaches for the knife to kill his son (Gen. 22:10–11), so Lot's angelic visitors rescue the beleaguered Lot and blind the Sodomites only after the Sodomites have rejected Lot's desperate offer and threatened to rape Lot himself (Gen. 19:9–11). Reading the story of Lot some twenty-five hundred years after it was written, we will probably never understand why any man who could offer his virgin daughters to a gang of rapists deserves to be rescued while his wife is salified for simply looking back at two burning cities (Gen. 19:26). But the story prompts at least one inference: within the book of Genesis, as in the New Testament, nothing matches the moral value of hospitality, and hospitality, like charity, covers a multitude of sins.

JAEL AND SISERA, THE LEVITE AND HIS CONSORT

To move beyond the book of Genesis, however, is to see something quite different. In spite of the principle seemingly exemplified by the stories of Lot and Abraham, the moral value of hospitality is hardly decisive throughout the Old Testament. On the contrary, as McNulty argues, it cannot stand against the post-Genesis consolidation of Israel as a monotheistic nation bent on defending itself against other nations and their gods.[21] The most startling evidence of the change is what Jael does to Sisera after admitting him to her tent as her guest. As a general serving under Jabin, the king of Canaan, Sisera had played a leading role in subjugating Israel for twenty years. When Barak led the Israelites to rout his army at last, Sisera fled on foot to the tribe of Heber, which was trusted not only by the Israelites but also by Sisera because Jabin had forged "friendly relations" (Judg. 4:17) with this tribe. So Sisera threw himself on the hospitality of the Heberites. Exhausted, thirsty, and shivering, he was taken in by Heber's wife Jael, who gave him milk, covered him up, and evidently agreed to conceal his presence from any Israeli pursuers who might come after him. But while her guest slept, she took up a hammer and a tent peg and fatally "drove the peg through his temple into the ground" (Judg. 4:21).

By Abrahamic standards of hospitality this is a flagrantly treacherous act. But by post-Genesis standards it becomes heroic. Since "the laws of peace were abrogated in time of war," as one modern commentator (Schenk) notes, Jael is celebrated for her deed by Deborah, prophetess of Israel, who had roused the tribes of Israel against Sisera and who calls Jael the "most blessed of tent-dwelling women" (Judg. 4:24). Nothing more vividly reveals that in the passage from wandering to settlement, the exemplary hospitality of Abraham and Sarah has been replaced by xenophobic nationalism. "Where Sarah is blessed for her nomadic hospitality," writes McNulty, "Jael is blessed for having anchored the nomadism and openness of stranger reception to the foundation of Yahwist fidelity. Significantly, Jael pins the warrior to the ground with exactly the same gesture used to pin a nomadic tent to its foundation: the fatal tent peg is made to anchor and thereby transform and redeem the potential for errancy inherent in hospitality" (McNulty 41).[22]

Jael's treachery is justified, therefore, by what it does for the nation of Israel. Yet later on in the book of Judges nothing can justify what is done to the unnamed consort of the Levite when she and her husband are guests in the Benjaminite city of Gibeah. At first the Levite, a man from the highlands of Ephraim, is twice favored with gracious hospitality. During a sojourn with his father-in-law in Bethlehem, where he goes to retrieve his estranged *pelegesh* (secondary wife or concubine), he is pressed to stay more than a full day longer than he intended. Then, when he stops at Gibeah on his way back to Ephraim with his servant and consort, now evidently reconciled to him, he is offered food, drink, and shelter by a fellow Ephraimite who has settled in Gibeah: an old man who spots the Levite sitting in the city square (Judg. 19:1–21). But when the "perverted" men of Gibeah behave like Sodomites, the Levite's host reacts much as Lot did. Like the Sodomites, the Gibeahites demand the chance to rape the old man's guest; in response, to deflect them from his guest, the old man offers them both his virgin daughter and his guest's consort. But when they ignore his offer, as the Sodomites ignored Lot's offer, no angels intervene to punish them. Instead, the Levite seizes his consort and turns her out for the Gibeahites to rape all night long. In the morning, after she has returned to the house and fallen at the doorway, the Levite finds her there dead, sets her corpse on his ass, takes it home, cuts it into twelve pieces, and distributes them to the Israelites so as to rouse them against the men of Gibeah (Judg. 19:22–31). In response, the tribes of Israel each send a tenth of their armies to requite Gibeah for its "wantonness," and on the third day of battle, after losing forty thousand men in the first two, they kill more than twenty-five thousand of the Benjaminites and destroy all their cities (Judg. 20:1–48).

To interpret this story, we must first determine what actually happened or what is said to have happened. Though the unnamed woman plays a crucial part in the story, we never hear her speak and do not know precisely what her relation to the Levite is. While the King James Version calls her a concubine who "played the whore against him," the Hebrew word *pelegesh* can also mean "secondary wife," as noted above, and her marital status is confirmed by later references to the Levite as her husband and to her father as his "father-in-law" (v. 3). Furthermore, following at least one Greek text and the Latin Vulgate, the New English Bible says that she had left her husband not in lust but "in a fit of anger" (Gunn 243, 245; Martin, *Judg.* 199–200). The difference between the two sharply affects what commentators have made of her story. For the seventeenth-century English Calvinist preacher Joseph Hall, the Levite's woman got just what she deserved: "She had voluntarily exposed herself to lust," he wrote; "now is exposed forcibly. Adultery was her sin; adultery was her death" (*Contemplations* [1615], qtd. Gunn 253). But few other commentators have dispatched her so briskly. Long before feminist critics such as J. Cheryl Exum noted that a prostitute would not have returned to her father's house, John Milton made precisely the same point, and "in classical Jewish sources," according to David Gunn, "the rabbis generally fault the husband's harsh nature" (Exum 83; Gunn 251, 245). So perhaps the only way we can imagine justifying what happens to her is to assume, as Exum suggests, that her "assertion of autonomy is tantamount *in the narrator's eyes* to an act of harlotry" (Exum 84, emphasis added).

What the narrator sees is itself problematic. Resolutely refusing to condemn the Levite for anything he does to his wife, the narrator of Judges leaves us to do the judging. Nowhere in the story itself does anyone fault the Levite, not even when he cuts up the body of his former wife, orders the pieces distributed throughout Israel, and tells the assembled Israelites that he has done so. Though the Levite calls "such a deed" unprecedented (19:30) and the Israelites demand to know how "this crime" occurred (20:3), the Levite's story of what happened to his wife leads them to blame everything on the Benjaminites and take vengeance only on them: "The Benjaminites," writes Exum, "are punished for siding with the rapists and would-be murderers. The mutilation of the woman's body by the Levite . . . is neither redressed nor explicitly censured" (Exum 86).

Yet the narrative gives us ample means to judge the Levite by comparing his version of the story with the narrator's. For instead of simply saying that the Levite told the assembled Israelites what happened, without recapitulating what we already know, the narrator records the Levite's testimony: "To Gibeah, which belongs to Benjamin, I came with my consort to spend the night; but the citizens of Gibeah rose against me, and at night surrounded the house against me. Me they intended to kill, and my consort they ravished, so that she died. Then I took hold of my consort, and cutting her in pieces, I distributed them through all the country in the possession of Israel; for they had committed a foul and carnal deed in Israel" (20:4–6).

The Levite truthfully admits what he did to his consort's dead body after leaving Gibeah. But he misrepresents almost everything that happened there. First, he fails to mention that he and his fellow travelers, consort and servant, were offered food and shelter in Gibeah by an old immigrant from Ephraim. Then he claims that the men of Gibeah wanted to kill him, though we know very well that they wanted to rape him. Having suppressed all reference to homosexual lust, he likewise elides any mention of what his host proposed or what the Levite himself did to facilitate the ravishment of his consort. Instead he defines himself and his consort alike as the helpless, passive, guiltless victims of brutal aggression.

These glaring differences between the Levite's testimony and the narrator's story of his sojourn in Gibeah surely do not spring from accident or careless-ness. On the contrary, I believe they are meant to challenge and provoke us, to drive us back to the narrator's account of just what the Levite and his host actu-ally did. Only after carefully considering their speech and actions can we judge them confidently or, what amounts to the same thing, can we understand what the narrative as a whole implies about them.[23]

Consider first the host's response to the Gibeahites' demand that he surrender his guest to be raped. If the duty to protect one's guest trumps all others, as in the story of Lot, and if the ancient Israelites thought homosexual rape grossly humil-iating, as we have seen, then we can readily understand why the host might feel driven to the kind of desperation already displayed by Lot. But to compare his words with Lot's is again to see glaring differences. While Lot offers his two daughters to the sexually ravenous Sodomites, the old man offers to the Gibeahites both his daughter *and* the consort of his guest. Quite apart from his willingness to give up his daughter, the host implies that his guest's consort is not

herself a guest and is therefore entitled to none of the special protections that
hosts are traditionally bound to provide. In the eyes of this particular host, the
only person worthy to be called a guest and treated as such is the Levite, the man
who has actively entered the old man's house (19.23) and thus deliberately placed
himself under his protection. To assault such a man, says the host, would be an
act of depravity. But the Levite's consort, having no rights or even a will of her
own, is as expendable as the host's daughter. So even while deploring and forbidding "a deed so carnal" as homosexual rape, the old man sanctions heterosexual
rape, urging the Gibeahites to do "what [they] like" to the women (19:24).[24]

In recycling Lot's offer as the prelude to a night of gang rape, the narrative
intensifies the shock of what follows and hence obviates the need for any
comment on its brutality, which only the morally blind could fail to see. Like
Lot's guests, the old man's guest feels bound to do something when a menacing
mob rejects the offer made by his host. But while Lot's guests save both him and
his daughters from sexual assault by blinding their attackers, the Levite seizes
his consort and throws her to a wolf pack of men who drain her life along with
her sexual dignity, leaving her only enough strength to make her way back to
the door of the house and die "with her hands on the threshold" (19:27): the
cruelest imaginable parody of crossing a threshold to hospitable refuge. In the
morning, when her husband opens the door of the house to go out and continue
his journey, the sight of this dying appeal for refuge and comfort draws a reaction so pitiless that we can instantly see why she left him in the first place: " 'Get
up,' he said to her, 'and let us be off' " (19:28). Is the Levite's mutilation of her
corpse any more appalling than this command addressed to what he construes
as her malingering, still-living self?

This is one of the many questions raised by the sequel to this story, a sequel
that both concludes the book of Judges and relentlessly challenges our power to
judge its central figures. No one in the sequel, including the narrator, blames
the Levite for anything he says or does. On the contrary, it has been argued, the
Israelite tribes go to war against Benjamin "to avenge crimes against a man and
his property" (Exum 80). Yet that is not what the Israelites say about their *casus
belli*. Pointedly ignoring the Levite's claim that the Gibeahites sought to kill
him, they aim "to requite Gibeah in Benjamin for *all the wantonness* which
they committed in Israel" (20:10, emphasis added). This statement unmistakably implies that the Israelites deplore rape of any kind, whether homosexual or
heterosexual, and that either one justifies their war.

Instead of righting wrongs, however, the war compounds them. Though
God repeatedly urges the Israelites to attack Benjamin, they lose forty thousand
swordsmen in the first two days of battle. After they win on the third day by

killing all but six hundred of the Benjaminite men and destroying their cities, they swear that none of them will give his daughter in marriage to a Benjaminite: an oath that almost exactly reverses the old man's offer of his own daughter to the men of Gibeah. But to save the tribe of Benjamin from extinction, the Israelites spare the four hundred virgins of Jabesh-Gilead after they have killed all its males and married women, and they give the virgins to the Benjaminites. Last, since the Benjaminites still need two hundred more virgins, the Israelites tell them to ambush and seize the girls of Shiloh when they come out to dance in the annual festival there. "As the Book of Judges draws to a close," writes Exum, "male violence reinscribes the story of female violation, with Israelite men repeating on a mass scale the crimes of the men of Gibeah" (Exum 86).

The crimes of those men involve and include the crime against hospitality committed at Gibeah by the host and the guest, who together contrive to betray a woman wholly dependent on their protection.[25] Though neither host nor guest is individually punished, their single act of treachery to a female guest plunges all of Israel into a bloodbath of war and an orgy of abduction. As Richard Bowman observes, this story of rape and its catastrophic aftermath conveys a "judgment on the people [of Israel] as a whole for allowing a climate of violence in which events such as these take place" (Bowman 42).

BETWEEN THE TESTAMENTS: ROMAN HOSPITALITY

The fact that such catastrophic violence springs from the flagrant abuse of a guest may suggest that in the world of the Old Testament, nothing is more dangerous to flout than the requisites of hospitality. On the other hand, the story could also be taken to exemplify the perilous nature of hospitality itself as a bridge thrown across a gulf of strangeness. It is no accident that the very word *hospitality* contains all the letters of the word *hostility*, for embedded in the history of the former is the overcoming and transformation of the latter. I wish to examine this process briefly now, with particular reference to Roman hospitality, before considering its relation to the radically new concept of hospitality that emerges from the New Testament and the Acts of the Apostles.

In primitive societies, hospitality originates as a defense against xenophobia. Anthropologists have discovered that primitive peoples instinctively fear strangers, endowing them with the magical or religious power to inflict harm. Repeated exposure to strangers can alleviate this fear. After many contacts with white men the Bushmen of the Kalahari Desert and the Tasadays of Mindanao in the Philippines may no longer think of their pale-skinned visitors as mysterious and menacing. But like a wild beast, strangeness can never be fully domesticated. As

Ladislaus Bolchazy notes, the word for *stranger* in primitive languages often signifies *enemy* as well.[26] Among the early Romans *hostis* meant both enemy and stranger; by the first century BCE *hostis* had come to mean only an enemy.[27]

To see a stranger as an enemy is to feel one of three urges: to attack, to propitiate, or to disarm. "Some peoples," writes Arnold van Gennep, "kill, strip, and mistreat a stranger without ceremony, while others fear him, take great care of him, treat him as a powerful being, or take magico-protective measures against him" (van Gennep 26). Joseph Conrad's *Heart of Darkness* memorably dramatizes two of these impulses. When the steamboat bearing Marlow and his crew of natives nears the Inner Station on the fogbound Congo River, they are suddenly attacked in a hail of arrows and spears, one of which kills the native helmsman. In other words, their unseen assailants treat all strangers, black or white, as enemies.[28] But when Marlow reaches the Inner Station, he discovers that what the natives fear is precisely the *loss* of another stranger, Mr. Kurtz, whom they have come to worship as an omnipotent being entitled to human sacrifice.

Between these two extremes of murderous aggression and craven self-abasement lies "apotropaic hospitality" (Bolchazy III): rituals calculated to tame or neutralize the threat posed by the stranger. As James Frazer notes, primitive peoples who come to realize that they need to meet certain kinds of strangers, such as traders and messengers, also need some way of "disarming" the stranger: deactivating his supposedly maleficent powers or washing away any pollution caused by his presence (Frazer). Even now, many of us reenact this process every Halloween when we offer treats to ward off tricks that would otherwise be played on us by would-be ghosts—a word derived from the Indo-European *ghostis*, "stranger"—at the very doors of our houses (Visser 94–95).[29] Among peoples who believe that strangers belong to foreign gods—a belief strongly implied by the very first of the Ten Commandments given to Moses, "You shall have no other gods before me"—all strangers threaten the gods or God of those who receive them "unless properly purified and initiated" by rites of passage (van Gennep 26–28).

In the epics of Homer, however, Zeus avenges any harm unjustly done by either hosts or guests to each other. Though called the god of guests, he is also, through the agency of Odysseus, the avenging protector of hosts. Just as Polyphemos pays a terrible price for devouring some of his guests, the presumptuous suitors of Penelope pay a terrible price for abusing the hospitality of the long-absent Odysseus, who paradoxically returns *as* a stranger and whose eventual slaughter of the suitors is clearly sanctioned by Zeus along with his daughter Athene. Likewise, we are told in the *Agamemnon* of Aeschylus that when the Trojan prince Paris abducted the wife of Menelaus, his host at Mycenae, Zeus

Xenios sent the Greeks against Troy to punish the whole city.[30] Stories like these suggest that whether the host or the visitor is protected by a known god or a strange one, the power that may be activated on his behalf commands respect at the very least. In meetings between complete strangers, therefore, hospitality springs from the urge to disarm the stranger of his presumed bad will and in so doing minimize the likelihood that he would harm the host (Bolchazy 6).

It would be hard to find such a motive in the alacrity with which Abraham serves his three angelic visitors, but he is obviously awed by them, and the story of Lot and the Sodomites just as plainly shows what angelic power can do to those who threaten guests. In the New Testament, as we have seen, Christ himself warns of dreadful retribution for those who fail to entertain the apostles, even if they don't harm them (Mark 6:11). But as Bolchazy notes, the distinctively Christian concept of one's duties to strangers emerged at a time when the Graeco-Roman world had moved beyond apotropaic hospitality. Perhaps as early as 399 BCE, nearly four centuries before the birth of Christ, Romans began to offer the *jus hospitii*, or the right of hospitality, to foreigners from communities that were linked to Rome by treaty. Just as Zeus was the god of hospitality to the Greeks, or at least to Homer's Greeks, Jupiter was the god of hospitality to Rome, the source of the jus hospitii (Bolchazy 26). A foreigner protected by this right was no longer a mere stranger or foreigner, a *hostis* or *peregrinus*; he was rather a *hostis petens*, a stranger seeking to be well received. Known for a time as *hos-pe(t)-s*, he eventually became *hospes*, a guest (Bolchazy 20).

By the first century BCE the jus hospitii had become a cherished ideal. Cicero called hospitality *sanctissimum*, more sacred even than friendship (*In Verrem* 2.45); Ennius termed the murder of a *hospes* a heinous crime (*Hecuba* 1247–48); Livy reports that a Roman named T. Quinctius Crispinus recoiled from "staining [his] hands with the blood of a guest-friend" even when the two met as enemies "in the thick of battle" (Livy 25.18.18). Most strikingly, in about the year 29 BCE, Livy began *Ab Urbe Condita*, his massive history of Rome, by making the otherwise unrecorded claim that Aeneas and Antenor survived the Trojan war "owing to long-standing claims to hospitality" (vetusti jure hospitii) as well as to their advocacy of peace (Livy 1.1.1).[31] Livy thereby initiates a history driven by the force of a new idea: the ideal of hospitality. Writing less than three decades before the birth of Christ, he repeatedly shows how this new ideal came to reform the lives of the Romans and their relations with other peoples. Once xenophobic, "the Romans . . . gradually developed altruistic motives for humane treatment of strangers, and . . . the *jus hospitii* prepared the Graeco-Roman world for the reception of the concepts of the brotherhood of man and the golden rule preached by late Stoicism and Christianity" (Bolchazy III).

Livy's history of Rome repeatedly bears witness to or simply affirms the emer-
gence of hospitality as a principle of human relations.[32] In the first book of *Ab
Urbe Condita*, which chiefly represents the xenophobic prehistory of Rome,
Tarquin's rape of Lucretia is represented as a grotesque violation of hospitality.
In Livy's narrative, Lucretia herself charges Tarquin with this crime on the
morning after the rape, when she speaks to her husband and his men. Though
graciously received and comfortably housed in a guest chamber ("hospitale
cubiculum"), Tarquin returned "hostis pro hospite"(hostility for hospitality)
and thereby ruined her as well as himself (Livy 1.58.2–8). Centuries later,
however, the jus hospitii saved the life of Hannibal. When Hannibal was invited
to a banquet given by two rich Capuans after the signing of a peace treaty
between Capua and Carthage, the other guests included not only the
Campanian leader of a party that had favored the treaty but also his son, who
had publicly opposed it. Putatively reconciled to Hannibal by his father and
invited to the banquet by Hannibal himself, the son nevertheless told his father
that he planned to assassinate the Carthaginian general, whereupon his father
told him plainly how outrageous that would be: "From the hospitable board
[ab hospitali mensa] to which you were invited by Hannibal with but two other
Campanians, do you rise with the intention of staining that very board with the
blood of a guest [hospitis sanguine]?" (23.9.4). Besides the characteristic set of
variations on his master word *hospitium*, the perspective from which Livy tells
this story gives it a revealing twist. As a Roman historian, he might have found
some way to disparage the champion of Rome's greatest enemy, and he might
also have sympathized with the treacherous son, who, by assassinating Hannibal,
sought to gain Rome's pardon for defecting to the Carthaginian side. But for
Livy, the jus hospitii supersedes all other obligations and political ends.

Livy's history of Rome, therefore, traces the process by which the militaristic
ideal of *virtus* gave way to the fundamentally humane ideal of hospitality, especially during the long peace imposed by Augustus just before the birth of Christ.
Ironically, Augustus himself personified militarism. The four virtues identified
with him, *pietas, virtus, clementia, iustitia*, were the means by which he
conquered and ruled the world.[33] But Livy shows that well before the time of
Augustus a quite different virtue had begun to shape human relations within
the Roman empire. *Hospitium* brought even strangers together peacefully.
Besides *hospitium publicum*, a treaty of hospitality that Rome periodically made
with an entire community, *hospitium privatum* bound individuals from diverse
communities to treat each other kindly even if their respective countries were at
war (Livy 25.18.5–9).[34] Though extralegal, it stood indefinitely, binding all the
descendants of those who entered into it unless it was revoked (Bolchazy 27).

Writing during the peace of the Augustan age, then, Livy presents hospitality as an ideal whose time had decisively come. "Now that the world was at peace," writes Bolchazy,

> virtus [valor] had lost its importance and would not be needed at all if peace . . . continued indefinitely throughout the world under the capable and benign Roman rule. . . . What was needed was an ethical quality that encouraged men to receive and treat each other kindly, though they met each other as strangers for the first time. The law of hospitality, which dictated such treatment and which by its contractual nature made the continuation of such humane and civilized treatment binding on one another indefinitely, answered the need of Livy's times. . . . Virtus was a soldier's virtue. Hospitium was a civilian's. As more men became civilians, the practice of hospitium was the more to be encouraged. (Bolchazy 66–67)

The practice of *hospitium* redefined human relations in what might well be called a proto-Christian way. Besides forestalling violence between those who met for the first time as strangers, it led them to meet as brothers, not as conqueror and conquered, patron and client, or master and supplicant. "The *jus hospitii*," writes Bolchazy, ". . . was based on the implied assumption of the brotherhood of man. A *hospes* was neither a *cliens* nor a *patronus*. He was viewed as an equal. While *clementia* dictated humane treatment of the conquered or of the subject, the *jus hospitii* encouraged humane treatment of every stranger who applied for hospitality, regardless of his relative social rank. . . . The *jus hospitii* dictated receiving a stranger because of his need" (Bolchazy 69). This did not mean that any needy stranger could find a welcome at every Roman house or that lavish hosts earned no particular credit for their benefactions. Cicero, for instance, treats hospitality as something rarified, a privilege meant for "distinguished guests" at "the homes of distinguished men" (*de Officiis* 2.18.64, qtd. and trans. Bolchazy 34). In addition, public buildings, fights, festivals, and public banquets in Rome were typically bankrolled by wealthy men bent on securing their status *as* patrons.[35] But Livy finds examples of truly open hospitality dating from centuries before his time. When the Etruscans came to Rome after being beaten and routed by the Arcini, he writes, the Romans welcomed them so warmly that some decided to make Rome their permanent home (Livy 2.14.9). Given this long-standing responsiveness to need among the Romans, it seems more than likely that the very word *hospes* (guest) comes not from *hostis potens*, as some have suggested, but from *hostis petens*, as I have noted. If we can trust Livy, who writes as an eyewitness of the Augustan age, Roman culture by the time of Christ had come to recognize the *hospes*—the *hostis petens*, the needy stranger—as someone to be greeted, fed, and housed.

HOSPITALITY IN THE NEW TESTAMENT

Hospitality in the New Testament springs from Roman soil. If Petronius's *Satyricon*, as we have seen, looks backward to Homer even while strangely aligning itself with the Christian ritual of Communion, the Roman concept of jus hospitii looks unequivocally forward to Christianity. Given Livy's account of what hospitality had become in the Roman empire, it is hard to imagine a soil more fertile for the seeds that would be planted by the teachings of Christ, who radically redefined hospitality in the process of making it central to his vision of the Kingdom of God. In the Old Testament hospitality is primarily a transaction that takes place within the world of God's chosen people. It is offered to God himself and to angelic visitors, as in the story of Abraham at Mamre; it is offered by one Israelite to another, as in the story of the Levite from Ephraim who stays first with his father-in-law in Bethlehem and then with a fellow Ephraimite in Gibeah.[36] But the second sojourn leads, as we have seen, to a gigantic war between the Benjaminites and the other tribes of Israel, and the stories of Judith and Jael show how readily they could sacrifice the claims of hospitality to the needs of their nation. Virtually nothing in the Old Testament suggests the possibility of generous interaction between Israel and the rest of the world. The only notable occasions on which Israelites stay with Gentiles are periods of painful captivity, first in Egypt and later in Babylon.

The New Testament marks a radical departure from this exclusivity as well as presenting a fundamentally new way in which anyone, Jew or Gentile, might reperform Abraham's entertainment of God.[37] Whereas God appears to Abraham as a man, Christ tells the apostles that all men stand in for God himself: "Whoever welcomes you welcomes me, and whoever welcomes me welcomes him who has sent me. . . . And no one who will give the humblest of my disciples even a cup of cold water because he is my disciple, I tell you, can ever fail of his reward" (Matt. 10:40–42). This is the corollary of what he says twenty-five verses before, where, as we have seen, he threatens disaster on the Day of Judgment for any town that declines to welcome his apostles (Matt. 10:14–15). In effect, he places hospitality at the very center of his teachings and makes it the pivot point for the starkest of choices. While a mere token of hospitality granted to the least of his disciples will gain salvation, *in*hospitality will incur a fate even worse than that inflicted on Sodom and Gomorrah (Matt. 10:15).

In making hospitality central to his teachings, Christ makes it universal: not a practice that circulates among the Jewish people alone, as in the Old Testament, but a form of welcome that must be made to cross all borders, ethnic, religious, social, and economic. Wherever he found exclusivism he ground it up. He took special delight in challenging the Pharisees at their own dinner tables precisely because they were rigorous lawgivers closely aligned with the *haberim*, the most pious of Jews, who strictly followed the Torah in their eating and who used dietary laws to distinguish themselves not just from Gentiles but even from ordinary Jews, the *Am-ha-aretz*, or "people of the land" (Koenig 17–18). In the first century CE, as John Koenig notes, traveling Jewish teachers were commonly invited into the homes of those who wanted to learn and were typically fed and housed in return for instruction (Koenig 17). But in sitting down with Pharisees, Christ confronted fellow teachers, and he seized these opportunities to give them radically new lessons in hospitality as well as healing.

During a Sabbath meal at the house of one Pharisee, for instance, he gives what amounts to a seminar on hospitality. First, noting a man suffering from dropsy, he asks his learned auditors if it is lawful to cure on the Sabbath. Getting no answer, he promptly heals the man, sends him away, and asks a rhetorical question: "Who among you, if his child or his ox falls into a well, will not pull him out at once on the Sabbath?" (Luke 14:5). The question exemplifies his rigorously pragmatic approach to all regulations: if they impede an act of kindness or rescue, they must give way. Likewise, he sweeps away all customs and conventions that might impede genuine hospitality, which demands both humility and an unconditional openness to human need.[38] When Christ finds the guests at the Sabbath meal picking out the best places to sit, he tells them not to do so, "for everyone who exalts himself will be humbled, but the man who humbles himself will be exalted" (Luke 14:11). This was a hard lesson to learn.[39] Even the apostles jockey for the best places and the highest status, prompting Christ to rebuke them. When James and John ask to sit on either side of him, "in your triumph," he tells them they can achieve greatness only by means of servitude, by giving their lives for others, as Christ himself had come to do (Mark 10:37, 43–45). At the Last Supper, when the apostles fall to quarreling about which of them should be ranked the greatest, Christ repeats the point. Instead of lording it over others like a heathen benefactor, he says, the apostles should strive to serve: "Whoever is greatest among you must be like the youngest, and the leader like a servant" (Luke 22:26). Acting like a servant himself, he insists on washing the feet of each apostle, as we have seen (John 13:4–15). In redefining by this means the relation between master and servant as well as the meaning and value of one's place at the table, he undermines the opposition between host and guest.

Here too Christ takes a major step beyond Roman hospitality. While the jus hospitii bridged the gap between the host as *patronus* or benefactor and the guest as supplicant, Christ plays guest and host by turns and sometimes simply ignores the line between the two. Instead of thanking his Sabbath-day host for the meal, for instance, he gives him advice so radical that probably not more than one Christian in a thousand has ever even thought of taking it. "When you give a luncheon or a dinner," Christ says, "do not invite your friends or your brothers or your relatives or your rich neighbors, for then they will invite you in return and you will be repaid. But when you give an entertainment, invite people who are poor, maimed, lame, or blind. Then you will be blessed, because they cannot repay you; for you will be repaid at the resurrection of the upright" (Luke 14:12–14).

This is probably the most unpalatable advice Christ ever gave. Among the many people I have known who consider themselves Christian, only one came anywhere near to taking even part of it. On Thanksgiving Day for many years she opened her dining room to anyone in her Vermont town who wanted a meal and had no other place to go. But on other occasions she did not hesitate to invite neighbors, relatives, and friends, including my wife and me, some of whom at least invited her in return. The history of all her invitations, in fact, would undoubtedly show that some of them were prompted by her desire to repay those who had first invited her. Should she have dismissed this feeling? could she have done so in good conscience? Though we no longer formally bind ourselves to each other by a pact of *hospitium privatum,* as the Romans did, most of us feel obligated to repay, if we can, those who have invited us. But implicitly Christ tells his host to shuck this obligation, to break the whole cycle of social reciprocity in favor of pure giving, that is, of hospitality prompted solely by the desire for repayment "at the resurrection of the upright."

Christ's words to his host, however, provoke none of the objections that readily occur to us. Instead, one of the other guests at the Sabbath meal feels moved to say, "Blessed is the man who shall be at the banquet in the Kingdom of God!" (Luke 14:15). In response Christ tells the story of a "great feast" that represents the kingdom. When the host's invitations were all declined, he sent out his servants to round up "the poor, the maimed, the blind, and the lame" (Luke 14:21–22). They would take the place of those he had invited, who symbolize the people that God originally chose but that now, insofar as the scribes and Pharisees represent them, spurn Christ's invitation to the Kingdom of Heaven.[40] The parable about the feast thereby becomes yet another assault on exclusivity, yet another way of saying that God's Kingdom is infinitely hospitable, open to all who enter it with good will.[41]

While giving lessons in hospitality Christ welcomed the kind of people whom the Pharisees scorned. When a Pharisee named Simon invited him to dinner, a prostitute walked in with a flask of perfume, stood at his feet, wet them with her tears, wiped them with her hair, and rubbed perfume on them—whereupon the Pharisee concluded that Christ could be no true prophet since he failed to recognize this wicked woman for what she was (Luke 7:39). But as Christ proceeds to show, Simon himself failed to recognize that she loved Christ enough to earn forgiveness for all her sins.[42] Just as important, she lovingly discharges all the duties Simon has neglected, that is, the duties of a host. "Do you see this woman?" Christ asks. "I came to your house; you did not give me any water for my feet, but she has wet my feet with tears and wiped them with her hair. You did not give me a kiss, but from the moment I came in she has not stopped kissing my feet. You did not put any oil upon my head, but she has put perfume on my feet. Therefore, I tell you, her sins, many as they are, are forgiven, for she has loved me so much" (Luke 7:44–47). Once again hospitality, like charity, covers a multitude of sins. The woman's hospitality expressed her love, without which her services would mean nothing.

Though Christ faulted the Pharisee for neglecting the duties of a host, he did not relish hospitality driven by a sense of duty alone. For this he gently chided Martha when, after welcoming him to her house, she complained of all the work she had to do for their guests while her sister Mary sat listening to the Master. "Martha, Martha," said Christ, "you are worried and anxious about many things, but . . . there is only one thing we need. For Mary has chosen the right thing, and it must not be taken away from her" (Luke 10:38–42). What then is the right thing here? If Christ faults the Pharisee for negligence, how can he commend the apparently idle Mary and chide her diligent sister—the very namesake of Martha Stewart—for slaving away in the kitchen over hot hors d'oeuvres? The answer seems to be that Christ does not measure hospitality only in terms of services rendered or material objects (like oil or perfume) offered. While Mary looks idle, her mind is at work. What she chooses to give this particular guest is her undivided attention, which surpasses anything else she might give him.

This story of two sisters invites comparison with a story of two brothers, also quite different in character, one dissolute and the other dutiful. The dissolute brother is better known as the prodigal son: a young man who has left home, squandered his inheritance, and returned in desperation, racked with hunger. By ordinary moral standards he deserves no reception at all, just the opposite of all that is due to his hardworking, obedient, stay-at-home elder brother. But this story turns conventional morality on its head. Merely by returning to his father, confessing his sins, and begging to be treated like a hired man, the ragged prodigal wins forgiveness expressed as lavish hospitality. Given new shoes, a ring,

and the best robe in the house, he is welcomed like a king, and even though his
elder brother has never been granted so much as a baby goat to eat with his
friends, the prodigal gets a feast for which a fatted calf is killed (Luke 15:11–29).
In short, the story seems to reward profligacy while stiff-arming industry, to the
bafflement and outrage of the elder brother.

We can readily understand his bafflement and outrage. But in spite of all the
perfectly good arguments on his side, he sounds like a Pharisee or at the very
least a prig. Just as Simon disapproved of Christ's gracious response to a prostitute, the elder brother fumes at his father's joyous welcome of a young man
"who has eaten up [his father's] property with women of the street" (Luke 15:30).
Gripped by jealousy, the elder brother fails to realize that he remains his father's
sole heir and will get everything the father has left (Luke 15:31). He also fails to
realize that for all his failings, his brother doubly deserves the reception he gets.
If home is "the place where, when you have to go there, / They have to take you
in," as Robert Frost has said, then *any* homecoming member of a household
deserves a welcome, and a joyous welcome if he returns from a land of spiritual
death.[43] "We had to celebrate and be glad," says the father to his elder son. "Your
brother was dead, and has come to life, and was lost and is found!" (Luke 15:32).

Since the parable ends here we do not know if the elder brother ever shed
his resentment. He might well have gone on sulking and feeling betrayed.
Christ's wide-open hospitality, in fact, must have felt like betrayal to those who
believed that they alone deserved the best places at God's feast, and they were
outraged to find them given to lowly outsiders. The Pharisees resented Christ's
open consorting with tax collectors above all. Though they were widely thought
dishonest, Christ called one of them, named Levi, to be his disciple (Mark 2:14),
invited himself to stay with another named Zaccheus (Luke 19:1–10), and entertained at Peter's house in Capernaum "many tax collectors and irreligious
people" (Mark 2:15–16). When the Pharisees asked why he dined in such disreputable company, Christ answered in much the same way as he spoke for the
prostitute: like a doctor who comes for the sick rather than the well, he "did not
come to invite the pious but the irreligious" (Mark 2:17).[44]

In the eyes of the Pharisees this hospitality to disreputables became still more
objectionable when compounded by what they saw as a second offense: irrever-
ence toward fasting. As guardians of Jewish law, especially dietary law, the
Pharisees scrupulously observed all fasts. When they and the disciples of John
the Baptist were keeping a fast on one occasion, Christ was asked why his disciples were not. He replied with a question: "Can wedding guests fast while the
bridegroom is with them? As long as they have the bridegroom with them they
cannot fast" (Mark 2:19–20). Implicitly casting himself as a host, he reminds us

of what he did at the wedding feast of Cana, where he ended a sudden drought at the tables by turning six stone jars of water into more than a hundred gallons of excellent wine (John 2:1–10), presumably enough for many feasts.[45] In other words, though he himself had once fasted for forty days and forty nights (Matt. 4:2), he saw no virtue in deprivation or mere sufficiency. Sometimes he relished excess. Unlike the rich man who threw mere scraps to the pockmarked beggar at his gate (Luke 16:19–23), Christ was bountiful. To feed the five thousand people who followed him to Bethsaida, he turned five loaves and two fish into food sufficient to sate them all with twelve baskets of leftovers (Luke 9:10–17).[46] While he was staying at Bethany in the house of Simon shortly before his arrest and crucifixion, a woman came in and poured an entire flask of costly liquid spikenard on his head, prompting onlookers to grumble about the waste of perfume that might have been sold for the benefit of the poor. Christ dismissed their complaints. "Leave her alone," he said. "It is a fine thing that she has done to me. For you always have the poor with you . . . but you will not always have me. She has done all she could; she has perfumed my body in preparation for my burial" (Mark 14:3–9).

Adumbrating as it does the imminent death of Christ, this episode ends darkly. But we miss the spirit of Christ's teachings on hospitality if we fail to hear the notes of joy and even playfulness they often sound. Noting, for instance, that the Pharisees and other experts in Jewish law refused to be baptized by John, he compares them to children sitting in the bazaar and calling out to one another,

> We have played the flute for you,
>   and you would not dance!
> We have wailed and you would not weep!

Glossing this pair of similes, Christ says, "For when John the Baptist came, he did not eat any bread or drink any wine, and you said, 'He has a demon!' Now that the Son of Man has come, he does eat and drink, and you say, 'Look at him! A glutton and a drinker!'" (Luke 7:32–34).

Since no simile walks on all four legs, it takes a little effort to follow the dance steps of meaning here. Just as the children are never satisfied with the response to their music and wailing, neither John nor Christ can ever satisfy the Pharisees and the legal experts, who suddenly become his auditors, "you." Because John took no bread or wine, Christ says to them, you called him possessed; because I eat and drink, you call me a glutton and a drinker. Both charges are caricatures, but rather than trying to refute them Christ simply reveals the impossibility of finding an alternative: you're damned if you fast and just as damned if you eat and drink. In which case, Christ implies, call me a pig and a lush. By thus styling himself, was he not ridiculing the hypocritical priggishness of the Pharisees, who took pains to clean their cups and dishes on the outside but within were "full of greed and self-indulgence" (Matt. 23:25)?

We can only guess. Since after his death the followers of Christ sought to distinguish themselves from the champions of Jewish orthodoxy, we do not know for certain just how many of the anti-pharisaical passages in the Gospels were actually spoken by Christ rather than simply put into his mouth by the evangelists. But in any case, the Christ of the Gospels is nothing if not generous to just about everyone *but* the Pharisees. Brooking no hypocrisy, no exclusion of disreputables, no jockeying for place, his vision of hospitality makes room for all, dissolving all enmities. "Love your enemies," he says (Luke 6:27), shortly before telling what a Samaritan did for a stranger on the road.

For most of us the word *Samaritan* automatically connotes goodness. But for the Jews of Jesus's time the Samaritans were anything but good. Just before the story of the Samaritan, in fact, we learn that when Christ and his companions wished to spend the night in a Samaritan village they were rebuffed, simply because they were headed for Jerusalem (Luke 9:53).[47] So the story of the Samaritan shows that loving one's neighbor, as Christ urges (Luke 10:27–28), may entail loving one's enemy.

This in turn means treating him hospitably, whoever or whatever he may be. When an expert in Jewish law asks Christ, "Who is my neighbor?" (Luke 10:29), Christ tells the story to say, in effect: anyone in need. The man who rouses the Samaritan's pity *may* be a Jew, but he is identified only as a traveler en route from Jerusalem to Jericho, a traveler who has been assaulted by robbers, stripped, beaten, and left for dead. Whoever this man is, his obvious and desperate need is willfully ignored by two Jewish travelers, a priest and a Levite who each cross the road to avoid him. By contrast, the Samaritan dresses and binds his wounds, sets him on a mule, and takes him to an inn, where he cares for him and then promises to pay all his expenses (Luke 30–36). The story shows, therefore, not that the Samaritan rescued a man whom he knew to be his enemy but that he was ready to help anyone in need. His conception of neighbor is comprehensive, compassionate, and unstintingly hospitable.

Nevertheless, while Christ's vision of hospitality calls for the greatest possible generosity to all, it is not blind to their failings. As we have seen, Christ faulted some of his hosts for negligence, chided guests who jockeyed for the best places, and vowed to punish dreadfully any town that refused to receive his apostles. Most important, he saw clearly that one of the apostles who dined with him at the Last Supper would betray him.

Scripture does not tell us who owned the house in Jerusalem that Christ requisitioned for the Last Supper (Matt. 26:18). But since Christ chose the venue for this supper and distributed the bread and wine consumed at it, he may be construed as its host. Perhaps uniquely in the recorded history of hospitality, this host foresees his own betrayal, and his foreknowledge stamps the whole event. All four versions of the Last Supper, which differ in many ways, highlight the imminence of treachery. In the Gospels of Matthew and Mark it is the first thing Christ mentions. "I tell you," he says to the apostles, "one of you will betray me! . . . The man who just dipped his hand in the same dish with me is going to betray me" (Matt. 26:21–23). When Judas asks, "Can it be I, Master," Christ says, "You are right!" (Matt. 26:25).[48]

The other crucial event of the Last Supper was the blessing, breaking, and distribution of bread, which became at once the iconic signature of Christ. Shortly after the crucifixion, when two of the apostles fell into step with a man they did not recognize while en route to the village of Emmaus, "their eyes were opened" to his identity just as soon as he sat down with them at a table, "took the bread and blessed it and broke it in pieces and handed it to them" (Luke 24:30). The breaking and eating of bread signifies what Paul calls *koinonia*, the primordial act of communion, the sharing of many in the body of Christ (1 Cor. 10:16–17). But Christ himself links this first communion with betrayal, especially when he identifies the traitor by the very act of giving him a piece of bread that he has "dipped . . . in the dish" (John 13:26).[49]

In speaking of the bread as "my body," Christ presents himself as the sacrificial victim-to-be, the metaphorical *agnus Dei* who has come to supplant the actual lambs that have up to now been sacrificed to God for consumption by the Jewish people. But this sublime gift of himself springs from an act of betrayal. Shortly after the Last Supper, when Christ and his disciples have gone to the garden of Gesthemane on the Mount of Olives just outside the city, Judas comes to Christ with a great crowd of armed men sent from the high priests and Jewish elders. As soon as Judas kisses Christ—a prearranged signal—the armed men seize him and take him to the house of Caiaphas, where a council of high priests and elders finds him guilty of blasphemy for claiming to be the Son of God. In handing him over to Pontius Pilate and demanding that he be crucified, they turn the host of the Last Supper into *hostia*, a sacrificial victim. By an exquisitely apt etymological accident, the survival of hostia in the Eucharistic *host*—the consecrated bread of communion—places the figure of the betrayed host quite literally at the very center of Christian ritual. When Paul tells the Corinthians how to practice this ritual, how to conduct "the Lord's Supper" at their meetings, he tells them to reenact what Christ did on "the night he was betrayed" (1 Cor. 11:23–24).

It is impossible to overstate the role of betrayal in the founding of the communion ritual, for the Last Supper, which is also the first Communion, primordially marks the intersection of hospitality and treachery. A trace of this intersection can be found even in a well-known Renaissance poem that seems to represent communion as a ritual of purely benign hospitality. In a richly illuminating analysis of George Herbert's "Love III" (from *The Temple* of 1633) Regina Schwartz argues that it stages communion as a loving conversation between a host and a guest. While the speaker, the reluctant invitee, balks at the threshold because he feels "guiltie of dust and sinne," Love, the irresistibly welcoming host, *"will not be refused"* (Schwartz 133). According to Schwartz, Herbert's poem evokes the covenant meal of Exodus, at which Moses and the seventy elders not only beheld with impunity a God who later declares that no one can see him and live (Exod. 33:20) but also "ate and drank" with him (Exod. 24:9–11). In assuring the guilt-ridden guest that he may look on Love with the very eyes that Love has made and "taste my meat," Love at last persuades, even compels, the speaker-guest to "sit and eat" and leave his guilt behind him, outside the door.

But can all his guilt be erased? Besides the speaker's own repeated references to it, the very structure of his dialogue with Love echoes the conversation in which the host of the Last Supper identifies his betrayer. In Herbert's poem the guest's repeated insistence on his guilt is met by a series of rhetorical questions. When the guest says he cannot look on Love, Love replies, "Who made the eyes but I?" Most tellingly, when the guest says he must bear the shame of his guilt, Love asks, "Know you not . . . who bore the blame?" The answer is the host as hostia, the sacrificial victim of the crucifixion. And the reassuringly rhetorical questions here invert the anxiously interrogative questions posed not by Christ but by every one of his apostolic guests in response to his prediction that one of them would betray him. When Judas finally asks, "Can it be I, Master?" and Christ says, "You are right!" he makes the prospect of treachery an essential part of the Communion ritual. Before being finally persuaded that he is worthy to sit and eat with Love, therefore, even Herbert's guest must be subtly reminded of this.

To return to the Last Supper itself, the sacrificial destiny of its host/hostia is prefigured not only verbally, by Christ's prediction, but also iconically, by his sharing of a wine that he identifies with his own blood: "For this is my blood which ratifies the agreement, and is to be poured out for many people, for the forgiveness of sins" (Matt. 26:28).[50] In Matthew's Gospel, which contains the fullest statement of what the wine signifies, Christ reaffirms his role as a sacrificial victim by plainly declaring that he will shed his blood to atone for many sins. But just after speaking of the wine as his blood and telling all the apostles to drink it, he says he will drink none of it himself. Do as I say, he says, not as I do.

Even though his first recorded miracle was to furnish over a hundred gallons of wine for a wedding feast, even though he wanted no one to fast in his presence, and even though he playfully flaunted his own reputation as a would-be "glutton and . . . drinker," this host will not touch the wine that he presses on his guests. He thus seems to crack the very koinonia he has forged. At precisely the moment when the sharing and eating of the bread have made the apostles one with him and sharers of his body, he isolates himself from them. While they drink the wine-made-blood that signifies his supreme sacrifice, he vows "never to drink the product of the vine again till the day when I shall drink the new wine in the Kingdom of God" (Mark 14:25).

Matthew's Christ softens this point by telling his apostles that he will drink the new wine "with you" (26:29). But Mark's more severe version, which is also more reliable (Koenig 39), underscores the sense of isolation Christ embodies even at this quintessentially communal gathering. Uncharacteristically, he vows to fast from wine on this night and for the rest of this life until, after his death and resurrection, he takes his place at the feast of God's Kingdom to come.[51] In the meantime he foresees not only the treachery of Judas but also the dereliction of all the other apostles. "You will all desert me tonight," he says, and when Peter vows never to do so Christ rightly predicts that Peter will disown him three times before cockcrow (Matt. 26:31–34). The great irony of the Last Supper, then, is that the host is betrayed not by Judas alone but by all of his guests. Mystified by Christ's accusation of Judas, they can hardly foresee how they too will fail him in time of greatest need.

A further irony of the Last Supper is that its spirit of communality, its koinonia, was best caught and taught not by any one of the twelve who attended it but by Paul, who became a follower of Christ only after his death.[52] Like Christ, Paul was by turns a guest and a host. In Corinth, for instance, he lodged with Gaius (Rom. 16:23) and with a pair of tentmakers named Aquila and Priscilla (Acts 18:1–3). Elsewhere he lodged with a Christian slave owner named Philemon, to whom he once boldly wrote, "Get ready to entertain me" (Phil. 22). In return he played host in Rome for two full years. Even when living under house arrest in rented lodgings he "welcomed everybody who came to see him" (Acts 28:30).

At times Peter could be just as willing as Paul to grant and accept hospitality. While staying in Joppa with a tanner named Simon he entertained two servants and a soldier who were sent to him from Caesarea by a Roman captain named Cornelius. Also, when Cornelius's emissaries asked him to return with them to the captain's house, he did so. "You know it is against the Law," he told the captain, "for a Jew to associate with a foreigner or to visit one; but God has taught me not to call anyone common or unclean. That was why, when I was sent for, I came without any hesitation" (Acts 10:17–28). Yet Peter's promptitude cannot mask the condescending tone of his speech, especially when compared with what Christ once said to a Roman captain in Capernaum. Needing help with a paralyzed servant but feeling unworthy to receive Christ "under [his] roof," the captain asks him simply to "say the word, and my servant will be healed." Instead of citing Jewish law and then making an exception to it, Christ says to his followers, "I have not found anyone in Israel with such faith as this" and promptly cures the servant (Matt. 8:8–11).

The limits of Peter's hospitality become still more obvious when he is compared with Paul. According to Paul himself, God commissioned him to preach to "the heathen," that is, the Gentiles, while Peter was "actuated . . . to be an apostle to the Jews" (Gal. 2:7–8).[53] So Paul not only dined with Gentiles but openly rebuked Peter for avoiding them. In Antioch, Paul writes, Peter "ate with Gentiles" until emissaries from the Jerusalem church came to tell him he was violating Jewish law, at which point "he began to draw back and hold aloof, for fear of the party of circumcision" (2:13). Though Peter himself elsewhere objects when the Pharisees of Jerusalem demand the circumcision of converts (Acts 15:7–19), he surrenders in Antioch to the strict observance of Torah, which forbade him to eat with Gentiles. Paul will not tolerate such exclusiveness. Like Christ, who did everything possible to combat it, he denounces it, even when practiced by Peter.

Just as dining with Gentiles played a vital part in Paul's conversion of them, communal dining played a central role in the life of the early church. Long before the erection of cathedrals and what we now call churches—buildings designed for worship by hundreds or even thousands of people—the word *church* (Greek *ecclesia*) meant simply the Christian inhabitants of a particular locality. What Paul called "the whole church" of Corinth, for instance, would periodically assemble in the largest hall or atrium of a private house, which could contain no more than forty people. The main event of this meeting was the eating of "the Lord's Supper" (1 Cor. 11:20): not just a wafer of bread and a sip of wine but an entire meal. This meal had to be consumed in a thoroughly communal way, with all participants sharing all food and drink. When Paul learned that some members of the Corinthian church were eating and drinking before others, he denounced them for betraying the spirit of the Lord's Supper. "When you hold your meetings," he wrote,

> it is not the Lord's Supper that you eat, for each of you hurries to get his own supper and eat it, and one goes hungry while another gets drunk. Have you

no houses to eat and drink in? Or do you mean to show your contempt for the church of God, and to humiliate those who have nothing? . . . Anyone who eats the bread or drinks from the Lord's cup in a way that is unworthy of it will be guilty of profaning the body and the blood of the Lord. . . . So, my brothers, when you come together to eat, wait for one another. If anyone is hungry, let him eat at home, so that your meetings may not bring down a judgment upon you. (1 Cor. 11:20–34)

From this passage Gerd Theissen plausibly infers that Paul is deploring a class conflict within the Corinthian church: a rift between rich and poor that shattered the harmony of its meetings.[54] According to Theissen, Paul believed that Christians should always eat and drink together as equals. Even if the poorer members of a Christian community brought nothing to a gathering, even if they had no food or drink to offer, they should never be made to suffer the humiliation of seeing richer members eat and drink all by themselves before anyone else. Plunging instantly and selfishly into their private hoards of food and drink, the wealthier Corinthians doubly betrayed the spirit of the Last Supper. They failed not only to share with others all they had brought to each meeting, but also to wait until the leader of the community had spoken the words of Christ over the bread. Since those words had made the breaking and sharing of bread among his followers signify koinonia, that is, participation in the body of Christ (1 Cor. 10:16–17), anything less than full sharing of all provisions would make the hoarders "guilty of profaning the body and the blood of the Lord."

Paul let no differences in wealth or status check the flow of hospitality between one Christian and another. In the very same letter that asks Philemon to "get ready to entertain" him, Paul also asks him to receive as a guest a Christianized young man who was once Philemon's slave: Onesimus. Now that Paul has entertained Onesimus even while under house arrest in Rome, where he became a second father to him, he sends the young man back to Philemon with the request that he be welcomed as if he were Paul himself. "If you regard me as a comrade," Paul tells Philemon, "welcome him as you would me" (Phil. 10–18). Significantly, the Greek original of "comrade" is koinonos, which can also mean "partner" or "sharer." In Paul's eyes Christian hospitality erases the distinctions between master and slave, benefactor and beneficiary, giver and recipient.

But how often was this ideal vision of Christian hospitality realized? Paul's first letter to the Corinthians sprang in part from his conviction that they had miserably failed to uphold it, and further evidence of just how difficult it was to preserve can be found in the *Didache*, or Teachings of the Apostles.

HOSPITALITY IN THE *DIDACHE*

First compiled in Greek about the year 120 CE, the *Didache* gratingly sounds what is perhaps the first note of exclusivity in the history of Christianity. Though Paul had once scolded Peter for refusing to eat with Gentiles, chapter 9 of the *Didache* firmly warns Christians not to share the Eucharist with any outsiders: "Let none eat or drink of your Eucharist but such as have been baptized into the name of the Lord, for of a truth the Lord hath said concerning this, Give not that which is holy unto dogs" (*Didache* [hereafter D] 9:5).[55] After thus excluding all non-Christians from any sharing of bread and wine, the *Didache* tells Christians how to receive traveling prophets. To some extent it echoes the teachings of Christ on this topic. Just as Christ told the apostles to depend on hospitality wherever they went (Matt. 10:11), the apostles tell Christians to receive "as the Lord" every apostle who comes to them (D 11:4). Likewise, since Christ told the apostles to "give without payment" and take no money with them (Matt. 10:8–9), the *Didache* says that any apostle who asks his host for money "is a false prophet" (D 11:6). But Christ also told the apostles they could each stay with "some suitable person" until they left his town or village (Matt. 10:11), and Christ himself stayed for extended periods at Peter's house in Capernaum. By contrast, the *Didache* vilifies anyone who stays for three days (D 11:5). It also assures Christian hosts that a wayfaring prophet "will not remain with you more than two or three days, unless there be a necessity" (D 12:2).[56]

Nothing is said to define "necessity" or to explain just when a wandering prophet can stay for three days without proving himself false. But the authors of the *Didache* clearly sought to strike a balance. Even in telling Christians how to receive a wandering prophet, they sought to limit the amount of hospitality such a man could expect and to reassure Christian hosts that they would not be indefinitely burdened by a freeloader. If the wandering prophet decided to settle in a specific community, he could and should work for a living at a craft or job of some kind (D 12:3–4). But since teaching is a vital part of his work and deserves some compensation (D 13:1), Christians should give each prophet who settles among them "the first fruits of every produce of the wine-press and threshing-floor, of oxen and sheep" (D 13:3) and "of money, of clothes, and of every possession, as it shall seem good unto thee" (D 13:7).

With this last admonition, which has no precedent in the teachings of Christ, the *Didache* moves from hospitality and ordinary employment into special maintenance, with all its potentiality for exploitation, privilege, disparity, and resentment. What has happened to the Pauline principle that all members of a Christian community share equally in its produce—at least when they meet to commemorate the Last Supper? Starting to build a fixed hierarchy even while saluting the unmoored authority of wandering prophets, the *Didache* equivocates, vilifying prophets who ask for money but also placing it among the many perquisites due to prophets-in-residence from their congregations, who are yet allowed some indeterminate discretion in doling it out ("as it shall seem good unto thee"). The *Didache* thus reveals the impossibility of perpetuating, even among Christians, the unreservedly open hospitality espoused by Christ and Paul: a hospitality that razes all barriers between insiders and outsiders, Jew and Gentile, hosts and guests, rich and poor.

I will not argue that Christianity ceased to promote this kind of hospitality after Paul died. Traces of it survive in *The Rule of Saint Benedict*, which was composed at Monte Cassino about the year 530. In this handbook designed for the guidance of monasteries, chapter 53 begins, "Let all guests who arrive be received like Christ, for He is going to say, 'I came as a guest, and you received Me'" (Matt. 25:35; *Holy Rule*, chapter 53). In quoting from the long passage in which Christ makes salvation itself depend on one's hospitality to all strangers (Matt. 25:31–46), this chapter, "On the Reception of Guests," strikes a note of generosity that perseveres to the end. The guest, it says, should be treated with "all kindness"; unless it's a principal fast day, "the Superior shall break his fast for the sake of a guest"; the abbot and the brethren shall together "wash the feet of all guests"; and special pains shall be shown to the poor and to pilgrims "because it is especially in them that Christ is received." At least among the Benedictines of Italy in the early sixth century, therefore, the spirit of inclusive hospitality exemplified by Christ and Paul seems to have remained alive and well.

Nevertheless, if Peter was the rock on which Christ founded the church, the *Didache* first furnished the locks on its doors, and in many ways the history of Christianity is the story of how it has perfected those locks. Among the many sects of Christianity, the only one that claims to be based on apostolic succession is also the only one that denies communion to all "non-Catholics," Christian or not, granting it only to those who have been officially received into the Roman Catholic Church. Though the word *Catholic* actually means "universal," it has come to mean "exclusive" and now signifies an institution that defines itself, in America, at least, largely by means of exclusion.[57]

In defining itself this way, the church forgets that Christ preached a gospel of radical inclusion. God's relation to humankind is often represented as familial, with God as the father to his people. But even a cursory survey of the Old and New Testaments shows how deeply the long story of this relation reflects a vision of God as host or guest, as giver or receiver of hospitality. Just as crucially, both testaments work to reaffirm and redefine the classical conception of the wayfarer as a figure protected by Zeus or Jupiter or even inhabited by divinity, as in Ovid's story of Baucis and Philemon. In the Old Testament, Abraham entertains three travelers who turn out to be angels and then God himself. In the New Testament, Christ says that whenever we take even the humblest stranger into our homes we are entertaining Christ. Appearing on earth at precisely the time when the *jus hospitii* had become a cherished ideal for the Romans, Christ put hospitality at the very center of his message and mission.

For this very reason his life on earth exemplifies the intersection of hospitality and treachery. In commemorating the Last Supper, the liturgy of the Eucharist recalls an evening of hospitality at which Christ was the host, dispensing bread and wine to his apostles. But that evening of *koinonia* is always identified as "the night on which he was betrayed," and Judas was not the only one who betrayed him. As Christ himself says, he was deserted that night by all of his followers, all of his guests, shortly before he became the *hostia*, the sacrificial victim. Furthermore, as Paul saw in Corinth, Christians who meet to evoke the Last Supper at a common meal betray its spirit whenever they fail to share their provisions equally, whenever the rich eat in such a way as to humiliate the poor. In the history of Christian hospitality, then, it is threatened not only by those who would betray a host or guest but also by anyone who fails to be truly receptive and generous toward the other: the poor, the alien, the complete stranger. To welcome the other is to risk being betrayed oneself, but that is precisely what Christ himself did at the Last Supper.

CODA: HOSPITALITY AND TREACHERY IN DANTE'S *COMMEDIA*

Dante wrote the *Commedia* some thirteen centuries after the New Testament appeared, but no one else has seen more clearly how treachery accosts hospitality at the very end of Christ's earthly life and thus exemplifies the worst kind of evil. In the vast, reverberating pit of the *Inferno*, the position of the circles occupied by the damned depends in each case on the viciousness of their sins. The deepest circle of hell, the circle of treachery, includes four concentric zones named for traitors, beginning with Cain and culminating in Judas, the most vicious of all. Just before the Judecca, the zone of Judas, comes Ptolomea (33.124), named for the betrayers of friends and guests.[58]

Dante's own experience might well have led him to rank this kind of treachery second only to that of Judas. Banished at the age of thirty-six or thirty-seven from his native city of Florence and threatened with execution if he returned, he was compelled for the rest of his life to rely on the hospitality of others, above all Can Francesco della Scala (called Cangrande, or top dog), who became the sole lord of Verona in 1311 and whose "magnificenze" Dante salutes in the *Paradiso* (17.85).⁵⁹ Though Cangrande treated him with exceptional kindness in Verona, Dante knew very well that no guest can long endure dependence without at least some sense of discomfort. In canto 17 of the *Paradiso*, where Cacciaguida, Dante's great-great-grandfather, foretells his exile from Florence, the poet discovers that he will have to learn the hard lesson of being a guest. "You shall learn," he is told, "how salt is the taste / of another man's bread and how hard is the way, / going down and then up another man's stairs" (17.58–60).⁶⁰

If not even the most generous and gracious of hosts can fully satisfy a guest, if the whole process of hospitality offers infinite opportunities for disappointment and strain, it likewise offers infinite opportunities for treachery. Ptolomea is probably named for the biblical Ptolemy, captain of Jericho, who prepared a great feast in the fortress of Dok for his father-in-law, Simon Maccabee, high priest and governor of the Jews, and for Simon's two sons Mattathias and Judas.⁶¹ When Simon and his sons were drunk, Ptolemy and his men gathered their weapons, attacked his three guests, and killed them along with some of their servants. "So," we are told, "he committed an act of great treachery" (1 Macc. 16:17).

In the *Inferno* this is precisely the kind of treachery confessed by Fra Alberigo, who calls himself, so to speak, a rotten apple. Sprung from the fruit of the evil garden ("de la frutta del mal orto," 33.120), he calls to mind the forbidden fruit of Genesis even as he anticipates the opening of Milton's *Paradise Lost*, where "man's first disobedience" is the metaphorical fruit of the literal fruit, the sinful outgrowth of "the fruit / Of that forbidden tree, whose mortal taste / Brought death into the world, and all our woe" (1.1–3). Alberigo's fruit was likewise deadly, and, like Satan, he played a double game. Though he belonged to a religious order, the Jovial Friars, that originally aimed to make peace among families and cities, he forgave insults only in order to avenge them in his own sweet time. In 1285, when Alberigo was one of the Guelph lords of Faenza (near Ravenna), a close relative named Manfred plotted to seize his political power. Struck by Manfred in the midst of a dispute, Alberigo pretended to forgive the blow as an act of youthful impetuosity, made peace with his kinsman, and later invited him and one of his sons to a banquet. When the host said, "Bring the fruit," armed men came from behind a curtain and butchered the guests (Singleton, *Inferno* 2: Com., 400, 621).

As a result, says Alberigo, he is now repaid with dates for figs ("riprendo dattero per figo," 33.120). Since dates were costlier than figs in Dante's time, this is Alberigo's sarcastic way of saying that for murdering his guests he is requited with something far worse (Hollander, *Inferno* Notes, 573). Stuck forever in ice, he cannot even weep because his eyes are locked in rigid veils ("duri veli," 33.112). But he can say enough to identify another treacherous host stuck behind him: Branca d'Oria, who killed his father-in-law after serving him dinner (Singleton, *Inferno* Com. 624)—and thus repeated the crime of the biblical Ptolemy.

The zones adjacent to Ptolomea hold figures whose treacheries evoke that crime obliquely. Though damned for political treason, for supposedly betraying Pisa in the course of negotiations with Florence and the Lucchesi, Count Ugolino della Gherardesca was himself betrayed by Archbishop Ruggieri degli Ubaldini, who had him imprisoned in the summer of 1288 and then cruelly mistreated him. Along with two of his sons and two of his grandsons, Ugolino was locked without food in the tower of Pisa, where all of them starved to death (Hollander, *Inferno* Notes 568). In Dante's poem the whole story of Ugolino's incarceration (33.22–75) savagely perverts the most basic ritual of hospitality: feeding and being fed. When first seen by Dante, Ugolino is chewing on the neck of the equally damned Ruggieri, his onetime host—if such a term can fit a man who locks up and starves his guests. Though Ugolino stops chewing to raise his head and tell his story, the story itself is all about eating. Seeing, Ugolino recalls, that his four boys were starving, he bit both his hands in agony, and thinking that he did so from hunger, the boys offered him their own flesh. Though he declined it—stopping short of Saturnian cannibalism—he knew that all he could do for his children was watch them die before he too expired. But having thus finished his story, Dante writes, Ugolino resumed his eternal chewing of the neck of Ruggieri, biting it "come d'un can" (33.78), like a dog.

In descending from the zone of Antenora to that of Ptolomea, Dante implies that treachery to guests beats even treason in its wickedness. It also draws a harsher penalty. As Alberigo explains, treacherous hosts are not only stuck forever in ice but often turned into zombies before they die, with demons usurping their bodies on earth while their souls go straight to hell (*Inferno* 33.124–32). Furthermore, just as the perversion of eating links the story of Ugolino to those of Alberigo and Branca d'Oria, it likewise informs the story of Judas, the most treacherous of all sinners—and all guests—in the underworld of the *Inferno*.

All this may help to explain why crimes against hospitality are punished so severely in the *Inferno*, why they drag their perpetrators to the very bottom of its lowest pit. Though the xenial host and the sacrificial host converge only in English, Dante's placement of the Judecca just below the Ptolomea prompts us to see the link between them and likewise the insidious kinship of all who betray their masters, benefactors, hosts, or guests.

BEOWULF AND GAWAIN:
MONSTROSITY, RECIPROCITY, SEDUCTION

In the literary history of hospitality, *Beowulf* takes us back to something like the world of Homer even while subtly evoking the New Testament, which it follows by about one thousand years. On one hand, in making his name by killing dragons and finally giving his life to defeat one who threatens his people, the eponymous hero of this Anglo-Saxon epic evokes Christ as the serpent-crusher, the self-sacrificing victor over the diabolically serpentine enemy of humankind.[1] On the other hand, in fighting on behalf of a Danish king who feeds and houses him and his men, Beowulf recalls the soldiers of Homer's *Iliad*, who were regularly entertained by kings such as Agamemnon in return for their services on the battlefield. Furthermore, since the Danish king once hosted Beowulf's father, his services to the king take their place in a history of hospitable exchanges like those we have seen in the *Odyssey*, especially in Telemachus's visits to his father's old friends.

The pagan ethos of *Beowulf* seems further confirmed when it is set beside *Sir Gawain and the Green Knight*, an Anglo-Norman, conspicuously Christian romance that was probably written around 1400. In the earlier poem Beowulf fights a series of monsters in the land of the Danes, returns to his homeland, the land of the Geats, to rule them for fifty years, and dies of wounds suffered in the act of fighting and killing a dragon. Sir Gawain fights no one of any consequence and does his most important business in the course of a single week. Though he beats back various savage adversaries, including dragons, while en route to a chapel, he does all this in a throwaway passage of just four lines (720–23). As a Christian knight he proves his virtue not by fighting but chiefly by resisting sexual temptation, then shows his frailty by scheming to save his neck from the axe of a giant he has promised to meet at the chapel on New Year's Day.

Can such a story resonate with *Beowulf*? Does the earlier poem share anything more with the later one than cryptic evocations of a Christianity that *Gawain* explicitly foregrounds? The short answer is yes. Different as these two stories are, each of its protagonists not only cuts off a head and proves himself a hero by the code of his time but also discovers how treacherous hospitality can be — especially when the reciprocal exchange of hospitable comforts gives way to deadly games of assault, retaliation, and seduction.

BEOWULF: THE MONSTERS AND THE GUEST

As an archetypal epic of heroism, *Beowulf* is punctuated by three great struggles of man against monster. But the world of the poem is something created by the rituals of hospitality and the requisites of reciprocity. As Marcel Mauss has shown, gifts are never free. Around the world and throughout human history a gift of any kind "obliges a person to reciprocate the present that has been received" (Mauss 9). When Beowulf sails with fourteen thanes from the land of the Geats in southern Sweden to the land of the Danes in northeast Denmark, he is not just selflessly offering his might and mettle to a king whose realm has been terrorized by a murderous monster. Beowulf and his men are King Hrothgar's guests, and at one point Beowulf is plainly called his *gaest* (1800).[2] For the duration of their sojourn in the land of the Danes, the king feeds and houses them in return for their services, more precisely for Beowulf's victories over two predators, Grendel and Grendel's mother.

In killing those monsters Beowulf is also requiting Hrothgar for hosting his father, Ecgtheow. We might overlook this point because Beowulf himself fails to mention it. On first presenting himself to Hrothgar, he calls himself the kinsman and retainer of Hygelac, king of the Geats; he says he has come because word of Grendel's terrible deeds has reached him; he lays out the record of his conquests, which includes his amazing triumph over monsters at sea; and he volunteers to crush Grendel in single combat. But Hrothgar's first reaction to all this is to recall that Beowulf's father was once his guest, in fact his needy supplicant. When Ecgtheow killed Heatholaf of the Wylfings, he felt compelled to leave the Geats, who could not harbor him without provoking war. So he sought refuge with Hrothgar, then the new king of the Danes, who settled his debts to the Wylfings by sending them ancient treasures as "wergild": recompense for the killing of Heatholaf.[3] In return, Ecgtheow swore oaths of fealty to him, and though Beowulf does not mention those obligations, we might well infer that he has come to discharge them.

Fittingly, he does so by defeating a monster who has savagely abused the hospitality of Hrothgar. Like the suitors who usurped the palace of Odysseus, Grendel has usurped Heorot, the great new feasting hall or guest hall ("gest-sele," 994) where Hrothgar entertains his warriors. As an uninvited guest one night, Grendel found them asleep after eating and drinking, seized thirty of them, took them away to his lair, and repeated his crime the very next day "until the greatest house in the world / stood empty" (H 145–46). Grendel is nowhere called a guest, but once he has driven off Hrothgar's men, once he has made it impossible for them to spend the night in the new guest hall, he becomes, with astonishing irony, a hall thegn ("*heal-thegn*," 142). Normally a hall thegn is one who seeks refuge from an intruder within a hall, where he spends the night as something between a guardian and a guest.[4] When Beowulf and his men spend their first night in Heorot, they are called *heal-thegnas* (719). It's ironic enough that this house of feasting and refuge for guests should have become so dangerous that no Dane will sleep in it. What doubles the irony is that Grendel treats this hall as his own merry refuge, the place where he feasts with the greatest of pleasure—and with no fear of resistance—on whomever he finds there. As he comes to Heorot on the night Beowulf and his men first sleep there, he behaves in some ways like a normal guest eagerly anticipating a grand party. From a distance he gladly ("gearwost") discerns the flashing fretwork of this gold-hall ("gold-sele," 715–16). Then, after he easily opens the bolted door and catches sight of the men sleeping inside, his heart laughs at the prospect of a hearty feast ("wyst-fylle," 734). Grendel thus savors the pleasures of hospitality even while shredding its rules.

Though it may seem absurd to speak of Grendel and hospitality in the same sentence, the poem treats all of its monsters *as if* they were hosts or guests, as if they could be judged by the standards of reciprocity that govern human inter-course. Just as Homer highlights the barbarity of Polyphemos by casting him as the worst of all possible hosts, *Beowulf* highlights the monstrosity of Grendel by casting him as the worst of all possible guests. In fact he spurns all obligations. By invading Heorot and devouring or carrying off the men he found there, he has already—before Beowulf arrives—savaged his hosts, and we also learn that he has made no recompense for any of his murders, that he has paid no "wergild," or death price (*fea*, 156), such as Hrothgar paid for the crimes committed by Beowulf's father, the man who became his guest. In short, Grendel has placed himself outside all laws of positive reciprocity, all laws requiring beneficial recompense for gifts received or violence inflicted. Nevertheless, he insists on enjoying one of the chief privileges of civilized life: feasting in a guesthouse.

Monsters may also host their prey, as we learn from Beowulf himself. On the first night the Geats feast in Heorot, a Dane by the name of Unferth plays his own version of Get the Guest. Enviously sneering at Beowulf for losing an eight-day swimming race against a young companion named Breca, Unferth predicts that Beowulf will lose to Grendel because "no one has ever / outlasted an entire night" with him (H 527–28). In reply Beowulf says not only that he was "the strongest swimmer of all" (H 534), stroking for five days and nights while bearing a sword and wearing a coat of mail, but also that he killed nine sea-monsters who sought to devour him:

> Time and again, foul things attacked me,
> lurking and stalking, but I lashed out,
> gave as good as I got with my sword.
> My flesh was not for feasting on,
> there would be no monsters gnawing and gloating
> over their banquet at the bottom of the sea.
>
> (H)

> [Swa mec gelome laðgeteonan
> þreatedon þearle. Ic him þenode
> deoran sweorde, swa hit gedefe wæs.
> Næs hie ðære fylle gefean hæfdon,
> manfordædlan, þæt hie me þegon,
> symbel ymbsæton sægrunde neah.]
>
> (559–64)

Anticipating a feast ("fylle") in their own domain, looking forward to sitting down at a banquet ("symbel") laid out on the ocean floor, Beowulf's murderous hosts had planned, like Polyphemos, to devour their guest. But he foiled them.

Having killed nine of those monsters with his sword, Beowulf firmly believes he can vanquish Grendel. Even as he takes the mead-cup offered to him by Wealhtheow, Hrothgar's queen, he proclaims his unwavering aim:

> I had a fixed purpose when I put to sea.
> As I sat in the boat with my band of men,
> I meant to perform to the uttermost
> what your people wanted or perish in the attempt,
> in the fiend's clutches. And I shall fulfill that purpose,
> prove myself with a proud deed
> or meet my death here in the mead-hall.
>
> (H)

[Ic þæt hogode, þa ic on holm gestah,
sæ-bat gesæt mid minre secga gedriht,
þæt ic anunga eowra leoda
willan geworhte, oþðe on wæl crunge,
feond-grapum fæst. Ic gefremman sceal
eorlic ellen, boþðe ende-dæg
on þisse meodu-healle minne gebidan.]
(632–38)

It is hard to imagine a more dramatic example of the reciprocity presupposed by the hospitality of a king. Taking the cup from the queen, Beowulf pledges his service to the king, and immediately after the Danish king entertains him and his men at a feast, the newly arrived guest risks his life against a monster who has terrorized the Danish kingdom.

But as if the level of terror were not already high enough, as if fighting Grendel "in single combat," as he has promised (H 426), were not daring enough, he insists on fighting him without weapons of any kind, including the sword he used to kill the sea-monsters in the race with Breca. Why? Aside from some bizarre notion of fair play, which makes him want to prove himself just as strong as Grendel by eschewing any unfair advantage over him (677–78), why would Beowulf opt to use only his bare hands?[5] And why does he respond at first so passively to Grendel's sudden appearance at Heorot? Playing possum, he simply watches Grendel grab and eat one of his men before he catches the monster's outstretched arm. Strange as these decisions seem, both of them might be explained in terms of hospitality.

If Grendel is an uninvited guest, as the poem implies, Beowulf may be watching to see not only how he would attack his prey, as we are explicitly told (738), but also what kind of a guest he is. In other words, Beowulf acts only after he sees that Grendel has savagely abused the hospitality of Heorot. Furthermore, Beowulf's way of thwarting Grendel evokes a handclasp: a gesture which, as we have seen in both the *Iliad* and the *Aeneid*, signifies hospitality. When the monster has eaten every bit of his first victim and then reaches for Beowulf himself "mid handa" (746), with his hand, Beowulf stops him by seizing that hand hard enough to make its fingers crack, "fingras burston" (760). Grendel can jerk himself free only by leaving behind his whole arm and dragging his fatally wounded body back to his lair. The monster's chief weapon then becomes Beowulf's trophy. Placing Grendel's hand, arm, and shoulder under Heorot's roof (833–35), Beowulf shows that he has broken the power of one who used his own hands only to destroy, never to signify a bond of friendship or hospitality.

We all know the shock of a fingerbone-cracking handclasp, when what should be a friendly moment of manual contact becomes a power play, a stroke of one-upmanship, a none-too-subtle assertion of imagined superiority. This passage turns such an encounter into a matter of life or death. A traditional gesture of hospitable greeting becomes a means of mortal combat that is literally hand to hand.

Again and again the story of Grendel's visit to Heorot stages the contest between man and monster as a battle of hands. Immediately after feasting on a sleeping warrior, biting into his bone-frame ("ban-locan," 742), drinking his blood, and devouring every bit of him, even his feet and hands ("fet ond folma," 745), Grendel reaches out to grip Beowulf "mid handa" (746). Startlingly enough, the poet does not speak of a paw or claw, as Seamus Heaney does (747); instead he uses a word that is almost the same as its modern English descendant. And lest we take "handa" as a metaphor for claw, we are also told that the fiend ("feond") reached out for Beowulf "mid folme" (748): with a hand, the very word just used for the hands (plural) of the man Grendel has devoured.[6] James Rosier counts sixty-six references to hands in this poem, ten of them used in narrating Beowulf's fight with Grendel (Rosier 10). Beowulf fights with his "mund-gripe" (753), a handgrip tighter than anything Grendel has ever endured. It makes the monster's "fingras" crack, as I have noted, and as he struggles to break free he knows his fingers' power is locked in Beowulf's grip ("wiste his fingra geweald / on grames grapum," 764–65).[7]

This does not mean that Beowulf simply holds the monster steady. The violent struggle of these two hall-wardens ("ren-weardas," 770), as they are called, might have leveled the building had it not been braced with iron bands, and many a gold-studded mead-bench actually crashes to the floor. But through it all Beowulf holds the monster literally in hand—"be honda" (814)—until his arm and shoulder are ripped from his body and then displayed along with the "hond" (834) under the roof of Heorot. All three parts of Grendel's grip ("Grendles grape," 836) thus become a wonder to the Danes. But what thrills King Hrothgar above all is the sight of Heorot's golden roof decorated with "Grendles hond" (927).[8]

So where does this take us? Let me frankly admit a gap here, a lacuna in my argument. Beowulf's lethal gripping of Grendel's hand, I believe, radically subverts the traditional meaning of the handshake even as Grendel's way of feasting shreds the rules of hospitality by turning Hrothgar's guests—collectively Grendel's hosts—into food. But while prompting this hypothesis, the poem stops short of clinching it with any passage in which, as in the *Aeneid*, a hand-shake signifies a bond of true welcome and trust between a host and a guest.

Awkwardly enough (for my purposes), the hands of Hrothgar and Beowulf are never said to meet.[9] When the newly arrived Beowulf tells the king that he has come to grapple with Grendel, Hrothgar promptly invites him and his men to feast, but he does not touch his new guest. Even when they part for what Hrothgar knows will be the last time, and with burning heart the old king tearfully kisses and embraces the young warrior, no mention is made of their hands.

But if hands are never said to join in greeting, they can nevertheless play a beneficent role. On the morning after Grendel's mother invades Heorot, kills one of the men sleeping there, and reclaims her son's bloody hand ("cuþe folme," 1303) Beowulf is summoned to the king from his separate lodging. When he arrives with his band of hands ("hand-scale," 1317),[10] he learns that Grendel's mother has made a feast ("fylle," 1333) of a man named Aeschere to avenge Beowulf's mortal grasping ("clammum," 1335) of her son. In mourning Aeschere, who was his favorite counselor, the king movingly recalls the touch of his generous hand:

> So it seems to thanes in their grief,
> in the anguish every thane endures
> at the loss of a ring-giver, now that the hand
> that bestowed so richly has been stilled in death.
>
> (H)

> [þæs þe þincean mæg þegne monegum,
> se þe æfter sincgyfan on sefan greoteþ,
> hreþerbealo hearde; nu seo hand ligeð,
> se þe eow welhwylcra / wilna dohte.]
>
> (1341–44)

As a man who used his hands not to fight but to dispense treasure, to please and comfort other men, Aeschere seems to have personified the kind of trust that is traditionally signified by a handshake. Taken by surprise and then beheaded, as the Danish warriors later learn (1420–21), he had no chance to fight with a hand that now lies still.

Is it too much to argue that Aeschere's benevolent hand takes the place of a handshake we never see, and thus evokes (indirectly, to be sure) the bonds of hospitality that are undermined by Grendel's murderous hand and Beowulf's lethal grasping of it? I do not know, but I can confidently state a related point. When Beowulf descends to the lair of Grendel's mother ("Grendles modor," 1258) to avenge the murder of Aeschere, the story of their encounter is explicitly couched in terms of hospitality betrayed. After Grendel's mother runs off to the fiery lake where she lives and plunges to the bottom, Beowulf joins Hrothgar and the Danes in tracking her down. Though they are all horrified to find the severed head of Aeschere on the slope leading to the lake, Beowulf dons his armor, takes up a sword named Hrunting that has been loaned to him by Unferth (who thus makes amends for taunting the brave guest of the Danes), and dives into the lake, taking a full day to reach the bottom. Then he becomes the monster's "gist" (1522), her guest.[11]

To catch the full irony of this term, we must realize that Grendel's mother is called both a "brim-wylf" (1506) and a "mere-wif" (1519), a sea-wolf and a sea-monster. Rosier reads the rare "brim-wylf" as a transformation of "brim-wylm" (1494), the brimming sea-flood that engulfs or overwhelms Beowulf as he dives into the monster's lake.[12] Beowulf thus becomes the guest of a monster whose name grimly echoes his own: a *wylf* of the deep. In Germanic mythology the devil often takes the name or shape of a wolf, and both Grendel and his mother are linked to hell (Rosier 13). We might also recall that wolvish hostesses turn up again in the later literature of hospitality. When King Lear's daughter Goneril scolds him for letting his knights misbehave in her household, where they are all her guests, he fiercely predicts that Regan will "flay thy wolvish visage" (*King Lear* 1.4.329). And in a much later play, Edward Albee's *Who's Afraid of Virginia Woolf?* (1962), Martha is both a hostess and a monster, as her husband George calls her: a woman who not only humiliates him in front of their two young guests but also gets the man of the couple by rousing his lust and then exposing him as a sexual flop (Albee, 157, 189). In the very last lines of the play, when George gently sings the title song (Martha's little parody of "Who's Afraid of the Big Bad Wolf?"), she admits that she herself is afraid of Virginia Woolf—of the she-wolf inside her.

Returning to Beowulf's encounter with Grendel's mother, the flip side of the monstrosity revealed by a superficially civilized woman of the mid-twentieth century is the superficial hospitality of a medieval monster. When Beowulf swims into her ken, she seizes him in a horrid grip ("atolan clommum," 1502). But since she cannot pierce his coat of mail with her loathsome fingers ("laþan fingrum," 1505), she escorts him—the verb is "baer," meaning "bore" (1506)—to her lair at the very bottom of the lake. At first sight this lair seems irresistibly inviting. It's an underwater hall ("nið-sele," 1513) or vaulted chamber ("hrof-sele," 1515) so watertight that it flickers with the bright blaze of firelight ("fyr-leoht," 1516).[13] Only after taking all this in does Beowulf start swinging his sword and bringing it down on the head of his monstrous hostess, at which point he finds that it won't cut into her. More precisely, we are told,

the guest found
that the light of battle [his sword] would not bite.

[gist onfand
þaet se bealdoleoma bitan nolde.]
(1522–23)

This is the first explicit reference to Beowulf's status in the monster's lair. Only now, after he has perceived its superficially hospitable features, is he identified as her "gist." But with supreme irony he is called a guest just as he is striving to kill his hostess. Furthermore, he uses his sword in a way that subtly recalls Grendel's manner of feasting. When Grendel caught up the sleeping warrior in Heorot, he bit the bone-frame, "bat ban-locan" (742). Here Beowulf's sword would not bite—"bitan nolde"—into the body of Grendel's mother. Does the echo mean anything? Neither Beowulf nor any other man in this poem is ever said to feast on a monster, let alone a man. Quite so. But in striving to make his sword bite into a creature who has been implicitly cast as his hostess, he shows how the monsters of this poem have sabotaged the rules of hospitality for all.

In place of the mutually beneficial reciprocity that links hosts and guests, the monsters have initiated a pattern of assault and revenge wherein hosts and guests take turns reciprocating each other's crimes. Sprung from the seed of Cain, whose murder of Abel caused God to banish him from humankind, Grendel is a hellish fiend ("feond on helle," 101) who fiercely resents the merry-making of revelers in Heorot, a place to which he will never be invited.[14] Denied any hope of ever enjoying the hospitality of God or man, he kills thirty Danes and one of Beowulf's men. In retaliation, Beowulf mortally wounds him, which leads to more mayhem. On the very morning after Hrothgar holds a feast to celebrate Beowulf's victory over Grendel, he tells Beowulf that Grendel's mother has avenged the wounding of her son by revisiting Heorot, again as an uninvited guest, and killing Aeschere. In turn, Beowulf sets out to kill the mother, thereby sustaining the brutal reciprocity that both recalls and radically undermines the benign exchanges typically made between hosts and guests.

When Beowulf's sword fails to cut the monster, he throws it away, trusts again to the might of his grip ("mund-gripe mægenes," 1534), and flings her to the ground. In retribution ("andlean," 1541)—even the rhythm of their fight is reciprocal—she takes him in a ghastly clutch ("grimman grapum," 1542) of her own that makes him stumble, drops down on her hall-guest ("sele-gyst," 1545), and draws her dagger to avenge her son, "hire bearn wrecan" (1546). Once again Beowulf is called her guest at the very moment when they are locked in mortal combat, and the poet's account of it is couched in the language of treacherous hospitality. While Beowulf is at first a guest bent on killing his hostess, he is now her potential victim, the guest she aims to get.

But the setback is momentary. Saved from death by divine power and his impenetrable coat of mail, Beowulf sees among the hitherto unmentioned weapons of the monster's lair a matchless sword so big that he alone can wield it (just as Odysseus alone can string the great bow). With it he promptly slashes through the neck of his hostess and then, finding Grendel on his deathbed, decapitates him: fit recompense for the severed head of Aeschere. As Beowulf tells his men afterward, he thereby avenged ("wreac") the slaughter of the Danes (1669–70).

Coming as it does at the midpoint of the poem, this double dispatch of the monsters who have up to now been terrorizing Daneland and fiendishly undermining the rules of hospitality seems cause for rejoicing, especially since the Geats who have waited nine hours for Beowulf's return have almost lost hope of seeing him again when he swims to shore. Their gladness anticipates the joy of the feast that will be held to celebrate Beowulf's victory and to restore the hospitality of Heorot, where the Geats, above all Beowulf, are rewarded by their royal host. "Ga nu to setle, symbel-wynne dreoh" (1782), says Hrothgar to Beowulf. "Go to your seat, enjoy the banquet," which is what "symbel" means once more.

By now, however, the poem has already shown how unstable such meanings can be. At the first of the three feasts held in Heorot, the feast that celebrates Beowulf's arrival, Hrothgar sets an example for all by eagerly consuming the "symbel" (619), meaning "banquet." But in describing his battle with the sea-monsters, Beowulf has just used the very same word for the meal they had planned to make of him (564), and this murderous sense of the word prefigures what Grendel will do right after the royal feast. The poet's account of the second feast likewise uses words that soon betray their original meanings. When Beowulf's killing of Grendel prompts Hrothgar to shower him with precious gifts and to offer him another "symbel" (1010), we are told that all of the glorious warriors, Geats and Danes alike, sit rejoicing at the feast ("fylle gefaegon," 1014). But the very next morning, the grief-stricken Hrothgar tells Beowulf that Grendel's mother is even then "fylle gefaegnod" (1333), rejoicing at the feast she is making with the corpse of Aeschere. This startling echo reinforces the note sounded near the end of the poet's account of Hrothgar's feast:

> That was a delectable feast;
> the men drank their wine; fate they knew not,
> grim destiny.

> [þaer waes symbla cyst;
> druncon win weras. Wyrd ne cuþon,
> geosceaft grimme.]

> (1232–34)

Even without knowing what awaits Aeschere on the night of this feast, the revelers might have been troubled by the song of Hrothgar's minstrel, his "scop." In the story told by this song, hospitality is sabotaged not by monsters seeking vengeance but by men, specifically by a Danish warrior named Hengest. In a winter battle between the Danes and the Frisians that has been somehow provoked by the Jutes, the Danish king Hnaef dies along with many of the Frisians, forcing their king Finn to make a truce with Hnaef's retainer Hengest and the other Danish survivors. Since Hildeburh, Finn's queen, is both the sister of the dead King Hnaef and the mother of another Dane killed in the battle, she is dismayed by its outcome, and when Finn is eventually killed by the Danes, they take her back to her homeland. As a result, the song of Finn and Hengest is often read as evidence that women cannot effectively serve as peace weavers between rival tribes in the world of this poem.

But the crucial point of the story is hospitality betrayed. The second syllable of Hengest's very name points to his frustrating status in Finn's land. Once he pledges himself to peace there, he becomes Finn's implacably resentful "gist" (1138), a guest obsessed with vengeance. Though Finn honors the Danes with gifts and threatens death to his own men if they provoke their guests, nothing can long conciliate men forced to serve the killer of their king. Even Finn's gifts seem fated to rankle them, especially the gift of a hall that must be shared with the Jutes. As the bloodstained winter gives way to a spring that warms the land and brings two more Danish warriors, Guthlaf and Oslaf, from across the sea, the Danes decide to strike. With savage swordblows ("sweordbealo sliðen") they kill their royal host in his own home ("æt his selfes ham," 1147).

Since the song thus ends on a note of victory for the Danes, who crown their triumph by reclaiming Hildeburh for Denmark (as if she had been abducted by the Frisian king who married her), it moves the revelers at Heorot to joyous applause. But, catching again the impermanence of their joy, the poet hints of treachery to come. When, for instance, Hrothgar's queen Wealhtheow tells him that their guest hall has been purged ("gefaelsod," 1176) of all menace, she knows nothing of what Grendel's mother will do there right after the feast.

By the end of his life Beowulf knows only too well how monsters repay their enemies and how guests can betray their hosts. Sometime after Beowulf's return to the land of the Geats, when King Hygelac was killed in a battle with the

Frisians, Beowulf declined the throne, though it was eagerly offered to him, and instead deferred to Hygelac's young son Heardred, whom he served as counselor. With or without Beowulf's advice, Heardred made the fatal mistake of receiving and sheltering two brothers who had rebelled against their uncle Onela, king of the Swedes. As a result of Heardred's hospitality, he was slashed to death by sword blows ("sweordes swengum," 2386) when Onela came to punish his nephews in a battle that left one of them dead. But Onela was eventually made to pay for these deaths. After Beowulf became king of the Geats he furnished weapons and warriors to Eadgils, the surviving nephew, who avenged the death of his brother Eanmund by attacking the Swedes and killing Onela himself. Thus Onela's treatment of hospitality *as* treachery launches once again a brutal parody of hospitable exchange: a deadly sequence of assault and revenge.

In the whole poem, however, no act of treacherous hospitality matches what the Heathobards do while hosting the Danes. The story of this fateful entertainment is told by Beowulf himself as part of the report he delivers to King Hygelac on his return to the Geats, and the report stands out like a sore thumb. In Beowulf's account of his triumphs over Grendel and Grendel's mother, the story of the Heathobards' hospitality looks like a purely irrelevant digression, as can be seen from a bald summary of his whole narrative:

1. In single combat Beowulf avenged Grendel's ravaging of Heorot.
2. Before the combat, he greeted Hrothgar at Heorot, where he was seated beside the king's sons and treated to glorious revelry.
3. Hrothgar's daughter Freawaru is promised to Ingeld of the Heathobards, who will entertain her Danish countrymen soon after she marries Ingeld.
4. After Grendel came to Heorot and devoured a Geatish warrior named (as we learn for the first time) Hondscio, Beowulf seized Grendel's hand and held it until Grendel escaped without his hand.
5. Hrothgar gave Beowulf many treasures and told stories of his past life.
6. When Grendel's mother came to Heorot on the following night to avenge the fatal wounding of her son and carried off a wise old counselor named Aeschere, Beowulf tracked her to her lair at the bottom of a lake and then beheaded her with a sword.
7. Hrothgar gave still more treasures to Beowulf, who now offers them to King Hygelac.

Two of these items are out of order, and one of the two seems wholly misplaced. Though item 2 is chronologically first, Beowulf's victory over Grendel probably deserves to be mentioned first because it is the most famous of his feats among the Danes, known to half the world ("micel gemeting," 2001).

But item 3 looks totally out of place. It has nothing to do with monsters, with any of Beowulf's feats, or with anything that has already happened in the land of the Danes or anywhere else. Instead, Beowulf veers away from the story of his triumphs to predict what *will* happen when Hrothgar's daughter Freawaru marries Ingeld of the Heathobards. Why this digression? Why does Beowulf tell of Heathobards murdering Danes, of hosts murdering their guests? Attentively considered, the context reveals the answer. What looks like a digression actually shows the monstrosity of revenge in the world of humankind. It shows how the lust for revenge among men can sabotage hospitality just as brutally as Grendel's invasion of Heorot.

As Beowulf explains, Hrothgar has promised Freawaru to Ingeld so that she may weave a peace between their respective peoples. Though the Danish warriors have killed many Heathobards, the Heathobards will entertain the sons of those warriors when a Danish princess marries the Heathobard king. But as Beowulf says, the spear rarely sleeps for long after men have been killed. We know this ourselves from the story of what Hengest and his fellow Danes did to Finn when he was their host. Since this story is told by Hrothgar's bard ("scop") at the feast held to celebrate Beowulf's victory over Grendel, it adumbrates the much fuller story of how the Heathobards come to murder their Danish guests. As if he were himself a poet, Beowulf foresees just what will happen at the celebration of Freawaru's marriage to Ingeld:

> Think how the Heathobards will be bound to feel,
> their lord, Ingeld, and his loyal thanes,
> when he walks in with that woman to the feast:
> Danes are at the table, being entertained,
> honoured guests in glittering regalia,
> burnished ring-mail that was their hosts' birthright,
> looted when the Heathobards could no longer wield
> their weapons in the shield-clash, when they went down
> with their beloved companions and forfeited their lives.
>
> (H)

> [Mæg þæs þonne ofþyncan ðeodne Heaðobeardna
> ond þegna gehwam þara leoda,
> þonne he mid fæmnan on flett gæð,
> dryhtbearn Dena, duguða biwenede.
> on him gladiað gomelra lafe,
> heard ond hringmæl Heaðabeardna gestreon
> þenden hie ðam wæpnum wealdan moston,

oððæt hie forlæddan to ðam lindplegan
swæse gesiðas ond hyra sylfra feorh.]

(2032–40)

Here the visiting Danes enact a cruel parody of hospitable exchange. Unlike
Beowulf, who served Hrothgar faithfully as his honored guest and was lavishly
rewarded for his exploits, the Danish warriors have done nothing for their
Heathobard hosts. On the contrary, as the ensuing lines make clear, they have
simply inherited heirlooms snatched from the Heathobards on the field of
battle. If they or their fathers had been *given* these heirlooms, the wearing of
them would have signified one more chapter in a history of hospitable relations
between the Heathobards and the Danes. Instead, the Danish flaunting of
Heathobard spoils drives the Heathobards to remember how those treasures
were lost and who was killed when they were taken.

In particular, says Beowulf, the sight of a Dane wearing a wondrously decorated Heathobard sword will infuriate an old Heathobard warrior and goad him
to taunt a young one:

"Now, my friend, don't you recognize
your father's sword, his favorite weapon,
the one he wore when he went out in his war-mask
to face the Danes on that final day?
After Wethergelkd died and his men were doomed
the Shieldings quickly claimed the field,
and now here's a son of one or other
of those same killers coming through our hall
overbearing us, mouthing boasts,
and rigged in armour that by right is yours."

(H)

["Meaht ðu, min wine, mece gecnawan
þone þin fæder to gefeohte bær
under here-griman hindeman siðe,
dyre iren, þær hyne Dene slogon,
weoldon wælstowe, syððan / Wiðergyld læg,
æfter hæleþa hryre, hwate Scyldungas?
Nu her þara banena byre nathwylces
frætwum hremig on flet gæð,
morðres gylpeð, ond þone maðþum byreð,
þone þe ðu mid rihte rædan sceoldest."]

(2047–56)

No guest can safely wear a weapon snatched from the father of his host. In the last battle of the *Aeneid*, when the hero's spear pierces the thigh of the Rutulian king Turnus and thus forces him to the ground, he begs Aeneas to spare his life. But while pondering this plea, Aeneas sees on his shoulder the gleaming swordbelt that Turnus took from Pallas, beloved son of Aeneas's ally Evander. Instantly reminding Aeneas that Turnus has killed the young man, the very sight of the swordbelt drives Aeneas to plunge his own sword "deep in his enemy's heart" (12.950 / F 1110). Likewise, in the eyes of the young Heathobard warrior, the sight of a Heathobard sword worn by a Danish warrior will signify the killing of the man who once owned it. As the son of that man, the young warrior should have inherited it. Instead he must see it flaunted by the son of the man who killed, or helped to kill, his father. Hence, goaded by the old warrior to an irrepressible rage, the young one will avenge the death of his father by killing one of Freawaru's thanes—one of their Danish guests—and making his escape in a land he knows well.

The figure of the escaped murderer at the end of Beowulf's tale calls to mind Beowulf's own father, Ecgtheow, who fled the Geats after killing Heatholaf of the Wylfings. In Hrothgar Ecgtheow found a king who would pay his debt to the Wylfings—"wergeld" for the murdered man—in return for loyal service. Hrothgar thus reinscribed the murderer in the system of exchange that underlies hospitality as well as peace between one people and another. But Beowulf foresees no "wergeld" for the murdered Dane. He sees only love disintegrating between Ingeld and Freawaru, hatred erupting in the Heathobard king, and treachery cracking the bond of trust between hosts and guests.

During Beowulf's sojourn with the Danes, the bond of love and trust he forges with his royal host Hrothgar remains unbroken, and in his lifetime, we are told, he never betrays the spirit of a feast by attacking anyone: he "never cut down a comrade who was drunk" (H 2179–80). Yet Beowulf knows how readily feasts may be sabotaged by violence and hatred. Ostensibly a digression from his story of feasting with Hrothgar, his forecast of treachery between the Danes and their Heathobard hosts may be read as translating the violence of fabulous monsters into the brutal facts of human aggression. Just as Grendel's murderous invasion shatters the mood engendered by the welcoming feast, which Beowulf recalls as one of the happiest he has ever seen (2014–16), Beowulf sees how bitter resentment can turn human revelers, whether hosts or guests, into murderers. Alternating between the story of Grendel and the story of the murderous Heathobards, Beowulf shows that hospitality can be shattered quite as much by men as by beasts.

This alternation between stories of monsters and tales of men persists in the last third of the poem, when Beowulf returns to his native land and becomes its king. Here at first we see human reciprocity at its most benign. After telling King Hygelac how he vanquished Grendel and was lavishly rewarded by Hrothgar with gifts of his own choosing (including precious armor and four bay steeds), Beowulf offers these treasures to Hygelac, "upon [whose] grace / . . . all favor depends" (H 2149–50). Also, he gives Queen Hygd three horses and the glittering necklace he received from Hrothgar's queen, Wealhtheow. In return, Hygelac gives him a gold-chased, gem-studded heirloom, the finest sword in Geatland, plus seven thousand hides and a hall and throne. This exchange of gifts seems to restore the benign reciprocity that has been all but eclipsed by the lethal exchange of assault and revenge. In particular, Hygelac's gift of a sword that came to him from his father Hrethel shows how an heirloom should pass from one man to another: by royal largesse, not by murder and theft that bequeath more violence to the next generation, as in the case of the Heathobards and Danes.

Nevertheless, the long reign of the wise king Beowulf, who ruled for fifty winters, is punctuated by yet another story of men, monsters, and hospitality betrayed. The source of evil in the last part of the poem is once again a fabulous beast, but unlike Grendel, he is not driven by resentment of God's curse or by any motiveless malignity. Instead he is roused by the treachery of a human being: a runaway servant who has somehow offended his master. Unlike Beowulf's father, who found refuge with a generous king, this nameless refugee wanders by accident into a barrow guarded by a sleeping dragon and thereby becomes, as we are explicitly told, the dragon's "gyste" (2227). Finding within the barrow a hoard of treasures that had been left there three hundred years earlier by the last survivor of an exhausted race, the dragon's uninvited guest steals a gilded, gem-studded goblet, takes it back to his master by way of reparation, and thereby prompts his master to plunder the hoard.

This brazen theft, the antithesis of the treasure giving we have seen so often up to now, initiates yet another violent exchange of attack and revenge. Enraged by the taking of his treasures, the fire-breathing dragon one night incinerates the homes of the Geats, including Beowulf's hall, "the best of buildings . . . / the throne-room of the Geats" (H 2326–27). For the third and last time, therefore, the fearless Beowulf resolves to fight a monster, and again in single combat, not with an army. But here the narrator injects two stories that chronologically precede Beowulf's reign: the story of Hygelac's death in a battle that Beowulf heroically survived, and the story of Hygelac's son Heardred, who inherited the throne as a boy and ruled with Beowulf's advice. Heardred, as we have seen, was slashed to death for granting hospitality to a pair of Swedish refugees who had rebelled against their uncle.

These stories highlight various things about Beowulf: his extraordinary stamina in battle, his grace in deferring to Heardred, and his kindness to the Swedish refugees after Heardred is killed and Beowulf succeeds him. But the fate of Heardred also serves to reaffirm that hospitality in this poem can never wholly seal itself from treachery and peril. How could it be otherwise if a "gyste" can sometimes be an intruder, if guests may kill their hosts, if even the welcome guests of the superlatively kind and generous Hrothgar can be brutally feasted upon, as Hondscio is, or if the very words for feast and banquet (such as *fylle* and *symbel*) can be used to designate man-eating?[15]

Feasting turns likewise murderous in Beowulf's fight with the dragon. Grendel, we may recall, bit the bone-frame ("bat banlocan") of the doomed Hondscio, but later the Danish sword Hrunting wielded by Beowulf failed to bite into Grendel's mother. In Beowulf's final fight, his ancestral sword (Naegling) bites feebly ("bat unswiðor," 2578) into the dragon's bone. Then, after the sword sticks in the dragon's skull and snaps, the dragon seizes Beowulf's whole neck in his jaws, biting the bone ("biteran banum," 2692), bathing him in blood, and thus reenacting Grendel's way of feasting on Hondscio. With the aid of young Wiglaf, who plunges his sword into the dragon's belly, Beowulf kills the dragon, but the dragon has already, so to speak, devoured his life.

Beowulf spends the last of that life on one simple act. He tells Wiglaf to rummage the hoard of the now-stricken dragon and bring him the ancient gold and jewels so he can examine them before he dies. It seems a selfless gesture, for what the bleeding king sees at last is not something he craves for himself but something he has won for his people and for which he dutifully thanks God, the King of Glory. Nevertheless, he sums up his final feat as a life-consuming exchange:

> Now for a hoard of treasures I have sold
> The last of my life.

> [Nu ic on maðma hord mine bebohte
> frode feorh-lege.]
>
> (2799–800)

Echoing his words, the narrator simply says,

> Beowulf paid
> the price of death for that plentiful hoard.

[Biowulfe wearð
dryht-maðma dæl deaðe forgolden.]
(2842–43)

Beowulf dies to enact an exchange that may be seen as either heroic and self-less or rashly invasive: one more instance of hospitality displaced by violence. In subtly deploying the language of feasting for murderous ends, the story of the dragon fight resembles the stories of Beowulf's fights with Grendel and his mother. But unlike Grendel, who comes to Heorot as an uninvited guest, the dragon does not initiate his feud with humankind. The feud starts only when he is robbed by the nameless refugee. Wiglaf too is a robber of sorts, though he robs at his king's command. The ancient treasures brought to Beowulf's dying eyes may be seen as fit reward for his heroic self-sacrifice but also as something violently taken rather than graciously given in the course of hospitable exchange: one more example of the price to be paid for breaking the rules of hospitality.

In showing how the benign exchange of hospitality turns into a malicious cycle of assault and revenge and finally into the deadly trading of life for treasure, *Beowulf* shows as well the limits of reciprocity as a principle of socioeconomic relations. If receivers of gifts feel typically obliged to "give back more than [they] have received," as Mauss notes (85), *Beowulf* displays an economy in which nothing short of death can end the cycle of obligation. On the one hand, the hero can be read as a Christ figure giving everything for his people, sacrificing his life for them. On the other hand, he can be seen as paying a price, a "wergeld" even, for an act of thievery, a crime against hospitality perpetrated by an invited guest in the dragon's lair. Echoed by the narrator, Beowulf's final words make us wonder if he thinks the treasure worth his life. In a poem that makes no promises of eternal salvation, his only recompense, unknown to him, is the afterlife of fame enshrined in the poem itself.

GAWAIN AND THE GREEN KNIGHT: BEHEADING AND EROTIC HOSPITALITY

Since *Beowulf* seems to end on a note of self-sacrifice—the hero giving up his life for the sake of his people—it might be judged even more Christian than *Gawain*.[16] But even without the robber's provocation of the dragon and Beowulf's own admission that he traded his life for treasure, a "plentiful hoard," rather than for anything like Christian salvation, it is hard to link the two poems in terms of Christianity or to overlook the obvious differences between Beowulf's

heroism and the valor of a Christian knight. Gawain kills no one of any consequence during his journey, suffers nothing worse than a nick on his neck, and
returns to the Arthurian court with his youth and his health intact. Since his
reputation for chivalric valor chiefly depends on his capacity to resist sexual
temptation, it has no counterpart in the world of *Beowulf*. Compared with the
hero of that poem, he seems to seek his fame by totally different means.

Nevertheless, the stories of Beowulf and Gawain are clearly linked by
beheading. As Jeffrey Cohen has shown, both of them reflect a long tradition of
heroes such as Gilgamesh and David, who establish their manhood by decapitating an adversary (Cohen 173) and who each gain a fearsome authority by
displaying a severed head. When David shows the head of Goliath to the
Philistine army, he frightens the army away and "announces both a personal
and a political coming of age, the birth of a heroic and a national identity"
(Cohen 173). Beowulf fights for the Danes rather than for his own people, but
he nonetheless savors a similar moment of triumph. After he kills the mother of
Grendel, chops off Grendel's gigantic head, and has it hoisted on a spear by
four of his men, he manifests his courage and glory by having the head dragged
into Heorot and thereby horrifying the queen and her court:

> In he came then, the thane's commander
> the arch-warrior, to address Hrothgar:
> his courage was great, his glory was secure.
> Grendel's head was hauled by the hair,
> dragged across the floor where the people were drinking,
> a horror for both queen and company to behold.
> They stared in awe. It was an astonishing sight.
>
> (H)

>   [ða com in gan ealdor ðegna,
> dædcene mon dome gewurþad,
> hæle hildedeor, Hroðgar gretan.
> þa wæs be feaxe on flet boren
> Grendles heafod, þær guman druncon,
> egeslic for eorlum ond þære idese mid,
> wliteseon wrætlic; weras on sawon.]
>
> (1644–50)

The corresponding moment in *Sir Gawain* comes at the beginning of the
poem, when the noble men and women feasting at King Arthur's court are
suddenly confronted by a gigantic Green Knight holding in his hand his own

talking head, which has just been cut off by Sir Gawain. Conceived by Morgan le Fay, mistress of Merlin the magician, the purpose of this ghastly spectacle was not just to horrify the queen and her company but to give her a fatal shock.[17] As ultimately explained to Sir Gawain himself by Lord Bertilak de Hautdesert, who was magically enabled to appear as the giant, Morgan aimed by means of this persona

> to have grieved Guinevere and caused her to die
> From gazing at that same person that spoke like a ghost
> With his head in his hand before the high table.[18]

> [to haf greued Gaynour and gart hir to dyʒe
> With glopnyng of þat ilke gome þat gostlych speked
> With his hede in his honde bifore þe hyʒe table.]
>   (2460–62)

To see how *Sir Gawain* evokes *Beowulf*, however, is also to see how radically it transforms the earlier poem—whether or not it was known to the author of *Sir Gawain*. Unlike Grendel, the Green Knight miraculously survives his beheading, and in doing so he manifests his own astonishing power, not that of Sir Gawain, who cuts off the giant's head at the giant's invitation and with an axe the giant gives him. In decapitating the giant, Gawain binds himself to present his own neck to the giant's axe a year hence. This second, future axe transforms the trophy value of the first even though, at Arthur's request, Gawain hangs it up over the dais of the feasting hall,

> Where all men might look on it as a marvel,
> And by the true evidence of it, tell the wonder.

> [þer alle men for meruayl myʒt on hit loke,
> And bi trwe tytel þerof to telle þe wonder.]
>   (479–80)

Hung up for all to see and wonder at, this potent souvenir of Gawain's encounter with the Green Knight recalls the fearful souvenir of Beowulf's battle with Grendel: the monster's "grape," or grip, meaning his shoulder and arm as a unit, which is likewise hung on high up near the roof of Heorot (833–36). But unlike Grendel's limb, which plainly signifies the power of the man who wrenched it from him, the Green Knight's axe signifies only his own power: the power to give, traditionally reserved to the king or the host, and the power to strike back.

This whole episode, then, raises serious questions about the significance of the decapitation, especially since the only other head cut off in the poem is that of a boar killed by Bertilak. While hosting Gawain during the Christmas week before his fateful meeting with the Green Knight, Bertilak kills the boar as Gawain lies in his bed and dallies, albeit chastely, with Lady Bertilak. This killing too recalls *Beowulf.* Just as the older hero kills the mother of Grendel in the depths of a lake by driving a sword deep into her neck (1492–1569), Bertilak catches the boar in the midst of a raging white stream ("In þe wyȝtest of þe water") and drives his sword deep into its heart (1583–94). Also, just as Grendel's head is borne in triumph to Heorot, the boar's huge head is hacked off, set high on a stake, brought back to a company of feasters, and then presented to Gawain himself, who feels bound to feign terror at it:

> Then they man-handled the huge head. The fine man [Gawain] praised it,
> And pretended that he was terrified in order to honor the lord.
> "Now, Gawain," said the good man, "this game is your own
> By the fine and faithfully bound bargain that you know."

> [þenne hondeled þay þe hoge hed, þe hende mon hit praysed,
> And let lodly þerat þe lorde for to here.
> "Now, Gawayn," quoþ þe godmon, "þis gomen is your awen
> Bi fyn forwarde and faste, faythely ȝe knowe."]

(1633–36)

Once again, however, the incidental parallels between the two situations serve to set off their fundamental differences. Unlike Beowulf, Gawain has fought no beast, and his response to the head is hardly heroic, let alone Beowulfian. Risking his masculinity, as he often does in this gender-bending poem, he plays the part of a frightened queen. But he has good reason to be unnerved by the spectacle of this "game," the centerpiece of a deadly game being played by the host on his guest. Proffered with the merry laughter ("laȝter myry," 1623) of the unflaggingly convivial host, the boar's head keeps the "forwarde," or bargain, that he earlier struck with Gawain: they have each sworn sincerely ("wyth trawþe") that after the host spends the day hunting and the guest dallying with the host's wife, they will "swap"—Bertilak's exact word— whatever they have gained (1108). Given the playfulness of Bertilak's tone, it seems more than possible that he is punning on *gome.* Also spelled *game,* this richly polysemous word could signify a warrior, a person (as in 2161, quoted above), a diversion (as in the "Crystemas gomme" proposed by the Green Knight, 284), an animal killed in a hunt, or sexual intercourse, the game of love.[19] We already know that from the lady of the house Sir Gawain has gained

two kisses, once just after she comes to his bedroom and another as she leaves
(1505, 1555). In response to the words of his host, therefore, he dutifully keeps
his part of the bargain:

> "It is truth," said the knight [Gawain], "and as surely true
>   [to confirm it]
> All my gain I shall give you again, on my honor."
> He clasps the lord around the neck, and graciously kisses him
> And soon after of the same [another kiss] he served him there.
> "Now are we even," said the knight, "in this eventide
> By all the covenants that we knit since I came hither
> By law."
>
> ["Hit is sothe," quoþ þe segge, "and as siker trwe
> Alle my get I schal yow gif agayn, bi my trawþe."
> He hent þe haþel aboute þe halse, and hendely hym kysses,
> And eftersones of þe same he serued hym þere.
> "Now ar we euen," quoþ þe haþel, "in þis euentide
> Of alle þe couenauntes þat we knyt, syþen I com hider,
> bi lawe."]
>
>   (1637–43)

The punctilious tone of this exchange—word for word, favor for favor, kisses
for kisses, and all according to "covenants"—masks the peril threatening
Gawain if he fails in any way to keep his part of the bargain. Bertilak seems the
most generous and convivial of hosts. He has welcomed a weary traveler to his
castle on Christmas Eve; he has fed and lodged and clothed him luxuriously;
and he has given him the company of his lovely wife, who on her first morning
visit to Gawain's bedroom has told him he is "welcum to my cors" (1237),
meaning, among other things, welcome to her body. But if he takes the lady up
on her enticing offer or fails to give Bertilak all he has gained from her, he risks
nothing less than losing his head to the axe of the giant he is bound to meet
on New Year's Day. Before King Arthur and all of his court, Sir Gawain has
pledged that he will abide the consequences of decapitating the giant, and in
words spoken by his own severed head the giant confirms that Gawain deserves
to be promptly repaid ("ȝederly ȝolden") on New Year's Day (452–53). This
"forwarde" of requital—one blow to the neck will repay another—frames the
whole narrative, including the compact of reciprocity struck between the host
and his unwitting guest during the week before his meeting with the giant.

Whether giant or host, Bertilak is a master of dangerous games. The
"Crystmeas gomme" of beheading that he offers to Arthur and his court (283)

may be just a spectacular magic trick, but the prospect of having to pay for it by exposing one's own neck to the giant's axe daunts every one of Arthur's knights until first the king himself and then Sir Gawain rise to the challenge. "Forwarde," meaning "bargain," sounds unnervingly like *forwird*, meaning "ruin or destruction," which is precisely where any bargain struck with the host or giant in this poem may lead. Long before the older couple in *Who's Afraid of Virginia Woolf?* play "Get the Guest" with a hapless young couple they have invited for drinks, Bertilak does all he can to get his guest.[20] When he says of the boar's head to Gawain, "This game is your own" (this gomen is your awen), he may well be saying, as Cohen observes, "This will be your head . . . should you fail the ordeals of passage" (Cohen 185).

But the word "ordeals" must be carefully unpacked. Gawain's ordeals differ so much from Beowulf's that no one in the world of Beowulf, including the anonymous author of the poem about him, could have seen anything heroic in what Gawain does or endures. Where is the heroism in decapitating a giant who offers you his neck and his axe, then picks up that head and with it reminds you that you must present your own neck to his axe a year hence? And how can the act of passively *enduring* death or the threat of death be heroic? The answer to this question comes only with the crucifixion of Christ, which has no demonstrable bearing on the ethos of *Beowulf* but which profoundly informs a poem that explicitly moves from one Christmas season to another. Nearly three centuries after the composition of *Sir Gawain*, the difference between Beowulf and Gawain was implicitly stated by Milton in a passage that effectively classifies knightly heroism not with the latter but with the fighting prowess of the former. In the invocation to book 9 of *Paradise Lost* Milton says that his "heroic song" will celebrate a new kind of heroism: not the "tedious havoc" of "fabled knights" in fictive battles—"hitherto the only argument / Heroic deemed"—but rather

> the better fortitude
> Of patience and heroic martyrdom
> Unsung.
>
> (9.25–33)

In Milton's poem, as in the Christian tradition, the supreme model of heroic martyrdom is the suffering of Christ, who utterly rejects the glory of mortal combat, who resists all temptation (including the temptation to conquer, except in vanquishing Satan), and who unresistingly submits himself to death on the cross. He thereby sets a standard that no human being can match but that a Christian hero is nonetheless expected to emulate. Unlike Beowulf, who proves his heroism solely by fighting and killing, the Christian hero must combine supreme patience—unresisting submission to suffering and death—with supreme self-control: the capacity to resist all temptation.

In *Paradise Lost*, Adam fails to resist the temptation of Eve when she urges him to join her in tasting the forbidden fruit. Though undeceived by the specious argument that Satan has fed her along with the fruit—that tasting it will deify the taster—he is unmanned by his passion for her, "fondly overcome with female charm" (9.999).[21] When Gawain himself finally succumbs to one of the temptations posed by Lady Bertilak, he complains that men have always been led into sorrow by women: "For so was Adam on earth deceived by one" (For so watz Adam in erde with one bygyled, 2416).

The impulse to hold women responsible for beguiling men richly complicates the role of women in the world of King Arthur and his knights, where Christian heroism is merely the foundation for a chivalric code riddled with contradictions. The code requires, for instance, that a knight revere a lady, above all his hostess, and obey her commandments. On her second morning visit to his bedroom Lady Bertilak tells Gawain that "courtesy" (cortaysy) requires a knight to claim a kiss from a lady (1491). When he says he has refrained to claim one lest he be denied, she says he could "constrayne" any woman he wanted if she were so "vilanous" as to refuse him (1493–97). In response, he commends her speech as "good," says that in his land it's unworthy of a knight to take a lady by force or against her will and also that he is at her commandment to kiss when she wishes ("at [her] commaundement, to kysse quen yow likez," 1499–1501).[22] Hard as it is to see the "good" of a speech that condones rape and vilifies any woman who spurns a knight's advances, it is harder still to reconcile Gawain's eventual vilification of his hostess with his chivalric deference to her and his acceptance of her secret gift, the green belt that she says will preserve his life against the Green Knight's axe. In the end she proves a handy scapegoat. When the Green Knight, a.k.a. Bertilak, reveals that Gawain has broken their compact by taking the belt without telling his host, let alone sharing it with him, Gawain curses himself for "cowarddyse and couetyse," the cowardly, covetous wish to save his skin (2374). But as soon as Gawain's confession moves Bertilak to absolve him, to restore the purity and innocence he was born with, Gawain promptly asks to be "excused" for his failing because, like a whole parade of men ranging from Adam to David, he was "bigyled" by a woman (2425–28).[23] As Bonnie Lander observes, Gawain fails to see that his attack on women wholly undermines the deference for them required by the chivalric code (Lander 54–55). Blind to this contradiction, he seems equally blind to the machinations of his host, who has ordered his wife to attempt the

seduction of their guest and who has no doubt schooled the guide furnished for
Gawain's trip to the Green Chapel: the guide who tries to scare him away from
it and assures him that he will keep the secret of Gawain's flight (2096–2125).[24]
Ignoring all this, Gawain bids farewell to his host as if Lord and Lady Bertilak
had both treated him impeccably:

> may good fortune betide you,
> And may he who grants all honors yield it to you fully!
> And commend me to that courteous [woman], your comely wife.

> [sele yow bytyde,
> And he ȝelde hit yow ȝare þat ȝarkkez al menskes!
> And comaundez me to þat cortays, your comlych fere.]
>
> (2409–11)

One might justify this language by arguing that the outcome of Bertilak's
Christmas game ("Chrystemas gomme" 283) not only confirms Gawain's status
as the most nearly faultless knight ("fautlest freke") who ever trod the ground
(2363) but also reveals in Bertilak a distinctively Christian willingness to forgive.
He has given the knight no more than what Gawain later calls a nick in the
neck ("nirt in þe nek," 2598) because, he says, Gawain's sin was venial:

> You lacked a little, sir, and loyalty you were missing;
> But that was for no wild work, nor wooing neither,
> But because you loved your life; the less I blame you.

> [yow lakked a lyttel, sir, and lewté yow wonted;
> Bot þat watz for no wylyde werke, ne wowyng nauþer,
> Bot for ȝe lufed your lyf; þe lasse I yow blame.]
>
> (2366–68)

Nevertheless, Bertilak's final words should give us pause. In light of the
emphatically Christian culture of these knights, his venializing of Gawain's sin
ignores both the Christian principle of self-sacrifice and the chivalric code of
courage built up over it. If Christ taught that "whoever wants to preserve his
own life will lose it" (Matt. 16:25), can the desire for self-preservation be treated
as a minor fault? As I have noted, Gawain himself condemns "cowarddyse and
couetyse," cowardice and the covetous attachment to life, as the worst of sins.
The chief purpose of Bertilak's game is to see if the pride ("surquidré," 2457) of
the Arthurian court is founded on courage, a bedrock principle of the chivalric
code. In the Middle Irish tale of *The Feast of Bricriu*, Cuchulainn answers the
beheading challenge of an ugly giant by decapitating him and then putting his

own neck on the giant's chopping block because he "would rather have death with honor" than fail to keep his pledge (par. 99, Henderson 44).[25] Gawain fails by scheming to save his neck, and though he censures himself for treachery and dishonesty ("trecherye and vntrawþe," 2383) he also asks to be excused, as we have seen, for being victimized by feminine wiles. In other words, just as he "shrank a little" (schrank a lytel) from the first fall of the Green Knight's axe (2267), he shrinks from taking responsibility for his cowardice, his disloyalty to his host, and his dishonesty in wearing the belt.

But are these truly serious sins? When Gawain dutifully reports them to the Arthurian court and says he will henceforth wear the green girdle as the sign of cowardice and covetousness ("couardise and couetyse") and as a "token of vntrawþ" (untruth) (2508–9), they all laugh loudly and resolve to wear the green band likewise in honor of Gawain. Its meaning thus changes drastically. No longer a sign of Gawain's disgrace, it becomes instead a souvenir of his sojourn with the Bertilaks and a sign of his contribution to the renown of the Round Table ("þe renoun of þe Rounde Table," 2519).

What happens to the shame signified by Gawain's belt exemplifies the radical instability of moral values in a world ostensibly governed by them. The Green Knight first appears on horseback at a Christmastide feast hosted by King Arthur, who will not eat at such a festive time until he has heard a tale of some marvelous adventure ("some mayne meruayle," 94) or seen two knights risk their lives against each other ("lif for lyf") in a joust (96–98). Even before the Green Knight enters the feasting hall, therefore, the death of a knight presents itself as simply a possible consequence of Christmas entertainment, and the Green Knight himself combines the terror of an executioner with the charm of an entertaining guest: just what the king has been waiting for. Unlike the ugly giant of *The Feast of Bricriu*, he is handsomely proportioned, well groomed, elegantly clothed, wholly unarmored, and weaponless except for the huge, menacing axe he holds in one hand. Welcomed by the king and hospitably urged to dismount and linger ("lenge") among them (252–54), he assures them that he comes in peace, which is signified by the holly branch he holds in his other hand (265–66). But the Christmas game he proposes is a game leading to death. Whoever takes up the giant's offer to behead him with the axe must give the giant the right to deal him another blow like it, and to lay him on a bier a year hence ("þe dom to dele hym an oþer / bar lay," 295–96). The unexpected guest proposes all this in the name of Christmas entertainment.

The stunned silence provoked by his challenge goads the giant to mockery. Taunting the knights for their dread ("drede," 315), he scornfully charges that one man's word has overthrown the renown of the Round Table. But has it? Only if we ignore the suicidal implications of the challenge. Is it cowardly for any mortal man to balk at beheading a giant who cannot be killed but demands the right to behead the mortal in return? Is it cowardly to refuse to play such a game—or merely wise? Whether or not this question roils the mind of anyone in the court, it fails to break their silence or dissolve the simpleminded polarization of courage and cowardice.[26] So the king feels bound to break the silence by taking up the challenge. In turn, Gawain feels equally bound to risk his own life—or give his life—for the sake of the king as well as of the court's reputation. His own reputation, he believes, will henceforth depend on his keeping the pledge he makes before all the court: to meet the giant a twelvemonth hence and take a "buffet" from him (381–85). In the parting words spoken by the Green Knight's severed head, Gawain must seek him out faithfully ("als lelly," 449) until he finds him. If he fails to go to the Green Chapel and bear such a blow as he has dealt to the Green Knight ("such a dunt as þou hatz dalt," 452), he will have to be called a "recreaunt" (456), a coward, a beaten man.

The gap between language and event, signifier and signified, is nowhere greater than here. Though Gawain has just made what seems a suicidal promise, he and the king both laugh and grin ("laȝe and grenne," 464) at the marvel they have witnessed, and, as noted above, the axe that is promptly displayed as a token of this marvel signifies not the conquering power of Gawain but the terror that awaits him at the end of the year, when the only alternative to cowardice is not to fight but simply to seek out and accept his own beheading.

In the week leading up to that ordeal of distinctively Christian heroism, Gawain must endure something that would have been equally incomprehensible to anyone in the world of *Beowulf*: the ordeal of temptation or, more precisely, of erotic hospitality. In the elegant castle of Lord Bertilak, which he comes upon after several weeks of strenuous tramping through the forested mountains and streams of North Wales, he is perfectly safe from the beasts he has had to fight along the way; he is not even expected to join his host in hunting but is left to enjoy the company of his lovely hostess in his own bedroom. What then is expected of him at Castle Hautdesert? Not the courage for which the knights of the Round Table are renowned, and not the "fierceness and ferocity" (grydellayk and . . . greme) they claim to possess but fail to display when the Green Knight challenges and then mocks them (312). On the contrary, the knights who welcome Gawain to Hautdesert see him chiefly as a model of courtliness. "Now," they tell each other,

shall we pleasingly see fine points of conduct
And the faultless words of noble discourse.
What power there is in inspired speech we may learn,
Since we have received that fine master of good breeding.
God has truly given us his good grace,
That grants us to have such a guest as Gawain,
When happy men shall sit
And sing of his birth [i.e., good breeding].
To instruction in fine manners
This knight now shall us bring.
I hope that whoever may hear him
Shall learn of love-talking.

["Now schal we semlych se sleȝtez of þewez
And þe teccheles termes of talkyng noble,
Wich spede is in speche vnspurd may we lerne,
Syn we haf fonged þat fyne fader of nurture.
God hatz geuen vus his grace godly for soþe
þat such a gest as Gawan grauntez vus to haue,
When burnez blyþe of his burþe schal sitte
and synge.
In menyng of manerez mere
þis burne now schal vus bryng,
I hope þat may hym here
Schal lerne of luf-talkyng."]

(916–27)

To the courtiers of Hautdesert Gawain exemplifies none of the virtues on which he chiefly prides himself. They do not speak of his courage or of the truth ("trawþe") and fivefold faithfulness signified by the endless knot of the pentangle emblazoned on his shield (619–34). They do not even mention his courtesy ("cortaysye"), which is bound by the pentangle to real virtues—generosity, friendliness, purity, and compassion (652–54)—but which can readily be attenuated to "courtliness."[27] Instead of such virtues or anything like them, the first thing the knights of Hautdesert hope to see Gawain demonstrate is "sleȝtez of þewez," which I have rendered as "fine points of conduct" but which might also be called tricks or sleights of conduct, tricks of the courtier's trade. Above all they hope to learn from him the language of seduction ("luf-talkyng").[28] Later on, when she comes to Gawain's bedroom for the second time, Lady Bertilak herself asks him to teach her "some tokens of true love craft" (sum tokenez of trweluf craftes, 1527), to engage her in "dalliance" (dalyaunce, 1529), and to instruct her in some "game" (1532), a word whose meanings range, as we have seen, from polite diversion to sexual intercourse. Eschewing the role of tutor in the art of love, Gawain defers to the social sophistication of his hostess. "In good faith" (In goud faýþe), he says, it is gracious of you to take such pains with so poor a man ("so pouer a man") and it comforts me:

> But to take on myself the task of explaining true love,
> And touch the themes of [romantic] texts and tales of chivalry,
> To you that, I know well, hold more skill
> In that art, by the half, than a hundred of such
> As I am, or ever shall [be], on earth where I live,
> Would be a manifold folly, my lady, by my troth.

> [Bot to take þe toruayle to myself to trwluf expoun,
> And towche þe temez of tyxt and talez of armez
> To yow þat, I wot wel, weldez more slyȝt
> Of þat art, bi þe half, or a hundreth of seche
> As I am, oþer euer schal, in erde þer I leue,
> Hit were a folé felefolde, my fre, by my trawþe.]

(1535–45)

Beginning with *faýþe* / faith and ending with *trawþe* / truth, two of the key terms in Gawain's conception of his own probity, his self-deprecating refusal to play the role of tutor in the art of "luf-talkying" seems to spring from an honest appraisal of his naiveté, his simplicity, his artlessness. While bent on upholding the Round Table's reputation for courage and faithfulness, he disowns any reputation for courtliness that might be thrust upon him, especially by a woman whose mastery of the "slyȝt," or tricks of seduction, far exceeds his own. Nevertheless, he reveals his art precisely in the act of denying it. In artfully deferring to Lady Bertilak's sophistication, he deploys what Lander calls "the convention of innocence" and thereby reveals it as something constructed (Lander 63). Confirming what the courtiers first said about him, Gawain proves himself a man of "slyȝt."

This is nowhere more evident than in his response to Lady Bertilak during her third visit to his bedroom, when she offers him the belt that she says will make him indestructible. Though reluctant to accept any gift from his hostess, he cannot resist the protective promise of this one:

It would be a jewel—a magic charm—against the jeopardy he was fated to meet.
When he reached the chapel to take his blow,
Might he have slipped away unslain, the trick were noble.

[Hit were a juel for þe jopardé þat hym iugged were:
When he acheued to þe chapel his chek for to fech,
My ȝt he haf slypped to be vnslayn, þe sleȝt were noble.]

(1856–58)

If Gawain considers this sleight or trick "noble," what has become of the noble prince ("prynce noble") whose perfect "trawþe" was signified by the pentangle (623–26)?[29] All such terms lose their stability, and "noble" comes to mean simply "sly." When Gawain conspires with Lady Bertilak to hide her gift from everyone else, including the host with whom he has promised to swap all his winnings, he seems little better than the fox who is even now being hunted by Lord Bertilak and using its "wyles" to elude his hounds (1700). Giving him the belt, she

> besought him, for her sake, to reveal it never,
> But to conceal it faithfully from her lord; the man agrees
> That never anyone should know it, indeed, but those two
>   for nothing.

> [bisoȝt hym, for hir sake, disceuer hit neuer,
> Bot to lelly layne fro hir lorde; þe leude hym acordez
> þat neuer wyȝe schulde hit wyt, iwysse, bot þay twayne
>   for noȝte.]

(1862–65)

Lady Bertilak speaks the language of "slyȝt": verbal tricks. When she begs Gawain to hide her gift from everyone and in particular to hide it "faithfully" (lelly) from her lord, she is asking him to betray his compact with his host in order to be "lel," or loyal and faithful, to her. This flagrant contradiction springs from the fact that she habitually uses "lel" to mean "devoted to a lady at any cost." On the morning of her second visit to Gawain's bedroom she tells him that she thinks him an expert on love because

> of all chivalric ideals one might choose, the chief thing praised
> Is the *loyal* game of love, the literature of arms;
> For to tell of this battling of these true knights,
> It is the documented token and text of their deeds,
> How men for the sake of *loyal* love have risked their lives,
> Endured for their paramours wretched times,
> And then avenged themselves by means of their valor and banished their cares,
> And brought bliss into a lady's bedchamber with charms all their own.

> [of alle cheualry to chose, þe chef þyng alosed
> Is þe *lel* layk of luf, þe lettrure of armes;

> For to telle of þis teuelyng of þis trwe knyȝtez,
> Hit is þe tytelet token and tyxt of her werkkez,
> How ledes for her *lele* luf hor lyuez han auntered,
> Endured for her drury dulful stoundez,
> And after wenged with her walour and voyded her care,
> And broȝt blysse into boure with bountees hor awen.]
>
> (1512–19, emphasis added)

Though Lady Bertilak says all this to buttress her request for tutelage in the art of "luf-talkyng," as noted above, she already seems to have mastered this art. In her conception of chivalry and its discourse, what moves a knight to fight is fidelity not to his king or his lord but only to the lady he loves and to the whole "layk," or game of passion, violence, and jeopardy created by the text ("tyxt") of romances, with their promise of bliss in a lady's bedroom to compensate for all the pain and misery required to reach it.

Earlier in the fourteenth century, Dante's Francesca told the pilgrim of the *Inferno* how she and her lover were led into adultery and then to death and damnation by reading of Lancelot's adulterous passion for Guinevere. Though Gawain never yields to sexual temptation and though neither he nor the lady could have read this story of an event that had not yet occurred at the time of his own adventure, they are each caught up in the language of romance, bound to the sliding signification of words at least as much as to any moral values they might signify. What does "lelly" (faithfully) mean when it modifies the act of hiding a gift from one's host and thereby breaking the terms of a promise? What does "trwe" (true) mean when it describes a knight willing to sacrifice all, including what he owes to his lord, for the sake of his passion? Lady Bertilak's way of using words like "lelly" and "trwe" resembles what a Chaucerian knight named Arveragus does with "trouthe" (truth) in *The Franklin's Tale*, written about the same time as *Sir Gawain*. During Arveragus's long absence in Britain, his wife Dorigen tells an infatuated squire named Aurelius that she will never be an untrue wife ("untrewe wyf," 984). But after she playfully promises to gratify Aurelius if he clears all the rocks from the shore of Brittany, he pays a "philosophre" to make the rocks disappear by "magically" calculating when a high tide will cover them. When her husband comes back to learn this from her, he says that she must keep her promise:

> I had rather be stabbed to death
> For the true love that I bear you,
> Than that you should not keep and save your truth.
> Truth is the highest thing that man may have.

[I hadde wel levere ystiked for to be
For verray love which that I to yow have,
But if ye sholde youre trouthe kepe and save.
Trouthe is the hyeste thyng that man may kepe.]

(1476–79)

What sort of "trouthe" compels a wife to be "untrewe"? Can she erase the contradiction by simply hiding her tryst in secrecy (like the rocks), as her husband demands? No: no more than Gawain can hide the belt that Lady Bertilak gives him and thus conceal the treachery ("falssyng") that Bertilak exposes when they meet (2378). To be sure, Aurelius is less exacting than Bertilak. While the lord humiliates Gawain for failing to keep his promise in full, Aurelius simply frees Dorigen from her promise and thereby seems to manifest what the narrating Franklin calls gentility ("gentillesse," 1524). But as D. W. Robertson has noted, "the squire bases his claim on the letter rather than on the 'entente' of a jocular remark" (Robertson 276). To say that a promise made in jest binds just as much as a promise made in earnest and that we must be equally "true" to both is to drain the word of all moral force. Something similar happens to "trawþe" in the world of *Sir Gawain*. Caught up in a "Chrystemas gomme" of beheading, goaded into a mortally perilous promise by a giant who cannot be killed but who threatens no more than the *amour-propre* of the Arthurian court, Sir Gawain feels bound to keep his promise lest he forfeit his "trawþe." Yet when Lady Bertilak asks him to tutor her in the art of "luf-talkyng," he swears "by my trawþe" that he could not possibly excel her in the "slyȝt" of that art—shortly before accepting the "slyȝt" of her gift and thus compromising the "trawþe" of his promise to share his winnings with his host.

But does he thereby become a treacherous guest, a man who deserves the gruesome fate of a traitor? Since Lady Bertilak's erotic pursuit of her guest alternates for three days with Lord Bertilak's hunting, and since the killing of each animal follows the lady's daily visit to Gawain's bedroom, W. R. J. Barron suggests that the flaying of the deer on the first day ("rent from its hide" / "rent of þe hyde," 1332) and still more of the fox on the third day ("stripped of his pelt" / "tyruen of his cote," 1921) could signify that Gawain is likewise "threatened with the rare but notorious penalty of flaying alive."[30] Barron himself finds this something of a stretch. Even though Gawain's covert acceptance of the lady's belt resembles the wiles of a fox, as already noted, "fears that the metaphorical hunt [in the bedroom] might end in a traitor's death," he writes, "must seem ludicrously exaggerated and unfounded" (Barron 53). But in a poem where a jousting knight may be killed to amuse a king, where beheading is a game, and where a giant's axe hangs like the sword of Damocles over the hero until the very end are such fears truly exaggerated? Or do they spring from the fact that Gawain is repeatedly imperiled by a host and hostess bent on luring him into treachery at the behest of a malevolent enchantress?

This may sound unfair to Bertilak, who seems to say in the end that he sought only to tempt the pride and thus, presumably, confirm the reputation of the Round Table (2557–58). But Bertilak acts for Morgan le Fay, who hoped to make Guinevere die at the sight of a severed head speaking, and he repeatedly uses his lovely wife to tempt their guest with her "cors." To see again how Lady Bertilak employs this polysemous word on her first visit to Gawain's bedroom is to see how dangerous she can be. Right after waking him up, sitting on the open side of the bed so that he is caught ("kaȝt," 1225) in it,[31] and assuring him that they are all alone in a locked room with her husband away, she tells him:

> You are welcome to my body,
> To make your own choice;
> It behooves me of necessity
> To be your servant, and I shall be.
>
> [ȝe ar welcum to my cors,
> Yowre awen won to wale,
> Me behouez of fyne force
> Your seruaunt be, and schale.]
> (1237–40)

Reading these lines as innocently as possible, we might construe Lady Bertilak as simply a hostess bent on chastely serving her guest. In welcoming him to her "cors," she offers to furnish personally whatever he needs during his stay. But the root meaning of "cors" (from the Latin *corpus*, body) is impossible to suppress, especially when it is spoken by a woman to a man lying in bed in a locked room containing just the two of them.[32] Also, since she has already declined Gawain's request that she let him get out of bed, she is patently not his "servaunt" in the normal sense of the word. Whatever else she means, then, is she not literally welcoming her guest to her body, inviting him to take her into his bed?

But "cors" imports peril as well as pleasure. As an alternate spelling of "curs," it can signify "curse," a meaning apparently missed by Gawain himself but still audible to us and surely audible to those who heard *Sir Gawain* read aloud — the way most of its audience would have experienced it some seventy years before the invention of printing. Underlying Lady Bertilak's dulcet tones, the grating sound of "curse" evokes the malevolence of Morgan le Fay, the withered

crone first shown leading Lady Bertilak by the hand (947) and later identified as
the source and brains of the dangerous game she and her lord are now playing
on Gawain.[33] Had Gawain accepted her seductive offer, he would indeed have
been cursed by her report of it to Lord Bertilak, and everything we know from
the rest of the poem tells us that their guest would have paid for his pleasure
with his head—if not his skin. The undertone of menace borne by "cors" thus
reinforces the threat intimated by each of the "forwardes" Gawain has struck,
the beheading compact (378) and the exchange of winnings (1105). As noted
above, the word used to designate each of these compacts sounds all too much
like "forwird," meaning "ruin" or "destruction."[34] Like the "lif for lyf" jousting
match customarily held to entertain the king on festive days (96–102), every
game played, bargain struck, or agreement sealed in this poem is potentially a
matter of life and death. Beneath the jovial gamesmanship of the host of Castle
Hautdesert lies a man poised and ready to kill his guest.

This does not make the guest himself wholly innocent. As Lander has
argued, Lord and Lady Bertilak together manage Gawain in such a way as to
expose the convention of innocence prevailing at Arthur's court (Lander 62–63).
As embodied by Gawain, the Arthurian convention of innocence entails a radically incoherent view of the female, whom he chivalrically idealizes as an
object of admiration and self-exoneratingly vilifies as an agent of temptation.
Beyond that, Bertilak's challenge also exposes the impulse to self-preservation
lurking behind the court's reputation for valor, its "surquidré." Gawain not only
acts like a fox in hiding Lady Bertilak's gift from his host; he also "swerves"
(schunt[s]) from the blow of the Green Knight's axe (2280) just as the fox earlier
"swerves from the sharp" (schunt[s] for þe scharp) blade of Lord Bertilak's sword
on his third day of hunting (1902).

Measured against Beowulf, who always lurks, however dimly, behind him,
Gawain seems almost a parody of his precursor. Beowulf fights the dragon after
leaving his men on the dragon's barrow ("beorge"), going under a cliff ("under
stan-cleofu"), calling out to the beast in rage, and drawing his sword (2529–65).
To meet his own challenger on the day appointed, Gawain rides along a ridge
with cliffs on either side, finds a barrow ("balgh bergh"), climbs to the roof of it,
hears what sounds like a scythe being sharpened on a grindstone, and calls out
loudly for whoever wants to meet him (2172–76). When the giant descends from
an overhead bank, Gawain doffs his helmet, kneels, and bares his neck to the
giant's axe. After swerving from the first blow, he holds steady for the second,
which misses him altogether, and then for the third, which nicks the skin on the
side of his neck and scatters blood on the snow. This stirs Gawain into his one
fleeting moment of traditionally heroic—one might almost say Beowulfian—

behavior. Springing away from the giant, donning his helmet, and drawing his sword, he says he has taken the blow he agreed to bear and will now strike back swiftly if struck again (2316–25). Armed and ready to fight, he plays the part of a gallant knight, a bold warrior. But his smiling adversary treats him like a star schoolboy getting one demerit. With absolute power to kill Gawain, he says, he has merely nicked him for covertly taking the lady's belt. Balked in his one and only effort to wield his sword like a traditional hero, Gawain is commended for his faultless ("fautlest," 2363) behavior in resisting nearly all temptations but chastised as well for showing less than perfect loyalty ("lewté," 2366) to his host and for clinging to his life. Strictly speaking, he fails to be either a Beowulfian or a Christian hero.

But does either Beowulfian or Christian heroism require the squandering of one's life? Even in scheming to evade the consequences of his "forwarde" with Lord Bertilak, Gawain himself unwittingly shows the folly of equating "trawþe" with fidelity to a suicidal bargain or risking one's life for the sake of a game. Gawain is flawed and blind to his failings, even after shamefacedly confessing his "cowarddyse and couetyse," but none of his failings match the ruthlessness of Bertilak in repeatedly sending his wife to seduce their guest and thereby make him deserve beheading. Whatever Gawain's disloyalty to his host, it is more than matched by the treachery Bertilak artfully weaves into the rich, luxurious fabric of his hospitality.

To read *Sir Gawain* against the background of *Beowulf* is to see how much their protagonists differ and how deeply Christianity shapes the values of the later poem. While Beowulf makes his name by killing predatory monsters and sustains it by ruling his people, Gawain proves his virtue chiefly by resisting something that never presents itself as a threat of any kind in the world of Beowulf: sexual temptation. Yet in spite of their differences, both poems show how treachery may undermine hospitality and, more specifically, how the benign exchange of hospitable comforts gives way to the malignant exchange of assault and retaliation. In *Beowulf* hospitality is literally undermined by the Heathobards' vengeful murder of their Danish guests and brutally parodied by the action of various uninvited guests: Grendel and his mother, who successively feast on the men of Heorot; Beowulf, who takes vengeance as the "gist" of Grendel's mother and later invades the dragon's barrow, biting him with his sword; and finally the dragon, who in turn fatally bites, or feasts upon, the hero. In *Gawain* hospitality is far more subtly threatened. First, an uninvited but nonetheless entertaining guest returns the hospitality of the Arthurian court by making one of its knights swear to visit him and bare his neck to the axe of his host. Then the lord of a castle who luxuriously lodges a weary traveler also does everything possible to catch him in an erotic trap that could cost him his life. That Gawain eludes the trap and returns from his journey unharmed, with no more than a scar on his neck and with most of his life ahead of him, makes an ending quite different from that of *Beowulf*, whose hero is mortally wounded in a final struggle after years of fighting and half a century as king. But in its own way, each poem shows how treachery can undermine hospitality.

4

STAGING HOSPITALITY: SHAKESPEARE

Every mans proper Mansion house and home [is] . . . the theatre of his Hospitality.

—HENRY WOTTON, *Elements of Architecture* (1624)

ORLANDO. I almost die for food, and let me have it!
DUKE SENIOR. Sit down and feed, and welcome to our table.

—*As You Like It* 2.7.103–4

Hospitality, like literature, is in many ways a child of its time. In the monstrous, vestigially pagan world of *Beowulf*, it is at once a reward for services rendered by visiting warriors and a system of reciprocity that can be either brutally parodied by man-eating "gists" or twisted into murderous revenge. In the more civilized as well as far more explicitly Christian world of *Sir Gawain and the Green Knight*, it hovers between supreme comfort and perilous seduction. By the time of Shakespeare's plays, written roughly two hundred years after *Sir Gawain*, it could entail two quite different things. On the one hand, it could take the quintessentially Christian form of charity: food for the starving, or shelter for the homeless, or both. On the other hand, as Wotton suggests, it could furnish an opportunity for ostentatious extravagance, for theatrically lavish display of one's wealth. In dramatizing both kinds of hospitality, Shakespeare bears witness to a notable shift.

In the early seventeenth century, at the midpoint of Shakespeare's dramatic career, the meaning of *hospitality* in England was undergoing a fundamental change. Traditionally it signified what we now call charity: "gifts to the needy, especially food, dispensed from the household and often in the household, at the householder's table."[1] When Duke Senior welcomes a hungry stranger to his woodland table in a play written at the very end of the sixteenth century, he is practicing this kind of hospitality, which is also plaintively described by

Katherina in *The Taming of the Shrew* after she has been "starv'd for meat" by
her new husband:

> Beggars that come unto my father's door
> Upon entreaty have a present alms;
> If not, elsewhere they meet with charity;
> But I, who never knew how to entreat,
> Nor never needed that I should entreat,
> Am starved for meat, giddy for lack of sleep;
> With oaths kept waking, and with brawling fed.
>
> (4.3.4–10)

Carried off by Petruchio right after their wedding and not even allowed to
stay for the wedding feast prepared by her father, the headstrong Katherina is
made to learn what she never knew before: to feel the pangs of hunger and
need, to entreat for hospitality of the most basic kind, and to appreciate it. Right
after Petruchio tells her, like a parent training an unruly child, that she must
thank him for the meat he offers her before she touches it, she says, "I thank
you, sir" (4.3.45–47).

Traditionally, hospitality meant not only food but shelter for needy travelers.
In Shakespeare's own county of Warwick, a survey of vagrants made in the 1580s
showed that most of them stayed in private homes (Heal 219). The poor and the
wandering thus received what Caleb Dalechamp called *Christian Hospitalitie*
in a book of that title published in 1632, and in the spirit of Christian charity
some families took exceptional pains to serve the poor.[2] In *King Lear*, Gloucester
offers just such hospitality when he finds the king on the heath in the midst
of a thunderstorm. Defying the "hard commands" of Goneril and Regan,
Gloucester tells Lear that he has sought him out "to bring you where both fire
and food are ready" (3.4.148–52).[3] Though Gloucester's "where" signifies his
castle rather than the hovel where he and the king end up, he promises no more
than basic comforts. In other words, in place of the extravagant reception that
would normally be granted a royal visitor, Gloucester offers the king little more
than he will soon offer to the apparently destitute Poor Tom: "In, fellow, there,
into the hovel: keep thee warm" (3.4.175).[4]

A hovel is better than nothing, and it may even be read as essentially theatrical: a nonce refuge comparable in its flimsiness and ephemerality to stage
furniture.[5] But within the world of the play it signifies the barest minimum of
shelter, and this startling substitution of basic charity for lavish entertaining
becomes even more startling when we realize that by 1605, when Shakespeare
wrote *Lear*, the traditional meaning of hospitality *as* charity was dying out. For

one thing, the widespread availability of inns and alehouses, pioneers of what is now called the hospitality industry, gave travelers an alternative to private shelter (Heal 204–5).[6] Also, the rise of public relief for the poor made individual householders feel less obliged to care for them (Heal 393). Partly as a result of these developments, the word *hospitality* came to mean not sustenance for the poor but entertainment, often lavish entertainment of the rich and influential.[7] One architectural writer of the sixteenth century defined the ideal house as a building divided between banqueting and daily living, with one side wholly reserved for "feasts and triumphs" (qtd. Heal 163). This turns hospitality into showmanship, which is what monarchs from Henry VIII through James I, in Shakespeare's own time, regularly expected from their country hosts.[8]

Underlying this expectation is the notion that nothing given to the monarch can possibly equal, let alone surpass, what flows from his or her immeasurable generosity. Receiving Duncan as a guest, Lady Macbeth declares that even if the services she and her husband might offer him were doubled or quadrupled, they could not possibly "contend" against the honors he has heaped upon them (1.6.14–20). This kind of contention recalls the primitive potlatch defined by Marcel Mauss: a system of exchange based on the tripartite obligation to give, to receive, and to reciprocate (Mauss 50). Among the Indians of northwest America, Mauss writes, the honor and prestige of a chief and his clan depend on

> the meticulous repayment with interest of gifts that have been accepted, so
> to transform into persons having an obligation those that have placed you
> yourself under a similar obligation. Consumption and destruction of goods
> really go beyond all bounds. In certain kinds of potlatch one must expend all
> that one has, keeping nothing back. It is a competition to see who is the rich-
> est and also the most madly extravagant. Everything is based on the princi-
> ples of antagonism and rivalry . . . . Everything is conceived of as if it were a
> "struggle of wealth" (Mauss 47).

The chief, therefore, manifests and maintains his dominance precisely by giving. "To give," writes Mauss, "is to show one's superiority, to be more, to be higher in rank, *magister*. To accept without giving in return, or without giving more back, is to become client and servant, to become small, to fall lower" (Mauss 95).

In the hospitable practices of sixteenth-century England as well as in the plays of Shakespeare, giving remains a competitive sport, but with a funda- mental difference. Unlike primitive chiefs, the monarch can never be equaled in giving, let alone surpassed. While English monarchs expected to be royally entertained, they did not wish to be overwhelmed, as Henry VII evidently was during a visit to the Earl of Oxford about the year 1500. Striding off through a passage formed by facing rows of the earl's liveried servants, the departing king reportedly said, "My lord, I have heard much of your hospitality, but I see it is greater than the speech. These handsome gentlemen and yeomen, which I see on both sides of me, are sure your menial servants." But when these "servants" proved to be mostly retainers, that is, men ready to fight for the earl if he needed them, he was fined fifteen thousand marks (Heal 48). He had not only challenged the magnificence of the king's own hospitality; he had crossed the line between making an impression and posing a threat (Heal 56). Quite aside from alarming a monarch, however, lavish hosts could run other risks—as Shakespeare demonstrates.

RUINOUS ENTERTAINING: *TIMON OF ATHENS*

In *Timon of Athens*, which may have been partly composed by Thomas Middleton and was probably written between 1605 and 1608, the title figure is neither a monarch nor the host of a monarch but nonetheless a lord bent on outspending everyone else, extravagantly reciprocating everything that is done for him or given to him. "He pours it out," says one of the lords invited to the feast he gives in act 1:

> Plutus, the god of gold
> Is but his steward; no meed, but he repays
> Sevenfold above itself, no gift to him,
> But breeds the giver a return exceeding
> All use of quittance.
>
> (1.1.275–79)

By the rules of the potlatch, Timon's extravagance would have secured his power and wealth. Giving more than anyone could ever return to him, refusing to be repaid under any circumstances, he would have proved his superiority to all others and made himself rich in obligations due.[9] But Timon is actually making himself poor. Spurning his welcome and scorning his meat, Apemantus ruefully sees

> what a number of men eats
> Timon, and he sees 'em not! It grieves me to see so many dip
> their meat in one man's blood; and all the madness is, he
> cheers them up too.
> I wonder men dare trust themselves with men.
> Methinks they should invite them without knives!

> Good for their meat, and safer for their lives
> . . . .the fellow that sits next him, now
> parts bread with him, pledges the breath of him in a divided
> draught, is the readiest man to kill him.
>
> (1.2.38–47)

Timon is virtually devoured by his guests. Echoing Matthew's account of the Last Supper, where Christ predicts that "the man who just dipped his hand in the same dish with me is going to betray me" (Matt. 26:23), Apemantus scents the imminence of treachery. But instead of being stabbed by one of the dinner knives that his guests have brought with them, Timon will be cut to the bone by their absolute refusal to reciprocate his hospitality.[10]

They turn merciless just as soon as they learn that Timon has bankrupted himself. When Timon's steward Flavius tells him that his coffers are empty, his land all mortgaged, and his provisions devoured by "riotous feeders" (2.2.154), he promptly discovers that his would-be friends, his regular guests, will not help him. The senators he has wined and dined reject his urgent plea for a thousand talents. Lord Lucullus, who has received many gifts from Timon and looks for yet another when Timon's servant arrives, has nothing to offer upon "bare friendship without security" when he learns that Timon needs fifty talents (3.1.38). Lord Lucius, right after telling two "strangers" that he would never deny a request from such a benefactor as Timon, promptly does so when Timon's servant appears to importune him.[11] This nauseating mixture of flagrant hypocrisy, stark ingratitude, and sheer fecklessness ("before the gods I am not able to do," he says [3.2.44]) prompts one of the strangers to say,

> Who can call him his friend
> That dips in the same dish? for, in my knowing,
> Timon has been this lord's father,
> And kept his credit with his purse,
> Supported his estate; nay, Timon's money
> Had paid his men their wages. He ne'er drinks,
> But Timon's silver treads upon his lip;
> And yet—O see the monstrousness of man
> When he looks out in an ungrateful shape!
>
> (3.2.59–67)

Besides evoking once again the treachery of Judas, the stranger at this moment discovers—finds out *and* reveals—precisely what will drive Lear mad in another play of Shakespeare: the monstrosity of ingratitude.

In this play it drives Timon to desperation and chicanery. Besieged by creditors he cannot possibly pay, he first cries out like a sacrificial victim ("Cut my heart in sums," 3.4.90), then summons his false friends to a second banquet. When they arrive, mumbling their pathetic apologies for having spurned his appeals, he seats them without ceremony at a table of covered dishes and bids them all, "Uncover, dogs, and lap" (3.7.77). As soon as they find in the dishes nothing but lukewarm water, Timon flings both the water and the dishes at these "detested parasites," drives them out, and denounces all feasting as a vicious mockery of friendship: "Henceforth be no feast, / Whereat a villain's not a welcome guest" (3.7.86, 94–95).[12]

Maddened in both senses, enraged and deranged by the monstrous ingratitude of his former guests, Timon calls down plagues upon Athens and flees in "nakedness" to the woods, where he may "find / The unkindest beast more kinder than mankind" (4.1.35–36). With the sole exception of his devoted servant Flavius, he hates all humankind ("I am Misanthropos," he says [4.3.53]), and he disowns all hospitality, even the traditional Christian kind:

> Hate all, curse all, show charity to none,
> But let the famish'd flesh slide from the bone,
> Ere thou relieve the beggar.
>
> (4.3.519–21)

Here as in several other passages, *Timon* clearly points to *King Lear*.

UN-CHRISTIAN HOSPITALITY: *LEAR*

In Shakespeare's later tragedies, which repeatedly show how treachery can sabotage hospitality, nothing exemplifies the violation of Christian hospitality more ruthlessly and vividly than *King Lear*. *Lear* chimes powerfully with *Timon*, which may have been written about the same time.[13] Like Timon, the old king is maddened by the fiendishness of ingratitude, above all of filial ingratitude, "more hideous . . . / Than the sea-monster" (*Lear* 1.4.237–38). Like the "naked" Timon, he forswears both human habitation and clothing, which he tears off while standing out on a heath in the midst of a thunderstorm (3.4.101). And just as the misanthropic Timon bans all Christian charity, Cornwall and Regan forbid Gloucester to help the desperate, houseless Lear in any way (3.3.1–5).

Gloucester himself extorts our pity too, for he seems a helpless victim of ruthless usurpation: a kindly old man grotesquely abused in his very own house for merely seeking to offer the simplest, most charitable kind of hospitality to a man he still regards as his king. But unlike the starving beggars spurned by

Timon, Gloucester is not wholly innocent, which is one of the many things that makes *Lear* so much more complicated than *Timon*. However touching they are, Gloucester's efforts to relieve the king straddle the line between simple charity and conspiring with a *foreign* duke—the Duke of Burgundy, Cordelia's husband—who seeks to avenge Lear's injuries by overthrowing England's present rulers, Albany and Cornwall.[14] Instead of secretly taking Lear into his house, he arranges for him to be escorted to Dover along with some thirty-five of his knights so that they might join the "well-armed" supporters of the king (3.7.14–19). Strictly speaking, given its ultimately insurrectionary purpose, Gloucester's act is treasonable.

The play reveals his treachery even while leading us to overlook it: to find him guilty of committing no more than the "crime" of hospitality. When suddenly seized and bound by order of Regan and Cornwall, he is dumbfounded by their assault on his position as host. "You are my guests," he says. "Do me no foul play, friends" (3.7.31). When they demand to know why the king was sent to Dover, Gloucester says he acted only because he could not bear to see the king treated so cruelly—shut out in such a storm as would have made Regan and Cornwall themselves open their gates to howling wolves (3.7.57–65). But Gloucester's impassioned hyperbole tends to make us forget that he has not opened his own gate to Lear. Instead, as he conspicuously fails to say when asked why the king has been sent to Dover, Gloucester has sent him there to join the forces gathered on his behalf. In other words, rather than risking surreptitious charity by taking Lear in, he has ventured to play an active part in the conspiracy against what he has just called his "guests." And in the end he cannot help alluding to this conspiracy. Outraged by the ruthlessness of Lear's daughter and son-in-law, he feels bound to say that he will "see / The winged vengeance overtake such children" (3.7.66–67). He thus gives Cornwall the perfect cue for blinding him and thrusting him out at his own gates.

The logic that makes Gloucester a traitor for merely helping his king, however, works only in a realm where hospitality has been criminalized and the king cast off by his heirs. Betrayed by his own son and driven from his house, Gloucester not only mirrors the plight of Lear but doubles the knot binding intrafamilial betrayal to repeated violations of hospitality. Betrayal within a family is the stuff of Aristotelian tragedy, but, as the story of Agamemnon's homecoming shows, intrafamilial betrayal may well entail the betrayal of a host or guest, and by itself the relation between hosts and guests is familial in both its intimacy and its potential for treachery. Nowhere else in Shakespeare's work are these two kinds of betrayal more tightly intertwined.

To see how Shakespeare motivates each kind of betrayal, we must be able to view Lear as well as Gloucester through the eyes of others. To Cornwall and Regan, Gloucester seems a traitor. To Goneril and Regan, Lear seems the most insufferable guest ever inflicted on any house. As soon as I learned, on my first reading of the play, that he planned to stay with each of them by turns for a month at a time (1.1.132–35), I thought instantly of my maternal grandmother. Widowed before I was born, she sold her house in Brookline, Massachusetts, when she was about seventy-five and then decreed that each of her married daughters (her sons were largely spared) should house her by monthly turns. So, two or three times a year, she would displace one or more of her grandchildren to take up residence in a bedroom where she expected (and regularly got) breakfast in bed before taking most of the day to dress for cocktails and dinner. She did not need nursing care, which came later, in a nursing home, and since she occasionally said amusing things as well as proving herself a crack shot with a BB gun (one day she neatly hit one arm of the weathervane on the top of our garage, making it spin), her entertainment value helped to alleviate her disruptive effect. But when I recall that my mother had to accommodate her while also feeding, housing, and managing eight children, I am freshly awed by my mother's stamina.

To be fair to both my grandmother and King Lear, I must recognize that for most people, old age eventually entails some kind of dependence. The folktale story of Lear's dividing his kingdom on condition that his daughters maintain him and his hundred knights seems bizarre, senseless, and prehistoric, but beneath it lies the commonplace fact that many elderly people need custodial care or at the very least some relief from the burden of keeping their own house, as my grandmother did. Before Congress established Social Security in 1935, older people in America often bargained with their children by trading the promise of an inheritance for love and care, both of which might be withdrawn if the property was conveyed too soon.[15] Social Security has slightly alleviated this problem but hardly covers the cost of care. To get it nowadays, elderly people of means sometimes hire professional caregivers at great expense or enter a continuing care community, which offers them a comfortable apartment and prepared meals plus nursing care whenever they come to need it.[16] In giving up their houses or a considerable chunk of their assets or both to buy this kind of maintenance, as often happens, they are doing something like what Lear did on a much more extravagant scale. He gives up all responsibility and everything he owns in return for continuing care.

But the care must be furnished by his daughters. Leaving aside the irrationality of the way Lear divides his kingdom—making the size and value of each share depend on which daughter can sound most sycophantic, banishing his dearest daughter just because she won't compete in the sycophancy sweep-stakes—consider what he expects Regan and Goneril to do for him every other month. To visualize what they faced when Lear came calling, I must reimagine my grandmother as a capricious, cantankerous old man trailing a hundred obstreperous young ones, all of them clamoring for food, drink, and lodging in my house. Under these conditions I would all too readily agree with Goneril when she tells her father,

> Here do you keep a hundred knights and squires;
> Men so disordered, so deboshed, and bold
> That this our court, infected with their manners,
> Shows like a riotous inn. Epicurism and lust
> Make it more like a tavern or a brothel
> Than a graced palace.
>
> (1.4.216–21)

Wholly undisciplined by Lear himself, who has apparently given up even his responsibility for his train, the hundred randy knights and squires disporting themselves in this house and infecting its servant girls resemble nothing so much as the suitors who took possession of Odysseus's house in his absence, wasting his food and debauching his serving maids.[17] Lear's men abuse Goneril's hospitality. Though he charges her with lying about them, hotly insisting they are "men of choice and rarest parts / That all particulars of duty know" (1.4.240–41), they may well be no better than a "disordered rabble," as Goneril calls them (1.4.231).[18] She quite plausibly fears that a body of men responsible only to the caprices of her father endangers her household (1.4.301–4). Whether Lear or Goneril exagger-ates, or whether both of them stretch a truth that lies somewhere in the middle, we might plausibly wonder, as Regan does, "How in one house / Should many people, under two commands, / Hold amity?" (2.4.247–49).

Nonetheless, these people are psychically essential to Lear as the vestigial sign of his royal status. In giving away his kingdom to Goneril and Regan, he not only demands that they take turns housing him and his hundred knights; he also declares that he will "retain / The name, and all the additions to a king" (1.1.135–36). The word "additions" signifies royal titles and honors: all the distinctions that follow him, as in his train. But it surely also includes all the men in his train as well, all those "added" to him so as to manifest and proclaim his importance wherever he goes. They embody his sense of royal identity. Just as he recoils when Goneril's steward calls him "my lady's father" (1.4.68) rather than "Your majesty," he rages at her demand that he dismiss half his followers "within a fortnight" (1.4.271–72) and promptly resolves to seek refuge for himself and all his men with the "kind and comfortable" Regan (1.4.283).

When he finds Regan at Gloucester's castle, however, she offers him neither kindness nor comfort. In the prophetic words of the fool, she tastes as much like Goneril "as a crab does to a crab" (1.5.15). Away from home and out of provisions, she says, she cannot entertain Lear until the end of the month, so till then he should shed half his train and return to Goneril (2.4.197–201). Lear's response to this plausible suggestion sounds wildly irrational. Rather than returning to Goneril with only half his train, he says, he would sooner live like a beast in the open air (2.4.202–6). But from Lear's perspective, stripping him of half his train means stripping him of his manhood—reducing him to what he later calls "a poor, bare, forked animal" (3.4.99–100). Only if we grasp this point can we understand why the gradual and relentless *subtraction* of his followers drives Lear to the brink of madness.

Throughout the scene in which this happens, the subtraction is made to sound perfectly rational. Why on earth does he need so many followers? Why a hundred? Or even fifty? Lear's train is not just disruptive; it's needless. As Goneril says, again quite rationally, "Why might not you, my lord, receive attendance / From those that she calls servants, or from mine?" (2.4.238–39).

Why not indeed? Since we already know that Goneril has ordered her servants to treat the king with "weary negligence" (1.3.12), and since he himself has felt the sting of Oswald's insolence (1.4.68), he has good reason to say that he cannot trust his daughter's servants. But instead he fights a losing battle over numbers, watching them trickle away like blood from an open wound. When he tells Goneril that he and his hundred knights can stay with Regan, she says not only (again) that she is not ready to receive him but also that even when she is, she'll take no more than "five-and-twenty" of his men (2.4.242–43). To which Lear responds, "I gave you all—" (2.4.244).

This is just the beginning of a lengthy statement about the terms of Lear's gift, but since the statement is promptly interrupted by Regan, we hear for a moment only these four words, which speak volumes about Lear's predicament. I have already quoted Mauss's observation that to keep face in primitive societies "one must expend all that one has, keeping nothing back." Yet if a king manifests his power precisely by displaying and dispensing his wealth, he cannot give all he has without forfeiting the power it signifies. In Tudor England this could not happen because whatever the king gave or received, he remained the ultimate creditor. In the Tudor economy of *Macbeth*, Macbeth tells Duncan, "Your highness' part / Is to receive our duties; and our duties / Are to your throne and state children and servants" (1.4.23–25). Like children to parents and servants to masters, subjects can never pay all they owe to a king, whose credit remains inexhaustible. But in the brutal, prehistoric economy of *Lear* the king wipes out his credit at a stroke. In reminding Regan that he gave her and Goneril "all," he obviously seeks to prick her comatose sense of gratitude by reminding her of all she owes him. But instead he unwittingly reminds her that he has nothing more to give, that he has lost all his credit, and that consequently she owes him nothing, either as his child or his subject. With no power to enforce the terms of his gift, the monthly maintenance of himself and his hundred knights, Lear must beg for hospitality; and as he does so the number of men he is allowed to bring with him soon shrinks to nothing.[19] On learning that Regan will take him with no more than twenty-five, he turns back to Goneril, whom he has earlier cursed for her ingratitude, because Goneril now seems comparatively generous:

> I'll go with thee.
> Thy fifty yet doth double five-and-twenty,
> And thou art twice her love.
>
> (2.4.253–55)

But with a little help from Regan, Goneril swiftly cuts him down to nothing:

> GONERIL.   Hear me, my lord.
>   What need you five-and-twenty, ten, or five,
>   To follow in a house where twice so many
>   Have a command to tend you?
> REGAN.   What need one?
>
> (2.4.255–58)

Perfectly rational and at the same time utterly ruthless, Regan's question drives her father to a pitch of desperation: "O reason not the need!" he cries:

> Our basest beggars
> Are in the poorest thing superfluous.
> Allow not nature more than nature needs,
> Man's life is cheap as beast's.
>
> (2.4.259–62)

Lear's desperation and pain are so poignant that they tend to make us forget what he is asking for. Accustomed to being lavishly entertained with all his followers, he cannot be satisfied with mere sustenance and shelter, which is what Christian hospitality would offer him. So he might have claimed that mere sustenance and shelter cannot fitly serve a king. Instead, he radically redefines

"need" for all humankind, beggars included. Need, he argues—and it *is* an argument, however desperate he sounds—cannot be reasoned, cannot be strictly
calibrated in terms of subsistence. What may keep us physically alive will not
sustain our sense of humanity. "Thou art a lady," he tells Regan,

> If only to go warm were gorgeous,
> Why, nature needs not what thou gorgeous wear'st,
> Which scarcely keeps thee warm.
>
> (2.4.262–65)

Gorgeously attired in some delicate fabric (perhaps silk?) whose rich design
feeds her craving for ostentation rather than warming her body, Regan personifies the need to display her own importance, which is surely akin to the need
defined by Lear: the need to preserve his dignity as a human being, something
more than a beast. Later on, when he and the fool and Kent discover what
seems to be a naked madman on the storm-lashed heath, Lear says,

> Is man no more than this? Consider him well. Thou ow'st the
> worm no silk, the beast no hide, the sheep no wool, that cat no
> perfume. Ha! Here's three on's are sophisticated! Thou art the thing
> itself; unaccommodated man is no more but such a poor, bare, forked
> animal as thou art. Off, off, you lendings! come unbutton here.
> [*Tearing off his clothes.*]
>
> (3.4.95–101)

In earlier explaining what he needs, Lear slides easily from accommodation
(housing) to accoutrement, for both serve to protect us from the elements as
well as to distinguish us from the lower animals, most of whom live unsheltered
as well as unclothed. In tearing off his clothes, Lear literalizes the metaphor
implicit in his earlier speech. By denying him shelter—more precisely by
refusing to house him with even one of his servants—Goneril strips him of his
dignity. He blends both meanings when he calls Edgar "unaccommodated," for
Edgar is both shelterless and naked, stripped down to what Lear calls "the thing
itself": animality. Yet Lear's final words here ("come unbutton here") complicate his own disrobing. Besides revealing that he, like Edgar, has retained the
distinctively human power to speak, they show that he still feels himself trailing
attendants, like pains from a phantom limb. Even as he tears off his "lendings"
(clothes made with material borrowed from animals), he orders a phantom
valet to unbutton his coat, for, as Kittredge shrewdly notes, he has probably
never before undressed himself (Kittredge, note to 3.4.102). Touching in its
irony, Lear's command is poignantly echoed at the end of the play, when with

his dying breath he asks Edgar to ease the constriction of his clothes: "Pray you, undo this button" (5.3.308).

Lear's argument with Goneril, then, turns on the crucial question of just how much he really needs. From Goneril's point of view it is "folly" (2.4.286) for him to think "unattended" means "unaccommodated," that is, to think her refusal to house any of his attendants would leave him naked. Rather than heartlessly driving him into a stormy night, she stands ready to shelter him just so long as he comes alone. "For his particular," she says, "I'll receive him gladly" (2.4.287). In spurning her hospitality rather than giving up his attendants, Lear punishes himself, and in the eyes of both Goneril and Regan he gets what he deserves. When Gloucester frets at the raging of the storm, Regan says,

> O sir, to wilful men
> The injuries that they themselves procure
> Must be their schoolmasters.
> (2.4.297–99)

But this smug dismissal of Lear and his needs betrays the ruthlessness that underlies Goneril's and Regan's version of hospitality. Willing to house Lear only on their terms, not his own, though they had earlier accepted them, they make no effort to accommodate his special needs or to dissuade him from plunging into the storm. On the contrary, taking their cue from Goneril, Regan and Cornwall each order Gloucester, as if he were their servant rather than their host, to bar his doors against the king and his "desperate train" (2.4.299–303). They do not even tell Gloucester that he may admit the king alone. A royal guest thus becomes a threatening outcast, and in the corrupted world of this play, where Edmund is rewarded for betraying his own father, Christian hospitality becomes an act of treason.

HOSPITALITY AND REGICIDE: *MACBETH*

Shortly after writing *King Lear*, Shakespeare took a further step in dramatizing the subversion of hospitality: *Macbeth*.[20] This theme is seldom thought to dominate the play. It seems driven instead by witchcraft, relentless ambition, and regicide, which has been called "close to the ultimate crime" in the age of King James: "a demonic assault not simply on an individual and a community but on the fundamental order of the universe" (Greenblatt, *Shakespeare* 2556). Yet to underscore the heinousness of this crime, Shakespeare fused it with something equally outrageous: the murder of a guest by his host. In Shakespeare's source for *Macbeth*, Holinshed's *Chronicles* (1587), Macbeth and his partisans are said to have killed Duncan near Inverness in the year 1040 (Holinshed 5:234). But Shakespeare reconstructs this event in terms of a much earlier story from the *Chronicles*: in 967 a Scot named Donwald, "kindled in wrath by the words of his wife," murdered King Duff when the king was his guest, lying in his own bedchamber.[21] In recasting Duncan's death, Shakespeare makes the violation of hospitality central to his play, which repeatedly evokes the rites and pleasures of conventional hospitality even as it undermines them. "In unmistakable ways," says Paul Kottman, *Macbeth* is "a play about hosting and being hosted, a play of guests that come when invited and ghosts, apparitions and witches that come regardless of invitation, to crash the party" (Kottman 93). No other play of Shakespeare says more about hospitality and the subversion of its rituals.

In the first act of the play Lady Macbeth receives two items of momentous news. First, her husband's valor on the battlefield has won him not only a new title from the king but also, from the reputedly all-knowing witches, the promise that he will eventually be king himself. Second, the king is coming to stay at her house. Her response to the second piece of news, though adumbrated by her response to the first, vividly shows how the ferocity of her ambition usurps the duties of a hostess. Both responses overturn anything one might expect to hear from a loyal wife and subject. Instead of rejoicing at her husband's success, she scolds him in absentia for his lack of nerve, for whatever scruples might impede his quest for the crown, and vows to pour into his ear the poison of her own ruthless determination.[22] This startling speech predetermines her response to the news that the king will be their guest that very night.

Surprisingly enough, however, her first reaction to this news makes her sound exactly like a dutiful hostess. When the messenger declares that the king is coming, she says,

> Thou'rt mad to say it!
> Is not thy master with him? who, were't so,
> Would have inform'd for preparation.
> (1.5.29–31)

What sort of preparation did a royal visit require? Since Shakespeare's play conflates two unrelated episodes from Scottish history, we might plausibly infer that his treatment of hospitality in medieval Scotland was at least subtly inflected by the hospitable practices of his own time, especially as they involved the entertainment of royalty. As we consider Lady Macbeth's response to the news that the king is on his way to her house, we should also know that in the England of Shakespeare's time the chief responsibility for the entertainment of guests in noble households fell on women. Assuming more control over their households than women did elsewhere in Europe, they are said to have "entertain[ed] all comers, conducting there [*sic*] guests to there chambers, carefull of there break-fasts, keeping them company at cards, with many more complements of this nature, whiche is not ordinary in other places and other nations" (qtd. Heal 179).

All this helps us understand why Lady Macbeth should think of "prepara-tion" just as soon as she learns that the king is on his way. Yet she doesn't even know how many mouths she has to feed. Her husband has sent no previous notice because he has received none from a king who has just abruptly invited himself to Macbeth's castle. "From hence to Inverness," he tells Macbeth, "And bind us further to you" (1.4.42–43). Having fought boldly, Macbeth now gains a further chance to oblige the sovereign by housing him for the night. Hospitality here is not a charitable gift to the needy but one of a series of exchanges in which the subject serves the king in return for honors and privileges, such as a new title.[23] Courtesy requires, however, that Macbeth define his hospitality as anything but onerous—"The rest is labour, which is not us'd for you!"—and also say that news of the king's approach will delight his wife (1.4.44–46). We need know nothing of hospitality in Shakespeare's time to catch the irony of this prediction. Would any woman whose husband suddenly sprang a royal guest upon her feel a surge of joy and not a wave of panic? How can she possibly prepare for his arrival in the time she has?

But as soon as the messenger leaves, Lady Macbeth gives not the slightest thought to such preparation. Instead of calling her servants to set the house in perfect order and cook up a sumptuous meal, she prepares *herself* by asking "spirits" to "unsex" her, to fill her with cruelty, to thicken her blood against remorse (1.5.38–42). At the same time, however, she knows that she and her husband must hide their murderous intentions behind the face of hospitality. Driven to kill, or rather driven to goad her husband into killing, she is no less bent on scripting his performance as a host. As soon as Macbeth arrives to say that Duncan will be spending just one night with them, she knows what each of them must do. "To beguile the time," she tells her husband,

> Look like the time; bear welcome in your eye,
> Your hand, your tongue; look like the innocent flower,
> But be the serpent under't. He that's coming
> Must be provided for; and you shall put
> This night's business into my dispatch,
> Which shall to all our nights and days to come
> Give solely sovereign sway and masterdom.
>
> (1.5.61–68)

Her speech exploits the language of hospitality for the most treacherous of ends. Not only does she tell Macbeth to hide his serpentine motives within a bouquet of "innocent"—literally harmless—geniality; with diabolical ambiguity, she says that the king "must be provided for." By the time she thus alludes once more to the conventional tasks of preparing for the arrival of a distinguished guest, we know that they have been thoroughly subsumed by her determination to kill him, so that all preparation for his entertainment is actually a prelude to and provision for his assassination.

Besides coaching her husband in the arts of hospitality, Lady Macbeth knows exactly how to welcome the king. When he mentions the "trouble" his visit may cause her, she assures him that nothing they do for him can equal what he is doing for them:

> KING.   See, see, our honour'd hostess!
>   The love that follows us sometimes is our trouble,
>   Which still we thank as love. Herein I teach you
>   How you shall bid God 'ield us for your pains
>   And thank us for your trouble.
> LADY.   All our service
>   In every point twice done, and then done double,
>   Were poor and single business to contend
>   Against those honours deep and broad wherewith
>   Your majesty loads our home. For those of old,
>   And the late dignities heap'd up to them,
>   We rest your hermits.
>
> (1.6.10–20)

In the art of exchanging courtesies, Lady Macbeth outdoes not just her husband but the king himself. Earlier, when the king says he will "bind" himself to Macbeth by staying with him, Macbeth graciously assures him that only what is *not* done for the king can be called labor ("The rest is labour, which is not us'd for you!" 1.4.44). In addressing Lady Macbeth, the king "teach[es]" her that entertaining a king is a labor of love for which she should thank him and urge God to repay him. In other words, rather than incurring an obligation the king is giving Macbeth and his wife a chance to express their love for him *as* work, which thereby becomes love and hence cause for gratitude.

Lady Macbeth knows only too well how to sound grateful. Though the king stops short of saying that he, like God, has already given his subjects everything they have to offer him in return, Lady Macbeth says virtually this much when she claims that nothing they might do for him could possibly equal what he is doing for them by "load[ing their] house" with honors. The difference between these two formulations, however, betrays her conviction that their gift of hospitality is bound up with exchange, that host and hostess alike have not only been prepaid for their labor but *are being* repaid for it in a progressive present that may continue indefinitely. Duncan himself tells Lady Macbeth that he will "continue our graces towards [Macbeth]" (1.6.30).

Unlike his wife, Macbeth says nothing to the king about his social duties, and in spite of Lady Macbeth's coaching he risks a breach of etiquette by leaving the dinner table before the king has finished his meal, which prompts the king to ask for him (1.7.29–30). Nevertheless, Macbeth's first soliloquy shows that he feels the full force of his obligations. Even as he contemplates murdering Duncan, he knows that doing so would brutally violate his duties as a host. Duncan is here, he tells himself,

> in double trust:
> First, as I am his kinsman and his subject—
> Strong both against the deed; then, as his host,
> Who should against his murderer shut the door,
> Not bear the knife myself.
>
> (1.7.12–16)

Macbeth feels so entangled by his ties to Duncan that he can hardly count them. Right after speaking of the "double trust" that binds him to the king as his kinsman and subject, he adds a third, as if it suddenly took him by surprise: he is the king's host. Given the power of a host, given his capacity to save or end the very life of his guest, royal or not, this position eclipses the importance of the other two. No other tie matches it in responsibility.

The viciousness of what he contemplates grows still more vivid when we see, or rather hear, just how much his soliloquy echoes the Gospel accounts of the Last Supper and Paul's words on sacrilegious communion. At the Last Supper, as we have seen, the host becomes the *hostia*, the sacrificial victim, after breaking bread and sharing wine with his apostles. In *Macbeth* the host himself is bent on murder, but with a royal victim "so meek" and "clear in his great office, that his virtues / Will plead like angels trumpet-tongu'd against / The deep damnation of his taking-off" (1.7.19–22). To kill a king of such Christlike meekness and virtue is bad enough, but to do so right after dining with him is the act of a Judas. "He that eateth and drinketh unworthily," writes Paul, "eateth and drinketh damnation to himself, not discerning the Lord's body" (1 Cor. 11:29). Drinking the "poison'd chalice" of his murderous intentions (1.7.13) even while hosting Duncan's last supper, knowing that his plans will lead to his own "deep damnation," Macbeth balks. Right after Lady Macbeth comes in to chide him for neglecting his guests, above all the king, he suddenly tells her, "We will proceed no further in this business" (1.7.31).

But Lady Macbeth makes quick work of his scruples. Once she explains how they can kill the king with the "very daggers" of his bedroom attendants (1.7.76) and blame it on them, he resumes his role as the quintessentially treacherous host of a model king who is also, strikingly enough, a model host. This too is a Shakespearean invention. Whereas Holinshed's Duncan is immature and ineffectual, Shakespeare's is both a strong, seasoned leader and a master of hospitality. On going to bed, the king sends a diamond to Lady Macbeth by way of Banquo, who delivers this news to Macbeth along with the jewel itself (2.1.11–15). The king thus shows that even though he comes as a guest he remains the host of the kingdom, the supreme dispenser of gifts, whether titles or precious objects.[24] His gifts and his capacity to give will always exceed whatever his nonce host and hostess can do for him. Though Macbeth and his lady were "unprepar'd" to entertain him lavishly, and though they gracelessly abandoned him in the middle of his meal, he offers a precious jewel to his "kind hostess" to signify his "measureless content" with her hospitality (2.1.14–16). He thereby proves himself a perfect guest, a man whose virtues will indeed plead like angels against his assassination.

But instead of brooding any longer on the heinousness of killing his royal guest, Macbeth envisions the instrument of it—a bloody dagger—and takes his cue from the howling of the wolf, who "with his stealthy pace, / With Tarquin's ravishing strides, towards his design / Moves like a ghost" (2.1.55–56). Macbeth speaks better than he knows. In alluding to Tarquin's rape of his hostess Lucrece, the subject of an early Shakespearean poem (see below), he prompts us to see that his killing of Duncan will radically destabilize his position as host in his own household, leaving him all too vulnerable to guests who come as ghosts.

Before the ghost of Banquo appears, however, Macbeth is startled by a succession of sounds. Guilt makes him preternaturally sensitive to anything he can hear, beginning with the bell that summons him to his bedtime drink with Lady Macbeth just before he kills Duncan (2.1.31–32, 62–63). Right after he kills him, even as Lady Macbeth fears the shrieking owl has awakened Duncan's men with the deed undone (2.2.3–4, 9–10), Macbeth's head becomes an echo chamber catching every sound that breaks the stillness of the night: the owl's scream, the crickets' cry, the soliloquizing voice of his wife, the last words of the king's doomed bodyguards, and the anguished cry of insomnia itself: "Sleep no more! / Macbeth does murder sleep" (2.2.8–15, 20–27, 33–34). Is it any wonder that Macbeth, not the wretchedly hungover porter, is the first to hear the knocking at his gate? Thomas De Quincey famously argues that the knocking marks the end of a "suspension and pause" in which "the world of ordinary life is suddenly arrested, laid asleep, tranced, racked into a dread armistice." The knocking, he says, makes us feel this suspension precisely by rending it and thus reactivating "'the pulses of life' in the ordinary world" (De Quincey 546). *But when do those pulses ever stop beating for Macbeth?* During the whole performance of the murder, when do his tormented ears ever gain "suspension and pause"? For him there is no such thing. Even as he tells his wife of the voice that has doomed him to sleeplessness, the knocking at his gate shows once again, he says, how "every noise appals" him (2.2.58).

The knocking actually signifies more than any other sound he has heard up to now: more than the scream of owls or the cry of crickets or even the voice of men doomed to die. While knocking normally marks the arrival of a visitor or guest who should be hospitably welcomed, it now betokens the advent of a shattering discovery: murder. When Macduff and Lennox, the knockers who have come to meet the king by appointment, find him murdered in his bed, Macduff cries, "Awake, awake! / Ring the alarum bell. Murder and treason!" (2.3.70–71). So ghastly is the news that for a moment it seems to horrify even the murderers themselves. "Woe, alas!" says Lady Macbeth, "What, in our house?" (2.3.84). Though Lady Macbeth has already proven her capacity to masquerade as a dutiful hostess, I find it impossible to say whether she is merely pretending to feel the enormity of murder in her own house or is honestly stunned by it. Macbeth likewise confounds our capacity to say just how much he may or may not be shamming desolation when he says that "from this instant / There's nothing serious in mortality" (2.3.88–89).[25]

But he might just as easily have said that in the new kingdom of Macbeth himself, there's nothing true in hospitality, no matter how lavish it becomes. In act 3, the modest meal served offstage to old King Duncan in act 1 is reenacted as a banquet served onstage by the new King Macbeth, now host of the royal palace. Since this way of inaugurating his reign also recalls what Claudius does shortly after murdering King Hamlet, we may usefully compare the two as hosts—or rather murderers masquerading as hosts.

Having gained their respective thrones by murder, both men seek to drape grief and horror with the iridescent tablecloth of festivity: Claudius with a nuptial feast at which "the funeral baked-meats / Did coldly furnish forth the marriage tables" (*Hamlet* 1.2.180–81), Macbeth with a banquet at which Lady Macbeth, still playing the hostess, presses him to be "bright and jovial among [his] guests" (3.2.28). Both men are confronted by guests who come as ghosts, though only Macbeth sees one at his table. While King Hamlet reappears as a ghost to his son alone, he is re-created before Claudius by the player king: just as King Hamlet was poisoned in the ear while sleeping in his garden, the player king is likewise poisoned before the very eyes of Claudius (3.2.241–42). By means of theatrical representation, then, the ghost of the old king appears to the new one as the centerpiece of an entertainment conceived by Prince Hamlet but also warmly approved by Claudius, who rejoices to learn that Hamlet has hospitably welcomed to the court a band of strolling players and who urges Rosencrantz and Guildenstern to "drive his purpose into these delights" (3.1.24–27). In the middle of the play, having thus encouraged the prince to host a production by the visiting players, Claudius suddenly finds himself entertaining, in effect, the ghost of the man he killed.[26]

No ghost of Duncan appears in *Macbeth*, but the ghost of Banquo literally comes to the banquet that is held to launch the reign of Macbeth. In joining the banquet he reminds us that hospitality in this play becomes another word for treachery, for it is only *as* a ghost that Banquo may attend the feast to which he is invited. Knowing what Macbeth and his lady have done to their royal guest in act 1, we know just what they intend—or at least what he intends—when they grandly invite Banquo as "chief guest" to their "solemn supper" and declare that his absence would leave "a gap in our great feast" (3.1.11–13). As Kottman says, "The violence perpetrated by Macbeth and Lady Macbeth is portrayed in Shakespeare's language as a kind of perverse hosting. Each time that Lady Macbeth and Macbeth plot a murder, they simultaneously plan the evening's hospitality. They twice withdraw together under the pretense of preparing the evening's entertainment" (Kottman 98). So it is that when he confers with his wife after commissioning the murder of Banquo, Macbeth sounds almost as much like a host as a killer. When Lady Macbeth prompts him to "be bright and jovial among your guests tonight" (3.2.28), he tells her to pay special attention to Banquo, to distinguish him "both with eye and tongue" and to join her husband in making "our faces visors to our hearts, / Disguising what they are" (3.2.31–36). These lines radiate irony. Not only does Macbeth seize the role of social director from his wife; he also tells her to single out that evening the very man he plans to kill beforehand. Though it is she who goaded him to kill the king, he cannot bring himself to tell her openly that he has ordered the death of Banquo. "Innocent of the knowledge," he says (3.2.46), she must act as if Banquo were indeed to be their "chief guest."

Macbeth speaks better than he knows, for before his very eyes Banquo will prove the centerpiece of the banquet from which he is brutally excluded. Displaced by murder, he will take the place of Macbeth himself at a feast chiefly characterized by its radical disorder. In killing the king, as Kottman notes, Macbeth has destroyed the foundation on which all hospitality in this kingdom rests (Kottman 97). Hence the absence of order in the seating of guests at what should be a rigorously formal ceremony. Even though Macbeth is launching his reign and proclaiming his new authority, he carelessly tells his nobles to sit down because they already "know [their] own degrees" (3.4.1). But Macbeth scarcely knows his own. Avoiding his official chair even while Lady Macbeth "keeps her state" on hers, he says he'll "play the humble host" by sitting "i'th' midst" of his guests (3.4.3–4, 9). Ironically enough, this fiercely ambitious man talks of taking a humble seat just after seizing the throne by murder; still more ironically, he takes no seat at all. Instead he walks off. Just as he earlier left Duncan in the middle of a meal, he now leaves the banquet to confer with one of the murderers lurking at the door and thus to learn that Banquo has been killed. But Macbeth cannot play both host and murderer without sacrificing one role to the other. Vexed by the news that Banquo's son Fleance has escaped, he inadvertently betrays his anxiety to his guests, as Lady Macbeth notices:

> My royal lord,
> You do not give the cheer. The feast is sold
> That is not often vouch'd, while 'tis a-making,
> 'Tis given with welcome. To feed were best at home,
> From thence, the sauce to meat is ceremony;
> Meeting were bare without it.
> $(3.4.31–36)$

At this point Lady Macbeth knows better than her husband what true hospitality is. Unless served with good cheer "while 'tis a-making," unless "vouched" with repeated invitations to eat and drink heartily, "the feast is sold" like a meal at a public house rather than hospitably "given with welcome." But Macbeth cannot even feign such welcome. Even though he has just counseled Lady Macbeth to join him in disguising their true feelings, he cannot take his own advice. He cannot manage his own impulses, much less gratify his guests.

Hence the simple act of sitting down to dinner with them becomes impossible. Having first left them without sitting down at all, he suddenly finds himself displaced by the ghost of his "chief guest" right after learning that the guest has been killed. Just as Macbeth contrives for a moment to sound like a gracious host, to wish his guests "good digestion" and to regret the absence of Banquo (3.4.38–43), the ghost of Banquo enters to take the place reserved for the new king. Since only Macbeth can see the ghost sitting in his place, only he can witness what he first takes to be a cruel joke played by one of his guests

("Which of you have done this?" he asks, [3.4.48]) and then construes as a silent accusation made by Banquo himself: "Thou canst not say I did it. Never shake / Thy gory locks at me" (3.4.49–50). Banquo's sudden arrival shakes Macbeth himself. As Kottman says, this unexpected guest breaks "one of the fundamental rules governing conventional hospitality: namely, the host ought to be in control of all entry into the house. . . . The entry of Banquo's ghost robs Macbeth, not only of his seat at the table, but of his position as *host* of the table" (Kottman 101). Macbeth cannot even play at hosting any longer. Obsessed with a ghost who usurps his place even as he has usurped the throne, he forgets his guests entirely, leaving his lady to keep them in their seats by assuring them he is having but a "momentary" fit (3.4.54).

But she cannot make him see that this ghostly guest is mere hallucination: the "painting of [his] fear" upon an empty stool (3.4.60, 67). Appalled though he is by the specter of a dead man glaring at him, he cannot help looking at it, and when the ghost leaves he insists to Lady Macbeth that he "saw him" (3.4.73). Besides affronting the commonplace conviction that death ends life, this particular ghost threatens to unseat him, in every sense, from the place he has just bloodily stolen:

> The time has been
> That, when the brains were out, the man would die,
> And there an end! But now they rise again,
> With twenty mortal murders on their crowns,
> And push us from our stools.
>
> (3.4.77–81)

Resurrection here becomes usurpation. The man who pushed the king from the throne now fears to be pushed in turn, by a man who rose again after twenty deadly wounds to the head. (Through Fleance, his descendants will reclaim the throne.)

Even now, however, Macbeth struggles to regain the poise of a host. With the ghost briefly gone and Lady Macbeth urging him to remember his guests, he brushes aside his "strange infirmity" as "nothing," pledges "love and health to all," promises to sit down, and calls for wine (3.4.85–87). But just as he pretends to wish that "our dear friend Banquo . . . / . . . were here" (3.4.89–90), his wish is granted by the reappearance of the ghost, who thereby goads him to contradict the wish he has just expressed: "Avaunt, and quit my sight! Let the earth hide thee! / . . . / Unreal mockery, hence!" (3.4.92, 106). Macbeth thereby shreds what is left of conviviality. Though the ghost obediently departs, Lady Macbeth tells him he has "displac'd the mirth, broke the good meeting / With most admir'd disorder" (3.4.108–9). Unhinged by an utterly unexpected guest, he can think no more of his other guests, whom Lady Macbeth now feels bound to dismiss without the slightest pretense of reluctance: "At once, good night. / Stand not upon the order of your going, / But go at once" (3.4.117–19).

In driving away their guests, Lady Macbeth does essentially what Macbeth himself does to all the noblemen around him. But besides driving them away, he drives them to end his tyrannous, bloodthirsty reign. When Macduff learns that his wife and all his children have been slaughtered by order of Macbeth, he joins Malcolm and an army of ten thousand English soldiers to overthrow the king and place Malcolm, son of Duncan, on the throne. This restoration of the rightful king rebuilds the trust that underlies all hospitality. In act 5, just before the battle that will crush Macbeth, Malcolm says, "Cousins, I hope the days are near at hand / That chambers [i.e., bedrooms] will be safe" (5.4.1–2). To this, Menteith instantly responds, "We doubt it nothing" (5.4.2). Having lived under a king who gained his throne by personally murdering one guest, tried to keep it by ordering the murder of another, and violated the castle of a third by having his family slaughtered there, the Scottish nobles yearn above all for a kingdom in which they and their families can sleep safely in their own chambers or as guests in the chambers of their friends. Nothing manifests the order or the violence of a kingdom more dramatically than the safety or peril of guests in its households. When Malcolm ends the play by inviting his thanes and kinsmen, now named earls, to see him "crown'd at Scone" (5.11.41), he implicitly assures them they will all be safely housed and hospitably entertained at his royal residence there.

In light of this ending and of what an English army does to restore the foundations of hospitable order in the Scotland of Shakespeare's play, it is startling to consider what English soldiers actually did in Scotland some eighty-five years after this play was written. In 1691, when all Highland clan chiefs were required to swear an oath of loyalty to the new king, William III, the only chief who refused was MacIain of Glencoe, elderly head of a small branch of the MacDonalds. On the first of February 1692 a division of troops from the Earl of Argyll's regiment reached Glencoe under the command of Capt. Robert Campbell of Glenlyon. Though the Campbells and the MacDonalds had feuded for centuries, the MacDonalds upheld the Highland tradition of granting hospitality to all visitors. Inviting the soldiers into their homes, they gave them food, drink, and lodging, and Captain Campbell was entertained by MacIain himself. But the MacDonalds' hospitality was cruelly requited. On the morning of February 6, shortly after receiving orders to kill every one of the MacDonalds under the age of seventy, Campbell's men slaughtered thirty-eight of them. Though it is hard to imagine anything more treacherous and brutal that guests could do to their hosts, the soldiers acted under orders devised by the secretary of state and approved by the king himself. The MacDonalds were victimized by neither brigandage nor clan warfare. They were cut down by deliberate English policy.

ENTERTAINMENT AND SEDUCTION: *THE WINTER'S TALE*

Turning back from an actual case of murderous guests to the staging of hospitality in Shakespeare, consider how the complex topic of entertainment is treated in *The Winter's Tale*, a late play far less bloody than *Macbeth* but in its own way just as disturbing. In act 1, Leontes, king of Sicilia, says the following about his wife's entertainment of Polixenes, king of Bohemia:

> This entertainment
> May a free face put on, derive a liberty
> From heartiness, from bounty, fertile bosom,
> And well become the agent; 't may, I grant;
> But to be paddling palms and pinching fingers,
> As now they are, and making practised smiles,
> As in a looking-glass, and then to sigh, as 'twere
> The mort o' the deer; O, that is entertainment
> My bosom likes not, nor my brows!
>
> (1.2.111–19)

As a virtual synonym for hospitality in Shakespeare's plays, the word *entertainment* can signify anything from the grand reception of a king to the modest feeding of a single visitor at a table in the forest, as in the banished duke's "entertainment" of Oliver near the end of *As You Like It* (4.3.141–42). Both kinds of entertainment, especially the humble kind, exemplify benign hospitality. But in the passage above, Leontes' abhorrence of his wife Hermione's "entertainment" of his old friend Polixenes reminds us that entertainment can be dangerous. Whenever a male guest is entertained by a woman, whether or not her husband is watching and whether or not she is chaste, she may find herself skirting the razor-thin line between friendship and seduction.

Etymologically, the word *entertain* means "hold between," for by way of the Old French *entretenir* it springs from the Latin *inter + tenere*. We have seen already that in the literature of hospitality the sexual implications latent in this lineage emerged well before Shakespeare's time. In Homer's telling, Paris ignited the Trojan war by abducting his hostess after sojourning with Menelaus and Helen in Sparta,[27] and when Odysseus returns to his kingdom he kills all of the would-be guests he finds in his palace because, among other things, they have been pressing their hostess to marry one of them. In the *Aeneid*, Dido breaks her vow of fidelity to her dead husband by taking her Trojan guest as her lover. In *Sir Gawain and the Green Knight*, Lady Bertilak offers her body, her "cors," to her husband's guest, though he chastely declines to take it. In later literature, as we will see, the relation between a hostess and her male guest is repeatedly eroticized. From *Wuthering Heights* to *Who's Afraid of Virginia Woolf?*, where the party games include Hump the Hostess, the hostess entertains her male guest in such a way as at least to rouse her husband's jealousy and sometimes to cuckold him.[28]

In Shakespeare's own corpus, Hermione has a notable precursor. Long before drafting *The Winter's Tale* in about 1610, Shakespeare wrote a narrative poem about a woman whose entertainment of a male guest leads to disaster. In *The Rape of Lucrece* (1594), a superlatively chaste wife pays a hideous price for entertaining Tarquin, her husband's comrade, while her husband is away. After she admits him to her house, feeds him, and gives him a bed for the night, he rapes her and thereby drives her to suicide.[29]

Hermione is neither raped nor killed by anyone. But she is ruthlessly punished by Leontes for the way she entertains Polixenes, whose very name includes the Greek word for what he is: their guest. When the impatient Polixenes rejects Leontes' demand that he prolong his stay, Leontes presses his hitherto "tongue-tied" wife (1.2.27) to bring their guest around. Ironically, her success in doing so prompts Leontes' suspicion. Though he does not openly accuse her until the second act, when he tells his court, "She's an adultress" (2.1.79), he suspects adultery as soon as he learns that this "kind hostess," as Hermione calls herself (1.2.61), has persuaded Polixenes to do what "at [Leontes'] request he would not" (1.2.89): prolong his stay. It does not matter that Hermione has spoken to Polixenes at her husband's request. In succeeding where he failed, she demonstrates a power of captivation that exceeds the power of one man's influence over another, which is always potentially political.[30]

Since a hostess oversees the threshold between the home and the world, her own power is likewise potentially political and becomes actually so when she petitions a foreign king. After first telling her husband how to keep their guest with them, she then speaks directly to Polixenes: "Yet of your royal presence I'll adventure / The borrow of a week" (1.2.38–39). This move is surely political. "In turning now to Polixenes," writes Julia Lupton, "perhaps even physically crossing over into his space, Hermione has *become public* by entering into persuasive speech" (Lupton, "H" 171). Furthermore, Hermione speaks more persuasively than her husband, who, she says, has charged their friend "too coldly" to stay (1.2.30).

In closely examining just what Hermione says to change the mind of Polixenes, Lupton quotes the speech she makes just after her first overture to him wins only a negative response:

> Verily,
> You shall not go: a lady's "Verily" 's
> As potent as a lord's. Will you go yet?
> Force me to keep you as a prisoner,
> Not like a guest: so you shall pay your fees
> When you depart and save your thanks. How say you?
> My prisoner? or my guest? By your dread "verily,"
> One of them you shall be.
>
> (1.2.50–57)

Lupton reads this speech as the exemplary expression of a host's or hostess's power to imprison his or her guests:

The guest is always a prisoner, not fully able to determine his own departure, fundamentally at the mercy of his host. (Recall Odysseus pining on the isle of Calypso, or Aeneas fleeing from Dido in the dead of night, or Ben Stiller in *Meet the Parents*.) The host extends special privileges to the guest precisely because the visitor is so thoroughly stripped of sovereignty and dignity in the household of another; the import of the return invitation is not to repay courtesy with courtesy but to match prison term with prison term, to subject oneself to the tyranny of someone else's off-brand coffee, unfamiliar toilet, or weird, jowly hound. What Hermione reveals in the very decorum of her extended courtesy are the risks inherent in hospitality, and the terror of that revelation in turn puts *her* at risk, up for interpretive reprisal. (Lupton, "H" 175)

In this provocative analysis of Hermione's speech, Lupton rightly stresses its coerciveness. Besides giving Polixenes a false choice (whether guest or prisoner, he can't leave), she commands him to stay ("You shall not go") in language "as potent as a lord's": language rivaling and challenging the potency of her own lord, himself a king, as well as of their royal guest. In flaunting its own potency even as it crosses the line between "tongue-tied" female silence and male expression, Hermione's speech does indeed threaten her guest with one of "the risks inherent in hospitality," namely, the risk of being trapped by one's host or hostess. Besides Calypso's entrapment of Odysseus, which Lupton cites, one might also recall the plight of Odysseus and his men in the cave of Polyphemos, where they are quite literally prisoners until Odysseus cunningly contrives their escape.

Nevertheless, in claiming that the guest is "*always* a prisoner . . . fundamentally at the mercy of his host," Lupton overstates her point. What would Dido herself have said to the claim that she held Aeneas at her mercy, and not the other way around? In leaving, even at night, he obeyed the gods ("Not of my own will do I seek Italy," he told her [4.360–61]) but resolutely defied her desperate longing to keep him. Likewise, Odysseus has no trouble leaving the lavishly hospitable Phaeacians, for they speed him on his way just as soon as they learn he is determined to get home. Not even Polyphemos can keep his Greek guests *always* at his mercy—but only until Odysseus outwits him. And the same is true of his sojourn with Circe. Indeed, we need not even stray from Shakespeare's text to see Lupton's generalization punctured. If the guest is "always a prisoner, . . . fundamentally at the mercy of his host," how could Polixenes reject Leontes' command that he stay?[31]

What all these examples suggest is that the risk or threat of hospitable entrapment, whether physical, emotional, or psychological, is not at all the same as the predictable certainty of it. To grasp this point is to see how Hermione's speech to a reluctant guest straddles the line between the certainty of male command, with all the powers of enforcement, and the unpredictable outcome of female seduction (remember, for example, that Lady Bertilak succeeds just minimally). By the time Hermione speaks, male command has failed, for in the face of Leontes' refusal to accept any "gainsaying" of his demand for a further stay (1.2.19), Polixenes has promptly gainsaid it. He can be kept from leaving only by means of a courtesy that opens itself, however innocently and unwittingly, to be construed as seductive.

To begin with, consider the terms in which Hermione rejects her husband's way of coaxing Polixenes to stay. "You, sir," she says, "charge him too coldly" (1.2.29–30). By "charge" she means command or exhort, as when Olivia tells the brawling Toby, "Hold, Toby! on thy life I charge thee, hold!" (*Twelfth Night* 4.1.27). In complaining that Leontes "charge[s]" their guest "too coldly," she implies that she can speak less imperatively and more warmly—though she ends up speaking far too warmly for her own good.

To say that she speaks less imperatively than Leontes, however, is to understate the sophistication and agility with which this hitherto tongue-tied hostess adapts her rhetorical strategy to the task at hand. Her first speech offers nothing but a variant of the gambit Leontes has already tried in vain: bargaining. After Leontes first insists that Polixenes stay a week and then offers to settle for half that time, Hermione offers a month of Leontes' time in exchange for just a week of Polixenes':

> When at Bohemia
> You take my lord, I'll give him my commission
> To let him there a month behind the gest [i.e., time]
> Prefix'd for 's parting. . . .
> . . . You'll stay?
>
> (1.2.39–44)

Here she presumes not only to bargain with Polixenes but to govern the movements of Leontes, who must come and go on *her* commission. But in ending with a simple question—"You'll stay?"—that can be answered yes or no, she makes it all too easy for Polixenes to say the latter, repeatedly:

> No, madam.
> Nay, but you will?
> I may not, verily.
> (1.2.45–47)

Here is Hermione's cue to change her strategy from bargaining and begging with impotent questions ("Nay, but you will?") to something superficially similar but fundamentally different: flirtation by means of rhetorical questions that barely conceal her coercive intent. Reconsider her second speech to Polixenes:

> Verily,
> You shall not go: a lady's "Verily" 's
> As potent as a lord's. Will you go yet?
> Force me to keep you as a prisoner,
> Not like a guest: so you shall pay your fees
> When you depart and save your thanks. How say you?
> My prisoner? or my guest? By your dread "verily,"
> One of them you shall be.
>
> (1.2.50–57)

Snatching up his "dread 'verily,'" she plays it like a pipe: first in the imperative mood ("Verily, / You shall not go"), then in the indicative ("a lady's 'Verily' 's / As potent as a lord's"), then in the simple interrogative ("Will you go yet?"), and finally in the rhetorically interrogative: "[Will you] force me to keep you as a prisoner, / Not like a guest[?]" With that cunning question she poses as the "force[d]" subject of her guest's will even while flexing the muscles of her own, forcing *him* to choose between alternatives that will, in either case, keep him from doing what he has repeatedly said he wants to do. As Menelaus says in the *Odyssey*, the truly considerate host or hostess never detains a visitor who yearns to leave but rather "speed[s] the parting guest" (15.75–76 / F 15.84–85).[32] Though doing just the opposite, Hermione shifts the burden of rudeness from herself to her guest, who promptly accepts it: "To be your prisoner," he says, "should import offending; / Which is for me less easy to commit / Than you to punish" (1.2.57). Polixenes knows very well that he need not be *either* her prisoner *or* her guest, that he is free to leave without saying another word. But she traps him rhetorically—and flirtatiously. Her threat to jail him if he won't remain her guest makes him feel that he risks offending her and that he can avoid the risk only by remaining her guest.

If Hermione thus contrives the perfect rhetorical means of detaining her restless guest, may we infer that this innocent and cruelly wronged heroine, as she proves to be, somehow evokes the manipulative power of a Iago? Of course not. Meaning no harm at all to Polixenes, she is simply doing her best to fulfill her husband's wish. But as soon as she masters Polixenes, is there nothing disingenuous in the claim that she thereby ("then") becomes his "kind hostess" or—when she has just outwitted him—in her plan to question him "of my lord's tricks and yours when you were boys" (1.2.60–61)? She has just played a flirtatious trick of her own on her guest, and she goes on to imply that she and Polixenes' queen devilishly stole their husbands' virginity (1.2.80–86). To see that even a "kind hostess" can be too kind—too cunning, too manipulative in pressing a guest to stay—is also to see how the playfulness of her manner with Polixenes borders on seduction, comes just close enough to rouse within Leontes the green-eyed monster of suspicion. Furthermore, her speech to Polixenes is so persuasive that it reminds Leontes of the only other time she has spoken so potently: when, after holding him off for "three crabbed months," she told the ardent young man she would be his "for ever" (1.2.105). To the eyes of suspicion, a hostess who can speak to her guest with all the potency of a woman newly in love looks lascivious. Even Hermione's giving of her hand to their guest in a perfectly conventional sign of hospitable welcome becomes a gesture of "paddling [i.e., caressing] palms and pinching fingers" that turns hospitality into seduction, the kind of "entertainment" Leontes cannot bear to see (1.2.113–21).[33]

Consequently, though Leontes finally comes to see his error and to be reconciled with his wife, all the suffering he inflicts on her as well as others in the play, including himself, springs from his groundless yet arguably explicable suspicion that his wife has betrayed him with their guest or, in other words, that any hostess who entertains a man must be somehow inviting him into her body as well as her house.[34]

I would hardly want to argue that such a suspicion—or such a hypothesis— explains the events of the play as a whole, which at last regenerates Leontes' love for the wife he has so cruelly wronged. I must likewise recognize that Shakespeare's plays are now and then punctuated by acts of genuine hospitality. Just as the generosity of Alcinous and the tender kindness of Eumaeus shine out against all the treachery that Homer's hosts and guests inflict upon each other, Shakespeare now and then stages hospitality at its most benign. In act 4 of *The Winter's Tale* itself, as Lupton notes, the peasant hostess fondly remembered by the old shepherd, her widowered husband, exemplifies a "rustic hospitality" that "welcomed all, served all" (Lupton, "H" 172–73 / *WT* 4.4.55–57) and thus set an example that he urges Perdita to follow in entertaining Polixenes and Camillo. Under much more vexing conditions, Leonato remains a model host in *Much Ado About Nothing*. As governor of Messina he receives his lord Don Pedro with suitable grandeur, gives a masquerade to honor the two young noblemen who come with him, and grants permission for one of them, Claudio, to marry his daughter Hero. Even on their blighted wedding day, when Claudio mistakenly accuses Hero of infidelity, Leonato grimly takes the word of his guests. Though he threatens to fight Claudio, he seeks only to make the boy suffer, as Antonio suggests (5.1.40–41), and specifically to make him see the apparently murderous effect of his slanderous words. Furthermore, Leonato's would-be "revenge" against Claudio is an act of supreme hospitality. Having invited him back to his house and made him agree to marry Leonato's niece, he presents Claudio with a masked young woman who, as soon as Claudio swears to marry her, reveals herself as the resurrected Hero. Then, along with the wedding of Beatrice and Benedick, that of Claudio and Hero calls for another lavish party, another opportunity for Leonato to play the gracious host.

Still more than Leonato, the banished duke of *As You Like It* exemplifies hospitality at its most disarmingly kind. Near the end of act 2, when the famished Orlando discovers the duke and his followers seated around a table of fruit in the Forest of Arden, he draws his sword and threatens death to anyone who touches the food before he does. But the duke's kindness instantly subdues him. Melting the steel edge of his belligerence, it prompts him to remember his old servant Adam, who must be fetched and fed before Orlando will touch any of the food offered to him. When Orlando returns with Adam, the duke welcomes them both.

This victory of gentleness over aggression shapes the whole play. At the very end, when Orlando sees that a lioness threatens his brother Oliver, who has treated him viciously, he saves his brother's life. As Oliver himself reports to Rosalind,

> Kindness, nobler than revenge,
> And nature, stronger than his just occasion,

Made him give battle to the lioness,
Who quickly fell before him.

(4.3.127–30)

Capping this kindness, Oliver says, Orlando led him "to the gentle Duke, / Who gave me fresh array and entertainment" (4.3.141–42). Once again, it is precisely by his hospitality that the duke reveals his nobility of character and his right to repossess the crown that his usurping brother, "converted / . . . from his enterprise," returns to him at last (5.4.150–54).

Nevertheless, just as entertainment turns perilous in *The Winter's Tale*, Shakespeare's plays reveal the very worst that hosts and guests can do to each other. In doing so, they also demonstrate that hospitality is something born to be staged. When Henry Wotton writes that every man's house is "the theatre of his Hospitality," he reminds us that, conversely, the theater can readily re-create a room in a house, such as the one in which Macbeth hosts the dinner invaded by the unexpected ghost of a missing guest. In scenes like this Shakespeare truly *stages* hospitality, as he often does elsewhere: in the second banquet scene of *Timon*, when Timon flings lukewarm water and empty dishes at guests, whom he calls "detested parasites"; in the begging scene of *Lear*, when the king turns vainly back and forth from one hostess to another—from Goneril to Regan—in quest of refuge for himself and his men; in the first act of *The Winter's Tale*, when Hermione gives her guest Polixenes a handshake that may be construed as either innocently hospitable or covertly seductive ("paddling palms and pinching fingers"); in the final feast of *Titus*, when Titus hospitably urges his imperial guests to eat and then reveals that Tamora has just "daintily" consumed the flesh of her own sons. To experience such scenes is to feel the full force of Wotton's metaphor, to see hospitality as well as treachery theatricalized.

But Shakespeare is hardly alone in staging hospitality, which has captured the attention of so many other playwrights that the topic deserves a book of its own. (Near the end of this one I briefly examine the New York dinner party staged throughout a recent play called *Omnium Gatherum*.) Beyond its often stunning theatricality, we may ask, what makes Shakespeare's treatment of hospitality distinctive of its time? I began this chapter by suggesting that his plays reflect a shift in English hospitality from charity to the theatrically lavish display of wealth, which in Tudor England was the indispensable sign of power. The impact of this shift is most obvious in *Lear*, where, in surrendering all his property, the king also gives up his power to entertain, to play the host, and becomes instead a homeless mendicant dependent on the charitable hospitality of his daughters. Yet he is so wedded to the trappings of royalty ("all th' addition of a king") that he cannot bear to be entertained without his train or, in other words, without some special expense and display on the part of his hosts or hostesses. Though Lear cannot reconcile this contradiction, his relentless attack on the notion that man's "needs" can be met by mere subsistence—a little food and the rudest of shelters—destabilizes the opposition between charity and power-proclaiming or power-confirming entertainment. Recalling the ancient Greek king who returned to his land disguised as a beggar in order to test the hospitality of his people, he implicitly asks if it is charitable to treat him as if he were no more than a beggar.

Macbeth likewise highlights the bond between hospitality and power, the power to rule and the power to entertain in such a way as to proclaim one's authority. Just as Lear loses the latter as soon as he gives up the former, just as the division of his kingdom means he can no longer play either the host or the lavishly welcomed guest, Macbeth shows that he is utterly unworthy of the crown by first abusing and then grossly mismanaging the power of a host. Even before he murders Duncan, neither he nor Lady Macbeth gives any serious thought to the "preparation" of a lavish welcome for the king, and during the dinner itself he leaves the table before the king has finished eating—to plan the murder of his royal guest. Afterward, at the banquet held to inaugurate his reign, he assigns no places to his guests (even though they are all members of his new court), takes no seat at all for himself, walks out (again) in the middle of the meal to discuss the murder of a guest, returns to find his own place taken by the ghost of that guest, twice fulminates against an apparition that none of his other guests can see, and thus—as Lady Macbeth herself tells him—breaks up the party. Uninvited and utterly unwanted, like a beggar in the night, the ghost of Banquo has dared to enter the house and sit in the very seat of its master. As a result, even after pretending to wish that his "dear friend Banquo" were among them, Macbeth drives the ghost away just as pitilessly as Goneril and Regan drive Lear into the storm: "Avaunt," says Macbeth, "and quit my sight!" Macbeth cannot play the host in any sense and certainly has no room or charity for unexpected guests.

Shakespeare's plays, then, test the very meaning of hospitality in his own time. Besides staging hospitality in ways that fully display its theatricality, and besides revealing the worst as well as the best that hosts and guests can do for and to each other, Shakespeare shows what happens when charity gives way to power as the motive for acts of hospitality. Driven by the quest for power and the urge to manifest it, hospitality in *Macbeth* turns not just uncharitable but also ruthless, treacherous, and murderous. And while *King Lear* complicates the opposition between charitable hospitality and lavish entertainment, it also reveals the brutality of a world in which Christian hospitality is considered treasonous and charity shrinks to the vanishing point.

5

———————◆•◆———————

WORDSWORTH, COLERIDGE, AND THE SPIRIT OF PLACE

European romanticism is customarily defined by its sentimental return to a nature that classical poets are thought to have experienced directly and by its advocacy of revolution in politics, literature, and society.[1] But nature and revolution did not always mix. Though Wordsworth and Coleridge at first embraced and celebrated the liberating energies of the French Revolution, they later deplored its violence: not only its shedding of human blood but its assault on a nature they had newly discovered as something like a paradise on earth. Central to their experience of nature was a reawakened sensitivity to the genius loci, the genius or spirit of place that might hospitably welcome a visitor but was also capable, like Homer's gods, of avenging crimes against that hospitality. In *The Prelude*, his autobiographical epic, Wordsworth recalls what soldiers of the newborn French republic did to a shrine of hospitality in the Alps—the Convent of the Chartreuse. In a play called *The Borderers*, Wordsworth tells a comparable story about hospitality violated: corrupted by the protorevolutionary Oswald, Marmaduke commits a crime against hospitality that he can expiate only by eternal wandering. In turn the story of Marmaduke's end is reenacted by Coleridge's mariner, who is doomed to wander eternally for "inhospitably" killing a bird held sacred by the Polar spirit.

WORDSWORTH: MONASTERIES IN THE REVOLUTION

In the opening lines of *The Prelude*, his life story in verse, Wordsworth tells us what he felt one day in the fall of 1799 as he returned to the English Lake District, where he was born and raised, after sojourning in London.[2] Though literally inspired by the breeze on his cheek and by a delicious sense of release, he sounds a little uncertain, for the exhilaration of this free-spirited, birdlike wanderer, newly "escaped / From the vast city," must contend with pedestrian queries about where he will alight. If "the earth is all before" him (l. 14), he could be retracing the journey of Milton's Adam and Eve, newly exiled—not escaped—from Paradise, whose "world was all before them" as they entered it "with wand'ring steps and slow" (*PL* 12:646–48). But even before evoking the plight of Adam and Eve, Wordsworth asks the question that sooner or later springs to the mind of almost every traveler gone for more than a day: "What dwelling shall receive me?" (l. 10). The ensuing questions, especially the one about where he will make his home, imply that he plans to settle somewhere rather than staying anywhere as a guest, but they also imply that he expects to be hospitably welcomed by nature and humankind alike. He thus invites us to consider him as host, guest, and poet of a hospitality always liable to violation.

Romantic hospitality heightens this liability by its very openness. According to Peter Melville, the essence of romantic hospitality lies in something approaching Derrida's absolute hospitality: in the act of welcoming "the desta-bilizing singularity" of the stranger, in embracing "the stranger's ultimate resistance to accommodation" (Melville, *RH* 8). If romantic hospitality can denote any welcoming of a stranger, as Melville implies throughout his book, this formula surely applies, as he argues, to such figures as the Wedding Guest of Coleridge's "Rime" (*RH* 111–13). Also, Melville rightly observes that Coleridge once described his writing process as an act of "promiscuous hospitality" in which the poet opens the doors and windows of his mind to revelation (letter of circa 1826, qtd. *RH* 110). But romantic hospitality entails more than domestic reception, more than the entertainment of visitors in one's home or habitus, and more than a willingness to accommodate strangers. To study what Wordsworth and Coleridge do with sacred sites like the Convent of the Chartreuse and with the spirit of place itself is to see that the romantic literature of hospitality is at least as preoccupied with the violation of hospitable trust as it is with absorbing the strangeness of the other.

Consider how Wordsworth treats hospitality in various accounts of his walking trip through France in the summer of 1790, five years before he met Coleridge. On July 27 of that year, after he and a college friend named Robert Jones had spent three weeks tramping from Calais to Chalon-sur-Saône, they boarded a boat bound down the River Saône to Lyons. Most of their fellow passengers were *fédérés*: delegates returning from the Festival of the Federation, which had been held in Paris on July 14 to mark the first anniversary of the storming of the Bastille and the outbreak of the French Revolution. The *fédérés* gave "the lonely pair / Of Englishmen" their first taste of revolutionary conviviality.[3] After spending just one day with them, Wordsworth writes, he and Jones were invited to their supper table:

> In this blithe company
> We landed, took with them our evening meal,
> Guests welcome almost as the angels were
> To Abraham of old. The supper done,
> With flowing cups elate and happy thoughts
> We rose at signal given, and formed a ring
> And hand in hand danced round and round the board;
> All hearts were open, every tongue was loud
> With amity and glee. We bore a name
> Honoured in France, the name of Englishmen,
> And hospitably did they give us hail,
> As their forerunners in a glorious course;
> And round and round the board we danced again.
> (*Prelude* 6:401–13)

To be welcomed thus is to savor hospitality at its most irresistible. Besides feeling something like the angels fed by Abraham (see chapter 2 above), Wordsworth probably knew that Milton had once been similarly welcomed in Italy, where the young literary prodigy from England struck the Italians as "non Anglus, sed Angelus" (Gordon 77). But Wordsworth does not traffic in stale Latin puns. As Englishmen, he and Jones are almost literally *angeli* — messengers from the nation where, just over a hundred years before, the "glorious" revolution of 1688 had deposed a tyrannical king and brought new power to the English parliament, forerunner of the new French National Assembly.[4] Welcomed like angels and as *angeli* of English freedom, Wordsworth and Jones might have tasted something like the joy of redemption itself, whirling around in what must have seemed a dance of heavenly joy.

Yet even this heavenly dance featured *tours jetés* of revolutionary violence. Just before the passage quoted above, we are told that some of the *fédérés* on the boat "flourished with their swords as to fight / The saucy air" (1805 *Prelude* 6:400–401). They would soon flash arms in earnest. In 1792, six years before starting work on *The Prelude*, Wordsworth briefly recalled in verse what he and Jones found when they attained the first goal of their tour, in effect of their pilgrimage.[5] After three weeks of steady marching, he and Jones reached the Carthusian Monastery of the Grand Chartreuse near Grenoble in the French Alps, where they were hospitably lodged on the nights of August 4 and 5. But in

Descriptive Sketches Wordsworth reports that he found this hospitable sanctuary freshly invaded by soldiers of the newborn French Republic. Mantled up to now in "a death-like peace" rent only by the roar of the torrent and the buzz of the cicada,

> The cloister startles at the gleam of arms,
> And Blasphemy the shuddering fane alarms; . . .
> The cross with hideous laughter Demons mock,
> By angels planted on the aerial rock.
> The "parting Genius" sighs with hollow breath
> Along the mystic streams of Life and Death, . . .
> Vallombre, 'mid her falling fanes, deplores,
> For ever broke, the sabbath of her bow'rs.
> (DS [1793] 60–79, in PW 1.46)

Wordsworth wrote these lines during his second visit to France, when he spent the spring and summer of 1792 in Blois, on the River Loire. What he had learned about the revolution by the spring of 1792 clearly informs his account of what he found at the monastery in 1790. Though he probably saw there only a small contingent of troops on a "domiciliary" or protective visit, he conflates this event with the armed occupation that took place in May 1792.[6] He thus darkens the remembered light of what he elsewhere calls the "golden hours" of the French Revolution in its youth (1805 *Prelude* 6:353).

This is a curious move. Even allowing for the fictive reshaping of the past that distinguishes autobiography from chronicle, why should this impassioned young supporter of the revolution have decried its violence as early as 1792? Part of the answer lies in the brand of revolutionary politics Wordsworth embraced among the Friends of the Constitution in Blois, who were far less radical than their Jacobin counterparts in Paris. According to Kenneth Johnston, their leader, Bishop Henri Gregoire, sought "to reform past ecclesiastical abuses with republican virtues" but also welcomed voices calling "for moderation and tolerance" (Johnston 301). It is precisely the absence of these two qualities that Wordsworth laments on the banks of the River Loire, where—in the spring and summer of 1792—he walked and talked with Michel Beaupuy, an aristocratic, idealistic young officer who yearned to wipe out poverty and the abuses of privilege. If we can trust Wordsworth's account of those walks in book 9 of *The Prelude*, first drafted in 1804 and later revised, his enthusiasm for the revolution did not keep him from feeling pained by the sight of a ruined "convent"—that is, monastery—unroofed by "violence abrupt" and shorn of its cross, "a sign / (How welcome to the weary traveller's eyes) / Of hospitality and peaceful rest" (1850 *Prelude* 9:466–78).

In lamenting the violation of monastic hospitality, Wordsworth conflates two different sights and two different periods. The ruined monastery he saw on the banks of the Loire in the spring or summer of 1792 recalls the Alpine monastery where he and his weary fellow traveler found hospitality in the summer of 1790. Knowing that republican soldiers occupied the Chartreuse in May 1792 and promptly expelled its monks, Wordsworth represents it as the victim of assault so imminent as to be virtually visible in 1790, even in a monastery far from the Chartreuse. And what he sees in this imminent assault is a crime against hospitality.[7]

The armed assault on monastic hospitality shocked Wordsworth so much that he recalled it more than once: first in the lines quoted above from *Descriptive Sketches*, composed in 1792, then in a lengthy passage from "The Tuft of Primroses," composed in the spring of 1808, and last in a passage composed for book 6 of *The Prelude* sometime between 1816 and 1819. In "The Tuft of Primroses" he imagines himself and Jones, "a Fellow-pilgrim," reaching "the solemn haven of Chartreuse / . . . for timely rest" just before it is invaded:

> and are we twain
> The last, perchance the very last, of men
> Who shall be welcom'd here, whose limbs shall find
> Repose within these modest cells, whose hearts
> Receive a comfort from these awful [i.e., awesome] spires?
> Alas! for what I see, the flash of arms,
> O Sorrow! and yon military glare;
> And hark, those Voices!
> ("Tuft" ll. 513–21, *PW* 1:360)

In Wordsworth's eyes monasteries furnish both a refuge from the world *and* hospitality for the weary traveler, whose bodily need for nightly rest—something expressed in the very opening lines of *The Prelude*—comes to signify the pilgrim's need for a site of spiritual rest, contemplation, and renewal.[8] When the traveler becomes an armed soldier bent on occupying the monastery and expelling its monks, the voice of Nature itself—the Christianized spirit of this place—condemns the violation:

> "Stay your impious hand":
> Such was the vain injunction of that hour
> By Nature uttered from her Alpine throne. . . .
> Let this one Temple last—be this one spot
> Of Earth devoted to Eternity.
> ("Tuft," ll. 537–45, *PW* 5:361)

In this poem, however, Nature speaks with a double voice. Strangely enough, it is only in a poem written in 1808, long after he turned against the French Revolution for its bloodthirstiness at home and aggression abroad, that Wordsworth first claims to have heard an Alps-enthroned Nature *praising* the revolution: saluting the revolutionary zeal of the French patriot and hailing the "mighty Passions of the Time" *before* exhorting the French troops to "spare / This House, these courts of mystery" ("Tuft," ll. 547–54, *PW* 5:361). Yet why should Nature—Wordsworth's Nature—voice any sympathy for the passions of men who trample on its sacred precincts, who render its protests "vain"? Partly, I think, to articulate Wordsworth's lasting ambivalence toward the revolution, but also to contrast the passions of the *time*, the turmoil of this moment in history, with the indestructibility of the monastic ideal, which somehow perseveres even in ruin. A little earlier in the poem Wordsworth commemorates all of the now "crush'd" medieval monasteries of France and England, including Tintern Abbey (the subject of his first major poem), which

> to this day beholds
> Her faded image in the depths of Wye;
> Of solemn port smitten but unsubdued
> She stands.
> ("Tuft," ll. 470, 477–80, *PW* 5:359)

In the final version of *The Prelude*, written some years after "The Tuft of Primroses," the double voice of a Nature torn between admiration for revolutionary zeal and veneration for the monasteries it has crushed becomes the voice of the poet's own heart. Conflating lines drawn from *Descriptive Sketches* as well as "Tuft," Wordsworth tells what happened soon after he and Jones left the boisterous *fédérés* who so "hospitably" welcomed them to their festivities in Lyons. Just two nights later they reached the Convent of the Chartreuse, the first object of their pilgrimage, to find its "awful *solitude*" rent by armed men flashing arms and bent on expelling the monks (1850 *Prelude* 6.404–26). While Nature once again implores the troops to "stay [their] sacrilegious hands," it is now the poet's heart that wrestles with "conflicting passions." Hailing "the patriot's zeal" and even the "discerning sword that Justice wields," his heart nonetheless venerates the "courts of mystery" where "shining cliffs" and immortal woods—"forests unapproachable by death"—furnish a perfect natural setting for transcendent meditation signified by the all-transcending cross, "stand[ing] erect, as if / Hands of angelic powers had fixed it there" (1850 *Prelude* 6.430–86).

It is painful to remember seeing a cross that has survived "a thousand storms" at precisely the moment when it is threatened by the "rage of one State-whirlwind" (1850 *Prelude* 6.486–88). And the pain of this remembered sight complicates the irony of Wordsworth's position as a Protestant pilgrim at a quintessentially Catholic shrine. Looking ahead to his graduation from Cambridge University, Wordsworth was not just a youthful heir to the Enlightenment; he was also expected, at the time of his one and only visit to the Chartreuse, to be preparing himself for a career in the ministry of the Church of England. In light of that fact, writes Johnston, he should have been "predis-posed to regard the monastery as a living relic of Catholic superstition" and corruption (Johnston 197). Why then does he commemorate it so fervently?

The answer, I think, springs not just from Wordsworth's tendency to identify the monastery with the transcendent immortality of Alpine nature, but also from something he had personally experienced and for which he remained permanently grateful: hospitality to the weary traveler who could seldom afford to buy his lodging, solace at once for body and soul. And his shock at the violation of that hospitality by soldiers of the French Republic holds the key, I believe, to his one and only play, *The Borderers*.[9]

Written in 1796–97, several years after *Descriptive Sketches* but two years before he started work on *The Prelude*, the play dramatizes Wordsworth's critique of Godwinian rationalism. In *The Prelude* he would claim that this rationalism idolized "human reason's naked self" and thereby licensed the passions to do their work without ever hearing "the sound of their own names" (1805 *Prelude* 10:807–18).[10] Well before voicing this critique in his poem Wordsworth voiced it in drama. Rather than dramatizing the revolution directly, however, he set his play in 1265, when monasteries offered refuge to the needy. But to Wordsworth they signified a refuge from rationalism. If *The Prelude* shows the brutality of the French Republic by backdating its military occupation of the Chartreuse, *The Borderers* attacks the ideology of the revolution by anachronistically placing a protorevolutionary intellectual in the age of monasteries.

As Wordsworth explains in his preface to *The Borderers*, he wrote it to show that once we have shed "the obligations of religion and morality," reason can lead us into hideous crimes (*Borderers* 66). Personified by the protorevolu-tionary Oswald, it misleads Marmaduke (originally called Mortimer), who captains a band of outlaws in the borderlands of England and Scotland but still feels moved by "gentleness and love" (168) until he is emotionally amputated by Oswald.[11] Cut off from "human feelings," as he says himself (1327–29), shorn of compassion for the blind and feeble old Herbert, Marmaduke leaves him alone to die in a desolate wasteland after promising to lead him to the refuge of a monastery. When he and Oswald find him at a hostel, where his dutiful daughter Idomenea has left him with instructions that he be well cared for, they offer to guide him to "quiet lodging" at "the Convent," later identified as "Stone-Arthur Castle" (352–57, 2197). But his first night's lodging under what Herbert trustingly takes for their "kindly" protection of him (825) is actually the dungeon of a half-ruined castle, and instead of leading him to the hospitality of the monastery, Marmaduke abandons him to its antithesis: a place "without house or track, and destitute / Of obvious shelter, as a shipless sea" (1389–90).

I Iere Marmaduke serves the wishes of Oswald, who leads him to think the worst of the virtuous Herbert. But unlike Oswald, who was himself once duped into killing an innocent man, Marmaduke cannot stifle the pangs of remorse, cannot pass beyond them "into a region of futurity" ruled by reason alone (1817–73).[12] On the contrary, he can never forget his crime. Knowing he has presumptuously cast the would-be "guilty" Herbert on the judgment of Heaven, he plainly admits his own guilt to Idomenea. "Through me, through me," he says, "Thy father perished" (2182–83).

In leaving a blind old man to die after promising to guide him to the convent, Marmaduke commits a heinous crime. To expiate it he will not seek relief in "a Convent," as Oswald did when he learned that his own victim was innocent (1766), and he will not commit suicide. Instead he will wander the earth without finding hospitality anywhere:

> No human ear shall ever hear me speak;
> No human dwelling ever give me food,
> Or sleep, or rest: but over waste and wild,
> In search of nothing, that this earth can give,
> But expiation, will I wander on—
> A Man by pain and thought compelled to live,
> Yet loathing life—till anger is appeased
> In Heaven, and Mercy gives me leave to die.
>
> (2314–21)

Personified by Oswald, rationalism demands that Marmaduke sacrifice his humanity by committing a crime against hospitality: a crime he can expiate only by eternal wandering. He thus prefigures both the crime and the punishment enacted by one of the most famous wanderers of English romantic poetry, Coleridge's ancient mariner.

WORDSWORTH, THE SPIRIT OF PLACE, AND COLERIDGE'S "RIME"

Coleridge begot his mariner in the spring of 1798, just a few months after Wordsworth had completed the original version of *The Borderers*. During a walking tour in Somerset that Wordsworth, Coleridge, and Wordsworth's sister Dorothy took together, the two poets conceived the idea for a poem about a man compelled to wander because of a crime he has committed at sea. Forty-five years later, Wordsworth claimed that key elements of the poem had come from him. While noting that it was "founded on a dream, as Mr. Coleridge said, of his friend Mr. Cruikshank," Wordsworth took credit for proposing the story of vengeance taken for the killing of a bird. "Suppose," he remembers saying to Coleridge, "you represent [the mariner] as having killed one of these birds on entering the South Sea, and that the tutelary Spirits of those regions take upon them to avenge the crime."[13] In the second edition of the poem, which appeared with the *Lyrical Ballads* of 1800, the killing of the bird is explicitly identified in the "Argument" as a crime committed "in contempt of the laws of hospitality" (Coleridge, *CP* 500). Though the "Argument" does not appear in later editions of the poem, the marginal notes Coleridge added after 1800 make it absolutely clear that the mariner killed the bird "inhospitably" (79–82 gloss). Why does hospitality loom so large in Coleridge's conception of the poem? And why should the murder of the bird break its laws?[14] So far as I can tell, no commentator on the poem has adequately answered either of these questions.

To do so we must consider what else Wordsworth contributed to the poem before Coleridge took full charge of it. As Paul Magnuson has shown, its plot was anticipated by the Salisbury Plain poems that Wordsworth wrote in the 1790s, in particular by the second of them, "Adventures on Salisbury Plain" (hereafter "ASP"), written between 1795 and 1799.[15] In this revised version of an earlier poem, a homecoming soldier becomes a sailor who has been press-ganged into two years of hard labor at sea and denied his pay. Dismayed by the prospect of returning empty-handed, he robs and kills a traveler near his home and then takes flight over the rainswept plain of Salisbury. After wandering in desperation, pausing at Stonehenge, and glimpsing no sign of a cottage inn or even firelight anywhere in the oceanic gloom, he comes at last to a ruined "Spital" revealed by a clouded moon:

> It was a spot where, ancient vows fulfill'd
> Kind pious hands did to the Virgin build
> A lonely Spital, the belated swain
> From the night-terrors of that waste to shield.
> But there no human being could remain;
> And now the Walls are named the dead house of the Plain.

> ("ASP" 184–89, in *SPP* 128)

Once, as its name suggests, a ho*spit*able refuge from the terrors of the night, the spital has become a dead house, a ruin for derelicts like the sailor himself. Racked by irremediable guilt, he takes no solace from the story told by his chance companion of the night: a woman who has lost her entire family and voyaged to America, where she found brief refuge only in a hospital ward and around a gypsy campfire. Having returned to wander in her own country, she somehow remains capable of feeling revived by the light of dawn when it breaks over the ruin. But nothing she says can cheer the guilt-ridden sailor, and no hospitality can soothe him. Though the two of them make their way to breakfast at a rustic inn, it is precisely the housewife's hospitality there that leads to the sailor's undoing. When she kindly accommodates a dying woman who passes by in a horse-drawn cart, it turns out to be the sailor's wife, forced from her home because her blue-vested husband is thought to have murdered a man found near her door. Her story shatters him. Though she strives to comfort him with her dying words, he cannot even break the bread that has been put before him. Wishing only to be dead, he gives himself up to be hanged.

And to be re-created by Coleridge. Haunted by guilt for murder and compelled to wander, Wordsworth's sailor plainly anticipates the ancient mariner. But at the same time, his deeds evoke two key stories of hospitality and betrayal in the New Testament. By robbing and killing a traveler near his home, the sailor inverts the hospitality of the good Samaritan, who rescues and finds lodging for a traveler that has been robbed, beaten, and left to die. The good Samaritan is reborn in the housewife who takes a dying traveler into her cottage, but when the sailor cannot break the bread she offers him and wants only to die, he reminds us of Judas, who hanged himself after betraying the breaker of bread at the Last Supper. Neither vicious nor treacherous by nature, the sailor is far more sinned against than sinning. But in shattering the rules of hospitality enshrined in the story of the Good Samaritan, he dooms himself to a life of misery and a death that recalls the end of Judas.

In subtly evoking the New Testament, this poem exemplifies one of the major strands of Coleridge's "Rime." In the first of its seven parts, the mariner and his shipmates hail the albatross "as if it had been a Christian soul" just before the mariner "inhospitably" kills it (ll. 65, 80–81, and gloss), and the whole poem can be read as a story of salvation meant to answer Wordsworth's story of suicidal despair. Instead of killing himself, the mariner frees himself from death-in-life by learning, with the help of his "kind saint" (l. 286), to love and bless all living things.[16] But Christianity alone cannot explain the poem. As Jerome McGann showed many years ago, the "Rime" weaves together Catholic theology and Broad Church Protestantism with pagan superstition and philosophy. Because Coleridge believed that pagan bards and the authors of scripture all participate in what McGann calls "a process of continuous spiritual revelation," the poet binds his Christian scheme to something manifestly pagan yet also amenable to reinterpretation within the Christian scheme: the spirit of place (McGann 50–51).

Homer and Virgil each treated place as something sacred to a god or guarded by a spirit. In the *Odyssey*, Odysseus and his men pay a terrible price for slaughtering cattle on the island of Helios, because all of its sheep and oxen are sacred to the god of the sun. As if to forestall a comparable fate, the first thing Aeneas does when he lands with his men in Latium is to pray to the "genium loci" (7.136), the genius or guardian spirit of the place. What then happened to this genius? In Milton's ode "On the Morning of Christ's Nativity" (1629), the birth of Christ is said to have banished it "from haunted spring and dale" (l. 184). But in "Lycidas," written eight years later, Milton hails the spirit of a drowned fellow poet as "the Genius of the shore" (l. 183), and even after the Enlightenment had done its best to banish every kind of superstition, the romantic poets fed their imaginations on the genius loci. In *Marriage of Heaven and Hell*, a prophecy steeped in biblical allusions, Blake recalls that "the ancient poets animated all sensible objects with gods or geniuses, calling them by the names, and adorning them with the properties, of woods, rivers, mountains, lakes, cities, nations, and whatever their enlarged and numerous senses could perceive" (plate 11).

Wordsworth knew almost nothing of Blake's poetry, but he shared Blake's desire to reactivate the "enlarged and numerous senses" of the ancient poets. Mourning our insensitivity to nature—to the heaving beauty of the moonlit sea and the coiled fury of the winds—he yearns to see and hear them as the ancients did:

> Great God! I'd rather be
> A Pagan suckled in a creed outworn;
> So might I, standing on this pleasant lea,
> Have glimpses that would make me less forlorn;
> Have sight of Proteus rising from the sea;
> Or hear old Triton blow his wreathèd horn.
> ("The world is too much with us," *PW* 3.18)

In this sonnet of 1802 or later (published in 1807), Wordsworth casts his animating impulse in the subjunctive mood, wishing he could *see* figures such as Proteus and Triton rather than knowing them only as mythological names, relics of a creed outworn. But in the late 1790s Wordsworth treats the spirit of place as a vital part of his childhood. In the earliest version of *The Prelude*, written in the fall and winter of 1798–99, he remembers feeling that "a huge cliff, / As if with voluntary power instinct" deliberately stalked him one night as he rowed across a moonlit lake in a shepherd's boat taken without permission (Two-Part *Prelude* 1.108–15). Guarding boats is not the usual duty of a genius loci, but Wordsworth is not mining classical tradition here. Instead, plunging into the well of his own memories, he calls to mind first his sense of guilt—the "troubled pleasure" of unauthorized borrowing—and then what he saw as he steadily rowed the boat away from the shore. Facing the stern, dipping his oars "in cadence" while steadily guiding himself by watching the top of a ridge near the shore, he suddenly notices a cliff that *seems* to rise up from behind the ridge—"till then / The bound of the horizon"—and then, "with measured motion, like a living thing" stride after him (1.88, 99–114). By describing precisely what he saw and did as well as what he felt, he shows how he himself made the cliff appear to rise "with measured motion" by steadily rowing away from the shore and thus changing the angle of his vision so that he gradually saw more of the cliff. But the frightened boy does not know his own powers, does not realize that the cliff is animated by his own "enlarged and numerous senses"—what Wordsworth will later call his imagination. As a result, he turns with "trembling hands" back to the shore, and for days afterward struggles mentally "with a dim and undetermined sense / Of unknown modes of being" (1.120–22). Only in retrospect—in the lines of his poem—does he construe this experience as evidence that by a combination of physical exertion and imaginative projection he has roused the spirit of the place to admonish him.

I stress Wordsworth's fascination with the spirit of place because I believe it holds the key to the concept of hospitality that informs the "Rime." Consider again the genesis of Coleridge's poem. About the time Wordsworth wrote of the cliff as if it were "a living thing," the home of an admonitory spirit, he urged Coleridge to write a poem about the "tutelary Spirits" of the South Pole, and specifically about a man who rouses them to vengeance by killing a bird of the region and thus, as Coleridge himself said, breaking "the laws of hospitality." Can such laws apply to an uninhabited region, where—as David Simpson observes—"the Mariner is spared the ethical challenge of encounter with other human societies" (Simpson 156)? Yes—but only if we recognize that for Coleridge and Wordsworth alike the genius or spirit of a place is its *host*. To seize anything from the place or to attack any living thing within it violates hospitality and thereby provokes a retaliation that typically takes the form of pursuit. In the 1817 edition of the "Rime" the storm blast of part 1 becomes a winged pursuer: "He struck with his o'ertaking wings, / And chased us south along" (ll. 43–44).[17] The personified storm prefigures both the visible bird who benignly follows the sailors and, once the bird is shot, its invisible avenger. Just as Wordsworth's boyhood self is stalked by the rising cliff and then, after he steals a bird from another's trap, by "low breathings" (1799 *Prelude* 1.43–47), Coleridge's mariner is relentlessly pursued by the Polar Spirit.

In Wordsworth's poetry the invisible host of a place sometimes finds more subtle ways of revealing its presence and power. In "Nutting," written soon after Coleridge first composed the "Rime," Wordsworth remembers a boyhood day on which, having set off in quest of hazelnuts, he comes upon a "virgin" grove of hazel trees ("Nutting" ll. 16–21, *PW* 2:211–12).[18] After eyeing "the banquet" (25) laid out by an unseen host, indolently playing with the flowers, resting his cheek on a mossy stone, and relishing the murmur of a stream, the boy suddenly drags both branch and bough to the ground; as a result, "the shady nook / Of hazels, and the green and mossy bower, / Deformed and sullied, patiently gave up / Their quiet being" (45–48). What startles him in retrospect is the power of this passivity, the pain that is quietly inflicted on him by a mutilated host. Unless he "now confound[s his] present feelings with the past," he says, the sight of the ruined bower sank his exultation:

> Ere from the mutilated bower I turned
> Exulting, rich beyond the wealth of kings,
> I felt a sense of pain when I beheld
> The silent trees, and saw the intruding sky.
>
> (50–53)

Paradoxically, in the very act of violating the hospitality of the grove he discovers what he reveals in the end to Dorothy: that "there is a spirit in the woods" (54–56). Wordsworth's final affirmation, then, springs directly from the memory of the pain that opened his mind and heart to his invisible host.

Together with memories such as that of being stalked by a cliff, this episode gave him what must have felt like immediate access to powers that somehow remained alive within his consciousness. Empiricism could not validate them. As educated men conversant with modern science as well as literature, Wordsworth and Coleridge both knew that they could not demonstrate the existence of a spirit of place. But both also knew the poetic value of this idea, and when Coleridge turned Wordsworth's suggestions into the "Rime," he made the spirit of place a vital part of it. He also explained, years after writing the poem, just what he hoped to do with its supernatural elements. As we learn from the *Biographia Literaria*, he aimed "to transfer from our inward nature a human interest and a semblance of truth sufficient to procure for these shadows of imagination that willing suspension of disbelief for the moment, which constitutes poetic faith" (*BL* 2:6).

This richly complex sentence tells us how to read the poem. On the one hand, as McGann observes, Coleridge acknowledges that we presumably enlightened readers no longer believe in such things as demons and specter-barks, that we reject them as primitive superstitions. On the other hand, as McGann notes, "the 'true' reality of all external phenomena, whether 'real' or 'delusion,' is [for Coleridge] inward and subjective" (McGann 65). In other words, as Coleridge says just before the above passage, supernatural phenomena are "real . . . to every human being who, from whatever source of delusion, has at any time believed himself under supernatural agency" (*BL* 2.6). Accordingly, the stalking cliff made itself inexorably real to the imagination of Wordsworth's boyhood self and to the memory of the poet he became. For him as for Coleridge, the genius loci is no dead relic of classical tradition but a spirit of place—a host of place—that can be experienced now within the world of poetry. If we suspend our disbelief in supernatural phenomena, then, we gain "an imaginative construct which offers limitless opportunities for symbolic interpretation" (McGann 65).

As an imaginative construct, animism remained alive for Coleridge. Given the range of texts he deploys in the "Rime," from the writings of an eleventh-century Neoplatonist to the seventeenth-century diction of its glosses, McGann argues that Coleridge's poem bespeaks the continuity of a belief in animism that neither Christianity nor the Enlightenment could obliterate in the history of thought, let alone of literature. But supposing that the Polar Spirit retains at least its "power of signification" (McGann 59), what links it to the Christianity of the poem? The answer, I think, is that both are linked to hospitality.

In the first part of the poem, next to the stanza in which the mariner and his shipmates hail the albatross "as if it had been a Christian soul, / . . . in God's name" (64–65), Coleridge's glosser—that is, the fictive author of the glosses—writes that the bird was received "with great joy and hospitality." In other words, the mariner and his shipmates become hosts of the bird by feeding it. "It ate the food it ne'er had eat," and at "the mariner's hollo ͏ " it came "every day, for food or play" (67, 73–74).[19] But the bird is more than a guest. As the only living thing in a world of fog and ice inhabited by neither man nor beast, it comes to the mariners, circles them, witnesses their liberation from the grip of the ice, and follows them, thereby forging a bond of mutual trust and aid. In return for food and friendly greetings, it seems somehow responsible, if only as "a bird of good omen," for the splitting of the ice and the "good south wind" that springs up behind the ship to drive it north around the Horn.[20] But after nine days the mariner, who is now our narrator, suddenly shoots the bird with his "cross-bow" (81–82) and thus, in the words of the gloss, "inhospitably" kills it.

The motive for the killing has been variously explained. On a material level, William Empson suggests that the mariner probably shot the bird for food (Empson 300). On a demonological level, Raimonda Modiano argues that the mariner reincarnates Cain, subject of an aborted "poem" (in prose) that Coleridge wrote shortly before the "Rime."[21] Since the Cain and Abel of this poem are each favored by rival deities, Modiano contends that in the "Rime" evil actions may spring from the whims of supernatural agents acting through "human hosts" (Modiano 205). Like Cain and Abel, who are *each* persecuted by gods who disfavor them, the mariner is driven to act and then punished for doing so, "guilty and innocent, . . . sacrificer and sacrificed" (Modiano 206). On this reading, then, the mariner has no motive of his own.[22] As Wordsworth says in his note on the "Rime" in the second edition of *Lyrical Ballads*, the mariner "does not act, but is continually acted upon" (qtd. Coleridge, *CP* Notes 497).

But Modiano's reading ignores a major point: the genius or spirit who persecutes the mariner is not a personal god using anyone as its host but is itself the host or spirit of a place, a genius loci.[23] Only in this light can we understand why the mariner should be said to have killed the bird "inhospitably." But we also need the light shed by Coleridge's conception of the mariner as a version of the wandering Jew.[24] Barely suggested by the Gospel of John, where Christ seems to predict that the disciple who betrayed him will not die until the Second Coming (John 21:20–23), the legend of the wandering Jew dates from the early thirteenth century, when an Armenian archbishop who was visiting the monks of St. Albans Abbey in England reportedly answered a question about Joseph of Arimethea. At the time of the crucifixion, the archbishop said, Joseph was a thirty-year-old Jewish shoemaker named Cartaphilus who would not let Christ rest while carrying his cross. When Christ paused for a moment Cartaphilus struck him and told him to move faster. "Why dost Thou loiter?" he asked. Looking back at him sternly, Christ said, "I shall stand and rest, but thou shall go on till the last day." After the crucifixion Cartaphilus was baptized a Christian under the name of Joseph, led a virtuous life of frugality and Christian piety, and looked forward fearfully to the Second Coming of Christ, "lest at the last judgment he should find him in anger, whom, when on his way to death, he had provoked to just vengeance."[25]

Later versions of the legend modify it. In an anonymous ballad called "The Wandering Jew" (hereafter "WJ"), which Coleridge must have known from Thomas Percy's *Reliques of Ancient English Poetry* (1765), the jew will not let Christ sit down on what he considers *his* stone:

Being weary thus, [Christ] sought for rest,
 To ease his burthened soule,
Upon a stone, the which a wretch
 Did churlishly controule;
And sayde, Awaye, thou king of Jewes,
 Thou shalt not rest thee here;
Pass on; thy execution place
 Thou seest nowe drawest neare.

And thereupon he thrust him thence;
 At which our Saviour sayd,
I sure will rest, but thou shalt walke,
 And have no journey stayed.
 ("WJ," ll. 25–36)

The fate of the jew in this ballad prefigures the fate of the mariner. Like the jew, he is made to pay for one rash act with endless wandering. As the jew moves "From place to place, but cannot rest / For seeing countries new" ("WJ," ll. 67–68), the mariner "pass[es], like night, from land to land" (586). The mariner also resembles the wandering jew of other sources known to Coleridge. The "glittering eye" (13) with which he holds the wedding guest and the "agony" (583) that periodically forces him to tell his tale recall the hypnotic eye and agonized life of the wandering jew in Matthew Lewis's *The Monk* (1796), which Coleridge not only reviewed but drew upon for his portrayal of Cain.[26] Likewise, the mariner's detaining of the wedding guest recalls the wandering jew's disruption of a wedding celebration in Friedrich Schiller's *Der Geisterseher* (1787–89), the fragmentary romance from which Coleridge took the plot for his play *Osorio* (1797).[27] But Coleridge does not simply follow his precursors; he creates a new character who swerves from the legendary old one. Unlike the jew of the ballad, who drives the weary Christ away from the stone he "controule[s]," the mariner lets the wedding guest sit "on a stone" (17) while he tells his tale.

In thus alluding, albeit cryptically, to the legend of the wandering jew, this small but significant detail implicitly defines his sin as a crime against hospitality. Whether or not the "wretch" of the ballad drove Christ from his own door, he would not let him rest, and the stone that he "churlishly controule[s]" is at least a resting place, if not a front step.[28] In remaking the legend of the wandering jew, Coleridge redefines inhospitality in terms both Christian and pagan, theological and animistic. By killing the bird with his crossbow, the mariner symbolically reenacts the crucifixion, as the voice of one of the Polar Spirit's "fellow demons" later implies:

> By him who died on cross,
> With his cruel bow he laid full low
> The harmless Albatross.
>
> (399–401)[29]

The cruelty is twofold. Besides being crucified, so to speak, by means of a crossbow, the albatross is killed by a man who has lately been sharing his food with it, presumably sailors' hardtack or ship's biscuit, a singularly durable kind of bread. Hence the killing of the bird subtly evokes the betrayal of the host of the Last Supper even as it rouses to vengeance the host of the South Pole.[30]

The Polar Spirit's vengeance recalls what pagan gods and demons do to those who offend them, as I have noted. But Wordsworth's word for the spirit— or "spirits"—of the pole is "tutelary" rather than retaliatory. While the Polar Spirit kills all of the mariner's shipmates and subjects the mariner himself to a living death of loneliness, stagnation, and thirst, his ultimate aim—if we can judge it by the effects of what he does—is to guide the mariner back to the communion table of life, to reawaken the love of life that first led him and his mates to welcome and feed the bird. In turn, the mariner "teach[es]" his tale (590) to a wedding guest, yet another figure with biblical significance.

What should we make of this figure? On the one hand, the mariner's insistence on keeping a man from attending the wedding of his brother—he is "next of kin" (6) to the bridegroom—violates all the norms of hospitality.[31] On the other hand, it reminds us that not everyone invited to the wedding banquet in Christ's parable (Matt. 22:1–14) proves fit to attend it. When the king's first invitations are ignored or brutally declined (by those who kill his messengers), he tells his servants to invite anyone they can find on the roads. But when one of these last-minute guests arrives without wedding clothes and cannot explain his failure to wear them, the king has him bound hand and foot and thrown out into the darkness, "there to weep and grind his teeth."

Why is such a trivial offense so harshly punished? If Christ elsewhere says that messengers of the word such as John the Baptist do *not* wear fine clothing (Matt. 11:7–10), will the kingdom of heaven have a dress code? No, says Augustine, who shrewdly observes that if the wedding garment had been a material object, the servants would have noticed its absence before inviting the man who came without it. "The garment that was looked for," writes Augustine, "is in the heart, not on the body; for had it been put on externally, it could not have been concealed from the servants. Where that wedding garment must be put on, hear in the words, 'Let your priests be clothed with righteousness' [2 Chron. 6:41]" (Augustine, Sermon 40 #4). The wedding garment, he goes on to say, "is charity out of a pure heart" and "faith with love" (Sermon 40 #6).

"Extend your love then, and limit it not to your wives and children. Such love is found even in beasts and sparrows" (Sermon 40 #10).

Whether or not Coleridge knew Augustine's sermon on Christ's parable, he plainly reveals his understanding of it in "Dejection: An Ode," where he writes that

> we receive but what we give,
> And in our life alone does nature live:
> Ours is her wedding garment, ours her shroud!
>
> (47–49)

Coleridge transfers the wedding garment from the guest to the world, or from us to nature. But the presence or absence of this garment depends on how we see the world, just as the appearance of the water snakes in part 4 of the "Rime" depends on how the mariner sees them. Shrouded with his revulsion, they strike him as "slimy things" (238); clad in his admiration, in the "rich attire" of flashing colors that suddenly disarm his loathing, they turn into "happy living things" of indescribable beauty, and with the aid of his "kind saint" he unconsciously blesses them (278–87). Robert Penn Warren long ago noted that the mariner sees the beauty of the snakes by the light of the moon, which for Coleridge symbolizes the creative imagination.[32] But according to the gloss, the moon and the stars together fascinate the mariner because, unlike him, they are *traveling:* "In his loneliness and fixedness he yearneth towards the journeying Moon, and the stars that still sojourn, yet still move onward; and everywhere the blue sky belongs to them, and is their appointed rest, and their native country and their own natural homes, which they enter unannounced, as lords that are certainly expected and yet there is a silent joy at their arrival" (263–66 gloss).

In what is surely the most lyrical of his comments, the glosser speculates on the diurnal rhythms of movement and rest. As a "fixed" spectator, the mariner yearns for and perhaps envies the movement of the moon and the stars, which are here called both sojourners *and* travelers headed home to "their appointed rest" in "their native country" of blue sky. The language is at once figurative and baffling. But if we can suspend our disbelief in the notion that stars *move* from darkness into the blue sky that obscures them and thus—shall we say?—puts them to bed for *their* night, they become homecoming travelers welcomed with joy: the most honored of guests.[33] Thus they are doubly removed from the mariner. Though he will soon be liberated from his fixity and supernaturally transported back to his native land, he will never be welcomed to any home. Like the wandering jew and Wordsworth's Marmaduke, he is doomed to travel as long as he lives without sojourning, without appreciable rest.

Passing "like night, from land to land" (586), he finds no hosts, only listeners whom he compulsively holds whenever he feels compelled to retell or "teach" his tale. In so doing, what he teaches above all else is the price to be paid for breaking "the laws of hospitality" by violating the spirit of a place. This unstated lesson supersedes the overt one about the value of love for all living things ("both man and bird and beast," 613), for this overt lesson hardly explains why the mariner keeps his listener from proceeding to the wedding feast and joining the guests whose "loud uproar" (591) catches the ear of the mariner himself near the end of the poem. Instead of joining a wedding feast or urging his listener to do so, the mariner would far rather walk "to the kirk / With a goodly company" (603–4) and pray. His preference should not surprise us. Since he regained his ability to pray just as he blessed the snakes and freed his neck from the bird that had been hung around it, he identifies prayer with the consummate joy of release from the living death of stagnation. But no such joy irradiates the end of the poem. Neither he nor the wedding guest joins either celebration or congregation. As the mariner leaves, presumably for yet another land, the wedding guest "turn[s] from the bridegroom's door" as if he had been "stunned" (621–22).

The ending of the poem, therefore, hardly confirms its ostensible moral. While the mariner's final words equate prayer at its best with love for all living things and thus suggest a community of love, the vision of community disintegrates into the separate solitudes of the mariner and the wedding guest going their different ways alone. While the curse of the mariner's shipmates is said to be "finally expiated" (442 gloss) by his suffering at sea, the final dispersion of the mariner and his listener implies that the mariner's crime against hospitality can never be fully expiated, let alone dissolved in the social joy of a wedding, the traditional way of resolving the conflicts in literary narrative.[34] Even if the wedding guest now wears the Augustinian garment of charity after hearing the mariner's tale, he cannot join a communal celebration of love. Just as disturbingly, the mariner himself leaves without spending so much as a night in the home of his listener. Having broken the laws of hospitality, he can never be received as a guest.

In representing the relation between humankind and the spirit of place, Wordsworth and Coleridge reconstruct the meaning of hospitality in ways that take us back to the epics of Homer and Virgil. In modern and early modern literature, such as Shakespearean drama, hospitality generally requires a home or castle with a threshold dividing the outer world from the inner one; whether benign or treacherous, hospitality begins only when that threshold is crossed.

But even in the modern era Kant defines hospitality as a matter of borders rather than thresholds: when a stranger "arrives in the land of another," the law of universal hospitality gives him the right "not to be treated as an enemy" (*Perpetual Peace* 320). In turn, Kant's formulation looks backward, for it recalls what Virgil's Aeneas and his men assumed when they landed on the shores of Carthage: "hospitio . . . harenae" (1.540), the right to land on the beach without being harassed. In the *Aeneid*, as I have noted, this essentially political concept of hospitality coexists with a belief in the apolitical spirit of place, for the first thing Aeneas does when he lands with his men in Latium is to pray to the "genium loci" (7.136). He thus recalls the world of Homer, in which travelers pay a terrible price for offending the gods or spirits of particular places. Not only do the men of Odysseus forfeit their lives for slaughtering, on the island of Helios, cattle sacred to the god; to the end of his life Odysseus is made to pay for blinding Polyphemos, who, for all his brutality, was both the host of Odysseus on the island of the Cyclopes and the son of Poseidon, god of the sea. In cursing Odysseus, Polyphemos begs his father to ensure that even if Odysseus gets home at last, he returns as "a broken man—all shipmates lost" (9.533 / F 9.593)—like Coleridge's mariner. And again like the mariner, Odysseus is made to travel in order to teach. Even after reclaiming his wife, his palace, and his kingdom, he cannot expiate his crime against hospitality without making a final journey to plant an oar as a sign of Poseidon among "a race of people who know nothing of the sea."[35]

Besides reviving the genius loci, Wordsworth and Coleridge link it to domestic hospitality, to the host of an enclosed habitation with a threshold that can be crossed. In the eyes of Wordsworth, the Chartreuse is a site inherently sacred as well as monastically sanctified, consecrated as much by its Alpine loftiness as by the cross that marks it as a refuge for the traveler, "a sign / . . . / Of hospitality and peaceful rest." To Coleridge likewise, the cross subtly marks the intersection of habitational hospitality with the hospitality of place. The very first verb used of the albatross is *cross*. In a desolate world of cracking, howling, roaring ice, we are told, "At length did cross an Albatross" (63). By internally rhyming "cross" with an "Albatross" that is hailed "as if it were a Christian soul," this line anticipates a later stanza that externally rhymes "the harmless albatross" with "him who died on cross" (part 5), thereby associating the victim of the mariner's crossbow with Christ crucified. But besides this overdetermining cluster of Christological meanings, "cross" also signifies cross*ing*, which is what the bird first does: by flying behind or in front of the ship, it crosses the invisible boundary separating the immediate world of the ship, the sailors' nautical home, from all that surrounds it. (In part 4, when the moon is shining on the ship, what can be seen "within [its] shadow" [277] clearly looks different from what can be seen "beyond the shadow" [272]). In crossing the invisible threshold of the mariners' nautical home, the albatross becomes a guest whom they welcome and feed. But the crossing of the albatross also reminds us that the mariners themselves have long since crossed the invisible line of the equator, as we are told first by the Argument of the poem — "How a Ship having passed the Line was driven by storms to the cold Country towards the South Pole" — and then by the glosser of part 1: "The Mariner tells how the ship sailed southward with a good wind and fair weather, till he reached the line." While the moment of crossing is eclipsed by three deictic stanzas on the mariner as teller, the wedding guest as listener, and the sounds of the wedding, the poem sharply contrasts the brilliance of the equatorial sun shining straight down "over the mast at noon" (30) with the ferocity of the storm blast driving them "toward the south pole" (41–44 gloss). By the time the mariner kills the bird, the ship has already rounded Cape Horn, entered the Pacific Ocean, "and sail[ed] north-ward, even till it reaches the Line" (103–6 gloss).

In crossing that line, says the mariner, "we were the first that ever burst / Into that silent sea" (102–3): into the dead and deadening calm of the equatorial Pacific. Even after the mariner alone barely survives to be rescued by "the angelic troop," the glosser tells us that "the lonesome spirit from the south-pole carries on the ship as far as the line, in obedience to the angelic troop, but still requireth vengeance" (377–82 gloss) and again that "penance long and heavy for the ancient Mariner hath been accorded to the Polar Spirit, who returneth southward" (393–97 gloss). Broadly speaking, the line of an equator that crosses both the Atlantic and the Pacific oceans marks the threshold of the southern hemisphere, the realm of the Polar Spirit. By acting "in obedience to the angelic troop," the spirit demonstrates that the ancient mythology of the genius loci has been historically superseded by the doctrines of Christianity, but the Christian "penance" imposed on the mariner for killing the bird evokes the kind of vengeance that Poseidon took on Odysseus for blinding his host. Just as Polyphemos curses the ancient Greek voyager, each of the mariner's dying ship-mates curses him with his eye (another link to Homer's giant?), and even though this spell is "snapt" (442) when the shipmates are reanimated, he is made to wander endlessly and to suffer periodic bouts of burning agony that he can relieve only by telling his tale. To see how that tale suggests both the crossing of a threshold and the attack on a host is to see why Coleridge saw the mariner's deed as a crime committed "in contempt of the laws of hospitality." It is also to see what links this distinctively Coleridgean poem to what is distinc-tively Wordsworthian: the sanctity and vulnerability of the spirit of place.

6

ROUSSEAU TO STENDHAL:
THE EROTICIZED HOSTESS

So far in this book I have applied the term *seductive* to any hostess whose desire for a male guest prompts her to detain him or wish to do so. But in attaching the word to figures ranging from Circe to Hermione, from a heartless enchantress to a grossly mistreated wife, I have understated their diversity. Among the hostesses I have examined so far, the will to entrap a guest by means of seduction is seldom absolute and never irresistible for good. Once Odysseus has thwarted Circe's plan to turn him into a pig, her beauty keeps him dallying for a year. But she cannot hold him longer against his will, and though Calypso detains him for seven years, she cannot keep him longer than Zeus will allow. Nausicaa's desire for Odysseus is backed by all that her royal father can offer, but even then it is no match for his determination to get home.

In three other hostesses the will to entrap a guest is hardly more than an act of submission to divine power or the power of a host. Dido's passion for Aeneas is ignited by Juno, Venus, and Cupid, and she is powerless to detain him once Jupiter, via Mercury, tells him to leave; Lady Bertilak offers her "cors" to Gawain only because her husband has ordered her to test his virtue in this way; likewise, Hermione makes her would-be seductive, but actually decorous, overtures to Polixenes only because Leontes asks her to persuade him to stay.

Romantic literature further complicates the power struggle that seduction almost always initiates or entails. While Keats's Belle Dame seems to enact seduction in its most ruthless form (she is indeed *sans merci*), she is at first actively courted by her pale knight, and the other hostesses to be examined in this chapter are all vulnerable. Despite her powers of enchantment, even Keats's

Lamia cannot keep her guest and lover from exposing them both to the eyes of the public, and their life together is destroyed by just one pair of those eyes. Keats's Madeline fares much better, but she is dreaming of her lover at the very moment when he arrives, as an unexpected guest, to take her away. Coleridge's Christabel is praying for her lover when she too is surprised by an unexpected guest, but this one seems to offer a chilling combination of maternal love and demonic possession. Unlike Christabel, Byron's Haidée savors all the pleasure and power that a hostess can enjoy with a beloved guest, but her power and then her very life evaporate as soon as her absent father returns to take her guest away. Finally, Stendhal's Madame de Rênal scarcely knows how to manage Julien Sorel, a household servant of fiercely contested status whom she variously treats as her surrogate son and lover as well as her guest. Different as they are, all of these hostesses are eroticized, gripped by desires that make them vulnerable to guests whom they can never fully control.

COLERIDGE'S *CHRISTABEL*

In the opening lines of *Christabel*, a fragmentary Gothic ballad written at the end of the eighteenth century, a mysterious lady named Geraldine seeks the help of a baron's daughter named Christabel late one night at the very moment when—in the woods outside her father's castle—she is praying for "her own betrothed knight," an absent figure whom we never see but who has filled her dreams the night before.[1] Besides yearning for her lover, Christabel keenly feels the absence of her mother, who "died the hour I was born" (line 97), as she tells her unexpected guest.

As a young and motherless hostess, Christabel embodies some of the vulnerability to be found in two characters of French romantic literature. Though both are male rather than female, guests rather than hosts, and far more ambitious than she, they are also both, like her, young and motherless. One is the fictional Julien Sorel, whose employer, as noted above, becomes his surrogate mother as well as his hostess and mistress; the other is the real-life Jean-Jacques Rousseau, who at the age of fifteen found a surrogate "Mamma" in the twenty-eight-year-old divorcée Madame de Warens—a "charitable good Lady" newly converted to Catholicism—when he became her long-term guest in the Savoyard town of Annecy (Rousseau 40). In the *Confessions*, written in the late 1760s but published in 1781, Rousseau tells us that his actual mother died shortly after giving birth to him and thereby left him a legacy of guilt. "I cost my mother her life," he writes, "and my birth was the first of my misfortunes" (Rousseau 6). In Madame de Warens he found not only a surrogate mother but implicit absolution for the crime of matricide. "For me," he writes, "she was the most tender of mothers who never sought her own pleasure but always my good" (Rousseau 89). In the name of that good, more precisely "to rescue [him] from the perils of [his] youth," she took his virginity (Rousseau 162). But since she remained his surrogate mother as well as his hostess, he felt after sharing her bed "as if [he] had committed an act of incest" (Rousseau 165). He also knew she was sharing her bed at the time with another young man, and though he afterward enjoyed a few months of intense happiness alone with her, he was shattered when his place was eventually taken by a third young man.[2]

In approaching *Christabel* by way of the *Confessions* I do not mean to imply that Coleridge's poem owes anything to the influence of Rousseau's autobiography. Though Coleridge had read it or at the very least learned about it well before 1816, when his poem was published, *Christabel* sprang largely from the same source that engendered "The Rime of the Ancient Mariner": conversations about nature, imagination, and supernature that Coleridge held with Wordsworth in 1797 and 1798, when they were neighbors in the county of Somerset.[3] Having decided to collaborate on a volume of poems in "two sorts," and having agreed that Wordsworth would choose his subjects "from ordinary life," they also agreed that Coleridge would focus on "persons and characters supernatural, or at least romantic." But Coleridge sought to credibilize these "shadows of imagination" by dramatizing the reality of the human feelings they might provoke, "supposing them real" (*BL* 2:6).[4] In light of this aim, Rousseau's account of his sojourn with an actual hostess may shed some light on Christabel's relation to her Gothic guest.

First of all, since the mysterious Geraldine aims to take the place of Christabel's mother even while sharing her bed, and since Christabel herself becomes jealously fearful of Geraldine's power to attract her father, both stories of hospitality thrust a motherless young person into something like incest complicated by sexual rivalry. Second, to compare Coleridge's portrayal of Christabel's guest with Rousseau's account of his hostess is to see that the poet and the autobiographer each strive to parry categorical judgments of the lady in question. Describing a woman who draws a young man into a bed she has already been sharing with another, Rousseau foresees what the "already shocked" reader will think about her effect on her guest. The reader will judge, Rousseau writes, that "since she was possessed by another man, she was degrading herself in my eyes by sharing herself" and thus cooling his affection for her (Rousseau 164). But calling this judgment "wrong" (164), Rousseau explains her motives sympathetically. Similarly, Coleridge checks our impulse to classify Geraldine as evil even while giving her traits that signify it.

Categorically, Geraldine recalls Duessa, the duplicitous witch of Spenser's *Faerie Queene*. When Geraldine tells Christabel that she is a noblewoman abducted by five warriors who will soon return and that she now begs Christabel's pity on "a wretched maid" (77–101), she echoes what Duessa (calling herself Fidessa) tells the Red Cross Knight just after he kills the Saracen who has been traveling with her. Posing as the "sole daughter of an emperor" (1.2.22), Duessa claims that the Saracen abducted her and that his death now leaves her "miserable" and craving of pity (1.2.26). Later on, when this would-be "fair lady" (1.2.35) is stripped of her rich garments, she is revealed as "a loathly, wrinkled hag" of unspeakable filth (1.8.46).

The surpassingly beautiful Geraldine likewise reveals something unspeakable when she undresses before going to bed with Christabel:

> Behold! her bosom and half her side —
> A sight to dream of, not to tell!
>
> (246–47)

Yet this very passage helps to show why Geraldine cannot be classified as just another Duessa. While a manuscript version of the poem says that Geraldine's bosom and half her side "are lean and old and foul of hue" (*CP* 169n1), Coleridge withheld this line from all published versions of the poem because he did not wish to brand her as unambiguously evil. "Geraldine is *not* a Witch," he wrote, "in any proper sense of that word."[5]

So what is she? In one of the nine marginal notes he made in a presentation copy of the poem in 1824, Coleridge comes close to branding her. Explaining Christabel's silent revulsion at seeing her father embrace their guest on the morning after the two women have slept together, he writes, "Christabel then recollects the whole, and knows that it was not a Dream, but yet cannot disclose the fact, that the strange Lady is a supernatural Being with the stamp of the Evil Ones on her" (qtd. *CP* 174n2). Does this mean that Coleridge thinks Geraldine innately evil? Or merely that she bears the stigmata of evil beneath the veil of her beauty?[6] And if Geraldine is evil, does the poem tell the story of how Christabel defeats her? According to James Gillman, who housed Coleridge as his guest for the last eighteen years of the poet's life, the story of *Christabel*

> is partly founded on the notion that the virtuous of the world save the wicked. The pious and good Christabel suffers and prays for
>> 'The weal of her lover that is far away' [l. 32],
> exposed to various temptations in a foreign land, and she thus defeats the power of evil represented in the person of Geraldine. This is one main object of the tale. (Gillman 283)

But the poem itself hardly confirms this version of its plot. Whether Christabel prays for the physical or spiritual welfare of her lover, whether he withstands temptation or simply the risk of being killed, she is never shown defeating Geraldine.⁷ On the contrary, Geraldine's story of abduction—told on the morning after her night with Christabel—wins the heart of Christabel's father, Sir Leoline, who wants to keep her with them until Geraldine's father can be sent for to meet him and the lady midway between their respective homes. This move cripples Christabel's powers as a hostess. Convinced that she has sinned by sleeping with Geraldine (369), dreading the malicious look in her "shrunken serpentine eyes" (590), and spellbound to silence about their night together in bed, she can only implore her father to send their guest away (604–5).⁸ But in doing so she flouts the rules of hospitality and infuriates her father:

> His heart was cleft with pain and rage,
> His cheeks they quiver'd, his eyes were wild,
> Dishonour'd thus in his old age;
> Dishonour'd by his only child,
> And all his hospitality
> To th'insulted daughter of his friend
> By more than woman's jealousy,
> Brought thus to a disgraceful end.
>
> (628–35)

These lines are doubly ironic. After hospitably taking the apparently exhausted and endangered Geraldine into her very own bed, Christabel now seems bent on stifling her father's hospitality. But she fails. In the final lines of the narrative proper (before the brief, reflective conclusion to the second part) Sir Leoline repeats his command that Geraldine's father be sent for, turns his back on his daughter, and leads forth Geraldine. In spite of Christabel's entreaty, he brings his hospitality to what seems to him an honorable end. Knowing nothing of what has transpired in Christabel's bed, he can only find her perverse: so inhospitable that she would have the lady sent away at once, and so jealous—even incestuous—that she cannot bear even to see him take the lady back to her father. If, as Sir Leoline thinks, his embrace of a lady guest provokes his daughter's jealousy, he is himself the object of desire by two women competing for his favor, and the incestuous curve of Christabel's desire makes it, one is tempted to say, even more serpentine than Geraldine's.⁹

Serpent imagery permeates the poem in ways that further complicate the task of judging either of its women. While Christabel sleeps in the arms of Geraldine, Bard Bracy dreams, as he explains in the morning, that a dove whom

Sir Leoline calls Christabel is caught in the coils of "a bright green snake" (537). The iconographic message of the dream is obvious, but even though Geraldine bears the shrunken, malicious eyes of a serpent on the morning after her night with Christabel, we find conflicting signals elsewhere. Ironically enough, Sir Leoline salutes their guest as "Lord Roland's beauteous *dove*" (557, emphasis added), and when he takes her in his arms, it is Christabel who sounds like a snake, inhaling "with a hissing sound" (447) and repeating the hiss when Geraldine looks askance at her (575–79). The hissing in turn suggests that Geraldine has come to possess and corrupt her. "The maid, devoid of guile and sin," says the narrator,

> I know not how, in fearful wise
> So deeply had she drunken in
> That look, those shrunken serpent eyes,
> That all her features were resign'd
> To this sole image in her mind
> And passively did imitate
> That look of dull and treacherous hate.
>
> (587–94)

This passage represents Christabel as the passive, helpless victim of Geraldine's manipulation. But if she is utterly passive, can she be good? Can she "save the wicked" or defeat evil, as Gillman suggests, merely by suffering? Or can she thus atone "for the wrongs committed by her absent lover," as Humphry House claims (House 129)? Coleridge himself allegedly said as much. In 1870, long after his death, his son Derwent reported what the poet had meant to do with his unfinished poem. According to Derwent, the sufferings of Christabel were to have been represented as vicarious, endured for "her lover far away" (qtd. House 127). Yet William Ulmer notes that while he was writing *Christabel*, Coleridge dismissed in his own words the doctrine of the atone- ment, the notion that Christ's suffering "should prove an adequate Satisfaction for the Sins of the whole World" (Coleridge, *L* 1795 205). "As a Unitarian," Ulmer writes, "Coleridge believed in a human, exemplary Jesus whose Crucifixion and consequent Resurrection . . . pointed the way that others must take on their own" (Ulmer 402). Since Coleridge also declared that we develop virtue "by Experience alone" (*L* 1795 108), Ulmer plausibly infers that "Christabel's sufferings become morally purposive only insofar as they contribute crucially to her own progress to virtue" (Ulmer 404).[10]

What then does Christabel's response to Geraldine tell us about her moral progress? The passage just quoted offers a small clue. Before passively imitating

Geraldine's malevolent look, Christabel actively—and "deeply"—drinks it in. She thus seems more than ready to consume the influence of Geraldine after actively taking her into her father's castle and lifting the "weary weight" of her guest over the threshold of its gate (126–27). Does Christabel thereby hoist the uncanny weight of her own unconscious?[11] Karen Swann puts the question another way: "Who is Geraldine, and where does she come from? Possibly, from Christabel" (Swann 155). Consider where and when Geraldine first appears. As Christabel prays in the middle of the night beneath a huge oak tree in the forest near her father's castle, Geraldine leaps up from the other side. Her story of how she got there is hardly plausible. If she was abducted by five warriors, as she claims, why did they leave her all alone without any restraints beneath a tree—let alone the tree that becomes Christabel's prie-dieu? If a nightlong ride with the warriors left her so exhausted as to be "scarce alive" (93), how does she manage to keep up with Christabel's "hurrying steps" (109) as they go to the castle? Given the implausibility of Geraldine's story, we might well take the hint proffered by Swann. When Geraldine appears, Christabel is praying for her lover in the middle of the night because she dreamed about him on the previous night, and her dreams, we are told, "made her moan and leap, / As on her bed she lay in sleep" (CP 29–30).

Though the moaning and leaping could well express her fear of what might happen to her lover, any woman dreaming of her lover while lying in bed must be equally susceptible to desire.[12] In *The Eve of St. Agnes*, written three years after *Christabel* was published, Keats explicitly links prayer, dreams, and desire in a ritual wherein "young virgins might have visions of delight / And soft adorings from their loves receive" if they go to bed without supper, lie "supine," and "require / Of heaven with upward eyes for all that they desire" (ll. 47–54). Christabel's wishes are not nearly so open, and unlike Keats's heroine, whose erotic dreams are consummated by her lover (an unexpected guest in her bedroom), Christabel never sees the man she prays for. But under the circumstances, she can no more keep suppressed desires from leaping up inside her than Saint Theresa could insulate her spiritual ecstasies from sensual arousal— as Coleridge himself pointedly observed.[13] Leaping up in the middle of Christabel's prayers, Geraldine embodies instincts that Christabel cannot openly acknowledge even to herself. As Ulmer observes, Geraldine "moves through the poem virtually as an allegorical figure of sexual desire" (Ulmer 387).

Does this itself make her evil? If Christabel must advance to womanhood, might not Geraldine signify the liberation of her sexual energies, as some critics have argued? Might not Christabel's reception of this unexpected guest imply her acceptance of womanhood? The problem with this line of argument is that not even Geraldine herself claims to be unequivocally good. On the contrary, she speaks of her own disfigured bosom as a moral stigma that Christabel will come to know through nightlong contact with "this mark of my shame, this seal of my sorrow" (258). In acknowledging her moral disfigurement, Geraldine shows that she is "divided within," as Ulmer says, a compound of "predominant evil qualified by residual good" (Ulmer 388). But in the very act of baring the mark of her shame Geraldine tells Christabel that its touch will silence her, that she will be compelled to suppress in the morning what she has learned about Geraldine's corruption at night. She will be allowed to say only that she has charitably received Geraldine as her guest. "For this is alone in / Thy power to declare," says Geraldine:

> That in the dim forest
> Thou heard'st a low moaning,
> And found'st a bright lady, surpassingly fair:
> And didst bring her home with thee in love and charity,
> To shield her and shelter her from the damp air.
>
> (261–66)

Nowhere else is Geraldine more duplicitous. Taking Christabel in her arms, she resolves to spend the night infecting her. But infecting her means silencing her about the infection, letting her speak only of hospitality in the traditional sense of Christian (Christ-able) charity. Thus the would-be agent of sexual liberation becomes the instrument of a suppression far more painful and insidious than anything Christabel has experienced so far.

Superficially, the evil Christabel is made to suppress is the ugly sight of Geraldine's bosom, the disfiguring "mark" made visible when she undresses for bed. But to find the moral evil signified by this physical sign, we must probe the triangle of links between Christabel, her guest, and her dead mother. On the one hand, as Geraldine herself perceives, Christabel's mother has become her "guardian spirit" (206) and is now a source of renewal for her guest. When Geraldine sinks to the floor of Christabel's bedroom, Christabel revives her with a drink of wildflower wine made by her mother, and Geraldine stands up to assure her hostess that she, Christabel, is beloved by "all . . . who live in the upper sky" (221). On the other hand, Geraldine usurps the place of Christabel's mother. Right after asking Christabel if her mother will pity this "maiden most forlorn," learning that she died in the hour of Christabel's birth, and seconding Christabel's wish that she could be with them now, Geraldine "with alter'd voice" takes command of Christabel by banishing a spirit whom only Geraldine can see: "Off, wandering mother! Peak and pine! / I have power to bid thee flee" (199–200). The sudden eruption of arrogance from a woman still down on the floor — she has not yet finished the wine — suggests nothing so much as the altered voice of demonic possession: a voice like that of Milton's Satan, who vehemently defies the power of God even while prostrate and chained to a burning lake in the first book of *Paradise Lost*. But if Geraldine's "residual good" is here choked by demonic possession, she nonetheless mingles good and evil with what can only be called diabolical subtlety. Right after assuring Christabel, in what sounds like her good voice, that Christabel is beloved by the heavenly spirits, Geraldine says of them,

> for their sake
> And for the good which me befel,
> Even I in my degree will try,
> Fair maiden, to requite you well.
> But now unrobe yourself; for I
> Must pray, ere yet in bed I lie.
> (223–28)[14]

Ostensibly the good Geraldine promises to reciprocate Christabel's hospitality and demonstrate her own piety with a bedtime prayer. But "requite" can mean retaliate as well as reward, and in telling Christabel to disrobe she is telling her to expose her body to the spellbinding touch of Geraldine's tainted flesh. When Geraldine takes Christabel in her arms and presses her to her bosom like "a mother with her child" (289), she reminds us that Christabel's mother did not live to embrace her infant daughter. At the same time, by treating Christabel as an infant Geraldine threatens to forestall a sexual maturation already retarded by Sir Leoline, who still sees her as a child "so fair, so innocent, so mild" (612). But unlike the wildflower wine of Christabel's mother, which rejuvenates Geraldine, Geraldine's bosom infects Christabel with a corrosive compound of guilt and fear. It not only reminds her of the maternal breast that Geraldine's cannot supplant and of her own responsibility for her mother's death; as the point of contact between two grownup naked bodies, it also prefigures the sexual experience of marriage, which Christabel may well dread.[15] Now sex confronts Christabel on every side. While she has undoubtedly tried to atone for the death of her mother by serving the emotional needs of a father who never remarried (Ulmer 389), she cannot fully replace her mother without entering her father's bed. Like Hamlet's hatred of Claudius, whose usurping marriage to his mother makes him visualize their coupling "in the rank sweat of an enseamed bed, / Stewed in corruption" (3.4.93–94), Christabel's resentment of Geraldine for embracing her father comes all too close to Oedipal—or, more precisely, Elektral—jealousy. In the eyes of Sir Leoline, Christabel's sin against hospitality springs from something "more than woman's jealousy"; it comes from a possessiveness both incestuous and irrational. Unable to wait for Bard Bracy to notify Geraldine's father, or to see her own father escort their guest back to a meeting point, Christabel begs him to send her away at once.

Thus our reluctant hostess is both eroticized and repressed. The whole poem, it has been argued, reflects a concept of original sin that rejects the notion of inherited guilt but nonetheless admits the depravity of the human will. Though Coleridge did not think humankind responsible for Adam's sin, he did believe, at the time he wrote *Christabel*, that from birth "our organization is depraved, & our volitions imperfect; and we sometimes see the good without *wishing* to attain it, and oftener *wish* it without the energy that wills & performs."[16] For this reason, innocence does not make Christabel good any more than experience makes Geraldine evil. Christabel must prove her goodness through suffering and moral growth. But she fails to grow because she cannot make room for a guest who threatens to undo the family structure she has built around her absent mother. Since she evidently thinks herself and her father equally responsible for her mother's death (he by impregnating her, she by being born), she has constructed a family founded on the absence of sex, with a father who has never remarried and a daughter whose lover is absent. By taking a sexually experienced woman into her bed, Christabel allows Geraldine to rouse desires that she has long suppressed but that she must acknowledge and organize if she is to become a woman. In jealously resenting Geraldine's power to attract her father and in contesting his hospitality by vainly demanding that she be sent away, Christabel reveals that she lacks the energy and will to realize her wishes, to move beyond repressed desire for her father into open desire for her lover. The result is a paralysis of will that literally ends her story. She has no way to grow and therefore nowhere to go.

KEATS: *THE EVE OF ST. AGNES*, "LA BELLE DAME," *LAMIA*

In one respect the heroine of *The Eve of St. Agnes* recalls Christabel. Coleridge's heroine prays for her faraway lover one night after dreaming about him in bed the night before; Madeline deliberately undertakes a pseudoreligious ritual one evening so that her lover may adore her, in her dreams, while she sleeps. But Madeline's admirer proves much more than a dreamy phantom. Unlike Christabel's far-off fiancé, Porphyro lives nearby, and while her parents entertain "a thousand guests" at a lavish party rocked by "silver, snarling trumpets" (31–33), he comes to her house in secret as an uninvited guest. Detested for his lineage by every "blood-thirsty" man in the house (99), he braves the threat of death to catch one sight of Madeline: to "gaze and worship all unseen" (80) on the very evening when, by convenient coincidence, she has been fasting and praying for "visions" (47) of him.[17] With the help of an old servant named Angela, who hopes that "good angels" will protect Madeline (125, 142), he hides in her bedroom closet just before she reaches it so that he may "see her beauty unespied / And win perhaps that night a peerless bride" (166–67). Angela also helps this uninvited visitor to play the host in his enemies' house. After she stores in the closet "all cates and dainties" for a private feast (173), he sets a table of sumptuous delicacies beside Madeline's bed before gently awakening her with music far tenderer than the bray and boom of clarion and kettledrum at the party. Playing on her own lute an old Provençal ditty called "La belle dame sans mercy," he rouses her to a "soft moan" (294) and then a plangent appeal ("Give me that voice again, my Porphyro," 312) that lead him in turn to enter her dream ("Into her dream he melted," 320), her body, or both.[18] In any case, he takes her off with him. Undetected by the "bloated wassailers" (346), leaving "the Baron. . . . / And all his warrior-guests" to "be-nightmar'd" by witches and demons (372–74), the lovers fly away into the storm and "o'er the southern moors" to Porphyro's home (351).

Written in the early winter of 1819, soon after Keats had reached an "understanding" with Fanny Brawne on Christmas of 1818, *The Eve of St. Agnes* retells the story of *Romeo and Juliet* with a happy ending. Though Madeline is said to have been "hoodwink'd" by superstition when she undertakes her ritual (70), and though she herself claims to have been "deceived" by Porphyro (332) after he awakens her, she nonetheless ends up leaving home with the man she loves. From the perspective of the raucous revellers, Porphyro doubly betrays the baron's hospitality, first by coming uninvited to his house and then by abducting his daughter. But since the poem makes us care only for the lovers, we readily forgive them. We may even read the poem as a wish-fulfilling answer to *Christabel*, which could have furnished Keats with some of its medieval details (Allott 451). Like Christabel, Madeline is a baron's daughter who dreams of her lover and who is joined in bed by an unexpected guest. But unlike Christabel's guest, who leaves her feeling violated, stifled, jealous, and paralyzed by contradictory urges, Madeline's guest gratifies her desires by waking her and taking her away.

Two months after writing *The Eve of St. Agnes*, Keats used the title of the "ancient ditty" that Porphyro sings to Madeline as the title of a love poem ending in desolation. If we wonder how such a poem could be linked to the title of a song that helps to join the lovers of the *Eve*, we should remember the story told by the impassioned singer of Coleridge's "Love," a poem Keats could have read in *Sybilline Leaves* (1817). In "Love," the impassioned singer wins Genevieve as his bride by rousing her pity with the song of a knight driven fatally mad by the scorn of the woman he loves. In Alain Chartier's medieval poem *La Belle Dame Sans Merci* (1424), a lover who fails to melt the marble heart of his beloved after lengthily pleading with her ends up tearing his hair in anguish and then dying.[19] In the *Eve*, we learn nothing about Porphyro's ditty beyond its title, and under the circumstances he could not have sung more than a highly condensed version of Chartier's poem. But like the singer of "Love," Porphyro uses a song about a scorned lover to melt the heart of his lady and thus "win . . . a peerless bride."

The story told in Keats's short ballad "La Belle Dame Sans Merci" is almost entirely new but preserves a crucial feature of Chartier's tale: the lover's anguish at the end.[20] Written on April 21, 1819, and slightly revised for publication in Leigh Hunt's *Indicator* for May 1820, the ballad begins with three stanzas addressed to the "wretched wight" whose woebegone pallor and solitude in a place of wintry desolation prompt the question, "What can ail thee [?]"[21] In response, the wight tells a story of seductive hospitality. But rather than being just victimized by a woman's wiles, he recklessly courts her. Meeting a beautiful, long-haired, wild-eyed, light-footed lady in a meadow, he sets her on his steed, spends the day gazing obsessively at her while she sings "a fairy's song," and adorns her with flowers. Only when they make love does she actively enchant him. She looks at him, sweetly moans, finds him exotic foods, and tells him "in language strange" that she loves him "true" (27–28). Like an apostle suddenly blessed with the gift of tongues, the enchanted wight instantly grasps the meaning of her strange words and just as quickly succumbs to her. While it is he who initiates their affair by setting her on his steed, it is she who *takes* him "to her elfin grot" as her guest (29). Yet he remains her accomplice, not just her dupe, as Keats's revision of lines 31–33 makes plain. In the original version (written on April 21, 1819) the knight says that after he shut "her wild wild eyes / With kisses four," she "lullèd" him to sleep (31–33). In the revised version (published 1820) he says that he shut "her wild sad eyes— / So kiss'd to sleep. / And there we slumbered on the moss" (31–33).

The revision not only makes the "sad"-eyed lady more sympathetic but also acquits her of narcotizing the man. As Jerome McGann notes, they fall asleep together, which delimits her sway ("Keats," 442). Only when he dreams does the speaker see how he has been caught:

> I saw pale kings, and princes too,
>   Pale warriors, death-pale were they all;

> Who cry'd—"La belle Dame sans mercy
>   Hath thee in thrall!"
>
> I saw their starv'd lips in the gloom
>   With horrid warning gaped wide
> And I awoke, and found me here
>   On the cold hill side.
>   (revised version 37–44)

Here Keats reshapes the relation between dreaming and waking that he had forged in *The Eve of St. Agnes*. In that poem Madeline's dream-vision of Porphyro transcends the real man, who disappoints her at first when she awakens to see him:

> Her eyes were open, but she still beheld,
> Now wide awake, the vision of her sleep:
> There was a painful change, that nigh expelled
> The blisses of her dream so pure and deep.
>   (298–301)

Compared to the man of her dream, Porphyro himself is "pallid, chill, and drear" (311), like the wretched wight on the cold hillside. When the voice of Madeline fires him so ethereally that he *melts* into her dream, he seems to erase the line between flesh and erotic phantasm. But when he afterward tells her that what they have just done was "no dream," she is far less dismayed by the shock of being awakened than by the threat of being abandoned:

> "No dream, alas! alas! and woe is mine!
> Porphyro will leave me here to fade and pine.—
> Cruel! what traitor could thee hither bring?
> I curse not, for my heart is lost in thine,
> Though thou forsakest a deceived thing;—
> A dove forlorn and lost with sick unpruned wing."
>   (328–33)

Realistically, Madeline knows she has been deceived, or self-deceived: that she has let a real man into her bed as if he were a dream or part of one. But what matters more than any dream now is his living company. Without it she would be forsaken and forlorn, like (once again) the hapless wight or Virgil's Dido. With it she awakens, literally and figuratively, into conjugal bliss. In words that echo the Song of Songs, Porphyro tells her, "Awake! arise! my love, and fearless be, / For o'er the southern moors I have a home for thee" (350–51).

Dreaming and waking work altogether differently in "La Belle Dame." While Madeline's dream seems at first to transcend reality, to surpass anything Porphyro can offer her awakened self, nothing can match, let alone surpass, what the Belle Dame offers the man *before* he falls asleep and dreams a nightmare that prefigures his rude awakening. The death-pale kings, princes, and warriors of the dream—all the powerful men unmanned by enchantresses ranging from Homer's Circe to Spenser's Duessa—foretell his wakening "alone and palely loitering" on a cold and barren hillside. While Madeline trades a dream of love for the blissful reality of conjugal possession, the wretched wight trades a nightmare of entrapment for the painful reality of desolation.

In its subtle blending of hospitality, dreaming, seduction, and treachery, "La Belle Dame" anticipates a poem that much more fully explores the relation between a young man and an enchanting hostess. Set in the ancient Greek city of Corinth, written in the summer of 1819 (the last great summer of Keats's poetic life), and published in July 1820, *Lamia* tells how its eponymous heroine lures a handsome young man to her secret dwelling and also shows how an uninvited guest brings disaster to their wedding feast.

In the original version of the story, *lamia* is a generic term denoting a serpentine vampire who takes delight in fattening up and feeding "upon young and beautiful bodies, because their blood is pure and strong." When a philosopher named Apollonius learns that one of his pupils plans to marry an apparently rich and beautiful woman, he boldly intervenes. Warning the young man that he is "cherishing a serpent," he joins the guests at a wedding feast furnished by the bride, denounces its rich food and furnishings as mere phantasms (which they prove to be by vanishing), compels the bride to admit she is a vampire, or "lamia," and thereby "save[s]" his pupil (Philostratus, *Life of Apollonius* 4.25).[22] In Keats's poem Apollonius likewise attacks the bridal hostess of the wedding feast, but besides showing how the philosopher's medicine kills the pupil it is meant to save, Keats transforms her so radically that we cannot tell for certain just who or what she is.

She embodies antitheses. Rather than masquerading as a woman to hide an essentially serpentine nature, she first appears in a serpent form that may have been merely inflicted on a creature essentially human and female. "I was a woman," she tells the god Hermes; "let me have once more / A woman's shape, and charming as before" (1.117–18).[23] But can we trust a serpentine figure to tell the truth about what she once was? Or is she actually a serpent asking to be disguised as a woman? We have no way of knowing for certain. Nor can we reliably judge her temperament. Though she is called at one point "cruel" because she knows how to tantalize men (1.190), she sounds altogether pitiable—"Ah!

miserable me!" (1.41)—when she first begs Hermes to make her a woman "once more" so that she might catch the eye as well as the ear of Lycius, whom she ardently desires. (His very name—pronounced "*lish*ous"—sounds like "delicious," subtly evoking the man-consuming hostess of Philostratus's tale.) Yet Lamia is no mere beggar. She knows how to bargain with Hermes, who has been smitten by a nymph that Lamia has made invisible so as to protect her from sexual predators. In exchange for Hermes' services, Lamia offers to let him see the nymph, trading the nymph's privacy for her own advantage. But since the "fearful sobs" (1.138) of this suddenly exposed creature soon give way to blooming acquiescence at the touch of Hermes' hand, and since the nymph flies off with him into what promises to be a life of dreamy bliss, Lamia seems not so much exploitative as artful, skilled in the art of gratifying desire: Hermes', her own, and perhaps even the nymph's.

Besides getting just what she wants by giving Hermes just what he wants, she demonstrates her power in nothing so much as in her all-consuming hospitality, her power to make Lycius what Odysseus was for Calypso: some indeterminate blend of guest, lover, and (at first) unwitting prisoner. Consider how she demolishes the possibility of his becoming her host. Once she captures him, once she sees, after catching his eye for the first time, that he adores her, she spurns any hospitality he might offer her. Unlike Ovid's Jove and Mercury (the Roman Hermes), who eat and drink happily in the humble cottage of Baucis and Philemon, or Milton's angel Raphael, who contentedly dines with Adam and Eve, Lamia insists that nothing in Lycius's world, not even its air, could suit a "finer spirit" such as hers (1.280). But she is merely testing her power. As soon as he turns pale and sick with pain at the prospect of losing her, she kisses him, renews "the life she had so tangled in her mesh" (1.295), and then leads him through the streets of Corinth to her own house. "Blinded" by her beauty (1.347), he also blinds himself to the "quick eyes" (1.374) of his teacher Apollonius, whom they pass en route to her house, so that instead of being either invisible or hidden, like the nymph, Lycius is both unseeing and visible, hence doubly vulnerable. Lamia's hospitality thus becomes absolutely exclusive. Ensconced within "a place unknown" to anyone but herself and Lycius and a few Persian mutes (1.388–90) and cocooned in a "purple-lined palace of sweet sin" (2.31), she and he are "shut from the busy world, of more incredulous" (1.396).

But not sealed from it. Since Lamia's palace is not soundproof, she cannot fully imprison her guest. Though nobody else can see or hear them, *they* can hear the world beyond their walls, and the sound of trumpets from that world catches Lycius's ear. In *The Eve of St. Agnes* Porphyro mutes the snarling trumpets of the raucous party by filling the intimate space of Madeline's bedroom with the tender vibrations of her own lute accompanied by his song. By contrast, "a thrill / Of trumpets" reminds Lycius of the "noisy world" he has forsaken (2.27–28, 33), and he wants it back. When Lamia mourns that he has emotionally "deserted" her, that like a banished guest she herself must "go / From [his] breast houseless" (2.44–45), he assures her he is even now striving "to entangle, trammel up and snare" her soul in his (2.52–53). But in spite of this desire, he insists on making his "prize" possession public (2.57), showing her off to friends and foes alike, rousing the "hoarse alarm" (2.61) of their shouts as her bridal car wheels through the streets of Corinth.

Lamia's dismay at this prospect goads him into something so far seen only in her: cruelty. As she tearfully begs him to change his mind, he sadistically takes "delight / Luxurious in her sorrows" (2.73–74) and compels her—masochistically loving his "tyranny" (2.81)—to do what he wants. With one crucial exception that I shall consider in a moment, she even gives him full charge of the guest list for the wedding feast.

Thus initiated, the wedding feast held in Lamia's palace differs sharply from the wedding feast of Coleridge's "Rime," which represents a "natural," waking alternative to the mariner's nightmarish encounter with a whole cast of super-natural creatures. Lamia's wedding feast is a production wrought by magic. Dreading the guests "who will come to spoil her solitude" (2.145), she aims only to "dress / [Her] misery in fit magnificence" (2.116). "Subtle servitors" flitting about on wings create a "haunting music" that somehow supports the "faery-roof" of the "glowing banquet room" (2.121–23), and under a canopy woven from the branches of an artificial glade, twelve round tables are each adorned with the statue of a god, encircled by silk couches, lit by a stream of lamps, set with cornucopias of food and wine in golden vessels, and perfumed by fifty censers whose wreaths of smoke are "mimicked" (2.180) by mirrored walls. All of this opulence amazes the guests because they have no idea where it comes from or how it could suddenly appear on a street they had long known well. The wedding feast of this poem is not a natural occasion but a supernatural feat.

Since Lamia shapes the whole celebration to "dress" her misery, it also serves as a stupendous disguise, a way of shielding her privacy when the "herd" of Lycius's kin (2.150) invades her house. As Paul Endo says, "She minimizes the risk of exposure by orchestrating her appearance," dazzling her guests with the richness of her furnishings and dulling their senses with 'merry wine'" (2.205–11, Endo 119). But just as Lamia cannot keep Lycius from the madness of showing "to common eyes these secret bowers" (2.149), she cannot control his guest list, and neither of them can bar an uninvited guest who soberly surveys

the feast "with eye severe" (2.157). Unlike the other guests, who surrender themselves to the world created by Lamia, Apollonius comes to conquer it by seeing
through it. As he tells himself with a chuckle, "'Twas just as he foresaw" (2.162).

In fixing his eyes on Lamia herself, Apollonius stares down a figure who has
up to now maintained her power by seeing more than others do and by manip-
ulating what they see. Catching the ear of Hermes at the beginning of the
poem, Lamia tells him that in a dream of the previous night she "saw" him
sitting sadly on an Olympian throne and then flying to Crete in quest of a
nymph that Lamia alone can make visible to him by breathing "upon his eyes"
(1.124). When Hermes in turn gives her the power to assume or—as she says—
reclaim the woman's shape she once had (her core identity remains inscrutable), all her serpentine features vanish, and she becomes "a full-born beauty
new and exquisite" (1.172), ready to catch the eye of Lycius. Gifted with a "scien-
tial brain" (1.191) that rivals that of Apollonius, capable of disentangling "bliss
from its neighbor pain" (1.192), she knows exactly how to present herself to a
young man whom she first saw by means of a dream when he was racing a
chariot in Corinth. Lest he think her a goddess endowed with supernatural
powers of vision, she tells him—after they meet—that he first captured her
heart while lounging outside the temple of Venus in Corinth, where she saw
him leaning against a column on the eve of the feast of Adonis: an irresistibly
erotic place and time. Though she coyly wonders "how his eyes could miss / Her
face so long in Corinth" (1.310–11), she specializes in seeing without being seen
and lives in "a place unknown" (1.388)—a house that cannot be found by
anyone but herself and her mutes. By contrast, Lycius is "blinded" to the wiles
of a would-be "real woman" who has not only managed to spy on him all the
way from Crete to Corinth but who also, "by a spell" (1.345), makes three
leagues shrink "to a few paces" (1.346) when she takes him from the hills near
Cenchreas (the port of Corinth) to her house in the city.

As the two pass Apollonius, the all-seeing Lamia perceives that Lycius blinds
himself from the "quick eyes" (1.374) of the sage, a man whose features she does
not recognize and whose penetrating gaze she fears. Here is the first challenge
to her powers of seeing and knowing, for she knows that she has *been seen* and
possibly found out by a man she does not know. The second challenge comes
when Lycius's attention is caught by the sounds of the outside world. "Ever
watchful" and "penetrant" (2.34), Lamia infers that Lycius has mentally deserted
her, that he no longer controls his every thought and impulse. By way of
answer, he gazes into her eyes, "where he [is] mirrored small in paradise" (2.47):
where, in other words, he can narcissistically see his face reflected in each of
her pupils. Yet even while implicitly saying that he has eyes only for her and

explicitly claiming that he yearns to possess her more deeply, Lycius insists that they hold a wedding feast, that they open their hidden house to guests, that they make themselves visible to a whole crowd of people Lamia does not know. She relents on one condition. Proud to see but fearful of being seen, more precisely of being detected, she tells Lycius he may invite anyone he wants except for Apollonius. From him, she insists, she must be "hid" (2.101).

But since Apollonius comes anyway, Lycius's power to invite—the quintessential power of a host—is doubly balked. On one hand, for reasons Lamia will not explain, she forbids him to ask his old teacher. On the other hand, for reasons Apollonius does not explain, he makes Lycius accept him as a guest:

> "'Tis no common rule,
> Lycius," said he, "for uninvited guest
> To force himself upon you, and infest
> With an unbidden presence the bright throng
> Of younger friends; yet must I do this wrong,
> And you forgive me."
>
> (2.164–69)

He "must" come uninvited for reasons that emerge only after his piercing scrutiny of Lamia—looking through her "like a sharp spear" (2.300)—has killed her loveliness. In "fix[ing] his eye, without a twinkle or stir / Full on the alarmèd beauty of the bride" (2.247), he drains the power of her own eyes, so that Lycius can no longer find anything like his reflection in them. Gazing entranced upon them rather than looking through her, as Apollonius does, he finds "no recognition in those orbs" (2.260), and her whole face turns "a deadly white" (2.275). Only now, after compounding the social sin of crashing a wedding feast by turning the bride into an "aching ghost" (2.294), does Apollonius tell Lycius why he has done so:

> "Fool! Fool!" repeated he, while his eyes still
> Relented not, nor moved: "From every ill
> Of life have I preserved thee to this day,
> And shall I see thee made a serpent's prey?"
>
> (2.295–98)

As the teacher of Lycius, Apollonius aims above all to make him see, more precisely to see through appearances—such as the image of his own face in Lamia's eyes—rather than being entranced by them. "According to Apollonius," Endo observes, "to not see is to prove a 'fool.' It is to expose oneself to the seeing of others" (Endo 115). Yet Apollonius's cure for what he takes to be Lycius's blindness kills the patient. As soon as he repeats the word "serpent," Lamia vanishes and Lycius dies.

An earlier passage in the poem prompts us to read this moment allegorically, to see Apollonius's murderous scrutiny of Lamia as the slaying of poetry by "philosophy," meaning "natural philosophy," or what we now call science. The earlier passage, in fact, seems to express what Keats personally felt about science. While drinking with Charles Lamb at a now-famous dinner party given by Benjamin Robert Haydon on December 28, 1817, he reportedly agreed with Lamb that Isaac Newton "had destroyed all the poetry of the rainbow, by reducing it to the prismatic colours," and he went on to drink "Newton's health, and confusion to mathematics" (Haydon 1:269). In the spirit of that heady moment, and with a little help from William Hazlitt, who had written that "the progress of knowledge" tends "to clip the wings of poetry,"[24] the narrator of *Lamia* laments the dissolution of the once awe-inspiring rainbow ("she is given / In the dull catalogue of common things," 2.232–33) and ruefully observes,

> Philosophy will clip an Angel's wings,
> Conquer all mysteries by rule and line,
> Empty the haunted air and gnoméd mine —
> Unweave a rainbow, as it erewhile made
> The tender-personed Lamia melt into a shade.
>
> (2.234–38)

This passage seems to make science the enemy of poetry as well as of festive hospitality: it was at a dinner party that the poet who wrote these lines drank "confusion to mathematics." But to take their ostensible message as the key to the whole poem is to overlook what Keats had come to think of "philosophy" by the summer of 1819. More than a year after Haydon's dinner party and shortly before writing *Lamia*, Keats soberly observed that "our reasonings . . . though erroneous . . . may be fine — This is the very thing in which consists poetry and if so it is not so fine a thing as philosophy — For the same reason that an eagle is not so fine a thing as a truth."[25] So the eagle wings of poetry deserve to be clipped, or at any rate are *eclips*ed by philosophy? If the author of *Lamia* had come to believe that philosophic truth excels poetry, we can only infer that the lines of poetry quoted above express the viewpoint of Lycius, that they represent what he sees (or fails to see) as co-host of a feast woven by magic in the "haunted air" of Lamia's palace. What *is* the truth here? Is Lamia truly "tender-personed"? We already know, as Lycius does not, that to gain her own ends she willfully sacrifices the privacy of the nymph. We also know, as Lycius does, that this "cruel lady" makes him suffer the fear of losing her just after she first captures his attention (1.290–91). At bottom what is she? We can no more seize her psychic core as victim or victimizer—"some penanced lady elf, / Some demon's mistress, or the demon's self" (1.55–56)—than we can fix the kaleidoscopic dazzle she first presents to us in her serpent skin: "Striped like a zebra, freckled like a pard, / Eyed like a peacock, and all crimson barred" (1.49–50). She defies us to define her.

But for this very reason, Apollonius's fatal penetration of her woman's shape cannot unequivocally signify the victory of philosophic truth over poetic beauty, mystery, and illusion. For one thing, Apollonius is himself a magician. As Endo says, this "agent of disenchantment is not without his own rationalistic magic" when the "hungry spell" of his merciless gaze devours Lamia's "loveliness" (Endo 121, *Lamia* 2.259). Whether or not she is a demon, he attacks her with what Lycius calls "demon eyes" (2.289). So as Endo says, Apollonius's "weapons are rational versions of the evil eye and the magic spell. . . . In *Lamia* reason is just as magical as romance in its need to discipline attention" (Endo 121).

We see this point more clearly in light of a second one. When Apollonius deconstructs the beauty of Lamia, he aims to show that she is fundamentally serpentine, that beneath her woman's loveliness lies nothing but a snake. But we do not know this for certain. What we know is that when Lamia first appears as a serpent with a woman's mouth, she tells Hermes that she was *once* a woman and now yearns to "have *once more* / A woman's shape" (1.117–18, emphasis added). We also know that just before she assumes or regains that shape, "the serpent" she has been loses all its brilliance and then "suddenly" disappears (1.146–66). When Apollonius kills the loveliness of Lamia by staring at her, she likewise disappears, vanishing "with a frightful scream" (2.305). *But she does not complete the circle of her metamorphoses.* She does not turn back into a serpent. Unlike the mortal Lycius, who dies, she leaves us with no final certainty about who she is or where she has gone. We do not know if Apollonius's vision of her identity is the final truth or simply one more way of seeing her, one more futile effort to fix her indeterminacy.

Apollonius's role as the would-be bearer of final truth is further complicated by the fact that he comes to the wedding feast as an uninvited guest, an unwelcome intruder. As such, he can readily personify the invasion of poetic beauty by the "cold philosophy" that makes "all charms fly" (2.229–30). But if he himself is a character within the poem, is he altogether alien to poetry? The mere fact that the poem admits him or hosts him—just as Lycius admits him, however uneasily, to the wedding feast—suggests that his role may be in some sense poetic. For a hint of this role, consider the opening lines of part 2, just after Lycius has moved in with Lamia:

> Love in a hut, with water and a crust,
> Is—Love, forgive us!—cinders, ashes, dust;
> Love in a palace is perhaps at last
> More grievous torment than a hermit's fast.
> That is a doubtful tale from fairy land,
> Hard for the non-elect to understand.
> Had Lycius lived to hand his story down,
> He might have given the moral a fresh frown,
> Or clenched it quite; but too short was their bliss
> To breed distrust and hate, that make the soft voice hiss.
>   (2.1–10)

The complexity of this passage rivals that of the one on philosophy. A coolly unsentimental couplet on the privations of love in a hut is followed by a "fairy land" tale of love in a palace. But instead of being lovely (the predictable converse of the first couplet), love in a palace is said to be "perhaps at last" more torturous than life on a starvation diet. If "fairy land" can accommodate such a tale, if the torments of love in a palace are even harder for the "non-elect" to understand than the pains of love in a hut, the elect must be anything but sentimentalists and dreamers.[26] If they can see beyond the bliss of brand-new lovers living in a palace, they must also be able to see, as Apollonius does, beneath the charm of Lamia's loveliness. Even before Apollonius crashes the wedding feast, Lycius begins to indicate that Lamia will not always enchant him, that the pleasures of living with her will eventually cloy. As Odysseus discovered with Calypso, not even the charms of a beautiful woman can long keep restlessness at bay, can stop the ears of Lycius to the sounds of the outside world or stifle his urge to advertise and publicize his trophy—a touch of self-promotion that might even be called Byronic in its modernity. Here lie the seeds of "distrust and hate." In sparking the couple's first fight, which goads Lycius to a "fury" that Lamia calms only by masochistically bowing to his "tyranny" (2.78–81), Lycius's demand for a wedding feast—his insistence on hosting his friends—shows that he is all too ready to sacrifice her privacy for his own gratification: exactly what the serpentine Lamia did with the nymph. Even if Apollonius had never crashed the wedding, how long would it be before Lamia's "soft voice" started to "hiss" with smoldering resentment, before she started acting just like what she nearly became when Lycius got so angry that he looked like Apollo "in act to strike / The serpent" (2.79–80)? In this light, Apollonius is something of a savior. He comes along just in time to save the couple's bliss from degenerating into hatred. In a crash course on seeing, the wedding crasher teaches his love-blinded, "non-elect" pupil just where love in a palace can lead.

This does not mean that Lamia is essentially serpentine or that all love—in palace, hut, urban condo, or suburban house—is doomed to degenerate. In poetically compressed form, *Lamia* shows only what erotic bliss may "perhaps at last" become and where erotic hospitality may lead. In rapid succession Lycius becomes Lamia's lover, then her house guest, then the tyrannous sacrificer of her privacy, and finally her co-host at a wedding feast she dreaded to hold. Forged out of conflict and the "misery" of the bride (2.116), this joint exercise in hospitality destroys him and at the very least banishes her. Once again it shows that the pleasures of hospitality may be as fleeting and perilous as the pleasures of love.

BYRON: JUAN AND HAIDÉE IN *DON JUAN*

Like Keats, Byron treats erotic bliss as something to be ended before it has time to degenerate. In *Don Juan*, the satiric epic he began writing in 1818 and thereafter published in irregular groups of cantos until his death in 1824, Byron commends the brevity of love—specifically the love enjoyed by his eponymous Spanish hero and Haidée, the young lady who finds and revives him when he turns up alone and exhausted on the shore of a small Greek island after barely surviving a Mediterranean shipwreck. There they briefly taste Edenic joy. But just as the cohabitation of Lycius and Lamia does not last long enough "to breed distrust and hate," Byron's lovers, we are told, "could not be / Meant to grow old" or "trail / A long and snake-like life of dull decay" (4.62–63, 70–71).[27] Long before they might have stooped to anything like serpentine hissing, they are irrevocably separated.

They meet in what might be called Homeric fashion. As the only daughter of a rich, slave-trading pirate who has built himself a grand house on the island, Haidée recalls Homer's Nausicaa, the island princess who found, revived, and fell in love with the shipwrecked Odysseus. Unlike Nausicaa, however, Haidée falls in love with a man her own age, and she tells her father—her only surviving parent—nothing about him. Finding Juan "almost famish'd, and half drown'd" (2.1028) and knowing that her father would have spiked hospitality with treachery ("would have hospitably cured the stranger, / And sold him instantly when out of danger," 2.1039–40), she and her maid Zoe take "their guest" (2.1045) to a cave, where they place him on a bed of furs, warm him with a fire, and feed him a good breakfast.

At this point Juan turns into something like what Rousseau became for Madame de Warens: a mother's child. Though he has already savored his first affair (with a married woman) and has proven his stamina by surviving a shipwreck, his exhaustion rouses all of Haidée's maternal instincts. As she gazes fondly at him, he "sweetly" sleeps the day away "like an infant" (2.1139). As she bends over him, he lies "hushed as a babe upon its mother's breast" (2.1178), and while he eats the food she eagerly brings him, she watches him "like a mother, [and] would have fed / Him beyond all bounds" (2.1258–59).

In watching over her visitor both maternally and erotically, Haidée recalls something of the passion with which Sophocles' Jocasta received the guest who turned out to be truly her son, and who eventually gave his name to the complex that paradigmatically eroticizes the love between sons and mothers. Though hospitality is seldom recognized as a factor in the Oedipus complex, we do well to remember that Jocasta was Oedipus's hostess as well as his mother, and that whenever a hostess entertains a male guest, he may arouse maternal affection as well as sexual desire. But to be infantilized or, so to speak, filialized as Juan is, the male guest must be young, passive, sexually uninitiated, or all three. When Porphyro comes to see Madeline, it is she who sleeps and he who watches with an ardor uninflected by any kind of paternal affection: an ardor that may all too readily cross the line from watching to ravishing. In pictorial examples of the "sleepwatch," as Leo Steinberg calls it, power belongs to the watcher. "Whether the intrusion is tender or murderous," he says, "the one caught napping, victim or beneficiary, is the butt of the action. Sleep is the opportunity of the intruder" (Steinberg 99). In Shakespeare's *Rape of Lucrece*, Tarquin rapes his hostess right after drawing the curtains of her bed and gazing enraptured on every feature of her sleeping form: her lily-white hands, rosy cheek, golden hair, blue-veined breasts, coral lips, and dimpled chin.[28] In *The Eve of St. Agnes* Porphyro is structurally the guest but performatively the host in charge of doling out delicacies to Madeline, and it is he who decides to enter the dream of this sleeping young woman by "melt[ing]" into it.

But when the male guest of a hostess is young, relatively passive, sexually inexperienced, or all three, he tends to be not so much her prey as her lover and child combined. In Rousseau's account of his sojourn with Madame de Warens, she becomes both his "mamma" and the taker of his virginity—in an act that feels to him like incest. In the final chapter of Joyce's *Ulysses*, Molly Bloom feels equal amounts of lust and maternal solicitude for Leopold's guest Stephen Dedalus, whom she would dearly love to adopt as both a surrogate for the infant son she has lost and a bedmate she will titillate "till he half faints under me" (*U* 18.1364). Even in the *Aeneid*, where Dido holds the power to receive and entertain her shipwrecked visitor, Venus ignites the queen's desire for her guest by making Cupid impersonate his son Ascanius.

Unlike those three hostesses, Haidée is a virgin when her visitor arrives. In watching the sleeping Juan as rapturously as a mother gazing on her sleeping child, she clearly feels a mixture of maternal affection and desire. But besides her virginity, her enraptured way of watching Juan sleep adds something different, for sleep in this passage is not just infantile but ominous. No one granted a pleasurable sight, says the narrator, not even "an Arab with a stranger for a guest," can feel such joy "as they who watch o'er what they love while sleeping" (2.1564–9). Something more than maternal tenderness is at stake here. While reminding us that Arabs traditionally entertain their guests with great care, this passage also evokes what is probably the oldest story of sleepwatching we have: that of Psyche and Cupid. When Psyche dares to light a lamp so as to see for the first time the sleeping form of a lover who has been visiting her only in the dark, she accidentally spills a drop of burning oil on his shoulder, wakes him up, and thereby drives him off, leaving her suicidally desolate.[29]

Whether or not the story of Juan and Haidée is meant to evoke the story of Cupid and Psyche (who end up reunited after many ordeals), Juan's sleeping form subtly prefigures the end of their affair. "Helpless," motionless, and "hushed into depths beyond the watcher's diving," Juan lies before her "like Death without its terrors" (2.1571–76). This is almost oxymoronic. With the obvious exception of orgasmic dying (as in John Donne's "We die and rise the same" in "Canonization"), death is the enemy of life, which has up to now revealed itself to Juan by a sequence of sudden changes: from boyish mischief making to first arousal, from the pleasures of a married woman's bed to the perils of being discovered by her husband, from love to sudden separation, from shipwreck to recovery. Having already taught us that no one can escape time, that the only alternative to aging is death, the poem makes us feel the evanescence of the lovers' joy even while lyrically celebrating it.[30] By the time we reach the beginning of canto 4, we know that their would-be "changeless" bond (4.121) cannot survive the return of Haidée's father Lambro, who has been off at sea so long that Haidée has forgotten him—even though he owns the island and is therefore Juan's absentee host.

In returning, Lambro seems to tread the footsteps of Homer's homebound island king. Like the returning Odysseus, he finds himself unrecognized and presumed dead, his house occupied by men gluttonously feasting on his provisions and grossly abusing his hospitality. One of the drunken revellers, in fact, tells him that the "dead" old master (Lambro himself) has been succeeded not by his daughter but by her guest and lover, the "new" master (3.341–44). But unlike the villainous suitors of Homer's Penelope, this new master, the would-be usurper, is the hero of the poem. So by the logic of romance in this romantic epic, his nemesis must be a villain. Even though the old pirate truly loves his daughter ("The only thing which kept his heart unclosed / Amidst the savage deeds he had done and seen," 3.451–52) and is fully entitled to repossess his own house (as Odysseus reclaimed the kingship of Ithaca), he forfeits our sympathy by seizing Juan, selling him into slavery, and driving Haidée into a despair that kills both her and her unborn child.

Lambro thus shatters what the lovers have come to regard as a "changeless" bliss. Though he returns at the beginning of canto 3, he holds off striking until canto 4, when they least expect him. Blissfully oblivious to a threat we know is coming, they are "alone once more" in "another Eden" after the party breaks up (4.73–74), as if they could indefinitely sustain the paradisal ecstasy of first love. But when they fall asleep together, Haidée is "shaken" by "the mystical Usurper of the mind" (4.235–36): a dream that puts her through a sequence of horrors. After being chained to a seaside rock and battered by fierce waves, she is released to make her bloody-footed way over a graveled beach in quest of a sheeted form that repeatedly eludes her. Then, while standing in a cave walled with marble icicles, she drips tears that freeze to marble as they fall to her feet, where Juan lies "wet, and cold, and lifeless" (4.265). Finally, she is awakened in a way that brutally reconstructs Juan's first experience of her. When the ship-wrecked Juan awakens on the beach where Haidée and Zoe find him, she seems a dream come true: "And slowly by his swimming eyes was seen / A lovely female face of seventeen" (2.895–96). But as Haidée in her own dream watches the face of the dead Juan, it grows to resemble the face of her father, which is just what she awakens to see: a nightmare come true, an "ocean-buried" father "risen from death, to be / Perchance the death of one she loved too well" (4.284–85).

But chance has its own agenda. Though Haidée offers to die with Juan, neither is killed. Even after slashing two of Lambro's twenty men with his sword, Juan is merely wounded, stowed in a boat bound for Constantinople, and then sold as a slave to a Turkish sultan whose wife, yet another *maman* of sorts, nearly lures him into her bed. So unlike Lycius but like Rousseau, he survives the pain of losing his beloved hostess. It is she who falls, weeps, rises, flies "at all she [meets], as on her foes" (4.532), and finally starves herself to death. Wrenched from a guest-turned-lover who is made to sail on in spite of himself, our would-be Nausicaa reenacts, without a funeral pyre, the fate of the Carthaginian hostess who could not bear to relinquish her Trojan guest.

STENDHAL'S *RED AND BLACK*: JULIEN AND MADAME DE RÊNAL

Since Byron's *Don Juan* furnishes epigraphs for seven chapters of *Red and Black* (1831), Stendhal prompts us to see his protagonist Julien Sorel as yet another variation on the legend of Don Juan, whose very name is echoed by Julien's. But Julien Sorel and Byron's Juan both differ in one important way from the legendary don. Unlike the jaded, heartless seducer best known from Mozart's *Don Giovanni* (1787), Julien and Juan first appear to us as virginal and vulnerable, young men needing the guidance of older women. At sixteen Juan is sexually initiated by a lovely married woman of twenty-three who leads him into temptation even while vowing to withstand it. Something similar happens in *Red and Black*. When the nineteen-year-old Julien first presents himself to Madame de Rênal, he looks so tearful and nervous that she takes him at first "for a girl in disguise" (21). Deprived of a mother, routinely beaten by his brothers, and despised by his sawmill-owning father, he badly needs a mother's love. So it is hardly surprising that this dreamy, bookish, teenage peasant should be aroused by a lovely bourgeoise who, we soon learn, is also an heiress. And it is probably no coincidence that the twenty-eight-year-old Madame de Rênal is just the age at which Madame de Warens—nearly an anagram of Rênal—first met the teenage Rousseau, whose *Nouvelle Héloïse* Julien later mines for its impassioned rhetoric and with whom Julien is later compared.[31]

I hasten to say that Julien matches neither of his precursors. Neither Juan nor Rousseau treats the object of his desire with anything like the embittered class consciousness that Julien brings to Madame de Rênal or with anything like his Napoleonic ambition to conquer her, to "cut down this fine lady's contempt for a laborer just liberated from the sawmill."[32] This fiercely aggressive ambition, which lurks just beneath his girlish, timid exterior, plainly sets him off from both of the others. In addition, he comes to the Rênals' household in order to work for them. Unlike Rousseau and Juan, who are both essentially guests of Madame de Warens and Haidée, Julien comes to Madame de Rênal because he has been hired to tutor her children.

Nevertheless, Julien crosses the line between tutor and guest on the sultry day of his very first meeting with Madame de Rênal, when—even while promising that he would never "lift a hand" to strike her children—he boldly lifts her own hand and carries it "to his lips," thereby drawing her "completely bare" arm out from beneath her shawl (24). The gesture is so transgressive that the lady shortly scolds herself "for not having grown indignant quickly enough" (24). But in getting away with this gesture, Julien plainly shows that he will not tolerate the status of a household servant. Even Monsieur de Rênal, the self-important factory owner who treats him with unrelenting arrogance, insists that everyone call him sir and fits him out with a tailor-made suit. More significant, Madame de Rênal soon feels maternal toward him. As their affair progresses, we are told, she sometimes "had the illusion of loving him like her own child" (77). And when he is eventually tried for attempting to kill her, he tells the jury that she "had been like a mother to me" (387).

As her lover and would be son, Julien achieves with her the kind of intimacy that guests ranging from Aeneas to Rousseau have gained with their respective hostesses. If Julien never quite becomes the guest of Madame de Rênal, she treats him much like one, and elsewhere his command of Latin is so much admired that he is invited to a dinner in his honor by Monsieur Valenod, the director of the Verrières poorhouse, who hopes to hire him away from Monsieur de Rênal. But dinner with the Valenods, along with other public officials and their wives, proves to be a painful experience. Julien winces to think that the splendid furnishings and rich food laid out to "astonish" him might have been bought out of funds committed to feed "the poor inmates" on the other side of the dining room wall.[33]

The thought of their hunger makes him choke, and when Valenod orders the singing of one of the poor men stopped, his hospitality becomes morally toxic. "Maybe," Julien's conscience tells him, "you'll get a place worth twenty thousand francs, but while you gorge yourself on rich foods, you'll have to shut the mouth of an [inmate] who's trying to sing. You'll give banquets with the money you've stolen from his miserable pittance, and while you're eating he'll be more miserable than ever!" (111). Yet it is not only Valenod's heartlessness— and its possibly contagious effect—that repel Julien. He is also galled by the vulgarity of his host and hostess, who boast of having bought their wine at the bargain price of "nine francs a bottle direct from the grower" (111). Does this boorishness trouble Julien even more than Valenod's heartlessness? Julien prompts us to think so when he concludes that he is not so much morally as *socially* superior to all the others at this dinner. In departing, we read,

> he saw himself as a complete aristocrat, he who for so long had been irked by lofty smiles and arrogant airs which he sensed behind all the polite phrases addressed to him at M. de Rênal's. He could not fail to notice the extraordinary difference. I won't consider, said he to himself, that all this money was stolen from the poor inmates, who are even forbidden to sing! But would M. de Rênal ever take it on himself to tell his guests the price of every bottle of wine he set before them? (113).

This passage reeks of irony. Having first exposed the fecklessness of Julien's sympathy for the starving inmates (a "weakness" like that of yellow-gloved conspirators who never do anything to change the world), the detached, worldly narrator now reveals that this young peasant has become a snob. Up to now, he has detested Monsieur de Rênal for his bourgeois pride of ownership, as when he tries to stone a little peasant girl for daring to cut through a corner of his orchard. Suddenly, however, Julien sees Rênal as a perfectly well-mannered host: the source of the *politesse* that Julien has already imbibed from him and that has made Julien a "complete aristocrat" fully qualified to despise the vulgarity of hosts and hostesses such as the Valenods.

But Julien has scarcely begun his ascent to aristocracy, much less completed it. Though learnèd, shrewd, and eloquent enough to rise within the church (a route he pursues for a time in a seminary), he can never vanquish his revolutionary passion, which makes him resent and distrust all upper classes, bourgeoisie and aristocracy alike. Yet as his final thoughts about the Valenod dinner illustrate, he is anything but a revolutionary hero. His first moment of glory comes when he is placed in the honor guard for the king's visit to Verrières. Dressed in a freshly tailored sky-blue uniform furnished for him by Madame de Rênal, who has also got him his place, and riding a horse he can barely control, he manages by sheer good luck not to fall off as the burst of a little cannon frightens his horse out of line. "From that moment on," we are told, "he felt himself a hero. He was one of Napoleon's orderlies in the act of charging a battery" (81). Stendhal thus aims his irony directly at Julien himself, the would-be Napoleonic revolutionary who has been outfitted by an heiress, who can barely stay up on his horse, and who glories in the very act of paying homage to a king. Later on, when the father of Mathilde de la Mole gives him a commission as lieutenant of hussars and a new aristocratic name, he suddenly imagines that his true parentage, hitherto obscured, has at last been recognized, that he is not really the son of a peasant after all. "Is it actually possible, he asked himself, that I might be the natural son of some aristocrat exiled among our mountains by the terrible Napoleon?' (360). The secret admirer of Napoleon now identifies himself with one of the emperor's worst enemies.

This self-contradictory version of the prince-in-disguise myth is the final consequence of Julien's first transgressive urge: crossing the line between tutor and amatory guest just after first crossing the threshold of Madame de Rênal. In some ways his sojourn in her bourgeois mansion is merely a stage in his social ascent. After falling "desperately in love" with her and rousing her to swear she would risk eternal damnation for the love of him (72, 92), he leaves her: first for the seminary in Besançon and then—supposedly "forever" (177)—for the grandly aristocratic household of the Marquis de la Mole in Paris, where he is once again treated as something between an employee and a guest.

Thanks to the intervention of his mentor, the Abbé Pirard, he is hired as secretary to the marquis at a starting salary of a hundred louis.[34] But he is also made to understand that he will be offered the friendship of the marquis' two grown children, the elegant Count Norbert and the beautiful Mathilde, both nineteen.[35] On his second day at work copying letters in the library, Norbert invites Julien to ride with him, and afterward he joins the marquis's family for dinner, which soon becomes a regular occurrence. Finding him "an original," the marquis treats him "like a son" (200) and dresses him accordingly, giving him a blue suit for evening wear. Whenever he wears it, the marquis says, he will see him as "the son of my friend the old duke [de Retz]" (219).

Nevertheless, Julien feels "completely isolated" (210). Much as he likes the genial marquis, who treats him with nothing like the arrogance of Monsieur de Rênal, he never forgets that he is a servant who wears a black suit by day and, in that capacity, cannot accept favors meant for "the man in the blue suit" (222). Family dinners stupefy him. Talking one day with the Abbé Pirard, he asks, "Is dining every day with the marquise one of my duties, or are they doing me a favor?" (203). Though the abbé calls it "a great honor," Julien finds it "the most painful part of [his] job" (203) because no one at the table is allowed to talk about anything interesting, let alone anything revolutionary. In the presence of the marquis himself, who deplores the past revolution and firmly supports the restored monarchy, Julien must suppress both his revolutionary politics and his irreligion: "his fanatical admiration for a name [Napoleon] that enraged the marquis, and his own perfect unbelief, which hardly suited a future clergyman" (220).

At the same time, Julien's loathing of reaction and conformity piques the interest of Mathilde. When she overhears him telling the abbé that he finds dining with the family "painful," she gladly perceives he was not "born on his knees" (204). Later on, seeing him talking with a Spanish count who has been sentenced to death in his own country (the only distinction that "can't be bought," Mathilde thinks), she tells herself that he acts "like a prince in disguise" and excitedly wonders if he might become "another Danton" (230, 234). Mathilde's greatest fear is not revolution but boredom. On meeting Julien in the library just after becoming his mistress, she glares at him and flails herself for having yielded "to the first comer." But when he draws an old medieval sword from the wall and seems to threaten her before replacing it, she is thrilled to think that she was "on the verge of being killed by [her] lover!" (281).

In spite of such moments, Julien soon learns that Mathilde can be "beaten" (343) only by a man capable of controlling his feelings, courageously keeping them in check. Yet as Henri Martineau long ago observed, passion always trumps calculation in the soul of Julien (Martineau 448). When Mathilde brings him news that he is to marry her (she is already pregnant), become an officer, and gain a title, he gives full license to his feelings: "His joy knew no bounds. It can be estimated from the ambition of his whole life, and from the passion he was now feeling for his new son. . . . Now at last, he thought, the novel of my career is over, and the credit is all mine" (359). Abandoning all checks on his feelings, Julien triumphantly asserts that he has ended the novel of his life, the would-be chivalric romance of his quest for glory and a princess. But the novel of his life is not yet ended, for catastrophe lies just ahead. "In the midst of these transports of unbridled ambition," a letter from Mathilde tells Julien that "all is lost" because her father has received a letter from Madame de Rênal saying that Julien is nothing but a fortune-hunting seducer (361). In response, Julien sets out to kill the only woman he has ever truly loved, his passionately maternal hostess, at once his redeemer and betrayer.

His plunge from exaltation into attempted murder epitomizes the radical instability of his condition, the unpredictability of a life driven by a relentless ambition that vaults him upward again and again only to throw him down. When we see him for the very first time in this novel, he is straddling a roof-beam in his father's sawmill — and reading. Entranced by a book about Napoleon that is suddenly dashed into the stream by the hand of his brutal father, he is just as suddenly cuffed so hard that he nearly falls into the machinery below. This little episode prefigures his whole life. Straddling a horse in the honor guard and imagining that he is charging a battery at Napoleon's command, he barely escapes falling when the noise of a cannon frightens his horse. Later on, just after Mathilde persuades her father to give him a commission and an aristocratic name, he tumbles from the height of this glory into the machinery of intrigue. The letter from Madame de Rênal, we learn, was actually written by a priest who made her copy it out in her own hand. Then, after Julien is arrested and imprisoned, Mathilde's elaborate scheme to save him is sabotaged by Valenod, who leads the jury to condemn him. In the end, it is the blade of Dr. Guillotine's machine that makes Julien's head drop, completing his fall from the roof beam into the machinery.

In falling, however, he does not simply surrender to the law of gravity. He wills his own death. Once he is arrested and jailed for attempted murder, he forsakes ambition. By the time of his trial he feels only remorse for trying to kill his surrogate mother and contempt for the bourgeois members of the jury. After forfeiting any chance of reprieve by requesting the death sentence for what he calls his "atrocious, and . . . *premeditated*" crime, he says to the jury,

Gentlemen, I have not the honor to belong to your social class, you see in
me a peasant in open revolt against his humble station. . . . I see before me
men who . . . are determined to punish in me and discourage forever a certain class of young men—those who, born to a lower social order, and buried
by poverty, are lucky enough to get a good education and bold enough to
mingle with what the arrogant rich call good society.

There is my crime, gentlemen, and it will be punished all the more
severely because, in reality, I am not being judged by my peers. I do not
see in the seats of the jury a single rich peasant, only outraged *bourgeois*.
(387–88)

Here again Julien sounds revolutionary. But he does not speak for the poor,
the peasantry, or any other class of people. His "class of young men" is a class of
one. No one but he in this novel has risen from the peasantry to the aristocracy,
has been repeatedly treated as a guest at the dinner table of a marquis.
Though he implies that rich peasants *would* be qualified to judge him, he hates
the only rich peasant we know—his own father. At once peerless and powerless,
Julien self-destructively assumes an aristocratic contempt for the bourgeoisie.
He cares only for the one other person who cannot be classified, who will
not judge him, and who loves him with the indestructible devotion of a
mother: Madame de Rênal. In the end, he returns to his first love with "profound
gratitude" (395) for all she has given him: sacrificing her respectability,
taking the place of the mother he lost, surviving his attempt to murder her,
and totally absolving him. Julien fails as a Napoleonic hero, as another Don
Juan, as a revolutionary upstart, as a prince in disguise. He succeeds only in
discovering, just before he is executed, what it means to be unconditionally
loved.

The true story of Rousseau's affair with Madame de Warens and the fictional
story of Julien's affair with Madame de Rênal (itself based on the true story of a
seminarian in Stendhal's time) furnish bookends for what might be called a
little library of erotic hospitality in romantic literature. Erotic hospitality knows
no generic bounds. Having already played a conspicuous part in Virgil's *Aeneid*
and *Sir Gawain and the Green Knight*, it resurfaces in the autobiography of
Rousseau, the supernatural romances of Coleridge and Keats, and the realist
fiction of Stendhal. This is not to say that its romantic practitioners simply
reenact the story of Aeneas and Dido. On the contrary, they rewrite it. In
Byron's *Don Juan* the heroine evokes Dido by starving herself to death when
her guest and lover is forcibly taken from her, and in Stendhal's *Red and Black*
Madame de Rênal dies of grief three days after the execution of her own guest

and lover. But neither of the two young men is driven onward by a divine destiny; each is racked with longing for the woman from whom he is irrevocably sundered.

As for the other hostesses treated in this chapter, none follows Dido into anything like self-immolation. When a desolate Rousseau leaves Madame de Warens for the last time, she has already found a new bedmate. In Keats's *Lamia* it is not the hostess of the wedding feast who dies (she disappears) but her guest and lover Lycius, who cannot live without her. And in *Christabel* the eponymous heroine radically reconstructs the figure of the hostess. After sleeping with a female guest who usurps the place of her dead mother, taints her with a serpentine sexuality, binds her to silence, and rouses the sympathy of her father, Christabel is stricken with impotent jealousy. Balked at expressing her sexual desires, especially her desire for her father, she enrages him by her flagrant inhospitality to their guest. When he overrules her by taking Geraldine's hand, Christabel is psychically paralyzed.

Part of the reason for which erotic hospitality assumes such a variety of forms in the romantic period is that each of its participants is shaped by a distinctive historical context. Byron's Juan is a good example. Though he evokes both Homer's Odysseus and Virgil's Aeneas, though he takes his very name from the Don Giovanni of Spanish legend, Juan is a lovable *naif* who is made to expose by contrast the vices of European society in the aftermath of the Restoration, when erotic hospitality—and the re-creation of paradise on earth—could last only as long as slave trading and property owning could be kept at bay. Stendhal's Julien, a Juan fired and reforged by Napoleonic legend, is inconceivable without his revolutionary class consciousness, which makes him see almost every hospitable gesture, erotic or not, as an act of insufferable condescension. By contrast, Rousseau's prerevolutionary affair with Madame de Warens is untainted by political animus, but his account of it is nonetheless shaped by its contextual frame: the story of how a motherless young man born into a battle of conflicting religions gradually liberates his mind as a prelude to launching an intellectual revolution that makes him reviled in his native land, forcing him—like the banished Dante—to know the salt taste of another's bread as the uneasy guest of David Hume in England.[36] Even the plight of a romance heroine such as Christabel can be traced in part to the cultural impact of the French Revolution. Paralyzed by the conflict between her desires and the law of the father, who enforces the laws of hospitality, Christabel exemplifies what Mary Wollstonecraft laments in *Vindication of the Rights of Woman* (1792), a sequel to her defense of the Revolution against Edmund Burke, where she decries the subservience that parents impose on their daughters.[37]

7

FIELDING TO JAMES: DOMESTICITY, MATING, POWER

"Was it for this, Count Morano," said Montini, in a cool sarcastic tone of voice, "that I received you under my roof, and permitted you, though my declared enemy, to remain under it for the night? Was it, that you might repay my hospitality with the treachery of a fiend, and rob me of my niece?"

—ANN RADCLIFFE, *The Mysteries of Udolpho* (1794)

In *The Mysteries of Udolpho* a wealthy nobleman named Montini marries the aunt of the orphaned heroine, Emily St. Aubert, tries to force the girl to marry his friend Count Morano, changes his mind when he learns that Morano is ruined, and then takes the two women off to his castle. When Morano turns up there late one night, Montini admits him as a guest but is soon after outraged to find Morano in Emily's bedroom about to abduct her. Drawing swords, they fight until Morano is severely wounded and then, by Montini's order, carried out of the castle.

Among representations of hospitality in English fiction, this episode exemplifies treachery in what might be considered one of its simplest forms: a man's designs on the niece of his host prompt the two men to fight until the guest is made to bleed and then hauled away. Crude as it is, I cite this episode not only because it vividly displays the intersection of hospitality and treachery, but also because it is motivated by a combination of revenge and passion: Morano's quest for revenge against Montini springs from his unrequited desire for Emily (who, incidentally, prefers another man). The whole episode thus entails a set of conditions and forces that we shall see much more deeply as well as much more subtly probed in novels ranging from Jane Austen's *Pride and Prejudice* to Henry James's *The Portrait of a Lady*. While generally eschewing violence, novels such as these reveal again and again how much the desire for a mate is bound up with domesticity, power, and hospitality.

In his book on domesticity, Michael McKeon defines it in terms of privacy, the public realm, and the novel. As "a species of modern privacy," McKeon argues, the story of domesticity "can only make sense within the more general story of modern privacy and its separation out from the realm of the public" (McKeon xxi). The novel—or more precisely the "domestic novel" commonly thought to have been launched by Samuel Richardson's *Pamela* (1740)—affirms this separation by focusing on the private realm of domestic space, the lives that people live inside their homes.[1] At the same time, McKeon contends, the novel reveals the public, political significance of "private, domestic relations," as in the conflict between Richardson's rebellious heroine and her tyrannical master, Mr. B. (642). But in his complex argument about the ways in which novelists ranging from Richardson to Austen subtly domesticate the world of public affairs, McKeon overlooks the role of hospitality. If the domestic novel not only reflects "the problematic separation out of self from society" but also strives to reconnect the two, as McKeon concludes (717), we cannot fully understand this process without examining the transactions of hospitality in English fiction. For it is in such moments of threshold crossing that the public world meets the private one, that society, in the form of friends and strangers alike, meets the separated, domesticated self.[2]

To set the stage for my examination of hospitality in five nineteenth-century novels (three English, one Russian, and one American), I will briefly consider two developments that helped pave the way for the domestic novel: the shift from romance and Christian allegory to secular realism, and the shift from battlefield heroism to moral heroism, the kind of fortitude or "heroic heat," as Elizabeth Barrett Browning calls it, that may be radiated by a woman as well as a man, especially when acting as a host, hostess, or guest. In classical epic, we have seen, episodes of hospitality now and then punctuate warfare, as in Priam's visit to Achilles' tent and Aeneas's sojourn with Dido. But the heroism of Achilles and Aeneas does not spring from what they do as hosts or guests. Only with the advent of Christian romance—and specifically with *Sir Gawain and the Green Knight*—does heroism manifest itself in the context of hospitality, specifically in the heroically virtuous self-control of a guest who resists the seductive overtures of his hostess.

Nevertheless, Christian romance kept militant heroism very much alive. In book 1 of Spenser's *Faerie Queene* the Red Cross knight meets various kinds of hospitality but can prove his moral heroism only by fighting. Whether the hospitality is treacherous (as in the House of Pride) or rehabilitative (as in the House of Holiness), it is never more than a pretext for or prelude to knightly combat. At the House of Holiness, where the all-but-despairing knight is revived by a host of allegorical counselors ranging from Fidelia to Contemplation, the whole process of therapeutic hospitality simply prepares him to play the hero again by fighting and killing the dragon who has captured the parents of Una.

In *Paradise Lost*, written some seventy years after Spenser died, Milton sought to demilitarize heroism. Lamenting that wars and the "tedious havoc" of "fabled knights / In battles feigned" have been "hitherto the only argument / Heroic deemed," he offers instead "the better fortitude / Of patience and heroic martyrdom" (*PL* 9.28–32). Yet this claim is somewhat misleading. In Milton's epic as in Christian tradition, the paradigm of heroic martyrdom is Christ, but before suffering death on the cross (an event merely prophesied, not enacted, within the narrative scope of the poem), Milton's Christ wins a glorious victory over Lucifer and his followers on the battlefields of heaven. Furthermore, even though the whole story of the war in heaven is told to Adam by the angel Raphael while visiting him and Eve as their guest, what Adam shows Raphael is not so much heroism as courtesy and deference. Adam's heroism has nothing to do with his hospitality toward Raphael. It lies rather in his doomed struggle to reconcile his duty to God with his devotion to Eve.

To find Christian heroism in the context of hospitality, we might turn to Milton's younger contemporary John Bunyan, whose *Pilgrim's Progress* (1678) appeared just a few years after the second edition of *Paradise Lost*. Early in part 1 of Bunyan's allegory Christian seeks hospitality while en route from the City of Destruction to Mount Zion. After scrambling up the steep hill called Difficulty as his two companions veer off in easier but morally disastrous directions, he defies the warnings of Mistrust and Timorous, who tell him of dangers and lions ahead, and presses on even after the sun has set. As a reward, it seems, for his heroic perseverance and courage, he finds "a very stately Palace" (38), where he asks for lodging. Though he soon learns that the house "was built by the Lord of the hill, on purpose to entertain . . . Pilgrims" (39), the hospitality offered him is anything but unconditional—even discounting his status as a pilgrim. First interrogated by the Porter, who then tells a virgin named Discretion where he has come from and where he is headed, he is promptly asked (by her) for the same information again, and then further interrogated about his journey as well as his name. Only after answering several questions is Christian given something to drink, and only after still more lengthy questioning is he finally given something to eat.

Besides grilling their pilgrim guest, the keepers of this would-be hospitable refuge aim to arm him for battle. At dinner Christian learns from a trio of hostesses—Piety, Prudence, and Charity—that the Lord of the Hill "had been a *great Warriour*" (43). Since he is also said to have lost "much blood" and to have died "on the Cross," the Lord is obviously Christ, and a forgivingly hospitable Christ at that, "willing . . . to receive into his favour" even those who "in time past had offered great affronts to his Person and proceedings" (44). Nevertheless, this Lord remains a great warrior. On the morning after his first night at the palace, Christian is shown records of what has been done by the Lord's servants, who, as we are told in Paul's letter to the Hebrews, "subdued Kingdoms, . . . waxed valiant in fight, and turned to flight the Armies of the *Aliens*" (Heb. 11.33–34, qtd. 44). In Paul's letter this Old Testament history of warfare makes up just one small part of a long discourse on the essentially nonmilitaristic virtue of faith ("our conviction about things we cannot see," Heb. 11.1). But Old Testament warfare is what stands behind the armory that Christian is shown on his second day at the palace. Here are displayed not only the "Sword, Shield, Helmet, Brest plate" that the Lord of the Hill has "provided for Pilgrims," but also the weapons with which Israel's champions slew their enemies, including the very hammer and nail that Jael used to kill her guest Sisera (44). Ironically enough, then, the house built by a Lord of the Hill who stands for Christ is a monument to Old Testament nationalism, to a xenophobic Israel that construed all strangers as enemies and renounced hospitality in favor of war.

Some seventy years after *Pilgrim's Progress*, Fielding's "history" of a foundling, a.k.a. *Tom Jones*, tells what might be called the story of another progress toward moral perfection: how a good-hearted, impulsive, sexually adventurous young man from Somersetshire learns in the course of his travels to London and back how to be worthy of a lovely young lady whose very name, Sophia, signifies the wisdom he achieves at last. In some ways *Tom Jones* is also another story about fighting. Since Fielding sets it during the Rebellion of 1745, when the Jacobites made their last, abortive effort to retake the English throne for Bonnie Prince Charlie, Fielding might well have placed his protagonist among the forces of the king, which at one point Tom offers to join as a volunteer foot soldier.[3] But instead of fighting for the king, he is provoked into seeking a duel when an ensign named Northerton jestingly slanders the virtue of Sophia and then throws a bottle at his head. Though Tom burns to defend the honor of the lady he loves, he asks himself a question that Bunyan would have found absurd: Can a Christian fight? "How terrible must it be," says Tom, "to anyone who is really a Christian, to cherish Malice in his Breast, in Opposition to the Command of him who hath expressly forbid it?" (1.383).[4] Whether or not he would have fought Northerton, who escapes before he can do so, Tom never joins the army, and thereafter strives to reconcile heroism with Christian compassion.

In doing so, he turns from the glories of the battlefield to the comforts of domesticity.[5] Instead of fighting the rebellious enemies of England, he fights on behalf of hospitality. Paradoxically, his first adversary is also his first host, an octogenarian misanthrope called the Man of the Hill, who is considerably less welcoming than Bunyan's Lord. After climbing "a very steep Hill" (1.443) on a moonlit night and seeking shelter and warmth in the house they find there, Tom and his companion, Partridge, gain entrance only after paying the old housekeeper, who tells them they must leave before her absent master returns because he "keeps no Company with any Body" (1.446). But Tom cannot believe her master would scold her for "doing a common Act of Charity" (1.446)—sheltering a stranger and thereby offering a distinctively Christian kind of hospitality. Furthermore, when a signal from the master just outside the door is accompanied by the voices of ruffians threatening to kill him, Tom leaps up to drive them away with a broadsword he finds in the house. He thus turns the misanthropic homeowner—temporarily, at least—into a grateful host who welcomes his "Deliverer" as his guest (1.448).

The long story of the old man's life—he's called only Jack (1.462)—is a chronicle of misbehavior and betrayal, but it includes an episode that evokes two of the most remarkable stories of hospitality in the New Testament: those of the Good Samaritan and the prodigal son. When young Jack finds a robbed, battered man on a London street one night, he takes him to a tavern and sends for a doctor, who proves another good Samaritan: "a very generous, good-natured Man, and ready to do any Service to his Fellow-Creatures" (1.468). But even as the doctor takes the injured man to an inn and offers him money, the man himself recognizes Jack as his son, and Jack in turn recognizes his father, a gentleman farmer in Somersetshire whom he has neither seen nor written to for many months. Though Jack has not, like the prodigal son, squandered his inheritance, this younger son of a prosperous man had to leave Oxford penniless after being caught stealing from a fellow student, and he has cut himself off from his father in shame. But the father now rejoices to see him. Having sought only to find his son and come up to London for the sole purpose of doing so, he makes no "Mention of the Crime" (1.469) that kept the young man from corresponding with him, and thinking that he "partly owed his Preservation to my Humanity," Jack recalls, he pronounced himself "more delighted than he should have been with my filial Piety, if I had known that the Object of all my care was my own Father" (1.469). Jack is thus rewarded with paternal love for behaving like the Good Samaritan, and at home he finds something like the welcome that greeted the returning prodigal. After reaching home with his father, who recovers in a few days, Jack is "provided with all the Necessaries of Life" (1.470).

Nevertheless, Jack remains a weird amalgam of Christian compassion ("Humanity") and embittered misanthropy. Though his elder brother (after the death of his father) leaves him more than enough to live on, though he claims to have learned from scripture that Christianity "softens and sweetens" the mind and leads to "eternal Happiness" (1.471), and though he gratefully receives Tom as his guest, he sees all of humankind through the lens of betrayal, which he suffered not only from his first mistress and first friend but also from a game-ster whom he had just saved from drowning. As a result, in words reminiscent of both John Calvin and Jonathan Swift, he finds humankind corrupted by "Dishonesty, Cruelty, Ingratitude, and accursed Treachery" (1.484).

Yet the man—or rather the host—he has become by the age of eighty-eight is best revealed by what he does on the morning Tom leaves him. Shortly after Jack leads his guest to the summit of Mazard Hill to enjoy the view, they hear the screams of a woman rising from the forest below. Though Tom runs down to rescue her from her tormenter (the loathsome Northerton, whom he throttles and ties up), the old man does nothing for this battered woman, whose plight he has witnessed "with great Patience and Unconcern" (1.497). When Tom returns with her, Jack offers no hospitality. Rather than taking the woman into his house, he tells Tom how to find the nearest town, Upton, which is said to offer "all manner of Conveniences" (1.497) but which is also about six miles distant (1.497n). Without Partridge, who is told to follow them, Tom and the woman must walk there.

It is Tom, then, who emulates the Good Samaritan by taking the battered woman to the Upton inn, where he braves the wrath of the landlady and the blows of her broom to gain a room for this half-naked and therefore seemingly disreputable female. Furthermore, Tom secures a room for her without, so far as we can tell, landing a single blow himself.[6] When a sergeant appears to iden-tify the battered woman as the wife of Captain Waters, the landlady promptly apologizes for abusing her and insists on letting the woman borrow her clothes. While she and Tom are then served a lavish meal, the irresistibly seductive Mrs. Waters deploys against her handsome young rescuer *"The whole Artillery of Love"* (1.511), with the result that he is shortly afterward found in her bed. In a manner hardly authorized by scripture, let alone by his love for Sophia, Tom is thus rewarded for his Samaritan kindness to a woman in distress. No longer a man who simply fights and kills on behalf of his lady, or anyone else, Fielding's hero is a pacific champion of hospitality, a man who suffers blows without retal-iation and will not rest until the battered woman he has rescued is granted shelter at the inn. Fittingly, the weapons of mortal combat, sword and pistol, give way here to the weapons of desire, the artillery of love.

I will not claim that Tom's behavior unambiguously exemplifies moral heroism, since he is not only "humane," as Mrs. Miller says later, but also, in his various susceptibilities, all too human.[7] He would surely not have met the criteria for heroism required of Sir Gawain. But Fielding's protagonist plays a crucial part in the domestication of heroism, which inevitably moves it into the domain of hospitality proper: not inns and lodging houses but actual homes, such as we have already seen in Stendhal's *Red and Black* as well as in romantic poetry. Since the domestication of heroism lays the groundwork for the representation of hospitality in nineteenth-century literature, I would like to look more closely at the first as prelude to a closer examination of the second.

DOMESTICATING HEROISM

> Nay, if there's room for poets in this world
> A little overgrown, (I think there is)
> Their sole work is to represent the age,
> Their age, not Charlemagne's,—this live, throbbing age,
> That brawls, cheats, maddens, calculates, aspires,
> And spends more passion, *more heroic heat,*
> *Betwixt the mirrors of its drawing-rooms,*
> Than Roland with his knights at Roncesvalles.
> —ELIZABETH BARRETT BROWNING, *Aurora Leigh* (1857; *emphasis added*)

> There is no real, no profitable campaign,
> except that waged in the drawing rooms.
> —MATHILDE TO JULIEN IN STENDHAL,
> *Red and Black* (1831), trans. Robert Adams

Could *Aurora Leigh* owe a debt to Stendhal? Strikingly enough, the reckless, beautiful aristocrat who redefines heroism for Julien Sorel in the world of the French Restoration seems to anticipate what Barrett Browning's heroine says to justify her literary goal: her ambition to write an epic in the seemingly unheroic age of the later nineteenth century. Throughout the century the topic of heroism vexed poets and novelists alike, for it was inextricably bound up with the question of whether or not the epic as a genre could survive. In one sense, as Herbert Tucker has magisterially shown, nineteenth-century poets answered this question with a resounding affirmative—by generating epic poems right through the century. But in doing so, Tucker observes, the poets also veered away from the bloody strife of ancient epic into bloodless *paragone* of cultural, pedagogical value, such as parliamentary debates (Tucker 27–28). In books 2 and 8 of *Aurora Leigh*, which Tucker takes to be an epic, Aurora and her cousin Romney Leigh debate the condition of England, and in book 5 the heroine undergoes a more personal *paragone* when the host of a grand house party leads her to Lady Waldemar, who now expects to become Romney's wife. Though Aurora has already spurned his proposal, she resents Lady Waldemar for driving him away from the poor but devoted Marian Erle. As a result, Lady Waldemar's "cold and bright" smile at the party pries almost nothing from Aurora. As the lady condescendingly speaks of Aurora's "literary toil" and sneers at the "wretched girl" whom Romney "never loved," Aurora periodically answers "yes" or "no" while standing "still, and cold, and pale . . . / As a garden-statue a child pelts with snow / For pretty pastime" (*AL* 5.988–1026). Nevertheless, it is Aurora who wins out in the end, partly by leading Romney to respect her literary work, and it is she who marries him.

Tucker persuasively argues that *Aurora Leigh* makes the "hydraulic" power of poetic imagination, in all of what was called its Spasmodic turbulence, serve the cause of social justice and women's rights, including the right to "epic spokesmanship" (Tucker 379–80). But in domesticating heroism, the poem also joins a trend that had been under way for decades. In the opening words of the first canto of *Don Juan*, which first appeared (with canto 2) in 1819, Byron declares that he "want[s] a hero" even while admitting that the "gazettes" are full of them—full of military and political notables who are "exceedingly remarkable at times / But not at all adapted to my rhymes" (1.23–24). This is part of a little joke that begins in the first stanza, where Byron breaks up the suave Hispanic monosyllable of his chosen hero's name by forcing it to rhyme with "new one" and "true one" so that it becomes a clunky *Joo-wan*.

Heroism is thus made to hang on pronunciation. In the wake of Waterloo, which Byron had scornfully called a "king-making victory" (*Childe Harold's Pilgrimage* 3.153), he finds no one who can be called heroic in the traditional sense. Admiral Horatio Nelson, "once Britannia's god of war," has been "quietly inurn'd" (*CHP* 1.25, 28); Napoleon (though he remains a hero to Julien Sorel) has become "nothing—save the jest of Fame" (*CHP* 3.328); and the English duke who won the battle of Waterloo but is not even mentioned in Harold's prolonged ruminations on it (*CHP* 3.17–45) appears in *Don Juan* only as "Wellesley" beside "Vernon, the butcher Cumberland" and a slew of other figures whose heroism means not much more than fleeting celebrity (*DJ* 1.9–12).[8] In *Childe Harold* Byron graciously salutes the bravery of his cousin Frederick Howard, who died at Waterloo (*CHP* 3.257–61), but since Howard died on behalf of what Byron has already called a "king-making victory," he cannot exemplify anything like the heroism of "true Glory's stainless victories," such as the ancient Greek victory over the Persians in the battle of Marathon (*CHP* 3.609–10).

In the mock-epic world of *Don Juan*, then, the bigger joke initiated by the little one about heroes and rhymes is that while Byron's protagonist joins the siege of Ismail in cantos 7 and 8, he shines not so much on the battlefield as in the bedroom. Like Stendhal's protagonist, whose very name echoes his own, he is a conqueror of ladies. But in a radical twist on the heartlessness of the legendary seducer, he strives to remain faithful to every woman he has loved, especially Haidée. When Gulbeyaz, the sultana of Constantinople, asks him to make love to her, he declines at the risk of his life because "he could not yet forget" Haidée (5.987). Knowing that the enraged sultana may have him killed at any moment, he stands

> *heroically* . . . resigned,
> Rather than sin—except to his own wish:
> But all his great preparatives for dying
> Dissolved like snow before a woman's crying.
> (5.1125–28; emphasis added)

Poor Juan. Bought as a slave by order of the sultana and dressed like one of her female attendants so as to hide his masculinity from the eyes of the sultan, he is a peculiar kind of hero: a nonce transvestite whose fidelity to one woman keeps him from succumbing to another—until her tears of self-pity melt his resolution. The sultan arrives just in time to forestall the likely consequence, but Gulbeyaz's desire for Juan recalls in some ways the erotic hospitality proffered by heroines ranging from Dido through Lady Bertilak, Rousseau's Madame de Warens, and Stendhal's Madame de Rênal. Though Juan at first rejects what he self-righteously calls sexual enslavement—"The prison'd eagle will not pair, nor I / Serve a sultana's sensual phantasy" (5.1007–8)—her invitation, especially when lubricated by her tears, turns him into something between a guest and a toyboy.

Thus domesticated as well as sexually destabilized, if not literally seduced, Juan offers one example of what happens to heroism in nineteenth-century English literature. At once domesticated and feminized, it moves from the battlefield to the drawing rooms and bedrooms of hospitality, where women themselves can radiate "heroic heat" as hostesses or guests.[9] Near the end of George Eliot's *Middlemarch* (1872), Dorothea resolves to rehabilitate the reputation of Dr. Lydgate, who has been suspected of involvement in the death of a man hated by Lydgate's benefactor. When she goes to call upon Lydgate, she finds his wife Rosamond talking intimately with Will Ladislaw, the very man whom Dorothea thought to be in love with her. In spite of this shattering indication that Will loves Rosamond, Dorothea casts herself as Lydgate's champion, determined to clear his name with everyone of importance she knows:

She felt power to walk and work for a day, without meat or drink. And she would carry out the purpose with which she had started in the morning, of going to Freshitt and Tipton to tell Sir James and her uncle all that she wished them to know about Lydgate, whose married loneliness under his trial now presented itself to her with new significance, and made her more ardent in readiness to be *his champion*. She had never felt anything like this triumphant power of indignation in the struggle of her married life . . . and she took it as a sign of new strength. (535, emphasis added)

Dorothea's heroism, then, is emphatically domestic, played out within the various drawing rooms she visits as a guest.[10] She resolves, heroically, not only to clear Lydgate's name but also to "save Rosamond" by assuring her of Lydgate's integrity and warning her against the sort of attachment that "murders . . . marriage" (545, 550). As a reward for her heroism, Dorothea learns from Rosamond that Will loves Dorothea alone, and it is she who ends up as his wife.

In two conspicuous ways, however, Dorothea's marriage to Will suggests that whatever new kind of heroine she might have come to be has been preempted by the role of a familiar old one: the lady in distress who is rescued by a man. The marriage she "save[s]" is essentially loveless, and even though she does what she can to salvage Lydgate's reputation, he feels bound to leave Middlemarch, abandon his pioneering research on tissues, gain a practice lucrative enough to feed Rosamond's expensive tastes, and die "prematurely" (575). Practically speaking, then, the only positive result of Dorothea's heroism is marriage to a man who has all along sought to rescue her from her suffo-cating first husband, Casaubon. During his first substantive conversation with Dorothea, which takes place in Rome at the apartment she and her husband have taken for their honeymoon, Will is pleased to find her alone but dismayed to find her married to his desiccated old drudge of a cousin.[11] In Will's mind, the situation has all the ingredients of romance, including a tantalizing opportunity for himself. "She must have made," he thinks,

> some original romance for herself in this marriage. And if Mr. Casaubon had been a dragon who had carried her off to his lair with his talons simply and without legal forms, it would have been *an unavoidable feat of heroism* to release her and fall at her feet. But he was something more unmanageable than a dragon: he was a benefactor with collective society at his back, and he was at that moment entering the room in all the unimpeachable correctness of his manner. (145, emphasis added)

This passage seems to evoke the romance plot only to show it trumped by the structures of socioeconomic realism: the would-be monster is not only

Dorothea's legal husband but also Will's cousin, benefactor, and potential host, since Dorothea has already told Will that she is sure her husband "will wish you to dine with us" (142). But in Will's imagination, Dorothea is a woman yearning to be rescued. She will remain so even after the death of Casaubon, for by ensuring that she will forfeit her considerable inheritance if she remarries, he goes on clutching her with the legal talons of his dead hand. Arguably, perhaps, Dorothea performs a heroic act of self-sacrifice by giving up her "position and fortune" to marry "an ardent public man" who wins election to Parliament with the aid of her "wifely help" (576).[12] But as the narrator observes at the end, Dorothea's wifehood stops far short of reenacting what has been earlier called the "epic life" of Theresa, the sixteenth-century Spanish saint whose "passionate, ideal nature" led her to "the reform of a religious order" (xiii). Supposedly, however, the fault is not in Dorothea but in her times. Whether a nineteenth-century Englishwoman strives to reenact the reforming zeal of St. Theresa or the "heroic piety" of Antigone, we are flatly informed that "the medium in which their ardent deeds took shape is for ever gone" (577).

But was it? As more than one commentator has lately noted, this crushingly negative view of what might be done by a woman in nineteenth-century England blinds itself to at least two examples of extraordinary achievement by women whom Eliot certainly knew. In 1852, many years before writing *Middlemarch*, she met Florence Nightingale, who had already become a nurse, who would shortly lead a team of volunteer nurses to treat men wounded in the Crimean War, and who in 1860 founded the first secular nursing school in the world at St. Thomas' Hospital in London.[13] A prolific writer herself (her collected works fill sixteen volumes), she called *Middlemarch* in print "a work of genius" but nonetheless decried its defeatism. Soon after reading it, she lamented, also in print, that Eliot could "find no better outlet for the heroine, . . . *because* she cannot be *St. Teresa* or an *Antigone*, than to marry an elderly sort of literary imposter and, quick after him, his relation, a baby sort of itinerant Cluricaune . . . or inferior Faun."[14] Instead of claiming, Nightingale writes, that the modern world gives women no space for heroic action, Eliot could have cited the example of Olivia Hill, who founded the Charity Organization Society and dramatically improved the lives of London's poor. Eliot must have known about Hill, says Nightingale, because the son of Eliot's common-law husband, George Lewes, married Olivia's sister Gertrude in 1864 (Nightingale 5:12–13). And besides Hill, Eliot could have cited the example of Nightingale herself.

Instead, she ends her novel on a note that once more confirms the domestication of heroism in nineteenth-century English literature. As the heroine of what Eliot calls the "home epic" of marriage (573), Dorothea becomes not only a wife but a mother, thereby fulfilling what Eliot is said to have considered "the highest form of duty of which most women were capable" (Flint 165). Dorothea diffuses her influence, we are told, in "unhistoric acts" (578) that presumably include the kind of thing she did for Rosamond when she came to call upon her after seeing her with Will.[15] And while we can only speculate that these "unheroic acts" included hostessing, we know that she is Will's hostess during their first important conversation in Rome. We also know that right after she promises him a dinner invitation, he does everything he can to discredit his host-to-be in the eyes of Dorothea by disingenuously regretting Casaubon's neglect of German scholarship in his research on mythology. In short, Will's heroic plan to rescue Dorothea from the talons of this dreary old dragon begins with a bloodless but "annihilating" act of treachery aimed at his host (144).[16]

This particular act of treachery exemplifies what hospitality becomes in much of nineteenth-century fiction: a prelude to mating, a threat to marriage, or—as we will see in the fiction of James and Hardy—a prelude to marital disaster.

HOSPITALITY, MATING, USURPATION: *PRIDE AND PREJUDICE*

In scholarship on English fiction, hospitality is nowhere more conspicuous by its absence than in studies of Jane Austen's *Pride and Prejudice* (1813), which might be considered the first major novel about hospitality and mating in nineteenth-century England. In the hundreds of books and articles on this novel that have appeared in the past seventy years, the salience of hospitality in its pages is a truth, so far as I can tell, universally ignored. But hiding in plain sight, the practice of hospitality raises questions from the start. In the very first chapter Mr. Bennet reveals that he has called upon Mr. Bingley, the wealthy bachelor who has just moved into their neighborhood, and has thereby opened the way for the Bennets to invite him to dinner and present their daughters to him. Though Bingley soon returns Mr. Bennet's visit by spending ten minutes with him in his library, he sees nothing of the daughters and then declines the Bennets' dinner invitation because he is off to London. Furthermore, though he promptly returns from London with his friend Darcy, his two sisters, and his brother-in-law, and though he spends nearly all of volume 1 in the Bennets' neighborhood, the Bennets never get around to having him to dinner before he decamps again.[17] Has anyone ever asked why?

A possible answer is that the Bennets need not whet or feed his appetite for their daughters because they can see him and his sisters at various other places. In chapter 6 we are told that Bingley's sisters "returned" a visit that "the ladies

of Longbourn"—surely including Elizabeth and Jane Bennet—have paid to
them at Netherfield (14); and we also learn that since dancing with Bingley at
the Meryton assembly, where he clearly showed a preference for her, and then
seeing him at his own house, Jane has "dined in company with him four times"
(16). But where? If they dined together at the Bennets' house, we would surely
have been told; if they dined together in other peoples' houses, that might help
to explain why the senior Bennets leave Bingley uninvited.

But why does Mrs. Bennet miss a perfect opportunity to invite him after Jane
and Elizabeth have spent nearly a week in his house? When a rainy-day horseback ride to Netherfield leaves Jane too sick to come back that night, Elizabeth
joins her there the next morning, and on the following morning Mrs. Bennet
arrives with her three younger daughters. Having no wish to see Jane recover
"immediately" (28), Mrs. Bennet wants her to stay at Netherfield as long as
possible—to maximize her chances with Bingley. So instead of leading off by
thanking Bingley for his hospitality, she tells him, after seeing Jane in her sick-
room, that Jane is "too ill to be moved," that "we must trespass a little longer on
your kindness," and also that she hopes he "will not think of quitting [Netherfield]
in a hurry" (28–29). Why does she not then fuel this hope by giving him one
more reason to stay—in the form of a renewed invitation to dinner? Though
she is said to be eventually "profuse" in acknowledging Bingley's kindness to
Jane (29) and later "repeat[s] her thanks" for it, "with an apology for troubling
him also with Lizzy" (31), she makes no move to reciprocate his hospitality. On
the contrary, she is delighted when her youngest, the irrepressible Lydia, tres-
passes on it even further by boldly insisting that Bingley keep his "promise" to
give the ball that he had merely "talked of giving" during the Meryton assembly
(31, 8). But why do the Bennets simply compound their social debts to Bingley
instead of trying to pay them off?

A simple answer—besides the variety of social gatherings just noted above—
is that Mrs. Bennet can think of nothing, for the moment, but of keeping both
Jane and Bingley at Netherfield as long as possible. But a deeper reason, I think,
springs from the fact that hospitality in this novel is more than usually bound
up with property, possession, and power. All three are conspicuously embodied
in Lady Catherine de Bourgh, who never condescends to be the guest of
anyone. Once upon a time, we learn, she paid Mr. Collins a visit in his "humble
parsonage" to oversee the alterations he was making and "even . . . to suggest
some herself" (45); and late in the novel she enters the Bennets' house just long
enough to complain about its park and its sitting room, "not very politely"
decline all offers of food, and then take Elizabeth into a "little wilderness"
outside so as to try to bully her into promising she will not marry Darcy (226).

Otherwise, Lady Catherine behaves as if nothing but abject homage could ever reciprocate her hospitality, which she proffers like coins to a lackey.

Lady Catherine turns hospitality into a kind of tyranny. Aided by the grandeur of her furnishings and the luxury of her "exceedingly handsome" dinner, she aims to intimidate as well as to dominate her guests. At her table one evening (along with Charlotte and Collins), Elizabeth finds that "nothing was beneath this great Lady's attention, which could furnish her with an occasion of dictating to others" (107) — or humiliating them. While interrogating Elizabeth at length about her family, the lady remarks, "Your father's estate is entailed on Mr. Collins" (107), meaning that Collins will inherit the estate from her father as his nearest male relative in the next generation. After thus reminding Elizabeth that she and her sisters will be disinherited, the overbearing hostess deplores the folly of their all having been raised without a governess, wonders that none of them learned to draw or play the piano and sing, and presses Elizabeth to give her age. In recompense for the luxurious dinner, then, Lady Catherine strives to discomfort her guests as much as possible.

But Elizabeth is no lackey. In refusing to be ruled by Lady Catherine, as when she declines to say how old she is or to practice the piano at the lady's house, Elizabeth not only anticipates her spirited response to Lady Catherine's later attempt to bully her; she also heightens by contrast the obsequious servility of Collins, who agrees "to everything her Ladyship [says]" (109), lavishly praises all she does, and tutors his own house guests in the art of subjecting themselves to her. Dress simply, he tells them, for Lady Catherine "likes to have distinction of rank preserved" (105). But Mr. Collins's servility toward Lady Catherine is matched by the self-importance with which he treats others, especially the Bennets. This is nowhere more evident than in his first letter to Mr. Bennet. Heedless of the old adage that guests and visitors stink in three days, Collins invites himself to "trespass on [their] hospitality" (43) for nearly two weeks.[18]

For all the absurdities of Collins's prose, Mr. Bennet's way of revealing this prospect to his family implicitly defines him as a usurper. On the very morning after Jane's return from her convalescence at Netherfield, when she and her mother might well have been planning to reciprocate Bingley's hospitality there, Mr. Bennet declares, with characteristic slyness, that he has "reason to expect an addition to our family party" — "a gentleman and a stranger" (41). Though Mrs. Bennet instantly infers that her husband has invited Bingley to dinner, she is wrong: instead of playing host to Bingley, they must submit themselves to someone whom none of them has seen but who radically destabilizes their right to Longbourn and hence the very basis of their hospitality. Collins not only displaces Bingley, the guest whom Mrs. Bennet has been eager to invite; he also preempts the privilege that virtually defines the host and hostess as such—that is, the privilege of deciding whom to invite, of choosing one's guests. In coming uninvited to stay with the Bennets, Collins prefigures what he will do when Mr. Bennet dies, which is—in Bennet's own words to his family—"turn you all out of this house as soon as he pleases" (42).

The brutality of this prospect belies both the cavalier tone in which Mr. Bennet mentions it and the conciliatory balm that seems to ooze from Collins's letter. In this letter—and in his whole approach to the Bennet family— I find more than a trace of the suitors in Homer's *Odyssey*. Like them, Collins invites himself, and when he speaks of his desire to make "every possible amends" for disinheriting the Bennet daughters (43), he intimates what he soon openly reveals: that he will seek to marry one of them. Courting a single young woman, of course, is not the same as courting the wife of a man who may still be alive, and inheriting property by entailment is not the same as simply taking it by force or raw presumption. But while Collins does not actively seek the death of his host, he anticipates it with at least as much ardor as he brings to the process of courtship. In the *Odyssey*, each of the suitors aims to marry the wife of a man whom they suppose to be dead and then vainly attempt to kill as soon as they discover him alive and among them. Though Collins threatens no one with violence (except for the wildly overstated "violence of [his] affection" for Elizabeth [72]), he is more menacing than he seems. In professing a wish to marry one of the Bennet daughters so as to save her from eventual destitution, he is comically masquerading as a knight in shining armor come to rescue a lady in distress. But behind his comic mask, he is a usurper: a suitor whose quest for a woman is inextricably bound up with his desire for her father's property, and hence, inevitably, her father's death. Consider how he proposes to Elizabeth: "The fact is, that being, as I am, to inherit the estate after the *death* of your honoured father, (who, however, *may live many years longer*,) I could not satisfy myself without resolving to chuse a wife from among his daughters, that the *loss* to them might be as little as possible, when the *melancholy event* takes place—which, however, as I have already said, *may not be for several years*" (72, emphasis added).

No suitor for a woman's hand could more ardently voice his longing for her father's property. In the space of a single long sentence expressing his intention to "chuse a wife from among [Mr. Bennet's] daughters," Collins first of all reminds Elizabeth that he is "to inherit the estate" and then refers *five times* to the prospect of her father's death, which gets tantalizingly closer even as he speaks; from "many years" it shrinks to "several years" at the end of the sentence. (Given the length of Collins's speeches, one might begin to wonder if

Mr. Bennet will survive even to the end of this one.) As much as—if not more than—Collins's pride in being patronized by Lady Catherine, the prospect of inheriting Longbourn gives him fantasies of power: a debased version of the power normally exercised by a host. Though he is a guest in the Bennet house, he talks to Elizabeth as if he already owned it, with favors to dispense or withhold. Having reminded her that she will inherit (when her mother dies) just "one thousand pounds in the 4 per cents" (72), a paltry income of forty pounds a year, he threatens her, when she declines him, with a spinsterhood of indigence. "Your portion is unhappily so small," he tells her, that not even her "manifold attractions" may gain her another proposal (73).

Collins's fantasies of power—his grossly overestimated valuation of what he has to offer as the heir to Longbourn and its future host—infect everything he does as both a suitor and a guest. On his arrival at the Bennets' house, he tells Mrs. Bennet that he has come "prepared to admire" her daughters, and he promptly proceeds to admire the whole house: "the hall, the dining room, and all its furniture" (44). Though he seems to behave like a polite guest, Mrs. Bennet can see through his flattery. "His commendation of every thing would have touched Mrs. Bennet's heart," we are told, "but for the mortifying supposition of his viewing it all as his own future property" (44–45). The irony is both manifest and latent. Given Collins's fascination with the prospect of Mr. Bennet's death, the word *mortifying* here fires more than just a figurative charge. Quite simply, Collins's designs on Longbourn entail the death of its present host. For all the would-be stupidity that makes her an object of ridicule to everyone around her, Mrs. Bennet nearly grasps this crucial point even before their self-invited guest arrives. Is she truly "beyond the reach of reason," as we are told, when she rails "against the cruelty of settling an estate away from a family of five daughters, in favour of a man whom nobody cared anything about" (42)? Such railing is irrational in the eyes of Jane and Elizabeth, who have tried in vain to educate her on "the nature of entail" (42). To them she must seem invincibly ignorant. But as Jean Fergusson Carr has shown, Mrs. Bennet enacts "the polemics of incomprehension" by daring to speak more radically and truthfully than Elizabeth can (Carr 74). Paradoxically, rage sharpens her powers of perception. While Mr. Bennet takes at face value the "peacemaking" overtures made by Collins's letter of self-invitation, Mrs. Bennet sees right through them. Even before hearing her husband read the would-be conciliatory letter aloud, she calls it hypocritical and adds, "I hate such false friends. Why could not he keep on quarrelling with you, as his father did before him?" (42). Mrs. Bennet clearly perceives that this son of her husband's old antagonist can never be their true friend or true "guest" (47). As a vulture circling the mortal body of her husband, a usurper waiting to seize their house from herself and her disinherited daughters, he can never be anything but a treacherous guest.

All this helps to explain, as suggested above, why the Bennets do not have Darcy or Bingley to dinner until late in the novel, when both men return to Netherfield after a full year spent away from it, mostly in London. So long as Collins occupies the Bennets' house he implicitly preempts their power of possession and their freedom to entertain any other guests. In volume 1, therefore, the Bennets never manage to reciprocate Bingley's hospitality to Jane; instead they trespass further on his hospitality by attending the ball he gives at Lydia's bold insistence. Once there, Mrs. Bennet proves herself a presumptuous guest. Since the Bennets, plus Collins, are personally invited by Bingley himself, who calls on them for this purpose rather than merely sending "a ceremonious card" (58–59), Mrs. Bennet presumes that the ball is given in honor of Jane and likewise that Jane will soon be mistress of Netherfield Hall. To Elizabeth's acute embarrassment, her mother talks of nothing else to Lady Lucas during supper at the ball, prating "freely, openly" — for all to hear, including Darcy, who sits opposite them — "of her expectation that Jane would soon be married to Mr. Bingley" (67). As Carr notes, Mrs. Bennet embarrasses Elizabeth by saying "openly" just what Elizabeth herself has been thinking: that Jane would soon be happily "settled in that very house" as Bingley's wife (67, Carr 75). Together with Collins's presumption in fawningly presenting himself to Darcy as an emissary of his aunt, Lady Catherine, Mrs. Bennet's presumption gives Darcy and Bingley's two sisters "an opportunity of ridiculing [Elizabeth's] relations," as she ruefully reflects (69). But to make matters worse, Mrs. Bennet is a lingering guest. Having earlier contrived to prolong Jane's stay at Netherfield by sending her off on horseback to catch cold in the rain, she now schemes to delay their carriages by "a quarter of an hour after every body else was gone, which gave them time to see how heartily they were wished away by some of the family" — namely, Bingley's sisters, who "were evidently impatient to have the house to themselves" (69).

Though she fails to realize this impatience, Mrs. Bennet nonetheless ends their visit in a manner surprisingly polite. For the first time she tries to reciprocate Bingley's hospitality by voicing "the hope of seeing the whole family soon at Longbourn" and urging Bingley in particular to eat "a family dinner with them at any time, without the ceremony of a formal invitation" (70). This informal invitation may be read, I think, in two ways. On the one hand, Bingley himself construes it as a gesture of genuine friendliness that he accepts with "grateful pleasure" and with a promise to join the Bennets for a meal as soon as possible after his return from a short trip to London (70). On the other hand, "a family dinner" is an ordinary meal. To ask him to such a dinner "at any time" is to presume that he deserves no special attention because he is already one of the family, all but married to Jane. This is precisely what Mrs. Bennet thinks as she leaves the house and foresees "her daughter settled at Netherfield in the course of three or four months" (70).

Bingley's failure to come back quickly from London and turn up for a family meal is due, we later learn, to the influence of Darcy, who persuades him to stay away from Netherfield, and especially from Jane and her family, for a full year. But in what might be called the moral universe of the novel, Bingley's long absence from Netherfield and from the Bennets' family table might also be seen as punishment for the presumption Mrs. Bennet displays, and even flaunts, as Bingley's guest. If so, the punishment has its effect. Though Mrs. Bennet learns far less than either Elizabeth or Darcy does in the course of the novel, she learns at least enough to issue a special invitation in volume 3. When Bingley and Darcy pay a call on the Bennets three days after their return to Netherfield, she invites them both to a "large" dinner party on the following Tuesday (217): not an ordinary meal but a special event that proves the prelude, this time, to a marriage proposal for Jane. With Collins out of sight and his designs on Longbourn out of mind, Mr. and Mrs. Bennet can freely exercise the prerogatives of host and hostess, inviting whomever they wish to dine with their daughters and thereby presenting them to eligible men.

Equally noteworthy is Darcy's hospitality. After offending Elizabeth with a condescending proposal of marriage, one of the most important ways in which he shows himself "properly humbled" (237) is by proving to be a supremely considerate host. This is not at all what Elizabeth expects. When she and her uncle and aunt turn up as tourists at Darcy's ancestral estate, the artful elegance of its house and grounds makes her suddenly feel that "to be mistress of Pemberley might be something!" (156). But she saves herself "from something like regret" for her rejection of Darcy by reminding herself that even as mistress of Pemberley she would be denied the proprietary freedom of a hostess: since her uncle was not of the landed gentry, merely a businessman, she would "not have been allowed to invite" him and her aunt (157). For part of this train of thought, Austen surely drew on her own experience as the recipient (at the age of twenty-seven) of a proposal from Harris Bigg-Wither, the hopelessly doltish young owner of an almost irresistibly magnificent estate. Presumably feeling that it might indeed be something to be mistress of such a place, Austen let this prospect override her aversion to its owner, accepted his proposal, and then— after a sleepless night—turned it down. On reflection, obviously, she saw no hope that her suitor would ever be anything but a dolt.

But unlike Austen herself, who never found wealth leavened with graciousness and wit in the real suitors of her own experience, Elizabeth finds all three in Darcy, who also gives her the supreme pleasure of reforming him before they are married—perhaps the most improbable feature of this whole novel. Its ending is the quintessential stuff of romance. Having learned how to gild all his other assets with a sensitivity elicited by Elizabeth herself, Darcy furnishes this novel of would-be social realism with a hero fit to meet, if not surpass, every young woman's fantasy: a witty, charming, handsome, sensitive man with a London house, a country estate, and an income of ten thousand pounds a year.[19]

To show Elizabeth what her rejection of his proposal has taught him, Darcy does many things. Most dramatically, he salvages the reputation of the Bennet family by negotiating and funding the marriage of Wickham to Lydia, and it is precisely by thanking him for doing so that Elizabeth emboldens him to make his second proposal. But in no small part, the change in Elizabeth's view of Darcy springs from his hospitality. Speaking to Elizabeth during a party given at the Philipses in volume 1, even Wickham admits that Darcy's pride, which Elizabeth calls "abominable," has "often led him to be liberal and generous,—to give his money freely, to display hospitality, to assist his tenants, and relieve the poor" (55).

When Elizabeth comes to tour Pemberley with her aunt and uncle (on the assumption that Darcy himself is away), she finds fresh evidence that Darcy practices what I have earlier identified as Christian hospitality. Following, says the housekeeper, the example of his father, Darcy "will be . . . just as affable to the poor" (158). A little later, just after Elizabeth and her relatives, the Gardiners, unexpectedly catch sight of Darcy on the grounds of the estate, he politely asks her to introduce him to them; then, "with the greatest civility," he urges Mr. Gardiner "to fish there as often as he chose," offers him fishing tackle, and shows him the best places to fish (163). The morning after, he delivers a personal invitation. Coming with his sister Georgiana to the inn where Elizabeth is staying with her aunt and uncle, he asks all three of them to dinner at Pemberley on "the day after the next" (168).

This genuinely hospitable treatment of Elizabeth and her relatives surely constitutes part of the change in Darcy that touches her more deeply than anything else she has learned about him since rejecting his first proposal. Feeling "not only astonishment but gratitude," she sees that Darcy's reformation can spring only from his "ardent love" for her (169), which later prompts him to arrange the marriage of Lydia and Wickham. Only after that, when Bingley returns to Netherfield after a full year away from it and when both men call on the Bennets, does Mrs. Bennet ask them both to dine at Longbourn, and for the first time in the novel they both come.[20] Then, after a day of shooting with Mr. Bennet and one more dinner with the family, Bingley at last makes his proposal.

As a further effect of the Bennets' hospitality, Darcy's second proposal to Elizabeth might easily have come right after Jane accepts Bingley's. But not until Elizabeth thwarts Lady Catherine's attempt to intimidate her does she truly open the way for Darcy's move. In an obvious sense, Elizabeth's refusal to promise Lady Catherine that she will never become engaged to Darcy sends him—via Lady Catherine herself—a clear signal of her availability; as he later tells her, it taught him "to hope" (235). But in parrying the rudeness of a guest whose tyranny as a hostess she has already withstood, Elizabeth also reasserts the power of her family on its own ground: its power to choose its own guests and entertain them as it wishes. Lady Catherine threatens to undermine this power. Arriving without invitation or any prior notice (which even Collins had sent), deprecating the house and its grounds, spurning all refreshment, and interrogating Elizabeth outside the house, she does all she can to trash the Bennets' hospitality. Further, just as Collins threatens to usurp the Bennets' house by seizing it from their daughters, Lady Catherine threatens to usurp Elizabeth's power to choose a mate or even to receive Darcy as a guest. In her right to choose a husband, then, Elizabeth also reclaims the family's right to hold their house and entertain whomever they wish.

From beginning to end *Pride and Prejudice* turns on hospitality. To present their daughters to Bingley and Darcy, the Bennets must be able to entertain them. Yet instead of doing so, they are forced to entertain a guest who not only invites himself to their house but also reminds them at every turn that he is destined to possess it as soon as Mr. Bennet dies. Here and elsewhere hospitality tests and manifests character. While Lady Catherine's way of treating both her guests and her hosts is tyrannical, overbearing, and rude, Darcy's reception of Elizabeth's uncle and aunt prove him an impressively considerate host, and along with the housekeeper's commendation of his distinctively Christian hospitality, his way of hosting plays a crucial part in overcoming Elizabeth's resistance to him. Finally, together with Elizabeth's way of holding her ground against an intimidating guest, the Bennets' entertainment of Darcy and Bingley shows them to be in full possession of their own house, however finite that possession may be. And this long-awaited exercise of hospitality sets the stage for the marriage proposals that conclude the novel.

MONSTROUS INHOSPITALITY: *FRANKENSTEIN* AND *WUTHERING HEIGHTS*

Published in January 1818, Mary Shelley's *Frankenstein* appeared just five years after *Pride and Prejudice* but seems in every sense a world apart from it.

Unlike Austen's novel, which confines itself to the gentry of rural England, *Frankenstein* roams from Geneva and the Alps to the Scottish Hebrides and the Arctic. More important, its central figure is a creature so repulsive to everyone he meets that he can find a welcome nowhere—not even from his maker, Victor Frankenstein. Yet these radically different books have one thing in common. Like the vast majority of nineteenth-century novels, they both involve the quest for a mate. While *Frankenstein* is finally driven by Victor's quest for revenge against the creature, all of the creature's crimes against Victor—killing his little brother William and framing Justine Moritz for the murder, killing Victor's friend Henry and then Victor's bride on their wedding night—spring from the frustration of his desire for a mate. And Victor's thwarting of this desire is prefigured by his first act of inhospitality: abandoning his own creature just as soon as it comes to life.

To compare this act with what Mr. and Mrs. Bennet do in the first chapters of *Pride and Prejudice* is to see that hospitality plays a crucial role in the mating process. For all the comedy of their miscommunication, the senior Bennets both assume they are responsible for introducing their daughters to eligible men. In promptly meeting this responsibility by inviting Bingley to dinner, they show what hospitality can do. Conversely, Victor Frankenstein abdicates all responsibility to his creature by treating him with flagrant inhospitality. Having first run away just as soon as the creature comes to life in his laboratory one night, and then again when the creature comes to his bedroom, Victor rejoices the next morning to find his apartment empty and his bedroom "freed from its hideous *guest*" (60, emphasis added). In thus designating the result of his animating project, whom he also calls "creature" and "monster" (56–59), Victor implicitly contrasts him with Henry Clerval, the old friend who comes to visit him on the very morning after he rejects the creature and whom he is delighted to welcome as a guest. Victor's attitude toward the creature, therefore, is doubly ironic. In refusing to recognize the creature as in any sense his son, ward, or protégé, he reconceives him as a guest, a "hideous guest," as if he were an intruder, an uninvited guest.[21] So far from assuming any responsibility to care for him or find him a mate, Victor defaults on both obligations—first by twice running away from him, then by destroying the mate he had reluctantly promised him.

After the creature's story makes Victor see that he owes him "all the portion of happiness that it [is] in my power to bestow" (141), he agrees to produce a female just as hideous as the male, on condition that they will both abandon Europe forever. But when the creature comes to visit him one night in the remote Orkney Islands, where Victor has set up his laboratory, he drives away the visitor by tearing to pieces his work in progress, destroying "the [female] creature on whose future existence [the male] depended for happiness" (161). Victor feels perfectly justified in aborting the birth of a woman who "might become ten thousand times more malignant than her mate" and might engender "a race of devils" capable of terrorizing "the whole human race" (160–61). In light of this fearful prospect, he sees in the moonlit face at his laboratory window a look of "utmost . . . malice and treachery" (161). In actuality, however, the "ghastly grin" that "wrinkle[s] [the creature's] lips as he gaze[s]" on Victor (161) may actually have been no more ghastly or malicious than the grin that "wrinkled his cheeks" when he first came to Victor's bedroom in Geneva (57). The first grin suggests an infant eager to be loved; the second could be that of a guest expecting a friendly reception, and in this case the imminent gratification of his most pressing need. But to Victor, who has always found the creature horrible to look at, any grin would appear ghastly and hence malicious and treacherous as well.[22]

Once we detach ourselves from Victor's viewpoint, however, we can see that treachery, if not malice as well, is precisely what drives his response to the creature's visit, his willful destruction of what he had promised to make for a creature whose future happiness, he knew, depended on a mate. What Victor sees in the creature must be measured against the creature's own words. When the creature comes to Victor's isolated cottage, he belies what Victor has just said about him. Though enraged by what Victor has done, he sounds neither malicious nor treacherous but simply desperate for hospitality, aching to be welcomed with the only kind of gift that can satisfy his deepest need: "Shall each man," he cries to Victor, "find a wife for his bosom, and each beast have his mate, and I be alone? I had feelings of affection, and they were requited by detestation and scorn" (162). Only after Victor absolutely refuses to keep his promise does the creature vow revenge, which will take the form of yet another visit: "I shall be with you," he tells Victor, "on your wedding-night" (163).

In making this promise, the creature may remind us of two other wedding crashers: Keats's Apollonius and Coleridge's mariner. As an uninvited guest who is relentlessly hostile to all dreams, Apollonius claims to discern the serpentine core of Lamia at her own wedding feast, making her vanish and in turn draining her new husband of life. The mariner, with whom the Arctic-exploring Walton compares himself in the frame-narrative of *Frankenstein* (19), does not actually attend a wedding, but like the creature, he has known an agonizing loneliness, and it leads him to interfere with a wedding by detaining one of its guests. Paradoxically, the mariner alleviates his loneliness in a way that accentuates it, for as a celebration of love and hospitality the wedding of the "Rime" epitomizes everything from which the mariner, like the creature, feels excluded. But the creature never finds a truly sympathetic auditor. Unlike Coleridge's wedding guest, who is irrevocably "stunned" by the mariner's tale, Victor is "moved" by the creature's tale (141) only long enough to promise what in the end he fails to deliver. So the creature takes his revenge by strangling Victor's bride on their wedding night bed (now a "bridal bier" [189]), making Victor taste the desolation that the creature has known throughout his life.[23]

What turns this desolation into rage, what prompts the creature to declare "ever-lasting war" against all humankind (132), is precisely the monstrous inhospitality of the family whose domestic affections are so often contrasted with Victor's egotism.[24] After he is attacked by a crowd of villagers—his first painful experience of the "barbarity of man" (103)—the creature takes refuge in a hovel attached to a cottage. Since the French family living in the cottage show great kindness to each other and to their Arabian visitor Safie, they lead the creature to hope they will hospitably receive him too. In addition, they are predisposed to sympathize with any victim of treachery or exile because they have experienced both.[25] Though the creature learns all this while secretly observing the family from spring through autumn, he knows that his "unnatural hideousness" repels anyone who looks at him (128), so he decides to seek hospitality from the old blind father when his sighted children are off on a walk. Admitted to the cottage and its warming fire by this "kind host" (129), as the creature calls him, he tells the blind man that he seeks the protection of a family whom he "tenderly love[s]" but whose eyes are so clouded by a "fatal prejudice" that "where they ought to see a feeling and kind friend, they behold only a detestable monster" (130). Though the old man humanely offers to help him overcome this prejudice, the creature sobbingly collapses in fear of being yet again rejected. Hearing the steps of the returning children, however, he seizes the old man's hand (the hand of achingly desired welcome as well as protection), tells him that he and his family are "the friends whom [he] seek[s]," and begs him—clutching the old man's knees—to "save and protect" him (131). But the old man cannot do so. Once his children, Felix and Agatha, return with Safie to view him with indescribable "horror and consternation" (131), Felix tears him away from his father, dashes him to the ground, strikes him with a stick, and drives him away. Compounded by treachery, their monstrous inhospitality reenacts what Victor has already done to him and will do again.

In contrast to *Frankenstein*, Emily Brontë's *Wuthering Heights* features an outcast who is given nearly all that Victor's creature is denied. Unlike the creature, who is rejected by his creator, Heathcliff is adopted in early childhood by a man who finds him "starving, and houseless" in the streets of Liverpool (29), carries him back to his Yorkshire home, and treats him with special favor above his two children. Nevertheless, Heathcliff is an alien in this family. Nelly Dean first refers to him as simply "it" (29), and even his adoptive father, old Mr. Earnshaw, calls him a dark and diabolic thing, "as dark almost as if it came from the devil" (28). Since *Wuthering Heights* appeared in 1847, just two years after the Great Famine struck Ireland, Terry Eagleton has plausibly argued that Heathcliff might well have come from that "rebarbative world" (9), that he might have been one of the estimated three hundred thousand destitute Irish people who had landed in Liverpool by June 1847 (Eagleton 3).[26] Whether or not he was, Heathcliff *looks* to the putatively civilized world around him much the way Frankenstein's creature appears to everyone he meets. As Eagleton notes, Heathcliff is variously called "beast, savage, lunatic, and demon" (Eagleton 3). Nelly Dean does what she can to instill confidence in the growing boy (she once calls him "fit for a prince in disguise," 44), but when the grown Heathcliff foams "like a mad dog" at the dying Catherine, Nelly "[does] not feel as if [she] were in the company of a creature of [her] own species" (124). Even Catherine Earnshaw, who loves Heathcliff passionately, calls him an "unreclaimed creature, without refinement, without cultivation" (79). Isabella Linton goes further. Using exactly the term that Victor Frankenstein typically flings at his creature, she calls Heathcliff "Monster!" and wishes "he could be blotted out of creation, and out of [her] memory!" (133). Eagleton sums him up neatly. From his first appearance, he writes, "it is clear that this little Caliban has a nature on which nurture will never stick" (Eagleton 3).

Yet it is equally evident that Heathcliff has something forever denied to Victor's creature: the capacity to make women love him, or at least want him so much that they fight over him. When Catherine calls Heathcliff an "unreclaimed creature," she does so only in order to dissuade Isabella from trying to win his love, thereby revealing that even though Catherine is now married to Edgar Linton, she wants "no one . . . but [herself]" to be loved by Heathcliff (79). Furthermore, even though Isabella learns to see Heathcliff as a monster, she falls in love with him first, and even though he detests her, he marries her for the sake of what she may inherit.[27] Then, after she dies, Heathcliff uses the child of their union to lure young Cathy Linton into a marriage made to serve him, for it ultimately gives him the means of controlling all the property she inherits when her father dies, including Thrushcross Grange. Through property Heathcliff gains power. After three years of absence, perhaps spent "in the army," his "ferocity" grows "half-civilized," according to Nelly, "and his manner [is] even dignified, quite divested of roughness, though too stern for grace" (74). Having learned how to be cunning as well as halfway civil, Heathcliff acquires not only Thrushcross

Grange but also Wuthering Heights from Hindley Earnshaw, its feckless heir. It is as the owner of both properties that we first see him through the eyes of Lockwood, who is both his tenant at the Grange and his guest at the Heights.

In the first three chapters of the novel, then, Lockwood's visit to Wuthering Heights replays as comedy the explosive visits paid to Thrushcross Grange by the newly returned Heathcliff. Though we learn of the latter only in chapters 10–12, when Nelly tells Lockwood about them, Heathcliff's visits to the Grange occurred well before Lockwood's visit to the Heights, and the earlier visits illustrate what can happen when a married woman entertains her former lover in the presence of her husband.

Behind Heathcliff's first visit to the married Catherine stands the boyhood memory of his first meeting with Edgar, when the pampered, prissy boy comes to the Heights for Christmas dinner with his sister and mother. Just after Hindley decrees that Heathcliff must be banished to his garret for the duration of dinner lest he seize the tarts and steal the fruit, Edgar's sneering at the length of Heathcliff's locks — "like a colt's mane over his eyes!" (45) — goads Heathcliff into violent retaliation. After thrusting a tureen of hot applesauce into Edgar's face and neck, he is taken to his garret and beaten by Hindley, leaving him not only determined to "pay Hindley back" (47) but also, it is clear, lastingly resentful of Edgar.

When the grown-up, "half-civilized" Heathcliff comes to visit Catherine at Thrushcross Grange, this class-based animosity is revived by the question of just where their guest should be received. Though Edgar suggests that the kitchen would be "more suitable" for Heathcliff than the parlor, Catherine tells Nelly to set two tables in the parlor: one for Edgar and Isabella, "being gentry," and the other for Heathcliff and herself, "being of the lower orders" (74). Catherine mocks Edgar. Having defined both herself and her guest as lowly kindred spirits to be separated — but not banished — from Edgar and Isabella, she comically subverts her own insistence that Edgar and Heathcliff "must be friends" by seizing "Linton's reluctant fingers and crush[ing] them into [Heathcliff's]" (73–74). This mild collision of host and guest may prefigure the moment at which Edgar strikes Heathcliff in the throat. But for all the brutality of his impulses, Heathcliff, who sneeringly calls Edgar a "lamb" of cowardice "not worth knocking down" (89), is actually *less* violent than Edgar, whom he does not touch. Instead, during frequent visits to the Grange he discomforts both his host and hostess by courting Isabella, making Edgar fear both "the degradation of an alliance with a nameless man" and the possibility "that his property, in default of heirs male, might pass into such a one's power" (78). This is the real danger. In spite of his threats and his occasional violence (such as trampling

Hindley at one point), Heathcliff takes his revenge not by killing his enemies but by outsmarting them. Soon after being made to leave the Grange by servants armed with bludgeons, he elopes with Isabella, and as Edgar ruefully foresees, this will eventually enable him to gain Edgar's property.

Given this outcome, which has already occurred when the novel begins, Heathcliff plays two contradictory roles in the opening chapters: first as the landlord and therefore host of both Wuthering Heights and Thrushcross Grange; then as a destitute, helpless, alien *thing* at the mercy of his hosts, his adoptive family. Though the role of the mistreated child is many years behind him, and though much of the novel is taken up with Nelly's story of how he moved from one role to the other, Heathcliff never forgets what he has endured as a guest at both the Heights and the Grange. As a host he uses his power to avenge himself, directly or indirectly, on everyone who has humiliated him. In the order of the narrative, then, his first victim is a guest whose only crime is to belong to a class that Heathcliff identifies with his oppressors and enemies, especially Edgar Linton: the educated upper class.

Lockwood exemplifies this class. As a well-meaning but clueless representative of it, he is baffled by Heathcliff's style of entertaining, which parodies conventional hospitality in something like the way it is parodied in the *Odyssey* by Polyphemos's reception of Odysseus and his men. Odysseus enrages Polyphemos by presuming to enter his cave and partake of his cheeses during his absence. Though Heathcliff surely knows that eating a new tenant would put a crimp in his rental income, Lockwood's assumption that he should pay a courtesy call on his new landlord runs head on into a startling combination of hospitality and something like cannibalistic brutality. On one hand, Heathcliff utters his "Walk in" through gritted teeth and in a cursing tone (3); on the other, he orders a servant to take Lockwood's horse and bring some wine, and to Lockwood's eyes he seems "in dress and manners a gentleman" (5). But when Lockwood sits down on the hearthstone and tries to caress "a huge, liver-coloured bitch pointer," this "canine mother" of squealing puppies—the only mother of any kind to be found in the house—bares its teeth like a wolf bent on taking a bite of his leg, and Lockwood soon finds himself assaulted by "half-a-dozen four-footed fiends" until a servant intervenes to disperse them. Heathcliff then ventures to be slightly congenial. Though he makes no apology for dogs who "do right to be vigilant" and curtly asks only if Lockwood has been bitten, he urges his guest to "take a little wine" and frankly admits that "guests are so exceedingly rare in this house that [he] and [his] dogs . . . hardly know how to receive them" (7). Relaxing a little, in fact, he talks well enough that Lockwood feels moved to propose coming again the next day.

In this sequence of visits it is ironic that Lockwood, the presumed embodiment of conventionally civilized behavior, invites himself twice in a row to the house of his landlord. But larger ironies spring from the collision between what Lockwood expects on his return to the Heights and what he finds there. With Heathcliff out and no one answering his vain knocks on the door as snow begins falling ("churlish inhospitality" [7], he calls it), a coatless young man who appears in the yard eventually leads him around into the "cheerful apartment" where he had previously met Heathcliff and where he now finds a slender, lovely young blonde who will turn out to be the daughter of Heathcliff's dead Catherine but whom he takes to be "Mrs. Heathcliff," wife of his absent host.

Yet even before he can learn his mistake, this "amiable hostess," as he archly calls her, plunges him into further confusion. First she tells him he "should not have come out." Then, while reaching for the tea canisters on the mantelpiece, she asks him twice if he has been invited to tea. When he answers, "No, . . . You are the proper person to ask me" (9), he not only presumes she is his hostess but also implies she has neglected her social duty. In response, she flings the tea back in the canister and resumes her chair, destabilizing her guest. Unlike a familialized guest, a visitor apprised of the family structure that incorporates him or her, Lockwood is made to feel like a bewildered intruder, and when Heathcliff enters the room he compounds his guest's bewilderment. The young woman Lockwood euphemistically takes to be Heathcliff's "amiable lady" turns out to be not his wife, for if that woman survives at all, it is only as the "ministering angel" of Wuthering Heights (10).

When Heathcliff uses this phrase he is clearly thinking not of Isabella but of his long gone soul-wife Catherine. Later on, as Lockwood sleeps and dreams in Catherine's childhood bed after "get[ting] in" (8), which he vowed to do while knocking on the door of the Heights, the branch of a fir tree knocks on his window, and the ghost of Catherine sobbingly demands, "Let me in!" (20). In echoing Lockwood's words, she accentuates a startling reversal. Usurped in her own bed by an overnight guest/intruder who has invited himself to the house, the woman who might have been Heathcliff's living wife and hostess of his house becomes instead a ghostly outsider brutally denied admission when the dreaming Lockwood breaks the window, seizes her wrist, rubs it against the broken pane until it bleeds, and shouts, "Begone! . . . I'll never let you in" (20). Like Edgar Linton, who strikes the throat of his guest, the dreaming Lockwood abandons conventional civility when faced with a visitor who demands absolute hospitality, unconditional acceptance.

Lockwood here acts blindly. While casting himself in the dream as part of the household, a would-be host with the power to admit or exclude outsiders, he displays again the kind of ignorance he brings to everyone he meets at the Heights, starting with Cathy II. Finding that this young woman is not the wife of his host, he promptly concludes that she must be married to the shabbily dressed, rudely spoken young man, and just as promptly casts himself as her would-be savior. But unlike other guests bent on captivating their married hostesses, unlike (for instance) Paris in the house of Menelaus and Heathcliff himself in the Linton household, Lockwood vows not to tempt her, as if she could be tempted by a man who has so far roused only her *con*tempt. Judging himself much more attractive than the "boor" she has "thrown herself away upon," he tells himself, "I must beware how I cause her to regret her choice" (11). But Lockwood is wrong on three points. The young woman has no interest in him; she is not married to the boor; and this would-be lout identifies himself as Hareton Earnshaw, the name inscribed over the door of the house, which would normally signify his possession of it or at least the status of heir and host-to-be. No wonder Lockwood begins "to feel unmistakably out of place in that pleasant family circle" (11).

His sense of dislocation is intensified when a snowstorm compels him to spend the night in this circle. Since Heathcliff still considers his guest "a stranger" who cannot be trusted with "the range of the place while [Heathcliff] is off guard" (13), Heathcliff says that Lockwood must sleep with Hareton or the servant Joseph, as if that would not endanger one of them. When Lockwood decides to brave the storm instead and takes a lantern for the purpose, Joseph sends two "hairy monsters" flying at his throat, and though he ends up with no more than a nosebleed, they give him—to the mingled guffaws of Heathcliff and Hareton (14)—a fresh taste of Polyphemic hospitality. Humiliating as this episode is, Lockwood is still more discomforted by what the housekeeper offers him: a deceptively cozy bed set into the windowed closet of an upstairs room. When the ghost of its previous occupant leads him to cruelty and then a frenzied yelling that awakens his host in the middle of the night, Heathcliff is appalled to find Lockwood—"only your guest, sir" (21)—in a room that he had ordered never to be used. He is also enraged to think that Lockwood has actually communicated with the ghost of Catherine, whom Lockwood dares to call a "little fiend" (21).

Brontë thus interweaves guest and ghost, something we can trace all the way back to Homer's *Odyssey* and the ghost of the returning hero, a living revenant.[28] Long thought dead by the suitors, Odysseus returns as a beggar after twenty years, exactly the length of Catherine's ghostly wandering: "It's twenty years," she moans; "I've been a waif for twenty years!" (20). Just as the returning Odysseus is abused by the presumptuous suitors, the ghost of Catherine is brutally rejected by one who arrogates to himself the power of a host and who has no idea that this would-be intruder—this uninvited, unwanted guest—is the rightful possessor of the very bed he sleeps in. But Lockwood mistreats Catherine only in his dream, and her ghost can hardly take Odyssean vengeance on him. So he is merely ejected from Catherine's room and made to spend the rest of the night in the kitchen while Heathcliff lies down on Catherine's bed, throws open the window, and vainly begs the ghost to become a guest: "'Come in! come in!' he sobbed. 'Oh, do—*once* more! Oh! my heart's darling, hear me *this* time—Catherine, at last!'" (23).

This desperate appeal is richly ironic. Besides revealing the latent tenderness of a man who has up to now seemed an overbearing brute, its tone is radically contradicted by what Heathcliff says immediately afterward to Catherine's living daughter Cathy, whom he damns for worthlessly living "on my charity" (24): a permanent, permanently resented house guest. In yet another reversal, Heathcliff treats the departing Lockwood with hospitable civility by escorting him through the new-fallen snow from Wuthering Heights to the gate of Thrushcross Park. But Heathcliff's scowling at Cathy exemplifies the spirit in which he treats everyone *but* the ghost of Catherine. For him, Cathy is only the means by which he gained possession of two properties and thus avenged himself on the heirs of those who, except for old Mr. Earnshaw, would never cherish or respect him as a guest in either house.

The whole story of Cathy's involvement with Heathcliff's son Linton, which comes out late in the novel, parodically reenacts Heathcliff's desperate invitation to the ghost of Catherine: "Come in! Come in!" By luring Cathy into visiting Linton at Wuthering Heights, where her father most emphatically does not want her to go, Heathcliff proves himself a master of entrapment. Like Polyphemos, whose first act as a would-be host is to close the mouth of his cave with a gigantic boulder, he imprisons his guest as soon as she enters his house, which she does after a series of carefully staged meetings with Linton. He thus inveigles her into visiting this quivering vessel of self-absorption, who has been turned by Heathcliff into an agent of psychic extortion: "You must come, to cure me" (184), he says at one point, begging her to visit him again. When they meet at a predetermined spot on the heath near Wuthering Heights, Linton tells Cathy that his very life is in her hands, that he will be killed unless she consents—to what he does not say. By the time she learns, she and Nelly have both crossed "the threshold" of Wuthering Heights (204). As soon as they have done so "of their own accord," as Heathcliff later claims, he announces that he has "a mind to be hospitable today" (205), but before offering them tea he shuts the door and locks them in, imprisoning his guests.

As prisoners, they become his property, or rather his means to property. Free to drop all pretense of courtesy, Heathcliff tells Nelly he hates both Cathy and

Linton, slaps Cathy's head repeatedly when she tries to wrest the key from his hand, and—in spite of her desperate longing to return to her dying father—tells her she must marry Linton "or remain a prisoner" (209). Keeping her long enough to see them married, he ensures that the property of the dying Edgar Linton will pass to Heathcliff's son, Edgar's nephew and only male heir, whose death will shortly leave Heathcliff himself with all of Edgar's property. He will even get "Catherine's fortune" (214), which the dying Edgar fails to protect from his enemy's hands, and Cathy herself becomes Heathcliff's property after Edgar dies. In a brazen act of usurpation, he removes her from Thrushcross Grange so that he can fill it with a tenant and take her to Wuthering Heights as his servant. Having stripped her of her fortune, he insists that she earn her keep at Wuthering Heights.

In narrating all this to Lockwood, the tenant of Thrushcross Grange, Nelly Dean makes him an unwitting accomplice in Heathcliff's designs. It was to make room for Lockwood's tenancy that Heathcliff drove Cathy from her birthplace to become a parody of a house guest: a servant trapped at Wuthering Heights. Lockwood thereby takes his place among Cathy's adversaries. Having driven the ghost of Catherine from her own childhood bed, he is made to know that he has unwittingly usurped the house of her living daughter.

Yet the monstrosity of Heathcliff's hospitality exhausts itself shortly before he dies. Unlike Frankenstein's creature, whose quest for revenge drives him to kill everyone linked to his maker, Heathcliff cannot endlessly punish the children of those who once tormented him, much less kill them. On the contrary, though he hates Hareton as the child of Hindley and detests Cathy as the child of Edgar Linton, he cannot deny the family resemblance that links each of them to Catherine Earnshaw as, respectively, her nephew and her daughter. The moment he sees that their eyes resemble Catherine's, that Hareton looks "startling[ly]" like her, and that the face of love Hareton presents to Cathy is "the ghost of [Heathcliff's] immortal love" for her mother (245), he gives up his quest to destroy the two houses they would otherwise inherit. Sole possessor of those two houses, Heathcliff sees in Hareton the ghost of his youthful self, but also foresees the ghost he will become when at last this brutally abused and still more brutally abusive guest of the Earnshaws finally departs, leaving both his houses to their heirs and hosts.

TREACHEROUS LOVER, TREACHEROUS GUEST: PUSHKIN'S *EUGENE ONEGIN*

In 1825, midway between the first and third editions of *Frankenstein* and just one year after the final cantos of *Don Juan* appeared, a young Russian poet named Alexander Pushkin started writing what he called "a novel in verse in the manner of Byron's *Don Juan*" (qtd. Arndt xv). Boxed up not in Byron's ottava rima but in intricately rhymed fourteen-line stanzas, *Eugene Onegin* came from the hand of a sophisticated, polylingual aristocrat who not only admired Byron's poetry and thought *Don Juan* "a wonder" but whose long, exotic narrative poems, combined with his high-living style and his insatiable womanizing, had already made him the Byron of Russia. Though his protagonist looks more like Mozart's licentious don than Byron's *naif*, Byron's influence permeates Pushkin's novel about an aloof, disenchanted, precocious eighteen-year-old playboy who moves from St. Petersburg to the country, carelessly nets the heart of a lovely young woman named Tatyana, coldly rejects her overtures, kills a friend in a duel, wanders the world in remorse, and discovers too late that he loves her. Pushkin repeatedly likens this jaded wanderer to Byron's Harold (1.38, 4.44, 7.24); Byron's portrait hangs on the wall of Eugene's house (7.19); and *Don Juan* is one of his favorite books (7.22).[29]

But Pushkin sometimes makes Byron his foil. Lest the "mocking reader" claim that Pushkin's narrator takes his cue from the autobiographical core of *Childe Harold*, "that, like proud Byron, I have penned / A mere self-portrait in the end" (F 1.56), the narrator insists that "Eugene and I are souls apart" (A 1.56).[30] In the very first chapter they are literally separated by the narrator's confinement to the cultural wasteland of south Russia. Far from St. Petersburg, where Eugene has been the quintessential man about town, as well as from the country manor he has just inherited from his uncle, Pushkin's narrator plaintively cries, "When strikes my liberation's hour?" (A 1.50). Here he speaks for the poet himself in exile. Like Byron, Pushkin fervently supported liberalism and detested reactionary regimes, more precisely, czarism. Unlike Byron, who freely chose to leave England for good in 1816 and spend the rest of his life in Europe, Pushkin was confined to south Russia in the early 1820s because of writings that Emperor Alexander I considered seditious. In May 1823 he started work on *Eugene Onegin* and continued after returning to Moscow in 1826, when he was pardoned by the new czar Nicholas I for his suspected involvement in the abortive Decembrist Revolt of 1825.

Pushkin writes, then, under the continuing threat of censorship and prosecution, which partly explains why he completed only eight of his projected ten chapters.[31] It also explains why the poem revolves around the life of a jaded playboy and seems preoccupied with trivia. The suffocating repressiveness of Russia in the later 1820s must have been something like that of Restoration France in 1830, as evoked by Stendhal in *Red and Black*: "Provided one didn't joke about God, or the priests, or the king, or the men in power, . . . provided one said nothing good about . . . the opposition newspapers, or Voltaire, or Rousseau, or anything which involves the use of free speech; provided, above all, that one never talked politics, one could talk freely about anything whatever" (202). Applied to the world of *Eugene Onegin*, Stendhal's words help us understand the radically different ways in which Pushkin and Byron represent Rousseau. In the politically unfettered stanzas of *Childe Harold*, Byron salutes the intellectual father of the French Revolution as the inspired source of "oracles which set the world in flame / Nor ceased to burn till kingdoms were no more" (*CHP* 3.81). In the first chapter of *Eugene Onegin*, Rousseau appears only as part of a digression from the description of Eugene's dressing room, where a fingernail brush reminds the narrator that as a guest in the house of a famous French encyclopedist, Rousseau "could not conceive how solemn Grimm / Dared clean his nails in front of *him*" (A 1.24).[32] In other words, in verses watchdogged by the czar's censors, all one can safely say about Rousseau is that he was a prig.

Given the interdiction on politics and revolution in this novel, both are displaced by a pair of love stories involving two young men: not Eugene and the narrator but Eugene and a country squire named Lensky, whom Onegin comes to know shortly after moving into the country manor he has just inherited. In some ways Onegin and Lensky recall Darcy and Bingley.[33] Like Austen's pair, Eugene and Lensky are friends involved with—or at any rate juxtaposed with—a pair of sisters living in a country neighborhood; and like Bingley, Lensky is far more ardent than the Darcyish Eugene, who is at first cool to both sisters. But there the resemblance to Austen's characters ends. Not quite eighteen, Lensky personifies romantic passion to the point of caricature.[34] Convinced that fate has designated Olga Larin for himself alone (they have known each other since childhood, when their fathers "predestined" them for marriage), Lensky takes her as the muse for his ecstatic poetry of the moon and the starlit sky. But Onegin finds her stupefying, as dull as the "stupid moon you see," he tells Lensky, "Up in that stupid sky you honor" (F 3.5). Sated with passion himself, he scorns both Lensky's passion and its object, which reinforces his reluctance to attend the party held to celebrate the name-day of Olga's sister, Tatyana. Since Eugene has just told Tanya that he cannot return her love—the love she has dared to express in a letter to him—he has no wish to attend the party for her. But in accepting the Larins' invitation at Lensky's insistence, he sets the stage for disaster.

Arriving late to the party, with guests already dining, both young men are promptly seated right across the table from Tanya, who can barely conceal the storm raging within her. In response, Eugene seethes. Long since overdosed on the "tragico-hysteric" fits of women, he swears revenge for what he considers "Lensky's treachery" in dragging him to the party and exposing him to Tanya's hysterics (A 5.31). Maliciously, therefore, he flirts with Olga and repeatedly dances with her, rousing not only the "jealous anguish" of Tanya, as we later learn (A 6.3), but also the "jealous outrage" of Lensky (A 5.44), who leaves the party bent on settling their quarrel with pistols.[35]

The pistol duel is the turning point of the novel. When Onegin kills Lensky with a single, carefully aimed shot before Lensky can fire at all, the realization that he has killed him reignites Onegin's capacity to feel. For the first time in the novel he is racked with remorse:

> In his clenched fist the pistol grasping,
> His heart with rueful anguish filled,
> Onegin looked at Lensky, gasping.
> "That's that," his neighbor said, "he's killed."
> Killed! By the awesome exclamation
> Pierced through, Eugene in trepidation
> Departs the scene to summon aid.
>
> (A 6.35)

Near the end of the novel, it is precisely this moment of anguish that a somewhat older Onegin (now twenty-six) recalls in his own plaintive letter to Tanya. Just after he rediscovers her at a Moscow ball as the wife of a prince he has long known, the prince invites him to a party at his house, where all Onegin can do is sulk wordlessly before the "superbly poised," self-assured princess she has become (A 8.21). Freshly lovestruck and then repeatedly rebuffed in his ensuing efforts to reawaken her interest in him, he writes a letter in which his long-repressed passion, hitherto stifled as if by a censor, breaks out like the storm of a political revolution. Remembering, he writes, that her heartfelt overtures found him "afraid of love lest it betray me / Of that chill freedom that was mine" (A 211), he was also so shattered by the death of Lensky that "from all that I had ever cherished / I tore away my grieving heart" (F 201). Only then, when the realization that he had killed Lensky made him dimly perceive that he had also aborted the birth of his love for Tanya (all he had ever cherished), did Onegin rediscover his capacity to feel. Years of striving to bury his feelings by wandering the world alone, "estranged from men and discontented," have left him "tormented" (F 201), and he is now tormented only by his longing for Tanya. Echoing her long-ago letter to him, which ended by saying that she entrusted her fate to his honor (A 78), he ends by saying, "My lot is cast—you are the stronger, / And to your sentence I submit" (A 212).

But not calmly, we soon learn. Receiving no answer to his letter or to either of his follow-up messages, seeing nothing but "January frost" in Tanya's face when he encounters her at a large party, he goes to her house, finds her alone, and then—overwhelmed by contrition—falls at her feet. As a hostess receiving in the absence of her husband a man she once loved, Tatyana might well be tempted into adultery or at least a compromising relationship—like that of Catherine Earnshaw Linton with Heathcliff. But instead Tatyana takes her revenge for the "frigid glances" and "dreadful sermon" Onegin gave her years before (A 8.43), when he warned her to temper her longings lest men lead her astray. Now, she says, she would have preferred "that wintry speech" to "this dishonorable passion," this "squalid notion" he presents to her (A 8.45). Though she married without love, she says, and still loves Onegin, she will be faithful to her husband "all [her] life" (A 8.47).

If *Eugene Onegin* radically revises *Don Juan* by replacing Byron's impulsive, good-hearted naif with a bored socialite, the ending of Pushkin's novel (such as we have it) startlingly intersects with the ending of *Don Juan*'s canto 5. At the end of that canto the sultana no sooner melts Juan's virtuous resistance to her adulterous advances than the sultan arrives to cool their ardor and leave us forever wondering what might have happened if he had not then turned up. In Pushkin's novel Tanya's rejection of Onegin's adulterous advances is almost immediately followed by the arrival of her husband, but not before the typically cool, detached Onegin undergoes an emotional shock far worse than what the sultana made Juan feel. When Tanya declares that she will always be faithful to her husband and then leaves, Onegin stands

> Struck dumb as by a thunderbolt.
> Yet in his heart, what stormy ocean
> Of feelings seething in revolt!
> (A 8.48)

> [Как будто громом поражён.
> В какую бурю ощущений
> Теперь он сердцем погружён!]

Though the Russian lines actually refer to neither an ocean nor to revolt, the words громом (thunder) and бурю (tempest) plainly reveal that Eugene's heart (сердцем) has been plunged (погружён) into a violent storm. The man who sought to betray his absent host and erstwhile friend by seducing his hostess is suddenly made to lose the self-assurance that has largely defined his character up to now. As an uninvited guest, he is betrayed not by his host or hostess but by his own presumption, and it is in this state of radical disruption, this tempest of agonizingly frustrated desire, that the poem leaves him "forever" (A 8.48).

HOSPITALITY AND ENTRAPMENT: JAMES'S
THE PORTRAIT OF A LADY

Can Pushkin lead the way to Henry James? From the raging storm of Onegin's thwarted desire in a Moscow drawing room to the exquisite serenity of a summer afternoon teatime on the lawn of a grand old English country estate — the opening scene of James's *The Portrait of a Lady* (1881) — is decidedly a leap. And the leap is temporal as well as spatial, since James's novel first appeared fifty years after Pushkin finished *Eugene Onegin* and was then extensively revised for the New York edition of 1908.[36] Startlingly enough, however, the all-but-final scene of James's novel virtually recapitulates the ending of *Eugene Onegin*. When Caspar Goodwood implores the unhappily married Isabel to abandon her husband for him and then seizes her on the very lawn where we first met her, his desperately impassioned kiss is said to be "like white lightning" (489). But just as Pushkin's Tatyana spurns Eugene, Isabel spurns Caspar, as she has repeatedly done before, for a man she does not love.

By itself, this coincidence does not make *The Portrait of a Lady* Pushkinian. Since Caspar is no Eugene and Isabel no Tatyana, I would not place *Eugene Onegin* among the novels that must have fed the imagination of James as he shaped his own. But James's novel shares with Pushkin's at least one other feature. Starting with Isabel's first entrance at the country house of her aunt and uncle, where she lingers "near the threshold" just after appearing "in the ample doorway" leading from the house to the lawn (27, 25), nearly all its crucial events involve hospitality.

So far as I can tell, this point has escaped the notice of everyone who has written about *The Portrait of a Lady* up to now. Yet James adverts to hospitality at least seventy-eight times.[37] In so doing, he underscores the fact that hospitality governs nearly all relations in this novel. While spending several months at Gardencourt as a guest of her Aunt Lydia and Uncle Daniel Touchett, Isabel is captivated by Madame Merle, who has so carefully cultivated the art of charming various hosts and hostesses — with whom she spends nearly all of her time — that she has become in effect a professional guest.[38] But Madame Merle often acts like a hostess. At Gardencourt, where Daniel is an invalid, where Lydia keeps largely out of sight, and where even their witty and congenial son

Ralph, also an invalid, grants Isabel no more than "half-hospitality" by denying her access to his "private apartments" (61), Madame Merle quickly takes charge of entertaining the heroine, appropriating the power and influence of her hostess and hosts.

In Florence likewise, where Madame Merle receives "for a month the hospitality of [Lydia's] Palazzo Crescentini" (210), it is she who asks Osmond to "come and see" her at the palazzo so as to meet "the girl" she wants him to marry (208).[39] At this first meeting, where Madame Merle takes the place of her characteristically absent hostess, Osmond invites Isabel to come with her for tea in the garden of the hilltop villa where he rents an apartment, and it is while acting there the part of a host that Osmond first begins in earnest to seduce Isabel, to lure her—aesthetically and emotionally—into a world imperiously ruled by his pretensions to taste. And after their marriage, when they occupy (courtesy of Isabel's newly inherited wealth) their own palazzo in Rome, we see them chiefly as the host and hostess of Thursday evening receptions that are calculated to manifest, as intimidatingly as possible, the cultural superiority and social power of the host.

This foregrounding of hospitality goes hand in hand with what we have seen in such novels as Stendhal's *Red and Black* and Barrett Browning's *Aurora Leigh*: the shifting of heroism from the battlefield to the drawing room. James himself, who was seventeen when the American Civil War broke out but never served in it, had conquered London socially by the time he started work on *Portrait*.[40] The novel refers to the Civil War just once, when Isabel takes pleasure in imagining that Caspar "might have ridden, on a plunging steed, the whirlwind of a great war—a war like the Civil strife that had overdarkened her conscious childhood and his ripening youth" (106).[41] But even though Caspar, who is just too young for the war, has actually assumed the generalship of a cotton mill, his brand of heroism—"straight and stiff" as a steel breastplate— cannot vibrate with what Isabel considers "the deeper rhythms of life" (106). So she rejects him in favor of a man who not only has declined to join the fight for Italian independence but also is "not in business," as Isabel explains to Caspar (278).[42] Rather than wishing that Osmond had thrown himself into the whirlwind of war or commerce, Isabel admires the social heroism of Madame Merle, "armed at all points" and "completely equipped for the social battle. She carried her flag discreetly, but her weapons were polished steel, and she used them with a skill which struck Isabel as more and more that of a veteran. She was never weary, never overcome with disgust; she never appeared to need rest or consolation" (337). This is evidently the kind of temperament Isabel aimed to achieve even before meeting Madame Merle, when she sometimes yearned to be challenged so as to "have the pleasure of being as heroic as the occasion demanded" (54). Madame Merle herself commends Isabel for her stamina. When she tells Isabel that life will never "spoil" her, never "break [her] up," Isabel "receive[s] this assurance as a young soldier, still panting from a slight skirmish in which he has come off with honour, might receive a pat on the shoulder from his colonel" (164).[43]

Besides yearning to prove herself heroic in some social battle yet to be faced, Isabel prides herself on being "quite independent" (24), as Lydia describes her in a telegram sent from America to Daniel and Ralph.[44] Understandably, they are puzzled by the phrase. Does it mean she is morally self-determined, financially secure, unwilling to incur any obligations, or simply "fond of [her] own way?"[45] The old man rightly suspects that it means the last (whatever else it means), but we soon learn that it also means "oblivious to her dependence." On first meeting Lydia in Albany and being asked how much she and her sisters expect to get for their grandmother's house, Isabel says she hasn't "the least idea" (35) and also that she does not know how much she has inherited from her late father. She is equally oblivious of her social responsibilities to a visiting aunt who has traveled some distance to see her. Rather than asking Aunt Lydia to stay for dinner, let alone spend the night, Isabel simply lets her return at six o'clock to what Lydia calls her "horrid hotel" (37).[46] This fact alone underscores Isabel's fundamentally dependent relation to her aunt. Rather than assuming, even for one night, the power of a hostess, she simply agrees to be "taken . . . up" (30) as a long-term traveling companion and house guest; Madame Merle later calls herself and Isabel parasites.[47] Yet even while telling Ralph that Lydia has been "very kind" to her, Isabel says she is "very fond of [her] liberty" (30), and Lydia herself later tells Ralph how Isabel reconciles her love of independence with her state of dependence. "She seemed averse to being under pecuniary obligations," Lydia reports. "But she has a small income and she *supposes* herself to be travelling at her own expense" (48, emphasis added).

The Touchetts' hospitality seems calculated to keep this supposition alive by forestalling any sense of dependence, by sparing Isabel anything like the Dantean taste of salt bread, by making her feel—even before she learns of her legacy—absolutely free. To compare her with Fanny Price in Austen's *Mansfield Park*, for instance, is to see that while each of these relatively poor young women is "taken up" by a wealthy aunt and uncle who invite her to stay with them, Isabel suffers none of the constraint and disdain that Fanny endures among the Bertrams. Partly for this reason, perhaps, she rejects Madame Merle's claim that we are each defined by the "shell" of our circumstances—by our houses, furniture, and clothes (175). Yet when Isabel insists that "nothing that belongs to me is any measure of me," that "my clothes . . . don't express me" (175), she forgets that she is ineluctably defined by her status as a guest in a house that belongs to someone else as well as by clothes that someone else may have paid for. No house guest can ever be absolutely free, and the hospitality furnished to Isabel at Gardencourt subtly recalls some of the ways in which earlier guests in the history of literary hospitality have been seduced, or entrapped, or both.

Consider just three other nineteenth-century English novels in which hospitality becomes a seductive trap. In *Wuthering Heights*, as we have seen, Heathcliff lures Cathy II into visiting Linton so as to engineer their marriage and make Cathy his prisoner. In *Great Expectations* Miss Havisham invites Pip to Satis House precisely so that he may be captivated by Estella and ever after tortured by unrequited love. And in Thomas Hardy's *Tess of the d'Urbervilles* the eponymous heroine's attempt to "claim kin" with a wealthy family and perhaps marry one of them leads her into being hospitably received by Alec d'Urberville, who feeds her strawberries as a prelude to seducing her later on.[48]

Hardy's *Tess*, which—by the way—James despised, appeared ten years after *Portrait*, and neither *Wuthering Heights* nor *Great Expectations* influenced the making of *Portrait* in anything like the way it may have been shaped by *Middlemarch*, whose young heroine, like Isabel, willfully and disastrously marries a middle-aged man of vacuous "distinction."[49] Nevertheless, Isabel has to contend with seductive hospitality in its subtlest forms, and much of the novel is taken up with showing how, after first resisting it, she gradually succumbs.

Warburton's hospitality provokes her resistance. Though certainly not pressed into marriage by her hospitable aunt, who truthfully tells Ralph she has "no plan of marrying her" off (49), Isabel is nonetheless introduced to a man who strikes her first as a character straight out of a novel (27) and then as "a hero of romance" (66). With his six houses, fifty thousand acres, and an income of a hundred thousand pounds a year (72), Warburton makes Darcy look almost plebeian, and since he has not a particle of Darcy's arrogance (he all but quivers with sensitivity), he seems the embodiment of a young woman's dream. One of the ironies of *Portrait*, in fact, is that its heroine is almost immediately offered a far grander and much more agreeable version of the man whom Elizabeth Bennet accepts only after she has performed the doubly arduous task of overcoming her own prejudices and reforming him.

A further irony is that Isabel rejects Warburton's first proposal without ever accepting a later one. But the first hints of this rejection may be found in her response to his hospitality at Lockleigh, where he entertains her for lunch along with Ralph, Lydia, and his brother and sisters. When Warburton shows Isabel his moated castle after lunch, it moves her "as a castle in a legend" (75). But unlike Elizabeth Bennet, who is delighted by Darcy's estate, Isabel wants no more of Lockleigh. When its owner tells her she has "charmed" him, she is so alarmed at the prospect of "something grave" to follow that without even consulting her aunt she firmly forestalls all further invitations: "I'm afraid there's no prospect," she tells Warburton, "of my being able to come here again" (76–77). By telling her she has charmed him and thus hinting of his aspiration to charm or enchant her, he subtly betrays the trust of "a young lady who had confided in his hospitality" (78).[50] In the very last words of a chapter describing her only experience as Warburton's guest, the coldness with which she receives his promise to "come and see [her] next week" is said to emanate from "a certain fear" (78).

This instinctual fear—a fear of entrapment—helps to explain why she declines a proposal that "nineteen women out of twenty would have accepted without a pang" (101). She fears being caught in the web of someone else's "design," a word that suggestively evokes the calculations of the minister who invites himself to the Bennets' house "with the design of selecting a wife" (Austen 71). Just as Elizabeth, who in this case resembles the Jamesian heroine, resists entanglement in Collins's design, Isabel feels bound to resist Warburton's. "What she felt," we are told, "was that a territorial, a political, a social magnate had conceived the design of drawing her into the system in which he rather invidiously lived and moved" (95). The hospitality furnished to Isabel at Lockleigh is precisely designed to draw her in, which is why she declines to accept any repetition of it.[51]

Yet even as Isabel makes it unequivocally clear that she wants no more of Warburton's hospitality, her friend Henrietta Stackpole conspires to use the hospitality of Gardencourt against her. Eager to help Goodwood track down Isabel when she learns he has come to London, Henrietta covertly tells Ralph that inviting him to Gardencourt "would be an act of true hospitality" (110). But it is nothing of the kind.[52] Though Goodwood declines the invitation because he perceives it has been prompted by Henrietta, Isabel strongly feels "the sense of Henrietta's treachery" (136) later on. She feels equally vexed when Henrietta prompts Goodwood to visit Isabel one evening while she is alone at a London hotel. Though she rejects him again and feels heroic elation at having "refused two ardent suitors in a fortnight," she nonetheless resents Henrietta's attempt "to set a trap for her" (145).[53]

The trap set by Madame Merle is far more subtle. "Charming, sympathetic, intelligent, cultivated . . . rare, superior and preëminent" (163), this cunning old blackbird soon becomes a model for Isabel, who promptly falls under her spell.[54] Knowing she is welcome anywhere she goes, she has come without being invited, for she is not only "one of the most brilliant women in Europe," as Mrs. Touchett tells Isabel (169), but also the perfect guest, always ready to say, do, paint, or play on the piano whatever may engage or enchant the people around her. Aptly enough, this new guest at Gardencourt first catches Isabel's attention with what might be called her siren song: "something of Schubert" played with feeling and skill (150–51). To Isabel, her only fault is that she is "not natural," too glazed by custom, too perfectly socialized, too purged of "tonic wildness" (167).[55] Nina Baym suggests that while the Isabel of 1908 is more knowing than the original heroine, she is duped by her own subtlety (Baym 621). Alternatively, one might say, she is more susceptible to the way in which the Brooklyn-born daughter of an American naval officer, a veritable navy brat, has dis-Americanized herself.[56] Even while falling under the spell of Madame Merle, Isabel asks herself "what Henrietta Stackpole would say to her thinking so much of this perverted product of their common soil, and had a conviction that it would be severely judged" (165). Since James originally wrote "this brilliant fugitive from Brooklyn" (519), Baym cites the change to help argue that the later James turns a complex character into a shallow, exploitative swindler (624). This seems to me overstated. While the later version of the novel does indeed treat Madame Merle more harshly than the earlier one, Baym misses the irony in Isabel's epithet for her. Already enchanted by this exceptionally cultivated product of European experience, Isabel playfully imagines that Madame Merle would strike the all-American Henrietta as dis-Americanized and hence "perverted." But since Isabel often disagrees with her friend, we should hardly expect her to second Henrietta's nationalistic verdict on a Europeanized American, especially since Isabel herself has already taken Madame Merle as a model of Continental sophistication.

Isabel's epithet also challenges us as readers. Do we share what she suspects to be Henrietta's nationalistic view of Madame Merle? Or are we tempted at this point to feel at least something of Isabel's enchantment with her? She is, after all, virtually appointed as Isabel's tutor by the shrewd, practical Mrs. Touchett. Even while her husband is dying, she has asked Madame Merle to stay so that Isabel may come to know her: to know a woman whose tact her hostess finds superlative, whose behavior she calls faultless, whose knowledge she finds total, and who, she says, has done her "a favour" by coming even while so much in demand at "great houses" elsewhere (169). To see Madame Merle at this stage as nothing but a manipulative fraud is to see both Isabel and her aunt as a pair of fools, which is hardly fair to the intelligence of either. To see Madame Merle as an enchantress, however, and to see how she captivates Isabel, is also to see how artfully she usurps the power of their hostess.

Consider what she does with Mrs. Touchett's admiration for her. When Isabel tells Madame Merle that their hostess considers her perfect, the lady demurs, in part because she has already described herself, with engaging candor, as "shockingly chipped and cracked" (168). But instead of simply reaffirming this self-deprecating point, she decorticates Mrs. Touchett's compliment. "Having no faults, for your aunt," she tells Isabel, "means that one's never late for dinner—that is for *her* dinner. . . . It means that one answers a letter the day one gets it and that when one comes to stay with her one doesn't bring too much luggage and is careful not to be taken ill" (169–70). In thus trivializing her hostess's criteria for perfection, Madame Merle caricatures her, for we already know that Mrs. Touchett admires her guest for substantive virtues such as tact. But a little later, just after Mr. Touchett's death, Madame Merle compounds this caricature by silently sneering at Mrs. Touchett's selfishness. When Mrs. Touchett tells her she "never sacrificed [her] husband to another" (meaning a lover), Madame Merle says to herself, "O no . . . you never did anything for another!" (180), forgetting all the hospitality Mrs. Touchett has lavished on Madame Merle herself, not to mention nursing her dying husband and "taking up" her barely solvent niece. Since what Madame Merle says openly to Isabel falls far short of this silent indictment, Isabel fails to realize that "Mrs. Touchett's accomplished guest was abusing her" (170). But in freely and frankly deriding their hostess's criteria for perfection in a guest, Madame Merle prompts Isabel to consider the two of them as kindred spirits joined in "intimacy" (170), linked by their common disdain for the would-be triviality of Mrs. Touchett's values. Madame Merle thus contrives to shift Isabel's allegiance from their hostess to herself.

She is equally irreverent, if not downright derisive again, when speaking to Isabel of Ralph. He is lucky, she says, to have consumption (i.e., tuberculosis) because it's "his *carrière*; it's a kind of position. You can say: 'Oh, Mr. Touchett, he takes care of his lungs, he knows a great deal about climates.' But without that who would he be, what would he represent?" (171). After disposing of Ralph in this way, without a single reference to his status as their host or host-to-be (he is the heir to Gardencourt, as Madame Merle surely knows), she mentions Gilbert Osmond, for the first time, as a man likewise indolent but nonetheless "exceedingly clever, a man made to be distinguished," and "one of the most delightful men" she knows (171). This comment marks a turning point. In deprecating both their hostess and Ralph without a word of protest from Isabel and then describing a man whom she promises to introduce to her, Madame Merle assumes the social power of a hostess herself.

Fittingly enough, it is precisely as a host and "entertainer" (202) that we first see Gilbert Osmond. In his elegantly furnished apartment outside Florence, he briefly entertains the pair of nuns who have brought his daughter Pansy back from the Roman convent where for many years she has been schooled. While demonstrating his absolute mastery of Pansy, who sweetly obeys him and does nothing without his permission, Osmond courts the visiting nuns with a combination of flattery, flowers, and wit. After making them laugh at a little joke about gymnastics, commending them for what they have taught Pansy, and giving them two large bunches of roses that Pansy (at his command) has gathered for them, he gallantly tells them as they rise to depart that while there may be "good people everywhere," as one of them says, "there will be two less here" when they leave (200). But his courtliness barely masks his determination to have his own way, especially with Pansy. When one of the nuns starts to weep at the prospect of losing a girl whom they have come to regard as "our daughter," he scarcely comforts them: "'It's not certain you'll lose her; nothing's settled yet,' their host rejoined quickly; not so as if to anticipate their tears, but in the tone of a man saying what was most agreeable to himself" (199–200).

Showing no pity for the nuns, whom he has not even thanked for returning Pansy to him (he could have fetched her away from Rome himself, as Madame Merle has expected), or for his daughter, who later weeps at the nuns' departure, Osmond simply toys with the wishes of all three, plainly indicating that whether or not the nuns "lose" Pansy depends entirely on his pleasure ("what was most agreeable to himself") and his power as "their host."[57]

It is to this very power, the power of "her host" (204, 207), that Madame Merle appeals when she comes with her plan to put Isabel in Osmond's way, to set the stage for him to play host to her that he may court her. Even though Osmond receives Madame Merle coldly, with neither an extended hand nor a greeting as he lets her cross his threshold, she boldly explains her "ambitions" on his behalf (205), which require him to display to Miss Archer the "adorable taste" enshrined in his exquisite rooms (208–9). To lure her into those rooms he must first meet her at her aunt's palazzo, and even as Madame Merle invites him to do so she promises to "keep [Mrs. Touchett] out of the way" (209), wholly usurping her position as hostess. But she cannot dictate the impressions Osmond and Isabel make on each other. All she can do is stage with Osmond a worldly conversation that she hopes will impress Isabel, who silently declines to make any impression of her own. When Madame Merle tells her after the visit that she was "charming," that she once again proved herself "never disappointing," Isabel bridles, for she feels no obligation "to charm Mr. Osmond" (213). But with Madame Merle's prodding, he has charmed her enough that she accepts his invitation to visit him on his own ground, where he can use the full power of a host to deepen the first impression he has made.

Even before Osmond greets Isabel and Madame Merle, who escorts her, the hilltop villa containing his apartment makes an impression of its own: "There was something grave and strong in the place; it looked somehow as if, once you were in, you would need an act of energy to get out" (217). Obliquely confirming this visual hint of potential entrapment, Osmond self-deprecatingly calls himself "rusty as a key that has no lock to fit it" and hardly capable of turning the "very complicated lock" of Isabel's mind (221). But he aims to do precisely this—as a prelude to locking her up in the house of his own will.[58]

As a host, Osmond dominates Isabel. Though she seems the antithesis of the "submissive" Pansy (219), who is made to stand between her father's knees and lean against him when he talks, Isabel defers to him at almost every turn. Rather than thrusting herself forward with a man "evidently capable of distinguishing himself," she lets him entertain her with "his wit" (219–20). Some of it targets his sister, the self-invited Countess Gemini, whose vulgarity conveniently sets off his own exquisite taste. Shortly after Isabel and Madame Merle enter Osmond's apartment, the countess warns Isabel to avoid sitting in a particular chair because some of Osmond's chairs are "horrors" (219)—meaning, no doubt, horribly uncomfortable. But having already begun to consider aesthetic distinction the only standard of value here, Isabel says she sees no "horrors anywhere. . . . Everything seems to be beautiful and precious" (219). Aside from this tribute to Osmond's furnishings, which—somewhat ominously—sacrifice comfort to beauty, Isabel says almost nothing. Instead she silently listens as her "host [exerts] himself to entertain her" by describing her aunt as an "old Florentine" whose dry little face can be found in a fresco by Ghirlandaio (221–22). Then, when "her host" does not move even as the other two women walk out to the garden, she waits "with a certain unuttered contentedness, to have her move-ments directed" (223). But instead of directing her attention to his treasures at once, as she expects, he first asks her what she thinks of the "family tone" and then, without waiting for an answer, says that his sister is "comically" unhappy, that her husband is "horrid," and that "she's not grammatical" (223–24), meaning not refined. In confirming that Isabel has been taken "into the family" (224), as the countess has already said (222), Osmond appropriates her even while placing her on his own side of the family, the side that appreciates beautiful furniture (regardless of comfort) as well as the treasures he proceeds to show her. Without a break, in fact, he suddenly shifts from family matters to the picture Isabel has been studying while he talks. He scarcely gives her time to realize that in parsing his sister's vulgarity, he is exposing his own.[59]

At the same time, Isabel is afraid of exposing herself. Accepting Osmond's principle that life is "a matter of connoisseurship" but feeling daunted by his cultivation, she fears revealing "her possible grossness of perception" by admiring what she ought not to like or by ignoring "something at which the truly initiated mind would arrest itself" (226). For Isabel, therefore, the whole tour of Osmond's treasures becomes a rite of initiation that turns worldly, that is, vulgar, standards of judgment upside down. Just as an uncomfortable chair can be reevaluated as beautiful, a man who might be commonly judged worthless can be reclassified, in his own words, as "the most fastidious . . . gentleman" in the world (227). When Isabel concludes that it would be "uproariously vulgar" to question him, "to intimate that he had not told her everything" (228), she reveals how much his standards of judgment have overtaken her own. While it is only after many months and many more meetings that Isabel agrees to marry Osmond, he has already captivated her. From the slightly embarrassed way in which Isabel listens to "the master of the house" as he leans against the parapet of the garden while facing her, Madame Merle shrewdly infers that she has fallen in love with him (230).[60]

But Madame Merle has more work to do. To further Osmond's courtship of Isabel she betrays her Florentine hostess, who is clearly displeased by his sudden flurry of calls at her palazzo. When Mrs. Touchett tells Madame Merle that she wants him to stop coming because she suspects he is nothing but a fortune hunter, Madame Merle feigns ignorance of Osmond's intentions and promises to "investigate and report" them to her hostess (237).[61] But instead she takes charge of Osmond's strategy, quietly telling him—when they meet at the Countess Gemini's—that he must follow Isabel to Rome. In all of this we are never allowed to forget that Madame Merle is undermining the wishes of her hostess. Though her conversation with Osmond takes place at the countess's, it ends in the courtyard outside, where he helps his co-conspirator into "Mrs. Touchett's victoria . . . awaiting her guest" (244). And as Madame Merle sits in a carriage furnished by a hostess who (as her guest knows very well) deplores Osmond's pursuit of Isabel, she calmly hears him say that Isabel's "many ideas," the vital signs of her independence, "must be sacrificed" (244).

And so must her freedom. When Ralph learns of her engagement to Osmond, he tells her bluntly she is "going to be put into a cage" (288).[62] But well before the engagement, after Isabel returns from Rome to Florence, Pansy offers her a prevision of this cage. She calls on Pansy at the request of Osmond, who stays behind in Rome and who—after "incommod[ing]" her by confessing his love— asks her to call on Pansy, now alone at the villa, and "tell her she must love her poor father very much" (264–65). This is a curious and cunning request. Besides egoistically inverting what a truly affectionate father would say ("tell her that her father loves her very much"), Osmond seems bent on casting Pansy as a model of devotion for Isabel to follow, for Isabel too is being none-too-subtly urged to love Osmond very much. And when Pansy receives Isabel at the villa, she does so precisely as an imprisoned hostess. Her life is still ruled by her absent father, who—as she tells Isabel—"left instructions for everything" (269) and who has also placed her under house arrest. At the end of the visit, when Isabel walks with her to the door opening on the courtyard, "her young hostess stopped, looking rather wistfully beyond. 'I may go no further. I've promised papa not to pass this door'" (270). As different as Pansy seems from the emphatically independent Isabel, she prefigures the life that Isabel will soon be made to lead—as hostess in "a house of suffocation" (360).

The vestibule to this house is the pied-à-terre of another hostess. For it is during the three weeks Isabel "lodge[s]" with Madame Merle in Rome—the one and only occasion on which anyone is said to lodge with her—that Osmond lays conclusive siege to Isabel by seeing her daily (275). But once Osmond has won her, the only social role he plays is that of host, "master of the house," the Roman palazzo they inhabit. He alone rules it.

In part he rules by exclusion. As Ralph perceives, he strives "to tantalise society with a sense of exclusion, to make people believe his house was different from every other" (331). He picks the guests even for evenings that are nominally Isabel's. "Her house," we are told, "was not open to every one, and she had an evening in the week to which people were not invited as a matter of course" (330).[63] Among those who *are* invited, Isabel's power as a hostess is crimped. When Edward Rosier ventures to "cross [the] threshold" (308) of the palazzo to attend one of her Thursday evenings "on general principles of civility" (307), she tells him that she can't help him speak to Pansy, whom he desperately yearns to court.[64] Just before thus admitting her incapacity to further a courtship, which is precisely what Madame Merle did while usurping the role of hostess in Florence, Isabel has appeared to Rosier "framed in [a] gilded doorway . . . as the picture of a gracious lady" (310). The second phrase evokes not just the title of the novel but the opening picture of a much younger Isabel lingering "in the doorway" of Gardencourt when first seen by Ralph, crossing the threshold into a world of wealth and all the freedom it can provide.[65] "Over the years," writes Anthony Lane, "she has traded one doorway for another— stepping from frame to frame. . . . In between, the picture has become a prison" (Lane 72). In terms of hospitality, the girl who once stood as a guest on the threshold of limitless possibility has become not only a lady but a hostess caught in a gilded frame, yet another objet d'art in her husband's collection, powerless to do anything for her visitors but manifest his taste.

But if Isabel can do nothing for her young guest, Osmond uses all the power of a host, not to mention of a father, to thwart him. When Rosier goes up to shake hands with him as he stands facing the fireplace, Osmond gives him just "two fingers of his left hand" (312) without turning toward him, and when Rosier politely tries to engage this connoisseur by talking of Capo di Monte porcelain, Osmond says he cares nothing for it. Partly emboldened by the rudeness of his host, Rosier commits "a breach of hospitality" by directly appealing to Pansy, telling himself that the sacredness of hospitality is "infinitely" surpassed by the importance of love (311–12).[66] Yet even after managing to speak to Pansy alone in a small yellow room and prompting her to admit that she likes him, Rosier is balked. When he returns to the palazzo the following Thursday to tell Osmond that he hopes to marry Pansy, "the master of the house" denies that she loves him (319) and soon after lets him know that he is not welcome. After a while he comes no more, and by the end of the novel Osmond has contrived to banish him from Pansy's life.

Superficially, Osmond is far more hospitable to Caspar Goodwood, whom he assures that he and Isabel will "always be delighted to see . . . again" (420). But Goodwood pleases Osmond chiefly as a source of what Goodwood himself suspects is "private entertainment" laced with "a streak of perversity" (421). Listening to Osmond speak at length, Goodwood hears the voice of a "host [who] had won in the open field a great advantage over him" (421), who had taken full possession of the woman for whom Goodwood endlessly pines. Osmond preens himself on his possession. While unctuously assuring Goodwood that he speaks for Isabel, that they are "as united . . . as the candlestick and the snuffers" (420), he implies that he has not only snuffed her fire but also swallowed her voice. Nothing rankles Goodwood more than hearing "Osmond speak of his wife's feelings as if he were commissioned to answer for them" (421). In this appropriative voice, Osmond speaks so patronizingly of their admiration for Goodwood's success in escaping the "danger" of a "commercial" occupation that Goodwood can scarcely understand him (420–21). Wanting only to be alone with Isabel, he listens with "dull rage" (421). For perhaps the only time in the novel, he claims our sympathies (or mine anyway) by silently yearning to murder his host.[67]

Still more, Goodwood yearns to "penetrate" Isabel (425) when he finds her at last alone in the very room where Rosier risked a breach of hospitality by speaking privately to Pansy. Besides its obviously phallic implications, Goodwood's urge is psychological: he aches to know what lurks beneath the "clear hospitable smile" (424) with which she greeted him in the midst of the others, and especially what underlies Osmond's claim—as Goodwood reports it—that he and Isabel "adore each other" (426). Whatever the truth of that, Isabel is no Pansy. While that young hostess cannot even walk with Isabel past the door leading out of Osmond's apartment, Isabel walks with Goodwood from the large, still partly occupied salon (as the party is breaking up) to a small, empty room. But she barely opens the door to her heart. When he begs her to tell him if he may pity her for a pain she will not confess, she tells him only that he may "give a thought to it every now and then" (427). She speaks as from within a prison.

To her sister-in-law, Isabel's prison looks like the social center of the universe. Bored to death with a disagreeable husband in the now declining city of Florence, the countess envies the "brilliant life" she thinks Isabel must be leading at celebrity-studded parties in Rome (374). But when, after years of neglecting her, Osmond suddenly invites his sister to come for several weeks, she ends up caught in the middle of a struggle for power between her hostess and her host.

Why he invites her at all is a question not easily answered. The novelist needs her in Rome to reveal to Isabel that Madame Merle is Osmond's former lover and the mother of Pansy.[68] But what motivates Osmond? Since he thinks his sister coarse, as we already know, what does she have to offer him? Does he find her useful with lingering party guests, as when she regales a ring of gentlemen around the fire at midnight after he has disappeared without saying good-bye to any of them? In any case, she seems to offer Osmond yet another opportunity to display the power of a host, the power to make her feel "the insecurity of her tenure of her brother's hospitality" (443). When she objects to "poor Pansy's banishment" (443) just after Osmond sends his daughter back to the convent, Osmond threatens to banish the countess herself, and when she learns that Osmond has forbidden Isabel to go and see Ralph on his deathbed in England, she instantly foresees the end of dinner parties at their house.

Nevertheless, she yearns to see Isabel defy her brother's authority by going to England.[69] It is partly to speed this end that she tells Isabel how Osmond and Madame Merle have tried to use her: having declined to marry Madame Merle because she had no money, Osmond married Isabel for hers, and Madame Merle arranged the match so that Isabel would take care of Pansy. In making these revelations, the countess seems driven not just by the urge to undermine her brother but also by her jealousy of Isabel, the brilliant hostess, and above all by her resentment of Madame Merle, the equally brilliant guest. For all her ambitions to "marry a great man," the countess says, Madame Merle has managed only to bring Osmond and Isabel together and to become a professional guest: "Getting to know every one and staying with them free of expense"

(453). While we already know that her captivating charm has brought her a steady stream of invitations, the countess seems to insinuate that charm alone could not have kept her afloat. "No one knows," she says, "no one has ever known, what she lives on, or how she has got all those beautiful things" (453). What, we are led to wonder, did she trade for them?

We are never told; we can only imagine. But we *are* told how her buried anguish calls to Isabel just as soon as the countess tells her that Madame Merle long ago renounced "all visible property in [her] child." "Ah, poor, poor woman!" Isabel instantly responds (452).[70] By her own admission Madame Merle has just been "vile" to Isabel (434) by insinuating that Isabel kept Warburton from marrying Pansy. If Isabel can recognize the pain endured by the very woman who has been vile to her, are we not asked to do likewise? Unlike Osmond, who never admits wrongdoing, Madame Merle knows all too well what she has done to Isabel by leading her into marrying Osmond. On receiving him alone as "his hostess" in her Roman apartment (433), she tells him that even while avenging himself on Isabel for insubordination, for refusing to serve all his wishes, he has destroyed the soul of his former lover (434–35). It was precisely while acting as hostess to Isabel in this very apartment that Madame Merle finally delivered her to Osmond. But instead of thanking her for her efforts he shows only resentment. While we do not know what this brilliant guest has paid for her life of serial dependency, Madame Merle herself knows how little she has gained from her treachery as a hostess. Just after Osmond leaves, she asks herself, "Have I been so vile all for nothing?" (437).

What then of Isabel? If Madame Merle ends as a nearly tragic antiheroine, Isabel remains the heroine who, after going to see the dying Ralph, must decide whether to reclaim her independence or resume her place within the framework of marriage. Yet to state the alternatives in these terms is to miss their complexity. In returning to Gardencourt, she defies Osmond's wishes and manifests her independence. But since Gardencourt was the site of her longest experience as a guest, it cannot help but recall her period of dependency (she ends up staying in the same room she occupied before) as well as recalling the two men who, during that time, sought to possess her.[71] At Ralph's funeral she sees both Goodwood, who soon after begs her to leave Osmond for him, and Warburton, who soon after holds out once again the lure of hospitality, begging her to keep her "old promise" to revisit him at Lockleigh (484).[72] Furthermore, if marriage to Osmond is the final frame for this portrait of a lady, returning to that frame does not necessarily mean forfeiting her independence. Paradoxically, it is an act of self-assertion, for as she tells the importunate Goodwood, going back to her marriage partly means *getting away from him* (488). It also means ceasing to live as a guest at Gardencourt and at Henrietta's London lodgings, where she spends only a single night before starting for Rome. Finally, it means returning to a house where, in the face of her husband's treachery, she might well reconstruct her roles as wife, stepmother, and hostess.

In returning to Osmond, Isabel displays the kind of heroism we have seen in novels ranging from *Tom Jones* to *Middlemarch*. At once demilitarized and domesticated, it is a heroism arguably moral, such as we find in Tom when he hospitably cares for a battered woman and in Dorothea when—while visiting various houses as a guest—she becomes the "champion" of Lydgate's tarnished reputation. But just as Dorothea "saves" an essentially loveless marriage by urging Rosamond to stay with Lydgate, Isabel preserves her own marriage only by resolving to endure life—for the time being—with a man who has exploited and then tried to suffocate her. Whether or not she will ever exercise the power of a hostess, whether or not she will ever again receive Rosier as a guest to facilitate his courtship of Pansy, is a wide-open question.

In turn, this question reminds us that hospitality plays a crucial role in the process of mating as well as in the manifestation of power. In *Pride and Prejudice* the Bennets' capacity to find husbands for their daughters is subtly impeded by the ways in which the self-invited Collins radically destabilizes their possession of Longbourn and thus vexes their freedom and power to entertain eligible men. In *Frankenstein* Victor compounds his brutal inhospitality to the creature by willfully frustrating his desire for a mate, and this frustration is further compounded when the would-be supersensitive De Laceys brutally reject his anguished plea for their hospitality. In *Wuthering Heights*, Heathcliff avenges himself on all those who have thwarted his desire for Catherine by gaining possession of their houses and brutally abusing his guests, especially Cathy II, whom he entraps. And in *Eugene Onegin*, Eugene's resentment of what he takes to be the Larins' insidious hospitality—placing him directly opposite the woman whose love he has just rejected—leads him into dancing with Olga, goading Lensky into a fatal duel, and wandering the world until he ardently returns to the woman he rejected, only to find that this lovely Moscow hostess now rejects him.

From Pushkin's novel alone, of course, we cannot infer that hospitality is always sabotaged by treachery in nineteenth-century Russian fiction, let alone in all the novels of this period. In the middle of Tolstoy's *Anna Karenina* (1878), published just three years before James's *Portrait*, Prince Oblonsky holds an elegant dinner party at his Moscow home precisely in order to bring together his beautiful young sister-in-law Kitty and her longtime admirer Levin, a shy, country-dwelling landowner. Since Kitty has been pining with unrequited love for Vronsky, she has so far resisted Levin's yearning for her. But at Oblonsky's dinner table, when all the other guests are talking about the education of women, Kitty and Levin conduct "a kind of mystic intercourse" (Tolstoy 389), and after dinner, when Levin anxiously screws up his courage to speak to her alone in the drawing room, she accepts him.

This happy outcome of benign hospitality, however, cannot erase the fact that Kitty and Levin are minor characters in a novel whose titular protagonist ends in suicidal despair over the wretchedness of her marriage and the faithlessness, or at least the unreliability, of her lover. In James's *Portrait* likewise, the comic congeniality of the romance between Henrietta and Mr. Bantling—a romance initiated by the hospitality of Ralph Touchett, who invites them both to his parents' London house—cannot erase the misery experienced by Isabel Archer. If anything, her misery is exacerbated by the irony of its genesis. Treated with exceptionally benign hospitality by her uncle, cousin, and aunt, who presents her to Madame Merle only so that she may get to know a perfect model of refinement, Isabel is exquisitely seduced.

Together with the other novels I have examined here, then, *Portrait of a Lady* exemplifies the process by which the treachery of hosts and guests grows less violent, more subtle, and also, if anything, more disturbing. Just as heroism becomes demilitarized and domesticated, treachery learns how to strike without drawing blood. Though Frankenstein's creature takes murderous revenge for the inhospitality he suffers, Heathcliff kills no one, and while Eugene kills Lensky, his most treacherous acts as a guest are nonviolent: willfully igniting Lensky's jealousy by dancing with Olga and, much later, trying to seduce the wife of his absent host. Likewise nonviolent is Will Ladislaw's "annihilating" attack on the weakness of Casaubon's scholarship when, as a guest of Dorothea, he slays the would-be distinction of his absent host. Occasionally, violent urges still fire the blood of hosts and guests, as when Caspar Goodwood longs to kill his insufferably patronizing host. But no one in *Portrait of a Lady* is actually killed or physically wounded. Isabel is betrayed by those who know precisely how to manipulate a guest and disempower a hostess. And in thus showing how treachery may bloodlessly undermine hospitality, Henry James points the way to Marcel Proust.

8

PROUST'S HOSTESSES

Au sien de nos relations amicales ou purement mondaines, il y a une hostilité momen-
tanément guérie, mais récurrente par accès.

[At the heart of our friendly or purely social relations, there lurks a hostility momentarily
cured but sporadically recurrent.]

— MARCEL PROUST, Sodome et Gomorrhe / Sodom and Gomorrah

I begin with the sound of a bell.

Near the very end of Marcel Proust's À la recherche du temps perdu, as the
narrator (Marcel) views a roomful of once-familiar faces now disguised by wrin-
kles, white beards, and silvery moustaches at a musical party given by the Prince
de Guermantes, he hears within him—tinkled by the long fingers of memory—
the bell on the garden gate of his parents' country house at Combray, where he
spent the summers of his childhood.[1] Marking the departure of his parents'
dinner guest, Charles Swann, long after the boy has been put to bed, the sound
of the bell tells his sleepless ear that his mother will soon be climbing the stairs
on which he yearns to ambush her for a goodnight kiss instead of having to wait
until morning for it. Heard in recollection by an aging man, in the midst of the
conversational buzz of the party, the bell stirs painfully mixed feelings. It draws
him into the depths of his past self, his childhood self, a self so enamored of his
mother that he could hardly bear to let anything come between them. Bound
up with the narrator's earliest recollection, therefore, bound up with "the point
from which [he] might start to [measure himself]" (TR 450), is the experience
of hospitality as a kind of betrayal. Though Swann will go on to win the love
and admiration of the narrator, he first appears to the boy as a cruelly disruptive
guest: "the object of a painful preoccupation" because his coming to dine
meant that Marcel would be denied "the precious and fragile kiss that Mama

usually entrusted to me in my bed when I was going to sleep" (SW 23).[2] On this night she was not just his Mama. She was also Swann's hostess.

This conflict between his personal needs and the social rituals that tend to frustrate them resurfaces at the end of Proust's novel, when the enfeebled narrator (who nearly fell down a flight of stairs after visiting friends one evening) struggles to take up the task of writing the monumental novel we have just read. To begin this task he must forsake the self "which in the past had been in the habit of going to those barbarian festivals that we call dinner-parties" (TR 440) and must forget even such social duties as answering invitations and sending notes of condolence. All parties and social obligations threaten to sabotage the narrator's project, which demands every ounce of his ebbing strength. But having read the novel he has heroically contrived to write, we have come to see that social experience—specifically, the experience of being a guest—vitally informed his past self, the self he aims to retrieve in his search for lost time. At least half of Proust's novel treats dinner parties and receptions in exhaustive detail, sometimes filling well over one hundred pages to recount a single event.

In this as in so much else, the narrator's past reflects that of his author. No young man ever courted a Parisian society hostess more ardently than the young Marcel Proust. In the fall of 1888, when he was seventeen and in his last year at the elite Lycée Condorcet, he began attending the salons held by the socially prominent women he met through their sons, who were his classmates. "While remaining friends with the sons," we are told, "Marcel now preferred the witty, worldly conversations of their mothers. Bewitched by the glamor of society, whose refined milieu suited his delicate nature, he wanted to know the details of its history, ceremonies, family connections, and secrets. Eager to please and genuinely thrilled at having been invited by a society *grande dame*, he lavished flattery and huge, expensive bouquets of flowers on the women who invited him to the most elegant drawing rooms of Paris" (Carter 91). Soon enough Marcel's classmates found his behavior ridiculous. Convinced he was squandering his talent, they teased him for lusting after invitations and fawning over aristocratic titles (Carter 95). Hence Proust gained a reputation that proved hard to shake for the rest of his life, as he knew only too well. At the end of his great novel the narrator feels bound to start work on an "edifice" because he has "lived a life of idleness, of pleasures and distractions" (TR 442). As late as 1912 André Gide declined to publish excerpts from *Swann's Way* in *La Nouvelle Revue française* because at that time, as he ruefully admitted two years later, he thought of Proust as "belonging to the Verdurin clan: a snob, a dilettante socialite—the worst possible thing for our review" (letter of January 1914, qtd. Carter 563).

In hindsight Gide must have recognized the irony of this verdict. Chastising himself for having rejected a novel he now (in 1914) greatly admires, he encapsulates his earlier view of Proust with a phrase plucked from the novel itself: "the Verdurin clan." The clan is just one part of an infinitely complex society that Proust represents with supreme detachment, for he is no more defined or ruled by the clan than is his chief character, Charles Swann. But the novel unquestionably harvests the fruits of his social experience. However ridiculous it may have seemed to his classmates, Proust's assiduous cultivation of society hostesses played a vital role in his literary education, in forming a writer who would grow up to re-create the pretensions, anxieties, petty tyrannies, and subtle cruelties of social life in the Belle Époque.

Hospitality in Proust's novel is a topic hiding in plain sight. Yet as if lurking beneath the overt themes we know so well—time, place, memory, mortality, social status, lust, Dreyfusism, homosexuality in all its forms—it seems to have eluded the notice of all recent critics, who say virtually nothing about Proust's treatment of hospitality: of hosts, hostesses, and guests. Not one of these words can be found in the index to such capacious critical studies as Roger Shattuck's *Proust's Way* (2000) or in any other study of Proust known to me. A possible reason is that in the world of Proust's novel, hospitality is almost as pervasive as life itself, and therefore seems no more than a canvas to which Proust applies the exquisite hues of his prose, leaving the canvas itself invisible to the reader's eye. But the roles and rituals of hospitality in this work are all too visible to anyone who cares to notice them. Unlike the threads of a canvas covered by paint, they resemble the strands of a tapestry woven into almost every one of the major relationships traced by the novel.

Swann's relation to Odette, for instance, is mediated by hospitality at every turn. Introduced to her by an old friend at the theater, he soon finds himself captivated by her sudden fascination with him, by the thought that he owns her heart. For her sake, therefore, he becomes one of the faithful at the house of the Verdurins even though he can barely tolerate them and their guests. Introduced to the Verdurins by Odette herself, Swann soon learns that Madame Verdurin will happily feed their affair, in every sense, so long as it nourishes his fidelity to their hostess. But once Madame Verdurin sees his fidelity wavering, once he admits to knowing prominent people whom she detests because they would never stoop to socialize with her, she does all she can to break up the affair. At the end of a party in the Bois de Boulogne given not long after Swann dares to call the lofty La Trémoïlles "charming," Swann overhears her organizing a little soirée that will exclude him but include his rival Forcheville along with Odette. Worse still, aborting his plan to take Odette home and "persuade her not to go to Chatou the next day or to see that he was invited," Madame Verdurin insists on taking Odette as well as Forcheville in her own carriage (SW 295). Tramping home in a black rage, Swann foresees them listening to Madame Verdurin's pianist play the "Moonlight Sonata" after she urges Odette to make a little room for Forcheville beside her. "In the dark!" he says to himself. "The pimp, the procuress!" (SW 298) ("maquerelle, entremetteuse!" [CCS 282]). Proust may well have originated this epithet for a hostess, which could be read as a louche version of the role played by hospitable parents in the world of Jane Austen. In *Pride and Prejudice* Mr. and Mrs. Bennet invite a wealthy young bachelor to dinner so as to introduce him to their daughters and perhaps coax him into marrying one of them. In *Swann's Way* Madame Verdurin exploits the power of invitation to make and unmake liaisons and thus sustain her iron grip on a little clan that Swann now finds revolting. Mirroring the collapse of his affair, sinking in his eyes just exactly as Odette's sweetness turns to acid, the little clan ruled by its hostess becomes for Swann "the lowest thing on the social ladder, Dante's last circle" (SW 298).

Swann's epithet for a designing hostess recurs two volumes later, when the young Marcel is joined by Oriane, the Duchess de Guermantes, at a reception given by Madame de Villeparisis. Arriving late, just in time to see a large crowd pouring out of the drawing room after a play and discussing the imminent or perhaps already effected separation of the duchess from the duke, Marcel sits down in the outer room on a narrow bench, where he catches the eye of the duchess as she walks out with the crowd. Swerving aside, she smilingly sits down beside him on the little *bergère*, gathering up as she does so her huge gown of yellow satin embroidered with large black poppies. Her act is mildly erotic. Besides recalling the way Madame Verdurin squeezed Forcheville in beside Odette, it prompts Marcel to remind himself that with the aid of his mother's sage advice, he has overcome his onetime infatuation with the duchess and can now enjoy her company as a friend.[3] But his would-be graduation from the throes of adolescent desire merely heightens the erotic charge here, for he quickly sees how he and his seatmate must look to those still lingering in the outer room. Taking her place beside a young man, the grand and glittering duchess, he surmises, must lead them to suspect that he himself may be the cause of her separation from the duke. His wild surmise holds a kernel of truth. Though she soon makes it clear that he interests her chiefly as the good friend of her nephew, Robert de Saint-Loup, her eagerness to invite him to dinner—to play the hostess herself—is threaded with hints of seduction. Just after she sits down beside him, they are noticed by their hostess, the duchess's aunt. Mildly chiding Marcel for coming so late, Madame de Villeparisis then catches herself:

Et remarquant que je parlais avec sa nièce, supposant peut-être que nous étions plus liés qu'elle ne savait:

"Mais je ne veux pas déranger votre conversation avec Oriane," ajouta-t-elle (car les bon offices de l'entremetteuse font partie des devoirs d'une maîtresse de maison). "Vous ne voulez pas venir diner mercredi avec elle?" (CG 669)

[And noticing that I was talking to her niece, and concluding, perhaps, we were more intimate than she had supposed:

"But don't let me interrupt your conversation with Oriane," she went on (for the good offices of the procuress are part of the duties of the perfect hostess [literally: mistress of the house]). "You wouldn't care to dine with her here [literally: come to dine with her] on Wednesday?"] (GW 432)

The tone of the parenthetical comment is as disarming as its content. Though the narrator follows Swann in calling the hostess an *entremetteuse*, a procuress, he voices none of Swann's animus. Instead he unspools a film of irony so fine as to be almost invisible. Is he mentally teasing the hostess for acting like a pimp here, or simply commending her for divining what her guests desire? Furthermore, *pace* Scott-Moncrieff, the narrator does not say that procuring is the duty of the perfect hostess—*l'hôtesse parfaite*—but rather of the *maîtresse de maison*, literally, the mistress of the house. Since *maîtresse* can also denote a sexual partner (the Duke de Guermantes is said to mistreat the duchess "en tant qu'il avait des maîtresses" [CG 744], insofar as he kept mistresses), the word exemplifies the way in which the whole scene weaves sexuality into the language of hospitality. Even though Marcel claims to have shed his infatuation with the duchess, he perceives at once that by squeezing in next to him she seems to mark him out as her lover, not only in the eyes of the other guests but also of their hostess, who interrupts their conversation just long enough to invite Marcel to dinner "avec elle," with the duchess. Then, after he declines both this invitation and a follow-up from Madame de Villeparisis, who walks away, the duchess invites him to a small dinner party, which (surprise, surprise!) he agrees to attend.[4] The duchess says nothing to indicate that she wants Marcel for a lover, but within the context of the narrator's thoughts about the relation between a hostess and a procuress, the whole conversation suggests that the duchess is procuring him for herself.

To be sure, she does not literally seduce him. Throughout the novel this beautiful, glittering, idiosyncratically outspoken wife of a philandering duke never takes a lover or even, so far as we can tell, tries to do so.[5] But she personifies the far more subtle ways in which the social world of Proust's novel can

seduce and betray anyone—especially a writer, as the narrator finally sees—
who surrenders all of his time and energy to it. In and out of the luxurious
houses of the Guermantes family, the novel repeatedly shows what hosts and
guests can do to each other without resorting to either literal seduction (the
tactics of a Circe) or outright violence.[6]

THE DUCHESS OF GUERMANTES: SEDUCTION, EXCLUSIVITY, CRUELTY

To the young Marcel, the name Guermantes is a sliding signifier. At first it
denotes the castle near the village of Combray, a castle at the end of the
"Guermantes way" along the river Vivonne, where the young Marcel walked
with his parents. The lady of this castle is a genius loci. As forests have their
genies ("leur génies," CG 311) and streams their deities, Madame de Guermantes
inhabited "an imaginary landscape" that turns out to be moveable (GW 5, 8).
When Robert de Saint-Loup dispels the mystery of the castle by telling Marcel
that it was bought by the Guermantes family in the seventeenth century and has
since been tastelessly furnished, the locus of the duchess becomes her house in
Paris, the Hôtel de Guermantes, where she entertains an assembly of the faithful
("des fidèles," CG 315) made up of famous and poetic names ("des noms célè-
bres et poétiques," CG 315). The guests she invites to her dinners for twelve are
"comme les statues d'or des apôtres de la Sainte-Chapelle, piliers symboliques
et consécrateurs, devant la Sainte Table" (CG 331) ("like the golden statues of
the apostles in the Sainte-Chapelle, symbolic, dedicative pillars before the
Lord's Table," GW 27). In Marcel's first impressions of the duchess, then, the
classical myth of the genius loci, which figures so prominently in stories of
hospitality and violation, gives way to the founding icon of the Christian church,
which is neither the cross nor the punning rock of Peter/Petrus but the table of
the Last Supper, site of hospitality and betrayal, locus of the first communion,
precursor of the altar at which bread is commemoratively consecrated and
broken at Mass.

Oriane's table evokes the splendid altar of Sainte-Chapelle far more than the
ordinary table of the Last Supper. While Christ preached a gospel of universal,
unconditional hospitality, Oriane prides herself on the exclusivity of her guest
list as well as the elegance of her house. Perhaps, however, its smallness helps
to explain why she seats no more than twelve. Even though she is said to own
"la première maison" in the Faubourg Saint-Germain (CG 328), the original
Hôtel de Guermantes—the family mansion—is gone, leaving only a wing in
which she and the duke occupy an apartment at the end of a courtyard flanked

by shops and workrooms. Since Marcel and his parents occupy another apartment in this same wing, he can see her come and go regularly but remains insatiably curious about the mysteries of her house and especially of its dinner parties. Once the genius of a castle in Combray, the duchess is now the genius of the Faubourg Saint-Germain, and the line between Marcel and the Faubourg—that is, between Marcel and his neighbor—"seemed to me all the more real because it was purely ideal" (GW 26).

Yet as we have just seen, Oriane soon draws him into her ideal world by means that hint of both seduction and rivalry between herself and Madame de Villeparisis, who invites him twice in vain before Oriane scores on the first try. Late in the novel her tactics become even more transparent. Dumbfounded to see Marcel at a big party given by the Princess de Guermantes, who has arranged a recitation by a rising young actress named Rachel (once the mistress of Robert de Saint-Loup), Oriane tells him to come to luncheon "alone with [Rachel] in my house" (LTR 422), thereby reenacting the role of procuring hostess played earlier by Madame de Villeparisis. Before he can even reply to this invitation, however,

> Elle me vanta surtout ses après-déjeuners où il y avait tous les jours X et Y. Car elle en était arrivée à cette conception des femmes à "salons" qu'elle méprisait autrefois (bien qu'elle le niât aujourd'hui) et dont la grande supériorité, le signe d'élection selon elle, étaient d'avoir chez elle "tous les hommes." (LTR 603)

> [She went on to tempt me with the glittering prospect of her "afternoons": every day after luncheon there was X- and there was Y-, and I found that her views on these matters were now those of all women who preside over a *salon*, those women whom in the past (though she denied it today) she had despised and whose great superiority, whose sign of election lay, according to her present mode of thinking, in getting "all the men" to come to them.] (TR 422–23)

The quoted phrase echoes what Madame Verdurin long ago said to Marcel near the end of a dinner party at her rented country house, la Raspelière. Urging him to come again with his "cousin," which is what he slyly calls his present mistress, Albertine, she assures Marcel that his cousin will find at the Verdurin house "toujours des hommes intelligents" (SeG 359) ("always clever men").[7] In adopting Madame Verdurin's tactics, the duchess plainly shows that by the final volume of the novel she has been surpassed as a hostess by Madame Verdurin, who gained her own social supremacy and "sign of election" by inviting men who were truly clever, who had achieved distinction by their own efforts—especially in the arts—rather than by simply inheriting a title.

Few such men can be found at the table of the duchess when Marcel first takes a seat at it. But the phrase suggests what gives exclusivity its power: the magnetism of what is at once sought after and scarce. The second counts for little without the first. So far from distinguishing a hostess, a small group of guests may expose her social impotence. Late in the novel, the now-superannuated Berma (a thinly disguised Sarah Bernhardt) holds a tea party that unhappily coincides with a grand musical reception given by the new Princess de Guermantes, the former Madame Verdurin, who married the prince after the deaths of her husband and his second wife. When Berma's tea party draws not even one of her most loyal friends but only her daughter, her surly son-in-law, and a young man looking ceaselessly at his watch because he yearns to be at the reception, the result is disaster: "vide absolut et mort" (*TR* 575) ("an absolute and deathlike void," *TR* 386). Nothing quite so dreadful strikes any other hostess in the novel, but at least two of them feel high anxiety at the prospect of losing their guests. While the Duchess of Guermantes prides herself on setting an apostolic table for no more than twelve, knowing that scores of others yearn to sit there, Madame Verdurin—as we have seen—feels bound to guard her faithful against the ever-present threats of heresy, distraction, and defection.

Less autocratic but no less anxious over the success of her parties, Madame de Saint-Euverte casts an invitational net wide enough to catch just about everyone the duchess slights. When Oriane (later the duchess, now the Princesse des Laumes) meets Swann at a musical evening given by Madame de Saint-Euverte, she claims to know none of the other guests, who strike her as so many "figurants" (*CCS* 331)—"extras" rented for the night (*SW* 351)—even though they include her cousin, the much older Marquise de Gallardon. Desperate to talk to the beautiful young princess, who has neither invited nor visited her in the six years since the princess was married, the marquise clumsily tries to impress her by sneering at the Judaism of Swann, the only other guest the princess "knows" and likes. "O, I know he's intelligent," says the marquise, "but still and all, a Jew in the home of the sister and sister-in-law of two archbishops" (*SW* 347). She then tries to sacrifice Swann on the altar of her own would-be exclusivity. "Some people do claim," she says, "that Swann is someone whom one can't have in one's house, is that true?" To which Oriane answers, "Why . . . you ought to know, . . . since you've invited him fifty times and he hasn't come once" (*SW* 348).

Laughing wildly, Oriane skewers a hostess whose pretensions to exclusivity cannot mask her social impotence. At the same time, Oriane's witty riposte anticipates the social ironies that later spring from the controversy over Captain Alfred Dreyfus, the Jewish army officer whose conviction for treason in 1894 will split the social world of Paris right across, not along, the gulf between "clever" men and dunces, social stars and nobodies. As the Duke de Guermantes and his titled friends strive to close ranks against the Dreyfusards and their supposed attack on the army and the nation, Madame Verdurin slowly climbs to social stardom by drawing to her house all the clever people—poets, writers, artists, dancers—who just happen to be Dreyfusards. But first Madame Verdurin must be content with such "faithful" as Doctor Cottard, the dim-witted punster, and likewise Madame de Saint-Euverte must sometimes act like a recruiting officer whose energy never flags. In *Sodom and Gomorrah*, just after giving a dinner party attended by Oriane and the Duke de Guermantes, the madame not only attends the grand reception given by the (first) Princesse de Guermantes but also spends most of her time there rallying the guests she has invited to her own garden party on the following day. Though she regularly gets just the sort of fashionable people who impress the readers of society columns, her guests (we are told) come only out of a sense of duty, and every time she talks to anyone at the reception she feels bound to market her party by hinting at its "unimaginable attractions" (*SaG* 82). She must also endure the withering scorn of the Baron de Charlus, who—knowing Madame de Saint-Euverte can overhear him—tells another lady that her so-called "garden parties" (he uses the English phrase) are nothing but "invitations to explore the sewers" (*SaG* 117) ("des invites à se promener dans les égouts," *SeG* 99). Even after overhearing this remark, which was made to be overheard, she abjectly asks Marcel how she could have offended the baron, urges him to bring the baron to the party "if he feels remorseful," and says she doesn't wish "to appear to be begging my guests to come" (*SaG* 118), which is just what she has been doing.

In thus braving insults while recruiting guests, Madame de Saint-Euverte provides a telling contrast to Oriane, who not only makes it plain that she will not attend the garden party but decries the vulgarity of all large parties, even the reception given by the Princesse de Guermantes. "I cannot understand," she says to Marcel, ". . . how Marie-Gilbert can invite us with all these dregs" (*SaG* 83–84) ("toutes cettes lie" *SeG* 72). By contrast, since the narrator has already reconstructed one of Oriane's own parties in exhaustive detail, we know how exclusive they are. The dinner party to which she invites the young Marcel includes a small, largely titled group of superficially amiable people such as the Princess de Parme, a "little dark woman taken up with good works" but nonetheless armed with an impenetrable sense of her exalted station. Her bearing, we are told, seemed to express the lesson that one should give to the needy "as much as you can . . . . without forfeiting your rank . . . but of course never any invitations to your soirées" (GW 493–94). This radical rewriting of Luke 14, where Christ tells the Pharisee who has invited him to dinner that he should spurn the rich and invite only the "poor, maimed, lame, or blind" (14:13), complements the irony of what Marcel has already imagined about Oriane's dinner parties and later repeats: that guests seated like the apostles in the Eglise Sainte-Chapelle participate in a social version of the Last Supper ("une sorte de Cène sociale," CG 802). A "social" Last Supper is a meal reconstituted for the carefully selected members of a particular society. While Christ's breaking of bread signifies a hospitality that has been reenacted for millions of communicants over the course of two millennia, the Duke and Duchess of Guermantes serve their exquisite dinners only to a carefully chosen few.

Within this tightly drawn circle Marcel is charmed to the point of seduction. Shortly after he arrives, the duke graciously leaves him alone to study a collection of paintings by Elstir, and though Marcel later learns that he has kept everyone waiting nearly three quarters of an hour for him, the duke signals the start of dinner timidly, so as not to make him feel responsible for the delay.[8] When he joins the other guests, the bare-shouldered ladies give him "long, caressing glances, as though shyness alone restrained them from kissing [him]" (GW 489). And even though Oriane never makes an erotic overture to Marcel or anyone else, she somehow radiates the scent of availability or at the very least blurs the line between hospitable warmth and pheromonal heat. In the world of the Guermantes this heat is just barely suppressed. "On feignait d'ignorer," writes the narrator, "que le corps d'une maîtresse de maison était manié par qui voulait, pourvu que le «salon» fût demeuré intact" (CG 716) (One pretended to ignore that the body of a mistress of the house was handled by anyone who wished, provided the "salon" remained intact).[9] Here Proust not only exploits again the sexual implications of "maîtresse" but also reinforces them with the brutality of "manié": handled, touched, and fingered as if her "corps"—like the "cors" of Lady Bertilak, the equally seductive hostess of *Sir Gawain*—were an object made for manipulation, hardly a *virgo intacta*.

But no one mishandles this particular "maîtresse de maison" without paying a bitter price for doing so. As even her husband implies, she uses her seductiveness to dominate her guests, especially the young Marcel. Though Marcel is barely allowed to speak (except to us, in retrospect), the duke thinks he must be overwhelmed by the duchess's literary sophistication when she quotes a few lines of Victor Hugo. "This young man," he says, "must be quite captivated" (GW 573) ("subjugué," CG 787). Neither host nor hostess perceives that their young guest is actually disgusted by her taste in literature, which—he tells us—"was the opposite of my own" (GW 572).[10] Furthermore, as Marcel knows at least in retrospect, the duchess's highly opinionated knowledge of Hugo's poetry is just one of the weapons she wields against a guest who happens to be the freshly jilted ex-mistress of her husband.[11] Ostensibly solicitous as well as hospitable toward this Madame d'Arpajon, who has actually sought the duchess's sympathy for the duke's abandonment of her, the duchess quietly crucifies her. When the Princess of Parma remarks on Madame d'Arpajon's love of poetry after hearing her fervently praise Hugo's "imagination," the duchess replies—in a would-be undertone clearly meant to be overheard by the lady in question—that Madame d'Arpajon knows nothing of poetry, that "she's become literary since she's been forsaken," that "she's boring to a degree you can't imagine," that she gives the duchess a headache whenever she comes to see her, "and all this because Basin took it into his head for a year or so [to cheat on me with her]" (GW 569) ("de me trompailler avec elle," CG 783).[12]

In thus nailing Madame d'Arpajon to her dinner table, the duchess manifests the contempt she feels for any other woman who threatens her supremacy as a wife or her authority as a hostess.[13] Near the end of this attack on her husband's ex-mistress, she gratuitously insults her footman by calling his fiancée "une petite grue"(CG 783)—a little whore—because, she says, he has been sulking over the duchess's refusal to ask the young woman to tea. With this scathing phrase Oriane turns the knife in a wound she has already made. A little earlier, on the flimsiest pretext possible, she suddenly revokes a day off she had previously granted her footman so that he might visit his fiancée—a gesture which Marcel heard the footman extol as "the kindness of Madame la Duchesse" (GW 488). But when one of her guests offers to send her a dozen pheasants on the day after the dinner, presumably to reciprocate her hospitality, she insists on sending the footman to fetch them on the next day, his day off, even though the guest says that the day following "will be soon enough" (GW 558). Her kindness, then, is merely the prelude to willful cruelty. Though she implies that she will give some of the pheasants away to her servants and is therefore complimented on her kindness to them, she seems driven chiefly by her desire to punish the footman for his presumption in seeking an invitation from her as well as for mooning over a woman who, the duchess thinks, must be no better than a streetwalker.[14]

Furthermore, since she makes her withering comment while the footman is serving her guests, she upsets him so much that he more than once bumps the elbow of a young duke, prompting the man to smile at him. "This good humour," writes the narrator, "seemed to me to betoken kindness on the guest's part. But the insistency of his smile led me to think that, aware of the servant's discomfort, what he felt was perhaps a malicious amusement" (GW 569–70) ("un joie méchante," CG 783). Thus a guest subtly helps his hostess to torture her footman.

"La bonne humeur" (*CG* 783) is the last thing to be found in Oriane herself. Priding herself above all on her wit, she uses it to ridicule, punish, and humiliate anyone she dislikes or disdains. Whenever any mistress abandoned by the duke sought the sympathy of his duchess, who was ostensibly "known to be kind," the duchess would uncomplainingly give it and then assume that her "pity . . . for the unfortunate woman gave her the right to make fun of her, even to her face, whatever the lady might say" (*GW* 557). Not long after sneering at the emptiness of Madame d'Arpajon, the duchess mocks her failure to grasp the point of a naughty crack about Zola.[15] To be sure, Madame d'Arpajon deserves a chuckle at her dim-wittedness even as Madame Gallardon deserves a hearty laugh at her pretensions to exclusivity. But just before the duchess makes her crack about Zola, Marcel silently notes that the would-be "originality" of her ideas about literature thinly masks what strikes him as a good deal of stupidity (*GW* 576). Likewise, her celebrated wit is exemplified by nothing more than a clever pun, which makes one wonder just how far her mind surpasses that of the only other punster we have met so far: the tedious Doctor Cottard.[16]

Oriane's wit beats his largely in malice. After prolonged discussion of the duchess's pun, the duke recalls a "far wittier remark" she made a few days before the Guermantes' dinner party. When her cousin Zénaïde had expected her for lunch and Oriane sent a last-minute telegram to cancel her attendance, Zénaïde called her to say that the food would be excellent, and the duke himself, while telling the story, says her cousin's food is "of the very best." But Oriane thinks her cousin's portions are stingy. So when she learned that the lunch would include "seven little *bouchées à la reine*"—literally, "mouthfuls"—she said, "Seven little *bouchées!* . . . that means we shall be at least eight!" (*GW* 563). Though this prompts a hearty laugh from the Princesse de Parme, Oriane's joke springs from the willfulness of a capricious guest and the spitefulness of a jealous hostess. As the narrator observes, she ducked out of the lunch because "she liked people to know" she was hard to get, and she mocks her cousin because she cannot bear to hear the food of any other hostess praised above her own (*GW* 562–63). In saying, too, that her cousin has neither malice nor wit (*GW* 560), she strongly implies that malice is the engine of her own wit.[17]

THE POLITICS OF EXCLUSIVITY: THE DREYFUS CASE

Not long before giving the dinner party to which she invites Marcel, the Duchess of Guermantes turns up at an afternoon reception given by Madame de Villeparisis and attended by various others, including Marcel. When the topic of Dreyfus comes up, the duchess strives to prove herself once again original, wholly unbound by the opinions of anyone else or by any sense of duty to her social caste. Rather than standing for or against Dreyfus, she deplores the expectation that she should socially embrace everyone who thinks him guilty, spurns Jews, or both. She cannot bear the idea of having to entertain or even socially acknowledge "all the people one has spent one's life trying to avoid" just because "they're against Dreyfus" or "just because they're supposed to be right-thinking and don't deal with Jewish tradesmen" (GW 271). She also judges the men in the case by her own stylistic criteria. While deploring the "idiotic, turgid letters" Dreyfus writes from the island where he is confined, she admires the phrasemaking of Major Ferdinand Esterhazy (GW 273), who had been acquitted in 1896.[18] But none of this means that she supports Dreyfus, Jewish tradesmen, or Jewish people of any kind, with the notable exception of Swann, whose wit and charm evidently make his Judaism invisible to her. "I don't know any [Jews]," she says (GW 271).

More precisely, she and the members of her set know how to exclude Jews from those they socially "know" and entertain. Besides Swann, the duchess is well aware of at least one other Jewish person: the actress named Rachel, who is now the mistress of the duchess's nephew Robert. Though Rachel performed in the duchess's house "before anyone else's," the duchess now considers her "a perfect horror . . . . and besides grotesquely ugly" (GW 253–54). Rachel's name comes up at Madame de Villeparisis's reception because it is mentioned by a Jewish man not yet introduced to those around him: Marcel's friend Bloch, who has written a play that the madame would like to see performed in her house. When Bloch offers to put Rachel in the play, the madame declines because she thinks Robert is in the process of breaking up with her. Then Bloch shocks his hearers. When he tries to claim that Robert showed his good breeding by introducing Bloch to the son of Sir Rufus Israels, whom the Guermantes consider "a foreign upstart" ("étranger parvenu," CG 515), the company is dumbfounded (GW 247–48).[19]

Bloch himself is treated as an alien, or *étranger*, by almost everyone else at the party. In a private conversation his arguments for Dreyfus are judiciously weighed by Norpois, a French diplomat, but Bloch cannot "get him to pronounce on the question of Dreyfus's guilt" (GW 277), and elsewhere Bloch is simply rebuffed. When he presumes that a Belgian diplomat named d'Argencourt must be a Dreyfusard because "everyone is, abroad," the man answers, "'It is a question that concerns only the [French among themselves], don't you think?' . . . with that peculiar form of insolence which consists in ascribing to the other person an opinion which one plainly knows that he does not share since he has just expressed one directly its opposite" (GW 281–82). In the French original, "les Français entre eux" (CG 543) literally means "the French among themselves." By using this phrase, d'Argencourt plainly implies that Bloch is not one of them. Then, as Bloch blushes, d'Argencourt casts around the room a smile that is full of malice toward Bloch ("malveillant pour Bloch," CG 544) but that turns cordial when it comes back to Bloch "so as to deprive him of any excuse for annoyance at the words he had just heard, though those words remained just as cruel" (GW 282).

The hostess sharpens this cruelty. Just after d'Argencourt makes his cutting remark, she says something that the narrator cannot hear but that must, he says, have referred to Bloch's Judaism because her face betrayed "la gaîté curieuse et malveillante qu'inspire un groupement humain auquel nous nous sentons radi-calement étrangers" (CG 544) (the inquisitive, malevolent amusement that inspires a human group to which we feel ourselves radically alien). Proust's French is at once precise and provocative. Following a faulty text that reads "qu'inspiré," Scott-Moncrieff and his team say that the hostess's amusement is "inspired *by* a human group" (GW 282, emphasis added) — inspired, that is, by a group (of Jews) from which we feel ourselves alien.[20] But "qu'inspire" is active. As Proust wrote it, the sentence puts "us," *nous,* not among the anti-Semitic onlookers titillated by Jews and made to feel alien from them but among all those, Jewish or not, who are made to feel alien *by the sight of others enjoying a secret joke at our expense.* Here, in other words, we are asked to identify with Bloch as a guest betrayed.

In fewer than two pages Bloch is made to feel totally ostracized. Though Robert, a Dreyfusard himself for the time being, has previously assured Bloch that he can speak freely of Dreyfus to the Duke de Châtellerault, the duke says that he never discusses the case "except among Japhetics," meaning Jews.[21] At this remark, which prompts everyone but Bloch to smile at the duke, Bloch asks naively, "But how on earth did you know?" (GW 282–83). He gets no answer. And when he turns to question another guest, an archivist and nationalist fearful of revolution breaking out "at any moment," the man makes no reply but instead wonders "whether Bloch might not be a secret emissary of the [Jewish] Syndicate." He also reports on Bloch to their hostess, who is a "little afraid" of the archivist and fearful too that Bloch might somehow compromise Norpois (GW 283). Bloch is thereby sunk in the eyes of Madame de Villeparisis. By pretending to be asleep in her armchair when he says goodbye, saying nothing at all in response, and letting her "eyes betray no hint of recognition" (GW 284), she signifies that he is henceforth banished from her house.

Surprisingly, the banishment is soon revoked. When the bewildered Bloch calls on Madame de Villeparisis a few days later, she warmly receives him because she still wants to see his play performed in her house and because her would-be banishment of him was itself a little play, a scene staged to mollify the anti-Dreyfusards at her party. But her private kindness to Bloch hardly changes the way he looks to others. To nearly all he remains an *étranger*, as we can see from what the Baron de Charlus says about Bloch to Marcel:

> "It is not a bad idea, if you wish to learn about life . . . to have a few foreigners [étrangers] among your friends."
>
> I replied that Bloch was French.
>
> "Indeed," said M. de Charlus, "I took him to be a Jew." His assertion of this incompatibility made me suppose that M. de Charlus was more anti-Dreyfusard than anyone I had met. He protested, however, against the charge of treason levelled against Dreyfus. But his protest took this form: "I believe the newspapers say that Dreyfus has committed a crime against his country. . . . [But] the crime is non-existent. This compatriot of your friend [le compatriote de votre ami] would have committed a crime if he had betrayed Judea, but what has he to do with France?"
>
> I pointed out that if there should be a war the Jews would be mobilized just as much as anyone else.
>
> "Perhaps so, and I am not sure that it would not be an imprudence. If we bring over Senegalese or Malagasies, I hardly suppose that their hearts will be in the task of defending France, and that is only natural. Your Dreyfus might rather be convicted of a breach of the laws of hospitality" (GW 330) ("règles de l'hospitalité," CG 584).

Nowhere else in the novel is hospitality linked so explicitly to French nationalism. As a native of Alsace-Lorraine, a partly German-speaking region of France that was partially annexed by Germany after the Franco-Prussian war of 1870–71, Dreyfus might have been considered, almost literally, a borderline patriot. But for the baron, as for all the other anti-Dreyfusards we meet in this novel, it is Dreyfus's Judaism, not his Alsatianism, that makes him an *étranger* in his native land, the very land he has been serving as a French officer. In the eyes of the baron, no Jew can be French. Since Dreyfus and his "compatriot" Bloch must be citizens of Judea (as if it had been a nation before the founding of Israel in 1948), the only way they could betray their country would be to betray Judea. In France he has merely broken the rules of hospitality. This starkly hypocritical charge serves only to justify—or rather rationalize—the starkly inhospitable treatment of Jews. At Madame de Villeparisis's party we see what happens to any Jew, no matter how talented, who dares to expose his Judaism by speaking up on behalf of Dreyfus. He is unmistakably defined as alien, unassimilable, strange, incapable of ever becoming French, let alone of gaining admission to the world of the Guermantes. Though the hostess invited Bloch and clearly aims to nurture his talents, she is so intimidated by the anti-Semitism of her other guests that she feels compelled to signify his banishment from her house. In 1940 French publishers did something similar. Once Nazi troops had crossed the Maginot Line and occupied France, the publishers readily accepted a Nazi manifesto banning books by Jewish writers, who, "betraying the hospitality that France extended to them, unscrupulously pushed for war" (qtd. Rothstein 3). Evidently the baron's charge, which doubtless echoed one circulating through the Paris of Proust's time, endured to at least the middle of the last century.

While Bloch is made to feel that Jews simply cannot find genuine hospitality in Parisian society, a special exemption for wit and charm has opened all doors to Swann. But near the end of *The Guermantes Way*, when Swann is dying, they start closing even on him, as if to anticipate his banishment from life itself. Consider first what Marcel does two months after his dinner with the duchess. Early one evening in what is presumably the month of June (we later learn that spring is ten months off), he goes to see the Duke and Duchess de Guermantes to find out whether or not he can trust an invitation he has received to a reception given by the Prince and Princess de Guermantes. (The invitation, he fears, may be a bad joke.) Finding the duke alone, he soon learns that neither he nor the duchess will give him any help. This is partly because they dislike doing favors for anyone[22] and partly because they are caught up in preparations for a three-stage evening: a dinner party, the princess's grand reception, and, at 1:00 a.m., a fancy dress ball that will require a return to their house for the donning of outfits furnished and fitted by *costumiers*. Their craving for social pleasure trumps all other obligations. Just as the duchess tramples on the feelings of her footman, the duke not only declines to help Marcel resolve his little quandary but also rejects the news that his own cousin is dying because taking it seriously would compel him to give up his round of parties for the sake of a bedside visit.

All this sets the stage for the arrival of Swann, who has been asked by the duchess to bring proofs of his article on the coinage of the Order of Malta along with a photograph of the coins. Speaking to Marcel before Swann arrives, the duke is surprised that the history of Christian knights should pique the interest of a Jew. "It's astonishing," he says parenthetically, "the passion people of one religion have for studying others" (GW 664). Then he tells Marcel not to mention the princess's reception to Swann because Swann may not have been invited. Though the prince—the duke's cousin—"likes [Swann] immensely," says the duke, "now of course the Dreyfus case has made things more serious. Swann ought to have realised that he more than anyone else must drop all connexion with those fellows, instead of which he says the most regrettable things" (GW 668). In the eyes of the duke, then, Swann deserves the hospitality of the Guermantes only so long as he suppresses all trace of his Judaism and hence allows his host and hostess to forget that he is Jewish at all.[23]

Furthermore, brooking no demands on their sympathy and always expecting their self-esteem to be stroked, they tolerate the news of Swann's imminent death no more than they acknowledge his Judaism. When Swann tells the duke, in response to a question, that one of his paintings is not the work of an old master but rather a "bad joke" (GW 671), the duke seethes. When Swann declines the duchess's invitation to come with her and the duke to Italy and Sicily the following spring, she jealously reminds him that he has accompanied the "more highly favored" Madame de Montmorency on a trip to Venice and Vicenza, where he "showed her things she'd never dreamed of" (GW 687). When the gravely ill Swann says he has no more than four months to live, she insists he must be joking (as if his death were yet another bad joke), and though she vaguely perceives that "the dinner party to which she was going must count for less to Swann than his own death" (GW 689), she yields to the social imperatives of the duke. He then takes full charge. Since he insists that the imminence of an eight o'clock dinner gives them no more time for Swann (or, as we can see, for his imminent death), she starts to mount the carriage that awaits them until the duke catches her wearing black shoes with a red dress. At this point the rule of punctuality is trumped by the rule of color coordination, and the duchess must return to her room. "Even if we turn up at half past eight," says the duke, "they'll wait for us, but you can't possibly go there in a red dress and black shoes" (GW 690). Death itself finally becomes no more than a trope for boredom, social fatigue, or hunger pangs. "Il y a des soirs où on aimerait mieux mourir!" (CG 874), says the duchess ("There are evenings when one would sooner die!" GW 679). While she changes her shoes, doffing the color of mourning for the festive blaze of red, the duke tells Marcel and Swann to leave because "she's already tired, and [if she talks further with you] she'll reach the dinner-table quite dead" (GW 690). As for the duke himself, he must go because he is dying of hunger ("je meurs de faim," CG 884). But like Swann's Judaism, real death cannot be a guest in this household.[24]

At the reception given by the Prince and Princess de Guermantes, Swann's Judaism is at best a covert guest. On one hand, the duke has already told Marcel that the prince "has a fit if he sees a Jew a mile off" (GW 668), and as we later learn from the narrator, the prince's "anti-semitism . . . did not yield before any social distinction" (*SaG* 79). This rule of exclusion underscores another rule arbitrarily imposed on the princess, who sometimes cuts even her friends from her guest list so as not to annoy the Baron de Charlus, "who had excommunicated them" (*SaG* 56) ("qui les avait excommuniés," *SeG* 48) for some unstated reason: another telling allusion to the perversion of Christian hospitality. On the other hand, the prince makes Swann socially admissible by ingeniously de-Judaizing him. Knowing that "Swann's grandmother, a Protestant married to a Jew, had been the Duc de Berry's mistress," the prince entertained him on the false supposition that Swann's father was the duke's "natural son," making Swann himself "a gentile to his fingertips" (*SaG* 79).

Implied in this supposition is the assumption that Swann will bury his Judaism, and as the duke has told Marcel, this means dropping "all connexion" with the Dreyfusards. Precisely because he has failed to do so and has taken no trouble to hide his support for Dreyfus, the special attention shown him by the prince looks to others like a social death warrant. The dying Swann comes to the reception only because the prince has sent him a wire asking for a private conversation. When the prince "immediately carrie[s] him off, with the force of a suction pump, to the further end of the garden," some people say that the prince simply means "to show him the door" (*SaG* 65) ("de le mettre à la porte," *SeG* 56).[25] As if he had heard every word of their tête-à-tête, Colonel Froberville flatly declares that the prince "gave Swann a dressing down" and banned him from the house "in view of the opinions he flaunts" (*SaG* 88). Hearing this, the duke charges Swann with exactly the crime charged against Dreyfus himself by the Baron de Charlus: breaking the rules of hospitality. Given all he has received from society and especially from Oriane, the duke says, "he should have openly disavowed the Jews and the partisans of the accused" (*SaG* 89). Deploring Swann's "ingratitude" to himself and the duchess, the duke, we are told, "evidently considered that to denounce Dreyfus as guilty of high treason, whatever opinion one might hold in one's heart of hearts as to his guilt, constituted a sort of thank-offering ["un espèce de remerciement" (*SeG* 77)] for the manner in which one had been received in the Faubourg Saint-Germain" (*SaG* 89–90).[26] In the eyes of the duke, then, Swann's reawakened "sense of moral solidarity with the rest of the Jews" (*SaG* 104), as the narrator will call it, makes him a faithless guest, a betrayer of his host and hostess. He betrays them in taking the side of anyone who challenges the authority of France. Unlike Charlus, the duke once believed that a Jew *could* be a Frenchman but now finds himself mistaken: in spite of all their hospitality to Swann, he has bitterly repaid the nation, the Guermantes, and all of their set. "Ah!" says the duke, "il nous récompense bien mal" (*SeG* 77). But the duchess finds her own way to repay him. Feigning a schoolgirl melancholy, she says, "Yes, it's true, I have no reason to conceal the fact that I did feel a sincere affection for Charles!" (*SaG* 90). By using the past tense—"que *j'avais* une sincère affection" (*SeG* 77, italics mine)—she banishes him from her heart as well as her house.

Everything the duke says about the host of this reception prompts us to infer that he too will banish Swann from his house. But unlike the duke, whose superficial camaraderie barely masks his disdain, the prince is a man whose reserve shields a genuinely considerate heart. We glimpse him first through the eyes of Marcel. Relieved to be greeted with a smile by the princess, who thereby assures him that his invitation was no joke after all, he is nonetheless dispatched to find the prince and looks in vain for someone to introduce him. Shortly after the Baron de Charlus declines because Marcel has foolishly told him that the princess "was very nice to me" (*SaG* 63)—as if he did not need the baron's help at all—Marcel hears the voice of M. de Bréauté, a man whom he met at the duchess's dinner party and whose "bonsoir" now sounds "comme la voix d'un sauveur possible" (*SeG* 54) ("like the voice of a possible savior," *SaG* 63): a promise of social redemption, a sign of election. But when Bréauté finally presents Marcel to the prince, he does so with a lip-smacking, vulgarly ceremonial air, as if handing the prince with a word of recommendation a plate of petit fours ("en les recommandant, un assiette de petit fours," *SeG* 55). Like Homer's Odysseus in the cave of Polyphemos or Dickens's Pip at the Pumblechooks' Christmas dinner table, Marcel is a guest suddenly made to feel like food, or possibly, and very obliquely, like the savior who identified his own body with the bread eaten at the Last Supper. But the prince neither consumes him in any sense nor disdains him. Instead, showing that he already knows something of Marcel's family, he politely asks him if he plans to follow his father's career. Furthermore, his private conversation with Swann proves him to be anything but a devouring host. As Swann himself confidentially tells Marcel, the prince told Swann that he had come to share his view of Dreyfus. While he could not publicly support Dreyfus, he said, he had long suspected "grave illegalities" in the trial (*SaG* 122), and once he learned that the princess, like himself, had been having Masses said for the man, he decided to give Swann the pleasure of knowing "how closely akin" their opinions were (*SaG* 128).

What can be made of this breach in the Guermantean wall of anti-Semitic exclusivity? On the one hand, it seems to forecast a further breach. Just as the prince's conversion to Dreyfusism springs in part from the example of his wife, the Duke of Guermantes is converted, soon after the prince's reception, by an Italian princess and her two sisters-in-law, whom he meets at a spa. But neither conversion fundamentally changes the feelings with which titled Parisians regard the Jews. As Swann explains to Bloch, who eagerly wants the prince to sign a petition on Dreyfus's behalf, the prince will do no such thing, and Swann himself declines to do so because "he felt that his name was too Hebraic not to create a bad effect" and because he did not want to be associated in any way with antimilitarism (*SG* 130).[27] In one version of a passage on the German-born Princess of Guermantes, the anti-Dreyfusards take the prince's conversion as evidence that he has succumbed to the insidious influence of her "foreign blood" (*SG* 623). Xenophobia thus turns hospitality itself into a subtle form of treason.

MADAME VERDURIN: THE TYRANNY OF THE *PATRONNE*

With a little fudging, Proust's novel might be called a tale of four hostesses: the Duchess de Guermantes, the Princess de Guermantes, Odette de Crecy, and Madame Verdurin. While at first the duchess reigns as "goddess of the waters" in her palace on the Seine (*SaG* 163), she and the princess are gradually overtaken by the other two. Starting out as a mere *cocotte*, a loose chick, Odette reaches "le dernier échelon" (*SeG* 143) ("the top of the ladder," *SG* 168) as Madame Swann, gaining, to our surprise, "a reputation for profound intellectuality," drawing to her house not only a dazzling array of titled figures but also "all the fashionable dramatists and novelists of the day" and thereby beating out in vitality and excitement the predictable receptions given by the Princess de Guermantes, who together with the duchess ruled "an exalted world . . . in which people were beginning to lose interest" (*SG* 169). But Madame Verdurin tops them all. Unlike Odette, whose "sound" anti-Dreyfusism reassures society (*SG* 166), Madame Verdurin flaunts her Dreyfusism, which makes her salon "far more lively . . . than the faintly nationalistic . . . salon of Mme Swann." She also conspicuously sponsors the "new music" of Igor Stravinsky, the Ballets Russes, and the new leaps of Vaslav Nijinsky (*SaG* 165–66). This moment of glory "si longtemps et si vainement attendu par la Patronne" (*SeG* 141) ("so long and so vainly awaited by the *Patronne*," SaG 166) prompts us to infer that Madame Verdurin has at last fulfilled the meaning of her name as patroness of the arts, which may partly explain how she manages, two years after the death of her husband, to marry the widowed Prince of Guermantes and thereby become the queen of the Faubourg Saint-Germain, grandest of all hostesses.

But this way of defining her gradual ascent to social glory overlooks a crucial point: though it is possible in French to speak of patronizing the arts (*patronner les arts*), the word *patronne* denotes not a supporter of anything cultural but, as applied to living persons, the wife of a shopkeeper or the madam of a brothel.[28] In the latter capacity its connotations overlap those of *maîtresse*. As we have already seen, Madame Verdurin is something of a procuress, an *entremetteuse*, when she does all she can at her parties to promote an affair between Odette and Forcheville. Besides these sexual connotations, Patronne (always capitalized for her) links Madame Verdurin to the world of commerce from which the wealth of the Verdurins springs. As an avatar of the haute bourgeoisie, she longs to join the aristocracy and participate in its rituals of hospitality, but for much of the novel she is excluded from it, forced to make do with managing a set of "faithful" distinguished not by their titles or social status (even Swann's makes him suspect in her eyes) but by their loyalty to her. Used repeatedly of Madame Verdurin, then, *Patronne* suggests a hostess who somehow combines the ecclesiastical power ("pouvoir ecclésiastique," *LaP* 749) of a high priestess with the marketplace authority of a commercial boss.[29]

This kind of authority does not keep her from sometimes treating her guests with generosity and grace. En route for the first time to la Raspelière, the country house that she and her husband rent during the summer, Marcel "adore[s] the Verdurins" for sending a carriage to meet the train bearing him and his fellow guests (*SaG* 342). At the house itself she discharges in full the duties of the hostess ("les devoirs de l'hôtesse," *SeG* 386) by not only serving vintage wines and succulent dishes but also conveying her guests around the neighborhood so as to intoxicate them "with the purity of the breeze and the magnificence of the sights" (*SaG* 469). Yet even this gesture comes from a presumptuously grasping hand. Though the Verdurins are merely renting la Raspelière for the summer, Madame Verdurin would show the local sights "as though they were annexes (more or less detached) of her property, which you could not help going to see if you came to lunch with her and which conversely you would never have known had you not been entertained by the Mistress" (*SaG* 459)—more accurately, "received at the home of the Patronne" ("reçu chez la Patronne," *SeG* 387). The shift from one epithet to the other, from *hôtesse* to *Patronne*, reaffirms the essence of Madame Verdurin's character, the proprietary force of her hospitality even on property that is not her own.[30]

Combined with her status as a tenant, her need for the loyalty of the faithful, and her acute ambivalence toward the socially elevated bores of the aristocracy, Madame Verdurin's sense of proprietorship richly complicates her status as a hostess when she invites the Marquis and Marquise de Cambremer, who own the property rented by the Verdurins but who, as we know from other sources, are social pygmies in the eyes of the Guermantes.[31] Madame Verdurin feels conflicted about them on other grounds. On one hand, the prospect of entertaining them enchants her "for reasons of snobbery," reasons she cannot divulge to the faithful lest she forsake her doctrine that all aristocrats are bores. On the other hand, she hates dining with people who do not belong to her clan, know nothing of Richard Wagner, oppose Dreyfus, and bore her (*SaG* 327). Pretending, therefore, that her motives are purely mercenary, she says she will tolerate these bores just to get their lease renewed next year on better terms, such as lower rent and more privileges (*SaG* 327–28). The Cambremers expect just the opposite. While socially disdaining the Verdurins, the Cambremers accept their invitation only because they hope these tenants will "return again for many seasons" and renew their lease at "an *increased* rent" (*SaG* 328, 361, emphasis added). Instead of reciprocating the Verdurins' hospitality, then, the Cambremers aim to exploit it. But the Verdurins are equally exploitative. It is hard to imagine a sharper collision between the motives of hosts and guests.

When the Cambremers play host in their turn, they are promptly punished for their exploitative moves. Leaving the Verdurins out, they ask Doctor Cottard because of his "go" (his would-be liveliness) and his usefulness in case anyone takes sick in their house, but they do not ask his wife because they don't want to "start anything" with her (*SaG* 565). They also ask Charles Morel, a promising violinist now being kept by the baron, so that he can not only perform for them but also tell the baron afterward about the "brilliant" people he met at their house (*SaG* 565). Yet both of these would-be guests default. Furious that two members of her clan have been invited without her, Madame Verdurin dictates Cottard's stiff refusal ("We are dining that evening with Mme. Verdurin," *SaG* 566), which requites the Cambremers for slighting both the Verdurins and Madame Cottard. Morel, told by Charlus to avoid anyone named Cambremerde (Cambreshit), answers only at the last minute, when he telegrams his no. Then, when the Cambremers invite the baron—and belatedly Morel also—so as to impress a "top drawer" couple they have already secured, Morel accepts for them both at the baron's dictation but arrives alone to say that the baron can't come (*SaG* 570–71). In response, the Cambremers can do little more than seethe. Suspecting Madame Verdurin of plotting against them, they retaliate "tit for tat" by half-accepting her next invitation (sending Cambremer alone) and sneering at her social pretensions: just because she's renting our house, says Madame Cambremer to Marcel, she thinks "she should also be entitled to make friends with us" (*SaG* 573).

Here the marquise proves blind as well as hypocritical. Quite aside from the fact that she and her husband willingly accepted Madame Verdurin's first invitation for mercenary reasons, the marquise fails to see how formidable an adversary Madame Verdurin can be. Having earlier detached Odette from Swann when his devotion to her little clan wavered, she has just bullied one of her faithful—Brichot, the Sorbonne professor—into cutting his amorous ties with the marquise by ceasing to accept her lunch invitations. Madame Verdurin will not allow any one of her faithful to court—or be seduced by—another hostess. Though Brichot grieves so much at giving up the marquise that he endangers his sight, she has her way.

The Verdurins have no pity for him or anyone else. Just as the imminent death of a close friend or relative will not keep the Duke and Duchess of Guermantes from a round of parties, the death of a talented pianist well known to the Verdurins does not keep them from holding a party at la Raspelière, where Verdurin warns his guests not to disturb his "morbidly sensitive" wife by mentioning the pianist (*SaG* 344).[32] He died, Verdurin says, "at the right moment," like the lobsters grilled for their dinner, and they cannot be expected "to die of hunger because Dechambre is dead" (*SaG* 346). They show scarcely more sympathy to their living guests. Even after Brichot risks his eyesight for them, they laugh "publicly" at his pedantry, "even his infirmities," and though they regularly feed a poor ex-archivist named Saniette, who (says Madame Verdurin) "needs his dinners" because "he hasn't a penny in the world" (*SaG* 405) and is also very sick, they ridicule him to the point of torment whenever he tries to speak. To his face one evening Verdurin compares him to "the stupidest man I know" (*SaG* 387), and when Marcel tells Madame Verdurin that she has not been very kind to Saniette, she says he exasperates them by cringing like a whipped dog instead of striking back (*SaG* 405).

At the end of the evening Madame Verdurin is "particularly affectionate" to Saniette "so as to make certain of his returning next time," even telling him that her husband "enjoys your wit and intelligence" (*SaG* 433–34). But this is flagrantly contradicted by everything Verdurin has said to him, and they invite him only to torture him. Later, at a party held in their Parisian house, Verdurin tells his servants to keep Saniette waiting for last in a drafty cloakroom, wheezing and shivering and "fearful of catching cold" as he stands holding out his hat and coat (*CAP* 256). Then, on learning right after the party that he is penniless and owes nearly a million francs from bad bets on the stock exchange, Saniette suffers a stroke (*CAP* 369). It is hard to believe the Verdurins did not help drive him to it. Though Verdurin promptly decides to give him ten thousand francs a year for three years while concealing its source, this burst of charity hardly atones for what they have done to their longtime guest.[33]

Unlike Saniette, Marcel is on the whole treated courteously by the Verdurins. But he is also made to feel the heavy hand of Madame Verdurin's possessiveness, her eagerness to bind him to her clan and fill him with loathing for any other hostess. As he leaves la Raspelière, she tells him, "I'm counting on you not to fail me next Wednesday" (*SaG* 426) and warns him against other houses. "Féterne," she says, speaking of the Cambremers' estate, "is starvation corner," home of rats, where "you'll die of hunger" (*SaG* 429). Likewise, when she hears that Marcel is planning to attend a tea party with his alleged cousin Albertine and the baron at Rivebelle, she sneers at its "filth" and says, "That I don't want, I don't murder my guests, Monsieur" ("Ça je ne veux pas, je n'assassine pas mes invités, monsieur," *SeG* 360).

If this startling allusion to the long history of treacherous hospitality sounds overstated, it is equally startling to see how Madame Verdurin poisons Marcel's next visit to her. While traveling with Albertine in a hired car, he stops at la Raspelière because Albertine wants to meet the Verdurins. When Madame Verdurin, who was not expecting them, begs them to stay for tea, they refuse because they plan to travel on, at which point la Patronne, "unable to face the thought of leaving us, or perhaps of letting slip a new diversion, decided to accompany us" (*SaG* 464). From that moment Marcel's visit is "empoisonnée" (*SeG* 391), poisoned. After trying in vain to shake Madame Verdurin with a lie about a call they have to make, he insists he must be alone with Albertine. Only then does Madame Verdurin accept his departure "in a voice trembling with rage" (*SaG* 465), and even as they leave she calls them back to urge them not to "let her down" on the following Wednesday (*SaG* 466).

Madame Verdurin is relentless. Beneath her possessiveness, her hatred of rival hostesses, and her fear of relinquishing her guests lies the deepest of all her fears: that of being abandoned by her faithful, of losing rather than gaining the social ground she must traverse to become a leading light in Parisian society. But for Madame Verdurin it is not enough to keep her grip on the faithful or even to attract a galaxy of titled stars. She can be satisfied only when all of them acknowledge her as la Patronne, which is precisely what does not happen at the reception she holds in Paris for a set of guests selected by the Baron de Charlus.

The Verdurins first meet the baron when Morel brings him along to dinner at la Raspelière, where one of the guests, a sculptor, knows him only as a man of low morals, and the rest, including the Verdurins, know nothing his social position. Approaching Madame Verdurin with an affectedly fluttering, "lady-like" gait that belies his effort to "assume a masculine appearance," he displays "all the seductiveness of a grande dame."[34] In spite of this or perhaps because of it (since Madame Verdurin dismisses the warnings of the sculptor), the baron soon charms her. When he explains Brichot's reference to Maecenas, patron of Horace, by saying that Maecenas "was more or less the Verdurin of antiquity," she cannot "altogether suppress a smile of self-satisfaction" (*SaG* 407). When she asks Morel to play the violin, the baron accompanies him "in the purest style" for the closing passage of Gabriel Fauré's sonata for piano and violin (*SaG* 407). As a result, she hopes he will join the faithful and, while asking him how long he plans to remain on the coast, "tremble[s] lest he should be returning too soon to Paris" (*SaG* 411). It does not matter that he flaunts his effeminacy again when he declines a glass of orangeade with the revelatory sign ("signe révélateur," *SeG* 357) of "endless simperings and wrigglings of the hips" (*SaG* 423). This is trumped by a much more startling revelation of something like the divinity that Ovid's Baucis and Philemon discover in a guest who turns out to be Zeus or that Abraham discovers in guests who turn out to be angels. When Madame Verdurin asks the baron about the Duke of Guermantes, he "carelessly" replies that the duke is his brother, "leaving Madame Verdurin plunged in stupefaction and uncertain whether her guest was making fun of her, was a natural son, or a son by another marriage. The idea that the brother of the Duc de Guermantes might be called Baron de Charlus never entered her head" (*SaG* 425).[35]

Sometime after it sinks in, Madame Verdurin lets the baron, at his suggestion, issue the invitations for a musical party she and her husband hold at their newly acquired house on the Quai Conti in Paris. Since the party features Morel on the violin, the baron thinks it may be "useful" for Charlie to meet some people he has collected "from another sphere" (*CAP* 217) as well as "nice for the Verdurins to meet" them (*CAP* 217), for these are the titled figures she has been yearning to know. But in letting the baron invite them, Madame Verdurin abdicates her authority as Patronne. Or rather that is what the baron himself tells Marcel when the two of them meet en route to the party. At this party, says the baron, the Patronne is "disseized" ("dessaisie," *LaP* 725), which technically means illegally ousted. Though the baron acts with her permission, he dumbfounds her by taking full charge of her guest list. Having forbidden Morel to perform at another party she is giving for her own friends, he vetoes almost everyone she suggests for the musical party, even the Comtesse Molé, whom he calls a "little middle-class toad" (*CAP* 264), and some other aristocratic ladies Madame Verdurin had just met.[36] As a result, she feels riven. Though she owes the baron a debt of gratitude for drawing a crowd of titled guests who might never have come to her otherwise, she resents his usurpation of her authority in her own house. Also, since she cannot punish him by literally killing him ("ne pouvait le *tuer* pour la peine," *LaP* 735, emphasis added), she resolves to kill him socially by exposing a "serious defect in him which would honorably dispense her from showing her gratitude" (*CAP* 259).

Everything that happens at the party itself steels her resolve. On learning that the death of her close friend, the Princess Sherbatoff, has not led her to cancel the party, the baron says he is very glad of it for the sake of *his* guests ("à cause de mes invités," *LaP* 645).[37] When his duchesses start to arrive, they each show their "ill-breeding" by making straight for the baron as if he were giving the party, and then asking Marcel, in a voice Madame Verdurin can easily overhear, if he thinks they really need to get themselves introduced to her. At the same time, while the baron's "invités" push forward to congratulate and thank him as if he were "the master of the house" (*CAP* 278) ("le maître de maison," *LaP* 751), he never asks them to speak to Madame Verdurin, not even when they take their leave of him after Morel plays.[38] Worse still, the baron deliberately keeps a long line of people waiting to thank him while he talks with a lady who wants Morel to play for her own party but who is told she can have the baron's "protégé" only "through" the baron, who will take full charge of her guest list and make her exclude "all those who have ears and hear not" (*CAP* 304, 306).[39] Finally, while several of the baron's guests book Morel on the spot for parties of their own, none of them invites Madame Verdurin, and for her party they give all credit to the baron.

The baron then thoughtlessly twists the knife in her wounds. Though he has aimed throughout the party not to advance her social standing but to make the reputation of Morel, he is so intoxicated with the success of his protégé and so blind to her smoldering fury that he decides, out of decency (!), to invite the Patronne to share *his* joy—"voulut, par décence, inviter la Patronne partager sa joie" (*LaP* 778)—as if such an invitation could reciprocate the hospitality she has granted to both him and Morel, not to mention his fancy friends. He treats her with suffocating condescension. Only after congratulating himself on his power to draw such a glittering crowd and praising Morel for playing "divinely" does he assure his "dear Patronne"("ma chère Patronne," *LaP* 779) that like the page boy who armed Joan of Arc for battle, she too has played her part. But the invitation to share the baron's joy is the only one she gets in response to her party. Instead of inviting her to his own house or procuring any other invitation for her, the baron tells her that one of the duchesses who came to her party has booked Morel for a party to which the duchess, at the baron's request, will invite Monsieur Verdurin. The baron thus gives his knife a final turn. Since Madame Verdurin thought she had earned by her hospitality the right to approve or veto Morel's appearances elsewhere, "this civility to the husband alone was, although no such idea ever occurred to M. de Charlus, the most cruel insult to the wife" (*CAP* 313).

It is scarcely possible to overstate the enormity of this insult to Madame Verdurin as Patronne. In that capacity, as we have been repeatedly told, she expects the faithful members of her little clan to be wholly hers, all for their Patronne ("tout à leur Patronne," *LaP* 782). She would let the men have a mistress ("une maîtresse") or even a male lover ("un amant"), but only on condition that such a liaison had no social consequence outside her house ("hors de chez elle"), that it fed and sustained itself under cover of her Wednesdays (*LaP* 782).[40] Since she has already placed Morel among her faithful, she cannot let him go "into society, without her, under the Baron's aegis" (*CAP* 314). In taking ownership of Morel, therefore, the baron unleashes "that feeling of hatred which was in her only a special, social form of jealousy" (*CAP* 314).

For this flagrant abuse of her hospitality she takes brutal revenge. To punish Charlus as well as to reclaim Morel for herself, she tells Brichot to occupy the baron while her husband poisons Morel against him with a toxic cocktail of insinuations and lies. Clearly she yearns to kill him. While explaining her plan to Brichot, she predicts that Charlus "will be found murdered in his bed one of these days, as those people always are" (*CAP* 317): a thinly veiled expression of her murderous wish. But with dazzling hypocrisy she frames her attack on the baron as an act of self-sacrifice implicitly worthy of Christ. "Ask Brichot," she tells Marcel, ". . . if I don't know how to sacrifice myself ["me dévouer"] to save my comrades" (*LaP* 785). As the narrator reminds us, her would-be self-sacrificial demand that Brichot break off a succession of affairs—first with a laundress, then with Madame de Cambremer—nearly cost the man his eyesight and, "people said," drove him to morphine (*CAP* 317).[41] In spite of this, as Brichot himself explains to Marcel, he knowingly participates in sacrificing the baron to "traditional Morality" because their "excellente hôtesse" (*LaP* 786), a rare use of the term, has requested this "small service" of him (*CAP* 319). Brichot knows he is aiding and abetting a potentially fatal act of treachery to a guest. In keeping Charlus occupied, he says, while Madame Verdurin alienates from him "all that he loves, to deal him perhaps a fatal blow ["un coup fatal," *LaP* 787], it seems to me that I am leading him into what might be termed an ambush, and I recoil from it as from a kind of cowardice" ["une manière de lâcheté," *LaP* 787].[42] But as the narrator observes, he "did not hesitate to commit" the deed (*CAP* 320).

Insofar as the narrative itself can steer the sympathies of the reader, it now seems to shift them from Madame Verdurin to the baron, from the cruelly abused hostess to the abusive guest who has no inkling of the ambush that lies ahead of him. His fate excites great pity at least in Marcel, whose feelings flow to the side of what has suddenly become "the weaker party" and who can hardly bear "the thought of the sufferings that were in store" for him (*CAP* 328–29). But since Marcel does not know how to warn the baron, he cannot act on his sympathies. He cannot even fulfill his urgent need "to leave the Verdurins' house before the execution of M. de Charlus occurred" (*CAP* 351). Instead he stays to see Madame Verdurin drop the blade. Telling the violinist that his "degrading promiscuity" with a man of such "vile reputation" threatens to shatter his artistic future, Madame Verdurin stops at nothing: "In the intoxication of her rage she thought to aggravate still further the wounds she was inflicting on the unfortunate Charlie, and to avenge herself for those she herself had received in the course of the evening" (*CAP* 353).

Once again, as we have seen so often before, the benign reciprocity of hospitality given and returned gives way here to the malign reciprocity of a revenge that knows no bounds. Madame Verdurin spares no one, least of all Morel himself, in her determination to punish the baron and, just as important, to reclaim Morel as an artist bound to her alone as his Patronne: his hostess, cultural sponsor, and proprietess. Ironically enough, she tells Morel he can go on seeing the baron, but only at her house. Ironically, too, even as she schemes to repossess Morel, she tells him how possessively the baron speaks of him: not as "mon ami" but as "ma créature, mon protégé" and possibly even "mon domestique" (*LaP* 817–18), "my servant."[43] Finally, knowing that the baron has sought the Cross of the Legion of Honor for Morel and muddling the fact that he is the son of a valet who once worked for Marcel's uncle Adolphe (a fact Morel strives to suppress), she falsely claims to have heard the baron say "this evening . . . with screams of laughter" that Charlie wanted the cross "to please [his] uncle and [his] uncle was a flunkey" (*CAP* 358). She thus sets the perfect trap. When Charlus rejoins them to announce triumphantly that Morel is about to receive the cross, the baron unwittingly confirms Madame Verdurin's lies, which now seem to Morel the "indisputable truth" (*CAP* 360). "Leave me alone," he shouts at the baron. "I forbid you to come near me. . . . I'm not the first person you've tried to pervert" (*CAP* 360).

Everything we know about the baron up to this point prompts us to expect that he will retaliate with overwhelming fury, that he will avenge himself on both Morel and the Verdurins, above all on la Patronne, the hostess who has dared to take revenge on her presumptuous guest. Marcel himself expects this. But instead the baron stands "muet, stupéfait" (*LaP* 820), "speechless, dumbfounded, measuring the depths of his misery without understanding the cause, unable to think of a word to say" (*CAP* 360). Against all odds, against our settled conviction that he has grossly abused the Verdurins' hospitality, he becomes in this moment a pitiable victim, a guest betrayed: "Struck as if by the Revolutionary guillotine in this salon which he despised, this great nobleman (in whom superiority over commoners was no more essentially inherent than it has been in this or that ancestor of his trembling before the revolutionary tribunal) could do nothing, in the paralysis of his every limb as well as his tongue, but cast around him terror-stricken, bewildered glances, outraged by the violence that was being done to him" (*CAP* 361) ("par la violence qu'on lui faisait," *LaP* 821). Treachery at last spawns violence. In the world of Proust, unlike those of Homer, Dante, and Shakespeare, neither guests nor hosts literally try to kill each other, much less succeed in doing so. But as we have seen, the Duke and Duchess of Guermantes can ignore the imminent death of a friend for the sake of a party, and the Verdurins risk mortally wounding at least two of their faithful guests by mercilessly humiliating one of them and forcing the other to give up his mistress. So it should not surprise us that Charlie's words, which channel the venomous hatred of la Patronne, should feel to the baron like the blade of a guillotine. It does not matter that the baron himself fails to suspect Madame Verdurin, that he thinks someone else must have poisoned Morel against him. What matters is that at the end of this glittering reception given by a woman destined to become the reigning hostess of Paris, she contrives to savage one of her guests.[44]

Proust's novel, as we have seen, tracks the rise of one hostess against the slow decline of another. Each has her attractions. The Duchess of Guermantes can at times be witty, playful, and irreverent; Madame Verdurin can at times take exceptional care of her guests. But at crucial moments each proves willing to sacrifice others to her own pleasure or need for social power. Not even the imminence of Swann's death can distract the duchess from her parties or deflect her determination to take him with her to Italy, and Madame Verdurin's lust for vengeance against the baron and for complete social control of Charlie lead her to wound them both. If we are tempted to think that the baron had it coming, that he at least—if not Charlie—fully deserved the blow, we must reckon with the Queen of Naples, "a woman of great kindness" (*CAP* 366) who has already distinguished herself by befriending and thanking her hostess while all the other titled guests ignored her. On returning to Madame Verdurin's house to retrieve a forgotten fan, she learns that the baron has just been vilified. Vexed by his "vile detractors," she barely speaks to her hostess and burns "with shame on [the baron's] behalf that the Verdurins should dare to treat him in this fashion" (*CAP* 365). She then guides him out in a way that reveals by contrast the Verdurins' vindictiveness. Urging the baron to lean on her arm, she assures him that "it will always support" him (*CAP* 367).

Proust's most important characters live to surprise us. No matter what people have done, the narrator says, we "ought never to judge them by some memory of an unkind action, for we do not know all the good that, at other moments, their hearts may have suddenly desired and realised" (*CAP* 372). Who would have guessed that the spirit of vengeance would finally desert the baron? Struck down and exhausted by septic pneumonia, he speaks to his visitors of gospel parables, and "the Christian meekness into which his splendid violence had been transposed ... provoke[s] the admiration of those who came to his bedside" (*CAP* 368). Likewise, as I have noted, the Verdurins make amends for their relentless humiliation of Saniette by an act of secret charity, anonymously giving him a ten-thousand-franc annuity when they learn he has suffered a stroke. But none of these three characters undergoes anything like the sort of conversion that finally redeems, say, Dickens's Scrooge or his Miss Havisham. The "moral improvement" bred by the baron's pneumonia, we are told, "vanished with the malady which had laboured on its behalf" as he slides morally downward with steadily growing speed (*CAP* 369). As for the Verdurins, la Patronne explains why they make their gift to Saniette anonymously: if it is made public, she says, "we'll be expected to do it for others" (*CAP* 370). Besides thus carefully guarding their wealth, both of them keep an iron grip on their regular guests. Driven by the very jealousy that led Madame Verdurin to lay her trap for the baron, her husband does not "shrink from the basest falsehoods, from the fomentation of the most unjustified hatreds, in order to sever any ties among the faithful which had not as their sole object the strengthening of the little group" (*CAP* 372).

It would be too much to say that the fierce possessiveness of la Patronne and her husband exemplifies the kind of hospitality to be found in Proust's novel as a whole. Quite aside from the moments of genuine kindness shown by hosts to guests and vice versa—such as the Prince of Guermantes' confiding his Dreyfusism to Swann, or the Queen of Naples's gracious overtures to Madame Verdurin—the many ways in which the guests and hosts in this novel betray each other often stop short of violence and malice alike. Nonetheless, even their gentlest encounters can feel treacherous. Recall again the sound of the bell heard by the narrator as a child. Signaling the departure of a man who seemed to the narrator a cruelly disruptive guest, it is the novel's first example of how guests can wound their hosts or, more precisely here, the child of their hosts. That this disruptive guest will prove to be, for Marcel and for us, the most sensitive and considerate of all guests in this novel simply demonstrates the ubiquity and perhaps the inevitability of ruptured hospitality in this world: hospitality undermined by everything ranging from inadvertent insult and exploitative seduction to willful, ruthless, malicious revenge.

In Proust's novel moments of genuine communion between host and guest are as evanescent as rainbows. As in the passage where even the Queen of Naples cuts her hostess for abusing a guest, they soon fade into the light of common day; or rather into the haze of suspicion, jealousy, resentment, posses-siveness, exploitation, and anti-Semitism that virally invade and infect the social worlds of this novel. Written, like Joyce's *Ulysses*, during the first of the two greatest wars ever seen in the world, it represents a society in which hospitality is always and everywhere threatened by treachery.

9

JOYCE, WOOLF, CAMUS

"I cannot see any special talent but I am a bad critic."[1] Thus wrote Joyce of Proust in October 1920, when he was hard at work on the long Circe chapter of *Ulysses* and had evidently read no more than a few pages of *À la recherche du temps perdu*. What should we make of this comment? On the one hand, it is hardly surprising that a man preoccupied or even obsessed with the writing of his own monumental novel (and plagued with bad eyesight as well) could find no sign of special talent, let alone genius, in whichever of Proust's pages he may have scanned. On the other hand, some of their contemporaries ached to know more: to know what these two giants of modernism thought of each other, or, better still, might say to each other if they ever met. This is precisely what led Sydney Schiff, a wealthy English novelist and patron of the arts, to ask them both to a large, late-evening dinner party at the Majestic Hotel in Paris on May 18, 1922, one month after the second volume of *Sodome et Gomorrhe* appeared, a little more than three months after the publication of *Ulysses*, and six months before Proust died, leaving the last three titles of his magnum opus to be published posthumously from 1923 to 1927. But just as *Ulysses* ultimately shows how Bloom's hospitable intentions go comically awry, Schiff's hospitality was comically subverted by the incompatibility of his two distinguished guests.

Schiff himself might have stepped from the pages of Proust. Anticipating just the sort of party Madame Verdurin gives in the final volume of *À la recherche du temps perdu*, he and his wife Violet held the dinner to follow the première of Igor Stravinsky's ballet *Le Renard*, performed by Serge Diaghilev's Ballets Russes. Though Diaghilev, a little like Proust's Charlus, took charge of netting Stravinsky and Pablo Picasso, who were both involved with the ballet, the Schiffs invited Joyce, whom they had first met over a year before when he was giving readings from *Ulysses* at the Maison des Amis des Livres. Because they

knew very well that Proust almost never left the sanctuary of his cork-lined
bedroom, they did not formally invite him, but having already cultivated his
affection with some success, they let him know about the party a few days in
advance (Davenport-Hines [hereafter D-H] 29).

The one and only occasion on which Proust and Joyce were thus corralled
to meet turned out to be hardly a meeting of minds. Arriving well after midnight
and shabbily dressed (he apologized for having no evening clothes), Joyce
appeared to be drunk. Promptly seated on the right of the host with a glass of
champagne on the table in front of him, he put his head in his hands and said
nothing. Sometime between 2 and 3 a.m. Proust appeared "in exquisite black
with white kid gloves" (Clive Bell, qtd. D-H 28) and looking "as pale as a midafternoon moon" (Stravinsky, qtd. D-H 35). After snoring his way (so Bell
reports) through a tense exchange between Proust and Stravinsky on the topic
of Beethoven, Joyce began with Proust a conversation that has been variously
reported but that seems to have consisted chiefly of the word *no*.[2] Whether or
not they discussed their respective maladies, they each parried every effort made
to establish common ground between them.[3] When Proust asked Joyce if he
knew the Princess X or the Countess Y, Joyce said no. When Violet Schiff asked
Proust if he had read anything of *Ulysses*, Proust said no, and Joyce likewise
denied, not altogether accurately, that he had ever read Proust (Ellmann
508–9). Joyce told one inquirer simply, "Proust would only talk about duchesses, while I was concerned with their chambermaids" (qtd. Ellmann 509).

Since *Ulysses* has been called Joyce's wedding gift to a woman he met when
she was working as a chambermaid in a Dublin hotel, the remark is singularly
apt, and may be taken as one more sign of the barriers that blocked any real
communication between the two greatest writers of their time.[4] Joyce's manners
seem to have left Proust utterly cold. As the two men left the party, the Irishman
insisted on squeezing into a small cab Proust had booked for himself and the
Schiffs (it was driven by the husband of Proust's housekeeper). After Joyce lit a
cigarette and opened a window, Schiff made him stop smoking and shut the
window because the asthmatic Proust could stand neither fresh air nor smoke.
For Proust this was surely the last straw. During the short ride from the Majestic
to his apartment in the nearby Rue Hamelin, he "talked incessantly" (so Violet
Schiff reports) without saying a word to Joyce, who said nothing, and when they
reached the apartment Proust made it absolutely clear that he wanted only the
Schiffs to come up with him. Though Joyce evidently wished to come up too,
Proust's very last words to Joyce politely dispatched him: "Let my taxi take you
home" (D-H 44).

If Proust saw Joyce as little more than a slovenly lout whose famous book he had never read, what did Joyce feel about Proust? In a word, ambivalence. On the one hand, besides caring nothing for Proust's great ladies, Joyce envied him for the comfortable, cork-lined privacy in which he worked—so different from the porous "matchbox" where Joyce had to put up with "people coming in and out" (Ellmann 487, 509). He was also unimpressed with Proust's style. As a master of terseness who sometimes made a single word do the work of a sentence, he was put off by the elaborateness of Proust's constructions: "Proust, analytic still life," he wrote in a notebook. "Reader ends sentence before him" (Ellmann 509). In fairness and honesty, he might have noted that Proust's novel opens with a sentence of just eight words ("Longtemps je me suis couché de bonne heure" [For a long time I went to bed early]) and that nobody can read any one of the eight gigantic "sentences" in the final chapter of *Ulysses* without pausing for breath—or perhaps a good stiff drink—well before the end of it. But never mind. Something about Proust's work impressed him. He once told Samuel Beckett that he wished they could have met and had "a talk somewhere" (D-H 42), and on November 18, 1922, exactly six months after the ill-fated dinner party, he attended Proust's funeral (Ellmann 509).

If Joyce and Proust had ever had that talk, I like to think their conversation might have touched on the topic of hospitality. In late September 1906, when Joyce had composed most of the stories that would later appear in *Dubliners* (1914), he wrote to his brother Stanislaus that in portraying Dublin life so far he had "not reproduced its ingenuous insularity and its hospitality" (*Selected Letters* 110). Joyce's knife cuts two ways. As Karen Lawrence has noted, the city's "openness to strangers" is here "fissured in a location at once isolated and welcoming."[5] By late September 1907, a year after his comment to Stanislaus, Joyce had managed to reproduce both qualities in "The Dead," which became the final story in *Dubliners*. Hospitality here takes a proto-Proustian form. Since the annual dance held by the Morkan sisters in this story not only shows Dublin at its most hospitable but also in some ways anticipates the annual garden party held by Madame de Saint-Euverte in *Sodome et Gomorrhe* (1922), it seems a fitting place to begin investigating what Joyce does with hospitality.

HOSTING A GHOST IN "THE DEAD"

Hospitality takes two forms in "The Dead." On the one hand, the Morkan sisters' annual dance exemplifies what their nephew, a teacher named Gabriel Conroy, calls "the tradition of warmhearted courteous Irish hospitality," which "is unique so far as my experience goes . . . among the modern nations."[6]

Though warmhearted and courteous, however, the Morkans' hospitality is also conventional or, as Derrida would say, conditional. The sisters hold their party each year predictably in the season of Christmas; they prepare for their guests a cornucopia of food and drink; and though they open their doors to everyone they know, this clearly includes many people whom they socially or profession-ally owe, such as those who have paid them for music lessons. Gabriel's tribute to their hospitality is itself part of a carefully planned after-dinner speech that formally reciprocates the sisters for all they have offered. But after the party he himself is asked to furnish hospitality of a radically different kind. When his wife Gretta tells him she has always cherished the memory of a young man who died of love for her, she demands from him something like Derrida's absolute hospitality: the unconditional acceptance of a ghostly guest whose sudden inva-sion of their hotel room is not just wholly unexpected but fatally, so to speak, intrusive, chilling to death all prospect of the conjugal intimacy Gabriel has warmly anticipated.[7]

The revelation that sabotages this prospect is the last and most painful in a series of shocks that undermine his pleasure and confidence—first as a nephew made to play the role of appreciative guest, then as a husband made to play host, in a sense, to his wife's first lover. All of the shocks are administered by women. Lily, the young woman who answers the door and takes his coat, bitterly rejects his patronizing assumption that she will soon be getting married. "The men that is now," she says, "is only all palaver and what they can get out of you" (154). Second, because Gabriel has published a review of English poems in a pro-British Dublin newspaper, he is charged by Molly Ivors, a fellow teacher, with being a "west Briton" (163): a man who thinks of Ireland as nothing but a western province of Britain. Whether or not the charge is just, Gabriel feels no love of Ireland. Rejecting Molly's invitation to join a group excursion to the western part of it and thus to visit his "own land," including Gretta's hometown of Galway, he tells her he is "sick of [his] own country, sick of it!" (165), and when Gretta excitedly says that she would "love to see Galway again," he "coldly" tells her she can go there by herself (166). Molly's refusal to stay for dinner, which is surely prompted in part by Gabriel's obvious annoyance with her, leaves him free to regret in his speech that the "hypereducated" generation she exemplifies may lack "those qualities of humanity, of hospitality, of kindly humour which belonged to an older day" (177). Yet with his outspoken loathing of Ireland, his privately felt fear of speaking "above the heads of his hearers" (155), and his doing just that by alluding to the Three Graces and Paris, he prompts us to question his own congeniality. Though his speech finally pleases his aunts, he later sees that he is not so much a warmly appreciative guest as "a ludicrous figure, acting as a pennyboy for his aunts, a nervous wellmeaning sentimentalist" (191).

If the shocks delivered to Gabriel by Lily and Molly make it difficult for him to play the role of warmhearted guest, the role he had expected to play at the party, he is wholly unprepared for what Gretta tells him afterward in their hotel room, where he is suddenly made to play the role of host. As Louis Saint-Amour astutely observes,

> Such a suggestion may seem perverse, given that Gabriel extends welcome here not to a stranger but to his own wife, and only by extension to the memory she bears of a long-dead stranger. If staying with this scene seems strange, it is because hospitality narratives across a range of cultures emphasize welcoming the absolute, nameless stranger—the god, angel, ghost, mendicant, or refugee—rather than the familiar-become-strange. Against this grain, "The Dead" suggests that extreme alterity can take the form of an intimate whose disclosures vandalize the portrait of our intimacy; it suggests, by extension, that radical hospitality can be asked of us not only by the absolute stranger but also by the intimate who comes bearing absolutely strange news. (Saint-Amour 102)

In my introduction to this book I argued that hospitality reverses the uncanny by seeking to domesticate the stranger. But if the uncanny, or *unheimlich*, springs, as Freud says, from the return of the repressed, from "something familiar and old-established in the mind that has been estranged only by the process of repression" ("The 'Uncanny,'" 394), Gretta's revelation is surely uncanny. Something long established and long silenced within her is "absolutely strange news" to her husband: news that profoundly challenges his capacity to take it in, as a host might take in a guest.

To juxtapose this scene with other hospitality narratives, however, is to see more than just the contrast between welcoming a stranger and discovering the strangeness of an intimate. It is also to see what Joyce does with the kind of narrative in which a guest usurps, seduces, or is offered the wife of his host. In some cultures, anthropologists tell us, the "natural law" of hospitality not only allows but requires a guest to sleep with the wife of his host if he offers her to him.[8] In a novel called *Roberte Ce Soir* (1954), Pierre Klossowski reformulates this "law" within a modern, sophisticated European context. According to the narrator, the "Rule of Hospitality" appears on handwritten pages framed under glass and hung above the bed in the guest room of his uncle Octave, a professor of scholastics and the husband of Roberte. In language that deliciously parodies scholastic diction, the "Rule" explains precisely how the master of a house should serve his wife to a guest. Like Lot, who waited at the gates of Sodom for his two angelic guests to arrive (Gen. 19.2), "the master of this house . . . waits anxiously at the gate for the stranger he will see appear like a liberator upon the horizon" (Klossowski 12). But while Lot offered his daughters to the men of Sodom so as to keep them from raping his angelic guests, Uncle Octave's "law" requires the host to offer his wife to his guest. To achieve "an essential relation-ship" with his guest, the host "invites the stranger to penetrate to the source of all substances beyond the realm of all accident" (12), that is, to penetrate the host's wife. The host, we are told, grasps "the essence of the hostess" only by leading her into infidelity:

> For to possess the faithless one *qua* hostess faithfully fulfilling her duties, that is what he is after. Hence by means of the guest he means to actualize some-thing potential in the mistress of the house: an actual mistress in relation to this guest, an inactual mistress of the house in relation to the host. The essence of the host is proposed as a homage of curiosity to the essence of the hostess. Now this curiosity, as a potentiality of the hospitable soul, can have no proper existence except in that which would look to the hostess, were she naive, as suspicion or jealousy. The host however is neither suspicious nor jealous, because he is essentially curious about that very thing which, in everyday life, would make a master of the house suspicious, jealous, unbear-able. (13–14)

The last three words give the game away. To satisfy his curiosity about the "essence" of his wife's presumed desire to gratify their guest in every way and thus to actualize her potential as "mistress" of the house (in precisely the ambig-uous sense we have seen exploited by Proust), the master of the house must master his own impulse toward suspicion and jealousy. Likewise, we are told, "the angel . . . in the guise of a guest" must "fearlessly excite the host's curiosity by that jealousy and suspicion, worthy in the master of a house but unworthy of a host . . . let the host put the guest's discretion to the test, the guest make proof of the host's curiosity; . . . but let the guest take all due care lest this jealousy or this suspicion grow to such proportions in the host that no room is left for his curiosity" (15). This is quite a trick. Could any host whose jealousy and suspi-cion have been thus aroused keep them in check by means of *curiosity*? Though for Derrida the "Rule" seems to exemplify "absolute, hyperbolical, uncondi-tional hospitality" (*OH* 135), it strikes me as nothing more than an elaborate joke on would-be sophisticates who think they can transcend both bourgeois possessiveness and jealousy alike.[9] Besides turning the Lot story inside out, it wittily reconstructs *Sir Gawain and the Green Knight*, in which the host, as we have seen, seeks to gratify his curiosity about his guest's self-control, not about the "essence" of sexual hospitality in his wife. But the subtext of the "Rule of Hospitality" can be summed up in a three-word statement made by a well-known Parisienne of our own time who for fifteen years shared both her husband and herself with a variety of other partners. Under these conditions, she eventually discovered, "Jealousy is unavoidable."[10]

Joyce himself felt the keenest pangs of jealousy two years after writing "The Dead," when he was falsely informed that during his courtship of Nora Barnacle in the summer of 1904 she had been out walking at night with another man. "Were you fucked by anyone," he promptly asked her, "before you came to me?" (Letter of August 7, 1909, *Selected Letters* 158). So it is not surprising that notes of jealousy inflect Gabriel's reception of the ghost of Michael Furey. When Gretta tells him she "used to go out walking" with this Galway boy, he "coldly" says, "Perhaps that was why you wanted to go to Galway with that Ivors girl?" (190). Even after she has answered all of his questions and fallen asleep, he thinks, "Perhaps she had not told him all the story" (193).

So Gabriel's hospitality to the ghost of his wife's long-dead suitor is not quite absolute in Derrida's sense. But he is far more open than either of two other hosts who—unlike Klossowski's Octave—precede him in the history of literature. One is Odysseus, who slaughters his wife's living suitors for merely seeking to marry her as well as for abusing his hospitality. The other is Angel Clare, whose wedding night is poisoned by his wife's story of her former lover in a novel Joyce almost certainly knew: Thomas Hardy's *Tess of the d'Urbervilles* (1892).[11]

Whether or not Joyce was thinking of Tess's confession when he conceived Gretta's revelation, the parallels between the two situations are striking. Like Angel, who married a peasant woman that his mother thought socially beneath him (Hardy 128), Gabriel remembers that his mother had "sullenly" opposed his marriage to a woman she called "country cute" (162). Angel learns about his wife's lover just before he would have consummated his desire for her on their wedding night; Gabriel, named for an angel, learns of his wife's young suitor just before he meant to gratify his "keen pang of lust" in a reenactment of their wedding night.[12] In each case the man's sudden discovery of another man in his wife's past chills his desire for her to the point of death. "Not long after one o'clock" on the second night of Tess's and Angel's would-be honeymoon, when the newlyweds have been sleeping in different rooms, a sleepwalking Angel comes to her bed murmuring, "Dead, dead, dead," rolls "her in the sheet as in a shroud," carries her to a nearby Cistercian Abbey church, carefully lays her down in the stone coffin of an abbot, and then lies down himself on the ground alongside her (Hardy 193–95). Sometime past midnight after the party in "The Dead," where we learn, among other things, that the Trappist monks of Mount Melleray in County Waterford sleep "in their coffins . . . to remind them of their last end" (175), Gabriel ends up lying like a corpse beside his wife, who has fallen asleep: "He stretched himself cautiously under the sheets and lay down beside his wife. One by one they were all becoming shades" (193–94).

To set Gretta's revelation beside Tess's confession, however, is also to see revealing differences. Angel is far more snobbish about Tess's "decrepit" family (Hardy 182), far more rigid in his morality, and far less aware of his shortcomings than Gabriel is. More important, while Tess was seduced by her former lover, Gretta gives us absolutely no reason to believe that she gave her virginity to Michael Furey or that she has withheld anything from Gabriel, as he faintly suspects.[13] Just as important, while Tess's former lover is still alive at the time of her confession, Gretta's suitor has long been dead.[14] These two features of Gretta's past love life make it easier for Gabriel to accept her revelation and to receive, as I have suggested, the ghost of her onetime suitor. In the end, instead of feeling bitterly betrayed by an unexpected guest, Gabriel welcomes him.

The contrast with Angel's response to Tess's confession is sharpened by the fact that on Tess's wedding night, Angel's hospitality proves doubly treacherous. First of all, he takes her to a rented farmhouse that had once been part of a now-demolished mansion belonging to the family of the d'Urbervilles: the very family with whom her mother had originally told her to "claim kin" because her own humble name, Durbeyfield, supposedly derived from that noble one. The name of d'Urberville has already come to signify hospitality at its most treacherous. Tess's first attempt to visit the d'Urbervilles leads to her being warmly welcomed by a sham d'Urberville named Alec and then seduced, impregnated, and thus made "guilty" in the eyes of Angel—once he has learned her story (179). Even before she tells her story, what awaits her in this house is prefigured by the life-sized portraits of two middle-aged women on its walls, especially the face with "long pointed features, narrow eye, and smirk . . . so suggestive of merciless treachery" (170). When Angel playfully says, "Welcome to one of your ancestral mansions!" as he guides her into this haunt of what Tess herself calls "horrid women" (170), he unwittingly recalls the treacherous welcome Tess has already received from Alec. Likewise, when his own confession of having "plunged into eight-and-forty hours' dissipation with a stranger" (177) makes her believe he will welcome or at least forgivingly accept the confession she has been aching to make, her trust in his generosity is cruelly betrayed.

Gabriel's response to Gretta's revelation takes a fundamentally different turn. Though her story chills his desire for her, it does not kill his generosity, which is what she chiefly loves about him. Shortly after they enter their hotel room, when he tells her that on Christmas he loaned a sovereign to the alcoholic Freddy Malins, she kisses him for being so "generous" (189). Part of the reason for which Gretta has been so long secretly mourning the death of Michael Furey, I suspect, is that she may feel doubly responsible for it. He "died for" her, as she tells Gabriel (191), not only because he loved her but also because she was not quite generous, hospitable, and daring enough to let him into her house, let alone her bed, on the rainy night he came to see her at her grandmother's house. Having been told not to see him before she left for the convent school in Dublin, she nonetheless slipped out the back door of the house after hearing gravel thrown up against her window. But when she found "the poor fellow at the end of the garden shivering," all she did was implore him "to go home at once" and tell him "he would get his death in the rain" (192). Gabriel does much more. He not only pities Gretta for what she has lost but also honors the ghost of Michael Furey for dying "in the full glory of some passion" rather than "fad[ing] and wither[ing] dismally with age" (194). As he shares Gretta's very last vision of the boy, as he imagines that he himself "saw the form of a young man standing under a dripping tree," he welcomes this specter of utterly self-sacrificial devotion, and "generous tears" fill his eyes (193–94). He thus learns to offer something like absolute hospitality—but only at the moment when his own soul starts drifting toward the final threshold, when this ultimately welcoming host "approach[es] that region where dwell the vast hosts of the dead" (194).[15]

HOSTS AND GUESTS IN *ULYSSES*

Leopold Bloom is no Gabriel Conroy. Though he shares Gabriel's generosity, he is hardly ready for the grave. Even after communing with the dead in the "Hades" chapter of *Ulysses*, he radiates vitality. Bidding farewell to the rotting denizens of Prospect cemetery as he walks out through its gates, he says to himself, "Let them sleep in their maggoty beds. They are not going to get me this innings. Warm beds: warm, fullblooded life" (6.1004–6). Unlike the sepulchral bed Gabriel enters at the end of "The Dead," Bloom's bed will have been warmed, when he finally reenters it, not only by the full-blooded flesh of his wife Molly but also by a guest who is anything but a ghost: Blazes Boylan, man about town and concert promoter. Fully expected by both husband and wife, Blazes Boylan comes to Molly by appointment at four o'clock in the afternoon of Bloomsday—ostensibly to discuss the program for a concert tour of her soprano voice but actually to invade her bed and thus usurp the powers of his absent host, who, like the long-absent Odysseus, comes home to find incontestable evidence that his hospitality has been grossly abused.[16]

In this as in many other ways, Bloom resembles Odysseus/Ulysses far more than he does Gabriel Conroy. Likewise, the all-too-living Boylan recalls the presumptuous suitors of the *Odyssey* far more than he does the pitiable, self-sacrificing ghost of Michael Furey. If Gabriel can finally welcome this specter with generous tears of sympathy, Bloom has far better reason to feel something like the rage with which Odysseus strikes the suitors who have besieged his wife while abusing his hospitality. But Bloom is a radically reconceived version of Ulysses. No longer a legendary king, Mediterranean voyager, and fearless fighter, he is a middle-aged Dubliner who makes his living selling advertising space in a newspaper, who has never left his native city, and whose nautical experience includes—so far as we can tell—nothing but an excursion boat tour of Dublin Bay and a single bout of rowing with Molly in which, as she ruefully recalls, his totally inept management of the oars nearly swamped the boat (18.954–59). Just as remarkably, this reincarnation of a legendary warrior is a thoroughgoing pacifist, which is why he will never do to Blazes Boylan anything like what Ulysses does to the suitors.

Pacifism is one of several things Bloom shares with Stephen Dedalus, a fictionalized version of Joyce's younger self and a man who fleetingly becomes for Bloom a replacement for the son he lost in infancy. To understand just how these two enact the rituals of hospitality between themselves and with others, we must first of all realize that neither one ever resorts to violence. In the "Cyclops" chapter Bloom bravely challenges the virulent anti-Semitism of the citizen, but he never comes to blows with the citizen or anyone else, and he decisively rejects the idea of taking violent revenge on Boylan for bedding Molly.[17] A punch to the face knocks down Stephen Dedalus near the end of "Circe," but scorning what he calls the "noble art of selfpretence" (15.4412), he will not strike back with anything but words. In eschewing violence, Stephen and Bloom open the way to a kind of comedy we seldom find in Proust. In the world of Proust, hosts and guests betray each other without bloodshed but with subtle forms of cruelty. In *Ulysses*, where the citizen becomes the Polyphemic host of a pub, the worst he can do is throw a cracker box at the departing Bloom, and their final battle of words comically exposes the impotence of his rage.

Furthermore, Joyce's hosts and guests encounter each other in settings that have nothing to do with the formal entertaining so elaborately re-created by Proust as well as by Virginia Woolf in *Mrs Dalloway*. In spite of Joyce's conviction that Dublin life was distinguished by its hospitality, he seems to have concluded that he had written quite enough about its private parties in "The Dead." In all of *Ulysses* he has virtually nothing to say about them. Bloom briefly remembers meeting Molly at a musical party (11.726); Richie Goulding briefly remembers hearing Simon Dedalus sing at another party (11.778–80); and at somewhat greater length, Lenehan remembers a grand official dinner, an annual fund-raiser, held at the Glencree reformatory (10.536–49). But the only events that qualify as social gatherings in the time present of this novel occur in public places such as pubs, restaurants, and the brothels of Nighttown: venues (minus the brothels) of what has come to be known in our own time as the hospitality industry. In one of these venues Bloom encounters a man whose brutal inhospitality reenacts the monstrous behavior of Homer's Polyphemos. Otherwise, the hospitality of *Ulysses* is something either realized or undermined in private, intimate, nonviolent moments of contact involving just two or three people.

To begin with, the Stephen of chapter 1, "Telemachus," is nowhere near as threatened as Homer's Telemachus is at the beginning of the *Odyssey*. With Odysseus long absent and possibly dead, Telemachus must confront suitors usurping his father's house, devouring his father's goods, besieging his mother, and plotting to kill him if he helps his father return. Stephen faces no such threat in the tower he shares with Mulligan and Haines. Though genuinely frightened by the nightmares of Haines, who has spent all night "raving and moaning to himself about shooting a black panther" (1.61–62), Stephen is not living in his father's house, has no intention of looking for him, and does not even think about him until chapter 3.

Nevertheless, the single word "usurper" at the very end of chapter 1 has a double referent. It first of all points to Haines, the only Englishman of the trio, who personifies the English usurpation of a land they first invaded in the twelfth century and would not relinquish, even partially, until 1922, the year *Ulysses* appeared. As a budding anthropologist specializing in Irish culture, Haines is also the only one of the three who speaks the Irish language. But when he speaks it to the old Irish woman who comes to deliver the milk, she does not understand him because for nearly one hundred years the English have literally stolen the Irish language from their hosts by forbidding and suppressing its use. Thus the "stranger in the house," as the English came to be known in a phrase that Stephen later recalls (9.37), takes possession of it. The very "house" now rented by these three is a Martello Tower built to defend Ireland against the French a few years after the invasion of 1798, when a force of some one thousand French soldiers vainly sought to help the Irish rebels against their English masters. All this is vaguely noted by Haines himself, who tells Stephen condescendingly, "We feel in England that we have treated you rather unfairly. It seems history is to blame" (1.648–49).

Besides pointing to Haines, the word "usurper" may encapsulate Stephen's thoughts about Mulligan. In conducting a Black Mass, Mulligan usurps the role of a priest, and by flirting with the milkwoman as "her gay betrayer" (1.405), he may be trying to usurp Stephen's right to possess or express what this "lowly form of an immortal" symbolizes: "silk of the kine and poor old woman" (1.403–4)— the Athenean wisdom and withered beauty of Ireland. Mulligan also seeks to usurp Stephen's literary ambitions by drowning them in drink and pressing them into the production of readily marketable wisecracks like the one about the cracked looking glass of a servant: a "symbol of Irish art" (1.146). At one point he even plays Claudius to Stephen's Hamlet, urging this black-suited young man (who will not wear even gray) to "give up the moody brooding" for his recently dead mother because death is a "beastly thing" that "simply doesn't matter."[18]

But Mulligan cannot be defined by any one term. On the contrary, if he is paying the rent for the tower, as Hugh Kenner plausibly argues,[19] then he is rightfully Stephen's host, and the reason for Stephen's resentment of him must be sought in Stephen's perception of his position as Mulligan's guest. As Stephen leaves the tower with Mulligan and Haines, he is reminded that the key to the tower is Mulligan's. "He wants that key," says Stephen to himself. "It is mine. I paid the rent. Now I eat his salt bread" (1.631). This looks like a confusing sequence of thoughts. On one hand, Stephen seems to be telling himself that he deserves the key because he is paying the rent. But if Stephen is paying the rent, how can he be eating the salt bread of dependence, as the exiled Dante did when he was forced to accept the hospitality of Can Grande?[20] The four-sentence sequence here makes sense only if we construe the two middle sentences as *spoken by Mulligan* in words that simply take their place in the stream of Stephen's thought: "It is mine. I paid the rent."[21] Thus processed, Mulligan's words are bracketed by Stephen's anxious thoughts. As we have already seen, Dante's experience suggests that not even the most generous and gracious of hosts can indefinitely satisfy a guest. Outside one's immediate family and sometimes even within that family, any dependence on another's hospitality can all too soon grow intolerably irksome. At the end of the chapter Stephen ruefully tells himself, "I will not sleep here. Home also I cannot go" (1.739–40). This is the voice of the exile, of the discontented *xenos*, of the alienated guest. Unable to live any longer at home, he cannot pay the price that Mulligan's hospitality demands, for Mulligan is a treacherous host: the gay betrayer of Stephen as well as of the old woman who brings the milk.[22]

Meanwhile, Leopold Bloom must contend with a treacherous guest. At the very time when Stephen is brooding on the impossibility of either going home or trusting himself to the hospitality of Mulligan, Bloom is shocked by what greets him in the hallway of his home after he returns from a little shopping trip. Approaching his door, he thinks of breakfast and Molly:

> To smell the gentle smoke of tea, fume of the pan, sizzling butter. Be near her ample bedwarmed flesh. Yes, yes.
>
> Quick warm sunlight came running from Berkeley road, swiftly, in slim sandals, along the brightening footpath. Runs, she runs to meet me, a girl with gold hair on the wind.
> Two letters and a card lay on the hallfloor. He stooped and gathered them. Mrs. Marion Bloom. His quickened heart slowed at once. Bold hand, Mrs. Marion. (4.244–45)

The first part of this passage faintly echoes the first book of the *Odyssey*, where Athene tells Zeus that Odysseus is detained by Calypso and "straining for no more than a glimpse / of hearth-smoke drifting up from his own land" (F 1.69–70). In book 1 also Athene dons the sandals that carry her over the sea to Ithaca, just as Hermes will later don the sandals that carry him over the sea to Calypso. Rippling with these allusions, the brief middle paragraph here hovers somewhere between metaphor, erotic fantasy, and myth: a flash of sunlight figuratively imagined as a golden-haired girl running toward Bloom. But the strongest evocation of the *Odyssey* comes in the final short paragraph, where Bloom finds the letter addressed to Mrs. Marion Bloom. The phrase reminds us—or should remind us—that Bloom himself has been identified in the very first words of the chapter as Mr. Leopold Bloom (4.1). Leopold means "the people's prince" (Gifford 70), and the title of mister indicates that he is the man of the house and presumably the master of it as well. In the days when a married woman took the name of her husband, the normal way to address her on an envelope would be by Mrs. plus all of that name: Mrs. Leopold Bloom.[23] But the bold hand on this particular envelope thrusts the husband aside and goes straight for the name of the wife, and the bold hand, we soon learn, belongs to Blazes Boylan. Since Bloom already knows that Boylan has sexual designs on Molly, he knows full well what kind of music Boylan will make with her and just what his bold hand will be doing with her shortly after four. At the very instant when Bloom enters his house, then, he finds that his place in that house has been usurped by another man who threatens to lay hold of his wife and thus betray his hospitality. It is the first unmistakably Odyssean moment in the novel.

In a later Odyssean moment, Bloom becomes a guest, so to speak, in the cave of a modern-day Polyphemos.[24] In a pub called Barney Kiernan's he is treated first with hospitable generosity by a newspaperman named Joe Hynes and then with mockery and menace by a drunken, blustering, xenophobic ex-shot-putter known only as the "citizen." Since Homer's episode is itself a "parody of a hospitality scene" (Reece 126), as we have seen, Joyce's chapter doubles this parody. Homer's monstrous, man-eating host is outwitted by a guest who calls himself "nobody," gets the monster drunk, blinds him with a burning stake, slips past him out of his cave, and finally, as he sails away from the monster's island, goads him into throwing two huge boulders and calling on Poseidon to curse the voyager with disaster and misery on his voyage home. Bloom is likewise a nobody in the eyes of the citizen, and his burning stake is nothing but the "knockmedown cigar" (12.502) that he "prudent[ly]" takes in place of a drink (12.437). But aside from the cracker box, all the citizen can throw at him is contempt. Thinking himself the embodiment of Ireland, he decries everything he considers foreign, including the "syphilisation" inflicted by England (12.1197), whose very language he speaks, and he cannot imagine how any man of Bloom's persuasion could call himself Irish. Just as the Judaism of Drefyus makes him irredeemably foreign in the eyes of the Baron de Charlus, who thinks he has broken the laws of hospitality in a land that is not his own, the Judaism of Bloom makes him irredeemably foreign in the eyes of the citizen, who finds him an intolerable intruder. He does not know or care that Bloom has come to the pub for the purely altruistic purpose of conferring with Martin Cunningham about a widow's need for her husband's life insurance. As a Jew in a predominantly Christian society, Bloom is a victim of what Edward Said has called essentialism—the notion that each of us is essentially bound to the ethnic or religious category that fate and our genes have given us.[25] In the eyes of both the citizen and the narrator of this chapter, therefore, an Irish Jew is a contradiction in terms, an intolerable anomaly, an alien presence, a stranger in the house (12.1150–51).[26] All Jews are grasping, miserly swindlers, and all evidence to the contrary must be resolutely ignored, unseen, or twisted to fit the essentialist stereotype.

Consider the citizen's response when Bloom says, in response to a sneering question, that his nation is "Ireland. . . . I was born here. Ireland" (12.1431). To this perfectly reasonable statement the citizen has nothing to say. He just spits in the corner and wipes his mouth because he cannot stomach Bloom's claim to be Irish. It does not matter that Bloom has been working for the Dignam family in particular and for all of Ireland politically, as John Wyse Nolan reports (12.1573–77). It does not matter that he has drawn up plans for

Irish independence that are based on the political means by which Hungary won its independence from Austria (12.1635–37). None of this matters because nothing good for Ireland can come from a Jew. In the words of the narrator, who thoroughly shares the citizen's contempt for Bloom, "Gob, that puts the bloody kybosh on it if old sloppy eyes is mucking up the show. Give us a bloody chance. God save Ireland from the likes of that bloody mouseabout. Mr. Bloom with his argol bargol" (12.1577–80).

But Mr. Bloom has more than "argol bargol" for these myopic nationalists. He has something to say to them that he has never said before, even to himself. Like Odysseus, who tells Polyphemos at first that his name is *Outis*, "nobody," Bloom has up to now resolutely suppressed his identity as a Jew.[27] Buying a pork kidney, trying (in vain) to tell a joke on a Jewish moneylender, ignoring a flagrantly anti-Semitic slur, he has tried to pass himself off as a generic Irishman—one of the goys. But when the citizen literally spits on Bloom's claim to be an Irishman, he can take no more. While still in the pub, still in the cave of the Cyclopean citizen, he defiantly proclaims his Jewishness, as the narrator reports:

> —And I belong to a race too, says Bloom, that is hated and persecuted. Also now. This very moment. This very instant. . . .
> —Robbed, says he. Plundered. Insulted. Persecuted. Taking what belongs to us by right. At this very moment, says he, putting up his fist, sold by auction in Morocco, like slaves or cattle. (12.1467–72)

Bloom speaks not just for Moroccan Jews, but for himself. All day long in a variety of subtle and sometimes flagrant ways he has been persecuted and insulted, and even now Blazes Boylan is usurping his house and his bed and taking what belongs to him by right, his own wife. Yet in defiantly proclaiming his Jewishness, Bloom is definitely not calling for a Jewish state—for a new Zionist nationalism. When the citizen asks him if he's talking about the new Jerusalem, Bloom says simply,

> —I'm talking about injustice.
> —Right, says John Wyse. Stand up to it then with force like men.
> (12.1474–75).

Though the contemptuous narrator sneers at Bloom's supposed effeminacy (as the citizen does later), Bloom bravely presses on:

> —But it's no use, says he. Force, hatred, history, all that. That's not life for men and women, insult and hatred. And everybody knows that it's the very opposite of that that is really life.

—What? says Alf.

—Love, says Bloom. I mean the opposite of hatred. (12.1477–85)

Bloom fits no categories. He is not the miserly, grasping Jew of anti-Semitic legend; he is not a militant Zionist; he is not a belligerent nationalist of any kind. He is a pacifist, and if we wonder how a pacifist can possibly play the role of Ulysses, we must ask ourselves how that shrewd, judicious man of many turns — who was once himself a conscientious objector to war — would respond to three thousand years of misery wrought by the kind of ethnic hatred that has lately killed so many thousands in Bosnia, Kosovo, Africa, and the Middle East.[28] For everything there is a season, says the book of Ecclesiastes. To remember that Joyce wrote this novel from 1914 to 1921, during the greatest, bloodiest war the world had ever seen, is to see why his Ulyssean hero had to be much more than just another warrior. He had to be brave enough to take up arms against war itself — against "force, hatred, history, all that" — but also flawed enough to reveal that all pretensions to heroism, including his own, are subject to comic deflation.

Taken seriously or piously, Bloom is a champion of love in the face of hatred and a modern-day apostle: "a new apostle to the gentiles," as the citizen sneeringly says (12.1489). But as a practical man, Bloom is far less eager to preach the gospel of love than he is to practice it. Having mentioned the word *love*, he does not even try to define or explain it because he hasn't time: he must find Martin Cunningham to see about the insurance money for the Dignams. To Bloom, love means simply helping other people when he can rather than doing battle with them. But when drawn into battle with the citizen, he dares to identify himself with Christ, in a move that infuriates the citizen but also comically exposes the flaws in Bloom's own humanity.

Instead of simply pitting blind rage against calm self-possession, the final battle between the citizen and Bloom shows the latter carried away by something very much like the recklessness with which Odysseus taunts Polyphemos. Once Cunningham gets him out of the pub and on to a jaunting car, Bloom could have kept his mouth shut. But just as Odysseus foolishly taunts Polyphemos from his departing ship, Bloom taunts the citizen from the back of his departing car. When the drunken citizen waddles out the door and mockingly cries, "Three cheers for Israel!" (12.1791), Bloom calls out,

—Mendelssohn was a jew and Karl Marx and Mercadante and Spinoza. And the Saviour was a jew and his father was a jew. Your God. (12.1804–5)

Just as the normally prudent Odysseus goads Polyphemos into hurling boulders at his ship, the normally prudent Bloom gets so carried away by the urge to retaliate that he makes some comic blunders: Mercadante was not a Jew, and as Cunningham quickly says, Christ "had no father" (12.1806), that is, no earthly father. But Bloom is quite right about the Jewishness of Christ, and in driving this point into the blind eye of the citizen he is saying something more about his own identity. Just as the departing Ulysses boldly throws his identity at Polyphemos, Bloom finally tells the citizen, "Your God was a jew. Christ was a jew like me" (12.1808–9). In identifying himself and his Jewishness with Christ, Bloom drives the citizen to a truly Polyphemic rage:

> —By Jesus, says he. I'll brain that bloody jewman for using the holy name. By Jesus, I'll crucify him so I will. Give us that biscuitbox here. (12.1811–12)

The comedy here is supreme. In threatening to crucify Bloom for using the name of Jesus, which he has just done himself, the citizen threatens to reenact the crucifixion and thus confirm the identity that Bloom has suddenly and outrageously claimed: "Christ was a jew like me." At the same time, this drunken, flabby, onetime shot-putter impotently apes the brutality of Polyphemos when he reaches for the "biscuitbox"—the cracker box, that is— and tries in vain to hit the departing Bloom. He fails because he cannot see straight in any sense, and unlike Polyphemos, who calls down on Ulysses the wrath of Poseidon, all the citizen can do is to send his bloody mongrel Garryowen racing after the car.

Nevertheless, the joke is on Bloom as well as the citizen. If we are tempted to see Bloom as a prophet for his time, carried off in the car like Elijah borne to heaven in a chariot, we are quietly informed that he rose no higher than "a shot off a shovel" (12.1918). If we want to see him as Christ, we must reckon not only with his comic blunders at the end of this chapter but also with what he does in the very next one, where this "man of inflexible honour to his fingertips" (13.694), as Gerty McDowell imagines him, masturbates at the sight of her underclothes on Sandymount Strand. But in masturbating, Bloom not only reveals again his ordinary, unsanctified susceptibility to the pleasures of the flesh; he also seeks "relief" (13.940) from the anxieties bred by the knowledge that his very own house has been invaded by a treacherous guest. For even as he meditates on Gerty McDowell he cannot forget the sight of Boylan's letter on his hall floor ("Bold hand: Mrs. Marion," 13.843) or suppress the knowledge of what Boylan has done in his house and bed by now. "Funny my watch stopped at half past four," he thinks.

> Was that just when he, she?
> O, he did. Into her. She did. Done. (13.846–49)

Like Odysseus and Christ as well, Bloom is a betrayed host. But unlike either of them, he is also a fully aware cuckold: a man who foresees and telepathically witnesses the usurpation of his bed but feels powerless to prevent it. For Bloom, trying to foil Boylan's bedding of Molly—or Molly's own lust for Boylan—is as futile as trying to stave off the sexual initiation of his fifteen-year-old daughter Milly. By telling coincidence the morning mail has brought not only Boylan's letter to "Mrs. Marion" but also a letter from Milly (now working out of town) reporting that she has just met a young man who sings alluringly of "seaside girls." As Bloom ponders both letters, "a soft calm, regret, flowed down his back-bone, increasing. Will happen, yes," he tells himself. "Prevent. Useless: can't move" (4.447–50).

Yet Bloom is never paralyzed. Ever on the move—whether physically, psychically, or both—he struggles to endure and somehow prevail. In not only finding the letter from Boylan but actually delivering it to Molly's bed, he knows he is serving the will of an adulterous usurper and thus playing the victim, *hostia*, in the game that Edward Albee's George would later call Humiliate the Host (Albee 138). In the phantasmagoric world of "Circe," Bloom becomes an antlered flunky acting out—and thus working through—all the humiliations he has silently endured during the day. Hanging his straw boater on a peg of Bloom's antlered head, Boylan says he has come to conduct "a little private business with your wife, you understand?" (15.3763–64). When Bloom replies that "Madame Tweedy is in her bath" (15.3767) and thus surrenders even his nominal possession of her, Boylan heads for the bathroom. In urging Bloom to look through the keyhole and play with himself while Boylan "go[es] through her a few times" (15.3788–89), Boylan mockingly reminds Bloom of what he actually did in the early evening to relieve the pain of being cuckolded. But the relief is hardly more than a spasm. Nothing Bloom does all day can hide or heal the wound of knowing that his house has been violated, his wife usurped, and his hospitality betrayed by a grossly presumptuous guest.

The pain of the wound becomes physical when Bloom at last returns to his house, enters the front room, and promptly knocks his temple against a walnut sideboard that has been shoved in front of the door. (As the catechist verbosely tells us, the "projecting angle" of the sideboard "had momentarily arrested his ingress," 17.1285–86). Possibly the only thing worse than a guest who rearranges your furniture in your absence is a guest whose rearrangement literally strikes you in the head. Recalling the footstool flung at Odysseus when he returns to his household dressed as a beggar, the displaced sideboard is just one of many signs that a hostile guest, an intruding stranger, has arrogantly taken possession of Bloom's house as well as of his wife. And the signs of possession lead right up into the marriage bed, where Bloom finds the imprint of a male form and some flakes of potted meat, punning signs that Boylan has adulterously potted his own meat.

In the face of this treachery, what can Bloom do? Unlike the host defined by the "Rule of Hospitality" in Klossowski's *Roberte Ce Soir*, he has not tried to walk a tightrope wire of pseudoscholastic calculation. He has not set out to actualize the potential of his wife-as-hostess—or to satisfy his curiosity about that potential—by authorizing her adultery with their guest even while somehow controlling his jealousy and suspicion. As a host whose hospitality, like that of Odysseus, has been grossly abused in his absence, Bloom fantasizes about vengeance and specifically about wandering through the universe past "the fixed stars" and then, after "incalculable eons of peregrination," returning as "an estranged avenger, a wreaker of justice on malefactors, a dark crusader" (17.2013–21). But he eschews revenge and every other form of retaliation such as dueling or divorce (17.2201–2). He is not an avenging host, like Odysseus, but a man whose comic vision sees beyond vengeance. He vanquishes his jealousy, says the catechist, by meditating on the comedy of his presumption to exclusivity, smiling (hypothetically at least) at the notion that he is "the first to enter whereas he is always the last term of a preceding series even if the first term of a succeeding one . . . neither first nor last nor only nor alone in a series originating in and repeated to infinity" (17.2127–30). Ranging from Mulvey (Molly's first boyfriend) to Boylan through a long list of men who could not possibly have ever bedded Molly, the ensuing series of her would-be lovers is nothing but "a list of past occasions for twinges of Bloomian jealousy," as Kenner aptly notes.[29] Given the disproportion between a single act of adultery and the throng of lovers that might be conjured up by Bloom's jealousy and suspicion, given the "natural" force of a sexual desire that has been unnaturally frustrated by Bloom's sexual neglect of Molly for more than ten years (17.2178, 2282–84), and given also that adultery is "less reprehensible than theft, highway robbery, cruelty to children and animals" and many other crimes (17.2178–83), Bloom has good reason to reach, before he falls asleep at last, a plateau of what the catechist calls "equanimity" (17.2177). Whether or not he thus retakes his home, his bed, and his wife is a question that can be answered only by Molly's monologue, in which she reveals, as I have argued elsewhere, that Bloom is still the only man she truly loves, and that she has bedded Boylan only to reactivate Bloom's sexual desire for her—to "make him want me" (18.1540).[30]

While Bloom contrives to vanquish Boylan mentally, to drive this unwanted guest from the house of his mind, he yearns to make Stephen an almost apostolic guest. Having rescued this drunken, groggy young man from the clutches of the police after he is struck down by Private Carr, Bloom first steers him to the cabman's shelter (where the coffee is undrinkable and the buns inedible) and then to his own home at 7 Eccles Street, where he offers him a cup of Epps's cocoa served up with "supererogatory marks of special hospitality" (17.359), including an extraordinary measure of the cream "ordinarily reserved" for the breakfast of Molly (17.359–65). Since the cocoa that both men drink in "jocoserious silence" is "Epps's massproduct" (17.369), and since cocoa comes from a tree called Theobroma cacao, "God-food cacao" (Gifford 571), we might well construe this moment of hospitality as a secular communion, the true culmination of the Mass that is mockingly initiated by Buck Mulligan at the beginning of the novel.

Yet Bloom makes it quite clear that he wants much more than Stephen's company for a cup of cocoa. He wants the young man not only to spend the night but also to start living at 7 Eccles Street. And in what might be called the mainstream of Homeric tradition, where every hospitable action must be somehow requited, he expects something in return. He wants Stephen to furnish him with regular intellectual stimulation, to give lessons in Italian to Molly, to take lessons in singing from her, to become a professional tenor himself, and, with Molly's seductive mediation, to marry Milly. In becoming Bloom's son-in-law, Stephen would perfectly fill the painful gap left ten years ago by the death of little Rudy. And not incidentally, the marriage of Stephen and Milly would tie the meandering and sometimes tortured plot of this novel into a perfect bow of melodramatic resolution.

Yet Stephen forestalls this ending—and everything else Bloom so eagerly envisions—by "promptly, inexplicably, with amicability, gratefully" declining his invitation to stay (17.955). "Inexplicably," says the catechist, who pretends to know everything but cannot explain why Stephen turns Bloom down.

This could be Stephen's way of reciprocating what Bloom did some twelve years earlier, when the older man "in appreciatively grateful sincerity of regret" declined the boy's invitation to dinner (17.473–76). But Stephen has much stronger reasons for saying no now. Even before Bloom extends his invitation Stephen allegorically reveals what would happen to him if he accepted it. At Bloom's urging he sings a song about little Harry Hughes, an updated version of the "strange legend" (17.795–96) of a Christian boy named Hugh of Lincoln who was supposedly crucified by Jews about the year 1255. Why should Bloom want to hear Stephen sing such a flagrantly anti-Semitic song? Possibly he feels that their mutually instructive conversation about Judaism, Christianity, and Irish history has so fully melted all the barriers between them that nothing about either Christianity or Judaism can seem alien to either one. But the legend of Harry Hughes remains, nonetheless, a particularly gruesome story of hospitality and treachery. Having first driven a ball over the Jew's garden wall and then with a second ball broken all of the Jew's windows (an uncanny prefiguration of *Kristallnacht*, which occurred sixteen years after the publication of *Ulysses*), Harry is welcomed by *"the jew's daughter / . . . all dressed in green"* (17.813–14).[31] She then takes him by the hand, leads him deep into the house, and cuts off his head with a penknife.

Bloom and Stephen take this story in quite different ways. While the father of Millicent (Milly) wonders at the apparition of a Jew's daughter "all dressed in green" (17.830–31) and thus remade as superficially Irish, Stephen silently parses the fate of the predestined victim. "Once by inadvertence, twice by design he challenges his destiny. It comes when he is abandoned and challenges him reluctant and, as an apparition of hope and youth, holds him unresisting. It leads him to a strange habitation, to a secret infidel apartment, and there, implacable, immolates him, consenting" (17.833–37). At this point Stephen himself has already been led, consenting, to Bloom's basement kitchen. Whether or not the kitchen qualifies as a secret infidel apartment, Stephen has no intention of taking up residence "in the apartment immediately above the kitchen" (17.932–33), for he knows that in that place his literary ambitions would be gradually, implacably sacrificed to the cultural, social, and sexual needs of the Bloom family as well as to Bloom's fantasy of a singing career for Stephen that would somehow leave him—as Bloom has earlier told him with comic overconfidence—"heaps of time to practice literature in his spare moments" (16.1860–61). This is something like the hospitality offered to Odysseus on the island of Scheria, where he could easily have married the beautiful young princess and lived off the generosity of her royal father. But Stephen, like Odysseus, knows that even the most hospitable of hosts can end up by subtly betraying a guest.

Does this mean that neither *Ulysses* nor the *Odyssey* shows us perfect hospitality? If perfect hospitality must be absolute (in Derrida's sense), and if the perfect host may require nothing whatsoever in return, not even the name of his or her guests, then not one host in either epic qualifies. In the *Odyssey* even the great-hearted Eumaeus eventually demands to know all about the stranger he entertains (F 14.213–18), and long before inviting Stephen into his house, Bloom knows him as the son of his friend Simon Dedalus. But whether or not such knowledge—or the desire for it—injures hospitality, it is compromised by any pressure on a guest to stay. According to Menelaus, the ideal host must speed a parting guest just as readily as he welcomes an arriving one.[32]

As we have seen, however, Menelaus himself does everything he can to detain Telemachus, and Bloom likewise does what he can to detain Stephen.

When the young man declines his invitation to spend the night, Bloom makes various "counterproposals": that Stephen give Italian lessons to Molly, that he take singing lessons from her, and that he conduct "a series of static, semistatic and peripatetic intellectual dialogues" with Bloom (17.960–72). Though the catechist indicates that these proposals were finally accepted in some form, Bloom considers their realization "problematic": no more likely than that Bloom should turn out to be the father of a circus clown, or that a coin Bloom set floating "on the waters of civic finance" should ever come back to him (17.973–984). The counterproposals, then, serve chiefly or even exclusively to postpone the moment of Stephen's departure from Bloom's house.

When the moment comes, however, Bloom leads Stephen out of the house with the aid of a lighted candle. In so doing, he recalls what Moses did for the Israelites when he led them out of Egypt, out of "the house of bondage" (17.1022) where their pharaonic host had detained them far beyond their wish to leave. The phrase about bondage first pops into Bloom's mind much earlier, in the printshop of the newspaper that employs him, when the sight of a typesetter laying out words in reverse order reminds him of his father reading backward in the Haggadah "all that long business about that brought us out of the land of Egypt and into the house of bondage" (7.208–9). After thus ineptly reversing a crucial phrase from the book of Exodus, Bloom now steps decisively forward. Having tried to install Stephen in his own house of bondage, Bloom sets him free to the secret strains of the 113th psalm, "modus peregrinus: In exitu Israel de Egypto: domus Jacob de populo barbaro" (17.1030–31). Since this psalm is sung in Dante's *Commedia* by a hundred souls newly whisked to the foot of the mountain of purification (*Purgatorio* 2.46–48), it may remind us that Stephen recalls Dante's words about being a guest earlier in the day, just before leaving a towered domicile that had become unbearably oppressive. Rather than eating any longer the salt bread of Mulligan's exploitative hospitality, he privately resolves not to sleep again in the tower that night or at his family's home (1.739–40). Many hours later, he likewise resolves not to sleep in the house of Bloom but to become instead a wanderer, *peregrinus*, with no fixed destination for the night.[33]

When Stephen parts company from Bloom by stepping through the gateway of his garden, the two are precisely contraposed: Bloom as "centripetal remainer" grants "egress to the centrifugal departer" (17.1214). But before that decisive separation, Bloom and Stephen gaze together at the "heaventree of stars" (17.1039) commonly called "fixed" but "in reality evermoving wanderers from immeasurably remote eons to infinitely remote futures in comparison with which the year, threescore and ten, of allotted human life formed a parenthesis of infinitesimal brevity" (17.1053–56). About the time he wrote those words, Joyce told Frank Budgen that Stephen and Bloom in this chapter "become heavenly bodies, wanderers like the stars at which they gaze" (Budgen 257). Though Bloom will never understand why Stephen should spurn the comforts of living in the Bloom household, he has traveled far enough—mentally and physically—to know the attractions of wandering and the perils of homecoming. As much as anything else, this knowledge links him to the wandering Stephen even as the young man walks off into the night.

WOOLF'S CLARISSA: SEX, POLITICS, AND THE ROLES OF A HOSTESS

Virginia Woolf knew *Ulysses* far better than Joyce knew À *la recherche du temps perdu*, and though she once tersely judged it "a misfire" (D 2:199), she could never put it wholly out of her mind, especially when writing *Mrs Dalloway*.[34] Published in 1925, three years after *Ulysses*, Woolf's novel strikingly recalls its precursor. Just as *Ulysses* chiefly recounts the thoughts, feelings, and memories of two men wandering separately (for the most part) through Dublin on June 16, 1904, *Mrs Dalloway* chiefly recounts the thoughts, feelings, and memories of three characters separately making their way around London on a single day "in the middle of June" in 1923 (6).[35] But to say so much is hardly to say that Woolf apes Joyce, any more than Joyce apes Homer.[36] The many minds plumbed in *Ulysses* nowhere include the mind of a schizophrenic or of a hostess, which if anything evokes the world of Proust; and not even Proust unveils, as Woolf does, the inner life and childhood memories of a woman engaged in giving a party.[37] So whatever its debts to the example of *Ulysses*, *Mrs Dalloway* makes its own contribution to the literature of hospitality.

Consider first the roles played by Clarissa, the heroine and hostess of *Mrs Dalloway*, in light of erotic hospitality. In nearly every work of literature I have examined so far, a married woman who receives an unrelated man as her guest—whether or not she has a husband living with her—opens herself to the possibility of becoming his lover. At one extreme, in Klossowski's *Roberte Ce Soir*, the "Law of Hospitality" requires the host to offer his wife to his guest, and the host grasps "the essence of the hostess" only by leading her into infidelity. At the other extreme, the abduction or even courtship of a hostess can be disastrous: Paris's abduction of Helen infuriates his host and ignites the Trojan war, and the suitors of the *Odyssey* pay with their lives for merely seeking to undermine their hostess's fidelity to their absent host. Between these extremes lie many variations. At the bidding of Lord Bertilak, who seeks to test the honor of his knightly guest, Lady Bertilak offers him her "cors," literally her body. Leopold Bloom painfully tolerates Molly's entertainment of Boylan but also flashes a photograph of her to entice Stephen into becoming their long-term guest.[38] Far less tolerant, though still nonviolent, are the husbands of Catherine Linton and Dorothea Casaubon. Just as Cathy's reception of Heathcliff at Thrushcross Grange alarms Edgar, Dorothea's entertainment of Will Ladislaw in Rome vexes Casaubon. While Ladislaw brings to Dorothea nothing like the history of passion that Heathcliff reanimates in Cathy, both men make the husbands of their respective hostesses feel sexually threatened.

In Woolf's novel, as in Proust's *À la recherche du temps perdu*, which she adored, the sexual implications of hostessing are more subtle.[39] Neither of the leading hostesses of Proust's novel shows any inclination to take a guest as a lover, but since a Proustian hostess can be an *entremetteuse*, a procuress, Madame Verdurin sometimes leads her guests into affairs with each other, and, as we have seen, the way in which the Duchess of Guermantes first invites Marcel to her house is so seductive that it promptly leads everyone around them to suspect him of being her new lover. No comparable suspicion lights on the title figure in *Mrs Dalloway*. Her one and only memory of being sexually aroused involves a kiss bestowed by another woman in their youth, and at the time of this novel she is a pale, weakhearted matron of fifty-one who sleeps alone in a clean, white, narrow virginal bed in the attic of her house—lest she be disturbed by her dutiful husband Richard, a member of Parliament, coming home late from his work at the House. After a fashion, however, she plays the *entremetteuse* insofar as she displays to her guests the vernal charms of her seventeen-year-old daughter, who has been made to feel she must appear at the party, who looks to one young man "like a poplar, . . . like a river, . . . like a hyacinth" (140), and who, at the very end of the novel, has been so transfigured by her pink frock that for a moment her father does not recognize her. Furthermore, one of Clarissa's male guests, Peter Walsh, is a former suitor who loved her passionately and was shattered when she rejected him for Richard. Though Richard feels not at all sexually threatened by him (once jealous of him, he now "had a very great liking for the dear old fellow," 80), and though Clarissa tells herself she was right to have refused him for threatening to crush her independence, she cannot forget what she felt when she learned, years ago, that he had married a woman he met on the boat to India, where he now works for the colonial British administration: "She had borne about with her for years like an arrow sticking in her heart the grief, the anguish, and then the horror of the moment when someone told her" (8). Walsh was never her lover, and he has no hope of becoming so on the day of the party. Yet he can still gain fleeting access to her heart, and he does so as they sit together on her sofa during his private visit to her in the morning. When he bursts into tears over all his troubles, she draws him to her, kisses him, and briefly feels within her "silver-flashing plumes like pampas grass in a tropic gale" (36). She also remembers him as a man who could make *her* cry, and strangely enough, what made her cry was his calling her a "perfect hostess."[40]

What did this phrase mean? Thinking of Peter on the morning of her party because he had written to say he would be "back from India one of these days" (5), she recalls his once predicting that "she would marry a Prime Minister and stand at the top of a staircase; the perfect hostess, he called her" (8). Here the context illuminates the phrase. Though her husband is merely a member of Parliament who is not even in the cabinet, the prediction closely fits the events of the party ahead, when Clarissa will stand at the top of her staircase to receive the prime minister and then triumphantly display him to her guests. In thus linking the world of politics to the role of a hostess, Peter's prediction reminds us that by the beginning of the twentieth century the word *hostess* might well signify a woman of political heft, a woman who regularly entertained and thereby influenced political figures. In the real world of nineteenth- and early twentieth-century London, hostesses of this kind ranged from Gertrude Tennant to Lady Ottoline Morell, whom Woolf knew personally, whose husband sat in Parliament, and whose grand parties included prime ministers as well as literary figures and intellectuals. In Victorian literature the most conspicuous example of such a hostess is Anthony Trollope's Lady Glencora Palliser, whose husband became prime minister, who tirelessly entertained the politicians around him, and who on one occasion sabotaged the candidacy of a man who had hoped to become chancellor of the exchequer.[41]

From the beginning of her work on *Mrs Dalloway*, which grew out of a short story about the title character and a sketch called "The Prime Minister," Woolf conceived it as a narrative that would culminate in a party and in some way involve the prime minister.[42] On its face, then, it has the makings of a novel about society and politics, or about the politics of hospitality as practiced by a Georgian counterpart of Trollope's Lady Glencora, that is, by a lady with a house in Westminster, the seat of the British parliament. Early in the novel, just after Clarissa has bought flowers for her party at a shop in Bond Street, the backfiring of a motorcar thought to contain, behind its drawn blinds, the "Queen, Prince, or Prime Minister nobody knew" (14) prompts her to think of her party as a sort of rival to the one that is to be given that night at Buckingham Palace: "And Clarissa, too, gave a party. She stiffened a little; so she would stand at the top of her stairs" (15). But Clarissa does not see herself as a politically consequential hostess. She links her party to the palace event only because one of her guests—her old friend Hugh Whitbread, who has a "little job at Court" (7) and whom she has just met in crossing St. James's Park—has told her that he "of course" is coming but might be "a little late . . . after the party at the Palace" (7).

Besides his grand manner and his impeccable clothes ("he was almost too well dressed always" [7]), Hugh's condescending way of accepting her invitation helps to explain why "she always felt a little skimpy" beside him (7). She also feels skimpy beside Lady Bexborough, a model of stoicism who opened a bazaar just after learning that her favorite son John had been killed in the war. Large, stately, dignified, and possessed of a country house, she is "interested in politics like a man" (10). By comparison, Clarissa is a nobody. With her "narrow pea-stick figure" and her "ridiculous little face, beaked like a bird's," she feels "invisible; unseen; unknown" (10).

Partly this is because her girlhood self has largely disappeared into "Mrs Richard Dalloway" (10). As the wife of a dutiful but hardly brilliant conservative M.P. (she remembers her old friend Sally Seton saying he "would never be in the Cabinet because he had a second-class brain" [90]), she has no political ambitions for him and no serious interest in his parliamentary work. After he comes home at three in the afternoon, gives her a bunch of roses, and tells her he must return for a committee meeting on the Armenians or Albanians (she is not sure which), she realizes that "she cared much more for her roses than for the Armenians. Hunted out of existence, maimed, frozen, the victims of cruelty and injustice (she had heard Richard say so over and over again)—no, she could feel nothing for the Albanians, or was it the Armenians? but she loved her roses (didn't that help the Armenians?)—the only flowers she could bear to see cut" (90).

By this point it is perfectly clear that even though her party will include the prime minister, Clarissa Dalloway is not a political hostess. But if in passages such as this one she sounds politically insensitive or irresponsible, we must realize that elsewhere the novel satirizes the political pretensions of another hostess. On the day of the party, Lady Bruton holds a lunch for Richard Dalloway and Hugh Whitbread so as to solicit their help in writing a letter about emigration to the _Times_ of London. Though Clarissa is shocked to learn that Richard has been invited without her, this little party is an exercise in futility and pretension. When Lady Bruton tells Hugh and Richard that their old friend Peter Walsh is back from India after making "a mess of things," Hugh offers to write on his behalf "to the heads of Government offices" but knows that his letters will lead nowhere "because of [Peter's] character" (80–81). As for Lady Bruton's letter to the _Times_, its subject matter "was not to others the obvious remedy, the sublime conception" (82) that it was to her, and she herself is incapable of writing anything coherent about it.

Nevertheless, she likes to think she has played her part in the history of great events. In an alcove of her drawing room is a table on which one of her ancestors, General Sir Talbot Moore, once wrote in her presence, "with her cognisance, perhaps advice, a telegram ordering the British troops to advance upon an historic occasion" (80). Now Whitbread drafts in her presence a letter that reduces her "tangles to sense." Though he "could not guarantee that the editor would put it in" (83),[43] the prospect of its appearing fills her daydreams after lunch, when she rests on a sofa and "her hand, lying on the sofa back, curled upon some imaginary baton such as her grandfathers might have held, holding which she seemed, drowsy and heavy, to be commanding battalions marching to Canada, and those good fellows walking across London, that territory of theirs, that little bit of carpet, Mayfair" (84).

Lady Bruton dreams of wielding imperial power, sending troops to Canada and crushing resistance in India, from which the "news" (83) that plainly alarms her—in June 1923—would doubtless have headlined the struggle for Indian independence and the rise of Mahatma Gandhi. Later on at Clarissa's party, after privately conferring about India with the prime minister, Lady Bruton deplores the "folly" and "wickedness" of its resistance and declares herself ready to fight for the empire: "If ever a woman could have worn the helmet and shot the arrow, could have led troops to attack, ruled with indomitable justice barbarian hordes and lain under a shield noseless in a church, or made a green grass mound on some primeval hillside, that woman was Millicent Bruton" (134). With comic extravagance, Lady Bruton exemplifies the kind of imperialism Clarissa has no wish to share and the kind of hostessing she has no wish to practice. "Lady Bruton," we are told, "had the reputation of being more interested in politics than people," which surely helps to explain why "Clarissa always said that Lady Bruton did not like her" (79–80). As Lady Bruton herself reflects at the party, "They had nothing in common—she and Clarissa" (133).

COMMUNION, DIVISION, LIES

Clarissa's intentions, then, might be summed up by what she concludes when she returns from her flower shopping to hear the sounds and see the signs of preparation for the evening throughout her house: "All was for the party" (30). I suspect a sly pun here, for the party in question is clearly not political—the conservative party to which her husband and the prime minister belong—but strictly social, or at least as apolitical as it can be with a prime minister in attendance.[44] This does not mean that the novel itself lacks political force. On the contrary, as Suzette Henke has argued, it "tacitly questions tyrannical authority in all its forms" (MDCS 128), from the nationalism that sacrificed millions of lives in the first Great War to the soul-destroying rest cures inflicted on those, like Septimus Smith, who came home psychically shattered.[45] But Clarissa herself is not a political hostess; she is a woman who likes to give parties. Why?

The simplest answer is *life*. In response to Peter's complaint that she liked to collect celebrities and to Richard's complaint that the excitement of party giving endangered her heart, Clarissa says that she gives parties "simply" for the sake of life (91)—simply, in other words, to radiate life in a world shadowed by death.[46] To explain this point, she conducts an internal dialogue while resting on her sofa after lunch. If, she thinks, "Peter said to her, 'Yes, yes, but your parties—what's the sense of your parties?' all she could say was (and nobody could be expected to understand): They're an offering; which sounded horribly vague" (191).

The word "offering" in this passage, which is repeated a few lines later, leads Henke to conclude that Clarissa's party is a secular version of the Mass. "The offering of the Mass," writes Henke, "apparently constitutes a primary metaphor in Woolf's novel—with Septimus Smith serving as Christ the victim and Clarissa Dalloway functioning as 'high priest.' . . . She offers to her dinner guests not only physical sustenance but the spiritual nourishment of a communion sanctified by the death of Septimus" (MDCS 126). This claim is highly problematic. While Clarissa finally reads Septimus's suicide as a defiant "attempt to communicate," to find the mystical "centre" that in her own life has been every day "obscured . . . in corruption, lies, chatter" (137), she is all by herself when she reaches this insight *after* an evening in which she greeted every guest with the words, "How delightful to see you!" (124). Was she truly delighted to see Lady Bruton, who excluded her from her lunch party and who, as we know from Clarissa herself, dislikes her?[47] Was she truly delighted to see the Bradshaws, whom (we are told), "she disliked" (135)? She is hardly impressed by Sir William Bradshaw's kind of psychiatry, for, like the "love and religion" of those bent on making converts, she senses that it "would destroy . . . the privacy of the soul" (95). In any case, the Bradshaws bring her news of Septimus's death near the end of the party, after its peak, "when she escorted the Prime Minister down the room," when "her severity, her prudery, her woodenness were all warmed through" and when she and Richard and all their guests felt together "the intoxication of the moment" (129).[48] When the Bradshaws break their news, she is so far from intending her party as a sacrificial offering that her first reaction is private dismay: "What business," she asks herself, "had the Bradshaws to talk of death at her party? A young man had killed himself. And they talked of it at her party—the Bradshaws, talked of death" (136). In her solitary meditation on

Septimus's death, she discovers its power to communicate and then resolves to rejoin her old friends Sally and Peter. But in our hearing she says nothing whatsoever about Septimus's death to them or to any of her other guests. How then does she offer them "a communion sanctified by the death of Septimus"?

A further problem with this reading of the party is that it is not a "dinner," as Henke says, but a large party for *after-dinner* guests.[49] The only thing we learn of the pre-party dinner at the Dalloways' house is that near the end of it, two bursts of laughter from the dining room signify "the gentlemen enjoying themselves when the ladies had gone" (123)—telling stories no doubt unfit for ladies' ears. Quite apart from this clear-cut moment of gender division, the distinction between a dinner and a party matters because a hostess cannot manage the multiple conversations of a party nearly as well as she can manage a single conversation at the dinner table. At the beginning of the dinner in Woolf's *To the Lighthouse* (1927), Mrs. Ramsay sees that with everyone sitting separate, "the whole effort of merging and flowing and creating rested on her" as hostess (*TTL* 126). So when she sees that Mr. Tansley is bored and disgruntled, she finds a way of making him merge and flow. Broaching the prospect of a sailing trip to the lighthouse and then asking Tansley if he's a good sailor, she prompts Lily (with a significant glance) to ask him if he will take her to the lighthouse, and thereby leads Tansley to relieve "his egotism" by telling of his nautical adventures (*TTL* 138–39). At Clarissa's party, the closest we get to this kind of merging is her presentation of Peter Walsh to her spinster aunt, who first met him at Bourton years before and with whom, Clarissa says, he can "talk about Burma" (133). But Peter's name (at first) means nothing to Miss Parry, and it soon becomes clear that her interest in Burma extends only to its orchids, on which he has nothing to say. By this time, however, Clarissa can do no more, for she has already left them to tell Lady Bruton how much Richard "enjoyed his lunch party" (133), a statement that wholly conceals her "shock" at having been excluded from it (24).

In thus suppressing her own feelings as well as ignoring Peter's, she demonstrates what prompted him to call her the "perfect hostess" years before at Bourton, just after he realized, at the dinner table, that Clarissa would marry Richard Dalloway:

> Afterwards he could remember standing by old Miss Parry's chair in the drawing-room. Clarissa came up, with her perfect manners, like a real hostess, and wanted to introduce him to some one—spoke as if they had never met before, which enraged him. Yet even then he admired her for it. He admired her courage; her social instinct; he admired her power of carrying things through. "The perfect hostess," he said to her, whereupon she winced

all over. But he meant her to feel it. He would have done anything to hurt her after seeing her with Dalloway. (48)

Seen through the eyes of a suddenly rejected lover, Clarissa's hospitality—her way of hostessing—is a double-edged sword. Though Peter admires her social courage, he cannot forget how "her perfect manners" once enraged him by erasing the history of their friendship and thus goading him into retaliation. Whether or not she deserved to be wounded by a jealous lover whom she had good reason to reject, her hostessing required some sacrifice of empathy rather than, as at Mrs. Ramsay's dinner table, a tactful application of it. Hostessing takes a similar toll at Clarissa's party, where her way of managing its multiple and abbreviated conversations tends, in her own word, to "obscure" true communication. Amid the chatter and lies, it is not easy to find communion.

THE POWER TO EXCLUDE

Whether or not a party becomes a secular communion, it is bound to be exclusive as well as inclusive. Before Woolf wrote *Mrs Dalloway*, Proust had already described the exclusiveness of the dinners for twelve given by the Duchess of Guermantes, who, as we have seen, decries the vulgarity of all large parties. Compared to the duchess, Clarissa is far more open and hospitable in the range and number of people she invites. They include her poor, unfashionable cousin Ellie Henderson, who is herself mildly amused by the ordinariness of the prime minister even while admiring his effort "to look somebody."[50] She thus seems implicitly to link the great man to herself, for she too has tried to look at least presentable for this occasion. But with her "cheap pink flowers" and "a shawl thrown over her old black dress" (125), she knows she cannot afford to match the fashionable women at this party, let alone the prime minister in all his gold lace. She knows too that she was invited at the last minute, which leads her to suspect that Clarissa did not wish to invite her at all. As we learn elsewhere, Clarissa did so only because she was pressured by Mrs. Marsham, who "told Ellie . . . she would ask Clarissa," and by Richard, "who did not see the reasons against asking" her (88, 90). Having meant to exclude Ellie "on purpose," Clarissa had asked herself, "Why should she invite all the dull women in London to her parties? Why should Mrs. Marsham interfere?" (88). Possibly, what Clarissa may want for her party is not the solemn hush of a secular communion but something like the sheer buzz and heat of social excitement Woolf herself prized: "the ferment and fountain of noise" generated by a big crowd.[51] But whether noisy or subdued, Clarissa wants to confine her guest list to the upper classes or at least to people who can afford to dress smartly, whether or not she likes them. And has anyone ever noticed that her guest list includes not one of the one and a half million British servicemen who had been maimed in the recent war?[52]

Notwithstanding his present plight, Peter Walsh makes the cut not only as an able-bodied old friend but also as a lifelong member of Clarissa's class. To be sure, he is an unconventional one. By comparison with Clarissa and Richard, he's a man of no public importance, in his own words a "failure" (34). Back from India, needing a job, and scheming to obtain a divorce for the young woman he wants to marry (she's the wife of an army major), he feels himself an outsider to London society, where he knows virtually no one but Richard and Clarissa. He also prides himself on his independence. Just after Clarissa invites him to the party at the end of his morning visit to her, he prowls the streets of London as "a romantic buccaneer," an urban adventurer. "Careless of all these damned proprieties . . . and respectability and evening parties," he follows an attractive, vivacious young woman to her door (41–42).[53]

By evening, however, he has decided to attend Clarissa's party, for which he has come near to cadging his invitation.[54] Also, en route from his hotel he decides that "everybody" is dining out because he sees doors being opened for "a high-stepping old dame, in buckled shoes, with three purple ostrich feathers in her hair" and "for ladies wrapped like mummies" in brightly flowered shawls (122). But Peter's "everybody" does not include the "shindy of brawling women" that catches his eye on Clarissa's own street. The cabs rushing "like water round the piers of a bridge, drawn together, it seemed to him because they bore people going to her party" (122) do not hold anyone of the lower classes. In claiming that "everybody" in London is dining out or headed to a party like Clarissa's, Peter unwittingly accepts the social values he pretends to reject in the morning. He is part of an "everybody" that includes him but excludes, with one exception, anyone Clarissa finds unfashionable. "However ambivalently," writes Ching-fang Tseng, "Peter . . ., belongs to the world that Clarissa as 'the perfect hostess' embodies, to the ruling class in charge of the London synonymous with affluence, orderliness, and civilization" (Tseng 243).

Consider, then, two figures who most certainly do not belong to Clarissa's world and would never be invited to any of her parties. One is a nameless female vagrant stretched on her elbow in Green Park, where she catches the eye of Richard going home after lunch with Lady Bruton. As he passes her while bearing the flowers he has just bought for Clarissa, "there was time for a spark between them—she laughed at the sight of him, he smiled good-humouredly" (87). She laughs, perhaps, at what might be construed as an old-fashioned sign of courtship—a floral sign. But they speak not a word—"not that they would ever speak"—and even as a member of Parliament Richard feels powerless before her: "What could be done for female vagrants like that poor creature, . . . he did not know" (87).[55] It may be a stretch, but one answer to Richard's silent question appeared some eighty years before *Mrs Dalloway* in a poem by Wordsworth. In *Guilt and Sorrow* (1842), a revised version of "The Female Vagrant" (which appeared in the *Lyrical Ballads* of 1798), Wordsworth uses the story of a destitute woman, a female vagrant, to show the statesmen of England how corrupt and oppressive the nation has become. "For want," he writes,

> how many men and children die?
> How many at Oppression's portal placed
> Receive the scanty dole she cannot waste,
> And bless, as she has taught, her hand benign?
>   (st. 49)

Just before this stanza, the narrator has directed the female vagrant and another wanderer to a lowly cottage in a valley where they can find a hospitality denied them in grander houses: "Comforts by prouder mansions unbestowed" (st. 47). Essentially, Wordsworth says, the nation is inhospitable to the poor. It remained so in 1923, the year in which Woolf set her novel. Until the Vagrancy Act of 1935, wandering around "without any visible means of subsistence" was a criminal act punishable by jail time and hard labor, and while the so-called casual wards of England and Wales offered shelter for the night, many of them were so filthy, crowded, and bare—with verminous mattresses at best—as to be scarcely fit for animals (Humphreys 135, 131). As Robert Humphreys notes, however, their "stubbornly fabricated inhospitality failed to deter the needy thousands who nightly claimed admission" to them in 1923, when unemployment stood at 12 percent (Humphreys 125–26). In London alone there were probably well over a thousand vagrants either forced into the squalor of a casual ward, sitting up on a hard bench in a charitable shelter, or simply sleeping in the street.[56]

So Richard's brief encounter with the female vagrant offers a fleeting glimpse of the world outside the London of the upper middle class, where hospitality means party giving, not—as it once did—the charitable provision of food and shelter to the destitute. I stress this point not to suggest that Clarissa should have invited the vagrant to her party or held a party for the homeless (she knows no vagrants and never sees one in her walks around London), but to indicate part of what her hospitality inadvertently excludes. She differs from Richard, who knowingly denies the vagrant any kind of hospitality by telling himself he has no idea, even as an M.P., what can be done for women like her. So far as we can tell, Clarissa knows nothing of such women, and the people she invites to her party are strictly limited to those who occupy at least the upper middle class. With the exception of Ellie Henderson, who is thrust upon Clarissa at the last minute, all of her guests are either respectable academics like Professor Brierly or wellborn, well dressed, and well-to-do.

As such, they exclude not only the vagrant but also Miss Kilman. Curiously enough, though Clarissa's party has been construed as a secular communion, the only explicit reference to communion in the novel is to the liturgical Communion that Clarissa's daughter Elizabeth regularly attends with Miss Kilman (11), her private tutor in modern history.[57] "They were inseparable," we are told (11), until Clarissa lures Elizabeth to her party, which could not possibly include Miss Kilman because, among other things, she tortures Clarissa by perpetually wearing "a green mackintosh coat" (11).

To be sure, Miss Kilman (whose very name sounds murderous) might well prove the death rather than the life of any party she attended. Embittered by degrading poverty and ill treatment—she was turned out of school during the war because of her German background—she resents anyone of wealth and privilege like Clarissa. In return, though Clarissa wants to "make allowances for her," she hates "not [Miss Kilman] . . . but the idea of her," as a kind of vampire sucking up "half [her] life-blood" (11). Their mutual loathing comes to a peak in the early afternoon, when Miss Kilman decides to take Elizabeth off to shop. Sensing that Miss Kilman yearns to overcome, ruin, and humiliate her in a "religious victory," Clarissa is shocked by this would-be Christian who lacks "kindness or grace," who makes no effort to please, and who has "taken her daughter from her!" (94).[58] Just now, however, Miss Kilman is merely taking Elizabeth to the cut-rate Army and Navy Stores, where Clarissa herself would never dream of shopping.

We are thus reminded that to Clarissa, one of the most repulsive things about Miss Kilman is the way she dresses. Clarissa herself realizes that she has inflated Miss Kilman's malignity, turning her into a monster of her own imagining.[59] The hateful "idea of her," Clarissa reflects, "undoubtedly had gathered in to itself a great deal that was not Miss Kilman" (11). When she tells herself that Elizabeth and Miss Kilman are "going to the Stores" (94), she fears perhaps that Miss Kilman's execrable taste in clothes may lead Elizabeth astray. But as Elizabeth fetches her gloves, which clearly shows that she is now absorbing her mother's tastes, Miss Kilman's monstrosity shrivels.[60] Clarissa sees "how, second by second, the idea of her diminished, how hatred (which was for ideas, not people) crumbled, how she lost her malignity, her size, became second by second merely Miss Kilman, in a mackintosh, whom Heaven knows Clarissa would have liked to help" (94).

In turning from a target of hatred into an object of pity, Miss Kilman recalls another poor woman. Just a few pages after Richard ineffectually wonders what can be done for the female vagrant, Clarissa tells herself that she yearns to help Miss Kilman but offers nothing more than laughter "at this dwindling of the monster" (94). She most definitely does *not* offer her an invitation to her party. On the contrary, she uses the party to reclaim her daughter from Miss Kilman, who has spent the early afternoon "closeted" with Elizabeth in "nauseating" prayer (88).[61] Just how bad is Miss Kilman? With her suffocating piety as well as her sullen resentment of Clarissa and her abominable taste in clothes, she seems scarcely more eligible for an invitation than the female vagrant. But if Professor Brierly, a Miltonist, qualifies for the party, Miss Kilman's thorough knowledge of modern history, along with her position as Elizabeth's tutor, should count for something in Clarissa's social world. The chief reason it doesn't is that in the eyes of Clarissa, Miss Kilman threatens to make Elizabeth her own, and to contest this threat, Clarissa must invite her daughter alone. Yet in desperately shouting a reminder of the invitation at the very moment when the two women leave the house, she unwittingly flings it at both of them:

Off they went together, Miss Kilman and Elizabeth, downstairs.

With a sudden impulse, with a violent anguish, for this woman was taking her daughter from her, Clarissa leant over the bannisters and cried out, "Remember the party! Remember our party to-night!" (94)

Later on over tea at the stores Miss Kilman shows that she has heard the invitation and knows it is meant for Elizabeth alone. When she asks Elizabeth, "Are you going to the party to-night?" Elizabeth equivocates. Though she "did not much like parties," she "supposed she was going; her mother wanted her to go" (98). Warning the young girl that "she must not let parties absorb her," Miss Kilman sees that this one is already starting to draw Elizabeth into a world from which Miss Kilman will be forever barred. So her would-be disdain for parties shortly gives way to a self-pitying sense of exclusion. "People don't ask me to parties," she says. "Why should they ask me? . . . I'm plain, I'm unhappy" (99).

Plain, unhappy, poor, self-pitying, disagreeable, and execrably dressed, Miss Kilman personifies everything Clarissa does not want at her party, and when Elizabeth leaves her, Miss Kilman plainly sees that the party as well as Clarissa herself has "triumphed" by wrenching Elizabeth's youth and beauty from her (99). But in using the party to separate — or liberate? — Elizabeth from

Miss Kilman, Clarissa also cuts her daughter off from a source of intellectual stimulation and lures her into the conventional role of a blooming debutante: a hyacinth girl.[62] For all her failings, Miss Kilman not only knows modern history but also urges Elizabeth to do something professional with her life. Weighing this advice as she tracks the busy feet of crowds along the Strand, Elizabeth briefly decides to "have a profession," to "become a doctor, a farmer, possibly go into Parliament." But since "she was, of course, rather lazy," this fleeting ambition fades as soon as she remembers the party: "She must go home. She must dress for dinner" (102). She must sacrifice her fleeting ambition to the will of the woman who is at once her mother, her hostess, and—in a socially respectable way—her *entremetteuse*.

THE STRUGGLE TO COMBINE

In managing Miss Kilman and her daughter, Clarissa wields the elemental power of a hostess: the power to include, exclude, and divide.[63] Any argument for the unifying force of Clarissa's party—for its status as a secular communion—must first reckon with the people it leaves out, including Septimus Smith, who (in effect) posthumously crashes the party. Before turning or returning to Septimus, however, consider again why Clarissa gives parties. Thinking about what she means by the "life" she aims to nurture with them, she says to herself, "Oh, it was very queer. Here was So-and-so in South Kensington; some one up in Bayswater; and somebody else, say, in Mayfair. And she felt quite continuously a sense of their existence; and she felt what a waste; and she felt what a pity; and she felt if only they could be brought together; so she did it. And it was an offering; to combine, to create; but to whom?" (91).

Leonard Woolf once wrote that the society hostess manifests "a kind of artistic creativeness—the art of hostess-ship; the love of the exercise of power and prestige; the passion of the collector of anything from stamps to human beings" (A 4:101–2). Clarissa's version of hostessing is somewhat less aggressively conceived. Seeing herself as less a passionate collector than a mediator, she aims to assemble those who "continuously" inhabit the house of her mind but who live apart in the city, albeit in quarters fashionable enough to ensure their social standing. (No one living north of Regent's Park or south of the Thames—in Brixton or Clapham, say—would qualify.) The chief aim of her party, then, is to bring people together and thus presumably set the stage for a secular communion.

This motive for party giving has been theorized as essentially psychological. Unlike Henke, who reads Clarissa's party as a sacrificial offering, Morris Philipson construes it as a nonsacrificial opportunity for psychic reintegration. At a party, he argues, we put our best selves forward, opening ourselves to social encounters that may enhance rather than threaten our identity, our sense of self.[64] Psychologically, then, a party offers each of its guests the opportunity to host each other, risking disruption to "whatever degree of integration the personality has already achieved" in order to be "confirmed or confuted by others" (Philipson 127–28). So even though Clarissa does "not for a moment . . . believe in God" (24), her party, says Philipson, is analogous to a religious ritual: "For those who cannot take communion in the body of a church, there is no ritual comparable to that of a party. To lose oneself in something larger than oneself among people one respects is to experience social fulfillment" (Philipson 130–32).

In light of this theory, however, it is striking to see how often the people assembled by Clarissa fail to lose themselves in each other, fail to bond. Their incompatibility surfaces not only in her novel but in the set of six stories about Clarissa's parties that Woolf wrote at the same time as *Mrs Dalloway* but that were not published in full until long after her death, when they appeared as *Mrs Dalloway's Party* (1973).[65] As fictional investigations of what Woolf called "the party consciousness" in 1925 (*D* 3:12), they help to illuminate her novel by showing how often the guests at a party *resist* the hostess's or host's attempts to put them together, how often — in other words — party consciousness is a consciousness of rift rather than of union or communion. In "The Man Who Loved His Kind," for instance, the man of the title — an overworked, underpaid lawyer wearing meager, borrowed evening clothes — feels grossly outdressed by the people around him, whom he despises. Though he loves "humanity" (Prose 27), as exemplified by the old couple who thankfully gave him a five-pound check for his free legal services, he feels nothing in common with the young woman to whom Richard Dalloway introduces him. Stifling her efforts to talk about literature or beauty, he yearns to "decapitate" her (Prose 28), and they end up "hating each other, hating the whole houseful of people who had given them this painful, this disillusioning evening" (Prose 30). In "The Introduction" Clarissa presents a "shy charming girl" named Lily Everit to an insolent, arrogant young man named Bob Brinsley because, says Clarissa, "both of you love Shelley" (Prose 34–35). But when Bob wholly ignores Lily's interests and talks of nothing but himself and his own work, she feels like a butterfly whose wings have been torn off.

The next three stories do nothing to reassemble the butterfly. In "Ancestors" an old woman finds "the stuffy London room" where Clarissa holds her party intolerable by comparison with the Scotland of her childhood, where she ran wild among current bushes and "heard the most wonderful talk of her time" from her father and his distinguished guests (Prose 39). In "Together and Apart"

Clarissa presents the forty-year-old Miss Anning to the fifty-year-old Roderick Serle. Though she tells Miss Anning, "You will like him" (Prose 42) and though they soon discover that they each love Canterbury, Miss Anning buries her own love in the past ("Canterbury twenty years ago") and under a tame cliché ("Of course, whatever they do, they can't spoil Canterbury") so as to crush the spark of common feeling and leave the two of them nothing further to say (Prose 47–48). In "The New Dress" a poor woman named Mabel feels like a "dingy old fly" in her newly made but "idiotically old-fashioned" Empire dress (Prose 50–51) and fails to draw solace from anyone she meets. After one man tries to soothe her by "quite insincere[ly]" commending her appearance, she says to herself, "Lies, lies, lies!" (Prose 51), as if "the truth" of a party lay precisely and paradoxically in the revelation of its lies as such.[66] When another man won't overrule her self-deprecating comment on the dress ("It's so old-fashioned"), she feels that "he would like her to drown" like a fly (Prose 53). Then, after unsympathetically hearing another woman's story of her children's ailments, she leaves early, tells Clarissa she has "enjoyed [herself] enormously," and tells herself, "Lies, lies, lies!" (Prose 57)—a triplet that perfectly describes what she has just told Clarissa. Finally, in the last of the stories, "A Summing Up," Sasha steps into the Dalloways' garden with Bertram only because he could be "trusted, even out of doors, to talk without stopping" and thus to relieve her from doing so (Prose 58). Sitting at the far end of the garden, Sasha admires the beauty of a house and garden created "over [a] bog" and silently applauds the "society of humanity" Clarissa has gathered (Prose 60). But when she looks over the garden wall to see the "vast inattentive impersonal world" of London again, she no longer sees poetry or beauty anywhere, and the party seems "nothing but people in evening dress" (Prose 60–61).

The stories of *Mrs Dalloway's Party*, then, offer just one fleeting spark of contact in a social world otherwise riven by disillusionment, resentment, hatred, and emotional brutality. When Clarissa leads Lily to Bob in the hope they will kindle together "the most ancient of all fires" (Prose 35) and thus reenact her own first meeting with Richard, Bob simply plucks Lily's wings. Clarissa makes no matches in these stories nor even prompts a single friendly conversation of any appreciable length. For that reason we might infer that Woolf writes the novel precisely to move beyond the stories, to show how Clarissa succeeds in a project of social integration that repeatedly fails in *Mrs Dalloway's Party*. For Philipson, the party of the novel is a model of psychic integration: "A gathering together of separate individuals about a hostess through participation in a social entertainment is, in its turn, a reflection of each personality's attempt (or in Septimus Warren Smith's instance, failure of the attempt) . . . to gather together the disparate elements within each self into states of integration of relative stability and self-enjoyment. Thus, through the form of the novel itself, we are led to see not only that the self is a group but, complementarily, the group is a self" (Philipson 134).

But is the group an integrated self? Clarissa does not even try to promote any new friendships, much less make any matches; the closest she comes to either is intervening to rescue "little Jim Hutton" from the overbearing Miltonist (131). The party does bring together three old friends—Peter, Sally, and Clarissa herself—and Clarissa is clearly pleased to see the other two "[settle] down together" (135). But she also sees that Sally—whom she once knew as a fearless young woman—has settled into a wealthy, provincial matronhood, and her own talk with Peter, who has so far annoyed as much as engaged her, is deferred until after the end of the novel. Furthermore, she leaves both Sally and Peter to greet "the Bradshaws, whom she disliked" (135) not long after leaving Peter to speak to Lady Bruton, whom we know she also dislikes.[67] The superficial tone of inclusion is undercut by notes of exclusion. When Clarissa asks three men what they are laughing at, Sir Harry says he can't tell her. (Like the dinner table stories, it is not fit for the ears of ladies.) Even her intoxicating moment of social glory with the prime minister, when she leads him through the party like a mermaid "lolloping on the waves" (129), quickly fades into darker feelings; "these triumphs . . . had a hollowness" for her, and as she sees the P.M. down the stairs, "the gilt rim of the Sir Joshua picture of the little girl with the muff brought back Kilman with a rush; Kilman her enemy. That was satisfying; that was real. Ah—how she hated her—hot, hypocritical, corrupt; with all that power; Elizabeth's seducer. . . . It was enemies one wanted, not friends" (130). The deliberately excluded Kilman thus crashes into Clarissa's thoughts, almost as if crashing the party itself. Again and again this would-be integrative hostess must reckon with people she dislikes, people who disappoint her, people who won't share their jokes, people she hates, and people who don't get along.

COMMUNION AND SUICIDE

In this light, the supreme irony of the party is that its one moment of genuine communion links Clarissa with a man who is not only absent from the party altogether but who, as Philipson notes, has utterly failed "to gather together the disparate elements" of himself.[68] When Lady Bradshaw tells Clarissa that this former patient of Sir William has killed himself, Septimus Smith crashes the party posthumously, and Woolf splices what have been up to now the two antithetical strands of her novel: the story of Septimus's day as an epitome of his life and the story of Clarissa's day as an epitome of hers. Unlike Sally Seton,

Septimus is hitherto unknown to her as well as wholly unexpected, a ghostly guest who comes unbidden—like the ghost of Michael Furey in "The Dead"— but who craves absolute hospitality. In welcoming this uninvited guest, in letting him enter the depths of Clarissa's consciousness, which is far beneath her party consciousness, Woolf herself becomes a meta-hostess bridging the gulf between the hostess and her unknown guest.[69] Here Clarissa's mind proves far more supple than that of the Duchess of Guermantes, who, as we have seen, will not let even the imminent death of her beloved Swann check her relentless pursuit of social pleasure.

Though Woolf had not yet read *The Guermantes Way* when she wrote *Mrs Dalloway*, she most certainly knew what Katherine Mansfield—her close friend and rival—had done with the convergence of party giving and death.[70] In tracking the stages by which Clarissa responds to a party crasher whom at first she seeks to exclude ("What business had the Bradshaws to talk of death at her party?" [136]), Woolf re-creates what Mansfield does in "The Garden Party," a short story published to wide acclaim in 1922, just as Woolf was beginning her novel. In Mansfield's story, preparations for a catered garden party to be given by a family living in a house on a hill are suddenly disrupted by news of a terrible accident that took the life of a poor workman living with his wife and five children in a nearby village. When Laura, one of the daughters, wants to cancel the party out of respect for the dead man's family, her mother distracts her with the gift of a new black hat, and the party goes on. Afterward, when her mother sends her to the grieving family with a basketful of leftovers, Laura gets no thanks from the dumbfounded widow but takes comfort from the sight of the "peaceful" and "dreaming" corpse: "I am content," she says to herself, even while sobbing her way out of the cottage (Mansfield 260). "It was simply marvellous," she tells her brother, adding, " 'Isn't life—.' . . . But what life was she couldn't explain" (Mansfield 261).

In Mansfield's story a young woman vexed by the heartlessness of holding a party in the face of death finds a way to make the would-be peacefulness of death confirm her self-satisfaction, which has already been gratified by the gift of a new hat. By sending leftover food to the house of the widow, her mother practices hospitality at a distance and thus keeps death out of her own house. Clarissa's response to the news of Septimus's death is altogether different. Since the news comes in the middle of her party (or near the end of it), she can hardly cancel the event, but she leaves the crowd to enter alone "the little room where the Prime Minister had gone with Lady Bruton" (136). As if to confirm her indifference to politics, she goes there not to confer with the P.M., who has already left the party, but to receive her unexpected guest, whose suicide gradually unveils its import to her meditating mind. First she imagines what her own body would feel as it plunged, like his, from a window onto the rusty spikes of the railing below.[71] Then she rereads her whole party, and in particular one of her guests, in light of what Septimus has done. Knowing he has been treated by Sir William, she surmises that "the great doctor" has driven the young man to suicide by making his life intolerable. "To her" Sir William looks "obscurely evil, without sex or lust, extremely polite to women, but capable of some indescribable outrage—forcing your soul, that was it" (137). To Clarissa, Septimus's suicide was more than his way of thwarting Bradshaw's effort to subjugate his soul. It was a defiant "attempt to communicate" beneath or beyond the words typically exchanged at parties like hers (137). Just as the hollowness of Mabel's compliment to Clarissa in "A New Dress" ("I have enjoyed myself enormously") is instantly exposed by what she says to herself ("Lies, lies, lies!"), Septimus's suicide reveals by contrast the superficiality of everyday talk, including party talk, wherein the "thing . . . that mattered"—the independence of the soul—is "wreathed about with chatter, defaced, obscured in her own life, let drop every day in corruption, lies, chatter" (137). Clarissa communes more deeply with the ghost of Septimus than with anyone else who comes to her party. To this wholly unexpected guest she offers absolute hospitality.

But this does not mean that she too will take the fatal plunge. Though Woolf first conceived the novel without Septimus and planned to make it end with Clarissa's suicide, she then added Septimus as her "double" and transferred the suicide to him.[72] At the moment of Clarissa's greatest identification with Septimus, she speaks for him, translating his act into words, fulfilling his "attempt to communicate" without them. She feels "somehow very like him" (138). But she will not *act* like him. In spite of her claim that life is hopelessly mired in "corruption, lies, chatter," she chooses to live. As wife and hostess, Clarissa will not abandon either her husband or her guests. Having earlier construed Richard's midday gift of flowers as an attempt to communicate his love "without . . . speaking" (89), she sees that her present happiness, which she has more than once acknowledged, is "due to Richard" (137). It is also due to the hospitality of her mind, her openness not only to the ghost of Septimus but also to "the process of living" and all it presents, human and natural. When she goes to the window and parts the curtains to see the sky, she finds that the old woman in the room opposite is staring "straight at her" (138). Though Clarissa cannot tell for sure what the woman sees ("Could she see her?" 138), here is another unexpected guest, another test of her receptivity. Instead of promptly reclosing her curtains against the staring face, Clarissa accepts her possible gaze even as she fascinatedly watches her cross the room to draw her own blind before quietly going to bed. When Clarissa then sees the old lady "put out her light," she is reminded of a Shakespearean line that she read in the morning in a bookshop window and that has since been haunting her all day long: "Fear no more the heat o' the sun."[73] This Shakespearean valediction to a young woman thought to be dead now applies to an old one quietly rehearsing for the end of her life. Though "put out her light" recalls what Othello says just before killing Desdemona (*Othello* 5.2.7), the old woman threatens no violence to anyone, including herself. The extinguishing of her light at the end of the day prefigures a peaceful death quite unlike that of Septimus, and in so doing it offers the mind of the hostess another way of thinking about the shape of life.

Clarissa not only goes on living; she remains a hostess to the very end. Having welcomed into her mind two unexpected guests with their contrasting messages about life and death, Clarissa turns back to her party and in particular to Sally and Peter, who, during Clarissa's absence, conduct the longest conversation to be found in the novel. But it hardly leads to perfect communion among three old friends. Feeling "a real affection" for Peter (139), Sally still faults Clarissa for rejecting him, and though she knows that she owes Clarissa hugely for her frequent hospitality at Bourton during their youth (when Sally was penniless), she now resents both host and hostess alike: Richard for caring "only for dogs" and smelling "of the stables," Clarissa for snobbishly thinking that Sally "had married beneath her" and for never coming to visit her house near Manchester even though Sally had repeatedly invited them (140–41). Also, throughout her conversation with Peter, Sally knows he is "longing" to talk to their hostess and "thinking only of Clarissa" (142) as Sally rattles on about her husband, her five sons, and her suburban flower beds. Significantly, she is not with Peter when Clarissa returns to the party at the end. Persuaded by Peter that "Richard has improved" (144), she goes off to talk to their host—an act that might be construed as integrative except that it leaves her out of the final conversation between Peter and Clarissa—a conversation from which we too are excluded.

The final page of the novel, then, juxtaposes exclusion and inclusion, dispersal and severely limited communion. As the party breaks up, the rooms get "emptier and emptier" and "even Ellie Henderson was going, nearly last of all, though no one had spoken to her" (144). Yet Richard, who actually *had* spoken to her ("How's the world treating *you?*" he asked, 126), is now joined not only by Sally but also by his daughter Elizabeth, who comes over when she feels him looking at her with admiration. This leaves Peter alone with Clarissa at the very end, when her return fills him "with extraordinary excitement" (144).

Since the novel ends before either of them speaks and since we see Clarissa through Peter's eyes alone, we can only guess what is in her mind. She has just experienced the most intense feeling of communion that the party has so far offered her, but she achieves this feeling only by leaving the party to commune with the ghost of a newly dead man she has never met. The whole episode strangely rewrites the Last Supper. While Christ is betrayed by a guest who later hangs himself, Clarissa feels betrayed by *news* of a suicide, by "talk of death at her party" (136), until she realizes that the suicidal man was himself betrayed by one of her very own guests, the "obscurely evil" doctor who tried to crush the young man's soul (137). By the time she returns to the party, the doctor and his wife have left, which spares her the pain of telling another social lie, such as, "How delightful to have seen you."[74]

But how does Clarissa bridge the gulf between her solitary meditation on Septimus's suicide and the social life of her party, which is mired in such lies? I have suggested that the woman she sees through the window presents an alternative to suicide, a way of quietly ripening to old age. In returning to her guests and particularly to Peter, Clarissa returns to her life, which is finally inseparable from her duties as hostess and wife. However much she may feel that her life obscures the "thing . . . that mattered," the center of the self, the independence of the soul, she knows she cannot take her own life without betraying her husband, her daughter, and the last of her guests, Sally and Peter. If a novelist resembles a hostess, as Woolf says (see note 69), Clarissa herself deploys a novelistic power to assimilate and transform a set of radically disparate elements. At a party meant to celebrate "simply life" (91), she makes room for even a suicidal ghost and thus perfects the art of hospitality as an art of receptivity. In the end, the message she brings back to the party from her silent encounter with the ghost is simply her wordless presence "there" before Peter. If, as Philipson argues, "a gathering together of separate individuals about a hostess" reflects each person's effort to integrate the disparate elements within him- or herself (Philipson 134), the hostess's return to her family and friends reaffirms the integrative power of her own personality, which has found a way to practice the art of hospitality in the face of treachery.

HOSTING THE OTHER: CAMUS'S "THE GUEST"

In "The Guest," a short story that appeared in Camus's late collection *Exile and the Kingdom* (1957), we return to the hospitality of individual encounter: a single host struggling to understand a single unexpected guest. At the end of "The Dead," Gabriel strains to comprehend the ghost of Michael Furey, who suddenly enters the hotel bedroom where he had planned to make love to his wife. At the end of *Mrs Dalloway*, the hostess of a large party withdraws to commune with the ghost of a complete stranger whose suicide seems at first utterly alien to her festive mood. In Camus's story, the intruding guest is not a ghost, but he seems to come from another world, a world almost wholly alien to the teacher who receives him in the remote Algerian schoolhouse where he lives and works. Aside from being an Arab who speaks no French, the man has been arrested for murder, and the teacher has been ordered to guard him as a prisoner while escorting him to the police.

For this reason Camus's story might be approached by way of an earlier story that suggestively blurs the line between guest and prisoner: Frank O'Connor's "Guests of the Nation" (1931). Here the so-called guests are English hostages of the Irish Republican Army (IRA) during the time when it was fighting—with the help of young O'Connor himself—for the nation's independence. As the story opens, the two hostages and their IRA guards, one of whom is the narrator, have grown friendly enough to call each other "chum" and to play cards every night in the house where they are staying. Also, one of the "decent [English] chaps," as the narrator calls him, has learned Irish ceili dancing with the local girls, and the other one has warmed the heart of the cranky old woman of the house by silently anticipating her every wish, "walking in and out, like a ghost, without a word" and making her a "friend for life" by fetching "any little thing she wanted" (O'Connor 173–74). But as Eugene O'Brien observes, "friend for life" sounds an ominous note for a man fated to become the very ghost he is said to resemble (O'Brien 115). The phrase "like a ghost" darkly reminds us that the word *ghost* derives from the Indo-European *ghostis*, "stranger," which is also what the Latin *hostis* meant before it came to signify only an enemy.[75] When the IRA guards are ordered to kill the hostages in reprisal for the execution of four IRA men, the nation's guests complete their trajectory from primordial ghosts (strangers, potentially enemies) to chummy guests and back to ghosts of a different kind: dead enemies still haunting the memory of the narrator, whose comrade sees nothing but "a little patch of bog with the two Englishmen stiffening into it" while he himself feels only desolation, "like a child astray in the snow" (O'Connor 187). "Stiffening," which might once have described the Englishmen's sexual response to the Irish girls, now signifies the onset of rigor mortis. As O'Brien notes, the story is steeped in what Derrida calls "hauntology" (Derrida, *Specters* 39, O'Brien 115). Haunted by "the glorious dead"—the ghosts of the Irish nation—the IRA men feel bound to treat the other, no matter how chummy, as an enemy of that nation.[76] Yet the narrator is equally haunted by the memory of his ghostly guests, the other who can never be banished from the nation of his mind.

In Camus's story the chief character is likewise haunted by a prisoner he is suddenly ordered to guard. Called "L'Hôte," a French word that can mean either "the guest" or "the host," the story takes place in an isolated schoolhouse perched on a high, rocky, arid plateau in the mountains of northern Algeria. Though Camus gives no date for the time of the story (as he had when setting *The Plague* in the 1940s), it appeared when Algeria was still considered part of France but three years after Arab insurgents had launched their struggle for independence by attacking their French colonial masters on November 1, 1954, Toussaint Rouge, Red All Saints Day.[77] The Arab prisoner who becomes a guest in the story, then, embodies a potential threat to his host, a French schoolteacher named Daru.

Alone without his pupils, who have been kept away by a mid-October snow-fall, Daru looks out one afternoon to see a familiar figure on horseback: a Corsican gendarme named Balducci slowly climbing the slope that leads to the school and trailing by a rope behind him an Arab who walks with his hands bound.[78] When the two men reach the schoolhouse, Balducci explains that the Arab has killed his own cousin in a family squabble over grain, that he comes from a village already "beginning to stir" as part of a possible "revolt" against the French (G 92), and that Daru must deliver him to police headquarters in Tinguit, a two-hour walk to the east.[79] Daru is dumbfounded. Having been hired to feed French culture to his Arab pupils, he is suddenly conscripted by the French authorities to help enforce their laws against a nameless Arab murderer who says nothing, who (says Balducci) speaks "not a word" of French, and who might be part of a nascent insurgency, "a forthcoming revolt" (G 92–93). But Daru will not simply play custodian. Though he signs a receipt for the Arab, he will not agree to deliver him to police headquarters, and he treats him as his overnight guest. Unbinding the prisoner's hands, he serves him tea and—after Balducci leaves—a dinner of oilcake and omelette in his bedroom. Meanwhile they start to talk—in Arabic. "Are you hungry?" Daru asks the prisoner. "Yes," he replies. When Daru tells the prisoner he is not his judge, as the man had thought, but simply his guard "until tomorrow," the prisoner asks, "Why do you eat with me?" To which Daru replies, "I'm hungry" (G 99).

They play their roles with stark severity. Though Daru provides a folding bed and blankets for the man in his own bedroom, they never achieve anything like the chumminess of O'Connor's hostages and guards, and beyond the need for food and shelter, they cannot communicate. Looking at the prisoner, Daru cannot imagine him bursting with murderous rage at his victim. When the teacher asks, "Why did you kill him?" the man says only, "He ran away. I ran after him," and then asks woefully, "What will they do to me?" When the teacher asks, "Are you afraid?" and "Are you sorry?" the Arab stares back open-mouthed in bafflement, whereupon Daru simply tells him, "Lie down there" and "That's your bed" (G 100).

Daru here displays what Colin Davis calls "Levinasian generosity" toward the stranger. In Levinas's "ethics of hospitality" as Davis explains it, "the self recognizes the absolute otherness of the other, and rather than responding to it with violence, conceives an infinite responsibility toward it" (Davis, "Cost" 242). Even his "not questioning the Arab further," says Davis, "can be read as a recognition of the impenetrability of the other (rather than as an exasperated renunciation of the attempt to understand him)."[80] Without demanding that the Arab explain himself, he feeds him and gives him a bed for the night.

But Daru is not simply a host. Unlike O'Connor's IRA men, who guard or host what the Irish have traditionally called "strangers" (the English colonizers of their land), Daru is a French colonizer living in Algeria, and to that extent is a guest of all its natives. Since *hôte* can mean, as noted, either "host" or "guest," Derrida argues that the word may be applied to either character in either sense. In the ambiguity or rather polysemy of *hôte* he finds the key to the story. Its colonizer, he writes,

> is a *hôte* of a certain type. He is *chez lui* [at home]; he is an *autochton* [native] . . . but he is *chez lui chez l'autre* [at home in the home of the other], in the home of the Arab. He is also the host and the prisoner whom he holds hostage. . . . "*Son hôte*" [H 52] signifies *l'hôte accueillant* [the welcoming host] just as well as the *l'hôte accueilli* [host as guest, the host welcomed as a guest]. Daru decides, alone, isolated by his responsibility, not to turn over his *hôte* [host as guest] whose *hôte* [guest] he himself is, because he is in Algeria in the Algerian's home.[81]

Is Derrida right? Though it fully exploits the double meaning of Camus's title word by neatly deconstructing the opposition between host and guest, colonizer and colonized, this quintessentially Derridean explanation of Daru's decision finds scant warrant in the story itself, where his motive seems at first purely visceral. When Balducci tells him that the Arab has slit his cousin's throat as if it were that of a sheep, Daru is suddenly revolted, not only by this man but by all men and "leurs haines unlassables, leur folie du sang" ("their tireless hates, their blood lust," H 50 / G 93). What churns his stomach is fresh evidence of man's bloodthirstiness, of hatreds "unlassable" because they are endlessly revived by fresh attacks that must be requited, whether by personal or official retaliation, throat slitting, or execution. In flatly refusing to hand the prisoner over to the law, even at the risk of insulting Balducci and perhaps the authorities as well, Daru is refusing to play any part in sustaining the cycle of hatred and retaliation that repels him. But in fairness to the spirit of Derrida's reading, I must admit that Daru's impulse also underscores the impossibility of taking sides in the war now brewing between the colonizers and the colonized or even of upholding the opposition between them. On one hand, Daru feels not so much threatened by the Arab, however murderous, as oppressed by French officialdom; on the other hand, the Arab has not attacked anyone French but has rather killed his own kinsman. If he is no better than any other man, no less bloodthirsty or barbarous, he is perhaps no worse, which by itself could explain why Daru insists on treating him as a human being in need of food and shelter for the night, a guest in the most elementary sense of the word.

Further weakening the opposition between the two men is Daru's sense that each of them is indissolubly bound to this pitiless land, a desert cruel enough "même sans les hommes" (H 48), even without the men who make it crueler. Having been born here, Daru feels exiled everywhere else (G 88), and to that extent he finds in his guest a kindred spirit. "Dans ce désert," he thinks,

> personne, ni lui ni son hôte n'étaient rien. Et pourtant, hors de ce desert, ni l'un ni l'autre, Daru le savait, n'auraient pu vivre vraiment. (H 52)

[No one in this desert, neither he nor his guest, mattered. And yet, outside this desert neither of them, Daru knew, could really have lived.] (G 98)

This thought comes to Daru just after Balducci leaves him alone with the prisoner, who has been told to wait in the classroom while Daru lies on the couch in his bedroom. Though Daru hopes the Arab will escape and thereby relieve him of the need to make any decision about him, the Arab is called "son hôte" for the first and only time in the story, and immediately afterward, when Daru finds him still in the classroom, he invites him into the bedroom to eat and sleep. Here, it would seem, Daru takes the greatest possible risk. In the spirit of something like absolute hospitality, he puts away in a desk drawer of the classroom the revolver Balducci has left for him and then spends the night sleeping unarmed in the same room with a murderer.[82]

The peacefulness of this night, therefore, suggests the triumph of humanity over barbarity, generosity over hatred, hospitality over hostility. As he hears the breathing of his nonce roommate, Daru even senses "une sorte de fraternité" (H 55): a sort of brotherhood he associates with comrades who cast off their armor for the night "dans la vielle communauté du songe et de la fatigue" ("in the ancient community of dream and fatigue") (H 55 / G 102) but that also evokes—for us at least—the holy trinity of the French Revolution: *liberté, égalité, fraternité*. As a teacher of all things French in the land of the Arabs, Daru must know that the yearning for liberty, equality, and fraternity could fire the hearts of Arabs oppressed by their French colonial masters just as readily as it fired the hearts of *le peuple* in the age of Louis XVI.

But Daru feels nothing of the kind. Instead of feeling touched or thrilled by a sense of fraternity, he is bothered by the presence of another man in a room where he has slept alone for a year. The presence of the Arab bothers him also, we read, "parce qu'elle lui imposait une sorte de fraternité qu'il refusait dans les circonstances présentes" (H 55) ("because it imposed on him a sort of brother-hood which he refused in the present circumstances"). To read the word "frater-nité" in this context is to see its meaning instantly erased. Though Daru and the Arab are both men of the desert who could live nowhere else, though they are both sleeping and breathing together unarmed in the same room, and though Daru is treating this man as his guest, he rejects "fraternité" just as strongly as he has already rejected the role of prison guard.

Does this rejection constitute a betrayal? Lawrence Kritzman argues that it does, that Daru "betrays the very principles to which he appears to subscribe" by refusing to take full responsibility for a man who seems unable to make his own decision (Kritzman 573). But just what are Daru's principles? On the one hand, he seems to have embraced the Arabic tradition of hospitality, which requires him to house and feed anyone, even an enemy or murderer, who comes to him for shelter. On the other hand, he will take no side in the nascent war, and he will condone no one's bloodlust, neither French nor Arab. To act *for* the Arab, to deliver him from custody and even the prospect of execution, would amount—in Daru's exquisitely scrupulous conscience—to taking sides. It would also preempt what Daru evidently takes to be the Arab's fundamental right to make his own decision as a man, not the cultural child of a paternalistic master, no matter how enlightened or benevolent.[83]

If these are indeed Daru's principles, he does not betray them. On the morning after their night together, he serves them by doing everything he can for the Arab short of usurping his freedom to decide. Having led him from the plateau down to a plain, having given him a package of food and a thousand francs, and having shown him the way east to the police station in Tinguit, Daru also shows him a trail leading south to the land of the nomads, who, he says, will "take you in and shelter you according to their law" (G 108). In other words, Daru expects the nomads to offer the unconditional hospitality of Arabic tradition, something like what he himself has just offered to his guest. Clearly, he also expects the Arab to head for the nomads and is dismayed to see him choose instead the road to prison. Defying all efforts to understand him, the Arab remains an inscrutable mystery.[84]

The bitter irony of his final choice is capped by what Daru finds clumsily chalked on the blackboard when he returns to his classroom: "Tu as livré notre frère. Tu paieras" ("You handed over our brother. You will pay for this," H 58 / G 109). These few words resonate with multiple ironies. First of all, they are the first French words produced by any Arab character in this story, since the Arab prisoner speaks no French at all.[85] Like Shakespeare's Caliban, the Arab who wrote those words has learned to curse—or at least to threaten—in the language of his masters, which he may have learned as a boy in this very school-room. Second, "Tu as livré notre frère" cruelly echoes its very opposite, "Tu as libaré notre frère," which in turn evokes once more the revolutionary words *liberté* and *fraternité*. Whether or not Daru hears this echo, he has actually freed the Arab to make a decision which has been construed by his "brothers" as an act of helpless acquiescence to the custodial authority of Daru, the very man who eschewed such authority.[86] Finally, and most cruelly of all, Daru will be made to pay. Instead of being rewarded for his generosity, instead of seeing his hospitality repaid with kindness, he will be punished for it, perhaps even made to pay with his life. The benign reciprocity of traditional hospitality thus gives way, once again, to precisely what Daru abhors: the bloodlust of revenge.

To read the ending in this way is to see it through the eyes of Daru, for whom *the* Arab, generically speaking, is at best an inscrutable mystery and at worst an irredeemable brute.[87] But the ending looks different in light of the Algerian struggle for independence, which Camus vehemently opposed.[88] Though independence came just five years after his story appeared and two years after he died, the story implies that Arabs cannot govern themselves because they would not know what to do with the freedom to choose or how to construct any system of justice not based on revenge. But in willfully misconstruing what Daru sought to do for his guest, the nameless Arab author of the scrawled message may also be saying, at some level, "Tu ne peux pas libérer notre frère": You cannot free our brother because we must free ourselves from you. No matter what Daru does for his guest, he cannot help betraying the aspirations of a people bent on claiming the rights of a host in their own land.

CODA: *OMNIUM GATHERUM*

Consider, finally, the rights or the plight of an Arabian guest at an American table in a recent play called *Omnium Gatherum*. Midway through the play, which stages a post-9/11 dinner party in New York for a wildly heterogeneous group of seven, a furious row breaks out between two Arabian guests. When an intellectual named Khalid (a thinly disguised Edward Said) deplores terrorism, he is fiercely challenged by an Islamic fundamentalist named Mohammed. As a late arrival excitedly billed as a "terrorist" by Suzie, a ditzy hostess bent on spicing up her haute cuisine with a pinch of shock, Mohammed quickly acts up to his billing. When he tries to stab Khalid with a fork, he is tackled, slugged down, bound at the wrists, and gagged by three other guests, including a right-wing novelist and the ghost of a New York City fireman killed on 9/11 (Rebeck 61–62).

Who is more dangerous—host or guest? As provider of food and accommodation, the host is structurally more powerful.[89] "Who has but once dined his friends," writes Herman Melville, "has tasted what it is to be Caesar. It is a witchery of social czarship which there is no withstanding" (Melville 131). Like Homer's Aegisthus, Dante's Fra Alberigo, and Shakespeare's Macbeth, he or she can have his guests murdered. Like Vladimir Satsyuk in Ukraine, the host of the dinner at which Viktor Yushchenko unwittingly ingested dioxin on September 5, 2004, he can see his guests poisoned.[90] But the moment of near-violence in *Omnium Gatherum* reminds us that guests can be dangerous too. Just as important, it also reminds us that even the utensils we use every day of our lives—knives and forks—can uncannily serve to reactivate the violence repressed by table manners.[91]

This does not mean that we should all start eating with plastic utensils, as the airlines now require, at least in coach (do terrorists never fly first class?). Shortly after Mohammed is subdued, a guest named Julia takes the gag out of his mouth, which enables him to denounce the silencing of Arabs and the American-led slaughter of them in Afghanistan and Iraq and also to say—in response to a question from Khalid, his antagonist—that he is hungry. When Khalid finds a seat for him at the table and Julia unties his hands, he picks up a fork, which "*for a moment . . . looks like a weapon in his hands.*" But instead of attacking anyone he starts to eat with it and finds the food "very good" (67). For a few moments a group of fiercely disputatious but nonetheless nonviolent people is reconstituted under the sign of food served and eaten at a common table: a site of potential violence but also, now as of old, a sign of potential *koinonia*. "This will be a compassionate universe," says Khalid,

> or it will cease becoming altogether! Let America strive to become the, the size of a true hero, like our friend the firefighter! Let our assistance be brave and supernatural!
> TERENCE [another guest]: And how would you go about doing this?
> KHALID: By feeding everyone!

(69)

Of course this is not a practical answer. Even if we could feed everyone on earth, we could no more banish the threat of treachery between hosts and guests than we can stifle the aggression that feeds unending wars. But at the end of Suzie's dinner party, which evolves from haute-cuisine pretentiousness into a drunken shouting match, Khalid's impassioned outcry reminds us that everyone needs to eat, that eating together can be an alternative to (as well as opportunity for) attacking each other, and that Suzie, for all her ditzy pretentiousness, is doing her part to practice hospitality. If what she offers falls far short of the absolute kind, she has nonetheless dared to bring the other to her table.

EPILOGUE

Since this book has chiefly considered the worst that hosts and guests can do to each other in works of literature ranging from ancient times to our own, I wish to say something more about why literature tends to slight hospitality at its best. One reason, as I noted in the introduction, is that literature feeds on conflict. Eschewing harmony and contentment, it thrives on discontent, restlessness, jealousy, resentment, hatred, suspicion, desire, frustration—everything that ignites conflict and thereby motivates plot. Without, for instance, the suspicions maliciously roused by Don John, Shakespeare's *Much Ado About Nothing* would be not much more than a lavish house party punctuated by a set of practical jokes.

But a second reason for the recurrence of treacherous hospitality in Western literature springs from the kinship between hospitality and love. Like love, hospitality breeds physical intimacy, the sharing of bed and board under a single roof. In Camus's "The Guest," the colonial French teacher feels "une sorte de fraternité"—a sort of brotherhood—with the Arab prisoner who shares his bedroom for a night. Such a feeling may approach the unconditional receptivity of Derrida's absolute hospitality, his radical antidote to the xenophobia of our time. But as Daru hears the breathing of his nonce roommate in the night, he can never forget that his guest is not only an Arab and a murderer but also an intruder sharing a room where Daru has slept alone for a year. Brotherhood, therefore, is something he feels has been imposed upon him, and physical proximity to his guest merely sharpens his sense of unease. Likewise, when a hostess makes a lover of her guest, as Dido does with Aeneas, she heightens the vulnerability that all hospitality entails. In receiving a guest, as in taking a lover, one risks betrayal. Either way, one opens oneself to what Proust called the hostility lurking "at the heart of our friendly or purely social relations," to the subtle or open wounds that may be inflicted by anyone operating at close range—within the charmed circle of trust.

At the end of chapter 8, I concluded that Proust's great novel represents a society in which hospitality is always and everywhere threatened by a treachery that does its work without ever resorting to open violence. Likewise, in the fictions of Joyce, Woolf, and Camus as well as in *Omnium Gatherum*, treachery undermines hospitality without drawing a single drop of blood. Yet in slight collisions, such as what the homecoming Bloom endures from rearranged furniture, in stifled rage, in threats of murder ("tu paieras"), and in numberless other expressions of resentment, fear, mistrust, retaliation, and contempt, we have seen how much the other—whether ghost, Jew, Arab, adulterous intruder, estranged old friend, or misunderstood new one—complicates the rituals of hospitality by threatening the host. And we have also seen how guests such as Stephen Dedalus can construe even hospitable overtures as potentially suffocating.

Along with *Omnium Gatherum*, then, these modern fictions—novels nearly of our time and a short story written when I myself was a teenager—cast new and profoundly disturbing lights on the ancient encounter between host and guest. In most of the literature of hospitality stretching from Homer to Shakespeare, from Odysseus's slaughter of the suitors through Judas's betrayal of his host as *hostia* to Macbeth's killing of Duncan, treachery and retaliation—the dark double of benign reciprocity—take violent forms. The hosts and guests of romantic literature can likewise prove murderous, as when Coleridge's mariner kills the albatross, avian host of the Antarctic, and when Stendhal's Julien shoots his lovingly hospitable mistress and mother surrogate. For the most part, however, the hosts and guests of nineteenth-century fiction betray each other with much less violence but often with equal or greater malice and pain. To study what happens to the rituals of hospitality in the history of literature is to see that even as treachery becomes less violent, the fabric of trust woven between host and guest becomes, if anything, more delicate, more vulnerable, more liable to be rent by the slightest of psychic wounds. Who can measure the desolation Daru must feel when he learns how his hospitality to the Arab may be repaid? How can he grasp his relation to a man who is at once a stranger, his guest, and his host? The absolute hospitality that Derrida posits is a noble ideal, but as we have seen so often in this book, every literary encounter between a host and a guest is bound by conditions and charged with risk. When the hosts and guests of Albee's *Virginia Woolf* play Get the Guest, Hump the Hostess, and Humiliate the Host, they play just three of the games that menace host and guest alike in modern literature.

Which is not to say that nothing good ever comes of hospitality in Western literature. In the *Odyssey* the generosity with which Eumaeus receives the homecoming Odysseus, whom he takes to be a wandering stranger, is moving enough to bring tears to the eyes of a reader—or at least to the eyes of this one. In the world of Proust, the Queen of Naples treats with perfect grace a hostess whom far too many other guests ignore. In Tolstoy's *Anna Karenina* Prince Oblonsky gives a dinner party in order to set the table for a marriage proposal that is happily accepted. But again and again the literature we have examined shows how even the best of hospitable intentions may go awry. In James's *Portrait* the extraordinarily hospitable Touchetts seek only to enhance and enrich the life of a heroine whom they unwittingly lead into a marriage of suffocation. In *Mrs Dalloway* Clarissa may strive to nurture a secular communion at her party, but in the end she breaks free of its "corruption, lies, [and] chatter" only by communing with the ghost of a man whose suicide has brought death itself into her party as an uninvited, wholly unexpected guest. And in Proust's novel, the Queen of Naples's graciousness to her hostess dies as soon as she learns that Madame Verdurin has savaged the Baron de Charlus.

I began this book by suggesting that hospitality reverses the *unheimlich*, the uncanny: while the uncanny exposes the threatening strangeness of what has been hidden by custom, familiarization, and domestication, hospitality yearns to domesticate the stranger, to take him in as if he were part of the family, to vanquish and absorb his otherness. But as Camus's story suggests, the otherness of the stranger can never be wholly assimilated, and the secular communion wrought by hospitality—the warm, joyful, convivial sharing of board and household—is never wholly safe against subversion. Like the Last Supper itself, the founding instance of liturgical Communion, it is always vulnerable to one or more of the infinitely variable forms that treachery can take.

Does literature ultimately teach us, then, that the rewards of hospitality are not worth the risk? By no means. For all its risks, we can no more dispense with hospitality than we can live without love, which is just as vulnerable to subversion and betrayal. Even now, a dozen years after Half and Susanne Zantop opened their door to the two young men who killed them, I salute the generosity of their gesture. If welcoming a stranger means exposing oneself to mortal danger, it also means opening one's heart and home to the possibility of new light, as Abraham discovered when his unexpected visitors turned out to be angels and then God himself. In the New Testament likewise, Christ declares that every time we invite a stranger into our homes, we welcome Christ himself (Matt. 25:35–36). But from secular literature we learn how to relinquish guests as well as how to receive them. Though Alcinous and Arete would love to see the wandering Odysseus marry their daughter and settle down with them, they speed him back to his native land. Likewise, though Leopold Bloom would love to see Stephen marry his daughter Milly and settle down at 7 Eccles Street, he leads him out of "the house of bondage" with the aid of a lighted candle. Besides reenacting what Moses did for the Israelites and evoking the "modus peregrinus" psalm sung by the newly redeemed souls of Dante's *Purgatorio*, Bloom's candlelit farewell to Stephen at the gateway of his garden recalls to me the moment indelibly stamped on the memory of the narrator of À *la recherche du temps perdu*: the moment when, during his childhood, the sound of a bell signaled that his parents' dinner guest was leaving by the garden gate of their country house. While the bell once signified for the narrator the disruptiveness of an intruder who came between him and his mother, turning her into a hostess, it ultimately comes to signify, for us as well as for him, the kindest and most considerate of all guests in the novel. Let us end, then, with the light of a candle and the sound of a bell.

NOTES

INTRODUCTION

1. For the complete story, see Zuckoff and Lehr.
2. Derrida, "H," 361. Over thirty years ago J. Hillis Miller proposed that the critic could be considered a host: not the literal accommodator of guests but the metaphorical accommodator of texts that may thereby become parasites within the body of a critical essay ("The Critic as Host"). More recently, Miller has considered Joyce's treatment of hospitality in the literal sense ("Irish Hospitality").
3. For a thoroughgoing account of Derrida's writings on hospitality, especially in relation to contemporary problems of immigration, see Still.
4. Alternatively, *host* and *guest* may both derive from the Indo-European *ghostis*, "stranger." In Old French *hoste* could mean either "host" or "guest," as the modern word *hôte* does now (Visser 91). But this line of etymology fails to explain the origin of *hospitality*.
5. All together, ancient Greek has fifteen words rooted in *xen-*. They include *xenodiaktes* (murderer of a guest) and *xenodaites* (devourer of guests or strangers).
6. *OH* 25. By contrast, Emile Benveniste treats all hospitality in terms of a pact that imposes "precise obligations" (Benveniste 94), and Margaret Visser writes, "Reciprocation is an essential part of the social system. Accepting a dinner invitation usually means promising to ask your hosts to a meal sometime later; eating together with members of a group proves loyalty to that group, and signifies a willingness to serve its interests in the future. Every society pressures guests to become hosts in their turn. Resistance may result in unpopularity, ostracism, even withdrawal of aid when times become hard" (Visser 84).
7. "The sweetest Christian duty," writes Louis Massignon, is "welcoming the other, the stranger, the neighbor who is closer than all our close ones, without reserve or calculation, whatever it costs and at any price" (letter of September 8, 1948, qtd. Derrida, "Hostipitality" 371).
8. "As a Jew," Saul Bellow once observed, ". . . I have long been aware . . . of the unparalleled hospitality of [America] to all the branches of humanity" ("A Jewish Writer in America").

337

9. Levinas, *Totality and Infinity* 156. According to Colin Davis, Levinas's "thought revolves around a primordial encounter between the self and other in which the self recognizes the absolute otherness of the other and, rather than responding to it with violence, conceives an infinite responsibility toward it" (Davis, "Cost" 242). In making his case for a radically new kind of hospitality, Derrida also recalls Hannah Arendt's analysis of the plight of stateless Europeans in the years before the Second World War. In *The Origins of Totalitarianism*, Derrida observes, "Arendt shows that one was witnessing the massive displacement not of exiles but of populations with no status and no state guarantees, which constituted a kind of call for pure hospitality" (*Manifeste pour l'hospitalité* [Grigny: Editions Paroles d'Aube, 1999] 100, qtd. Carroll 814n).

10. The same law prevails among the Arabs of Iraq. On April 11, 2003, shortly after the American invasion began, Saddam Hussein and his two sons found shelter with a wealthy businessman named Mudher al-Kharbit in his palatial compound west of Baghdad. Though Hussein had repeatedly tried to kill al-Kharbit, who had been working with the CIA to overthrow him, Arab tradition required al-Kharbit to receive his enemy and thus risk the lives of his family. On the night he received the dictator and his two sons, American bombs meant for Hussein missed him and killed instead al-Kharbit's brother Malik and twenty-one others, including children (Worth A6).

11. In December 2001 the Pentagon released a videotape of Osama bin Laden conversing with a Saudi sheik and several members of Al Qaeda at a dinner party that had been held the previous month in the city of Kandahar in southern Afghanistan. While the guests around him eat and drink, bin Laden explains, in a printed translation of his recorded remarks, how the destruction wrought by the attacks of 9/11 exceeded his expectations (www.september11news.com/OsamaEvidence.htm).

12. Many years ago I made this point to a class of about sixty students by asking them, first, "What happened to Elpenor?" and then "What happened to Agamemnon?" The first question stumped nearly every student in the room, but the second raised at once a forest of arms. So far as I can recall, every student knew the answer.

13. In a lecture given at Salamanca in 1539 (published 1557) a professor of theology named Francisco de Victoria used this passage as "one 'proof' of the universal principle that obliges everyone to welcome harmless visitors" (Waswo 745).

14. According to Derrida, justice differs from law because it cannot be codified, calculated, enforced, or universally applied ("Force" 233–45). To buttress the point that "law is always an authorized force" ("Force" 233), Derrida cites Kant, who argues that law "depends . . . on the possibility of an external coercion which can coexist with the freedom of everyone in accordance with universal laws" ("Introduction" 134). Elsewhere, however, as I have already noted, Derrida equates "the law of hospitality" with "absolute hospitality," and he distinguishes this singular *law* from the plural *laws* of reciprocity and mutual obligation that constitute conventional hospitality (*OH* 77). By the word *justice* in "Force of Law," I take it, he means something like what he calls "the law of hospitality" in *Of Hospitality*.

15. In "On a Supposed Right to Tell Lies from Benevolent Motives" (1797), Kant defends himself against Benjamin Constant's claim that "a duty to speak the truth, if taken unconditionally, and in isolation, would make all society impossible." Schwarz, who

quotes Constant, argues that "Kant's justification of his position against Constant is conclusive, if some key points of his argument are not overlooked" (Schwarz 62).

16. Kant's concept of hospitality, for instance, is highly conditional: one may not mistreat the stranger, he writes, "so long as he peacefully occupies his place" (*Perpetual Peace* 320). In Kant's world of peace, as Peter Melville aptly observes, "the other who approaches the border of the state presents itself in the eyes of the nation as a risk" (Melville, RH 90).

17. Qtd. Freud, "The 'Uncanny,'"375. Freud quotes Schelling from Daniel Sanders's *Wörterbuch der deutschen Sprach* (1860).

18. The Center for Immigration Studies estimates that in 2010–11 there were approximately eleven million illegal aliens in the United States (http://cis.org/node/3877#36).

19. A particularly gruesome case of such exploitation, however, entailed the false promise of a prolonged stay. "In 2006," reports the *New York Times*, "a company called Signal International hired 500 skilled metalworkers from India, under the H-2B temporary guest worker program, to repair oil rigs after Hurricane Katrina." Though the workers were promised green cards and though they paid as much as twenty thousand dollars to travel to Mississippi, they soon learned they would get no green cards, could not work for anyone else, and were trapped in their labor camps ("Editorial: A Bitter Guest Worker Story").

20. On the concept of the immigrant as guest, which I treat only occasionally in this book, see Still 191–92 and Rosello.

21. Not surprisingly, the title of Conrad Hilton's story of how he built his hotel empire is *Be My Guest* (1984).

22. Too late for consideration here, a study of the ethics of hospitality in late Victorian fiction has just appeared (Hollander).

23. In what follows I occasionally mention the games of treacherous hospitality played in Albee's *Virginia Woolf*: Get the Guest, Hump the Hostess, and Humiliate the Host. As for Keaton's film, the title proves deliciously ironic when a young woman invites Willie (Keaton's character) to dine at the house of her father and brothers. Though they detest him because they have long feuded with his family, the father decrees that by the rules of "our hospitality" he must not die in the house. To the sons this means they can kill him anywhere else.

CHAPTER 1. CLASSICAL HOSPITALITY

1. For this point and for the rest of this paragraph I am deeply indebted to an unpublished lecture by Edward Bradley. Also, I cite Fagles's translations of the *Iliad* and *Odyssey* as F followed by his line number(s), which are different from those of the original.

2. For more on this point, see the introduction and my discussion of Camus's "The Guest" in chapter 9.

3. Just before the first battle of the *Iliad*, for instance, Agamemnon invites "the best men" of the Greeks, including Odysseus, to feast on an ox (2.400–409). "It would appear," writes van Wees, "that the highest-ranking men in a community are engaged in a cycle of mutual invitations to feasts" (van Wees 171). But in the *Odyssey* the suitors disrupt

this pattern from the start by consuming the goods of Odysseus " 'without recompense' to their absent host," as Telemachus says (1.376–78; van Wees 171). My thanks to Edward Bradley for alerting me to the distinction made here.

4. Fagles deftly renders Homer's *xenos* as "your sworn friend / your sworn host" because it means "friend with whom one has a treaty of hospitality" (Berry 471). Depending on the context, *xenos* can mean either "guest" or "host," though ancient Greek had another word—*xeinodokos*—which meant only "host."

5. "While the lavish entertainment of visitors was a special tradition in Thessaly," Lattimore notes, "the hospitality of Admetus goes far beyond this and is no merely sociable virtue. Rather, this is the old Homeric *xenia*. It is one of the steps by which society progresses from savagery to civilization, when strangers make a willing, immediate, and permanent agreement to be friends" (Lattimore, Introduction to *Alcestis* 7).

6. When Heracles arrives he sees that Admetus is in mourning and knows that Alcestis has offered to die for him but is told only that the dead person is a female stranger. Though Heracles hesitates to enter a house of mourning in any case, Admetus insists on his doing so.

7. Christ likewise promises that those who are hospitable to guests who cannot repay them "will be repaid at the resurrection of the upright" (Luke 14:12–14). See also Mark 9:40 and Matthew 10:40–42.

8. A similar warning was made by an inscription on the pass issued to travelers bound for Beijing under the Yuan dynasty of the Mongol Empire in thirteenth-century China. Roughly translated, the inscription runs as follows: "By the strength of Eternal Heaven, / Edict of the Khan / He who does not respect / Shall be punished" (Watt 10–11).

9. Unlike Derrida's "law of hospitality," which he equates with absolute hospitality (see introduction), this law is enforced with rewards and punishments.

10. Later on, Odysseus himself realizes that it would have been better to leave at once, as his men had urged (9.228).

11. Something similar happens near the beginning of John Huston's film *Key Largo* (1948). When a hotel run by James Temple is suddenly taken over by a fugitive gangster named Johnny Rocco, Rocco tells Temple, his daughter, and their visitor that none of them can leave. "Do you mean we're your prisoners?" Temple angrily asks, to which Rocco replies, "Let's just say you're my guests."

12. When Polyphemos asks who he is, Odysseus twice calls himself "*Outis*," "nobody" (9.366–67). Later on, right after the monster is blinded and the other Cyclopes swarm up to ask why he has awakened them, he says, "No one [*me tis*] is trying to kill me" (9.408, trans. Dawe 380), prompting them to leave and Odysseus to relish the pun on *me tis* and *metis* (cunning): "Laughter filled my heart," he remembers, "to think how nobody's name—my great cunning stroke [*metis*]—had duped them one and all" (9.413–14 / F 461–63).

13. On December 26, 1501, something like what Agamemnon describes actually happened in Fermo, Italy, at the house of Liverotto da Fermo. Shortly after his uncle Giovanni Fogliani generously received him and a hundred attendants and then lodged him in his house, Liverotto invited his uncle and the leading men of Fermo to "a most

solemn banquet." When they had all eaten and enjoyed the entertainment, Liverotto led them to a "secret place" where they were no sooner seated than killed by soldiers who suddenly came out of hiding (Machiavelli 34). In Egypt some 300 years later, Muhammad Ali used the same stratagem to break the power of the Mamluks. Descendants of slaves brought to Egypt in the tenth century by Fatimid caliphs, the Mamluks had become a warrior caste that ruled Egypt for more than 250 years until the Ottoman Turks captured Cairo in 1517. Though the Mamluks no longer ruled the country, they remained strong enough in the early nineteenth century to thwart Ali's plans for building a European-style army. So in 1811 he invited about seventy-four of them to a banquet at the Cairo citadel and had them all massacred as they left (Cleveland 65–67).

14. He reaches Calypso's isle after lightning shatters his ship and his companions drown, leaving him to drift for nine days with his arms around the ship's keel (7.249–54). He reaches Scheria after a wave shatters the raft he made at Calypso's direction; riding one of its beams for two days and nights, he is thrown by a wave against the face of a cliff but with the help of Athene manages to swim to the mouth of a river (5.365–69, 388–89, 424–42).

15. Unless noted otherwise, translations from the *Aeneid* are mine.

16. She is driven by a threefold jealousy. As Knox notes, she resents the Trojans because they descend from Dardanus, son of Zeus and her rival Electra; because Zeus made the son of a Trojan prince, Ganymede, his specially favored cupbearer; and because Paris, the Trojan prince who abducted Helen, awarded the apple of contention to Aphrodite rather than to herself (Knox 16–17).

17. According to Williams, "dona ferentes" actually means " 'making offerings,' that is to say religious offerings to Minerva [the Roman Athena] as goddess of Troy" (Williams 1.220). The Greeks thus sought to make amends for the theft of the Palladium, a small sacred statue of a fully armed Athena that safeguarded Troy from its shrine on the heights of the city but was stolen by Diomedes and Ulysses, infuriating the goddess. The horse is not a gift to the Trojans (as Charles Beye privately informs me), but Laocoon implies that it is, and virtually all translators of this line, including Robert Fagles, construe "dona" as "gifts."

18. The word "veneno" (venom) also links the two passages. Venus tells Cupid to deceive Dido with venom: "fallasque veneno" (4.688), presumably the figurative poison of lust. In Aeneas's account of Laocoon's doomed effort to warn the Trojans against the wooden horse, the sea-borne serpents who seize and bind him and his sons also strike him literally with black venom, "atroque veneno" (2.221). Incidentally, if my "tricks" and "treats" sound too much like Halloween, note that Virgil too uses double alliteration in "dona" and "dolis."

19. Dido herself wanted the flaming pyre to be the last thing Aeneas saw of her: "hauriat hunc oculis ignem crudelis ab alto / Dardanus et nostrae secum ferat omina mortis" / "Let the cruel Dardan's eye consume this fire from the deep, and bear with him the omens of our death." (4.661–62).

20. After the horse appears, Sinon (a Greek agent) craftily tells the Trojans that he has run away to escape being sacrificed, that he hates the Greeks, and that they built the horse

to make amends for stealing the statue of Pallas Athene from its shrine (2.132–84). But as if the horse were a gift to the Trojans, he urges them to take it into their city (2.192–94), and he himself is accepted as a permanent guest. "Quisquis es," says Priam, ". . . noster eris" (2.148–49). "Whoever you are . . . you will be ours." According to Warde Fowler, the bond between hosts and guests in ancient Rome was "stronger . . . than any other but that of the relation of father and son" (*Aeneas at the Site of Rome*, 91, qtd. Austin, *Quartus* 4.323).

21. Joyce once said of Ulysses, "The tank is his creation. Wooden horse or iron box—it doesn't matter. They are both shells containing armed warriors" (qtd. Ellmann 436).

22. Literal and metaphorical fires light Aeneas's whole narrative. Awakened to the sight of houses burning and the Sigean straits reflecting the flames, he learns that Sinon has been insolently scattering fire even as armed men pour out of the horse (2.310–12, 328–29). Attacking the palace of Priam, the Greeks throw flames on the rooftop (2.478). Running down Priam's son Polites within the palace, Pyrrhus is "ardens infesto vulnere" (burning with the wound he will inflict). Then, just after fatally spearing Polites, he buries his sword in the side of Priam, who dies gazing at "Troiam incensam" (2.555), Troy ablaze.

23. As Austin notes (*Quartus*, 4.669), this comparison of Dido's suicide to the immolation of a city looks backward and forward at once: to the destruction of Troy, freshly depicted on the walls of her new temple, and to the eventual destruction of Carthage itself.

24. Only after he leaves Dido and returns to his ship does he feel the force of his love for her ("magno . . . labefactus amore," 4.395) as if for the first time.

25. Though I will not even try to say how much freedom Aeneas has, it is clearly circumscribed, if not preempted, by the gods. In the *Aeneid*, says Knox, the gods "preside over the world of the heroes. . . . As in Homer, the passions and actions of the gods affect the actions and passions of the heroes on earth" (Knox 16). The supernatural influence on Dido's passion for Aeneas is abetted by her sister Anna, who urges Dido to detain Aeneas. "Be lavish with your hospitality," she says, "and weave pretexts for loitering" (4.51).

26. By thus arranging a "marriage" of Aeneas and Dido, Juno aims to ally the Trojans with the Tyrians so as to keep the Trojans from founding a kingdom in Italy. But Venus knows that Jupiter will never allow this (4.90–128).

27. Austin calls *hospes* "a sad word here; Aeneas is now no more than what he was when first they met" (Austin, *Quartus* 4.323). According to Servius, Virgil read these lines to Augustus with great feeling "ingenti adfectu" (qtd. Austin, *Quartus* 4.323).

28. Long on rational argument, which Aristotle called the *logos* of rhetoric, Aeneas's speech fails to deliver either *pathos* or *ethos*, emotional appeal or a sense of personal values. "Its effect," writes Spence, "is of weakness, since it fails to engage the emotions of the audience and raises questions about the moral integrity of the speaker" (Spence 92).

29. These lines may well express the feelings Aeneas has up to now struggled to repress. But his language also shows that he has mastered them. The imperative "desine" is commanding, and even though he claims to be acting against his own desires, his final

word, "sequor," is decisive. By thus ending his speech in the middle of a line that has been left unfinished, he plainly indicates that his mind is inalterable. He has nothing more to say to Dido. If his speech sounds cold and formal, writes Williams, "this is not because he feels no emotions but because he has decided that he must control them" (Williams 362).

30. She herself tells Anna later: "The faith promised to the ashes of Sychaeus has not been kept" (non servata fides cineri promissa Sychaeo, 4.552).

31. Having lost hope in the survival of Troy, Priam had secretly sent him—along with a great load of gold that the Thracian king took from the dead boy. The king killed him when Troy fell.

32. In Sicily they are likewise terrified by the monstrosity of the Cyclops, whose merciless man-eating is described by a terrified eyewitness to it, and in the Ionian Strophades they are revolted by the Harpies, who foul every dish the Trojans try to eat and curse them with the prospect of a hunger so fierce it will drive them to eat their own tables (3.257). The eyewitness to the Cyclops's man-eating is a Greek suppliant named Achaemenides, who sailed with Ulysses to and from Troy but was left in the Cyclops's cave when the Greeks sailed off two months before Aeneas arrived. Now, ravenous from a starvation diet of roots and berries, he begs to be taken away by the Trojans or killed. His account of the Greeks' ordeal in the cave is a much-compressed version of Homer's story. We learn only that after the Cyclops ate two of the Greeks, the rest speared his one huge eye while he lay stupefied and vomiting (3.623–36).

33. As Williams notes, the poem ends not with the triumph of Aeneas—as it might so easily have done—but with "the pathos of Turnus' death" (*Aeneid* 2.503). Likewise, Beye treats Turnus as "a tragic epic hero . . . whose valiant defense of his land, wild impetuosity, and anger at defeat bear traces of the two exemplars of tragic epic behavior: Achilles and Hector" (Beye 242). On the ongoing debate between optimistic and pessimistic readings of Turnus's death, and on the opposition between rational *pietas* and the *furor* within Aeneas himself, see Hardie 99–100.

34. *Ab Urbe Condita* 1.57–58. It is difficult to know whether Livy is recording historical fact or transmitting legend. The story of Lucretia is also told in Ovid's *Fasti* and—as noted below in chapter 4—retold in Shakespeare's *Rape of Lucrece*.

35. The story of Lucretia is conspicuous by its absence from the list of figures and historical references that, according to Beye, Dido evokes in the "experienced reader." Besides Nausicaa, Calypso, and Circe (mentioned above), they include Cleopatra, Medea, Carthage as the enemy of Rome, and Ajax, who, like Dido, dies by his own hand and keeps a bitter silence in the underworld (Beye 233).

36. I quote the text of Petronius by chapter and line number(s). Unless otherwise indicated, all translations are mine.

37. Heseltine, "Introduction," Petronius, xvii.

38. In the first chapter of *Finnegans Wake* Annie likewise offers the "flowerwhite bodey" of her dead husband as a meal for the mourners, but the corpse vanishes before they can "sink teeth" through its "pyth" (FW 7).

39. According to James Jeffers, 1 million sesterces in ancient Rome equaled 250,000 denarii, which, he calculates, was worth about $12.5 million.

40. This might be seen as a variation on any kind of hospitality that detains a guest, as we have seen in both the *Odyssey* and the *Aeneid*. In mid-nineteenth-century America, Henry David Thoreau judged extravagant entertaining *in*hospitable. Confident that "abstinence . . . was never felt to be an offence against hospitality" when a crowd of visitors came to his little house on Walden Pond (he never fed them), he was repelled by ostentatious hosts. "For my own part," he wrote, "I was never so effectually deterred from frequenting a man's house, by any kind of Cerberus whatever, as by the parade one made about dining me, which I took to be a very polite and roundabout hint never to trouble him again" (95). See also his conclusion to *Walden*: "I sat at a table where were rich food and wine in abundance, and obsequious attendance, but sincerity and truth were not; and I went away hungry from the inhospitable board. The hospitality was as cold as the ices" (219). On ostentatious hospitality in the mid-twentieth century, see Ludwig Bemelmans's report on a visit to William Randolph Hearst's San Simeon around 1943 (Bemelmans).

41. Smith notes that by the middle of the second century BCE there was a dish known as the "porcus Troianus" because it was stuffed with various creatures (Smith 134).

42. Smith writes that "animam ebulliit" is "a colloquial expression" meaning "has breathed his last" (Smith 99). But given the immediately following reference to bubbles, "ebulliit" is surely more than a dead metaphor. It evokes a boiling pot, an apt allusion to the kitchen.

43. In part 6 of the film *Monty Python's The Meaning of Life* (1983), a gigantically fat man waddles into a restaurant and eats an enormous meal. Persuaded to follow this by eating one last "wafer-thin" mint, he literally explodes, scattering his entrails all around him.

44. P. Fedeli, "Petronio: il viaggio, il labirinto," *MD* 6 (1981), qtd. Connors 38–39.

45. For a modern (and grotesque) remixing of food, death, and anthropophagy, see the ending of Peter Greenaway's film *The Cook, the Thief, His Wife & Her Lover* (1989), in which Georgina, the well-bred wife of a restaurant-owning gangster (the thief), persuades the chef to cook the body of her lover, a bookshop owner whom the gangster's thugs have tortured to death by force feeding him pages from his own books. Confronting her husband at the restaurant with the cooked and naked body of her lover, Georgina makes him eat and gag upon the penis—"a delicacy," she calls it— before shooting him in the head.

CHAPTER 2. BIBLICAL HOSPITALITY

1. Unless otherwise indicated, I quote the Old Testament from *The Complete Bible: An American Translation*. See Bible in the bibliography below.

2. Derrida, "Hostipitality" 369, drawing on Louis Massignon, "The Three Prayers of Abraham." "With good reason," writes Robert Alter, "the Jewish exegetical tradition makes Abraham figure as the exemplary dispenser of hospitality. Extending hospitality . . . is the primary act of civilized intercourse" (Alter 86n).

3. As Alter notes, "The narrator at once apprises us of the divine character of Abraham's guests, but when Abraham peers out through the shimmering heat waves of the desert noon (verse 2), what he sees from his human perspective is three 'men'" (Alter 85n).

Nevertheless, Abraham's response to them exemplifies what Derrida calls "absolute hospitality" only if we presume he knows nothing at all about them, a point that several ancient commentators do not accept.

4. McNulty xlv, 40. In the later books of the Old Testament, prophets such as Ezekiel strive "to neutralize" the "'lawless' quality of absolute hospitality" by stressing "the need to exclude categorically all reception of strangers"—not just gods but all strangers, human and divine (McNulty 35). Ezekiel condemns the welcoming of Egyptians, Philistines, Assyrians, and Chaldeans as whoredom and adultery (Ezekiel 16:26–32).

5. "And *they* said unto him [Abraham], Where is Sarah thy wife? And he said, Behold, in the tent. And *he* said, I will certainly return unto thee according to the time of life" (Gen. 18:9–10, emphasis added).

6. See Ambrose, "On His Brother, Satyrus," qtd. ACC 61. As McNulty notes, Christian iconography turns the three guests into an "Old Testament Trinity," exemplified by Andrei Roublev's fifteenth-century depiction of Abraham's hospitality (McNulty 14). But regardless of what that hospitality is later seen to prefigure, the doctrine of the Trinity does not surface until the New Testament, long after Abraham's time.

7. Homilies on Genesis 4.3 (ACC 62); Caesarius of Arles repeats the point in his Sermon 83.5 (ACC 62).

8. *City of God* 16.29 (ACC 62).

9. Clifford Ackley writes that the gesturing hand of the central figure "authoritatively" signifies God's announcement that Sarah will miraculously give birth to a son (Ackley 214). But since God makes that announcement only after Abraham has performed all the duties of a host, the gesture could just as easily be God's way of thanking Abraham for washing his feet: another distinctively human transaction.

10. Judith Still aptly notes that Old Testament hospitality, as exemplified by Abraham, "has a great deal in common" with the hospitality practiced by the most virtuous of Homer's hosts, who receive the stranger "without demanding his name" (Still 68). But in both cases the stranger may turn out to be divine.

11. In Luke 9:3–5 he says much the same, but without threatening to damn the inhospitable.

12. This point is also noted by Origen. For all of his comments cited here, see Homilies on Genesis 4.2 in ACC 64–65.

13. According to Still, critics such as René Schérer and Jonathan Dollimore have "celebrat[ed] the hospitality of the Sodomites as a particular way of embracing the foreigner" (Still 72). I think those critics are nuts.

14. Gen. 19:3; Caesarius, Sermon 83.3 (ACC 66). Dunn and Rogerson note that Sarah makes her cakes "with flour usually reserved for sacrifice" (*ECB* 53). On the other hand, we are told that Lot "prepared a feast" for his visitors (Gen. 19:3). Can a feast be made with unleavened cakes alone?

15. Cleveland Bible Commentary on Genesis 19, www.christiancommunitychurch.us/clevelandcommentary/Gen19.html.

16. Though Alter finds the latter explanation too pat (Alter 92n), I believe it furnishes at least part of an answer to the questions raised by Lot's proposal. Robert Polhemus states that Lot "opts to sacrifice his own female flesh and blood, and he chooses, for God's

sake, the safety of his visitors and his sacred duty of hospitality over the life of his girls" (Polhemus 2). Like the hospitality of the Levite (examined below), Lot's hospitality raises for Still "the question how far you should go for a guest" (Still 76), but she does not answer the question.

17. The second episode and its cultural heritage have been thoroughly explored by Robert Polhemus, who is chiefly occupied with this "narrative of incest" (5) rather than with Lot's hospitality.

18. By contemporary standards of fairness, for instance, it is impossible to justify paying all workers the same regardless of how many hours they have each worked. Yet this is precisely what Christ approves in the parable of the laborers (Matt. 20:1–15).

19. McNulty argues that all three of Lot's women—wife as well as daughters—serve purely instrumental roles in his preservation, thus ensuring that this relative of Abraham can take his place "in the genealogy of the book of the patriarchs." Rather than being a distinct character, she contends, Lot's wife signifies the part of him "that cannot separate itself from the iniquity of Sodom but must be 'seized by the hand' [Gen. 19:16] and forcefully compelled to go" (McNulty 16). Likewise, McNulty construes Lot's offer of his virgin daughters "as a sacrifice of 'himself'" because they are his property. "The father's ability to 'dispose' of his female dependents is due not only to historical factors, but to the structural requirements of the hospitality act in Genesis. Like his wife, Lot's daughters are not merely property, but instrumental 'things' mediating the host's relation to the divine" (McNulty 20). Insofar as "the essential discontinuity and lack of reciprocity interrupting the relation between host and [divine] guest" requires of the host "a fundamental loss or renunciation," as McNulty contends (22), Lot's offer may be construed as "structurally" necessary. But in my view, this does not absolve him of responsibility for having made it.

20. In *Nouveau traité de la civilité qui se practique en France parmi les honnêtes gens*, published in 1671 and frequently republished thereafter, Antoine de Courtin argues that Lot's offer exemplifies the principle of virtually limitless sacrifice: a host, he says, must be ready to sacrifice for his guest his own life and whatever is even dearer than that ("sacrificier sa vie et ce que l'on a de plus cher pour lui"). See Marie-Claire Grassi, "'Sous l'ombre de mon toit': l'hospitalité dans le manuel de civilité d'Antoine de Courtin," in Montandon 14.

21. Even in Genesis, the sons of Jacob betray the Gentile Shechemites after accepting what might be called their hospitality. When the sons' sister Dinah is raped by Shechem, the son of prince Hamor, Hamor tries to make amends by telling them that if they will let their sister marry Shechem, they can "make [their] home" in the city of the Shechemites and intermarry with them (Gen. 34:9–10). Though Dinah's brothers agree on condition that all the Shechemite males be circumcised, the brothers strike as soon as the men have been made "sore" by this operation. Avenging themselves on the whole city for Shechem's violation of their sister, the sons not only kill Shechem and Hamor and every other man in the city but also take all its wealth and capture its women and children (Gen. 34:25–29).

22. In chapters 11–13 of the deuterocanonical book of Judith, a beautiful Hebrew widow from the city of Bethulia commits an act of comparable treachery while a guest of

Holofernes, the general who served the Assyrian king Nebuchadnezzar. Having gained admission to Holofernes' tent by dressing seductively and posing as a traitor to her own nation, she sits with him at a feast, eats and drinks (though only from her own provisions), and waits until all his servants have left and he falls into a drunken sleep. She then beheads him with his own sword, bags the head, and carries it off to her own people, whose ruler, Ozias, praises her as lavishly as Deborah praises Jael. "Blessed art thou of the most high God above all the women upon the earth," he says (Judith 13:18).

23. I am alluding here to Wayne Booth's well-known distinction between the narrator and the implied author, where the latter is the sum of inferences that can be drawn about the meaning of a work of literature—regardless of what we may know about the actual author or what is overtly said by any narrator identified as such within the work itself (Booth 74–75). Exum's account of how the would-be misogynistic "narrator" judges the woman makes no allowance for the judgment of the implied author.

24. Mieke Bal likewise notes that the old man objectifies the women (Bal 122).

25. This point has hardly escaped the notice of earlier commentators. As long ago as the fifteenth century, Denis the Carthusian found the Levite and his host both culpable: if it's wrong to commit a venial sin to keep someone else from committing a mortal sin, he argued, how much worse it is to "expose someone else to adultery or rape" (qtd. Gunn 246).

26. Bolchazy II (from his introduction, paginated in Roman caps). As will soon become obvious, my discussion of Roman hospitality is greatly indebted to Bolchazy's highly informative book on the subject.

27. According to Cicero, "he who would properly have been called 'a fighting enemy' (*perduellis*) was called 'a guest or stranger' (*hostis*) . . . for *hostis* [now meaning "enemy"] meant to our ancestor what we now call 'stranger' (*peregrinus*)." *De Officiis* 1.12.37, qtd. and trans. Bolchazy 19). I have already noted the various meanings of *xenos* in ancient Greek.

28. "Killing of strangers," writes Bolchazy, "has . . . been observed in many primitive societies where strangers are automatically regarded as enemies, or viewed as spirits hostile to the native deities, or considered magically dangerous" (Bolchazy 1). He also notes that Homer's *xenos*-devouring Polyphemos has real-life counterparts described by later writers: "Herodotus and Euripides report that the Tauri used strangers for human sacrifice. Strabo says the Scythians devoured the flesh of strangers and used their skulls as drinking cups" (Bolchazy 2).

29. Since *ghostis* denoted "stranger," the words *ghost* and *hostis* share a common ancestor, and in literature ghosts may become guests (see chapter 9 below).

30. Horace likewise faults Paris for violating the laws of hospitality, calling him a "famosus hospes" (an infamous guest) (*Odes* 3.3.26).

31. Bolchazy notes that even though this point is generally accepted ("satis constat"), no other known explanation for Aeneas's survival matches Livy's (Bolchazy 43).

32. Livy uses some form of the word *hospitium* 129 times in his extant corpus (Bolchazy 61).

33. These virtues—piety, valor, clemency, and justice—were inscribed on the *clupeus* (shield) of Augustus, and in the opening paragraph of *Res Gestae*, the chronicle of his reign, the acts in which he displayed these virtues are called "acts of the Deified

Augustus by which he placed the whole world under the sovereignty of the Roman people" (Bolchazy 77).

34. Regarding *hospitium publicum*, Rome granted covenants of hospitality to the Liparaean pirates (Livy 5.28), to the town of Caere after the Gauls sacked Rome in 390 BCE (Livy 5.50.3), and to the town of Tarentum (Borchazy 109n21).

35. Some may have been motivated less by self-aggrandizement than by a sense of civic obligation. "What began as a desire on the part of the rich to make ostentatious display of their wealth increasingly came to be seen as a duty imposed upon wealthy citizens by their cities" (Veyne 107). But whatever the motive, wealthy patrons distinguished themselves from their beneficiaries, and at the lavish private banquet of Petronius's *Satyricon*, as we have seen, the host makes it repeatedly clear that he alone is running the show.

36. In Leviticus God tells Moses that he and his fellow Jews "must treat the proselyte who resides with you like the native born among you . . . for you were once aliens yourselves in the land of Egypt" (Lev. 19:34). But a proselyte is hardly a complete stranger; he or she is an apprentice to Judaism, in training to becoming a full member of the Jewish community.

37. In the New Testament this remains a touchstone of true hospitality. In response to the Roman captain who says he is unworthy to receive him, Christ says that "many will come . . . and take their places at the feast with Abraham, Isaac, and Jacob, in the Kingdom of Heaven" (Matt. 8:11), and when the beggar named Lazarus dies at the gate of the inhospitable rich man, he is "carried away by the angels to the companionship of Abraham" (Luke 16:22).

38. As I have noted, Derrida defines "absolute hospitality" in similar terms. Unlike "conditional hospitality," it "requires that I open up my home . . . to the absolute, unknown, anonymous other, that I *give place* to them . . . without asking of them either reciprocity (entering into a pact) or even their names" (*OH* 25).

39. But easier than some of Christ's other lessons in hospitality—insofar as it refers strictly to one's place at the dinner table. Even in our own time, however, grand dinner parties can generate a high degree of anxiety about who sits where. In the summer of 2005, just after the beginning of a dinner for 350 hosted by the Italian fashion designer Valentino at his chateau outside Paris, his partner, Giancarlo Giametti, discovered that the name of an important guest had been left off the master list and not assigned a seat. Furious at the oversight, Giametti himself removed one of the head table guests and found a seat for him elsewhere in order to make a suitable place for the hitherto forgotten VIP (Specter 134).

40. "But alas for you, you hypocritical scribes and Pharisees, for you lock the doors of the Kingdom of Heaven in men's faces, for you will neither go in yourselves nor let those enter who are trying to do so" (Matt. 23:14).

41. "The images of God's kingdom that predominate overwhelmingly in Jesus' teaching," writes John Koenig, "are those associated with the production of food and drink or homelike refuge for God's creatures" (Koenig 27).

42. He makes this point by means of a parable about the moneylender who cancels debts owed by two men. Since one owed him ten times more than the other, the man with the larger debt will feel "more attached" to the moneylender (Luke 7:41–44).

Conversely, the prostitute shows greater love for Christ than the Pharisee does because she has more sins to be forgiven (Luke 7:47). In each case, love varies according to the quantity of sins/debt that has been forgiven or that needs to be forgiven.

43. In Frost's poem "Death of the Hired Man" (ll. 118–19) a farmer speaks the quoted words to his wife, describing a man whom they formerly employed and who has come back to die because he has nowhere else to go. In response to the farmer's words, the wife redefines *home* in terms even more apposite to the prodigal's return. "I should have called it," she says, "something you somehow haven't to deserve" (ll. 119–20).

44. And Zaccheus, like the prostitute, wins the praise of Christ for his generosity when he promises to give half his property to the poor (Luke 19:9).

45. The Greek text says that each jar held two or three *metretas*. Since a *metreta* equaled about nine English gallons, each jar could hold at least eighteen gallons. So once filled, at Christ's request, with water that turned into wine, the six jars held over a hundred gallons of it.

46. Here we might be reminded of the overwhelming abundance with which Trimalchio fed his guests. But there is a big difference between stuffing a few people to the point of abdominal explosion and feeding five thousand with leftovers enough (perhaps) for fifty more.

47. Koenig notes that "unlike Mark and Matthew, Luke allows Jesus no regular headquarters in Peter's house in Capernaum. Moreover, from 9:51 to 19:28, in the so-called 'travel narrative' unique to the Third Gospel, he portrays him as one constantly on the road, sometimes finding hospitality with others . . . sometimes experiencing rejection" (Koenig 86–87).

48. In Mark and Luke likewise, Christ identifies Judas as "one of the Twelve, who is dipping his bread in the same dish with me" (Mark 14:20–21) and one whose hand "is beside me on the table" (Luke 22:21–22). For John's version, see below.

49. This is precisely the moment depicted in the most famous of all paintings of the Last Supper, where Judas, sitting slightly to the left of Christ, is shown with his hand hovering over a piece of bread. In the words of Leo Steinberg, Leonardo's *Ultima Cena* "conflates the ritual and the episodic; conflates as well the two natures of Christ, whose earthly peril aggrieves the disciples, while his divinity manifests itself in his shape, in his gift, in their faith, in the responsiveness of their perspective, in the beholder's perception" (Steinberg, *Last Supper* 53).

50. Mark's version (14:24–25) omits the final phrase. In Luke's version, which puts the wine sharing before the bread breaking, Christ says nothing about his blood (22:17); and in John's version of the Last Supper, which is far longer than any other (chapters 13–17), Christ neither breaks bread nor shares wine—though he does tell the apostles, "I am the vine, you are the branches" (16:5).

51. Koenig sees the abundance of this heavenly kingdom prefigured in the emphatically vinous language of Genesis 49:10–12, where a messianic king launches his reign by washing "his garments in wine and his vesture in the blood of grapes," and "his eyes," we are told, "shall be red with wine" (Koenig 40).

52. As a young man named Saul who worked for the high priests of Jerusalem, he approved the stoning of Saint Stephen, the first Christian martyr, and ruthlessly harassed "the

Lord's disciples" until he was struck blind en route to Damascus and then regained his sight by the hands of Ananias — at which point he was "filled with the Holy Spirit" and became a staunch defender of Christ (Acts 9:1–20).

53. In Acts, however, God says of Paul to Ananias, "This man is the means I have chosen for carrying my name among the heathen and their kings, *and* among the descendants of Israel" (Gal. 9:15, emphasis added). If Paul is chosen to preach to Jews as well as heathens, the division of labor between him and Peter is not so clear. See also Acts 15:7, where Peter tells the apostles and elders in Jerusalem that God chose him to preach to "the heathen" (Acts 15:7).

54. "It can be assumed," writes Theissen, "that the conflict over the Lord's Supper is a conflict between rich and poor Christians" (Theissen 145–74, qtd. Koenig 66–67).

55. I quote the *Didache* by chapter and line number from Milavec's edition of it (see Bibliography).

56. This seems to be an early version of the apothegm retailed by Ben Franklin and Charles Lamb: fish and visitors stink after three days.

57. During the United States presidential campaign of 2004, for example, the Roman Catholic bishops of the state of Colorado threatened to excommunicate any Catholic who voted for John Kerry. Though Kerry himself is a practicing Catholic and was the first to be nominated for president by a major political party in forty-four years, the bishops opposed his candidacy simply because he did not — and does not — believe that abortion should be recriminalized.

58. In naming the zone of Judas "Judecca," Dante alludes to the name of the quarter (Judeca, Judaica) within certain cities (such as Venice) where Jews were required to live apart from the Christian population.

59. Dante's first host in Verona was Cangrande's older brother Bartolommeo, the "gran Lombardo" who ruled the city from 1301 until his death in 1304 and whose "cortesia" to the poet is handsomely acknowledged in the *Paradiso* (17.70–78).

60. According to Hollander, all commentators agree that this passage "refers to the bitter taste of bread (or anything else) eaten in bitter conditions" (*Paradiso* Notes 423). But it may also allude to the fact that in Florence bread is traditionally baked without salt, possibly because the Florentines learned to like it that way after 1100, when the Pisans blocked a shipment of salt destined for Florence. Alternatively, one commentator suggests that the salty taste may come from the exile's tears, and another, Henry Wadsworth Longfellow no less, finds an echo in Shakespeare's *Richard II*, where Bolingbroke says he has eaten "the bitter bread of banishment" (3.1.21). I cite both comments from Hollander's *Paradiso* Notes 424.

61. Dante's Ptolomea may also recall the Egyptian Ptolemy XII, brother of Cleopatra, who had Pompey murdered when the Roman general sought refuge in Egypt after his defeat at Pharsalia. But it is not at all clear that Ptolemy ever treated Pompey as a guest or led him to think he would be treated that way.

CHAPTER 3. BEOWULF AND GAWAIN

1. Just before expelling Adam and Eve from the Garden of Eden, God cryptically predicts that by sacrificing himself on the cross, Eve's "seed" — Christ, her descendant —

will eventually crush beneath his heel the diabolical serpent who led the pair into sin. To the serpent he says, "I will put enmity between you and the woman, And between your seed and her seed; He shall bruise you on the head, And you shall bruise him on the heel" (Gen. 3:15). Though sometimes called pre-Christian, *Beowulf* was written some eight hundred years after Christianity came to Britain and four hundred years after Gregory the Great sent Augustine to convert the Saxon kings of southern England, where he established a celebrated monastery in Canterbury. In the poem itself Grendel is called a descendant of Cain, which evokes the Old Testament, and other elements of the poem, such as Beowulf's fight with the dragon at the end, evoke the new one. Scholars also note that the final epithet for Beowulf at the very end of the poem is *lofgeornost*, "eager for fame," where *lof* can mean either "fame" or "heavenly glory." On the other hand, as Mitchell notes, *Beowulf* offers nothing that is "obviously and unambiguously Christian" (Mitchell 14). So it might be called crypto-Christian.

2. I quote the Anglo-Saxon by line number from Seamus Heaney, *Beowulf*. Translations quoted from this edition are marked H. Unmarked translations are my own.

3. On the Homeric precedents for Hrothgar's reception of a murderer, see the opening of chapter 1.

4. I am adapting Rosier's definition of this term (Rosier 8).

5. We later learn that no sword could ever wound Grendel because he has "conjured the harm from the cutting edge / of every weapon" (801–4). But none of Beowulf's men knew about this spell (800), and there is no reason to believe he knew about it either. Note also that in the song sung by Fitela when the Danes and Geats return from tracking the wounded Grendel to his lake, the Danish hero Sigemund uses a sword to kill a dragon (884–91).

6. According to Rosier, *folmu* usually means a hand of violence, a sinful hand, or a wounded hand (Rosier 12).

7. Literally, "he knew his fingers' power in the grip of the grim one." Heaney's translation—"The latching power / in his fingers weakened" (H 763–64)—is inaccurate here.

8. Words for hand likewise predominate in Beowulf's account of this fight to Hygelac, king of the Geats, when he returns to his native land. Describing the fight as "hondraes haeletha" (2072) (hand-fray of heroes), he says that Grendel would never have left Heorot "idelhande" (2081) (empty-handed). Having seized and devoured a man now identified as Hondscio, a name meaning "glove," he clutched me, says Beowulf, with "gearofolm" (2085) (ready hand), and beside him hung a huge glove ("glof," 2085) that he planned to fill with Beowulf and many of his men. For more on Hondscio, see Rosier 11.

9. Even outside *Beowulf*, the closest thing to a handshake in Anglo-Saxon poetry is the thegn's touching of his lord's knee in *The Wanderer*: "It seems to him in his mind that he is embracing and kissing his lord and laying his hands [honda] and head on his knee, as he sometimes formerly in the days of yore enjoyed the gift-throne" (trans. Robert E. Diamond; my thanks to Peter Travis for this example). The poet of *Beowulf* refers just once, in passing, to the role of hands in gift giving (see my comments on 1341–44 below).

10. The phrase, I take it, means something like what is now denoted by the word *hands* as applied to workers of various kinds, such as cowboys or sailors.

11. Heaney renders "gist" as simply "he." Strangely enough, he nowhere translates "gist" or "gyst" as "guest."

12. Rosier 13. Evidently the word "brim" could apply to lake water as well as seawater. Grendel's mother is also called a "grund-wyrgenne" (1518), which means "wolf of the deep."

13. Though the online *Anglo-Saxon Dictionary* (Oxford: Clarendon, 1898) glosses *nið-sele* as "a hall where one is exposed to the hatred of a foe," it has also been construed as "a hall low down, beneath the water." Given the context, the second meaning seems to me far more plausible than the first. The whole point of the passage is that this is a "neath"-cell: a cozy firelit dwelling underneath the water.

14. The Grinch who stole Christmas because he hated the merrymaking of the Whos is a sentimentalized version of Grendel, whose name strongly alliterates with his own.

15. In the words of Peter Travis, "The poem's vision may be so bleak that finally hospitality and homicide are two sides of the same Moebius strip, and not opposites: one evokes and replicates the other" (e-mail to author of June 5, 2007).

16. "It would be possible to argue," writes Hillis Miller, "that *Beowulf* is more Christian than *Gawain* on the grounds that the final fight with the dragon is Christ's gratuitous and unrepayable self-sacrifice for the sake of us sinners, in this case the idiot who stole the treasure" (e-mail to the author of October 17, 2008).

17. Though the shock does not kill her, Arthur feels bound to comfort her afterward: "Dear lady, today never dismay" (Dere dame, today demay you neuer, 470).

18. Unless otherwise indicated, all translations of passages quoted from *Sir Gawain* are my own, and my aim is simply to reproduce the meaning of the original as accurately as possible—with no pretense to elegance.

19. For all definitions of words in *Gawain* my source is the online Middle English Dictionary (MED) compiled by the University of Michigan (http://quod.lib.umich.edu/m/med/lookup.html).

20. In Albee's play, George goads his wife and their drunken young male guest into an offstage clutch that leaves the guest humiliated because of his temporary impotence.

21. In thus failing to meet the exacting requirements of Christian heroism, however, Adam arguably becomes a tragic or romantic hero, risking all for the sake of his devotion to Eve and his determination that from her state of being "mine never shall be parted, bliss or woe" (9.916).

22. When she asks him for a kiss on the first morning, he says likewise, "I shall kiss at your command, as becomes a knight" (I schal kysse at your comaundement, as a knyȝt fallez, 1303).

23. Bertilak's formulation also finesses the doctrine of original sin, which denies perfect innocence even to newborns.

24. Having rejected the guide's proposal, Gawain says nothing about it to Bertilak, who doubtless told the guide to tempt him into a further act of cowardice.

25. When Cuchulainn puts his head on the block, the giant lowers on his neck the blunt side of the axe, then tells him to arise as the best of all warriors of Ultonia and Erin, the

matchless embodiment of "valour, bravery, and truthfulness" (par. 102, Henderson 44). Like the Green Knight, the giant of this tale comes in disguise to test the mettle of warriors.

26. After Gawain beheads the Green Knight and leaves Camelot to meet him, however, some members of the court regret that such a promising man should lose his head to an elvish man for the sake of insolent pride ("an aluisch mon, for angardez pryde"). "Who ever knew," they ask, "any king to take such counsel / As knights in cavilling over Christmas games?" (Who knew euer any kyng such counsel to take / As knyȝtez in cauelaciounz on Crystmasse gomnez! 682–83). Why, they seem to be sensibly asking, should the king allow anyone to quibble over games with a man's head?

27. As already noted, Lady Bertilak links courtesy ("cortaysye") with the art of kissing.

28. Whether or not the courtiers see "luf-talkyng" in precisely these terms is debatable, but I think seductive language is what it denotes for the reader. Conor McCarthy notes, "MED glosses *love-talkinge* as having two (hypothesized) meanings: 'pleasing conversation' and 'courtly love talk.' The reference to *luf-talkyng* in 927 would seem initially to offer the broad meaning 'courteous conversation,' identical then to *talking noble*. But, seen retrospectively, *luf-talkyng* in line 927 would also seem to foreshadow the lady's attempts to verbally seduce Gawain, and so to have an ironic sense of 'conversation about love'" (McCarthy 157).

29. Ironically enough, Bertilak credits Gawain with nobility even after he surreptitiously takes the belt. As Gawain leaves Hautdesert, Bertilak says, "Now farewell, on God's behalf, Gawain the noble!" (Now farez wel, on Godez half, Gawayn þe noble! [2149]).

30. Barron 74. "Flaying occurs in the literature of both France and England," Barron notes, ". . . and in both there is the same persistent association with various forms of treason" (Barron 38).

31. When Lady Bertilak tells Gawain she will "imprison [him] here on the other side also" (happe yow here þat oþer half als, 1224), she evidently means that she will guard the only free side of his curtained bed, which is presumably placed against a wall on the other side.

32. Vantuono renders "cors" as "me" in the text of his translation and "companionship" in a footnote (Vantuono 70n). While both evade the strict sense of "cors," "welcome to me" is just about as sexually suggestive as "welcome to my body."

33. After the Green Knight reveals himself as Bertilak, he tells Gawain that Morgan has given him the enchanting power to challenge Gawain's wits ("witteȝ," 2459). The challenge, I take it, includes everything Bertilak does directly and indirectly (through his wife) to undermine Gawain's valor and self-control.

34. When Gawain reaches the chapel where he is to meet the Green Knight, he calls it "a chapel of misfortune, may ruin befall it!" (a chapel of meschaunce, þat chekke hit bytyde! 2195). He also calls it "the most cursed church I ever entered" (þe corsedest kyrk þat euer I com inne! [2196]), bitterly, if unwittingly, echoing Lady Bertilak's "cors."

CHAPTER 4. STAGING HOSPITALITY

1. Heal 393. In the sixteenth century Thomas Becon defined hospitality as "provision-making for the poor." *Works*, ed. J. Ayre, 3 vols. (Cambridge: Parker Society, 1843–44) 1.3, qtd. Heal. "In all discussions on hospitality in the 1590s," writes Heal, "it is the

affirmation of common humanity and neighborhood with the poor through the sharing of bread that emerges as the dominant trope" (Heal 129).

2. For Dalechamp, who obviously took to heart what Christ said about the makeup of guest lists (Luke 14:12–14), the entertainment of friends and neighbors did not count as hospitality at all; all Christians, he wrote, were bound to care for strangers (68ff.). In the sixteenth and early seventeenth centuries three generations of the Lewkenor family of Sussex proved especially generous to the poor. Sir Edward Lewkenor, who died in 1618, not only fed them regularly at his gates but also raised a building near his house for the sole purpose of feeding them three times a week (Heal 177).

3. I quote from the conflated text of the play in the *Norton Shakespeare*, 2479–553.

4. Likewise, in tearing off his clothes, Lear himself may be not just identifying himself with this "poor, bare, forked animal" (3.4.108–9) but also, by implication, offering to clothe him.

5. Julia Lupton notes that at the close of Lars von Trier's *Melancholia* (2011), characters facing the end of the world "*assemble [a] hut* out of found materials in order to *assemble within it.*" To Lupton, the hut exemplifies "softscape": "the use of timber, fabrics and foliage to build temporary structures for purposes of entertaining, refuge, worship, or protest." Since entertaining often takes place in "semi-sheltered gathering places" such as gazebos and partitioned spaces, Lupton argues that hospitality is very much like theater, where "portable or partial edifices support collaborative fictions sustained and constrained by actors, theater makers, audiences, and environment" (Lupton, SS). But this line of argument presupposes that hospitality means festive entertaining, which is precisely what a play such as *Lear* contests.

6. On the other hand, Heal also notes that up to 1700 "inns remained uncommon outside the large towns, and a tradition of private hospitality was fully sustained, at least in the Highlands. Even at the end of the seventeenth century, James Kirkwood noted that the stranger could "travail amongst them gratis" (Campbell 89).

7. "Under Elizabeth and James," writes Daryl Palmer, "hospitality and entertainment are nearly interchangeable terms, marking the accepted interdependence of householding and theater, domestic and political practice" (Palmer 3). Shakespeare, as we shall see, sometimes uses "entertainment" to mean modest feeding. But hospitality was not fully identified with "Liberal" or lavish entertainment until the latter part of the seventeenth century. In 1642 the preacher and scholar Thomas Fuller identified charity as one kind of hospitality (Fuller 2:153). By 1663, when the Countess of Bridgewater died, the two things had diverged: "The rich at her Table," it was said, "daily tasted her Hospitality, the poor at her gate her Charity" (qtd. Heal 393). Though not confined to the rich, hospitality came to mean something quite different from sustenance for the needy. *Christian Hospitalitie . . .*, the title of Dalechamp's book, suggests that *Christian* hospitality had to be distinguished from other forms of it, and by the end of the seventeenth century even the author of a book on Christian "Oeconomicks" could define hospitality as "a Liberal Entertainment of all sorts of Men, at ones House, whether Neighbors or Strangers, with kindness, especially with Meat, Drink, and Lodgings" (Wheler 173). As Heal observes, this definition does not include the giving of alms (Heal 17).

8. Heal 163. In statutes drafted for cathedrals that were founded or refounded about 1540, Heal writes, they were obliged to "keep hospitality" in the old Christian sense, that is, "to feed all comers" (Heal 263). But rather than banning all the ostentation of the Roman Catholicism he had renounced, Henry expected even clerical households to entertain him "with the old ceremoniousness and grandeur of the preceding age" (Heal 262). Likewise, according to Kottman, "Queen Elizabeth's court was noted for its ceremonious displays of hospitality, and she is noted for her manipulation of these ceremonies for political gain. Maintaining the 'prestation' of hospitality, especially as a debt owed to the crown, was of course a way of maintaining power, a way of putting the power of the gift in service of the law. In this way, hospitality becomes a law, becomes law" (Kottman 91).

9. When Ventidius inherits a fortune from his newly dead father and offers to repay the five talents Timon paid to get him out of jail, Timon won't take them (1.2).

10. The Norton editors observe that "Renaissance dinner guests brought their own silverware" (*Shakespeare* 2260n5).

11. He also seeks help from Ventidius, a man whom he bought out of prison when Ventidius was poor but who has since inherited a fortune (2.2.231–35). Though his servant's appeal to Ventidius is curiously undramatized, it is denied—just like all others (3.3.1–7).

12. In the London National Theatre production of *Timon* (2012), the lukewarm water was replaced by lumps of shit on each plate, and Timon (played by Simon Russell Beale) rubbed the shit on the head of one guest.

13. First performed at court in December 1605 and first published (in quarto) in 1608, *Lear* is generally thought to have been composed in 1604–5 (Greenblatt 2308), and according to Katherine Maus, "most scholars believe that *Timon of Athens* was "written between 1605 and 1608" (Greenblatt 2247).

14. Speaking to Edmund, whom he still mistakenly trusts, Gloucester says he has received a letter reporting a "power already footed" on behalf of the king. Though Gloucester says he wants only to perform an act of surreptitious charity ("privily relieve him") he also tells Edmund that "we must incline to the King"—i.e., take the king's side in the coming battle between him and his sons-in-law (3.3.10–13).

15. I refer here to the recent findings of Hendrik Hartog, who spent ten years studying old-age care in America in the decades before Social Security and who has written a book on the subject (*Some Day All This Will Be Yours* [Harvard, 2012]). Demolishing the sentimental notion that earlier generations in this country took good care of their elders without complaining or expecting anything in return, much of what Hartog discovered resembles the world of *King Lear*: "Older people negotiated with the young to receive love, to be cared for with affection, not just self-interest." But the bargains they struck "were often unstable and easily undone. . . . Wills would be left unwritten, deeds unconveyed, promises unfulfilled, because of the onset of dementia or the meddling of siblings. Or property was conveyed too early, *and then the older person would be at the mercy of a child who no longer 'cared'*—or who could not deal with the work of care" (Hartog, emphasis added). Many years ago I recall reading somewhere that when the daughter of the aging Somerset Maugham asked him to let her take over his house in France, he replied, "My dear, I have read *King Lear*."

16. Since Medicare does not cover custodial care, the high cost of private caregivers must be paid out of pocket or with the help of privately purchased Long-Term Care Insurance. According to Carol Levine, the director of the Families and Health Care Project of the United Hospital Fund, "at least 21 percent of the country's 48 million caregivers" now care for the elderly (Levine).

17. Though Goneril refers here to "a hundred knights and squires," Lear later calls his train "my hundred knights" (2.4.226), perhaps to make them sound more impressive.

18. For what it's worth, Goneril has earlier told Oswald that Lear's "knights grow riotous" (1.3.6) and to the consternation of some Shakespeare scholars, that is how directors like Peter Brook have shown them onstage.

19. Even in our own time the power of a guest can still be measured by the size of the following he or she is allowed to bring to a social event. On the night of the Academy Awards in 2001, when the dress designer Donatella Versace tried to bring her whole entourage into the VIP lounge of the InStyle Elton John Oscar party, she was "turned back for having too many guests. After five minutes of confusion and loud Italian, she decided to proceed with a single guest." "Tribal Customs of Oscar Week," *New York Times*, February 26, 2006, Sunday Styles, 2.

20. Probably written in 1604–5, *King Lear* was performed at court in December 1605 (Greenblatt, "King Lear" in Shakespeare 2308). *Macbeth* "is usually dated 1606," chiefly because the term "equivocator" (2.3.11) seems to be an allusion to Henry Garnet, the author of *A Treatise of Equivocation*, who in late 1605 was executed for his part in the Gunpowder Plot (Greenblatt, "Macbeth" in *Shakespeare* 2555–56).

21. Holinshed 5:234. But the historical Macbeth was likewise fired up by his wife. According to Holinshed, she "was very ambitious, burning in unquenchable desire to beare the name of a queene" (Holinshed 5:269).

22. She aims, she says, to "pour [her] spirits in [Macbeth's] ear" (1.5.24), which echoes what the ghost of King Hamlet tells his son in a play probably written in 1606 (Greenblatt, Shakespeare 1659), about the time Shakespeare wrote *Macbeth*. During his afternoon nap, says the ghost, Claudius stole up to him with "cursed hebona in a vial / And in the porches of my ears did pour / The leperous distilment" (*Hamlet* 1.5.62–64). With slight variations, then, Shakespeare uses a single trope to signify first what was done to a victim of usurpation and then to a half-unwilling instrument of it.

23. Hospitality thus distinguishes itself not only from charity but also from trade. According to Marcel Mauss, participants in the "prestation" of hospitality exchange more than commodities and wealth. "They exchange rather courtesies, entertainments, rituals, . . . and feasts" (Mauss 64). Though Mauss here describes a system of exchange between groups, much of his formula applies to individual hosts and guests. "Nothing 'real,' no 'things of economic value,'" writes Kottman, "change hands when someone extends, receives and repays the kindness of hospitality" (Kottman 90). Strictly speaking this is false, since a meal and a bed for the night were things of value bought and sold at inns and alehouses in Shakespeare's own time. But the king's favor—something anyone who hosted might hope to gain—is impossible to calibrate or commodify. As Kottman says, the gift of hospitality "generates a profit of 'fantasies' (or phantasies), phantoms and phantasms. . . . [It] means a continuous profit instead of a single, one-time return" (Kottman 90).

24. As Kottman observes, "Every word that King Duncan utters in the play relates in some way to receiving subjects or to being himself received; his role is to speak of and extend hospitality. The King not only sanctions conventional hospitality, but he presides over it as if he were to do nothing else. The King is King as host" (Kottman 97).

25. On the other hand, he is quite obviously shamming when he claims that his love for Duncan drove him to kill the king's would-be murderers: his bodyguards (2.3.105–15).

26. My son Andrew Heffernan, a professional actor who has played both Hamlet and Macbeth, suggestively links "The Mousetrap" to the final duel. "Hamlet," he says, "hosts 'The Mousetrap' in the third act, which is an accusation of murder masquerading as evening's entertainment; Claudius hosts the duel in Act 5, which is murder masquerading as a sporting event" (e-mail of June 6, 2007).

27. When Telemachus comes to see Menelaus after Helen has returned to him, she recognizes him as the onetime baby left "at home when all you Achaeans / fought at Troy, launching your headlong battles / just for *my* sake, shameless whore that I was" (4.144–45 / F 4.160–62).

28. In *Entertaining Mr. Sloane* (1964) Joe Orton takes this kind of seduction one step further: a young man who comes to live as a tenant in the home of a middle-aged woman ends up getting seduced by the woman and also rousing the lust of her brother, who blackmails him into sexual servitude. (My thanks to Peter Saccio for this example.)

29. Hospitality and rape converge still more gruesomely in *Titus Andronicus*, Shakespeare's first tragedy, in which a brutal rape is requited by a bloody feast. Early in the play the sons of the empress Tamora rape Lavinia, daughter of the Roman general Titus, and cut off her tongue and hands. In the fifth act, masquerading as Revenge, Rapine, and Murder, Tamora and her sons offer to take vengeance on Titus's foes—the empress and emperor Saturninus—if he will give a banquet for them at his house. Knowing just who his disguised visitors are, he agrees, dismisses Tamora, cuts the throats of her sons, and then welcomes to his feast the empress and emperor. After urging them to eat, he tells the emperor what he has done with Tamora's sons. "Why," he says, "there they are, baked in this pie; / Whereof their mother daintily hath fed, / Eating the flesh that she herself hath bred" (5.3.59–61). When he punctuates this sentence by killing Tamora, Saturninus kills him, goading Titus's son Lucius to kill Saturninus in turn. Titus's feast thus becomes a bloodbath for himself and his enemies alike.

30. "He understands her persuasive speech," writes Lynn Enterline, "not as obedience to his desire . . . but as a force that eclipses his own" (Enterline 198).

31. In thus questioning this part of Lupton's argument, I must also say that her article as a whole is so rich and provocative that it caused me to rethink my own approach to the *Winter's Tale*, and I fully agree with her conclusion: "Shakespeare probes the scene of hospitality for its dramatic potential, that is, for the kinds of action and the forms of self-exposure that we risk each time we set the table" ("H" 185).

32. Ironically, however, Menelaus does all he can to detain Telemachus.

33. Leontes also describes her shaking the hand of Polixenes as "virginalling / Upon his palm" (1.2.125)—as if she were playing the piano-like "virginals" even while scarcely behaving like a virgin. Lupton finds her verbal overtures to Polixenes perfunctory.

Arguing that Hermione is "inherently reserved" (she "held [her] peace" [1.2.28–29] until Leontes exhausted his persuasive powers) as well as "in the late, unromantic stages of second pregnancy," Lupton asks, "does a woman in this condition really *want* to entertain her husband's friend for an extra week?" (H 169). But if Hermione "shakes off her virtuous reserves" in appealing to Polixenes, as Lupton contends (174), can she do so even while masking her wish to see him go?

34. Lupton seems to imply something like this when she suggests that we think of Leontes' seemingly unmotivated jealousy "as in part structural, as no longer requiring the agency of a Iago" (H 176). The link I draw here has also been forged in reverse. "Inviting a man into your body," writes Mary Ellen Strote, "is a little like inviting a guest into your house" (Strote 36).

CHAPTER 5. WORDSWORTH, COLERIDGE, AND THE SPIRIT OF PLACE

1. In the first part of this sentence I allude to Friedrich Schiller's *On Naïve and Sentimental Poetry* (1800).

2. I take at face value the opening lines of *The Prelude* (1850 1.1–14). Though the editors of the *Prelude* say he was almost certainly "in the Lake District when he wrote these lines," he represents himself as newly released from the "vast city" (l. 7) and making his way into the country. The editors also suggest that "city" may partly refer to Goslar, Germany, where Wordsworth spent the winter of 1798–99, but the "vast city" that truly captivated Wordsworth in the 1790s was London. See *Prelude* 28n2 and Heffernan, "Wordsworth's London."

3. Wordsworth and Jones themselves had reached Calais on July 13, "the very eve / Of that great federal day" (1805 *Prelude* 6:356–57).

4. In the summer of 1790 Wordsworth could not foresee that France would reenact the decapitation of King Charles I. On January 20, 1793, when Louis XVI learned he was to be executed the next day, he asked a servant to bring him David Hume's *History of England* so that he might see how the English king had faced his execution (Blanning 196).

5. At one point Wordsworth calls himself and Jones "two brother pilgrims" (1850 *Prelude* 6:477).

6. See De Selincourt's note to the 1850 *Prelude* 6:425–26 (p. 557). The phrase "parting Genius" comes from Milton's Nativity Ode. "For Milton," writes Johnston, "the 'parting Genius' was the mythological spirit of the classical world, sadly departing before the new spiritual reality of Jesus Christ. But for Wordsworth, . . . [it] was now Christianity itself, and he the last among men who could appreciate its spiritual value even as its institutional forms disappeared" (Johnston 198).

7. The campaign against monasteries actually began in February 1790 (five months before Wordsworth reached France), when the National Assembly forbade monastic vows. And in April, three months before the *fédérés* welcomed Wordsworth and Jones like angels, the abbé Montesquieu conjured up before the National Assembly the specter of an angel hardly welcome. Debating a new set of laws, the Civil Constitution, that would turn clerics into public servants, he wondered if "the exterminating angel" was about "to pass over the face of this Assembly" (Schama 491). The Civil Constitution

passed the Assembly on July 12, just three weeks before Wordsworth reached the Chartreuse and imagined hearing the "hideous laughter" of demons at its aerial cross: a cross "by angels planted" as a sign of monastic hospitality.

8. On the theme of the halted traveler in Wordsworth's poetry, see Hartman 3–30.

9. Below I cite the preface of the play by page and the text (of 1842) by line number(s).

10. In *Enquiry Concerning Political Justice* (1793) William Godwin argued that everything must be tried by "the standard of reason," that nothing must be tolerated simply because it is ancient, long revered, or long unquestioned (Godwin 90). It is no exaggeration to say that reason was idolized by the revolutionary French Republic, especially when the Jacobins ruled it. In November 1793 Parisians held a Festival of Reason in the Cathedral of Notre Dame, renamed the Temple of Reason (Schama 778).

11. The quoted words are applied to Marmaduke by Idomenea when her father Herbert calls him a "wild Freebooter" (207). By this time Herbert has already ordered Marmaduke to stay away from her.

12. Later, Oswald tells Marmaduke, "You have cast off the chains / That fettered your nobility of mind" (2248–49).

13. From notes dictated to Isabella Fenwick in 1843 (qtd. Coleridge, *CP* Notes 498–99); Coleridge's comment appears in Dyce 185. Eight years before, Wordsworth told Dyce that he had suggested the shooting of the albatross (which he had read about in Shelvocke's *Voyages*) and "the re-animation of the dead bodies, to work the ship"; also, he reportedly said, he composed six lines of the poem: the stanza beginning "He holds him with his glittering eye—" (ll. 12–16 of the final version) and the second part of the first stanza of part 4, "And thou art long, and lank, and brown, / As is the ribb'd sea-sand" (ll. 226–27 of the final version). (Letter of Dyce to H. N. Coleridge, qtd. *CP* Notes 498.)

14. In a quite different context, Coleridge charged that Napoleon had disrespected Britain's "constitutional Laws and Rights of Hospitality" during the Peace of Amiens (*F* 1:266)—possibly referring to Napoleon's demands that Britain evacuate the island of Malta.

15. See Magnuson 78–81 and Stephen Gill, "Introduction," *SPP* 9–12. "ASP" is a revised version of "Salisbury Plain," written in 1793–94. Neither version was published in Wordsworth's lifetime, but a third version appeared as *Guilt and Sorrow* in 1842.

16. Questioning Jerome McGann's contention that *The Rime* has a Christian plot and "ultimately redemptive meaning" (McGann, "Meaning" 60), Raimonda Modiano argues that such a reading ignores the despair expressed by the mariner—especially in recalling that his agonizing loneliness was unrelieved by providential aid: "And never a saint took pity on / My soul in agony" (ll. 234–35, Modiano 191–92). But besides the mariner's echoing of Christ on the cross ("My God! My God! Why have you forsaken me?" [Matt. 27:46]), Modiano fails to note that shortly after he bemoans the heartlessness of all saints, his "kind saint" *does* pity him (l. 286). Only at the very end of the poem, I believe, does the Christian answer to the mariner's guilt break down (see below).

17. Unless otherwise noted, I quote from the 1817 version of the poem as reprinted in 1834 (*CP* 167–86 and Notes, 504–5), and all numbers cited are lines of the poem.

18. After starting its life as a passage composed for *The Prelude*, this poem was published separately in 1800.

19. "The mariner's hollo" is evidently something generalized, as in Blake's phrase, "the harlot's cry."

20. Lines 67–74 and gloss. Coleridge thus *contra*-motivates the killing of the bird. In Shelvocke's account of the episode that prompted Wordsworth to suggest a poem about "*shooting an albatross*" (qtd. Coleridge, *CP* Notes 498), "a disconsolate black Albatross" that hovers near a ship for several days is shot by an officer who imagines "in one of his melancholy fits . . . that it might be some ill omen" and who is sure that its death will bring a fair wind (Shelvocke 19). In the "Rime" nothing is said to explain or justify the shooting until after it occurs, when the mariner's shipmates at first denounce him for killing a bird that brought a fair wind and then commend him for killing one "that brought the fog and mist" (ll. 93–102).

21. Published in 1828, it consists of a prose fragment marked canto 2 (see *CP* 218–23).

22. In a contribution to Southey's *Omniana* (1812), Coleridge himself wrote that finding the motive for a particular action is both impractical and unimportant. "Rather seek to learn what his objects in general are. What does he habitually wish, habitually pursue? and thence deduce his impulses which are commonly the true efficient causes of men's conduct" (Coleridge, *Literary Remains* 1.297, qtd. *Magnuson* 58–59). In the "Rime," however, we learn nothing of what the mariner habitually wished or pursued before he shot the bird, and everything that happens to him afterward results from the shooting.

23. In a passage with which I wholly agree, however, Modiano writes, "The killing of the Albatross reflects at some level the Mariner's need to ascertain the sacred boundaries of this unknown environment and it does release spiritual forces, just as the ravaging of the bower in Wordsworth's 'Nutting' establishes the presence of a 'spirit in the wood.' In this sense both acts bear a certain resemblance to sacrificial practices, in that it is precisely through violence that the sacred is instantiated" (Modiano 206).

24. "He was in my mind the everlasting wandering Jew—had told this story ten thousand times since the voyage, which was in his early youth and 50 years before" (Coleridge, N 1.2, Note 45).

25. Recorded in 1228 by Roger of Wendover in *Flores Historiarum*, the passage is quoted in Paris, 5.340–41.

26. See Fulmer 800 and Coleridge, *BL* 2:33n. In "The Wanderings of Cain," the protagonist has a "fierce and sullen eye," and "his countenance [tells] in a strange and terrible language of agonies that had been, and were, and were still to continue to be" (*CP* 220).

27. Fulmer 800, 803. Written in 1797 but rejected for the stage, the play was rewritten as *Remorse* in 1812 and performed the following January at Drury Lane (Coleridge, *BL* 1:26n).

28. Fulmer takes it as the latter. "Inhospitality," he writes, "is precisely the sin of the Wandering Jew, who refused succor to Christ when He passed the unfortunate man's door" (Fulmer 806). The early sources for the legend make no mention of the Jew's house, but insofar as hospitality entails the provision of rest, the stone of the ballad signifies it.

29. On the other hand, the hanging of the Albatross "Instead of the cross" (141) around the mariner's neck has been construed as "an ironic reversal of the crucifixion. The cross-like brand of sin, which is also a promissory indication of retribution to be made, is in direct contrast with the symbol of the innocent Christ" (Fulmer 807). But the figure of Christ crucified traditionally signifies his willingness to atone for the sins of human-kind, including the sin of killing him, and those who wear the cross identify them-selves with suffering and atonement, which is precisely what the "harmless" Albatross comes to signify when it becomes part of the "penance" inflicted on the mariner (401, 409–10). Since the albatross sinks "like lead into the sea" when it falls from the mari-ner's neck (291), Modiano argues that its death further subverts the Christian myth by negating the resurrection (210). But the poem does not offer a tidy scheme of correspondences, and not all of its Christian elements hang from the bird itself. The resurrection, for one, is evoked by the reanimation of the mariner's dead shipmates in part 5.

30. Critics averse to Christian readings of the poem have sometimes argued that the shoot-ing of the albatross signifies the evils of the slave trade. For J. B. Ebbatson, the killing of the bird symbolically rehearses "the crux of colonial expansion, the enslavement" and murder of "native peoples" (Ebbatson 198, qtd. Modiano 185). Likewise, Malcolm Ware argues that Coleridge's way of describing the specter-bark identifies it as a slave ship (Ware 589–92). Yet while both of these interpretations are possible, neither—unlike the Christian/animist reading—is explicitly authorized by the poem.

31. For variations on this point, see Melville *RH* 18, Fry 17, and Simpson 153–54.

32. Warren 87. To show how imagination can modify "the truth of nature" in poetry, Coleridge memorably observed "the sudden charm, which accidents of light and shade, which moon-light or sun-set [diffuse] over a known and familiar landscape" (*BL* 2.5).

33. Though Coleridge surely knew that stars were fixed, he elsewhere describes them as mobilized—to the eye—by the clouds through which he saw them: "those thin clouds above, in flakes and bars, / That give away their motion to the stars" ("Dejection," 31–32, *CP* 308).

34. They are thus resolved in "Love" (*CP* 275–78), a ballad Coleridge probably wrote in November 1799. On the disruption of the wedding in the poem, see Simpson 165; on the narrator's refusal to affirm at the end "the sacrificial benefit of a united commu-nity," see Modiano 210.

35. In Hades, Tiresias tells him he must carry his oar inland until he meets people who cannot recognize it, then plant it in the earth "and sacrifice fine beasts to the lord god of the sea, / Poseidon" (F 11:121–30).

CHAPTER 6. ROUSSEAU TO STENDHAL

1. *Christabel* (Coleridge, *CP* 187–205), ll. 27–28. Hereafter I cite the poem by line numbers alone.

2. The first, Claude Anet, died soon after she began sleeping with Rousseau, who lived alone with her in Chambéry from the summer of 1736 to September 1737. During his absence from then until early 1738 for medical treatment, his "place [was] taken" by a

wig maker's boy who had managed to make himself noisily indispensable in household jobs of all kind, including that of warming Mamma's bed (Rousseau, *Confessions*
219–20).

3. On Coleridge's objections to Rousseau's philosophy, see Chris Rubenstein, who
argues that *Christabel* itself is a covert critique of Rousseau's novel *Emile*. On the
other hand, while comparing Rousseau to Luther in a periodical essay written for
The Friend and published October 5, 1809, Coleridge writes that Luther's table talk
"to a philosophic mind, will not be less interesting than Rousseau's Confessions"
(*F* 2:115).

4. *Credibilize* is a verb coined by Coleridge. Lecturing on *Hamlet* in 1813, he noted the
"credibilizing effect" of the word "again" in the first question asked about the ghost:
"What, has this thing appeared again tonight?" (1.1.19) (Coleridge, *Shakespearean
Criticism* 1.18).

5. Written in the presentation copy given to Derwent Coleridge in 1819 and quoted in
PP 159.

6. In 1828 Coleridge reportedly said, "Geraldines character is that of *apparent* innocence
but of real *malice*" (qtd. *CP* 177n). If this statement is quoted accurately, he must have
thought her innately evil, but we must weigh it against all the other evidence, especially the poem itself.

7. By the end of the poem, as Magnuson says, she "has been rendered utterly passive"
(Magnuson 96).

8. As she joins Christabel in bed, Geraldine says, "In the touch of this bosom there work-
eth a spell, / Which is lord of thy utterance, Christabel!" (255–56). In his marginal
note of 1824 on these lines, Coleridge writes, "As soon as the wicked Bosom, with the
mysterious sign of Evil stamped thereby, touches Christabel, she is deprived of the
power of disclosing what has occurred" (qtd. *PP* 169n4).

9. According to Peter Melville, Christabel's "greatest failure" is that "she fails to recognize her other self in Geraldine" and hence to welcome that self (Melville, RAM 114).

10. Or as Magnuson succinctly puts it, her "restoration must come from within"
(Magnuson 96).

11. According to Coleridge's marginal note of 1824, "The strange Lady may not pass the
threshold without Christabel's help and will" (*CPP* 166n4).

12. During the night in which she sleeps with Geraldine, we find her "Fearfully dreaming,
yet I wis, / Dreaming that alone, which is— / O sorrow and shame!" (282–84). In the
only other point at which the poem suggests something unspeakable, Christabel sees
Geraldine's "bosom and half her side— / A sight to dream of, not to tell!" (246–47). It
is hard to escape the conclusion that Christabel's dreams are themselves unspeakable—or at least unspeakable in decorous words.

13. In his *Philosophical Lectures* Coleridge writes that "a maiden so innocent and so susceptible" as Theresa could hardly fail to "mistake, and often, the less painful and . . .
sometimes pleasurable approaches to bodily deliquium . . . for divine transports, and
momentary union with God—especially if with a thoughtful yet pure psychology you
join the force of suppressed instincts stirring in the heart and bodily frame, of a mind
unconscious of their nature and these in the keenly-sensitive body." (*L* 1818, 2, 466).

14. In 1819 Coleridge noted that this passage "must . . . be changed, for the same reason" as lines 79–101, which he called "flat" (*CPP* 165n1, 168n9). But he revised neither passage.

15. Besides her virginal fear of sexual experience, which may perfectly well coexist with desire for it, Christabel knows only too well that childbirth might kill her.

16. Letter of March 1798 to George Coleridge (*CL* 1.396), qtd. Ulmer 381–82. During the time he composed *Christabel*, Ulmer notes, Coleridge was influenced by Joseph Priestley's conception of Original Sin and specifically by his "rationalist denial of vicarious sin" (Ulmer 381).

17. Unless otherwise indicated, I quote the poem by line number(s) from Keats, *CP* 229–39.

18. Keats's language about the dream is self-contradictory, for Porphyro is said to have "melted" into it after it has been called "a midnight charm / Impossible to melt as iced stream" (320, 282–83). For a thoroughgoing critique of the notion that Madeline and Porphyro are joined metaphysically rather than physically, see Stillinger, "Hoodwinking." More recently, Stillinger has identified fifty-nine ways of interpreting the poem, ranging from human love and masturbatory ritual to scopophilia and the crisis of feudalism (*Reading* The Eve 35–77, 147–49). But since no one has so far tried to gloss the poem in terms of hospitality and treachery, I venture to hope I am hereby adding, briefly, a sixtieth.

19. Richard Roos's mid-fifteenth-century translation of Chartier's poem remained popular for well over a century, but it was often attributed to Chaucer. According to Leigh Hunt, Keats may have found it in the 1782 edition of Chaucer's *Poetical Works* (Allott 500–501n).

20. By "new" I mean independent of Chartier's plot. Keats's poem, says Allott, "is obviously connected to K's feelings about Fanny Brawne and is strongly influenced by memories of Spenser's fatal enchantresses in *The Faerie Queene* and by various traditional ballads expressing the destructiveness of love" (Allott 500n). It would probably be impossible to identify all the sources that flowed into the making of any poem by Keats, but I can't help wondering if the eyes of the lady in this one—"her eyes were wild" (16)—owe something to the twice-mentioned "wild eyes" of Dorothy in Wordsworth's "Tintern Abbey" (ll. 119, 148), a poem Keats knew very well.

21. I quote from the *Indicator* version in Bush 201–2. Most editors of Keats, including Stillinger, print the original version, which was first published in Richard Monckton Milnes's *Life, Letters, and Literary Remains of John Keats* (1848) from a copy made by Charles Brown. But since the *Indicator* version is the only one Keats published, Jerome McGann argues that it "most closely corresponds to the author's final, active intentions" ("Keats" 441).

22. Richard Burton's digest of this story, which was probably Keats's source for it, defines "a lamia" as simply a serpent and makes no reference to its feeding on human flesh (*Anatomy* 3.2, qtd. Keats, *CP* 359). But otherwise Burton's version essentially follows that of Philostratus.

23. I quote the lines of this two-part poem by number from Keats, *CP* 342–59.

24. "On Poetry in General" (1818) in *Works*, ed. P. P. Howe (1930–34), vol. 9, qtd. Allott 645.

25. Journal-letter of February–May 1819 in *Letters*, ed. H. E. Rollins (1958), vol. 2:80–81, qtd. Allott 645.

26. In *The Fall of Hyperion*, which Keats started in July 1819 while he was working on *Lamia*, the prophetess Moneta scolds the poet for being a dreamer and insists that

> The poet and the dreamer are distinct
> Diverse, sheer opposite, antipodes.
> The one pours out a balm upon the world,
> The other vexes it.
>
> (1.199–202)

The problem with Moneta's antithesis, however, is that she herself is a character within the poet's dream.

27. I quote the poem by canto and line number(s) from McGann, *Byron* 373–879.

28. In *Cymbeline* likewise, Iachimo spies on the sleeping Imogen, including the "cinque-spotted" mole on her left breast (2.2.38), but only so that he can later "prove" he has ravished her.

29. Apuleius 121–23. Misled by her sisters into thinking that her unseen husband is a monstrous serpent, she had planned to cut his head off with a sharp razor until she saw that he was a beautiful god (Apuleius 119–21).

30. Right after describing the blissful plighting of their hearts ("to their young eyes / Each was an angel, and earth Paradise," 2.1632), the narrator asks himself if Juan has forgotten Julia—his first lover, whom he swore he would never forget—and then playfully chides himself for his inconstancy.

31. On meeting a young woman in Besançon just before he enters the seminary there, Julien dazzles her by reciting passages from Rousseau's novel (Stendhal 132). Later, at a glittering ball in Paris, the aristocratic Mathilde de la Mole commends his wisdom by saying that he views "all these balls and parties like a philosopher, like Jean-Jacques Rousseau" (Stendhal 229).

32. Stendhal 24. Adams's aptly cutting metaphor does not appear in Stendhal's "diminuer" (*Rouge* 52), which means simply "lessen" or "reduce," but "cut down" surely serves the spirit if not the letter of the passage. Apropos Julien's ambition, his favorite book is Emanuel Las Casas's *Mémorial de Saint-Hélène*, which Adams calls "a keystone of the Napoleonic legend" (Stendhal 13n), and he also loves to read Napoleon's bulletins of the Grand Armée (Stendhal 44). When he succeeds one evening in taking and holding the hand of Madame de Rênal, he believes he has carried out *"a heroic duty"* (Stendhal 44).

33. Adams translates Stendhal's "pauvres détenus" (*Rouge* 166) as "poor prisoners." But since men housed in a poorhouse are not really prisoners, I use "inmates," which is the term Adams himself uses for them in a later passage (113, quoted below).

34. Presumably this was his annual salary. In 1862, thirty-one years after *Red and Black* first appeared, a hundred Louis d'or was worth two thousand francs, and since a day's pay for a fan maker was three francs (www.chanvrerie.net), Julien's starting salary was about double that. He is also told that his salary may be quadrupled, "raised in time to eight thousand francs" (188).

35. Though never explicitly identified as twins, they are each said to be nineteen years old (Stendhal 188, 198).

36. Fleeing arrest after the publication of *The Social Contract* and *Principles of Political Right* in 1762, he left Geneva first for Bern and then Môtiers, where his house was stoned on the night of September 6, 1765. After taking refuge at Hume's house in Wootton, Derbyshire, where he wrote much of *The Confessions*, he began to suspect that Hume and others were plotting against him. Though he covertly returned to France under the name "Renou" in 1767, he was not legally admitted before 1770.

37. "[G]irls, from various causes, are more kept down by their parents, in every sense of the word, than boys. The duty expected from them is, like all the duties arbitrarily imposed on women, more from a sense of propriety, more out of respect for decorum than reason" (155). In *A Vindication of the Rights of Men* (1790), Wollstonecraft not only attacks the institutions Burke had defended in *Reflections on the Revolution in France* (1790). She also anticipates her second *Vindication* by attacking the inequality of a society founded on the passivity of women, which Burke's argument presumes.

CHAPTER 7. FIELDING TO JAMES

1. Starting with Aphra Behn's *Love-Letters Between a Noble-Man and his Sister* (1684), the first wave of English novels—written mostly by women such as Behn—exemplify what has been called "amatory fiction" (Ballaster). But as McKeon notes, Richardson and Fielding launch a second wave of English fiction not so much by rejecting the "sexual profligacy" of the first (as some critics claim) as by turning their attention from the explicitly public realm to the politically charged "secret history" of domestic life (McKeon 641–42). On the relation between the novel and the history of "personal writings" such as the diary, see Hunter, *Before Novels* 303.

2. What Julia Lupton says of Shakespeare's plays also applies to the novels I shall examine here: they "consistently draft hospitality as the social script that opens the household to the risk of politics" (Lupton, H 165).

3. "Fielding," writes Fumiko Takese, "wants to sublimate the individual character, such as Tom at a particular time, the 1745 Rebellion, to 'Man in History'" (Takese 42).

4. Battestin notes that Fielding himself abhorred dueling and that a recurrent theme of Fielding's *Amelia* (1751) is "the irreconcilable opposition between Christian principles and the modern code of honour" (Fielding 1.383–84n).

5. On the diminishment of the hero in *Tom Jones*, whose protagonist recalls not Homer's Odysseus but rather his Telemachus, as filtered through François Fénelon's *Télémaque* (1699), see Hunter, *Occasional Form* 130–35.

6. After Susan the chambermaid challenges Partridge "to single Combat" (1.503), he gives her "a Black-Eye" and gets in return some fists and nail scratches in the face (1.507). But Tom is never said to land a blow at the inn, and since the swordfight he had planned to have with Northerton never took place, his only act of violence against another man is to beat Northerton to the ground and tie him up, leaving him well enough to scamper off soon after. By contrast, the sergeant embodies a comic pugnacity: "The only way when Friends quarrel," he says, "is to see it out fairly in a friendly

Manner, as a Man may call it, either with a Fist, or Sword, or Pistol, according as they like" (1.507).

7. Late in the novel, when Tom has been arrested for murder, Mrs. Miller sums him up to Squire Allworthy as follows: "I do not pretend to say the Young Man is without Faults; but they are all the Faults of Wildness and of Youth; Faults which he may, nay I am certain he will relinquish, and if he should not, they are vastly over-ballanced by one of the most humane tender honest Hearts that ever Man was blessed with" (2.878).

8. The full name and title of the English duke was Arthur Wellesley, Duke of Wellington. Some years ago, in response to an exam question about the Waterloo stanzas of *Childe Harold*, one of my students wrote, "Remarkably enough, Byron writes not a word about the English general who won the battle, Duke Ellington."

9. The quoted phrase exemplifies the sexual energies of *Aurora Leigh*, in which, writes Tucker, the "peak experiences are all eroticized" (Tucker 380). Comparing Browning's poem with Erasmus Darwin's much earlier *Botanic Garden*, Tucker observes, "Both poems propose subversively sexualized alternatives to the martial origins of cultural grandeur that prevail in traditional epic" (Tucker 380n56).

10. Christine L. Krueger, who has written a book on nineteenth-century women preachers, informs me that besides "the long-standing Protestant practice of narrating the soul's struggle with sin in epic terms (e.g. *Pilgrim's Progress*), . . . much Methodist and Baptist activity moved that struggle into specifically domestic settings and made 'heroic,' or at least 'saintly' figures out of the ordinary folk who conducted prayer meetings and classes in their homes—and often morphed into preaching and prophesying. George Eliot's aunt, Dinah Morris, was one such figure" (e-mail of June 28, 2013).

11. "Old" is relative. When Casaubon marries Dorothea, he is said to be "over five-and-forty," but also "a good seven-and-twenty years older than" Dorothea (26), who is "not yet twenty" (2).

12. Since Sir James and the other grandees of Middlemarch "never ceased to regard Dorothea's marriage as a mistake" (577), Kate Flint has recently observed that the "uneasiness expressed both within the text, and by critics both Victorian and modern, about the suitability of Ladislaw as a husband for Dorothea, testifies to George Eliot's refusal to provide an orthodox romantic closure in *Middlemarch*, despite her narrative's valorization of her heroine's fate" (Flint 172). If such a closure requires the heroine's marriage to a wealthy man, such as Elizabeth's marriage to Darcy at the end of *Pride and Prejudice*, Flint is right. But in giving up wealth and property for a life of modest prosperity with the man she loves, and thus defying the bourgeois values of her friends and relatives, not to mention the wishes of Casaubon, Dorothea is gratifying urges that are surely more romantic than otherwise—whether or not they are also heroic. Hillis Miller calls her decision historic precisely "because it is based on ardor, not prudence" (Miller, "Conclusion" 140).

13. When she and her aunt Mai met Eliot in the summer of 1852, Nightingale was "much pleased with her" (letter of July 16, 1852, qtd. Nightingale 5:774n).

14. *Fraser's Magazine* (1873): 567, Nightingale 5:12–13. Something like a leprechaun in Celtic mythology, the cluricaune is an idle dandy—not a figure with whom Ladislaw can be justly identified. But this hardly invalidates Nightingale's main point.

15. Glossing the word "unhistoric," Hillis Miller writes of Dorothea, "Her effect on those around her exceeded the public power of naming that makes the writing of grand histories possible. The result is that her influence cannot be measured except hypothetically" (Miller, "Conclusion" 137). One might also say it cannot be measured except fictively.

16. By shaking Dorothea's faith in Casaubon's intellectual distinction as well as by rousing Casaubon's jealous resentment of his influence over Dorothea, it could be argued that Will at the very least hastens his death.

17. At the end of the chapter in which Bingley is reported to be suddenly off for London, Mrs. Bennet consoles herself by thinking that he "would be soon down again [in their neighborhood] and soon dining at Longbourn," where "he had been invited . . . to a family dinner" (81). But there is no prior reference to this invitation, and it is only when Bingley returns to Netherfield after an absence of "about a twelvemonth" that Mrs. Bennet decides to ask him to dinner again (212–13).

18. Since he plans to arrive by four o'clock on a Monday afternoon and stay "till the Saturday se'night [seven nights] following," and since this stay will require his "absence [from his parish] on a Sunday" (43), his stay will be twelve nights altogether.

19. Mrs. Bennet's raptures over this prospect attest to its fairy-tale perfection: "A house in town! Every thing that is charming! . . . Ten thousand a year! Oh, Lord! What will become of me? I shall go distracted" (243).

20. In issuing the invitation, she reminds Bingley that when he went to town the previous winter, he had "promised to take a family dinner with [them], as soon as [he] returned" (216). But no such promise was ever made in our hearing or seeing.

21. Peter Melville notes that since the lab is linked by a passageway to Victor's apartment and bedroom, "this connectedness makes the laboratory a potential guest-space. . . . Witnessing the creature's coming to life as a second subjectivity in the [bed] room, Victor is made aware that he is no longer simply at-home with himself, but is now forcibly made host to another within the most private of his domestic spaces" (Melville, MIH 181).

22. Because the novel reveals far more of the creature's inner life than any film does, it allows us to see how Victor's loathing of the creature's appearance may distort his perception of the creature's inner life. Film versions of *Frankenstein* represent the creature chiefly as Victor sees him, that is, from the outside (see Heffernan, "Looking").

23. "Know," he tells Walton, "that, one by one, my friends were snatched away; I was left desolate" (191). Since the creature claims to be Victor's "master" who must be obeyed (162), I have elsewhere argued that he rapes the bride before killing her, exercising "in his own murderous way the traditional right of a *feudal* master: the *droit de seigneur*, the lord's right to take his vassal's bride on her wedding night" (Heffernan, "Looking" 195). While the creature brutally gratifies his frustrated desire for a mate, Victor seems capable only of necrophilia. Having left Elizabeth alone in their room at the inn while he prowls its corridors in quest of the creature, he touches her for the first time only after her death, when he embraces "with ardor" what proves to be her corpse (189). He thereby reenacts the dream he had right after animating the creature—the dream in which he embraces an Elizabeth who turns into the corpse of his mother.

24. In certain bifurcated readings of *Frankenstein*, as O'Rourke notes, "the De Laceys commonly serve as the idealized foils to Victor's selfish vanity" (O'Rourke 113).

25. When the creature thanks old De Lacey for offering to help him, the old man says, "I and my family have been condemned, although innocent; judge, therefore, if I do not feel for your misfortunes" (130).

26. Emily Brontë started writing *Wuthering Heights* in the autumn of 1845, which is just when the famine struck. Though her brother Branwell's visit to Liverpool occurred in August of that year, Eagleton notes that "there would no doubt have been a good many impoverished Irish immigrants hanging around the city; and it is tempting to speculate that Branwell ran into some of them and relayed the tale to his sister" (Eagleton 3).

27. Right after telling Cathy he would beat Isabella daily if they ever lived together, he observes, "She's her brother's heir, is she not?" (83). Though Cathy tells him that "half-a-dozen nephews" (i.e., her own would-be sons) "shall erase her title, please Heaven!" and though Heathcliff agrees to "dismiss" for the time being the question of his marrying Isabella (83), he plainly reveals his reason for later doing so.

28. The French word *revenant* can mean either "one who returns after an absence" or "one who returns from the dead." In chapter 9 of Joyce's *Ulysses* Stephen calls Shakespeare "a ghost by absence" (*U* 9.147) because he was absent from Stratford for twenty years while he lived and worked in London. "What is a ghost?" says Stephen. "One who has faded into impalpability through death, through absence, through change of manners" (*U* 9.147–49).

29. With the exception of Tanya's letter to Onegin and his to her, both of which depart from Pushkin's regular stanzaic form, I cite the poem by chapter and stanza numbers, and I quote translations by the translator's initial: F for Falen, A for Arndt.

30. Though Pushkin ignores the differences between Byron and Harold, Byron himself admitted that he had failed to draw a convincing distinction "between the author and the pilgrim" in the first three cantos of his poem and decided to abandon the effort altogether in the fourth (Byron 146). Also, when Pushkin's narrator claims that he and Eugene are "souls apart," he seems to forget the bond they formed. As he has just told us, they became "good friends" because "we both had drunk from Passion's chalice: / In either, life had numbed all zest; / Extinct the glow in either breast" (A 1.45).

31. Fragments of both chapters survive; fragments of the tenth, which was to have treated Pushkin's part in the Decembrist conspiracy, are "written in Pushkin's private cipher and not completely decoded" (Arndt xv). He stopped work on the poem in 1831, eight years after starting it.

32. While staying with Baron Frédéric Melchior Grimm, Rousseau found him one morning cleaning his nails with a special brush—"a work he continued proudly in front of me" (*Confessions*, book 9, 392). Though Pushkin implies that Rousseau was offended by Grimm's breach of propriety, he was actually deploring Grimm's foppish devotion to grooming. In a footnote to his lines on this episode, Pushkin waggishly defends Grimm as "ahead of his age: nowadays, all over enlightened Europe, people clean their nails with a special brush" (qtd. F 230n15).

33. Since Pushkin knew something of English fiction (the heroine of *Eugene Onegin* reads the novels of Richardson, 2.29–30), he could have known *Pride and Prejudice*, though I have found no evidence that he did.

34. In a poem written on the night before fighting a duel to defend his claim to Olga, Lensky wonders if she will weep over his grave, and he imagines himself calling her to join him in death. He writes, the narrator tells us, like one of the "Romantics," and he falls asleep "upon the fashion-word 'ideal'" (A 6.23).

35. At the age of thirty-eight Pushkin himself challenged a French baron for paying too much attention to his wife, Natalya Goncharova, and was mortally wounded in the resulting duel.

36. Unless otherwise indicated, I quote by page number(s) alone from the 1908 text edited by Robert Bamberg (Norton). When I refer to the Oxford edition of this text, I cite it as *PL/O*. The extent of James's revisions has led one critic to conclude "there are two *Portraits*, not one" (Mazella 597), and another to argue that the later James transforms his original story "into a drama of consciousness" (Baym 620). But James's treatment of hospitality, I believe, remains largely unchanged in the later version.

37. Not including the use of "ask" to mean "invite," I count fifteen references to *hospitality/hospitable*, eleven to *hostess*, fifteen to *host*, five to *guest*, twenty-three to *invite/invitation*, seven to *entertain/entertainer*, and two to the crossing of a threshold.

38. On leaving Gardencourt after a long stay there, she tells Isabel she is "going to six places in succession" to visit "old friends" (177). Since Madame Merle almost never invites anyone to her own pied-à-terre in Rome, she reminds me of a charming old friend who was once chided for failing to reciprocate the many invitations he accepted. "Oh," he said, "I like to entertain people in their *own* houses."

39. In the end, Isabel realizes that Madame Merle has "made a convenience" of her, and Mrs. Touchett promptly agrees: "So she did of me! She does of every one" (475). As a veteran guest, Madame Merle herself has already told Isabel that the English are "the most convenient in the world to live with" (169).

40. The second volume of Leon Edel's biography of James is aptly subtitled *The Conquest of London, 1870–1881*. Unlike Henry and his elder brother William, their younger brothers Wilkie and Bob "were forced into the army and sent South. Both were injured and traumatized by their war experience, and lived out desperate post-war lives, disregarded first by their father and then by their guilty elder siblings" (Luckhurst viii).

41. Furthermore, though preoccupied with the distinctively American concept of independence, the novel alludes just twice to the condition of those nominally emancipated during the war. In discussing "American ladies" with Henrietta early in the novel, Lydia calls them "the slaves of slaves," meaning "the companions of their servants—the Irish chambermaid and the negro waiter. They share their work" (89). Later on, describing her train trip around America with Mr. Bantling, Henrietta tells Isabel that "he was always ordering ice-cream from the coloured man" (410).

42. As "a man of forty" (197) in the mid-1870s, when the novel is set (chapter 36 occurs "in the autumn of 1876" [301]), Osmond is easily old enough to have fought in the third war of Italian independence (1866), but as he tells Isabel, he "could do nothing in Italy—I couldn't even be an Italian patriot" (227). In eschewing business as well as

war, Osmond may reflect the temperament of James himself, who once professed himself utterly incapable of plumbing the mystery of "the American business-man" (James, AN 193). But while Osmond has been said to represent the "hidden side" of his fastidious, acutely self-conscious creator (Edel 3:18), he shares nothing of James's ambition, industry, and capacity to imagine the feelings of others, especially women.

43. By contrast, as we later learn, Edward Rosier lacks the martial might to win Pansy. Though he thinks himself "heroic" to risk the poisonous air of a Roman November in hopes of seeing her (301), and though he bristles with "military resolution" to see her at a party even after her father has forbidden her to dance with him, he strikes Isabel as always smelling "so much more of heliotrope than of gunpowder" (365).

44. Later Isabel herself tells Caspar Goodwood, "If there's a thing in the world I'm fond of, . . . it's my personal independence" (142).

45. Since Lydia's telegram ("Taken sister's girl . . . two sisters, quite independent") is care-lessly worded, Ralph does not know whether "quite independent" describes Isabel alone or all three sisters, so he refers to "their own way" (24).

46. On a later visit to New York, Lydia is invited to dinner "four times" by Isabel's sister Lily, and she went once (473).

47. "We're mere parasites," she tells Isabel, "crawling over the surface; we haven't our feet in the soil" (171). Though she's referring to American expatriates generally, she might just as well be describing their condition as long-term guests, especially of the Touchetts.

48. While most critics now seem to assume that Alec rapes Tess, the evidence for seduc-tion, which includes an explicit reference to Alec as the "seducer" of Tess (238), seems to me decisive. For more on this point, see Heffernan, "Cruel Persuasion," which can be found on the Victorian Web as well as in print.

49. For James's estimate of *Tess*, see his letter of February 17, 1893, to Robert Louis Stevenson. While recognizing the public acclaim for Hardy's novel, James nonethe-less insisted that "she is vile," presumably referring to both the novel and its heroine (qtd. Elledge 388). On the other hand, the reading of the pre-European Isabel includes "the prose of George Eliot," whose *Middlemarch* began to appear in *Harper's Weekly* on December 16, 1871 (42 and n.).

50. According to the OED, the word *charm* originally meant "sing [magic] into," as in two other French versions of the Latin, *in-cant-ation* and *en-chant-ment*: "chanting or reci-tation of a verse supposed to possess magic power or occult influence" (OED 1.383).

51. When Warburton and his sister come to lunch at Gardencourt shortly after Isabel rejects his proposal, she repeats her refusal to visit him again. Pressed by his sister to "come to Lockleigh again" but seeing in her eyes "the reflexion of everything she had rejected in rejecting Lord Warburton" (including "a deep security and a great exclu-sion"), she says, "I'm afraid I can never come again" (120).

52. As a journalist bent above all on gathering material for the press, Henrietta scarcely understands what "true hospitality" is. When she tells Isabel that she is working on a letter about Gardencourt for an American newspaper called the *Interviewer*, Isabel tells her, "My uncle won't be delighted—nor my cousin either. They'll consider it a breach of hospitality" (82).

53. In refusing two suitors, we read, "she had tasted of the delight, if not of battle, at least of victory; she had done what was truest to her plan" of remaining independent (145).

54. Luckhurst notes that "merle" is French for blackbird and that idiomatically "*un fine merle* means a deep or cunning old bird" (*PL/O* 587). Her name also evokes the magic, enchanting powers of the legendary Merlin, counselor to King Arthur.

55. James may well be alluding to the "Spring" chapter of *Walden* (1853), where Thoreau proclaims, "We need the tonic of wildness. . . . We can never have enough of Nature" (Thoreau 209–19).

56. By contrast, as we learn early on, long residence in England had left Daniel Touchett with "no intention of disamericanising, nor had he a desire to teach his son any such subtle art" (43).

57. Though he goes on to tell the nuns that Madame Merle will help him decide whether or not Pansy will return to them "at the end of the holidays," Madame Merle describes this as Osmond's "pleasantry; I decide nothing," she says (202).

58. Later on, when Osmond first declares his love for Isabel, the pang of dread she feels seems to her like "the slipping of a fine bolt—backward, forward, she couldn't have said which" (263).

59. Isabel faintly suspects something is wrong here. Wondering why Osmond asks her what she thought of his sister, Isabel takes it as "a proof that he was interested in her" (i.e., Isabel herself) but also finds it "a little singular he should sacrifice his fraternal feeling to his curiosity [about Isabel]. That was the most eccentric thing he had done" (225). But Osmond is far less interested in what Isabel thinks than in taking charge of her thoughts.

60. Since Osmond is not the master of the villa but merely a tenant in one of its apartments, the narrator's phrase evidently signifies the way in which Madame Merle sees him, which doubtless accords with the way he sees himself.

61. Mrs. Touchett takes this to mean that Madame Merle will serve the wishes of her hostess. After Isabel becomes engaged to Osmond, her aunt tells her that Madame Merle "has deceived me. She had as good as promised me to prevent your engagement" (283).

62. The Countess Gemini is equally blunt. "I never congratulate any girl on marrying," she tells Isabel. "I think they ought to make it somehow not quite so awful a steel trap" (300).

63. Later on, the noninviter is explicitly identified as Osmond. When Goodwood comes to Florence, Isabel feels bound to invite him "to her Thursday evenings, of which she had grown very weary, but to which her husband still held for the sake not so much of inviting people as of not inviting them" (411).

64. A little later, however, she gives him a little encouragement after Osmond tells him that Pansy has given him up. "She has not given you up," says Isabel (319).

65. Isabel lingers "in the doorway" only in the first edition of the novel; in 1908 she stands, as already noted, "near the threshold."

66. But he never wholly forgets the first. Even while telling Pansy privately that she is "very dear" to him, he tries "to believe that there was after all such a thing as hospitality" (313).

67. He "had at times grimly wished he were dead and would have liked to kill him" (421).
68. Though James considered letting Madame Merle herself reveal this, he decided that making it come from the countess was "better on many grounds" (*Notebooks*, qtd. *PL*, ed. Bamberg 641).
69. Earlier, just before she goes to Rome, we are told of her eagerness "to see Osmond overtopped" (376).
70. She thus echoes what she says to herself earlier after learning that Madame Merle had arranged her marriage to Osmond. Even after reflecting that her would-be friend had been "deeply, deeply deeply" false, Isabel softly exclaims, "Poor, poor Madame Merle!" (431–32).
71. Except for giving her the chance to see Ralph one last time, Gardencourt has now lost its appeal for Isabel. After she arrives, she is made to wait a long time in the drawing room for her aunt, who—when she at last appears—makes Isabel wonder if she "resembled more a queen-regent or the matron of a jail" (472).
72. This promise is Warburton's invention. As already noted, Isabel tells him at the end of her only visit to Lockleigh that there is "no prospect" of her returning, and when Warburton's sister later urges her to "come to Lockleigh again," Isabel replies, "I'm afraid I can never come again" (120). Though Warburton is engaged to another woman, he still seems bent on courting Isabel by means of hospitality.

CHAPTER 8. PROUST'S HOSTESSES

1. "For a few seconds . . . I had difficulty in recognizing the master of the house and the guests and why everyone in the room appeared to have put on a disguise . . . which changed him completely" (*TR* 286). In the opening sentence of *A Death in the Family* (1957), his posthumously published autobiographical novel, James Agee reverses this trope: "We are talking now of summer evenings in Knoxville, Tennessee, in the time that I lived there so successfully disguised to myself as a child."
2. The narrator is unequivocally named just once, when Albertine salutes him in a note as "My darling dear Marcel" (*CAP* 172). I use Marcel to refer to the narrator when he acts as a character.
3. As a young man, Proust himself fell in love with a society hostess named Genevieve Strauss, the mother of his school friend Jacques Bizet. Lovely, witty, and flawlessly complexioned, she became one of the models for the Duchess de Guermantes (Carter 86, 91–93).
4. We know this for certain only because the duchess's last words to him are, "I look forward to seeing you on Friday" (*GW* 439). Marcel is so caught up in speculating on his relations with the whole Guermantes clan—more precisely with the duchess, the duke, and M. de Charlus—that he never tells just what he said in response to her invitation.
5. Though the Baron de Charlus tells Marcel that beneath the duchess's "legendary purity" lurked "an incalculable number of love-affairs" antedating those of the duke, the narrator says he "had never heard any gossip to this effect" from any other source. His own "affair" with her took place only in his imagination. Catching her eye as a boy in the church at Combray, he thought for a moment she was sending him "glances of

love" but later "realised that they were merely the gracious looks that a sovereign lady . . . bestows upon her vassals" (*TR* 418).

6. In other words, Proust's novel stops well short of what happens at the end of Evelyn Waugh's *Scoop* (1938), where X kills himself because he is not invited to a party.

7. Though Scott-Moncrieff et al. translate the French inaccurately as "lots of clever men" (*SaG* 426), the duchess's "tous les hommes" echoes the first syllable of Madame Verdurin's "toujours." The phrase "signe d'election" is also applied to guests of Madame Verdurin en route to la Raspelière. Amidst the crowd on the train they are taking, they are marked not only by full evening dress but also "by a certain air of assurance, elegance and familiarity" (*SaG* 305), their "signe d'election" (*SeG* 259).

8. "It was the absence of grandeur in this gesture that disclosed the true grandeur which lay in the Duke's indifference to the splendor of his surroundings, in contrast to his deference toward a guest, however insignificant, whom he desired to honour" (*GW* 502).

9. My translation, with the help of Colette Gaudin (e-mail of June 29, 2009).

10. We are told earlier that even when she invited "great intellectuals" to dinner, she never talked with them of literature, science, or philosophy (*GW* 235). On the other hand, the duchess has also revealed—to Marcel's surprise—that she greatly admires the wit of Bergotte, a writer he considered "intellectual" and therefore "infinitely remote from" her realm (*GW* 239).

11. One of the least attractive features of the salons given by the Duchess of Guermantes, we are told, was the presence of "one or two extremely good-looking women who had no other right to be there but their beauty and the use that M. de Guermantes had made of them" (*GW* 553). We also learn that the duchess makes allies of the duke's mistresses because through them "she had obtained countless things which she wanted but which M. de Guermantes denied his wife so long as he was not in love with someone else" (*GW* 554). Observations like these clearly derive from the narrator's long familiarity with the duke and duchess rather than from Marcel's observations of them during his first evening in their house. Unlike Conrad's Marlow, for instance, who clearly distinguishes direct experience from retrospective interpretation, Proust's narrator does not consistently separate what he (as Marcel) sees and hears at a particular time and what later knowledge allows him to make of that experience in retrospect.

12. Here and elsewhere the bracketed words in a translation quoted from Scott-Moncrieff et al. are my own effort to render the French more accurately.

13. Earlier the narrator tells us that "the Duchess was bored by other women, if their princely rank did not give them an exceptional interest" (*GW* 235). But if, for this very reason, she typically invited men without their wives (*GW* 234), it would appear that her only reason for inviting her husband's ex-mistress is to humiliate her in front of him.

14. The word "grue," which literally means "crane" (the bird), figuratively denotes a prostitute standing around on the sidewalk like a crane, waiting for trade. Oriane is appalled to think she should ask this "grue" to leave her "fructueux trottoir" (profitable pavement) to have tea with the duchess (*CG* 783, *GW* 569).

15. When the duchess playfully claims that Zola is not a realist but an epic poet "of the sewers" who "hasn't enough capital letters to write the *mot de Cambronne*"

(a euphemism for *merde*, "shit"), Madame d'Arpajon exclaims, "He writes it with a big 'C.'" To which the duchess replies, "Surely with a big 'M,' I think, my dear," after shooting her husband "a merry glance which implied, 'Did you ever hear such an idiot?'" (GW 576–77).

16. On hearing her brother-in-law Charlus called "taquin," a teaser, she calls him "Taquin le Superbe" (CG 756), punning on Tarquin the Great, the seventh and last king of Rome. (Since the pun doesn't work in English, Scott-Moncrieff et al. approximate its effect with the phrase "Teaser Augustus" [GW 537].) It must be admitted that the pun nicely catches Charlus's pretensions to grandeur.

17. The link between these two qualities and social success is by no means clear or consistent in the novel as a whole. On the one hand, Oriane contrives to charm her guests, especially the Princesse de Parme, with comments that come across as titillatingly wicked or daringly "original." On the other hand, we are elsewhere told that Madame de Villeparisis in her youth antagonized people with "cutting taunts" and that even though her *Memoirs* displayed an "eminently social" graciousness, "certain literary qualities" are bound to impede social success (GW 209). As a generalization, this can be challenged by at least the example of Madame Recamier (1777–1849), to whom the narrator once alludes (SaG 317) and once refers (TR 420). Besides winning the admiration of Chateaubriand and Madame de Stael for her literary style, Madame Recamier charmed everyone who knew her, and Charles-Augustin Saint-Beuve said that she brought the art of friendship to perfection (Luyster viii–xii).

18. Much later, in 1930, extracts from the papers of the German military attaché assigned to Paris in 1894 exonerated Dreyfus and showed that Esterhazy was guilty.

19. The Duke of Guermantes is also appalled to think that anyone of Robert's class could support Dreyfus, as Robert (for a time) does. Though the duke claims to have "no racial prejudice" and to "move with the times," he says, "Damn it all, when one goes by the name of Marquis de Saint-Loup one isn't a Dreyfusard. I'm sorry, but there it is" (GW 268).

20. Yet not even "qu'inspiré" can justify the Scott-Moncrieff translation, since it presupposes a French text reading "qu'*est* inspiré *par* un groupement"—definitely not what Proust wrote.

21. Strictly speaking, however, Japhetics are descendants of Noah's son Japheth.

22. Earlier, toward the close of Marcel's first evening with the duke and duchess, Oriane refuses to speak to a general on behalf of her nephew Robert, now an army officer, even when the Princesse de Parme urges her to do so. Sharing her husband's "deep-rooted unwillingness to oblige . . . the Duchess had practically refused to recommend her nephew to M. de Monserfeuil. And," writes the narrator, "I saw in this an indifference all the more blameworthy in that I seemed to have gathered from a few words which the Princess had let fall that Robert was in a post of danger from which it would be prudent to have him removed. But it was by the genuine malice of Madame de Guermantes that I was revolted when, the Princesse de Parme having timidly suggested that she might say something herself and on her own initiative to the general, the Duchess did everything in her power to dissuade her" (GW 595). Later on, we learn, the duchess "often did things for [Marcel] that were far more difficult" than

getting him invited to the Princess de Guermantes's grand reception (*SaG* 72). But clearly she does not welcome *requests* for favors.

23. Later we learn that Oriane entertains at least two other Jewish guests: Madame Alphonse de Rothschild ("constantly to be seen in the house of Oriane") and Baron Hirsch, "brought to [her] house by the Prince of Wales" (*SaG* 79). But since this does not keep her from saying, "I don't know any [Jews]" (*GW* 271), as already noted, one can only conclude that, like Swann's wit, their high social standing makes their Judaism invisible to her.

24. In the very last words of *The Guermantes Way* the duke scornfully rejects Swann's claim to be dying by insisting that he is "sound as a bell. You'll bury us all!" (*GW* 620). In *Portrait of a Lady* Osmond likewise rejects Isabel's claim that her cousin Ralph is dying. "He was dying when we married," says Osmond. "He'll outlive us all" (444).

25. Later we are told that even the Duchess of Guermantes "dreaded the prospect of having to shake hands with Swann in these anti-semitic surroundings" and was relieved to learn (mistakenly, as it turns out) "that the Prince had refused to have Swann in the house and had had 'a sort of altercation' with him" (*SaG* 84).

26. A comic version of this ingratitude is exemplified by Colonel Froberville, who is married to a poor relative of the Guermantes and seldom invited anywhere. Though he and his wife and children would never miss the annual garden party of Madame de Saint-Euverte, they resent so much her "joy of self-satisfied pride" in giving it that every year they hope bad weather will ruin it (*SaG* 89). The colonel is also delighted to learn that the Duchess of Guermantes will not attend the party. "What a blow!" he says laughingly. "It'll be the death of her [the madame]!" (*SaG* 97–98).

27. More precisely, the petition is an appeal on behalf of Lt. Col Georges Picquart, who discovered evidence that proved Dreyfus innocent and incriminated Maj. Ferdinand Esterhazy. For this action Picquart had been dismissed from the army.

28. My thanks for this point to Colette Gaudin. At one point during a party at the Verdurins' the Baron de Charlus says that Horace's patron Maecenas "was more or less the Verdurin of antiquity" (*SaG* 407), but he says it chiefly to flatter his hostess, who has just made him fear that she will exclude him from another party to which she has just invited his boyfriend Morel. Also, we have already been told that the prospect of dining for the first time at the Verdurins' made the Baron de Charlus as fearful as a schoolboy going for the first time to a brothel ("un maison publique") and paying his respects to the madam—"pour la patronne" (*SeG* 298). *Patron* and *Patronne* may also denote the patron saint of a person or town, but obviously this sense cannot apply to anyone living.

29. In English usage the word *patroness* has no commercial connotations. At Almack's ballroom in Regency London, for instance, life was ruled by women known as lady patronesses, who also wielded great political influence. According to Cheryl Wilson, "the 'official' duty of the Lady Patronesses was to control the dance—to construct the narratives of the ballroom" (Wilson 68).

30. At one point she compares herself to various political, military, and religious figures— the Roman empress, the supreme commander of a legion, the Christ who demands that his adherents leave their parents and follow him (*SaG* 318). But the kind of power she asserts is consistently identified by the word *Patronne*.

31. The Baron de Charlus sneers at "tous les petits messieurs qui s'appellent marquis de Cambremerde" (*SeG* 475) ("all the pipsqueaks who call themselves Marquess of Cambershit"). In *Swann's Way* the Princess des Laumes tells Swann that the name Cambremer "ends just in time"—that is, before the "mer" becomes "merde"—"but it ends badly!" (*SW* 354).

32. Later, when Madame Verdurin is told at the beginning of a party in her Parisian house that her good friend Princess Sherbatoff has "died at six o'clock," she insists that the princess is merely ill, "thereby unconsciously imitating the Duc de Guermantes" (*CAP* 256).

33. In a variant passage, Saniette's slightly critical remark on Morel's playing enrages M. Verdurin so much that he throws Saniette out, whereupon the man has a stroke in the courtyard and dies a few weeks later, "only intermittently regaining consciousness" (*LaP* 802–3, my translation). Since the presumably final version of the novel has Saniette living to receive the Verdurins' largesse, it prompts the narrator to say that we should never judge people "by some memory of an unkind action" (*CAP* 372). But in discussing their gift to Saniette, the Verdurins show no sign of remorse, and what Madame Verdurin sincerely desires is protection from any further demands on their purse (see below). Proust, I suspect, sought to complicate our estimate of them without fundamentally changing it.

34. *SaG* 354. The word "ladylike" appears in the French text (*SeG* 300).

35. Nor the head of her husband, who had earlier assumed that the baron was wholly indifferent to titles. "Vous en êtes" (*SeG* 332), he says to the baron. "You are of *one of us*" in disdaining them (*SaG* 393), whereupon the baron casually lists his own titles, starting with Duke of Brabant (*SaG* 395). Later on, when Madame Verdurin wants to know if the baron is among those already invited for a carriage excursion, she asks him, "Are you one of them?" (*SaG* 1002) / "Est-ce que vous en êtes?" (*SeG* 359). Since the baron doesn't know that she's referring to an excursion party and evidently thinks she is alluding to his homosexuality, he sardonically calls it "a strange question" and declines to answer it (*SaG* 426). In both cases, a phrase used to solidify the baron's membership in the Verdurin circle simply underscores his distance from it.

36. The only one proposed by Madame Verdurin and also accepted by the baron is Saintine, "once the flower of the Guermantes set," who has made what the baron considers a socially disadvantageous marriage but whom the baron continues to see (*CAP* 260–61). Nevertheless, as we have seen, the guests for this party also include one of the least fashionable members of the faithful, the hapless Saniette.

37. Like the evening on which the Duke and Duchess of Guermantes ignore the imminence of death among their relatives and friends (including Swann) in order to attend a round of parties, this party is haunted by a death for which Madame Verdurin nervily declares that she "feel[s] no regret at all" (*CAP* 269). It is not immediately clear that the princess is dead. On entering the house, Brichot regretfully tells Madame Verdurin that she is "seriously ill," but shortly afterward Madame Verdurin says, "I don't mean to say that I wouldn't rather she were still alive" (*CAP* 270).

38. When the Queen of Naples shows exemplary courtesy to Madame Verdurin, she acts on her own initiative, with no prompting from the baron.

39. Just as the Princess of Parma implicitly rewrites the lesson that one should spurn the rich and invite only the "poor, maimed, lame, or blind" (Luke 14: 13), the baron twists for his own ends the words of Christ, who told his disciples that he spoke to others in parables because "hearing they hear not" (Matt. 13:10). Later on, however, the baron says it doesn't matter what Morel's audience hears "as long as they have tongues and can speak" (*CAP* 316), meaning spread his reputation.

40. The English parts of this sentence are my translation of the French. In revealing the crucial difference between *Patronne* and *maîtresse*, this passage clearly shows how misleading it is to translate both as "mistress," as Scott-Moncrieff et al. do (*CAP* 314).

41. Thus she resembles not Christ but the church, which, as the narrator notes, prefers "any sacrifice rather than a concession on orthodoxy" (*CAP* 318). She will stop at nothing to preserve the orthodoxy of her clan, to ensure the faithfulness of its members and root out heresy.

42. While Madame Verdurin planned at first to have her husband tell Morel about the baron, she herself completes the task of vilifying him.

43. In *Tess of the d'Urbervilles* (1891), Thomas Hardy's heroine recoils at the prospect of becoming what she calls the "creature" of the rich, seductive Alec: his mannequin, clothed with the "best" his money can buy (Hardy 60). Hardy himself perhaps alludes to Mary Shelley's *Frankenstein*, in which the character typically known as the monster is introduced as Victor Frankenstein's "creature" and poignantly identifies himself as such when he begs Victor to care for him (Shelley 56, 96).

44. This episode may partly explain why the narrator later calls dinner parties "barbarian festivals" (*TR* 1097) ("festins de barbares," *LTR* 617).

CHAPTER 9. JOYCE, WOOLF, CAMUS

1. Letter of October 24, 1920, to Frank Budgen (*L* 2:148).

2. See Ladenson on this point. The only "yes" or "oui" reportedly uttered by either of them was Joyce's response when Proust asked him if he liked truffles (Ellmann 508–9).

3. At different times, William Carlos Williams and Ford Madox Ford both claimed to have been told by Joyce that he and Proust discussed their headaches and stomachaches (D-H 41–42), but Violet Schiff told Richard Ellmann that the conversation never turned to these topics (Ellmann 508n).

4. But Joyce's remark also betrays his ignorance of Proust, whose immense novel shows considerable sensitivity to the feelings of servants, as we have seen. Proust was also thinking of servants in the early hours of the morning after the Majestic dinner, when he invited the Schiffs back to his apartment for more conversation there lest "the poor waiters" at the hotel be forced "to stay up and clean the room after we left and . . . get no rest as they had to be on duty early in the morning" (qtd. D-H 43).

5. Lawrence, "Confessions of Xenos." Joyce offers a glimpse of this paradox in one of the stories he wrote before "The Dead." Near the end of "A Painful Case," James Duffy realizes that by moralistically rejecting a lonely married woman who has offered him her love, he has driven her to suicide and deepened his own isolation. Looking out over Dublin one night from a hill in Phoenix Park, he sees the lights of the city burning

"redly and hospitably in the cold night" but knows that "no-one wanted him; he was outcast from life's feast" ("A Painful Case" 98).

6. "The Dead," 176. To some extent Gabriel here speaks for Joyce himself, who, shortly before writing this story, declared that so far as he could see, the "virtue" of hospitality "does not exist elsewhere in Europe. I have not been just to its beauty: for it is more beautiful naturally in my opinion than what I have seen of England, Switzerland, France, Austria, or Sicily" (*Selected Letters* 109; oddly, Joyce never witnessed the hospitality in Greece.) But as Hillis Miller observes, Gabriel's repeated use of the term "hospitality" makes it ironic, especially in light of the various things that threaten the warmhearted mood of the party, such as the bad cold of Bartell D'Arcy, who refuses to sing for the guests as a whole, and the discourtesy of Miss Ivors, who insists on leaving before dinner is served (Miller, "Irish Hospitality").

7. For the concept of Michael Furey as a ghostly intruder as well as for Joyce's possible debt to the ghosts of Dickens's "Christmas Carol," see Saint-Amour. Hillis Miller likewise construes Furey as a ghostly guest—the last of the dead, such as Patrick Morkan, father of the Morkan sisters, who are hospitably remembered by the living. "Most importantly," Miller writes, "the resurrection of the dead as ghostly guests within consciousness and memory as hosts is dramatized in the climax of the story, Gretta's memory of Michael Furey, who died at seventeen, for love of her" (Miller, "Irish Hospitality"). For more on ghosts and hospitality in Victorian and modern literature, see Thurston.

8. In regions such as Andalusia, North Africa, and the Arctic, "to attempt to sleep with the host's wife or *to refuse to do so* may either of them be infractions of a code of hospitality" (Pitt-Rivers 109, emphasis added). In southern Arabia and present-day Saudi Arabia, however, guests "of the same birth and descent" as the host may be offered "only unmarried blood-relatives of the host, i.e. daughter or sister . . . never the wife of the host" (Dostal 20–21).

9. For a quite different account of how Klossowski challenges "metaphysical notions of identity" in *Roberte Ce Soir* and the other two novels of *The Laws of Hospitality* (a trilogy published between 1954 and 1960), see McNulty 87–174.

10. I quote from Catherine Millet's interview with Laurel Ives in 2009. In her book Millet insists that none of her sexual adventures "ever affected" her life with her partner, Jacques Henric, and also that she would never have told him that his making love to another woman made her angry (Millet 114, 121). But on one occasion, when she asked him if he had gone to dinner with a particular young woman, he accused her of "masochistic jealousy," and she responded with arguments clearly driven by jealousy: "By principally surrounding himself with very young women he was stigmatizing my body, which was the body of a mature woman" (Millet 122).

11. In February 1928, shortly after the death of Hardy, Joyce was asked to contribute an essay on him to a special issue of the *Nouvelle Revue française*. He declined to do so on the grounds that he had not read Hardy in many years, but his letter to the editor plainly indicates that he had once read his novels (*L* 3:169–70), though without specifying which. In any case, Patrick Diskin has plausibly argued that "The Dead" echoes Hardy's *The Woodlanders* (1887), where Grace Melbury tells her husband Edred about

a former lover who, she tells a friend, "died for me!" (chapter 43). Diskin also notes that in both the novel and the story, "the lover meets his death as a result of exposure to rain following on a previous illness," and the wife's revelation changes "the attitude of the husband towards both his wife and her early lover" (Diskin 330–31).

12. *Dubliners* 187. Lusting for Gretta, he yearns to "make her forget the years of their dull existence together and remember only their moments of ecstasy" (186).

13. On the vexed question of whether Tess was seduced or raped, see Heffernan, "'Cruel Persuasion': Seduction, Temptation, and Agency in Hardy's *Tess*," in print and online. Jolanta Wawrzycka has suggested that Gretta herself may have been impregnated by Michael and "whisked away from her young lover to the convent where she could secretly give birth to a child" who was miscarried or born dead (Wawrzycka 71). This seems to me rather a stretch. Gretta's statement about Michael—"I was great with him at that time" (191)—surely does not mean that she was pregnant, for she could hardly be swollen "with" her lover. According to Margot Norris, Gretta's "great" here means "intimate, but more in a sense of intense emotional friendship than passion" (*Dubliners*, Norris 191n2).

14. The former point makes a crucial difference to Angel. "How can we live together," he asks Tess, "while that man lives?—he being your husband in Nature, and not I. If he were dead it might be different" (Hardy 190).

15. A comparable triangle emerges in Sándor Márai's novel *Embers* (1942), which Christopher Hampton adapted for the London stage in 2006. Having invited to his castle a friend named Konrad whom he has known since boyhood and often entertained but has not seen for more than forty years, a wealthy old general named Henrik carefully explains to his dinner guest just how this guest has betrayed him. Though they were once all but lovers (and perhaps that too), Henrik suspects that Konrad wanted to kill him the last time they hunted together on the general's estate; in spite of Konrad's talent, Henrik thought, the poor, slighted man hated him for his wealth and privilege, for being a "general favorite" (156). Also, right after Konrad broke off their friendship by suddenly leaving the hunt without explanation, Henrik learned that Konrad had been having an affair with Henrik's wife (now long dead) even while regularly savoring the intimate friendship and hospitality of them both. Yet in the end the host moves beyond the quest for revenge—his original motive—to something like empathy for his guest. "Do you believe," he asks him, "that what gives our lives their meaning is the passion that suddenly invades us heart, soul, and body, and burns in us forever, no matter what else happens in our lives?" (210). To which Konrad quietly replies, "Why do you ask me? . . . when you know that the answer is yes" (211).

16. In the early hours of the morning after Bloomsday, when Bloom finally enters the bed he shares with Molly, he finds not only "the presence of a human form, female, hers [Molly's]," but also "the imprint of a human form, male, not his [Bloom's]" (17.2123–25).

17. In the words of the catechist of "Eumaeus," Bloom concludes that adultery is "less reprehensible" than a great many other offenses rising in gravity to "criminal assault, manslaughter, wilful and premeditated murder" (*U* 17.2189–90). Bloom is also restrained by his awareness that since he and/or Molly first met Boylan in the shop of Bloom's tailor, George Mesias, they have each played host and guest to the other:

"hospitality extended and received in kind, reciprocated and reappropriated in person" (17.2170–72).

18. 1.235–36, 206–7. Mulligan thus coarsens and condenses Claudius's way of counseling the prince against "unmanly grief" (*Hamlet* 1.2.94). In a bizarre twist on the ghost's revelation that Hamlet's uncle has killed the prince's father, Mulligan has already told Stephen that "the aunt"—meaning Mulligan's aunt—"thinks *you* killed your mother" (1.88, emphasis added).

19. Kenner 55–56n. Given the size and number of Stephen's debts, which he himself tabulates in the next chapter (2.255–59) and which far exceed his monthly pay, it is simply inconceivable, as Kenner notes, that he could be paying the rent.

20. See *Paradiso* 17.58–60 and above, chapter 2.

21. Kenner attributes this point to Arnold Goldman.

22. It is hard to know for certain whether or not Mulligan is gay in the current sense of the word. Though he claims to be insatiably heterosexual (a *"Fertiliser and Incubator"* of young women, 14.660), he shows a possible trace of homosexual jealousy when he warns Stephen against the would-be advances of Bloom at the end of "Scylla and Charybdis": "Did you see his eye? He looked upon you to lust after you. I fear thee, ancient mariner. O, Kinch, thou art in peril! Get thee a breechpad" (9.1211).

23. So say several modern-day Dubliners with whom I have corresponded on this matter. But Terence Killeen writes as follows: "Married women, in correspondence, would be addressed by their husband's initial: in the case of Noreen's mother, for instance, she was addressed in letters to her as Mrs P. Donohue while her husband, Patrick, was alive. She became Mrs Mary Donohue after his death. So that was the basic principle until well after Bloom's day. The only proviso is that Molly, because of her professional career, might have been treated differently. She wouldn't have been known as 'Mrs L. Bloom' on stage. She'd probably have been called 'Marion Bloom.' So the letter from Boylan could be seen as a professional communication (as indeed it was, in more ways than one) and 'Mrs Marion Bloom' might have been just about excusable on that basis" (e-mail of October 14, 2010, to Michael Groden, who forwarded it to me). Alternatively, one might infer that Boylan is addressing Molly as if Bloom were already dead, just as the suitors of Homer's Penelope presumed that Odysseus was dead. (I owe this fascinating suggestion to George Lazarus.) Apropos the naming of widows in Joyce's Dublin, his immense cast of characters includes "Mrs. Florence MacCabe, relict of the late Patk MacCabe, deeply lamented, of Bride Street" (3.33–34). A further complication is that when Molly lost a pair of suede gloves, Bloom wanted her to advertise in the *Irish Times* for their return to "Mrs Marion Bloom" (18.256).

24. Strictly speaking, the citizen is hardly the host of the pub, since he neither owns it nor buys drinks for anyone in it. But since he clearly corresponds to Homer's Polyphemos, he is structurally the host in this episode.

25. Said critiques not just the imperialist reduction of native people to a particular essence but also essentializing acts of native self-definition provoked by imperialism. What Said writes about "post-colonial national states" largely applies to the xenophobic citizen's conception of a still-colonial Ireland. "The liabilities of such essences as the

Celtic spirit, *negritude*, or Islam," Said writes, "are clear: they have much to do not only with the native manipulators, who also use them to cover up contemporary faults, corruptions, tyrannies, but also with the embattled imperial contexts out of which they came and in which they were felt to be necessary" (Said 17). Though essentialism "is typically defined in opposition to difference" (Fuss xi), Said rhetorically asks, "Who in India or Algeria today can confidently separate out the British or French component of the past from present actualities, and who in Britain or France can draw a clear circle around British London or French Paris that would exclude the impact of India and Algeria upon those two imperial cities?" (Said 15). It is equal folly to think that Irishness can be purged of either its English or its Jewish ingredients.

26. "We want no more strangers in our house," says the citizen (12.1150–51). As already noted, "stranger in the house" is what the Irish traditionally called the English occupiers of their native land.

27. On Odysseus's use of "*Outis*," see chapter 1, note 12.

28. Speaking of Ulysses to his friend Frank Budgen, Joyce called him a "war dodger who tried to evade military service by simulating madness" (Ellmann 435). Joyce refers to a non-Homeric story: when Ulysses heard he would be forced to wander for twenty years if he went to Troy, he feigned madness by yoking a horse and an ox to a plough. But when Palamedes put his infant son Telemachus in front of his plough, Ulysses had to stop the plough and thus reveal his sanity (Hyginus).

29. In her totally uninhibited monologue, Molly refers to nothing more than heavy petting with any man she ever knew before Bloom. As a result, it is quite clear that Boylan is the only other man who has bedded her.

30. See Heffernan, "Joyce's Merrimanic Heroine," 757–58.

31. On the night of November 9–10, 1938, in retaliation for the assassination of a German diplomat by a German-born Polish Jew in Paris, SS stormtroopers and civilians attacked Jews and their houses throughout Nazi Germany and parts of Austria. During this rampage, which came to be called the Night of Broken Glass, they smashed windows, ransacked over sixteen hundred synagogues, destroyed buildings, killed ninety-one Jews, and took thirty thousand Jewish men to concentration camps, where more than a thousand died.

32. See *Odyssey* 15.68–74 and above, chapter 1.

33. "And this homelessness, beside which is the homelessness of Joyce himself, strikes us as a joyful tragedy in Stephen's freedom and solitude and exaltation" (Seldes in Deming 2:238). So wrote Gilbert Seldes in an extraordinarily perceptive review of *Ulysses* that appeared in the *Nation* on August 30, 1922.

34. On Woolf's profoundly ambivalent response to Joyce's novel, see Heffernan, "Tracking." In my opinion *Mrs Dalloway* confirms the truth of what T. S. Eliot wrote of *Ulysses* in 1923: "It is a book to which we are all indebted, and from which none of us can escape" (*Dial*, November 1923, in Deming 1:268).

35. Morris Beja plausibly calculates that *Mrs Dalloway* is set on June 20, 1923 (Notes 147). For an extensive analysis of the parallels between the two novels, see Richter. Leopold Bloom's peregrinations around Dublin have been often diagrammed (notably by Don Gifford), and on unnumbered pages right after his introduction, Beja diagrams "The

London of Mrs Dalloway," showing just where she goes in the city during the course of the day (Beja xxxiv–xxxv).

36. Even after enumerating all of the borrowings and parallels between *Ulysses* and *Mrs Dalloway*, Richter rightly declares, "They cannot be called imitation. Rather, it is a question of transformation, of Woolf taking ideas from Joyce and adapting them to the particular needs of her novel" (Richter 316).

37. Writing of *To the Lighthouse* (1927), Elizabeth McArthur notes that Woolf "endows her female characters with an interiority largely lacking in *Swann's Way*" by giving her two chief female characters, Mrs. Ramsay and Lily Briscoe, "strong interior voices, extensive imaginative vision, and creative agency" (McArthur 331). The same could be said of Clarissa Dalloway.

38. Though Bloom aims to pair Stephen off with Milly, as I have noted, he clearly stresses the attractions of Molly, and in her monologue she savors the prospect of a passionate affair with him (*U* 18.1363–65) if he becomes their long-term guest.

39. Apropos Woolf's adoration of Proust's novel, the first volume put her "in a state of amazement; as if a miracle were being done before my eyes. . . . One has to put the book down and gasp" (*L* 2.566).

40. "The perfect hostess he called her (she had cried over it in her bedroom), she had the makings of the perfect hostess, he said" (*MD* 8).

41. See *Phineas Redux*, volume 2, chapter 13, for Lady Glencora's management of Mr. Bonteen.

42. In notes dated October 6, 1922, she set down "thoughts upon beginning a book to be called, perhaps, At Home: or The Party." Its eight possible chapters would begin with a story called "Mrs Dalloway in Bond Street" (which she had just written) and "The Prime Minister" (which she was then working on and would finish by early November) and end with "The Party," on which she wrote, "all must converge . . . at the end" (qtd. Beja xi–xii). "Mrs Dalloway in Bond Street" (*CSF* 146–53) appeared as a story in *The Dial* (July 1923); "The Prime Minister" (*CSF* 316–23) was never published in Woolf's lifetime but furnished material for *Mrs Dalloway*.

43. And Richard, we soon learn, "didn't care a straw what became of Emigration; about that letter, whether the editor put it in or not" (85).

44. Diane McGee contends that Clarissa's "political function is a major and evident one" (McGee 131), and her party does include some political conversation. Besides Lady Bruton's private talk with the prime minister, Peter Walsh decides to go (he tells himself) "because he wanted to ask Richard what they were doing in India—the conservative duffers" (*MD* 119–20). But Peter also wants the latest news on theater, music, "and mere gossip" (119–20), and his main motive (unstated) is to see more of Clarissa—for reasons having nothing to do with politics.

45. Tseng likewise notes that the London of this novel is a city regulated by political power: "The synchronous order, manifestly punctuated by Big Ben's strokes, organizes the city's innumerable lives and activities into an imagined organism. Forged in Westminster, the solemn seat of power, this official temporality epitomizes the so-called "Concept-city" (de Certeau 95), the commensurate order of the time-space of the city. The ubiquitous strokes of Big Ben are analogous to the recurrent state

symbols such as the flag, the Queen, Buckingham Palace, the Union Jack, the British imperial dominions and the Prime Minister. Together, they signify the official social and political order imposed on the city dwellers of London" (Tseng 241).

46. In notes made on November 9, 1922, soon after she started writing *Mrs Dalloway*, Woolf wrote, "All must bear finally upon the party at the end; which expresses life, in every variety . . . while Septimus dies" (qtd. Henke, MDCS 146n24).

47. Lady Bruton also responds very coolly when, after her lunch, Richard asks her if she is coming to the party. "She might come; or she might not come. Clarissa had wonderful energy. Parties terrified Lady Bruton" (*MD* 84).

48. But for Clarissa even these moments of social triumph "had a hollowness" that does not touch the heart with anything like her "real" hatred of Miss Kilman as "Elizabeth's seducer" (*MD* 129–30).

49. "Our status outside the inner circle," notes Diane McGee, "is made clear by our not being invited to the pre-party dinner. The dinner remains so private that even the guest list is not divulged; we do not know which of the party guests were among the select few invited" (McGee 127).

50. As Morris Philipson has noted, the prime minister who comes to Clarissa's party is very different from the all-but-invisible and wholly inaccessible Very Important Person who is thought to be lurking behind the closed blinds of a motorcar in Bond Street on the morning of the party (Philipson 132).

51. According to Leonard Woolf, "The idea of a party always excited [Virginia], and in practice she was very sensitive to the actual mental and physical excitement of the party itself, the rise of temperature of mind and body, the ferment and fountain of noise" (*A* 4:98). While Clarissa seems a little alarmed by the decibels at her own party ("But the noise!" she said. "The noise!"), Professor Brierly assures her that this is "the sign of a successful party," and when she turns away to speak to Lord Gayton and Nancy Blow, who are silently standing side by side against the curtains, she seems to fault them for being too quiet: "Not that *they* added perceptibly to the noise of the party," she thinks (*MD* 131).

52. Aside from Septimus Smith, who presumably symbolizes all of those traumatized in any way by the war (but who is not invited to the party), the only reference made in the novel to soldiers or veterans in London is Peter Walsh's brief description of uniformed "boys" laying a wreath at the "empty tomb" in Whitehall (40). On the maimed British veterans of the First World War, see Nicolson. While Molly Bloom gives no parties in *Ulysses*, she throws a coin to a one-legged sailor crutching himself through Dublin (*U* 10:228, 251–53) shortly after he gets nothing from Father Conmee, who nevertheless thinks, "*but not for long*, of soldiers and sailors, whose legs had been shot off by cannonballs, ending their days in some pauper ward" (*U* 10:10–14, emphasis added).

53. Though his stalking adventure ends at this point, it recalls what Woolf would probably have called an "indecent" incident in the "Calypso" chapter of *Ulysses*, which she knew very well (she read the chapter three times; see Heffernan, "Tracking"). Waiting to buy a pork kidney for his breakfast and finding the "nextdoor girl" (his neighbor's servant) just ahead of him at the counter, Bloom wants to follow her home if he can,

walking "behind her moving hams. Pleasant to see first thing in the morning" (4.172–73). But the butcher takes so long that she slips away from him.

54. When Clarissa tells him she is having a party that night "which I shan't ask you to," he asks her why she wouldn't, and though she doesn't answer right away, she shouts the invitation after him as he leaves (*MD* 32–33, 37–38).

55. Though Richard has virtually nothing in common with Leopold Bloom, his brief encounter with the vagrant curiously resembles Bloom's much longer sighting of Gerty McDowell. In both cases a man and a woman who are complete strangers to each other communicate purely by visual signs, not words; in both cases there is "time for a spark between them"; and in both cases the man pities the woman both silently and ineffectually: on discovering Gerty's lameness, Bloom thinks, "Poor girl" (*U* 13.772) but does nothing to help her.

56. In 1910 at least 1,500 men and women seeking handouts gathered every night on London's Embankment, a short walk from Green Park, where Woolf's vagrant appears. Sleeping conditions in the casual wards were so bad that on one night in October 1913, 692 people, including 141 women, preferred either sitting on a shelter bench or sleeping in the street (Humphreys 116, 124). By 1930 the occupancy rate in casual wards throughout England and Wales rose to more than 13,000, and the total number of vagrants was probably four times that number (Humphreys 126). Given those facts, I think it reasonable to infer that on the night of June 20, 1923, when Peter Walsh wonders if "everyone" in London is stepping out to a party, well over a thousand vagrants must have been hungrily tramping its streets.

57. We later learn that just over two years previous, Miss Kilman had "turned into a church" where the sermon and service moved her to tears, and when she went to call on the preacher, Mr. Whittaker, he told her that "the Lord had shown her the way" (*MD* 93).

58. The passage is a little puzzling because Clarissa here reacts to what purports to be only the *thoughts* of Miss Kilman, not to anything the woman says or does openly.

59. We see Miss Kilman only from the outside and chiefly through the eyes of Clarissa. Even though *Mrs Dalloway*, like Joyce's *Ulysses*, democratically enters the consciousnesses of many characters, Anne Fernihough aptly notes that it never enters the consciousness of Miss Kilman, the "stereotypical embittered spinster" whose "mind is closed off from us" and who "remains in the mind as a 'type' rather than a fully individuated consciousness" (Fernihough 77–78).

60. Early in the day we are told that Elizabeth "cared not a straw" for gloves while her mother "had a passion" for them (*MD* 11). Just before she leaves with Miss Kilman, Elizabeth fetches her gloves simply because, we are told, she cannot bear to see Miss Kilman and her mother stand together in mutual hatred (*MD* 93). But the glove fetching nonetheless shows her mother's influence.

61. Suggestively enough, the loathsomeness of Miss Kilman comes to Clarissa's mind just as she is chafing at the thought of having to invite Ellie Henderson.

62. As already noted, one of her young admirers, Willie Titcomb, silently compares her to a hyacinth (*MD* 140). In T. S. Eliot's *The Waste Land* (1922), which Woolf knew well, the voice of what sounds like a young woman says, "You gave me hyacinths first a year ago; / They called me the hyacinth girl" (ll. 35–36).

63. By contrast Lady Bradshaw, who gives "large dinner-parties every Thursday night to the profession" (presumably her husband's medical colleagues and their wives), seems to have surrendered all power—social and otherwise—to her husband, with "the slow sinking, water-logged, of her will into his" (*MD* 72, 76).

64. "Between *protecting* yourself from being violated (by those who would 'force' another's soul) and *opening* yourself up to life-enhancing experience is created the tension of conflict between being yourself and becoming your best self. The former is retrospective; the latter is prospective" (Philipson 127).

65. The first of them, "Mrs Dalloway in Bond Street," appeared in *The Dial* in 1923, and Leonard Woolf published four of them in *A Haunted House and Other Stories* (1944). In 1973 they appeared as *Mrs Dalloway's Party*, edited and with an introduction by Stella McNichol (Hogarth Press). I quote them as reprinted in Prose 24–62.

66. "For a party makes things either much more real, or much less real, she thought; she saw in a flash to the bottom of Robert Haydon's heart; she saw through everything. She saw the truth" (Prose 51).

67. Apropos the Bradshaws, Peter tells Sally they are "damnable humbugs," which makes her laugh (*MD* 143). Different as they are or have become, the three old friends clearly share an aversion to Bradshaw.

68. But Septimus is not wholly cut off from others. One of the rare moments of true communication in this novel occurs when Septimus sees his wife, Rezia, trimming an "absurdly small" hat for Mrs. Peters. When he calls it "an organ grinder's monkey's hat," they laugh "together, poking fun privately like married people" (*MD* 107). Unlike the laughter raised elsewhere by stories that ladies are not allowed to hear, this joke is shared with the reader.

69. In "Character in Fiction" (1924), Woolf observes that a writer seeking to reach "his unknown reader" is like a hostess building a bridge to "her unknown guest" (*E* 3:431).

70. Just after Mansfield's death in January 1923, Woolf told her diary, "I was jealous of her writing—the only writing I have ever been jealous of" (*D* 2:227).

71. She thus reenacts Septimus's literalization of her own metaphor for stepping outside in the morning ("What a plunge!"), which itself reenacts her youthful plunging "into the open air" at Bourton (*MD* 5).

72. See Woolf's introduction to the Modern Library edition of *Mrs Dalloway* (1928) in *MD* 198. Like the Editor in Goethe's *Sorrows of Young Werther*, Clarissa survives to bear witness to the suicide of another. But while Goethe's Editor dispassionately records what Werther did and calmly transcribes what he wrote about his feelings up to the moment of his death, Clarissa can only imagine the feelings of Septimus, whose suicide she finds heroic.

73. In *Cymbeline*, this is the first line of a song that two brothers sing to Imogen when she appears to be dead after taking a potion (4.2.258–81).

74. As noted above, "How delightful to see you" is what she says "to every one" (*MD* 124) before the Bradshaws arrive. Before she can say it to the newly arrived Lady Bradshaw, however, she is interrupted by the lady's apology for being late (*MD* 135).

75. See Visser 94–95 and Derrida, *OH* 45.

76. O'Brien 116–20. Taking his cue from Derrida, *OH* 53–55, O'Brien notes, "The right to take life is a central factor in the creation of a nation. In O'Connor's story, the 'guests'

in question are doomed, despite the gradual relationship that dawns between both sets of very similar young men, to become transformed into ghosts by the end of the narrative" (O'Brien 121). To some extent, the IRA guards separately personify the conflict between sympathy for the hostages and nationalist "duty." While Bonaparte (the narrator) and Noble come to see the Englishmen as their chums, the other two— especially Jeremiah Donovan, the leader of the guards, who instigates the executions— has "no great love" for them (O'Connor 176).

77. Though their struggle was brutally suppressed by what Derrida calls the "state terrorism" of the French police, the French Parliament in the 1990s retrospectively construed the conflict as a "war" *on* "terrorists." But "the terrorists," Derrida writes, "were considered and . . . are considered in much of the world as freedom fighters and heroes of national independence" (*Philosophy in a Time of Terror* [2003] 131, qtd. Still 67).

78. This picture of the gendarme and his prisoner recalls Pozzo roped to Lucky in Samuel Beckett's *Waiting for Godot*, a play Camus surely knew. Published in October 1952, it was first performed in Paris two months later, four years before Camus wrote his story.

79. I refer to the English translation by Justin O'Brien as G (for "Guest") and to the French original as H (for "Hôte"). Translations followed by no page reference are my own.

80. "Cost" 250–51. Davis takes the story as a rewriting of Camus's early novel *L'Etranger* (1942). "Both texts," he says, "describe a confrontation between a white man and an Arab against a background of violence, and both are concerned with the authority of the law. . . . However, in [*L'Etranger*], Meursault's act of violence against the Arab is translated into an act of generosity. Meursault kills in order to submit himself to the law . . . whereas Daru rejects the law and refuses to follow the instructions transmitted to him by Balducci" (Davis, "Cost" 248). See also Jillian Beer, "Le Regard."

81. Derrida, "Etre Chez Soi" 255, trans. Carroll, "Remains" 820n13. All of Derrida's original words, including those in parentheses, are italicized. The explanatory words in brackets are mine.

82. Davis observes that in Camus's story, as in the ethical writings of Levinas, "hospitality entails an acceptance of risk. The guest may turn out to be a murderer or rapist (and so might the host). In the context of an ethics of hospitality, I can never be entirely sure who or what I am inviting in. . . . When Daru invites a murderer into his house, feeds him, and sleeps alongside him, he knows that he might literally be killed in his own bed" (Davis, "Cost" 251).

83. Kritzman himself notes that Camus's story challenges both paternalism and "the historically determined concepts of master and slave" (Kritzman 574). Philosophically, one might also say that Daru respects the Arab's existential freedom and will not compromise it—unlike, let us say, Tom Sawyer in Mark Twain's *Huckleberry Finn*, who takes full charge of Jim's "escape" from slavery after he has already been freed and in the process humiliates him.

84. Levinas insists that neither empathy nor sympathy can bridge the gulf between the self and the other, that "the relationship with the other is a relationship with a Mystery" (*Time and the Other* 75).

85. Though the prisoner speaks an Arabic that is rendered for us into French, we have no reason to believe that the words written on the blackboard were not originally French.

The chalker's use of "tu," the familiar form of "you," mirrors Daru's use of "tu" with the Arab from the start of their conversation, as in "Tu as faim?" (H 172). "Tu" plays no part in subordinating one man to the other.

86. A further irony is that their figurative "brother" has killed his nearly literal brother, that is, his cousin.

87. In "The Guest," as in *The Stranger*, Camus hardens the mystery by giving the Arab no name, as Still notes (177). The sense of desolation that grips Daru in the final words of the story, where he feels absolutely "alone" (G 109), suggests not so much a respect for the mystery of the other as the despairing conviction that all Arabs—like the Congolese natives seen through the eyes of Conrad's Kurtz—are brutes.

88. Noting this point, though with no specific reference to "The Guest," Edward Said argues that Camus's novels and short stories confirm and consolidate the legitimacy of French claims to Algeria (Said 216–19). While Derrida seems to commend Daru's sensitivity to the rights of the Algerian "in the Algerian's home" (see above), the story itself may be read as suggesting that native Algerians are incapable of governing themselves. Unlike French Algerian liberals, including Derrida, who backed Algerian independence, Camus is said to have "dreamt rather of a Franco-Muslim community in which cultural differences would be accepted within the framework of political equality, guaranteed by French sovereignty" (Baring 243).

89. Hospitality, writes Peter Melville, "founds itself on a certain inequity between the guest and the host, an inequity which the 'generosity' of a welcome both guarantees and aims to resolve." Structurally, the host enjoys a "hierarchical authority over the guest" (P. Melville 15). Jesse Browner defines this power in feral terms. The host, he writes, is like "a predator who has killed his prey and owns it," while the guest is like "a scavenger who finds his meal laid out for him by an unknown benefactor who may return at any moment to claim it" (Browner 11–12).

90. "Poisoning," writes Gail Bell, "is an up close and personal crime. The victim is deceived into swallowing a toxic dose concealed in a benign carrier like food or drink, thereby betraying one of the foundations of all social dealings between fellow humans, the assumption of benign intent. In Ukraine, the rules of hospitality demand that the guest eat and drink heartily at the host's table, even when he suspects him of ill intent" (Gail Bell 11). To my knowledge, it has not yet been established that Satsyuk was complicit in the poisoning of Yushchenko, who was then a candidate for the presidency of Ukraine, but the dinner took place at Satsyuk's dasha outside Kiev.

91. Margaret Visser notes that rules for the handling of utensils—such as the rule that knives must be set facing in toward the plate and must not be held upright—spring from the need to forestall the violence that might otherwise be done with them (Visser 98).

BIBLIOGRAPHY

Abel, Elizabeth. "Narrative Structure(s) and Female Development: The Case of *Mrs. Dalloway.*" In *The Voyage In: The Fictions of Female Development*, ed. Elizabeth Abel et al., 161–83. London: University Press of London, 1983.

ACC. *Ancient Christian Commentary on Scripture: Old Testament.* Vol. 2, Genesis 12–50. Edited by Thomas C. Oden and Mark Sheridan. Chicago: University of Chicago Press, 2001.

Ackley, Clifford S., with Ronni Baer, Thomas E. Rassieur, and William B. Robinson. *Rembrandt's Journey: Painter Draftsman Etcher.* Boston: Museum of Fine Arts, 2003.

Aeschylus. *Agamemnon.* Translated by Richmond Lattimore. *The Complete Greek Tragedies.* Vol. 1: *Aeschylus.* Edited by David Greene and Richmond Lattimore. Chicago: University of Chicago Press, 1992.

Ahl, Frederick. *Metaformations: Soundplay and Wordplay in Ovid and Other Classical Poets.* Ithaca: Cornell University Press, 1985.

Albee, Edward. *Who's Afraid of Virginia Woolf?* New York: Pocket Books/Giant Cardinal, 1964.

Allott, Miriam, ed. *The Poems of John Keats.* New York: Norton, 1972.

Alter, Robert. *The Five Books of Moses: A Translation with Commentary.* New York: Norton, 2004.

Ames, Christopher. *The Life of the Party: Festive Vision in Modern Fiction.* Athens: University of Georgia Press, 1991.

Anon. *Sir Gawain and the Green Knight.* Edited by J. R. R. Tolkien and E. V. Gordon. Revised by Norman Davis. Oxford: Clarendon Press 1967. Revised by David Seaman, University of Virginia Library Electronic Center, 1994.

Anon. "The Wandering Jew." *Miscellanies and Collections, 1750–1900* [from *Percy's Reliques*]. Vol. 2: *Ancient Songs and Ballads, Series the Second. Book III,* 1767.

Apollonios Rhodios. *Argonautika.* Translated by Peter Green. Berkeley: University of California Press, 1997.

Apuleius. *The Golden Ass.* Translated by Jack Lindsay. Bloomington: Indiana University Press, 1962.

Aristotle. "Poetics." *The Complete Works of Aristotle.* Vol. 2. Revised Oxford Translation. Edited by Jonathan Barnes. Princeton: Princeton University Press, 1984.

Arndt, Walter. "Introduction." Pushkin, *Eugene Onegin*, xiii–xxii.

Auerbach, Erich. *Mimesis: The Representation of Reality in Western Literature.* Translated by Willard Trask. Princeton: Princeton University Press, 1953.

Augustine. *Sermons on Selected Lessons of the New Testament.* Edited by Philip Schaff. Translated by R. G. Macmullen. New York: Christian Literature Publishing, 1886.

Austen, Jane. *Pride and Prejudice.* Edited by Donald Gray. 2d ed. New York: Norton, 1996.

Austin, R. G., ed. *P. Vergili Maronis Aeneidos Liber Secundus.* Oxford: Oxford University Press, 1964.

———. *P. Vergili Maronis Aeneidos Liber Primus.* Oxford: Oxford University Press, 1971.

———. *P. Vergili Maronis Aeneidos Liber Quartus.* Oxford: Oxford University Press, 1955.

———. *P. Vergili Maronis Aeneidos Liber Sextus.* Oxford: Oxford University Press, 1977.

Bal, Mieke. *Death and Dissymmetry: The Politics of Coherence in the Book of Judges.* Chicago: University of Chicago Press, 1988.

Ballaster, Ros. *Seductive Forms: Women's Amatory Fiction from 1684 to 1740.* Oxford: Clarendon, 1992.

Baring, Edward. "Jacques Derrida." *Critical Inquiry* 36:2 (Winter 2010): 239–61.

Barron, W. R. J. *Trawthe and Treason.* Manchester: Manchester University Press, 1980.

Bate, Walter Jackson. *John Keats.* New York: Oxford University Press, 1966.

Bayle, Pierre. *The Dictionary Historical and Critical of Mr. Peter Bayle*, 1734–38. 5 vols. New York: Garland, 1984.

Baym, Nina. "Revision and Thematic Change in *The Portrait of a Lady.*" James, *Portrait*, edited by Robert Bamberg, 620–34.

Beer, Gillian. "Le Regard: Face to Face in Albert Camus's 'L'Hôte.'" *French Studies* 56.2 (2002): 179–92.

Beja, Morris. "Introduction" and "Notes." Woolf, *Mrs. Dalloway*, xi–xxxii, 146–59, respectively.

Bell, Gail. "Murder He Ate." *New York Times*, December 19, 2004, News of the Week, 11.

Bell, Quentin. *Virginia Woolf: A Biography.* New York: Harcourt Brace Jovanovich, 1972.

Bellow, Saul. "A Jewish Writer in America—II" (1988). *New York Review of Books* 58.17, November 10, 2011, 29.

Bemelmans, Ludwig. "San Simeon, Circa 1943: The Castle Rocked." *New York Times: Fashions of the Times Magazine*, February 25, 2001, 147.

Benedict, Saint. *The Rule of Benedict.* Translated and edited by Carolinne White. London: Penguin, 2008.

Benveniste, Emile. "'L'Hospitalité." In *Le Vocabulaire des Institutions Indo-Européennes* 1:87–101. Paris: Minuit, 1969.

Berry, George Ricker. *The Classic Greek Dictionary.* New York: Follett, 1956.

Beye, Charles. *Ancient Epic Poetry: Homer, Apollonius, Virgil.* Ithaca: Cornell University Press, 1993.

Bible. *The Complete Bible: An American Translation. The Old Testament*, trans. J. M. Powis et al.; *The Apocrypha* and *The New Testament*, trans. Edgar J. Goodspeed. Chicago: University of Chicago Press, 1948.

"Bitter Guest Worker Story, A." Editorial. *New York Times*, February 4, 2010, A24.

Blake, William. *The Marriage of Heaven and Hell*. London: Oxford University Press, 1975.

Blanning, Tim. *The Pursuit of Glory: Europe, 1648–1815*. New York: Viking, 2007.

Bolchazy, Ladislaus J. *Hospitality in Early Rome: Livy's Concept of Its Humanizing Force*. Chicago: Ares, 1977.

Booth, Wayne. *The Rhetoric of Fiction*. Chicago: University of Chicago Press, 1961.

Bowman, Richard G. "Narrative Criticism: Human Purpose in Conflict with Divine Presence." In Yee, *Judges and Method*, 17–44.

Bradley, Edward. "The Face of Reconciliation: Beyond War and Other Forms of Murderous Violence." Lecture, 2007.

Bragg, Rick. "Afghan and Pakistani Tribe Lives by Its Guns and Honor." *New York Times*, October 21, 2001, 1, B5.

Brontë, Emily. *Wuthering Heights*. Edited by William M. Sale Jr. and Richard J. Dunn. 3d ed. New York: Norton, 1990.

Brooks, Peter. *Realist Vision*. New Haven: Yale University Press, 2005.

Brown, Huntington. "The Gloss to the Ancient Mariner." *Modern Language Quarterly* 6 (1945): 319–24.

Browner, Jesse. *The Duchess Who Wouldn't Sit Down: An Informal History of Hospitality*. New York: Bloomsbury, 2004.

Browning, Elizabeth Barrett. *Aurora Leigh*. 4th ed. (1859). In *The Works of Elizabeth Barrett Browning*, edited by Sandra Donaldson, vol. 3. London: Pickering and Chatto, 2010.

Budgen, Frank. *James Joyce and the Making of* Ulysses. New York: Smith and Haas, 1934.

Bunyan, John. *The Pilgrim's Progress*. Edited by Cynthia Wall. New York: Norton, 2009.

Bush, Douglas, ed. *John Keats, Selected Poems and Letters*. Boston: Houghton Mifflin Riverside, 1959.

Byron, Lord. *Byron*. Edited by Jerome McGann. New York: Oxford University Press, 1986.

Campbell, J. L., ed. *A Collection of Highland Rites and Customs*. London: Folklore Society, 1975.

Camus, Albert. "The Guest" [G]. In *Exile and the Kingdom*, trans. Justin O'Brien, 85–109. New York: Vintage, 1991.

———. "L'Hôte" [H]. In *L'Exil et le Royaume*, ed. Alain Schaffner. In *Oeuvres Complètes*, ed. Raymond Gay-Croisier et al., 4:46–58. Paris: Gallimard, 2008.

Caraher, Brian G. "Trieste, Dublin, Galway: Joyce, Journalism, 1912." In *Joyce on the Threshold*, ed. Anne Fogarty, 132–50. Gainesville: University Press of Florida, 2005.

Carr, Jean Ferguson. "The Polemics of Incomprehension: Mother and Daughter in *Pride and Prejudice*." In *Tradition and the Talents of Women*, ed. Florence Howe, 68–86. Urbana: University of Illinois Press, 1991.

Carroll, David. " 'Remains' of Algeria: Justice, Hospitality, Politics." *MLN* 121.4 (2006): 808–27.

Carter, William C. *Marcel Proust: A Life*. New Haven: Yale University Press, 2000.

Chase, Karen, ed. Middlemarch *in the 21st Century*. Oxford: Oxford University Press, 2006.

Chaucer, Geoffrey. "The Franklin's Tale." In *The Tales of Canterbury*, ed. Robert A. Pratt, 391–412. Boston: Houghton Mifflin, 1974.

Cicero, Marcus Tullius. *In Verrem Actionis Secundae*. In *Scripta Quae Manserunt Omnia*, ed. C. F. W. Mueller. Leipzig: Teubner, 1901.

Cleveland, William L. *A History of the Modern Middle East*. 2d ed. Boulder: Westview, 2000.

Cohen, Jeffrey Jerome. "Decapitation and Coming of Age: Constructing Masculinity and the Monstrous." In *The Arthurian Yearbook III*, ed. Keith Busby, 173–92. New York: Garland, 1993.

Coleridge, S. T. *Biographia Literaria* [*BL*]. Edited by James Engell and Walter Jackson Bate. 2 vols. Bollingen Series 75. Princeton: Princeton University Press, 1983.

———. *The Complete Poems* [*CP*]. Edited by William Keach. New York: Penguin, 1997.

———. *The Friend* [*F*]. 2 vols. Edited by Barbara E. Rooke. Bollingen Series 25. Princeton: Princeton University Press, 1969.

———. *Lectures 1795: On Politics and Religion* [*L 1795*]. Edited by Lewis Patton and Peter Mann. Princeton: Princeton University Press, 1971.

———. *Lectures 1818–19: On the History of Philosophy* [*L 1818*]. 2 vols. Edited by J. R. DeJ. Jackson. Princeton: Princeton University Press, 2000.

———. *Notebooks* [*N*]. Edited by Kathleen Coburn. New York: Pantheon, 1957–61.

———. *Poetry and Prose* [*PP*]. Edited by Nicholas Halmi, Paul Magnuson, and Raimonda Modiano. Norton Critical Edition. New York: Norton, 2004.

———. *Shakespearean Criticism*. Edited by Thomas Middleton Raysor. 2 vols. 2d ed. London: J. M. Dent, 1960.

Connolly, Arthur. *Journey to the North of India Overland Through Russia, Persia, and Affghaunistan*. 2 vols. London: Richard Bentley, 1834.

Connors, Catherine. *Petronius the Poet*. Cambridge: Cambridge University Press, 1998.

Conrad, Joseph. *Heart of Darkness*. Edited by Robert Kimbrough. 3d ed. New York: Norton, 1988.

Conradi, Peter. "The Metaphysical Hostess: The Cult of Personal Relations in the Modern English Novel." *ELH* 48.2 (1981): 427–53.

Conte, Gian Biagio. *The Hidden Author: An Interpretation of Petronius' Satyricon*. Translated by Elaine Fantham. Berkeley: University of California Press.

Coope, Lane. "An Aquatic in *The Rime of the Ancient Mariner*." *MLN* 20.4 (1905): 107–8.

Dalechamp, Caleb. *Christian Hospitalitie* . . . . Cambridge: Thomas Buck, 1632.

Dante Alighieri. *Inferno*. Translated by Robert Hollander and Jean Hollander. Introduction and notes by Robert Hollander. New York: Doubleday, 2000.

———. *Paradiso*. Translated by Robert Hollander and Jean Hollander. Introduction and notes by Robert Hollander. New York: Doubleday, 2007.

Davenport-Hines, Richard. *A Night at the Majestic: Proust and the Great Modernist Dinner Party of 1922*. London: Faber and Faber, 2006.

Davis, Colin. "The Cost of Being Ethical." *Common Knowledge* 9.2 (2003): 241–53.

———. "Diasporic Subjectivities." *French Cultural Studies* 17.3 (2006): 335–48.

Dawe, R. D. *The Odyssey: Translation and Analysis*. Lewes: Book Guild, 1993.

De Felice, John. *Roman Hospitality*. Marco Polo Monographs, 6. Warren Center, Penn.: Shangri-La Publications, 2001.

Deleuze, Gilles. *Proust and Signs*. Translated by Richard Howard. New York: George Braziller, 1972.

Deming, Robert H., ed. *James Joyce: The Critical Heritage.* 2 vols. New York: Barnes and Noble, 1970.

De Quincey, Thomas. "On the Knocking at the Gate in *Macbeth*" (1823). In *Norton Anthology of English Literature*, 7th ed., vol. 2, edited by M. H. Abrams and Stephen Greenblatt, 543–46. New York: Norton, 2000.

Derrida, Jacques. *Acts of Religion.* Edited by Gil Anidjar. London: Routledge, 2002.

——. *Adieu to Emmanuel Levinas.* Translated by Pascale-Anne Brault and Michael Naas. Stanford: Stanford University Press, 1999.

——. "Etre Chez Soi Chez l'Autre." In *Idiomes, Nationalites, Deconstructions: Rencontre de Rabat avec Jacques Derrida*, ed. Jean-Jacques Forte, 254–56. Casablanca: Editions Toubkai, 1998.

——. "Force of Law: The 'Mystical Foundation of Authority.'" Translated by Mary Quaintance. In *Acts of Religion*, 230–98.

——. *The Gift of Death.* Translated by David Wills. Chicago: University of Chicago Press, 1995.

——. "Hospitality, Justice, and Responsibility: A Dialogue with Jacques Derrida [HJR]." In *Questioning Ethics: Contemporary Debates in Philosophy*, ed. Richard Kearney and Mark Dooley, 65–83. London: Routledge, 1999.

——. "Hostipitality" [H]. In *Acts of Religion*, 358–420.

——. *Of Hospitality: Ann Dufourmantelle Invites Jacques Derrida to Respond* [OH]. Translated by Rachel Bowlby. Stanford: Stanford University Press, 2000.

——. *Specters of Marx: The State of the Debt, the Work of Mourning and the New International.* Translated by Peggy Kamuf. Introduced by Bernd Magnus and Stephen Cullenberg. London: Routledge, 1994.

Dickens, Charles. *Great Expectations.* Edited by Edgar Rosenberg. New York: Norton, 1999.

Didache, The. Text, translation, analysis, and commentary by Aaron Milavec. Collegeville, Minn.: Liturgical Press, 2003.

Diskin, Patrick. "Joyce's 'The Dead' and Hardy's *The Woodlanders*." *Notes and Queries* 30.4 (1983): 300–331.

Dostal, Walter. " 'Sexual Hospitality' and the Problem of Matrilinearity in Southern Arabia." *Proceedings, Seminar for Arabian Studies* 20 (1990): 17–30.

Dougherty, Michelle Ruggaber. "Virgil's Alecto as a Possible Model for Coleridge's Geraldine." *Notes and Queries* 52.4 (2005): 473–74.

Dyce, Alexander. *Reminiscences of Alexander Dyce.* Edited by Richard J. Schrader. Columbus: Ohio University Press, 1972.

Eagleton, Terry. *Heathcliff and the Great Hunger: Studies in Irish Culture.* London: Verso, 1995.

Ebbatson, J. B. "Coleridge's Mariner and the Rights of Man." *Studies in Romanticism* 11 (1972): 171–206.

ECB. *Eerdmans Commentary on the Bible.* Edited by James D. G. Dunn and John W. Rogerson. Grand Rapids: Eerdmans, 2003.

Edel, Leon. *Henry James.* 5 vols. Philadelphia: Lippincott, 1953–72.

Eggen, Dan, and Cheryl Thompson. "Angry Bush Orders Probe of 'Inexcusable' INS Action." *Washington Post*, March 14, 2002, A13.

Eliot, George. *Middlemarch*. Edited by Bert G. Hornbach. New York: Norton, 1977.

Ellmann, Richard. *James Joyce*. Rev. ed. Oxford: Oxford University Press, 1982.

Empson, William. "The Ancient Mariner." In *Argufying: Essays on Literature and Culture*, ed. John Haffenson, 297–319. Iowa City: University of Iowa Press, 1987.

Encyclopedia of Islam [*EI*]. Leiden: E. J. Brill, 1971.

Encyclopedia of Philosophy [*EP*]. 8 vols. Edited by Paul Edwards. New York: Macmillan, 1967.

Endo, Paul. "Seeing Romantically in *Lamia*." *ELH* 66.1 (1999): 111–28.

Ennius. *Tragedies*. Edited by H. D. Jocelyn. London: Cambridge, 1967.

Enterline, Lynn. *The Rhetoric of the Body from Ovid to Shakespeare*. Cambridge: Cambridge University Press, 2000.

Euripides. *Alcestis*. Translated by Richmond Lattimore. In *The Complete Greek Tragedies*, vol. 3: *Euripides*, ed. David Grene and Richmond Lattimore, 11–57. Chicago: University of Chicago Press, 1958.

Exum, J. Cheryl. "Whose Interests Are Being Served?" In Yee, *Judges and Method*, 65–90.

Fairbanks, Arthur, ed. and trans. *The First Philosophers of Greece*. London: K. Paul, Trench, Trubner, 1898.

Fedeli, Paolo. "Petronio: Il Viaggio, Il Labirinto." *MD* 6 (1981): 91–117.

Fergusson, Frances. "Coleridge and the Deluded Reader: 'The Rime of the Ancient Mariner.'" In Fry, *Samuel Taylor Coleridge*, 113–30.

Fernihough, Anne. "Consciousness as a Stream." In *The Cambridge Companion to the Modernist Novel*, ed. Morag Shiach, 65–81. Cambridge: Cambridge University Press, 2007.

Fielding, Henry. *The History of Tom Jones, a Foundling*. Edited by Fredson Bowers. Introduction and commentary by Martin C. Battestin. 2 vols. Oxford: Oxford University Press, 1975.

Flint, Kate. "George Eliot and Gender." In *The Cambridge Companion to George Eliot*, ed. George Levine, 159–80. Cambridge: Cambridge University Press, 2001.

Frazer, James. "Taboos on Intercourse with Strangers." In *The Golden Bough: A Study of Magic and Religion*. Salt Lake City: Project Gutenberg Literary Archive Foundation, 2003 (www.gutenberg.org/ebooks/3623), chapter 19, section 1.

Freud, Sigmund. "The 'Uncanny'" (1919). In *Collected Papers*, vol. 4. Translated by Joan Riviere. New York: Basic, 1959.

Frost, Robert. "Death of the Hired Man." In *The Poetry of Robert Frost*, ed. Edward Connery Lathem, 34–40. New York: Holt, Rinehart and Winston, 1979.

Fry, Paul, ed. *Samuel Taylor Coleridge, The Rime of the Ancient Mariner*. New York: Bedford/St. Martin's, 1999.

Fuller, Thomas. *The Holy State and the Profane State* (1642). Edited by M. G. Walten. 2 vols. New York: Columbia University Press, 1938.

Fulmer, O. Bryan. "The Ancient Mariner and the Wandering Jew." *Philological Quarterly* 66 (1969): 797–815.

Fuss, Diana. *Essentially Speaking: Feminism, Nature, and Difference*. New York: Routledge, 1989.

Gelder, Ann. "Wandering in Exile: Byron and Pushkin." *Comparative Literature* 42.4 (Autumn 1990): 319–34.

Gifford, Don, with Robert J. Seidman. *Ulysses Annotated: Notes for James Joyce's Ulysses.* Rev. ed. Berkeley: University of California Press, 1988.

Gill, Stephen. *William Wordsworth: A Life.* Oxford: Clarendon Press, 1989.

Gillman, James. *The Life of Samuel Taylor Coleridge.* Vol. 1. London: Pickering, 1838.

Ginsberg, Elaine K., and Laura Moss Gottlieb, eds. *Virginia Woolf: Centennial Essays.* Introduction by Joanne Trautman. Troy, N.Y.: Whitson, 1983.

Godfrey, Emelyne. *Masculinity, Crime, and Self-Defense in Victorian Literature.* London: Palgrave Macmillan, 2011.

Godwin, William. "From *Enquiry Concerning Political Justice and Its Influence on Morals and Happiness*" (1793). In *British Literature 1780–1830,* ed. Anne K. Mellor and Richard Matlak, 90–95. New York: Harcourt Brace, 1996.

Goethe, Johann Wolfgang von. *The Sufferings of Young Werther.* Translated by Bayard Quincey Morgan. New York: Frederick Ungar, 1957.

Gordon, George Stuart. *The Lives of Authors.* London: Chatto and Windus, 1950.

Green, Peter, ed. "Commentary, Glossary." In Apollonius, *Argonautika,* 201–360, 378–445.

Greenblatt, Stephen, et al., eds. *The Norton Shakespeare.* New York: Norton, 1997.

Gunn, David M. *Judges.* Oxford: Blackwell, 2005.

Hardie, Philip. *Virgil.* Oxford: Oxford University Press, 1998.

Hardy, Thomas. *Tess.* 3d ed. Edited by Scott Elledge. New York: Norton, 1991.

Hartman, Geoffrey. *Wordsworth's Poetry 1787–1814.* New Haven: Yale University Press, 1971.

Hartog, Hendrik. "Bargaining for a Child's Love." *New York Times,* January 14, 2012 (www.nytimes.com/2012/01/15/opinion/sunday/bargaining-for-a-childs-love.html?pagewanted=all).

Haydon, Benjamin Robert. *Autobiography and Memoirs.* Edited by Tom Taylor. Introduction by Aldous Huxley. 2 vols. New York: Harcourt Brace, 1926.

Heal, Felicity. *Hospitality in Early Modern England.* Oxford: Clarendon Press, 1990.

Heaney, Seamus, trans. *Beowulf.* New York: Farrar, 2000.

Heffernan, James A. W. *Cultivating Picturacy.* Waco: Baylor University Press, 2006.

———. "Joyce's Merrimanic Heroine: Molly vs. Bloom in Midnight Court." *James Joyce Quarterly* 41.4 (Summer 2004): 745–65.

———. "Looking at the Monster." *Critical Inquiry* 24 (1997): 133–58. Reprinted in Heffernan, *Cultivating Picturacy,* 179–200.

———. " 'Cruel Persuasion': Seduction, Temptation, and Agency in Hardy's *Tess.*" *Thomas Hardy Year Book* 35 (2005): 5–18, and the Victorian Web (www.victorianweb.org/authors/hardy/heffernan.html).

———. "Tracking a Reader: What Did Virginia Woolf Really Think of *Ulysses?*" *Parallaxes: Virginia Woolf and James Joyce Seventy Years After.* Ed. Sara Sullam and Marco Canani (Newcastle upon Tyne: Cambridge Scholars Publishing, 2014): 1–25.

———. "Wordsworth's London: The Imperial Monster." *Studies in Romanticism* 37 (Fall 1998): 189–211.

Heidegger, Martin. "Letter on Humanism." Translated by Frank A. Capuzzi. In *Basic Writings,* ed. David Farrell Krell, 213–66. New York: Harper and Row, 2008.

Henderson, George, trans. *The Feast of Bricriu*. Cambridge, Ontario: In Parentheses Publications, 1999.

Henke, Suzette."*Mrs Dalloway*: The Communion of Saints" [MDCS]. In *New Feminist Essays on Virginia Woolf*, ed. Jane Marcus, 125–47. London: Macmillan, 1981.

———. "'The Prime Minister': A Key to *Mrs Dalloway*" [PM]. In *Virginia Woolf: Centennial Essays*, ed. Elaine Ginsberg and Laura Gottlieb, 127–41. Troy, N.Y.: Whitson, 1983.

Heseltine, Michael. "Introduction." Petronius, *Satyricon*, ix–xlvi.

Hilton, Conrad N. *Be My Guest*. New York: Prentice-Hall, 1984.

Hogan, Patrick Colm. "The Epilogue of Suffering: Heroism, Empathy, Ethics." *SubStance* 30.94/95 (2001): 119–43.

Holinshed, Raphael. *Holinshed's Chronicles of England, Scotland, and Ireland*. London: J. Johnson, 1808.

Hollander, Rachel. *Narrative Hospitality in Late Victorian Fiction: Novel Ethics*. New York: Routledge, 2013.

Holy Rule of Saint Benedict, The. Translated by Leonard J. Doyle. Collegeville, Minn.: Order of Saint Benedict, 2001 (www.litpress.org).

Homer. *The Iliad*. Translated by Robert Fagles. New York: Penguin, 1990. Cited as F.

———. *The Odyssey*. Translated by Robert Fagles. Introduction and notes by Bernard Knox. New York: Penguin, 1997. Cited as F.

Horace. *The Odes*. Translated and edited by Colin Sydenham. London: Duckworth, 2005.

House, Humphry. *Coleridge: The Clark Lectures*. 1953; rept. London: Rupert Hart-David, 1969.

Hume, David. "Of Tragedy." In *Eighteenth Century Prose*, ed. Robert K. Root, Louis Bredvold, and George Sherburn, 647–52. New York: Nelson and Sons, 1935.

Humphreys, Robert. *No Fixed Abode: A History of Responses to the Roofless and Rootless in Britain*. New York: St. Martin's, 1999.

Hunter, J. Paul. *Before Novels: The Cultural Contexts of Eighteenth-Century Fiction*. New York: Norton, 1990.

———. *Occasional Form: Henry Fielding and the Chains of Circumstance*. Baltimore: Johns Hopkins University Press, 1975.

Hyginus. "Ulysses." *Fabulae* 95, trans. Mary Grant. Classical E-Text (www.theoi.com/Text/HyginusFabulae2.html#95).

Ives, Laurel. "The Jealousy Issue." *New York Times*, October 25, 2009 (http://women.timesonline.co.uk/tol/life_and_style/women/relationships/article6882487.ece).

James, Henry. *The Art of the Novel: Critical Prefaces* [AN]. Edited by Richard P. Blackmur. New York: Charles Scribner's Sons, 1934.

———. *The Portrait of a Lady*. Edited by Robert D. Bamberg. 2d ed. New York: Norton, 1995.

———. *The Portrait of a Lady* [PL/O]. Edited by Roger Luckhurst. New York: Oxford University Press, 2009.

Jeffers, James S. *The Greco-Roman World of the New Testament Era: Exploring the Background of Early Christianity*. Downers Grove, Ill.: InterVarsity Press, 1999.

Johnston, Kenneth. *The Hidden Wordsworth: Poet, Lover, Rebel, Spy*. New York: Norton, 1998.

Joyce, James. *Critical Writings*. Edited by Ellsworth Mason and Richard Ellmann. New York: Viking, 1959.

———. "The Dead." In *Dubliners*, ed. Margot Norris, 151–94. New York: Norton, 2006.

———. *Finnegans Wake* [*FW*]. New York: Viking/Compass, 1959.

———. *Letters* [*L*]. 3 vols. Edited by Stuart Gilbert (vol. 1) and Richard Ellmann (vols. 2, 3). New York: Viking, 1966.

———. *Selected Letters*. Edited by Richard Ellmann. London: Faber and Faber, 1975.

———. *Ulysses* [*U*]. Edited by Hans Gabler. New York: Vintage/Random House, 1986. Cited by chapter and line number(s).

Kant, Immanuel. "Introduction to the Theory of Right." In *Political Writings*, trans. H. B. Nisbet, 134. Cambridge: Cambridge University Press, 1991.

———. *Perpetual Peace: A Philosophic Sketch* (1795). In *Critique of Practical Reason and Other Writings in Moral Philosophy*, ed. and trans. Lewis White Beck, 306–45. New York: Garland, 1976.

Keats, John. *Complete Poems*. Edited by Jack Stillinger. Cambridge: Harvard University Press, 1982.

———. *Selected Poems and Letters*. Edited by Douglas Bush. Cambridge: Riverside Press, 1959.

Kempis, Thomas à. *Imitation of Christ*. Translated by Richard Whitford. Edited and introduced by Harold C. Gardiner. Garden City: Image-Doubleday, 1955.

Kenner, Hugh. *Ulysses*. Rev. ed. Baltimore: Johns Hopkins University Press, 1987.

Kierkegaard, Søren. *Fear and Trembling*. Translated by Sylvia Walsh. Edited by C. Stephen Evans and Sylvia Walsh. New York: Cambridge University Press, 2006.

Kittredge, George Lyman, ed. *King Lear*. 2d ed. Revised by Irving Ribner. Waltham, Mass.: Blaisdell/Ginn, 1966.

Klossowski, Pierre. *Roberte Ce Soir* and *The Revocation of the Edict of Nantes* [Paris: Editions de Minuit, 1953]. Introduction by Michael Perkins. Translated by Austryn Wainhouse (1969). Champaign-Urbana: Dalkey Archive, 2002.

Knox, Bernard. "Introduction." Virgil, *The Aeneid* (trans. Fagles), 1–41.

Koenig, John. *New Testament Hospitality*. Philadelphia: Fortress, 1985.

Kottman, Paul. "Hospitality in the Interval." *Oxford Literary Review* 18.1–2 (1996): 87–115.

Kritzman, Lawrence. "Camus's Curious Humanism, or the Intellectual in Exile." *MLN* 112.4 (1997): 550–75.

Kroeber, Karl, and Gene Ruoff, eds. *Romantic Poetry: Recent Revisionary Criticism*. New Brunswick: Rutgers University Press, 1993.

Krueger, Christine L. *The Reader's Repentance: Women Preachers, Women Writers, and Nineteenth-Century Social Discourse*. Chicago: University of Chicago Press, 1992.

Ladenson, Elisabeth. "A Talk Consisting Solely of the Word 'No': Joyce Meets Proust." *James Joyce Quarterly* 3 (Spring 1994): 147–58.

Lander, Bonnie. "The Convention of Innocence and *Sir Gawain and the Green Knight*'s Literary Sophisticates." *Parergon* 24.1 (2007): 41–66.

Lane, Anthony. "Out of the Frame." Review of Michael Gorra, *Portrait of a Novel: Henry James and the Making of an American Masterpiece* (New York: Liveright, 2012). *New Yorker*, September 3, 2012, 70–75.

Lattimore, Richmond. Introduction to *Alcestis*. In *Complete Greek Tragedies* 3:6–9.

———. Introduction to *Oresteia*. In *Complete Greek Tragedies* 1:1–31.

Lawrence, Karen. "Confessions of Xenos." Paper delivered at the 18th International James Joyce Symposium. Trieste, Italy, June 17, 2002.

Lee, Hermione. *Virginia Woolf*. London: Chatto and Windus, 1996.

Lelyveld, Joseph. "All Suicide Bombers Are Not Alike." *New York Times Magazine*, October 24, 2001, 49–53, 62, 78–79.

Lenormant, Amelie Cyvcot. *Memoirs and Correspondence of Madame Recamier*. Translated and edited by Isaphene M. Luyster. Boston: Roberts Brothers, 1878.

Levi, Primo. *The Black Hole of Auschwitz*. Edited by Marco Belpoliti. Translated by Sharon Wood. Malden, Mass.: Polity Press, 2005.

Levinas, Emmanuel. "No Identity." In *Collected Philosophical Papers*, trans. Alphonso Lingis, 141–52. Pittsburgh: Duquesne University Press, 1998.

———. *Time and the Other*. Translated by Richard A. Cohen. Pittsburgh: Duquesne University Press, 1987.

———. *Totality and Infinity: An Essay on Exteriority*. Translated by Alphonso Lingis. Pittsburgh: Duquesne University Press, 1969.

Levine, Carol. "Caring for Elderly Parents." Letter to the Editor, *New York Times*, January 18, 2012 (www.nytimes.com/2012/01/19/opinion/caring-for-elderly-parents.html).

Livy (Titus Livius). *Ab Urbe Condita*. Edited by C. F. Walters, R. F. Conway, et al. 5 vols. Oxford: Clarendon Press, 1914.

Lowes, John Livingston. *The Road to Xanadu: A Study in the Ways of Imagination*. Rev. ed. Boston: Houghton, 1930.

Luckhurst, Roger. "Introduction." James, *Portrait* (ed. Luckhurst), vii–xxvi.

Lupton, Julia Reinhard. "Hospitality and Risk in *The Winter's Tale*." In *Thinking with Shakespeare: Essays on Politics and Life*. Chicago: University of Chicago Press, 2011. Cited as Lupton, H.

———. "Shakespearean Softscapes: Hospitality, Phenomenology, Design." Manuscript, 2011. Cited as Lupton, SS.

Luyster, Isaphene M. "Introduction." Lenormant, *Memoirs and Correspondence*, v–xvi.

Machiavelli, Niccolò. *The Prince*. Translated by James B. Atkinson. New York: Bobbs-Merrill, 1976.

Magnuson, Paul. *Coleridge's Nightmare Poetry*. Charlottesville: University of Virginia Press, 1974.

Mallios, Seth. *The Deadly Politics of Giving: Exchange and Violence at Ajacan, Roanoke, and Jamestown*. Tuscaloosa: University of Alabama Press, 2006.

Mansfield, Katherine. *The Stories of Katherine Mansfield*. Edited by Antony Alpers. Oxford: Oxford University Press, 1984.

Márai, Sándor. *Embers*. Translated by Carol Brown Janeway. New York: Random House, 2001.

Martin, George R. R. *A Storm of Swords*. New York: Bantam Spectra, 2000.

Martin, James D., commentator. *The Book of Judges*. New English Bible. Cambridge: Cambridge University Press, 1975.

Martineau, Henri. "The Ending of the *Red and Black*." Stendhal, *Red and Black*, 446–53.

Massignon, Louis. *L'Hospitalité Sacrée*. Paris: Nouvelle Cite, 1987.

———. "The Three Prayers of Abraham" (1923). In *Testimonies and Reflections: Essays of Louis Massignon*, trans. Allan Cutler, ed. Herbert Mason, 3–20. Notre Dame: University of Notre Dame Press, 1989.

———. "Visitation de l'Étranger: Réponse à l'enquête sur l'idée de Dieu." In *Testimonies and Reflections*, 39–40.

Mauss, Marcel. *The Gift: Forms and Functions of Exchange in Archaic Societies.* Translated by Ian Cunnison. Introduction by E. E. Evans-Pritchard. New York: Norton, 1967.

Mazella, Anthony J. "The New Isabel." In James, *Portrait*, ed. Bamberg, 597–619.

Mbiti, John S. *African Religions and Philosophy.* London: Heinemann, 1990.

McArthur, Elizabeth Andrews. "Following *Swann's Way: To the Lighthouse.*" *Comparative Literature* 56.4 (Fall 2004): 331–46.

McCarthy, Conor. "*Luf-Talking* in *Sir Gawain and the Green Knight.*" *Neophilologus* 92 (2008): 155–62.

McGann, Jerome J. "Keats and the Historical Method in Literary Criticism" (1979). In Kroeber and Ruoff, *Romantic Poetry*, 439–64.

———. "The Meaning of the Ancient Mariner." *Critical Inquiry* 8:1 (Autumn 1981): 35–67.

McGee, Diane. *Writing the Meal: Dinner in the Fiction of Early Twentieth-Century Women Writers.* Toronto: University of Toronto Press, 2001.

McKeon, Michael. *The Secret History of Domesticity: Public, Private, and the Division of Knowledge.* Baltimore: Johns Hopkins University Press, 2005.

McNulty, Tracy. *The Hostess: Hospitality, Femininity, and the Expropriation of Identity.* Minneapolis: University of Minnesota Press, 2007.

Mehlman, Jeffrey. "Literature and Hospitality: Klossowski's Hamann." *Studies in Romanticism* 22.2 (Summer 1983): 329–47.

Melville, Herman. *Moby-Dick.* Edited by Herschel Parker and Harrison Hayford. New York: Norton, 2001.

Melville, Peter. "Coleridge's 'The Rime of the Ancient Mariner'" [RAM]. *Explicator* 63.1 (2004): 15–18.

———. "Monstrous Ingratitude: Hospitality in Mary Shelley's *Frankenstein*" [MIH]. *European Romanticism* 19.2 (2008): 179–85.

———. *Romantic Hospitality and the Resistance to Accommodation* [RH]. Waterloo, Ontario: Wilfrid Laurier University Press, 2007.

Miller, J. Hillis. "A Conclusion in Which Almost Nothing Is Concluded: *Middlemarch's* 'Finale.'" In Chase, *Middlemarch*, 133–56.

———. "Irish Hospitality: Parties in Joyce." Paper delivered at the 18th International James Joyce Symposium, Trieste, Italy, June 17, 2002.

———. *Literature as Conduct: Speech Acts in Henry James.* New York: Fordham University Press, 2005.

———. "Reading Proust's 'Rachel When from the Lord': Interpretation of the Wholly Other." *E-Magazine LiterNet* 15:2.(2001), accessed 2/21/2009.

———. "The Critic as Host." *Critical Inquiry* 3 (Spring 1977): 439–47.

Millet, Catherine. *Jealousy: The Other Life of Catherine M.* Translated by Helen Stevenson. London: Serpent's Tail, 2009.

Milton, John. *Complete Poetical Works*. Edited by Douglas Bush. Boston: Houghton Mifflin, 1965. I cite *Paradise Lost* [PL] by book and line number(s) and shorter poems (e.g., "Lycidas" and the Nativity Ode) by line numbers alone.

Mitchell, Bruce. "Introduction." In *Beowulf*, trans. Kevin Crossley-Holland, 1–29. New York: Farrar, 1968.

Modiano, Raimonda. "Sameness or Difference? Historicist Readings of 'The Rime of the Ancient Mariner,'" 1999. In Fry, *Samuel Taylor Coleridge*, 187–219.

Montandon, Alain, ed. *L'Hospitalité au XVIIIe Siècle*. Clermont-Ferrand: Presses Universitaires Blaise Pascal, 2000.

Nicolson, Juliet. *The Great Silence: Britain from the Shadow of the First World War to the Dawn of the Jazz Age*. New York: Grove, 2010.

Nightingale, Florence. *Collected Works*. Edited by Lynn McDonald. 16 vols. Waterloo, Ontario: Wilfrid Laurier University Press, 2001–.

Nouwen, Henri. *Reaching Out: The Three Movements of the Spiritual Life*. New York: Doubleday, 1975.

OBC. *Oxford Bible Commentary, The*. Edited by John Barton and John Muddiman. New York: Oxford University Press, 2001.

O'Brien, Eugene. "Guests of a Nation; *Geists* of a Nation." *New Hibernia Review* 11.3 (2007): 114–30.

O'Connor, Frank. "Guests of the Nation." In *Classic Irish Short Stories*, ed. Frank O'Connor, 172–87. Oxford: Oxford University Press, 1958.

OED. *Oxford English Dictionary*. Compact Edition. New York: Oxford University Press, 1971.

O'Rourke, James. *Sex, Lies, and Autobiography: The Ethics of Confession*. Charlottesville: University of Virginia Press, 2006.

Ovid. *Metamorphoses*, trans. Rolfe Humphries. Bloomington: Indiana University Press. Since the lines are unnumbered in this translation, I cite them as H with page number(s).

Palmer, Daryl W. *Hospitable Performances: Dramatic Genre and Cultural Practices in Early Modern England*. West Lafayette: Purdue University Press, 1992.

Palmer, Parker. *The Company of Strangers: Christians and the Renewal of America's Public Life*. New York: Crossroad, 1981.

Paris, Matthew. *Chronica Majora (c. 1300)*. Edited by H. R. Luard. London, 1880.

Perkell, Christine, ed. *Reading Vergil's Aeneid: An Interpretive Guide*. Norman: University of Oklahoma Press, 1999.

Petronius. [*Satyricon*]. With translation by Michael Heseltine. Revised by E. H. Warmington. Cambridge: Harvard University Press, 1975.

———. *Satyrica*. Translated and edited by R. Bright Branham and Daniel Kinney. Berkeley: University of California Press, 1996.

Philipson, Morris. "Mrs Dalloway, 'What's the Sense of Your Parties?'" *Critical Inquiry* 1.1 (1974): 123–48.

Philostratus, Flavius. *Life of Apollonius*. Translated by F. C. Conybeare. Loeb Classical Library. 2 vols. Cambridge: Harvard University Press, 1912.

Pincus, Walter. "Videotape Shows Bin Laden Laughing at 9/11 Pilots." *Washington Post*. Repr. *Lebanon, NH Valley News*, December 21, 2001, A10.

Pitt-Rivers, Julian. "The Law of Hospitality." In *The Fate of Shechem, or, The Politics of Sex: Essays in the Anthropology of the Mediterranean*, 94–112, 179–81. Cambridge: Cambridge University Press, 1977.

Polhemus, Robert M. *Lot's Daughters: Sex, Redemption, and Women's Quest for Authority.* Stanford: Stanford University Press, 2005.

Prose, Francine, ed. *The Mrs. Dalloway Reader.* New York: Harcourt, 2003.

Proust, Marcel. *À la recherche du temps perdu.* 4 vols. Edited by Jean-Yves Tadie et al. Paris: Gallimard, 1987–88.

———. *Du Cote de Chez Swann* [CCS]. *À la recherche* 1:3–420.

———. *Le Cote de Guermantes* [CG]. *À la recherche* 2:309–884.

———. *Sodome et Gomorrhe* [SeG]. *À la recherche* 3:3–515.

———. *La Prisonnière* [LaP]. *À la recherche* 3:519–915.

———. *Le Temps Retrouvé* [LTR]. *À la recherche* 4:275–625.

———. *In Search of Lost Time.* 6 vols. Translated by C. K. Scott-Moncrieff et al. London: Chatto and Windus, 1992.

———. *Swann's Way* [SW]. Translated and with an introduction and notes by Lydia Davis. New York: Viking, 2003.

———. *The Guermantes Way* [GW]. Translated by D. J. Enright, C. K. Scott-Moncrieff, and Terence Kilmartin. Rev. ed. *In Search of Lost Time* 3.

———. *Sodom and Gomorrah* [SaG]. Translated by C. K. Scott-Moncrieff, Terence Kilmartin, and D. J. Enright. *In Search of Lost Time* 4.

———. *The Captive* [CAP]. Translated by C. K. Scott-Moncrieff, Terence Kilmartin, and D. J. Enright. *In Search of Lost Time* 5:1–473.

———. *Time Regained* [TR]. Translated by Andreas Mayor, Terence Kilmartin, and D. J. Enright. *In Search of Lost Time* 6.

Pushkin, Alexander. *Eugene Onegin.* Translated by James Falen. New York: Oxford, 1995. Cited as F.

———. *Eugene Onegin.* Translated by Walter Arndt. 2d ed. rev. New York: Dutton, 1981. Cited as A.

Putnam, Michael. "Aeneid 12: Unity in Closure." In Perkell, *Reading Vergil's Aeneid*, 210–30.

———. *Virgil's Aeneid.* Chapel Hill: University of North Carolina Press, 1995.

Rebeck, Theresa, and Alexandra Gersten-Vassilaros. *Omnium Gatherum.* New York: Samuel French, 2003.

Reece, Steve. *The Stranger's Welcome: Oral Theory and the Aesthetics of the Homeric Hospitality Scene.* Ann Arbor: University of Michigan Press, 1993.

Reynolds, K. D. *Aristocratic Women and Political Society in Victorian Britain.* New York: Oxford University Press, 1999.

Richter, Harvena. "The *Ulysses* Connection: Clarissa Dalloway's Bloomsday." *Studies in the Novel* 21.3 (1989): 305–19.

Robertson, D. W. *A Preface to Chaucer: Studies in Medieval Perspectives.* Princeton: Princeton University Press, 1962.

Rosello, Mireille. *Postcolonial Hospitality: The Immigrant as Guest.* Stanford: Stanford University Press, 2001.

Rosier, James L. "Hands and Feasts in Beowulf." *PMLA* 78.1 (March 1963): 8–14.

Rothstein, Edward. "'Sorrow, Pity, Celebration: France Under the Nazis." *New York Times*, Arts and Design, April 26, 2009, 1/3.

Rousseau, Jean-Jacques. *The Confessions and Correspondence, Including the Letters to Malesherbes.* Vol. 5, Collected Writings of Rousseau. Edited by Roger Masters, Christopher Kelly, and Peter G. Stillman. Hanover, N.H.: University Press of New England, 1995.

——. *Oeuvres Complètes.* Pléiade Edition. Paris: Gallimard, 1959.

Royce, Josiah. *The World and the Individual.* 2d ser. New York: Macmillan, 1901.

Rubinstein, Chris. "Rousseau and Coleridge: Another Look at Christabel." *Coleridge Bulletin*, n.s. 1 (Winter 1992–93): 9–14.

Rutherford, Richard. "Preface to *Alcestis*, Explanatory Notes." *Euripides* 3–6, 167–70.

Safire, William. "On Language." *New York Times Magazine*, October 24, 2002, 34.

Said, Edward. *Culture and Imperialism.* London: Vintage, 1994.

Saint-Amour, Paul. "'Christmas Yet to Come': Hospitality, Futurity, the *Carol*, and 'The Dead.'" *Representations* 98 (May 2007): 93–117.

Schaeffer, Josephine O'Brien. *The Three-fold Nature of Reality in the Novels of Virginia Woolf.* The Hague: Mouton, 1965.

Schama, Simon. *Citizens: A Chronicle of the French Revolution.* New York: Knopf, 1989.

Schenk, C. E. "Jael." *Net Bible* (http://net.bible.org/dictionary.php?word=JAEL, accessed January 20, 2010).

Schwartz, Regina Mara. *Sacramental Poetics at the Dawn of Secularism: When God Left the World.* Stanford: Stanford University Press, 2008.

Schwarz, Wolfgang. "Kant's Refutation of Charitable Lies." *Ethics* 81.1 (October 1970): 62–67.

Scott, Bonnie Kime, ed. *The Gender of Modernism: A Critical Anthology.* Bloomington: Indiana University Press, 1990.

See, Rich. "Host and Guest." *CurtainUp: The Internet Theater Magazine of Reviews, Features, Annotated Listings* (2004): 1–3 (www.curtainup.com/hostandguest.html).

Seldes, Gilbert. "Review of *Ulysses*." *The Nation*, August 30, 1922. In Deming, *James Joyce*, 235–39.

Shakespeare, William. *The Norton Shakespeare.* Edited by Stephen Greenblatt et al. New York: Norton, 1997.

Shattuck, Roger. *Proust's Way: A Field Guide to* In Search of Lost Time. New York: Norton, 2000.

Shelley, Mary. *Frankenstein, or the Modern Prometheus.* Edited by Maurice Hindle. New York: Penguin, 1992.

Shelvocke, George. *A Voyage Round the World by the Way of the Great South Sea.* London: J. Senex, 1726.

Simpson, David. "How Marxism Reads 'The Rime of the Ancient Mariner.'" In Fry, *Samuel Taylor Coleridge*, 148–67.

Singleton, Charles. *Dante, The Divine Comedy: Inferno.* Vol. 2: *Commentary.* Princeton: Princeton University Press, 1970.

Smith, Martin S. "Commentary." In *Petronii Arbitri Cena Trimalchionis*, 51–212. Oxford: Clarendon Press, 1975.

Son, Youngjoo. *Here and Now: The Politics of Social Space in D. H. Lawrence and Virginia Woolf*. London: Routledge, 2006.

Specter, Michael. "Profiles: The Kingdom." *New Yorker*, September 26, 2005, 134.

Spence, Sarah. "Varium et Mutabile: Voices of Authority in *Aeneid* 4." In Perkell, *Reading Vergil's Aeneid*, 80–95.

Spenser, Edmund. *"The Faerie Queene,"* book 1. In *Edmund Spenser's Poetry*, ed. Hugh Maclean, 5–148. 2d ed. New York: Norton, 1986.

Starobinski, Jean. *Jean-Jacques Rousseau: Transparency and Obstruction*. Edited by Arthur Goldhammer. Introduction by Robert J. Morrissey. Chicago: University of Chicago Press, 1988.

Steinberg, Leo. *Leonardo's Incessant* Last Supper. New York: Zone, 2001.

———. *Other Criteria*. New York: Oxford University Press, 1972.

Stendhal. *Red and Black*. Translated and edited by Robert M. Adams. New York: Norton, 1969.

——— . *Le Rouge et Le Noir*. Edited by Michel Crouzet. Paris: Garnier-Flammarion, 1996.

Still, Judith. *Derrida and Hospitality: Theory and Practice*. Edinburgh: Edinburgh University Press, 2010.

Stillinger, Jack. *Reading* The Eve of St. Agnes: *The Multiples of Complex Literary Transaction*. New York: Oxford, 1999.

———. "The Hoodwinking of Madeline: Skepticism in *The Eve of St. Agnes*." In *English Romantic Poets: Essays in Criticism*, ed. M. H. Abrams, 448–69. 2d ed. New York: Oxford University Press, 1975.

Strote, Mary Ellen. "Mirror, Mirror, on the Wall." *Lear's* (June 1991): 35–36.

Swann, Karen. "'Christabel': The Wandering Mother and the Enigma of Form (1984)." In *Romanticism: A Critical Reader*, ed. Duncan Wu, 151–70. Oxford: Blackwell, 1995.

———. "Literary Gentlemen and Lovely Ladies: The Debate on the Character of *Christabel* (1985)." In Kroeber and Ruoff, *Romantic Poetry*, 1993.

Tacitus. *Complete Works*. Edited by Moses Hadas. Translated by Alfred John Church and William Jackson. New York: Modern Library, 1942.

Takese, Fumiko. "Some Considerations of The Man of the Hill in *Tom Jones*." *English Studies* 69 (February 1988): 37–47.

Theissen, Gerd. *The First Followers of Jesus: A Sociological Analysis of the Earliest Christianity*. Norwich, England: S.C.M. Press, 1978.

Thoreau, Henry David. *Walden* and *Civil Disobedience*. Edited by Owen Thomas. New York: Norton, 1966.

Thurston, Luke. *Literary Ghosts from the Victorians to Modernism: The Haunting Interval*. New York: Routledge, 2012.

Tolstoy, Leo. *Anna Karenina*. Translated by Louise Maude and Aylmer Maude. Introduction and notes by W. Gareth Jones. Oxford: Oxford University Press, 1998.

Tseng, Ching-fang. "The Flaneur, the Flaneuse, and the Hostess: Virginia Woolf's (Un) Domesticating Flanerie in *Mrs Dalloway*." *Concentric: Literary and Cultural Studies* 32.1 (January 2006): 219–58.

Tucker, Herbert. *Epic: Britain's Heroic Muse, 1790–1910*. Oxford: Oxford University Press, 2008.

Ulmer, William A. "*Christabel* and the Origin of Evil." *Studies in Philology* 104.3 (Summer 2007): 376–407.

van Gennep, Arnold. *The Rites of Passage.* Translated by Monika B. Vizedom and Gabrielle L. Caffee. Introduction by Solon T. Kimball. Chicago: University of Chicago Press, 1960.

Vantuono, William, ed. and trans. *Sir Gawain and the Green Knight: A Dual-Language Version.* New York: Garland, 1991.

van Wees, Hans. "Princes at Dinner: Social Event and Social Structure in Homer." In *Homeric Questions*, ed. J. P. Crielaard, 147–82. Amsterdam: J. C. Gieben, 1995.

Veyne, Paul. "The Roman Empire." In *A History of Private Life*, Vol. 1: *From Pagan Rome to Byzantium*, trans. Arthur Goldhammer, ed. Philippe Ariès and Georges Duby, 5–234. Cambridge: Harvard University Press, 1987.

Victoria, Francisco de. *De Indis et de Jure Belli Relectiones* (1557). Translated by John Pawlcy Bate. Washington, D.C., 1917.

Virgil. *The Aeneid.* Translated by Robert Fagles. Introduced and annotated by Bernard Knox. New York: Viking Penguin, 2006.

———. *Eclogues, Georgics, Aeneid I–VI* (1916); *Aeneid VII–XII. Appendix Vergiliana* (1918). 2 vols. Edited and translated by H. R. Fairclough. Revised by G. P. Goold. Loeb Classical Library. Cambridge: Harvard University Press, 1999–2000.

Visser, Margaret. *The Rituals of Dinner.* New York: Grove Weidenfeld, 1991.

Wanderer, The. Translated by Robert E. Diamond (http://research.uvu.edu/mcdonald/wanderweb/trans1.htm, accessed 2/12/2011).

Ware, Malcolm. "Coleridge's Spectre-Bark: A Slave Ship?" *Philological Quarterly* 40 (1961): 589–93.

Warren, Robert Penn, ed. *The Rime of the Ancient Mariner, with an Essay.* New York: Random House, 1946.

Waswo, Richard. "The Formation of Natural Law to Justify Colonialism, 1539–1689." *New Literary History* 27.4 (1996): 743–59.

Watt, James C. Y., ed. *The World of Khubilai Khan: Chinese Art in the Yuan Dynasty.* Exhibition Catalogue. New York: Metropolitan Museum, 2010.

Wawrzycka, Jolanta W. "Apotheosis, Metaphor, and Death: John Huston's *The Dead* Again." Spanish James Joyce Society. *Papers on Joyce* 4 (1998): 67–74 (www.radford.edu/jolanta/publications/Joyce%27sTheDead1998.htm).

Wheler, George. *The Protestant Monastery: Or Christian Œconomicks.* London, 1698.

Williams, R. D., ed. and annotator. *The Aeneid of Virgil.* 2 vols. London: Macmillan/St. Martin's, 1972–73.

Wilson, Cheryl. *Literature and Dance in Eighteenth-Century Britain: Jane Austen to the New Woman.* Cambridge: Cambridge University Press, 2009.

Wollstonecraft, Mary. *A Vindication of the Rights of Woman.* Edited by Carol Poston. New York: Norton, 1975.

Woolf, Leonard. *Autobiography* [A]. 5 vols. London: Hogarth Press, 1960–69.

Woolf, Virginia. *Complete Shorter Fiction of Virginia Woolf* [CSF]. Edited by Susan Dick. 2d ed. New York: Harcourt Brace, 1989.

——. *Diary of Virginia Woolf* [D]. Edited by Anne Olivier Bell and Andrew McNeillie. 5 vols. London: Hogarth Press, 1977–84.

——. *Essays of Virginia Woolf.* Vol. 3: *1919–1924* [E 3]. Edited by Andrew McNeillie. New York: Harcourt Brace, 1988.

——. *Jacob's Room.* Edited by Edward L. Bishop. Oxford: Blackwell/Shakespeare Head, 2004.

——. *Letters of Virginia Woolf* [L]. Edited by Nigel Nicolson and Joanne Trautman. 6 vols. New York: Harcourt Brace Jovanovich, 1975–80.

——. "Modern Novels (Joyce)." Woolf's Reading Notes on *Ulysses* in the Berg Collection, New York Public Library, transcribed by Suzette Henke. In Scott, *The Gender of Modernism,* 642–45.

——. *Moments of Being.* Edited by Jeanne Schulkind. 2d ed. New York: Harcourt Brace Jovanovich, 1985.

——. *Mrs Dalloway* [MD]. Edited by Morris Beja. Oxford: Blackwell/Shakespeare Head, 1996.

——. *Mrs Dalloway's Party: A Short-Story Sequence* [MDP]. Edited and with an introduction by Stella McNichol. London: Hogarth Press, 1973.

——. *Pargiters, The: The Novel-Essay Portion of* The Years. San Diego: Harcourt Brace, 1978.

——. *A Passionate Apprentice: The Early Journals 1897–1909* [PA]. Edited by Mitchell A. Leaksa. New York: Harcourt Brace Jovanovich, 1990.

——. *To the Lighthouse.* New York: Harcourt Brace, 1955.

Wordsworth, William. *The Borderers.* Edited by Robert Osborn. Ithaca, N.Y.: Cornell University Press, 1982.

——. *Home at Grasmere: Part First, Book First, of* The Recluse. Edited by Beth Darlington. Ithaca: Cornell University Press, 1977.

——. *Poetical Works* [PW]. 5 vols. Edited by Ernest De Selincourt. Oxford: Clarendon Press, 1940–49. 2d ed. of vol. 2 revised by Helen Darbishire, 1952.

——. *The Prelude.* Edited by Ernest De Selincourt. Revised by Helen Darbishire. Oxford: Clarendon, 1959.

——. *The Prelude, 1799, 1805, 1850.* Edited by Jonathan Wordsworth, M. H. Abrams, and Stephen Gill. New York: Norton, 1979. I quote the poem by book and line number(s) following the date of the version quoted.

——. *The Salisbury Plain Poems* [SPP]. Edited by Stephen Gill. Ithaca: Cornell University Press, 1975.

Worth, Robert F. "From a Beirut Cell, an Iraqi Watches as the U.S. Finally Takes His Advice." *New York Times,* April 2, 2008, A6/A14.

Yee, Gale A. *Judges and Method.* Minneapolis: Fortress, 1995.

Zuckoff, Mitchell, and Dick Lehr. *Judgment Ridge: The True Story Behind the Dartmouth Murders.* New York: Harper Collins, 2003.

INDEX

An expanded version of the index, including all literary characters mentioned in the book and scholars cited in the notes, may be found online at www.jamesheff.com.

World Trade Center attacks. *See*
    September 11, 2001, attacks
Wotton, Henry, 117, 147
Wuthering Heights (E. Brontë), 224–31,
    239, 250, 368n26

xenophobia, 4–5; etymology of, 3, 337n5;
    hospitality and, 55, 59–60, 271;
    immigration and, 10–11. *See also*
    nationalism; strangers
xenos: meanings of, 3

Yushchenko, Viktor, 331, 387n90

Zaccheus (biblical), 68, 349n44
Zantop, Half and Susanne, x, 2,
    3–4, 335
Zeus (deity): Agamemnon's story told
    by, 20; Calypso's hospitality and,
    170, 295; as god and protector of
    guests, 16–18, 19, 20; as god and
    protector of hosts, 60–61; hospitality
    conditioned by fear of, 6–7; Odysseus's
    prayers to, 24; as prefiguring Christ's
    hospitality, 78; rivals for, 341n16. *See
    also* Jupiter/Jove
Zola, Émile, 263, 373–74n15